Praise for **CONVERSATIO**

MW00697968

"Brilliant, really! David Crump has them while most books on Trial Pra reader authoritatively how it 'should' be done. Real, regular people teaching us what they want to know and how they want the Trial Lawyer to speak with them leads us straight to the vein of gold! Get this book and do this right!"

—*Kent Spence*
Spence Law Firm
Board Member, Trial Lawyers College
Past President and Board Member, Wyoming Trial Lawyers Association
Jackson, WY

"The heart of the American juror is the ultimate antidote to the relentless legal machinery — the 'cause of action' standards, the summary judgment procedures, the defense medical expert testimony, and the jury instructions that defense lawyers direct against our wounded people to deny them justice. Unlocking jurors' hearts and unleashing the antidote start in *voir dire* and continue through conversations with every witness who testifies and before the jury and in every argument made to the jury through the end of the trial. Trial lawyer David Crump's newest book *Conversations* gives useful examples of ways to start (and perhaps some ways not to start) communications to unlock the hearts of American jurors who decide civil damages trials. *Conversations* begins with the source — the initial beliefs, attitudes and experiences that jurors bring to trials that influence how justice ultimately will be delivered in their verdict."

— *John Budlong*
Past-President, Washington State Association for Justice
Tom Chambers Trial Lawyer of the Year 2006
WSAJ President's Award 2000
Member, Damages Attorney's Round Table
Edmonds, WA

"Outstanding! This is the only book of its kind on jury selection, providing an indispensable insight about genuine conversations with jurors like no other. I will use this book for the remainder of my trial practice, and I will recommend it to anyone who will be trying a case to a jury. It's a must have in the trial lawyer's arsenal."

— *Francisco A. Duarte*
Board Member, Washington State Association for Justice
Faculty, Trial Lawyers College
Seattle, WA

"DO NOT begin your next trial without first reading *Conversations*! This is the book every trial lawyer has been waiting for. Crump's indispensable approach resonates universally and applies to every case, including yours."

— *Scott P. Carness*
Editor-in-Chief, *Trial News* (2015-2017)
Edmonds, WA

"Finished the book. I thoroughly enjoyed it and believe it is an asset for any trial lawyer. I wish when I had started trying cases I could have read this book. I remember all the times I stumbled when confronted with hostility or an unexpected answer that made no sense to me and I had to stand there dumbfounded. If you are going to try cases, you should read this book well in advance and think about each section. Great to work with others as a guide for doing practice *voir dire*."

— *Jim Kytle*
Seattle, WA

"As a trial lawyer, Jury Selection is the most uncertain part of trial. 'Will I like this jury? And most importantly, will this jury like my client and me?' In *Conversations*, Mr. Crump has taken a giant step for trial lawyers in probing the inside secrets of jurors, and providing insights for my next Jury Selection."

— *Joe Cunnane*
Edmonds, WA

"David Crump has done a masterful job of providing a road map for the most challenging and important phase of trial practice. Selecting a jury is an art but, like all art forms, the practitioner must understand the fundamentals of the discipline before being able to express creatively. This book provides those essential fundamentals. Great read."

— *Paul Henderson*
Vancouver, WA

"*Conversations* should be mandatory reading before your next jury selection. I came away with a much better understanding of words and concepts that do or do not resonate with jurors. I anticipate reading my highlighted sections of this book before I sit down and draft my *voir dire* outline in any future trials. You simply cannot find this kind of insight into the minds of potential jurors anywhere else."

— Bruce J. Lambrecht
Spokane, WA

"I commonly tell clients that when you put your fate into the hands of 12 licensed drivers, the outcome is usually unpredictable. *Conversations* is a constructive reminder that this characterization is too cursory, and that every prospective juror (whether licensed or not) presents with a unique humanness and individual perspective which attorneys must at all times respect during *voir dire*. Moreover, if like most attorneys you don't try cases on a regular basis, *Conversations* is an engaging refresher course on human nature and effective communication skills that will positively aid you in your next trial."

— Andrew Bergh
Bainbridge Island, WA

"With his typical modestly, Mr. Crump shares the insights of a master trial attorney in a real, honest and enviably insightful way. I'd be comfortable putting anything important to me on the line before any jury he had a hand in sitting."

— James P. Moriarty
Cedar Rapids, IA

"*Conversations* provides an unfiltered insight into the thoughts of non-lawyers. It is an asset not only for jury selection but for understanding our own clients and other non-lawyers we come into contact with on a daily basis."

— Richard Downs
Kirkland, WA

"David has a novel approach to the maddening 'art' of attempting to understand the minds of our jurors. No lectures. No rules. Instead — through creative and well-thought-out questions to potential jurors themselves — he challenges us to address our own biases and views of the process. The result is a practical way to connect with a jury through a 'new set of glasses.'"

— David Ryder
Edmonds, WA

"Engaging potential jurors in a conversation and then just being able to LISTEN is a challenge for many attorneys. Mr. Crump's book will become a valuable tool in overcoming this challenge. It provides meaningful insights into the minds of jurors regarding what is important to them and what they want to see, hear and talk about. Every attorney should read it before he or she even walks into the courtroom."

— Tara L. Eubanks
Board Member, Washington State Association for Justice
WSAJ New Lawyer Award 2008
Edmonds, WA

"Trial attorney David Crump is, first and foremost, a listener. Fifty in-depth conversations with individuals from a cross section of ages, occupations and ethnic backgrounds, sharing their biases, inclinations and attitudes related to jury service. The result is a fascinating — and often surprising — insight into how people evaluate attorneys, litigants and the process itself. Highly recommended."

— O.R. Elofson, Ph.D.
Carnation, WA

"Wow! This will be a tremendous resource for the insight David Crump has provided to us as trial lawyers! He has gleaned and gathered information from everyday folks who may be serving on a jury in the near future. I don't have the time to interview or meet with this many people who may be jurors. David has done that work for us and helped show us what may be truly important to them – our potential jurors. Well done!"

— Ed Harper
Kirkland, WA

"I have tried over 180 jury trials, mostly criminal, a few civil. *Conversations* caused me to reflect upon my life in the courtroom and all the jurors that I have met. It reminded me that the vast majority of the folks who serve are good and want to do the right thing, but they are also human, with all of their biases and prejudices. These conversations will be echoing in my head the next time I pick a jury, or help another lawyer get ready for this most daunting of tasks."

— Dan Ambrose, Trial Lawyer
Co-founder of Trojan Horse Method
Santa Monica, CA

"*Conversations* is an invaluable read for lawyers who try cases. David Crump shares candid revelations from real people and real jurors. He offers insights which engage the mind and inspire the heart!"

— Liz Quick
Trial Lawyer, Quick | Law Group, PLLC
Board Member, Washington State Association for Justice
Kirkland, WA

"Coming from one who probably tries one case a year or every other year, *voir dire* has been the most challenging stage of the trial process. *Conversations* started off with the most important thing that some of us seem to overlook and that is, jurors are human. We sometimes get so caught up with the law, the facts of the case and the process that we forget that the ultimate decision lies with the 12 pairs of eyes watching and ears listening to our case. I've always wondered what it would be like to be a fly on the wall when the jury is deliberating. This book gives a sense of what that is like and what goes through a juror's thought process, whether it is relevant or irrelevant to the case at hand, and will certainly come in handy when I prepare for *voir dire*."

— Faye Wong
Mercer Island, WA

"Very revealing, candid conversations. There are pearls contained in these many interviews. I will turn to this book often preparing for *voir dire*."

— Brian Leonard
Edmonds, WA

CONVERSATIONS: JURY SELECTION

Also by the Author

Life by a Thousand Cuts

CONVERSATIONS:
JURY SELECTION

David L. Crump

Published by ICENET PRESS, Seattle, Washington

Copyright ©2016 by David L. Crump

All Rights Reserved

Printed and bound in the United States of America

ISBN: 978-0-9863162-2-7

FIRST PAPERBACK EDITION: March 2016

No part of this book may be reproduced or transmitted in any form or by any means,
electronic or mechanical, including photocopying, recording or by any information,
storage and retrieval system, without express written permission of
the author and publisher, except where permitted by law.

Interior layout & cover design by **idesign**

10 9 8 7 6 5 4 3 2 1

To every juror who serves with an open mind;
and to lawyers everywhere seeking justice for people, facing their fears
and "honoring the share".

Publisher's Note

This book is intended for those studying the law, embarking on a career or practicing in the legal profession. This book offers no legal advice and cannot substitute for informed consultation with one or more qualified legal professionals.

The reader is urged to consider all of the material herein as an adjunct to his or her own independent experience, judgment, skill and acumen.

The conversations herein are not intended for use in litigation.

The names and other specifically identifying details of the participants, with the exception of the author, are confidential.

The author and publisher expressly disclaim any liability or responsibility for loss or damage resulting from the use of this book or the information, ideas or opinions contained herein.

Acknowledgments

This book would not have been possible without the enthusiastic participation of the individuals who agreed to speak candidly about their personal, often closely-held thoughts, feelings, opinions, experiences and beliefs. Without exception, each person contributed something valuable and to them, I am grateful.

To the trial greats and sitting judges who graciously agreed to share their thoughts for this book, my sincere respect and appreciation for your time and contributions.

Thank you to the Washington State Association for Justice; the Trial Lawyers College; and the greats who have contributed to my professional development, notably Paul Luvera, Rick Friedman and Gerry Spence. Thank you also to Reed Schifferman, Eric Fong and John Budlong for your friendship and counsel.

Special appreciation goes to Rebecca Schade and Narrows Court Reporting for agreeing to be a part of this project. Becki transcribed every conversation flawlessly, often with distracting background noise. Thanks and appreciation as well to Terri Fisher and the Washington Court Reporters Association, and to Susan Selby who painstakingly helped edit portions of this book.

Finally, thank you to my amazing wife Natalie. She inspires me daily and makes all things possible with her love, generosity, caring and support.

A Note on Methodology

All participants were over the age of eighteen and were either registered voters or licensed drivers, meeting the threshold qualifications for jury service in Washington.

Every participant completed a written questionnaire requesting basic demographic information similar to what is asked of prospective jurors in Washington, attested that the information was true and correct and signed a release consenting to audio recording. A summary of the demographic data is found in the Appendix.

At the outset, every participant was asked to imagine "as if" they had received a jury summons; showed up to the courthouse; were grouped together in a courtroom with a panel of, variously, 40, 60 or 80 prospective jurors; and told by the judge that the case involved a person, the plaintiff, claiming injury caused by negligence of another person or entity, the defendant. At the conclusion, participants were paid twenty-five dollars.

What follows are the transcripts, nearly-verbatim, in the order conducted.

The conversations that make up the content of this book have been professionally transcribed from the original audio recordings. Errors of grammar and style, common to the conversational form, have been retained.

"*Every friend was once a stranger and if you know this, you have to understand that conversations are the beginning of connection.*"

— *Israelmore Avivor*

"*A tribe is a group of people connected to one another, connected to a leader, and connected to an idea. For millions of years, human beings have been part of one tribe or another. A group needs only two things to be a tribe: a shared interest and a way to communicate.*"

— *Seth Godin*

Foreword by Eric Fong

The search for justice eludes many a seeker. Today, like every day, a frustrated judge presides over a trial where a great injustice is perpetrated. She can see it, she can hear it and she can feel it, yet she is unable to stop it. This slow train wreck is evident to her the minute the lawyers start talking to the jury. Justice is yet again subverted by virtue of the fact that not all juries are created equal.

Who is the culprit for this injustice? Is it the judge's fault? Is it the jury's fault? Is it the system's fault? We all know the answer to this question, and it is what keeps us up at night; it is the lawyer's fault.

Going on 20 years of practicing law, I have talked to scores of juries and thousands of jurors. I've read dozens of books, and attended even more seminars. I've taught with the likes of Gerry Spence and Paul Luvera, to name but a few. I tried and watched cases with Nick Rowley. I count Rick Friedman as a dear friend, whom I do cases with and constantly pick his brain about the subject. Yet, in this one-of-a-kind book, I learned something that none of these experiences taught me; I learned the inner thoughts of jurors.

Conceptually, I fully grasped the notion that the minute a juror sees me, before I ever open my mouth, opinions and feelings are formed, opinions and feelings that will make or break my relationship with the jury, and consequently the outcome of the case. I fully appreciate the fact that the only way I will do my client right, is with honesty, genuineness and sincerity. My words must come from a feeling that I only get when I step back and listen with a calm mind and open heart. I must be totally in tune with that juror. If I react with intellectual analysis, half of the room will disagree with me. Right minds will always disagree on the same facts; look no further than the respective political parties that rule this country. But words governed by feeling, emotion, spirit and understanding resonate with all, political parties be damned.

And here is a fascinating revelation learned from the pages of this book; my eyes, ears and understanding of that precious moment are self-absorbed. Through this book, my understanding of what goes on in that moment is transformed. As much as I worked to listen, appreciate and respect the feelings behind the jurors' words, I only now realize how far I was from being in that moment. Through this book, my level of appreciation, connection with the jury and the depth of my awareness are all radically improved. As I read this book, I kept a log of quotes that opened my eyes to a better understanding of what it is like to be a juror, of their needs and beliefs. Through this insight, my ability to connect with the true feelings of that moment is enhanced.

So, if my main objective is to come out of *voir dire* with credibility, there is a more ambitious goal. There is an opportunity to prove myself as a worthy leader of a group whose sole function is the search for justice. At this moment, group formation, alliances, self-selection and de-selection naturally occur. At this moment, I am thrust to the forefront of this process; the formation of a justice family that necessarily needs a leader in its search for truth. Wouldn't it be great if the jurors saw me as that person?

To be sure, group formation, the will of individual beliefs versus those of a larger group and my standing as their leader is worthy of an entire bookshelf of study and a lifetime of learning and experiences. Nevertheless, contained in the passages of this book are countless real-life examples of what jurors need to hear and express to feel a part of that group. You will learn what they need from their leader and what they expect from a lawyer. As I compiled my list of lessons, I could not help but feel overwhelmed with the insights these folks gave me.

As much as I got out of the insights of jurors, I got as much or more out of the conversations with the judges and trial greats. With these chapters, instead of making a list of great quotes, I copied the pages whole, highlighted them, and put them in my trial notebook. These discussions contain far more than decades of experience from some of the most successful people imaginable; they contain original thought, insight and observations that only come from spontaneous creativity. The free-flowing conversations contain so many pearls of wisdom, scenarios I'd never considered and approaches I'd never thought of, that I find myself anxious to try a case so I may explore these new things.

Every book, lecture or program on the subject of picking a jury comes from the perspective of the presenter. This book turns that notion on its head, and seeks the perspective of others; the result is a treasure trove of information, ideas and insights. As such, if you are preparing your first case for trial, or you are heading into your 200th jury trial, you will learn far more than you ever expected from the passages of this book. Happy reading!

— Eric Fong
Port Orchard, WA

Introduction

Few lawyers can claim to be *voir dire* experts. My jury selection experience is limited to cases tried over a thirty-year career, augmented by review and study of many of the books, videos and DVD's readily available on the subject, as well as participation in "action-method" workshops with skilled facilitators and like-minded colleagues familiar with role-reversal and psychodrama. Study and practice, I've learned, are helpful, but there is no substitute for boots-on-the-ground experience.

Many lawyers have not tried enough cases, laying it all on the line in a real courtroom setting, with court-imposed time limits, clever and objectionable opposing counsel, worrisome clients, anxious selves and a roomful of less-than-enthusiastic potential jurors who rightly value their time, jobs and families far more than they have concern for our clients; who bring with them all manner of beliefs and opinions; and who may think of us as "sleazy" and "dishonest" "ambulance chasers".

Fortunately, there are trial lawyers who have proven, time and again, that meaningful jury selection can happen. We know it happens, in part, by the impressive verdicts these lawyers, the "trial greats", obtain, often enough in major cases, that it can be said these are not flukes. Having watched some of them in action, I am always relieved to learn that there is no magic, only good case selection, hard work, superb presentation, an understanding of people, an understanding of ourselves and a willingness to march into battle.

I've heard it said, "If you want to know what a jury is thinking, don't ask a lawyer." I didn't want to believe that. We lawyers are, after all, the masters of our professional domain. But the more I reflect on my own and my colleagues' experiences with juries, and my experiences and conversations with non-lawyer family members and friends, the more I come to understand the powerful truth of that statement. Too often, with potential jurors, I've paddled upstream, trying to convince, persuade and exclude rather than listen, learn and accept.

I set out to learn, in a qualitative, non-controlled way, some of what may be prevailing in the hearts and minds of a cross-section of the real decision makers – the potential jury-eligible members of our community. To that end, I took the most direct route I could think of: I simply asked, in a series of informal face-to-face conversations, what thoughts, impressions, feelings and expectations were evoked upon mention of such concepts as jury service; plaintiffs, defendants and their attorneys; civil lawsuits; auto accidents; medical negligence; bias, prejudice and open-mindedness; credibility, humanity and connection; accountability and deterrence; burden of proof; experts and expert testimony; pain and suffering; remedies, damages and money awards; and anything else that might naturally, spontaneously, flow from the encounter in the time given.

The participants in Part One of this book represent what I believe, for these purposes, is a reasonable sampling of a cross-section of the jury-eligible community: male and female; Black, Caucasian, Hispanic and Asian; young, middle-aged and old; single, married and divorced; husbands and wives; parents and grandparents; lesbian, gay and straight; employed, unemployed, retired and homemakers; individuals of all levels of education; people working in the public and private sectors; in for-profit and non-profit environments; and in high tech, low tech and no tech industries and in creative professions; military veterans and those with no military service; homeowners and renters; liberal, conservative and middle of the road political views; religious and atheist; individuals with prior jury service and no prior jury service; and those with and without first-hand past or present involvement in the legal system.

Part Two and Part Three provide, respectively, perspectives of two sitting superior court judges who observe on a daily basis, year in and year out, what may, and may likely not work best with our prospective jurors today; and of two proven trial greats, practiced and polished, with unquestionably impressive records of success.

Admittedly, the sample size is small and I do not suggest or presume that the contributions of the individuals, judges and trial experts, as set forth in this book, are anything other than what they are: their personal thoughts, feelings, values, opinions and beliefs as expressed to me in the moment.

In Part Four, I share my conclusions, takeaways and what I learned about what matters to jurors and what they believe and need in order to feel good about us, our clients and the civil justice system.

I invite the reader to reach his or her own conclusions. I can share, however, that I learned early in the process that every individual, no matter how they may have presented themselves or appeared at first, brought instructive insights to the table, and I was invariably rewarded when I found ways to engage, encourage and meaningfully connect with them. It may be this book's greatest lesson.

— David L. Crump
Seattle, WA

Table of Contents

Part One – **The Jury-Eligible Public**

Part Two – **The Judges**

Part Three – **The Trial Greats**

Part Four – **Conclusion**

Appendix

PART ONE – **THE JURY-ELIGIBLE PUBLIC**

1

BE HUMAN

Caucasian female, age 78, widow, one child and two grandchildren, Retired

I think you need to show that you are a person, that you are as human as you possibly can be, to represent yourself as a human being.

Imagine yourself in a jury panel, in a courtroom, with a lawyer standing before you, ready to speak to you and your fellow jurors in the jury selection process. Until then you've only heard from the judge. The judge then says ladies and gentleman, please give your attention to the attorney for the plaintiff who will begin what we call the *voir dire* or jury selection process. Can you imagine that, and tell me what you are thinking and feeling and what is important to you at that moment?

> *First I would look at your eyes and then I would look at your body movements. I would look at the overall presentation of yourself and consider how much truthfulness am I hearing in this; am I reminded of someone I don't trust – or the other way around?* **Do I have a connection to that person? Does that person have a connection to him or herself?** *No matter what, there's not much you can do if you resemble someone else, and I will try to listen very closely to what's being said.*

What do you think you would like to hear about my client?

> **I think it has more to do with you, who you are, than your client at that point.**

What do you think you would like to hear from me or about me?

> **I think you need to show that you are a person, that you are as human as you possibly can be, to represent yourself as a human being,** *but not with humor at this time because it's not a joking matter.*

How should I address the jury?

> *You should try to look at each one of them, scan them but don't linger. See their movements. Talk to each one of them, but don't linger.*

What can I avoid doing that might turn the jury against me?

> *Avoid using the words "lawyer" and "attorney". Don't use a note pad or pen.*

You should have someone else taking notes for you. Focus your attention on the people in the jury.

Is it helpful or appropriate to address a juror by their name?

If you can use their names when you talk to them that would be powerful.

What kinds of questions would be good for me to ask?

Do you, the juror, have a family? Have you or anyone in your family been through anything like this before?

I'm of the opinion that before I ask jurors to share openly with me I should share and disclose something about myself. In other words, I'll show you mine, then you show me yours. What would be a safe and appropriate share for me in this context?

I think you need to ask if I can be open-minded to your client and the case.

Can I ask if anyone has biases?

You can, but I may say that I do have biases but I choose not to talk about them.

How should I respond to that?

Just say thank you, I appreciate your honesty.

Anything else?

You should dress well.

Thank you.

2

SHOW THEM YOU'RE LISTENING

Caucasian female, age 32, single, Non-Profit Development, M.F.A. Creative Writing

Pleases, thank yous, eye contact. There's that famous thing about when somebody asks you a question, you show them you're listening by a handful of things: repeat the question back, you do whatever to explain, to show you understand, those sorts of things. Allow a conversation to be more like, I understand you, I understand what you're saying, and then you repeat it back. It allows that connection.

You've never been on a jury before?

No.

Have you ever been called for jury service?

No.

Would you like to be?

I'm curious. Although, you know, jobs and money – depending on where you work, they'll pay you your regular service. Some places won't. That freaks me out. I think the law only requires like $12 a day or something really small. I can't live off of that. So, I'm interested in doing it so long as my job will pay me.

Given what you know about lawyers and jury service, I'd like you to imagine that you are in a jury box. You know what a courtroom looks like, so imagine that you have been brought in, you and about 20 or 40 other people. Actually, let's narrow it down to forty, because sometimes it's that many or more. A lawyer who is representing a person who's been injured is going to stand up and talk to you. Before anything, tell me – if you envision yourself in that situation, what are you feeling at that moment?

Nobody's said anything. I think I'd be pretty neutral at that point, because nothing's happened yet.

Right. Not so much about the parties or the case itself, but about yourself in that situation, as an attorney is ready to stand up and is going to start asking questions of you and your fellow jurors.

None of the questions have started. I haven't been made uncomfortable. I don't get very nervous about that sort of thing, so unless they hit a really funny button I'm comfortable, fine.

What might be a funny button for you?

I imagine if I was feeling attacked by a person. I don't really have many secrets, so that doesn't seem like it would be a struggle. There's some stuff I don't usually share unless directly asked. In that situation, I can't imagine that would come up. But we'll see. I have been injured in situations, so in that situation, maybe I'd feel inclined.

What are your expectations about the jury process, as you're sitting there in the jury box, before all of this unfolds? What are you expecting will happen?

Everything I know about what would happen at that point I've learned in the movies, so my guess is they would ask questions and make judgments based on how they think it would favor their client best and that could mean anything from political leanings to mode of transit or situational information related to how that person was injured or lots of things.

If the attorney wanted to ask you about biases or prejudices, how would you feel about that and how would you like to be asked about that if that were going to come up?

That's fine. They should feel that right? They should go in, I would hope, knowing some of your biases. **I guess it would depend on what the biases are to be asked.** *If they were like, do you have any biases? Well, that's subjective and who knows. I know some of them.*

What if they were to ask about just your ability to be fair?

I think I am relatively fair. Does everybody think they're relatively fair?

Some more than others, I think.

I would be just a little bit more – that would be a very easy way to be asked the question. I would feel comfortable with that and that should really get the best results that way.

What do you think would get the best results with you?

For me, I think that would be fine. I think I can be fair. I think I can be objective. But I also think most people aren't really very self-aware. Maybe that's true for me, too. So, who knows what kind of results you get with a subjective self-reflective question like, are you a fair person?

If you were asked, do you have any biases or prejudices that might affect your ability to be fair in a civil case where someone is trying to get money for injuries, how might you answer that?

I feel a little biased in each direction. A friend of my father's is famous for getting money out of any situation he can and right now he's living quite handily after. But almost the entire time I've known him, he's gotten money from any employer or another and then gone out golfing. I mean, I got hit by a truck who wasn't paying attention and took a free right, and the cops declared it my fault because there was no witness. I was in the hospital and physical therapy for a long time.

That affected you.

Yeah. I – could have been so much worse than it was, but, you know, serious knee injury for about a year. I don't drive. I ride a bike, so that takes that out of commission – besides the daily impacts on my ability to live.

You no longer ride the bike?

No, I do now. But that took a while, I think about a year, to get back on full-time, really riding.

Is there anything we would need to know about you as an individual that would help we lawyers determine whether you would be a good juror on this particular case or not? Is there something we would want to ask you?

Well, I don't have any skeletons in my closet, if that's what you're getting at, but I don't really know.

Let me put it a different way. What do you think we might want to know about the other jurors in the pool with you?

*In this case, **if they'd ever injured somebody, been in a case like this or knew somebody who had sympathies in that direction.** And if we already know if they hired a lawyer or anything then that stuff's useful. **Health, jobs, medical biases,** probably.*

Tell me about your generation, your friends who are in your age group. How do they feel about the legal system and jury service and people who are injured and are seeking to get money for it?

My friends? I know at least two other people who've been injured in car accidents and they never have gotten money from that. It seems like maybe a sense of what's expected when you're – at least one of my friends was taken out of work for like three months, and you know, stuff like that. Most of my close friends really have respect for the legal system. One of my best friends is a lawyer but, you know. I have a great love for Ruth Bader Ginsburg, but a disappointment with failures of the law and political systems, legal systems, in general. Conceptually, one hundred percent behind it, but I think people in my generation mostly talk about movies and stuff.

In terms of justice or just movies in general?

Just movies in general. One of my friends is a lawyer and we do talk about politics sometimes, but I've never talked to my friends about the jury system and how they feel about it.

What would turn you off about a lawyer who's talking to you? In other words, what

might cause you to be defensive or to not like this particular lawyer? What, – if they were to say something or do something, might that be?

Being patronizing, being mean and kind of yelling; that wouldn't be very nice. So don't be mean.

How can a lawyer such as myself show you that he or she is human? What can they say or do to show you that they're human beings, not just lawyers?

You're talking in this weirdo jury selection process?

Yes.

I don't know from the outside, but what is the interaction like? Because if you go up and ask a question or sit down –

I have about 30 to 60 minutes to speak to the jury uninterrupted, and I can talk to everybody, and learn about them in a short period of time.

Pleases, thank yous, eye contact. There's that famous thing about when somebody asks you a question, you show them you're listening by a handful of things: repeat the question back, you do whatever to explain, to show you understand, those sorts of things. Allow a conversation to be more like, I understand you, I understand what you're saying, and then you repeat it back. It allows that connection. In a limited amount of time I'm sure it limits the amount of repeating you can do.

Would you want me to share something about myself if I'm asking you to tell me about your biases or prejudices?

Seems like a weird situation to do that. Maybe if there was a person who was having trouble coming forward with that sort of thing, it might be the kind of invitation that would work under their hand. If you were just like, hey, I hate Republicans, that would be weird. And then, situationally, that could be useful in getting the kind of information you want and building that rapport.

How do you feel about the concept of insurance in the context of we are seeking money but most often it's an insurance company that's paying for that. What are your thoughts? Your feelings about that?

Isn't that why we pay insurance companies? My feelings about insurance generally is sort of, well, it's kind of a scam. Spend $250 a month for your whatever, and then you use it once in your lifetime and – I know that's how they make money, but on the other hand, that's what it's there for. That's why you pay $250 a month or whatever you pay. I think that's fine. I think that's what they're there for. It's their job.

Going into a trial like that, even though the judge will tell you that insurance is not to be considered, do you think you know that the insurance is really what the target is?

No, I never knew they were the ones that paid up, actually. I mean, for certain things, like when I got hit by a car their car insurance covered my medical bills, it didn't cover any like life stuff.

You talked about insurance paying medical bills. We call those special damages because they can be specially identified. But the law allows another category called general damages for which there's no fixed standard. In other words, there's no formula for that. Some people, for whatever reasons, religious reasons, any personal reason, don't believe in that at all, don't believe that a person should sue their neighbor or their friend or anybody for money for physical pain and suffering. What do you think about that?

I think it's really complicated, and it really, really depends. It is a circumstance that allows for a lot of people to take advantage. I know some people really deserve it. I don't know. I'm not sure which is better, to have none or to have people taking advantage of the system.

Do you believe that jurors such as yourself are able, on a case-by-case basis, to police people taking advantage of that; to see that doesn't happen?

I hope so. Humans are imperfect. One would hope that 12 people sitting on a bench would have enough different experience that, for stuff like that, a balance would be seen. I think that was the original goal of the jury system to begin with. Obviously, time has shown us again that sometimes we screw up.

Are you thinking about a particular case in general?

In personal injury stuff, no, but there was DNA that just came back that had never been tested but proved a bunch of people that were on death row or in criminal cases and spent lifetimes in jail. So it's like, no, that was wrong – which, granted the jury couldn't know that.

Let me switch gears. We're still talking about civil cases and injured people. Instead of auto cases, let's talk about medical malpractice cases. How do you feel about people who believe that a doctor has caused a mistake that's injured them and have sued the doctor?

This, I think, concerns the same thing where if somebody made a mistake and a person's life is altered in ways that are just inconceivable, they absolutely should sue. There should be reparations, but I also think – I was in a bus that got into a car accident. A car ran a red light at an intersection and the bus ran right into it. Now when this happened, I was sitting there in a forward-facing seat and there was a gentleman in from out of the country standing in the middle who literally did a somersault down the middle of row. He was freaked out but fine. But then there was this older lady sitting there – and the contact was not that bad. We were coming from a full stop. Really not that fast.

There's a lot of momentum with a big bus.

The lady in front of me started saying we should sue, we should sue. You know, it didn't even bruise me. It wasn't that much. I felt bad for the guy who fell down the middle of the aisle, **but most people were just like that's just taking advantage of the situation.** *And I know that's not medical malpractice, but people take advantage of the situation. I don't have much faith in people en masse.*

If you were called on a jury, does your employer pay for your time?

I don't actually know. I know my last employer did. I've only been at this place for five months. Probably. They're generous about that sort of thing.

How do you feel about personal responsibility in the context of both the people who are bringing a case and the people who are having a case brought against them? How do you feel about rules and personal responsibility and the role that plays in the court system as a juror? Do you think – is it your sense that most cases are going to come down to a rule being violated or rules being violated and that's going to be how you determine who's right or who's wrong?

I should hope so. I take it no?

I agree.

I would hope so. **Not everything is black and white,** *so maybe there were two rules being broken, and then it gets fuzzy. But I should hope that most of that comes down to pre-existing known rights and wrongs.*

Sure. And if experts are there to help the jury on both sides, you'd listen to them?

Of course.

You said that you were in a car accident on your bike?

I was hit by a truck. And then a couple weeks ago, I was hit by a Porsche.

While on your bike? So you've had a couple of instances?

Well, one five years ago. A guy took a right turn across the bike lane – just wasn't paying any attention. I swerved, and he saw me in time to slow down and turn and he hit my fender, my rear-end fishtailed around, and I was fine, and my bike was fine. I don't know what magic happened to make that happen, because he was not going slow.

I drove here and a lady had been hit, the police were interviewing her and her bike was upside down. It's happening a lot.

It's occasionally very scary. But I really like riding my bike. I'm a happier person riding my bike, actually.

Do you believe that drivers of vehicles are not sensitive to bicyclists?

Oh, definitely.

Because we have these cases, bicyclists versus cars. There tend to be polarized opinions.

I don't think it's true for all. I think a lot of bicyclists are (expletives) too. The number of people I yell at every day is just – the other day I saw a motorcycle go in a designated bike lane, the opposite direction, to turn into his work. But didn't – I almost ran off the road and – flipped off by a motorcyclist. Definitely been yelled at by a number of cars, but I've also watched bicyclists run stop signs without slowing down or looking. There's fault on all sides.

Are there any political or religious or social affiliations about you that lawyers might want to know that would help them determine if you would be fair and impartial in a civil injury case?

You just want to know my political leanings, you know, I'm a raging socialist. I'm terrible. I used to belong to the ACLU and Red Cross and try to volunteer and that stuff. Working non-profit work. I work for Medic One.

Is there anything else that you'd like to share, maybe something that I didn't ask that you think is important, might be important to me or my readers?

You know, I don't know.

Thank you.

3

IT TAKES AWAY

Caucasian male, age 46, married, one child, Hyperbaric Technologist, Junior College

You want to be honest, but yet, you don't want to be selected in certain situations. It takes away from your home life to be in the selection process.

Imagine you're in a jury room with 20 to 40 other jurors; nobody's had a chance to be questioned yet. There's a civil case where somebody's been hurt and they're suing somebody to get money back for their injuries. As you sit there looking at the plaintiff's lawyer, who's going to stand up, who represents the injured person, what are you thinking?

First thing I think is what a snake. That's what I'd imagine. But at the same time you're torn because you know that they have to have some representation and that's what they're there for. You gotta be a psychologist sometimes with these people. They're anxious.

Tell me a little bit more about "what a snake"? What does that mean?

You know, a snake in the grass, kind of looking for an opportunity to represent somebody. I feel like I form an opinion on people initially and then I feel regretful after that.

What would you expect to hear that lawyer say?

Everything that the defendant's done.

Is there anything that lawyer could say to you that might change how you feel, initially?

Prior to – regarding the case?

Just when the lawyer's talking to you, to learn a little more about you before the trial starts.

I think my opinion would probably change a little bit depending on how they talk to you.

Is there a way that you could be talked to that might warm you up or give you a little more comfort with the individual?

Probably he would have to speak to me, because I have been in a court and you don't want to feel like you're just being torn apart on the stand to make somebody else win or lose.

At this time, what the lawyer's doing is talking to the jury to find out if there are people who might have some bias or prejudice, who might not be best to be on that jury for whatever personal reasons they have about it. Is there anything the lawyer could say to you that would make you feel more comfortable about that?

That's actually a tough one because I know a lot's going through your mind that you feel obligated to – **you want to be honest, but yet, you don't want to be selected in certain situations. It takes away from your home life to be in the selection process. I'm not sure. I don't know if you could change the way I feel or feel comfortable. I think it would be based on my own scenarios, my work, how much impact it would take out of time and money and also I think it would depend on how I view – I've actually looked at the person they're representing and formed an opinion upfront.** *I didn't want to, but you can't help it, you're human, based on maybe the way they look, act, and say things. So that would be tough depending on how I formed an opinion on that person they're representing.*

If the lawyer asked you, do you have any biases or prejudices that you're willing to talk about or admit to in this case, how would you feel? What might you say about that?

That's what got me off there last time. I said, yes, there is.

Are you willing to talk about it here?

It was a guy under the influence of an uncontrolled substance. The judge, they just gave us his story. He injured some people in a vehicle, driving, and ran into some innocent people.

This was a criminal case?

Criminal case. I looked at him and I formed an opinion. And the attorney didn't like my answer, because I flat out told him, I think he's obviously guilty, if he's – the judge just told you he was found under an uncontrolled substance and he injured people in a vehicle and two cops were the witnesses. How can he not be guilty of something? They booted me.

How did the lawyer respond to you?

He said, is there any minute possibility in your mind that this person, my client, can be found innocent, despite what's said in the courtroom? I said, not at this point.

Was he respectful to you in the questioning?

He was respectful. But I just was fighting myself the whole time, thinking you know what, I want to be honest, but yet, not disrespectful. **But let's face it, I didn't ask to be here.** *So that's what I had to do.*

Looking back on that, did you feel that was still the best thing to do?

It was the right thing for me to do, because I knew in my mind, I already knew where I sat on that case, and I think they did, too, obviously. But it wouldn't have been fair for me to not be non-biased to this guy either. And I didn't want to feel that way.

In the civil context, where you have a person who's been injured and they're suing someone else or a company, is there anything in your life that makes those kinds of cases something that you're okay with or not okay with? On general principles?

Yeah. Something I've heard on the radio about a case with McDonald's, involved a McDonald's napkin – sued McDonald's for not placing a napkin in his bag, caused him emotional distress, and he won. That was just a few months ago. So to me, that was just – my opinion. I don't know if it really did affect them that way, but I thought that was the most ridiculous thing I'd ever heard. I consider that really ridiculously frivolous. But probably most of the public would think that, that's why it made the radio. But then there's other scenarios where people tell me cases they were involved with and how it affected them, you know, wholeheartedly truthful and how detrimental it was to them financially or something else. So that's different to me. I see it differently.

How do you feel about the jury's ability to determine if the case is worthwhile or not? Let's say it's a case that justifies going through it. Do you think the jury, by the time they've heard the evidence, are going to do the right thing?

Ask that question again.

So we've got that McDonald's case, and that other McDonald's case; do you think that there are cases that are justified?

Yes.

On that gamut from McDonald's to righteous and everything in between, do you have a sense that if you're on that jury, you're going to get it right?

*I do. As people it's going to be human nature first to feel sympathetic. Or not. So it's going to sway you one direction or the other and **I think the first thing that people do is they size you up and see how credible you are as a person.***

Are you talking about the juror sizing up?

Sizing up the defendant or the plaintiff. Determining – they kind of position them, their views, on each one of those people and think, ah, he's a little shady, but I'm going with this guy right now until I hear further. That's how I see it. They don't see it the same way, other people.

And do you feel that's fair. Do you feel you do that with the lawyers, too?

Yes, probably based on personality. You kind of expect, even though it's not realistic, you expect people to think and see things the way you do. And when they don't, you start looking at them differently. It's the way they come across to you.

How do you feel, in general, about the notion that the law allows people to bring claims against those that injured them through some negligence or recklessness?

I feel there is definitely legitimacy to having that ability. My own scenario when I was in the toxic mold case – I was in and out of the hospital, hundreds of thousands of dollars in bills.

You've indicated a family member or close friend in law enforcement, legal profession, and the medical profession. Does that color how you feel as a juror when you're sitting in that courtroom?

No. I have to think about why I feel that way.

Any particular one we're talking about here?

I think because I'm not fanatic about law enforcement or medical and some people are really extreme. They're pro law enforcement. I think it doesn't make it neutral for them. It's all law enforcement. There's no other. It's black and white, no color in between. So I think they're too tainted that way.

Do you see yourself as an in-between person and non-black and white individual generally?

I try to be. I do. When it comes to the law and how things are – like the police – I've been troubled about all the shootings going on with the African American kids. None of us really know what took place in any of those events, but I think the news puts some false views out there or maybe some real views, I don't know.

We form opinions.

We do form opinions.

As you're looking at a lawyer, the one who represents the injured person, is there anything that lawyer can say or do right away to show you that he or she is human?

I think telling the jury a little bit about the person.

About the lawyer person, or the –

Lawyer's – who they're representing.

A little bit about who the attorney's representing.

Mm-hmm. **About them, their life, do they have kids and are they married. You know, this guy's – citizens who are being proactive in society, out working, are they trying to work – just a little bit of that. Their character stuff, I think, too.**

How about the lawyer talking about the lawyer, him or herself? Anything about the lawyer you'd like to know?

I think it would help if a lawyer told the jury about themselves, whether they're married and got kids, and maybe even one of their hobbies. Gives an inside view of the person, what they're representing as far as the law is concerning, but what about them as a person, too? I guess you can get a little too much, but –

Here's why I ask: a lawyer often will ask a juror about themselves, asking you to share a little bit about you. Some people believe if the lawyer's going to do that, the lawyer should share a little bit about themselves first. I'll show you mine and then would you show me a little bit of yours? A little self-disclosure. So I'm going to ask you about bias and prejudice, should I share a little of my own? How would you feel about that? Is that too much?

No. I think it's not. I think it'd be a good thing. It might even clear up a little bit of somebody's thoughts about forming opinions of these guys up front, and sticking to it. I think if they talk about themselves a little bit, maybe even say, oh, they're human. They're doing their job. They're representing what they're supposed to. They're only supposed to do the facts and that's it. I think that would help.

You've got 40 people in that courtroom who are prospective jurors. What do you think I, as the lawyer in the courtroom, needs to know about those people? In other words, what should that lawyer ask them?

I think it would depend on the case.

We're talking about a civil injury case; could be auto accident, could be medical malpractice, could be a workplace injury.

*I would ask if they'd ever sued somebody in a civil case for any amount or if it were pertaining to the same type of case. I would find out what they do for a living, because that might impact how they'll see the case. If they're an insurance adjuster; maybe they were the doctor for this guy, and you know, on the stand – and then maybe ask if they have family, kids. Are they married? **Get a little bit of character information on these people, what pushes their buttons, heartstrings, that kind of thing.** Because I think you can ask them two questions and know a lot more about somebody than they want you to know.*

What are those two questions?

Are you married? What's your favorite – what's your sport or hobby? Says a little bit. It tells me a lot about the person. I think that makes a big difference. I've had them ask different questions. Back in my case, one of the jurors went to my wife's family's church and knew her parents. But they let her stay on the stand. It was weird. That's something right there: do you know the people?

How do you feel about insurance being the primary target? In other words, money is the issue here.

I think the insurance should be the target if they're taking a monthly premium for some coverage and they don't produce what they said they were going to produce at the end. They met the criteria and they're still trying to find loopholes. For the case where I think somebody was reckless in a vehicle, arrested for reckless driving and hurt somebody or something, then I think the insurance should be liable for that, that person should be. But the same time, who's going to pay for the medical bills on the other end? I don't know. It's hard to say.

In injury cases, we have two kinds of damages. We have special damages, and they're all the costs that the person's incurred out-of-pocket. Medical bills, car repair, those kinds of things. And then we have a category called general damages where there's no fixed standard. In other words, pain and suffering. Every case is different because we have no rule about how much money is right in a given case. How do you feel about general damages and the idea that the lawyer – well, let's say, my client has had pain and suffering and that that's compensable under the law as well as those items that are specifically have been spent. How do you feel about money for pain and suffering as a component of a claim?

*I think I would have to see. **I would have to hear how it affected them, pain and suffering wise. Their relationship at home with their kids and their family, wife or spouse, you know. Their job. Show that they couldn't function in their job, they couldn't function at home, a few things like that. That's where I think you'd have to paint a picture, really, really clear.***

Do you think expert testimony can be helpful in these cases?

I think it could. Here's my brother-in-law's analogy. He's not suing anybody, but he recently was in Maui bodysurfing and took a header into the bank. Now he has a spinal cord injury. The minimal functions, and he's walking, but he can't lift his arms or move his hands. And I thought, wow, that's a case where, I mean, if it were a scenario where he was suing somebody for that, in that scenario, and somebody could say, well, he's not functional. An expert could say, he can't even change his own clothes, perform hygiene, and things like that. That to me is where that would come in.

Do you think that non-expert witnesses are helpful in those cases?

***I think they're probably just as significant because they're people that know them or work with them, are around them and witness their inabilities or lack of ability.** Things like that.*

Is there anything else that you'd like to add about anything I have overlooked? Something you'd like to share?

I was thinking about my own mold case. When you talk about pain and suffering, you know, I was thinking – we won one of the largest toxic mold cases in the country.

Was that a class action case?

No. Just my wife and son and I. God, we had news team after news team afterwards, how it impacted my life with everything. Everybody you thought was a true friend or family, they're jealous. That totally is real. But the other downside is, we had a lot of money, put a lot in a trust for my son, big trust. Pissed away a lot of money. Helped family with some money. It's never enough.

But I was looking back thinking, the biggest thing that stood out for me, I didn't even want to sue anybody. We were in an apartment, and I ended up in the hospital, just couldn't breathe. Found this problem and they said, hey, you need to call the health department, I think it's where you're living. The immunologist – pulmonologist. The first thing that I think about was, my son, who was only six, was he wanted to play, can we go out and play kickball and stuff. I lived on an inhaler. I couldn't even kick the ball, and I'd have to sit down on the steps. Living like that was miserable. Fighting – as a young man. So it's weird.

With your experience in that toxic mold case, as a plaintiff in a civil case, would that color the way you sit as a juror for a person who's also seeking some kind of a claim for injury?

It actually kind of makes me put the burden of proof on them, because I lived through it. And I know that when you've had a case, which we were in a position to have to seek legal counsel because the apartments were giving us hell. We just wanted to be moved out. So I know that people see money, and especially a news flash about it – I'd be more likely to screen the person on the stand about how credible they are with this up front, just based on this whole having been through that situation, it would probably make me feel that way.

Thank you. I appreciate it.

4

A GOOD SMILE

Caucasian male, age 68, divorced, two children, Counseling Psychologist/Vocational Expert, Ph.D. Psychology

I know the attorneys are there to convince me that their side is right. I'm not looking for them to change that, because that's the way the system is. So it gets down to real personal stuff. It's back to the, he's got a good smile. I think that goes a long way. Farther than you'd like to think it does.

With that framework in mind, my first question is, as the judge says that to you, what thoughts and feelings are going through your mind?

*It surprised me. I hadn't ever thought of this before but the very first thing that popped into my head was nothing to do with the facts of the case or trying to glean information about the plaintiff, but **it was all about the attorney**. And what it was specifically that came into my mind was doing a quick – but probably it'd be pretty long lasting – assessment of what kind of an attorney is this? Is this, for lack of a better phrase, an ambulance chaser that's a slimy guy? Or is this one of the really, truly, okay reputable ones that aren't like that. And I never really thought before about how quickly I'd make that determination, because for me, if it's a kind of a slimy ambulance chaser guy, which is very much the minority in my experience at least, but they are there, then they've probably lost already. So I'm looking at the way they're dressed and certainly the way they present themselves and just the way they use words. I'd be paying a lot of attention to that.*

I can ask this in two ways: I could say, how would a reputable attorney present themselves in terms of that attire? Or, how would a disreputable attorney look to you?

*I think of it from a perspective of the slimy guy. I would say I don't know how they'd look, because I've seen people who are terrible dressers and look pretty sloppy and miss big patches of hair on their face when they shave and they're still really good attorneys. **I don't know that I'd pay as much attention to look as exaggeration right off the bat, you know, that kind of dramatic presentation of the facts that's so polarizing.** But I've gotta say, there's no way to get around, whether you like it or not, for me – not so much the grooming or the way the person is dressed, but **those subjective intangibles in a person's presentation. It's like when you're talking to a used-car salesman.***

Do you have a sense the other 60 people in that room are approaching it likewise?

I would guess they're not. And I think my approach is partly by nature but it's partly because I work in a closely related profession. One thing I know – this is not certainly an absolute – is that **good attorneys tend to pick good clients,** *you know? And the bad ones tend to gravitate to the – anybody that wants to make a fast buck one.*

That's a great point. You wouldn't be the first person who has talked about the slimy lawyer as a male figure. Do you think that there are slimy female lawyers?

Sure. I think you just don't see them as much because, at least for me, they still in most venues are a minority. And considering my age, they were a much, much smaller minority 20 or 30 years ago, so you just didn't see them very much. Actually, the women attorneys I've known going back have been really good. They were people I'd trust with anything. They were competent, smart, honest. There just aren't as many of them. But I've certainly seen the slimy ones, too.

Do you think your training, your background as a psychologist and an observer of people and human interaction leads you to look at things differently than say the average non-psychologist?

In a way. I think I might look at people a little differently, probably a little more liberally, giving people the benefit of the doubt a little bit more until you get to know them, because I know how misleading it can be when you just hear something, or on an initial meeting when you're talking to somebody, they can give you a bad impression, and yet, that can be overridden with some time and depth. I don't know if that's a byproduct of training, though. That's where I might take issue. I think that's more of a hardwired personality feature than it is to do with my training. I think that's what probably attracted me to that as a profession. But it was probably always there. I think it would have been there whether I'd gone into something completely different.

How can I identify those people in the jury who are more likely to possess a capacity for giving the benefit of the doubt? Or instill in them a willingness to be open to giving the benefit of the doubt, early on? Is that even possible?

I don't know. You can never say it's not possible, but I think it's really difficult. One of the things I did a lot of way more than most psychologists in my career and it was – my primary emphasis – was group work. I've done so many groups. When I was in practice, I had multiple groups every week that were groups that went on for years. So I know how – even if I consider myself fairly open and liberal, I know how at the same time, I'm also kind of quick to form an initial impression and maybe a negative judgment about somebody. Or the other way around. People that at first glance, I really like them, but I know how much that can change. So for me, even if you're just talking about me alone, even if you got my honest evaluation of myself on the front end, you wouldn't know much yet because I haven't really seen the participants and the litigation enough to know.

Tell me what you have a sense, overall, of the other people in the room that are the potential jurors. What is your sense of that? Those people in general?

Well, because I've only done this once –

It doesn't have to be based on the experience that you had. It can also just be your sense of things "as if".

I certainly get to see juries, doing what I do, but you almost have to discount that because I don't see them for any length of time. I just come in, give my testimony, and go. I take their questions if they have them, but I would say that I've been kind of surprised at the quality of questions when I've been asked questions. I thought they were good questions. One stupid question, I can remember last time I had to do that. And I remember one juror that asked me a question that just didn't make sense. I tried to verify that, and finally the judge interrupted and said I don't understand that question at all. It doesn't make any damn sense to me either. So we stopped. But I've been surprised at the quality. But frankly, my bias going in is it's a low quality group of people in general. That's not my experience having done it.

When you say "quality," what metric are we using?

Well, from a social perspective. These were more blue-collar, tended to be older, more retired, not well-educated. Looked like NASCAR fans for the most part. But my actual experience – and that gets back to what you were asking earlier, too, because that is my impression, I think, often going in. And yet, I walk away with a completely different one by the end of the – whatever it is, even if it's a short – just me doing my testimony or if I'm part of the jury and sticking with it. **When I was on a jury, I was really impressed with how conscientious people were. They really wanted to do the right thing. And they really understood the implications of not doing the right thing.**

Do you have a sense one way or the other that potential jurors who express a real desire to be on the jury may likely have an agenda? Or are they just really interested in doing the service?

I don't know the answer to that.

Let me ask it this way: I once heard a great trial lawyer say, he generally distrusts those who express a strong interest in being on a jury - and he may be talking about criminal cases - because he felt that anybody who was in a rush to sit in judgment on another could not be trusted.

But that presupposes that that's the reason the person is so anxious to be on it is so that they can sit in judgment. I think for some people, it's certainly not the big bucks and it's certainly not that it's not a frustrating kind of maddening thing to sit through, to be on a jury, but I think for some people, it's a social obligation. I know I felt like that when I did it. I've been called probably four times, and I'd gotten out of it before – which I can do. I can easily get out of it. But then when I took the case that I did take, it was more a sense of social obligation. It wasn't to sit in judgment necessarily. I mean, that's part of it, I guess. You know you're doing that. But it's the right thing to do, and I would guess most people are like that, but it just feels like, I don't want to do it all the time and I've weaseled out of it since then because it's just too time-consuming for me when you're self-employed. When I did it I was employed. I got my salary whether I was sitting down there for a week or not.

As a prospective juror, what would you value the most in that moment? Are you valuing participating in the process as a civic matter, or are you valuing your time that's important to you? What is it that is of the most value to you that should be respected?

My first reaction is, it's going to change a lot kind of depending on when you ask me that during the course of the trial.

How so?

*Just as a for instance, one of the things as a juror and especially in a criminal trial like the one I was involved in, a fair amount of my time **I was really frustrated to be on the jury because the jury itself was constantly being dismissed.** We'd go sit in the damn jury room while attorneys argued motions and objections.*

Did any party pay for that result? The plaintiff or the defendant?

No, we felt like everybody was doing it. And the judge was doing it. And what you felt like was, it's not just the disruption and the inconvenience and all that and the awkwardness of going to a room where you're not really supposed to be discussing what happened – but of course you are – but it was that you felt – at least, I felt like I was being denied facts. That it would have been valuable for me to hear the arguments and hear how the judge ruled on the arguments. Because I'd get a real sense for things that I felt wasn't fair to me as a juror to hold me responsible and accountable for the decision we're going to make when I'm excused so constantly and just disrupted. But I felt like it wasn't fair to the, in this case, the poor old cab driver that got the (expletive) beat out of him or to the two guys that were charged with the crime. I thought, there's such a barrier between me and what feels like most of the information that was elicited during the trial. I felt like I was out more than I was in.

What do you think the average juror who's sitting there, the average potential juror, wants and needs in that moment?

I suppose that's going to be different for everybody, because some people want to be told what to think. Other people, it's the last thing they want. For me, it would be all about the more information I can get the better. It's so scripted in a trial, by both parties, that they are so –

Even in the jury selection?

*I think so. Yes, I understand why they do it and why that strategically makes sense. On the other hand, **I feel like the more information I can get, the more permeable the boundaries between me and the information, the better. And I feel like court is a process that often just by its nature is set up to provide*** *impermeable boundaries to a huge amount of information.* *Everybody wants to do their own spin. And I want more than just that. It's like when you're a therapist. It's great and critical that you get all the stuff from the person you're seeing, but after a while, it's really important to get family and other people to tell you what they think because you get a different perspective. And for me, my single biggest frustration with the process was I felt like, first of all, you've hamstrung me because I can't stand up and ask questions.*

In one of our early conversations, you mentioned this notion that you're observing as a potential juror that there are two sides who are coming in with more or less intractable positions that are different from one another.

Well, you always know that whatever A says is going to be opposed by B, just on general principles. That there's no – on either side, you just don't ever hear them say, hey, that's a really good – I never thought of that or – it just doesn't happen. And so you know that, yes, they've got relatively intractable positions, but not completely, because I think anybody's capable of retooling their argument halfway through if they have to. If you've got a loser you can come up with a new one.

How can the attorney who's attempting to put their case before you, and knowing that's a potential issue, address that in a way that puts you at ease or makes you feel better about that? In other words, the attorney knows that his or her position is diametrically opposed to the other attorney's position and that's the way it is coming in. What, if anything, can the attorneys say or do to acknowledge that? If they even need to?

You know, short of soliciting questions constantly from jurors – which I don't know if you can even do that – so that you can answer them as you go. And maybe just a couple of written questions in the morning and a couple in the afternoon that you can be a participant in, but I don't know if that's possible. And I don't know what else you could do, because it's just the nature of the process. It's not that I necessarily blame attorneys for being that way and being oppositional with one another, but it's just the way the system is built, so what could I ask an attorney or what would I want of an attorney that would make that less of a problem is pretty tough. Because it's less the attorney and more just the system to me. And to some extent, then we've gotta factor in the judge, because some of them can be real inquisitive and interesting and some can be (expletive) and opinionated.

As you're sitting there in that "as if" moment, what might the attorney say or do at the outset that would put you at ease in that moment, or conversely, what would they do that would make you uncomfortable in that moment?

They could show their hand enough that I would suspect them of being Tea Party members; that would bias me against them. Anything that they did like that. And for other people that would be gray. So I don't know. On the other hand, I really try to instinctively evaluate both the attorneys, their intellect, and I don't know *how you could fake that. **To some extent, their honesty, integrity.** I mean, it's like going in to buy a car. The nicest, most personable used-car salesman, the guy you really like or woman you really like, **they're still there to sell you a car.** I know it. I know that's the rule, and **I know the attorneys are there to convince me that their side is right. I'm not looking for them to change that, because that's the way the system is. So it gets down to real personal stuff. It's back to the, he's got a good smile. I think that goes a long way. Farther than you'd like to think it does.***

What about lines of inquiry or questions that the attorney could ask or avoid? Keep in mind that the purpose of *voir dire*, as the legal system would like it to be, is to find out if a juror has bias or prejudice, whether they can be fair and impartial. In that moment, are there questions or inquiry that attorneys can safely go down with you or are there lines of questioning that they must absolutely avoid when they're seeking to learn about bias or prejudice for suitability?

For me personally, there would be nothing I can think of that I'd either want them to or appreciate they avoided. There really isn't.

How about if they were to say, you know, I'd like to ask you if anybody here has any biases or prejudices towards civil lawsuits, for example. What do you think about a question like that?

I have an answer to it: I know what I think about civil lawsuits. I think for the most part they're a good thing, a necessity, a good way to settle differences, to hold people accountable. I think they can be misused. I don't know. It runs the gamut like it would for you, I think. No different. I wouldn't begrudge anybody asking me things that I think most people would think are a little too personal, like – I'm pretty atheist. I wouldn't mind that. That's, for most people, too personal. I wouldn't care. If it helps you, you know, me, I'm fine. So I don't know that I have any reservations that way.

Without getting into any specific biases or prejudices that you have – and I'm going to put out the position that I think we all have them in one way or another.

Of course.

But what's important, I think, for the lawyer, is to get people to tell us what those are if they're willing to do so without being offended by it.

And if they know them. I don't think you always exactly know it.

What strategies might be helpful in determining or getting people to open up and shine a light on some things that they're not all that aware of, in that environment?

*It's tough. Because **I think all you can do is just raise the issue, just like you're raising it here, and have people think about it for themselves.** I don't know that there's any script you could play back time after time, individual after individual and get that. **To me, it would be a good thing to talk about as an attorney, to say, look, we've all got biases.** To make it even worse, probably* *most of us,* **the things we're most biased about, are things we'd probably deny being biased about because we don't like to think of ourselves that way.**

Do you think there are better words than bias or prejudice to use when having that inquiry?

I like bias. I'm not saying there's not a better word if I really thought about it.

What about an attorney, before asking jurors to share some of their biases or prejudices, sharing something of him or herself – as they say, I'm showing you some of mine, and now, if you would show me some of yours – to keep the social contract balanced.

My initial reaction is don't do it. I'd have to think about that a little bit more, but I think you risk looking manipulative. Even if you can do it with the best poker face in the world, and even if everybody's crying at the end of it, I still think it feels a little manipulative. But that's – it's tricky.

If it were done, I imagine you'd say it would have to be 110% genuine.

Yeah. If it's not, then you risk creating an impression that you'll never change. And in a trial, they don't know you well enough and you don't know them well enough to do that. If it was a more intimate thing that was ongoing over months, years, that's another thing, like a group. **But to be too revealing too early, it looks attention-seeking. It looks manipulative to me. It makes me suspect.** *Not always. I mean, I think a lot of people could do it. And my initial impression probably would be, they're just trying to put me at ease. They're trying to give me examples that will make sense to me. And like you said, they're trying to balance the social nature of the whole thing. Still, in all, I don't know that it would. If it slips out in little bits during the course of the trial, that's another thing, that's where it might work, actually, pretty well. But to do it as a premeditated strategy, I'm going to show you what a good human being I am – because you're not going to talk about the bad (expletive) or whatever it is you do. No, I would say don't do that. But that might be just me.*

You've said that that smacks of manipulation, and so –

It feels like I'm being set up for something. I know you didn't say it on accident, but it's not –

Would you say that if you encounter something that smacks of manipulation it would beget resistance?

It could. Trial, it's like two competing car salesman, you know? It's nothing but manipulation. That's the nature of it. So just because it's manipulative, I think to some extent that's what you're there for is to manipulate on behalf of whoever's paying you. But it's the kind of manipulation. If it's an attorney that right or wrong you have the impression they're in it to suck as much money out of somebody else's hideous disfigurement as they can manage to, that's the kind of manipulation you'd hate. On the other hand, you'd really feel bad for the attorney's client that is going to be the victim of that in the end, along with the attorney. So, I don't know. The just being manipulated? No, I expect that.

Let's talk about the role – and again, we're still in this context of the jury selection process which as you know, is an all-too-short time period, maybe an hour per side, or two. Tell me, in general, your thoughts about the role that spontaneity plays in making a jury at ease or potential jurors at ease or comfortable.

In general, for me at least, being spontaneous is at least somewhat correlated that they're more open. In that sense, it's a good thing. On the other hand, again, it's like in a group. The first stage of a group is when people are just being introduced to each other and getting to know each other. And if you want to be a deviant in the group, enter that process, that beginning socializing process, and spill the beans about how you were assaulted as a kid and your parents were drunks and all that. You're going to be a deviant in the group right off the bat. So I think it's just not time for that. Especially, when you're talking to a jury, that's the very first thing that happens as far as the jury's concerned. **So I think yes, spontaneous is good, to not look rehearsed, to look like you're more in the moment. I think that's always a good thing.** *But whether I hold it against you or – I'm fine with that. Makes you more persuasive. I don't know. There's just too many variables to give a generalized answer to that.*

Do you think it's important if the attorney has memorized your name instead of referring to you by a number?

On the one hand, it wouldn't mean anything to me. On the other hand, I would think, wow, he really did that, huh? Without reading. That would be kind of a good thing. It would surprise me, but it would be, I guess, a good thing, because I'd think if you're taking the trouble to do that, you're serious. And it's impersonal but it's personal, too, at the same time. It's another one of those things that you could rightly say that's somewhat manipulative, but it's still – it's important to you. I don't see how it hurts you. I could see how it could help. I'm not saying somebody wouldn't be offended by it. God knows, you'd better get the pronunciation right. I don't know. I've not ever seen that done, but that probably would be a pretty good thing.

What's the best way for an attorney to ask questions of potential jurors about whether they have biases or prejudices or can be open minded?

My initial impression is like screening for a group. You don't do that with the group, you do that individually with people. I don't think you have the option. You might, I don't know.

We're asking a group, either I ask of the group a general question and ask for a show of hands or I zero in on a particular individual at a given time.

The problem with that is, then they're performing in front of group that they don't know and so you're going to get weird answers. Not as good, I don't think, as if you were going off in a little room on the side and talking to people individually. I suppose you can't do that.

No.

*You wouldn't do that in a group setting, where you're wanting people to work together to help each other and to really work, not just spout off opinions, but to really do things, and things that are comfortable and uncomfortable, that you don't get them together as a group of a hundred and then try to pick ten of them to make your group. You interview people one at a time, and you take a lot of time with them. Take two or three hours; I always did. It really does determine how your group is going to work if you're good at that and **you pick people that work well or have the potential to work well together.***

A luxury we don't have.

Yeah, and I don't know how you – just put myself in that position if that's the way I was going to form a therapy group is to send a letter out in the mail and $10 a day to a hundred people and then ask them as a group to just show their hands, I wouldn't know (expletive). I really wouldn't. I think you're going at it in a way that doesn't – I mean, maybe there's some way, if you can have them answer written things, maybe. But –

Given your professional experience and your educational background with groups, what stage is a group of potential jurors? What would you call that at that point? They haven't been selected to be the 12; they're just this group who are going through a selection process. Does that fit within any group dynamic we can read about or learn about?

Sort of. And sort of not.

I know it would probably be the early stage of a group formation.

Well, I think – no. The way you'd look at it in group theory, is that that group of a hundred people then is the group. And it's a group that doesn't last very long. It's just a group that lasts for an hour or two, because then it becomes another group that goes off on its own, and then you start all the stages. So you'd have to say that for the group of a hundred, they would go through, if it's really done right, they'd go through the same, whatever it is, five stages that any group would go through in a very short period of time. It's like structured groups, that they still go through those same stages of introducing and them kind of bonding and being real cohesive and then arguing and hating each other and then getting down to real work and then terminating as a group.

That's not happening in just this jury selection. All the stages?

*It can. **You'd really want to be aware of the stages. I can't think of anything as a facilitator of a group that's more important.** It's not that you jump in and offer your enlightened opinion on anything, it's that you understand what stage the group's in and really work with them accordingly. In other words, you* *don't push people at the start when they're just getting to know each other. You don't push them to be overly revealing or confrontive. You don't want that. You don't want to short circuit. You want them to move from stage to stage on their own steam. You don't want to influence that. Because if you do, it's going to (expletive) it all up and they'll never do anything well. So I think just being aware of where they're at at a given time is pretty helpful. But it's difficult with those huge numbers they work with in this short time. It's not even really a group. It's – I mean, it is, but –*

I've got a working hypothesis that much of what's being taught about the jury selection process for lawyers is dangerous and all that needs to be asked, especially given the constraints of time, is an open-ended question of the entire group: can you be, do you believe you can be, fair and unbiased in this case? If you can, raise your hand and say you can. I'll accept you. If you think you can't, I'll say thank you and ask the judge to excuse you. And just accept that group as it is, in the first 12 people. I may exercise my challenges peremptorily, if I wish. The point being, I'm going to end up with the same result whether I risk individual and group questioning or if I take them at their word.

The only thing I might do a little differently is not just let it go by saying, can you be fair or can you at least be aware of your biases and then be fair, at least in this particular case. **I think I might spend a little more time talking about what you mean by fair.**

What I would say is, can you let each side start at the same spot? Can everybody start at the same –

I think that's a good way to say it. But elaborating a little bit on that. Then I think you're right. I would agree with you there. Your chances are every bit as good of getting a fair jury doing it that way as trying to pick out who was raised in Alabama and loves Jesus and all those things. If you can get people to really think about that, which I think you could. I think you could get them to think – this is hard, because – I go back to my experience with that hate crime. These boneheads walk in with their shaved heads, and really, they had 666 tattooed on their necks and their heads. One of the first things I can remember thinking is, where's my guilty stamp? There's no question that these guys are a couple of (expletives). This isn't the first time they've been to court for a hate crime, and this isn't the first time they've beat somebody up. But to ask me, can I give them a fair trial despite the fact that they've got the look of everything you don't want. They were just – and their lawyers didn't look any better than they did. God, there's just such a bias going in. And it probably was – I think it was correct in the end. I think to be biased was okay, but I think it was the right decision. I still think, it probably wasn't fair to them.

Taking it further: does it even matter that the questions are asked? Could I dispense with this *voir dire* process and by – I'm going to get a percentage of stealth jurors that are tort reform jurors; I'm going to get a percent of jurors that probably are okay with these kinds of cases –

You know, it's so interesting, because to do it, to really test it, to scientifically test it, you'd have to actually do that in a real trial. And that's just like human subjects. You can't do some of that stuff. My sense is, I think you'd be okay.

I'm just as good with the first 12 as I am with any 12?

*Within limits. Maybe ruling out the people that are obviously crazy or, you know, really goofy that they wouldn't understand it. **I might go for a pool that's, to the extent I could, that's a little brighter, that's a little more introspective.** I think that always helps. I'd rather have that than a stupid group. But I think you'd be okay doing that.*

Do you think the potential jurors who are there ultimately want to get it right, regardless of which group of jurors are chosen for the trial?

I think so.

As they see it?

Of course.

Let's talk about money. Would you want a lawyer to talk to you about the fact that this is a case where money, dollars are being sought, and would you want to know how much at that selection stage this case is going to be about?

*Boy, that's a tricky one, isn't it? That **money can be so biasing** because if you just throw out a rough million dollars for something, which these days isn't much, then you're right there looking right into the headlights of that, oh, that's what you're in for kind of attitude. And I think it's rough. On the other hand, you gotta get them used to it at some point. They might as well know, because it's going to come down to that at some point. And you gotta get them thinking that way, because I think, especially older people, come into it thinking a couple thousand dollars is probably just fine. **So do you do that at the front end, maybe very lightly?** Maybe very, very, just breathe on it lightly, somehow.*

Do you have any suggestions on how to touch on that?

I was thinking of something that's really oblique. But you know, a lot of these personal injury cases, I'm not saying this one – I'm not saying not this one, but we're talking about millions of dollars. These are not inconsequential cases. These are hugely expensive cases to try. And the damages, when you really understand how deep they run, like vocational damages, I think people don't really think that through very well, usually. Maybe something oblique that's not about the specific case but just about personal injury or med mal or whatever it is in general. It's important too, maybe, because you realize, a lot of these cases, almost every case, you're talking about millions of dollars here that are at stake.

The role of money in these cases?

***I think you gotta mention it.** You don't have to, but somebody needs to. It's probably good to put people on notice that this isn't $2,000 we're talking about here.*

What about the notion that different juries, hearing the same set of facts, can and likely would reach different conclusions about value. Is that something that jurors need to be thinking about or talking about?

I would guess people know that. Unless you're really dumb.

What do you think the average potential juror needs to know, more than anything, in order to feel like a bonded member of the tribe with the plaintiff's lawyer?

Just to not underestimate how important their individual honest opinion is and how difficult it can be because your opinion might differ from everybody else in the room. *And you have to know that, and you have to be ballsy enough to stand up and say so at some point.*

You're talking about the juror?

Mm-hmm.

How should the lawyer best honor that share?

I think it's pretty easy to talk about that, because people have that – especially on the front end, that tendency to, you know, let's all get along, we're all in here together. We're a little jurors group, you know, all stuck in here. But I think that's the part that's hard for a juror, at least in my experience. You've got one or two people on a jury that are not necessarily the leaders of the jury. They might be the people that talk the most, though. And they're often, at least in my case, the jury I was on, I remember there were a couple of people with really strong opinions. It's not that they weren't good opinions, they were, but they persuade other people, the people that are quieter, just by the force of their personality, and I think that's the one thing that, if there's any one single thing, it's you've gotta look at this from such an individual perspective. And then you have to be willing to stand up and represent yourself as an individual, that you're not part of the herd.

The attorney, you mean? Or the juror?

*No, the juror. That's what I'm here for. It's not to agree with everybody else and just say, okay, you guys seem to have thought through better than I have or you guys worked in that field so you know more about it than I do. No, you really have to have your own questions and your own way of looking and then know from the start – **and I think, even to remind people of that occasionally during the course of the trial is that you've really gotta think this through for yourself. That's hard to do, because "groupthink" is a real thing.** People in a group, they all agree on what we agree on. And so we've all kind of compromised what we really think to come up with our group opinion. But no, I think at least a really big factor is, can you remind people how important it is for them to be individually accountable to what they're doing. Because, God, if you're wrong, you know? It's like you've sent, even if it's a civil case, it's comparable to sending somebody to prison who didn't do it. Or letting the person who did it go. It's such a big deal, and **there's so much human tendency to regress toward the mean***

in the group, whatever the group's mean is. *Well, you think it was terrible, and you think it was great, so I'm going to be in the middle. Well, that's not what you really think, you're just reacting to those things. And to me, it would be kind of important to talk about that, maybe even that way, to say, you're going to be in a group of 12, somebody in that group is going to be adamantly on one end of the extreme and somebody else is going to be on the other. And you can think you're doing the right thing by saying, I'm going to be right in the middle. But maybe that's the dead wrong thing. Maybe everybody should be on that side or everybody should be on that, but you've gotta maintain your individuality and yet work as a group. I think if you convince people of that, then they pay attention to what's going on, and they actually think about it instead of just being such a passive lump sitting in a jury box.*

What's the lawyer's role in facilitating that?

I think you keep reminding them of it, to have rehearsed that a little bit. To really have figured out how you tell the story in a straightforward, easy to understand way, and then you do it a couple of ways during the course of the trial just to remind them that they're not – because I think that it really is. There is some of that dynamic. But I think you get a group of 12 people and you've got one or two people on this end and one or two on this end, and then – but then the other eight in the middle, that's what they tend to do, then, is kind of huddle together in the middle or you'd come up with some half-assed –

What can I do in jury selection to bring that up?

I think you have to just say it. Because it's not going to help you select anybody, but at least you're taking the time to prepare whoever it is that gets on the jury for being a little more –

To remind them or to say what? To hold onto the strength of your convictions?

Well, to do it, to have convictions, you're going to have to pay attention. This isn't like watching a movie or TV where you get to rerun it, even though you can ask questions and other jurors, well, what did he say? You do it all the time. But yeah. To understand how important you are as an individual. Because the focus is usually on –

"You" meaning the jury?

But it's you, the individual juror, that's really important here. You know, if you have strong beliefs, I'd probably use it as an example, but if you're just going to say, well, this idiot's way on this end, this idiot's really an extreme here, so I'll be in the middle, you've done everybody a disservice if you do that. Because what you've done is you've tried the two extreme jurors; you haven't tried the case. You're just trying the members of the jury. I would think that's important, to me. And it's something I'd like to be reminded of at a trial. Because it's so easy to get caught up in the influence of the group.

Even before the group is ever convened to talk about the case during deliberation?

It's worth mentioning. It doesn't take much time.

You talked about the deviant. How can I best identify the unfavorable deviant or lightning rod early, early on?

*I don't think you can, in some gross ways. You can tell people that have some chronic, serious mental health issues; they usually look like it. But other than that, **I don't think you can, because it comes as a surprise,** no matter how many groups you've done. I've probably done, at least over a 20-year period, as many groups as anybody's ever done. I did a lot. And you can't. You think you know, at the start, and boy, that turns out to be so dead wrong so often. It's somebody you never saw. **Because you didn't see them. You get their façade. And some of them have great ones** and they're smart and they can pull it off, but eventually, it crumbles. So I don't think you know. I wouldn't say there's not somebody in the world who could figure out a way to do it, but I've never seen it.*

Do you think that an individual potential juror who talks a lot and often - monopolizing - is somebody I would likely not want to have on a jury?

Not necessarily, no, because you're gonna have them. Every group is going to – even if nobody in the group is like that in any other setting, somebody's going to be like that on the jury. It just will happen.

Let's talk about narcissists: people with no empathy. How do I identify them? Might they be good jurors? I would think they wouldn't be. Do you have a thought on that? And how would you identify?

It's not necessarily the narcissistic person doesn't have empathy; that's more of a sociopathic person that wouldn't have empathy. But in that general realm of personality disorders, would you want somebody who's very narcissistic? Probably not. Or really histrionic; maybe that's a better example, meaning somebody who has an inordinate need for affection and attention. In general, it'd be best to avoid that, I think, because they're a distraction. And not because you don't know what their opinion's going to be, but they have a need to be a distraction. So they want to turn the attention of the jury away from the facts of the case or the person or the whatever, and the stuff they are supposed to be paying attention to, to them. Narcissists generally, at least psychologically, it's kind of a pursuit of perfection, often. So it's not necessarily that they don't have empathy, but they want to be seen as a perfectionist, important.

What do you think about those types of people?

Well, I think there's some that you can actually identify going in.

Would they be good jurors or bad jurors, generally? Would they be favorable or unfavorable jurors, generally?

Unfavorable, I think. Because, A, they're reading everything as though it's them, for one thing. And B, they have that, not conscious, necessarily, but that huge need to be kind of a center of attention.

Does that mean a power struggle between the lawyer and the judge and everybody else with that juror, if they're struggling to be the center of attention? They're going to struggle to keep that throughout the trial as well? Even among the litigants and their attorneys and the judge and everyone else?

Yeah. So many women that come in with bright red dresses on, I want to stay away from them, because that's almost a dead giveaway for a histrionic woman. I'm sure there are parallels for men, but that's one that I've been aware of since day one of graduate school and I started thinking about it and then talking to people who were genuinely knowledgeable about personality disorders. If you look at women who dress in that bright red all the time, they're almost always pretty attention-seeking. If it's an extreme case, it's bad, but still. It's a little more of a distraction. So there's some things I'd watch out for; that'd be one of them.

What can I do to increase my chances of making this group, the ultimate jury, my jury? Or what must I not do to hurt my chances?

It's one I think we could answer in some generality, but it's tough because –

Is there a mindset?

Well, to me, the one thing that the attorney or the attorneys do or don't do that influences that would be the degree to which I perceive them as being genuine. I'm not saying I can't get fooled, because I can, but I'd say at least 7 times out 10 I won't get fooled. So maybe three. So if I see you, for instance, the attorney as being – A, not really giving a (expletive) one way or the other, it's just, this is what I do for a living and these are the arguments you make, or I'm in for the money because the oil change on my Mercedes is more expensive than your Pinto or whatever. That ain't going to play well. It has funny offsets though because I feel worse for the person you're representing. I feel like they're not getting a good square deal because look who they got. But I would say in general, that kind of gets back to the smile stuff. There's something about a genuine smile that is – a fake smile is enervated on different neural tracts than a spontaneous smile. You'd be hard pressed to find one in a million people who could describe the difference, but they all know it when they see it. So you can say, well, this lawyer's got a great smile, so I'm going to do this – well, that ain't gonna work. It's gotta be real. And it kind of carries over, at least for me. I think, okay, if you're an attorney representing someone that I respect and I think you're really being genuine, I assume, I don't think about it consciously, but I assume you exercise those qualities when you agreed to represent this person. That you did talk to this person for a lot of hours or looked into everything. You read all their stuff and you really thought through it and you believe in it. Whereas, the thing I think the defense guys have working against them is, they don't do that. They just – here's your morning case and here's your hourly wage. Make the same old tired arguments you make on every one. But I think that's the big deal. I think being a real – and it's hard to do that, I think. It takes some calming down all the time, some kind of almost meditative stuff at times to really do that until it comes so naturally you can't help it, you know? But to be just really a – kind of a genuine human being. It's hard to do that. It's risky.

Indeed.

(Expletive). People might not like you. And then what? And you've showed them who you are and they don't like you – oh, oh.

They may not like you anyway, so.

Well, that's a rationalization. I think it still is pretty crushing. You have to do it, but.

Well, I thank you.

5

CONTEXT HELPS

Hispanic male, age 52, single, Designer, B.S.

You go through this process, you don't really have a lot of insight into what's supposed to be done, how it's supposed to be done, who you're dealing with. To be honest with you, to a degree, it's intimidating. You're glad that you're in the jury pool and not on the other side, whether plaintiff or defendant. So I think any time the lawyer has an opportunity to put how he's going to interact with you or what his goal of interacting with you, in the context, it helps you understand better. I think that not only serves him, it serves the entire judicial process better.

You have served on a jury before?

I have.

What kind of case was that?

It was a medical malpractice case.

What was the negligence they were alleging?

It was something about a woman in labor and the system they had set up to check where she was in terms of giving birth and how that system apparently failed to inform the doctors. And then the doctor wasn't real available and at the time that she went into labor or actually started to have the kid, there were complications and the kid ended up with disabilities as a result.

How long was the trial?

It wasn't really all that long. It was like five days.

Did they settle?

Yeah.

So you never had an opportunity to hear all the evidence and go through the deliberation process?

No.

Was that the only trial you've been on?

That and then I've been on a lot of mock juries.

Do you recall the jury selection process where you were brought into a room with a hundred or so other jurors?

Yeah, it's a weird process in the sense that you feel that everybody – the feeling is they've done it before except you. And you're passed along this process with very little information, very little communication, and it's almost like you feel like cattle being herded into one room or another and you're doing your process as a citizen, but in terms of customer service, in terms of trying to engage with the demographic that serves a vital role in the judicial system, that leaves just a lot lacking. You don't really know what you're doing or what you're supposed to do and you just have to wait. You can't leave, you can't do anything. And there's a lot of system rules, but none of them are necessarily well-communicated.

How about when you were finally brought into the courtroom with all those other jurors? Do you recall that part of the jury selection where you're there being asked questions by the lawyers?

I remember being asked questions.

That's where I'd like to focus. What I'd like is if we could go into that "as if", as if you were in that room again or a similar room with a group of - probably in that case, they had close to a hundred people in the room - somewhere between 40 to 100, I'm guessing.

I don't think it was a hundred, but it was a lot of people.

What I'd like to know is, the very first thing when you're in that room and the judge says, okay, I'm going to have the plaintiff's lawyer talk to you now in jury selection, or *voir dire*, and then says, Mr. Attorney, go ahead - what are your feelings then? How do you feel about the lawyer or the lawyers in the case?

I wouldn't have any opinion on it. I don't know enough. **I have no context, other than I'm being called in to be a potential member of the jury.** *So, the case I don't have any opinion on. The court, this judge, or the lawyers, I have no opinion. It's a blank slate.*

When you look at the people, do you form a sense about people as you look at them?

That's funny you say that. I'm aware of this study that was done, I don't remember where. I think it was one of the California universities, that when you see somebody for the very first time you make several assessments of them whether they're like young or old or healthy or ill, whether they're educated or uneducated. In that sense I make assessments of people, but I think you don't really have anything to go off of until people start talking to you. And the questions they are asking you, obviously it's from the perspective they have and that's how you start to get some sort of context for them.

How do you feel – in that "as if" moment – about the other people in the room with you?

I have an affinity for them, because we're all in the same situation. So I identify with them more closely than anybody else in the courtroom.

Do you understand what the process of jury selection is to do at that point? What's your sense of what the lawyers are trying to accomplish?

I think they're trying to weed out whether you know anything about the case or have biases.

How do you think the lawyers can best determine if a particular juror has biases or not?

I don't know if you truly can, to be honest with you. I think the way the process is set up, it only has the capacity to detect biases that the person with the bias is unaware of themselves. So, if you ask me questions and I give you a candid answer, but if I have a bias, and I'm aware of that bias, and I seek to conceal it, I don't think a lawyer's questions are going to be able to filter that out.

I agree. It's very difficult. Would you be willing to disclose biases if you had them? Well, let me ask you this. Do you think that you bring biases with you into the courtroom?

I think we all have biases to one degree or another. To say that you don't have biases is kind of incorrect whitewashing to try to make yourself seem an elevated human being, but we all have biases. Your inability or your unwillingness to detect what they are is more of a sign of weakness than like, you know, negates whatever you think you're gaining by saying that you don't have any biases; you do. And that's what I learned, not so much by that one court case, but more through the mock juries that I've done that really, the lawyers in the mock juries are really interested, and it's not the same sort of structure, but they're really interested in knowing what your biases are, because it also might be the biases of jurors in their actual court case, and if you can understand what that potential might be, then you can think about how to address it if it should present itself in the court case.

If you were asked, do you have any particular biases in a civil case – personal injury, medical malpractice, and such – what particular biases do you think you bring to the table that lawyers might want to know about?

To me, questions like that are so vague that I can't, without context – you have to bring in specific context.

That's very helpful, because that tells me that I need to formulate better questions.

Real general questions for me are almost useless, because there's nothing about me that tends to – I don't perceive myself as being this person that has a broad box reply or perspective to situations. You have to tell me specifics, and then I can form an opinion and then tell you whether I think that I might have a bias or not.

We frequently encounter persons who don't believe civil cases should happen. Some religious groups say you shouldn't sue your neighbor, for example. If you're injured, you should just go on, because things happen. That would be, I think, some people's bias, for example. Another bias is, you can sue, but you shouldn't get money for pain and suffering. You should only get compensated for your actual out-of-pocket costs. How do you feel about those two issues?

Again, in general, suffering, I'd need more specifics in regard to detail, but it's not something, in general, I feel inclined to award somebody compensation for, right? It's not a default area that I think is just as valid as anything else. Or and again, what's the context? What really is this person's pain or disability, as a result of whatever happened? So I don't really have any biases like that, but I can see, and I've been experienced with other people that just don't really like the idea of large civil settlements. I think that skews their perspective. And I can kind of see that too, you know. I think one of the things that I've been exposed to via the mock juries is trying to – not myself so much, but I've seen it with other people that – if I'm not mistaken, in this State you can't award punitive damages, but yet other people really want to rack up what they give somebody as a punitive means even though you're telling them as a fellow juror that punitive damage, they can't do that. No, you've just got to make a statement. It's like, do you understand what punitive was? So that's like again, what the bias that somebody had but they're unaware of it, so they're never going to expose it because they don't even see what it is.

Right. Even though the judge tells them that the only compensation they can give is an award – but your experience in the mocks is that some people do want to be punitive. If it's deserved

Definitely. If they perceive it to be.

If I'm standing up before you, how can I show you that I'm a human being? What can I say or do in that context of the jury selection that shows you that I'm a human being?

I think it's important for a lawyer to be able to come across that way. It's funny, in that court case I was telling you about, the plaintiff's lawyer, by the time we were finished, I really had a dislike for him, even though I had sympathy for the plaintiff, and I would have awarded in favor of the plaintiff. And the defense lawyer, by the end of it, he really accomplished something that I never thought was possible in the sense that I've never been offended on somebody else's behalf, but by the end of my time with him, I was just so annoyed with that guy, actually I probably would have made a punitive award just because of how negative he'd left me with. And that's just kind of irrational. One of the things about the plaintiff's lawyer that kind of annoyed me was, this child was born into the world because of circumstances; he just got the short end of the stick. So one of the things that he wanted to be awarded was lost wages, which, you know, this is newborn. This child, A, is never going to have a normal life, right? So how's this kid – this kid's *never ever in the employment picture. Seeking lost wages has nothing to do with this child, but it came across as somebody who was kind of flashy, like a lot of jewelry and stuff like that. The kid's not a part of the process, like that's more for money that he's going to get, right? So the context was, I could understand him wanting to get the most for the plaintiff's family, but when he was making that presentation and there was real stylistic contrasts between him and the defense's lawyer. In the end, it seemed that facet of what he was asking for was more about him than anything else. I think the mother and the father were just so distraught over what had happened. They just couldn't. They can't get what they want, which is a normal child. The child that has a full life, potential for a full life ahead of him. The money would have meant nothing to them in that regards, they just wanted to make – we wanted the hospital to acknowledge that they had done something wrong, and we have to shoulder the burden of it. Obviously if you take these on-going medical expenses that that should be their financial burdens. But **that's a good example of how the lawyer, their personality started to frame how I perceived the court case, and the more I disliked the defense's lawyer, the more I was not going to go his way no matter what.***

How do you perceive lawyers getting paid in these cases?

That's a great mystery. In the mock juries I do, people have a wide range of assessments of what the lawyer gets. So people will make – settle on an award and then – certain discussion, well, you know, the lawyers are going to get about half of that or the lawyer's going to get a third of that. And then oftentimes, the numbers change as a result of that, right? Because then you look at it as what the plaintiff should get – and what the lawyer's taking out of it, and you might want to adjust that accordingly so you feel that the plaintiff is getting what they want them to get.

What about insurance and the role of insurance in these cases? Do you have a sense, when you come into this jury box that insurance plays a picture before it's ever talked about?

It does play a role in how the award is determined, but I can't say that I think it plays a large role or a well-defined role. I think everybody has a sense for stuff being awarded and oftentimes it's noted that, I think like medical expenses, what's been paid, stuff like that. It's a consideration, but I don't really think it has a profound impact. I think a lot of people are still somewhat unsure of what that really means. And also, no doubt with the mock jury, you're given a more concise presentation. You don't have all the info.

Or the opportunity to spend time with these folks day in and day out for five, six, eight weeks or more. Do you feel or have a sense, when a lawyer gets up to talk to you in this jury selection process, that it's appropriate for the lawyer to share or disclose something of him or herself to break the ice? Or to say, if I'm going to ask you to show me a little bit about your, say, bias or prejudice, that I will also share something. Do you feel that that's appropriate?

I think it is appropriate, and I think it helps people put things into context. It's not like there's only going to be a veteran juror or somebody that's been in court cases repeatedly and this is old hat for them. **You go through this process, you don't really have a lot of insight into what's supposed to be done, how it's supposed to be done, who you're dealing with. To be honest with you, to a degree, it's intimidating. You're glad that you're in the jury pool and not on the other side, whether plaintiff or defendant. So I think any time the lawyer has an opportunity to put how he's going to interact with you or what his goal of interacting with you, in the context, it helps you understand better. I think that not only serves him, it serves the entire judicial process better.** *Because then you can come into this with very little knowledge. I was a juror before I was a mock juror, so I didn't really know what to expect. I had no insights whatsoever, other than in perhaps watching television shows, and I'm not going to take that for real. So* **I think that if a lawyer – particularly understanding – in exposing himself in a personal – using it as a means to share the subtleties of potential biases, I think it's helpful for people to understand. It will give them a context. Because the one thing I do see is that, talking to another juror, there's like a priority in everybody's opinion. But when it comes to what somebody like a lawyer and the judge said, then that opinion, because of that role that person plays in the court case, usually carries greater weight. So a lawyer talking about biases will probably have greater significance to a juror than another juror saying, I think that's a bias, and here's why I think that's a bias, right?**

How about problem jurors - people who clearly don't want to be there or clearly want to make it difficult. How do you think the lawyers should handle that to not have the pool be upset with the lawyer or anger anyone on the jury? We don't want to alienate people.

Right. To be honest with you, that is probably the biggest challenge. I've never been in the presence of a problem juror, but I think, via these mock juries, exposed to people that I think they would have successfully weeded themselves through the jury selection process only to expose their problematic behavior later. So I don't know what you can do with that. My sense is that there's two camps of people. Those are people that wouldn't say anything about that problematic juror, and there's others that want to address it but don't know how. Because really, if you feel like to talk to the court about a fellow juror, or you know, even these mock juries, that's not something you want to do. It's really a confined sort of – that's the one thing that I learned from all those mock juries that I've done, even though they're not real judicial court cases, essentially the dynamic of hiring a group of strangers to try to work together is, I think, the same. It doesn't really change even though it's not an actual court case. And that dynamic is really interesting. It's very telling. It's just kind of weird. One of the things I've discovered is that often – it's never the foreperson, right, not that I couldn't do it, I just don't want to do it. But I often find that whenever the discussion starts on deliberations, there's so many people that, whatever the first couple initial discussions are, so many people, rather than saying what their opinion is will just go like, what he said, or I agree almost entirely with that person and they're not really contributing to the conversation. And I know this might be ethically wrong, but in the course of these mock juries, sometimes I just play the role of the Devil's advocate, having done it a lot, to get the discussion or just advocate a different perspective. And what's really weird about it is, sometimes I can sway people who have already, maybe they're doing like a round table sort of thing, you start here and just kind of say what you would want to say about the case without really going towards a jury verdict. And it's really weird, because then I'll get to the point and I will persuade people that have already spoken, and it wasn't so much that what I said was persuasive, I think it's just that all of sudden that there was a break in the collective mindset of continuity of like, what he said. And I really feel, I think people will agree with what other people have said, versus stating their opinion. Because you know, if you're waiting on somebody within that line to come up with a different perspective for you to agree with them, I don't think you're fulfilling your role as a juror, right? How can I do a 180 on the prevailing trend and persuade people that have already agreed with that, right? You must have had some sort of seed of doubt but you didn't want to articulate it.

The purpose of jury selection – the court's primary purpose – is to find out who may be biased or prejudiced. Lawyers also want to get their theory of the case out there first. In other words, they want to try and get an advantage by talking about, in some way, what their theory is and how their theory might be better than the other side's. What do you think about those two roles, and do you think it's appropriate for a lawyer to start trying to talk about anything other than bias and prejudice or fairness?

In the end, there's this idealized concept of what the judicial system is. It's about justice; it's about being fair. But really, it's a competition. You have two sides competing with one another to find for their clients. And I think everybody's painfully aware of that. So I don't think it's inappropriate that a lawyer tries to get a forecast on what the strength of their argument is. That's why they're there. We know that. So again, based off the bulk of the mock jury experience, you'll have lawyers present their evidence, their expert's testimony, and you go back in the deliberations and it's all basically a wash, because everybody'll, like, you know, here's what the defense said, here's what the plaintiff said: it's a wash.

Do you think having been a juror, or just in your sense of worldly experience, that I'd be wasting my time to do anything other than talk to the jury about bias, prejudice, and fairness and to get as many of them to articulate their own personal biases or prejudices?

No. Your job is multitude. One of your clients is the court. You have to serve the court, or the judicial process. But you also have to serve your client. So whether it's the defense or the plaintiff, either way, you're tasked to do both. So I don't really think it's unfair or out of context for you to seek insights into anything other than bias. Potential bias.

I'm mindful that the jury's time is important, and also, the courts give us painfully little time to talk about this large group of people and really attempt to get anything done, meaningful about –

I agree. I don't know how you guys do it.

One of the questions I'm asking myself is, do I really want to spend time doing anything other than just asking the jury as a group, do you think you can be fair? And if so, I accept that, and leave it at that rather than go through this tortured exercise.

*I do think it will probably benefit your perception among the jury in your interaction with them and being respectful of their time. **I think one of the things you really resent about being a juror is that you feel like you're captive to a process that you more than likely wanted to get out of but couldn't get out of, right?** And so now that you're a party of it, don't waste my time. I'm here, let's go through this as quickly as possible.*

Do you have a sense that those jurors that wanted to get out of it could find a way to?

Well, yeah. To be honest with you, you could just expose a bias that's not even real. You could use it as a way of red-flagging yourself to get out of the jury selection process.

Did you have an opportunity to hear the opening statements of the parties in the trial that you were in?

Yes.

I'm curious to know your thoughts about those opening statements and the technology, the presentations.

I think the opening statements are important because as a juror coming in with a blank slate, you might have only the slightest understanding of what the case is about, so at least it gives you a – if you looked at it as like two camps. Here's defense, here's plaintiff, what are you trying to get me to understand? And so an opening statement starts out great in that regards. In terms of the technology that's presented, what's odd about that is, I think that oftentimes – I used to – have you ever been to this thing called the PechaKucha?

No. How do you spell that?

That's a good question. I don't really know. P-e-c-h-a-K-u-c-h-a. It's Japanese for a discussion. But basically it's this forum where people show 25 slides at five seconds each or something like that, and you have a whole bunch – it's almost like TED Talks, kind of like that, right? But I used to coordinate and run some of those events. What I discovered about that, and it's kind of what I relate to the *court cases, is that **oftentimes people are so fixed in to the technology of their presentation that it becomes a crutch.** If there's something not right about it, there's a break in the continuity. **A lawyer is telling a story.** Rather than relying on a PowerPoint presentation or whatever visuals you have, **there's a greater effectiveness if you have continuity and a naturalness to your presentation** versus me being this sort of technology to try to tell your story for you. That's a great asset, but it could also be a crutch because sometimes it doesn't work, it throws people off.*

I find that it always doesn't work.

And then it throws people off, and the lawyer assumes that once you get it back up again, that the way you perceive it has a continuity that it doesn't have. It's broken. It's more of a liability than an asset. Ultimately, I often find what's so weird about it is this is your case, why have a presentation that's broken, that you don't know how to move forward? It tells me, do you really know what you're talking about?

That's very helpful. I struggle with technology. Some great lawyers keep things very simple. I tend to err on the side of simple rather than the side of having too much technology, because – I'll relate a funny story. I went to a conference on technology for lawyers and without fail, every one of the presenters had failures in their technology.

That's funny. It's ironic.

For an entire day. The crucial thing we're taught as lawyers, if we're to be good, is that we have to have rapport with our jurors, our judges, and everybody. Having sat through this trial, or part of it, and these mock juries, what are some prevailing behaviors you've observed that have been very helpful? Actually, let me back that up – that have not worked, that the attorneys have exhibited?

*Well, technology, for instance. Your presentation doesn't bring you closer to the jurors. I don't think lawyers understand this, but it can also be this thing that distances them from the lawyer, particularly from the jurors. When it doesn't work and their inability to bridge that gap – to go back to communicating to you, it becomes this challenge for the lawyer, not for the jury. Talking about the PechaKucha chats. What's interesting about PechaKucha, you'd have somebody come in, it might be an artist talking about their work and their slideshow breaks, and I'm, how do you not know your work? This is what you do, right? So if I was to give a great example of a good communicator, and it's very similar to law, is I'm really impressed with people like a Carl Sagan or a Brian Greene if you're talking to me about quantum physics. I don't know what they're talking about, but they still can take these really complex things and communicate it to me. You're seeing visuals, but you're not seeing these tight PowerPoints. **There's something innate in their ability to communicate that even though they're talking about really difficult complex things, they can do it in a way that's very personable. I think when you connect with that, you really have an*** *advantage over your competition in terms of trying to win your case.*

How important is the plaintiff's lawyer's caring for his or her client? And are you able to see that come through?

*That's a really good part. I'm glad you mentioned that. **I think it's only to your advantage to come across as really wanting to do right by your client. Not just win the case, because winning the case is often perceived as much about the lawyer as it is about the client. But if you can communicate somehow that you empathize emotionally with your client, that you feel has been wronged, and want to see the judicial process to get them justice, I think that's very persuasive.***

Do you have a sense that individually or collectively as a group you can sense if a lawyer is genuine and congruent – that the lawyer truly does care about the client, you will know that?

I think you do get a sense for that. I don't know if it's something I can articulate in terms of attributes, or if it's something you know when you see it.

You feel it.

Absolutely.

Well. Thank you.

6

WE'RE WATCHING

Black female, age 27, single, one child, Receptionist, College student

We're not just listening, we're watching.

I know you haven't been in a jury before – but let me explain that when you show up for a jury, you're – if you're selected for a case initially, you go through a round of questioning which is called jury selection. You are in a room with 20 to 40 other people who are going to be asked questions by the lawyers about their beliefs, like, do you have any biases or prejudices about people or about the legal system, about people who sue for money? My first question is, if you imagine yourself in a courtroom, in that panel and the lawyer gets up to talk to you, what do you feel when you're sitting there in that moment?

The first feeling? I think I feel a sense of assurance, because at that point, it's kind of about my beliefs, my thoughts and bias and me being willing to bring that honesty of who I am, or the essence of me to him. I first feel assured that I am who I am. I'm ready. I feel a sense of confidence, maybe, and just assurance, I think.

Do you have a sense that you would like to be on that jury? The reason I ask is that some people don't want to do jury service because it takes time out of their day or their work or their family obligations and doesn't pay very well.

I think as a person in this community, it's important for us to have a sense of helping one another. So giving back, me helping someone in their issues, I think would make me feel good. I think I'm more neutral, but I would love to, if needed, help someone. Whether that someone is the defendant or the plaintiff, you know, we don't know.

Do you feel like you've come in with any preexisting feelings stronger more for one side or another?

I don't think so, no. I think I'm straight neutral. I think.

Sure. That's what we'd like to have, are people who let all sides start out at the same starting line.

Definitely. Because prejudgments and our past experience has a way of shaping our thoughts and our vision of people, corporations, and things like that. But like you said, it's very important that we all have that same standard of a starting line.

If you imagine yourself in that room and these 20 to 40 other people in the room with you, what do you think they're sensing and feeling about that experience right now? And the people that are in the courtroom?

Probably don't want to be there, initially. Jury duty is commonly looked upon as – there's a negative connotation. It's boring, it's long. Before I knew what it was, I knew that it was bad because of how people talked about it. So my first thought would be, these people probably were dragged here. They had to be here. But me, I'm actually interested and I always wanted to be a lawyer. I'm in school now to be a psychiatrist, but who knows what may happen.

So you understand human behavior?

Well, I'm just starting off, but I believe I have a good sense of understanding of it.

Do you have a feeling one way or another about people using courts to sue other people for money if they've been hurt?

I do feel like the system is not completely a 50/50 type of thing. I believe it can be kind of easy for people to get money from corporations. I also believe it's easy for corporations to swindle people out of giving what is due. I believe it's not 50/50 on either side. I actually have an auntie – not by blood. But she goes to department stores and she fakes – she pours water on the floor and she'll fall. She tells me you have to wait for the ambulance to get there, so I've seen that side of it firsthand. And I just be like, oh, my gosh, Auntie. And then I've seen where corporations do a lot of sneaky things and they cause a lot of damage to people, whether it's psychological or physical and they don't want to be held accountable. Whether that's monetary or even just an apology. So both ways – that's why you have to be open, because you never know what you're in for.

Do you have a sense that after hearing all the evidence and listening to the witnesses, including the people who are being sued or are suing and the experts and talking to your jurors, that you would be able to do the right thing?

I want to say, yeah. But in a lot of cases, the law – I don't know. I can't say for sure yes. I would hope so.

When the lawyer first stands up to talk to you and the jury, is there anything a lawyer could say or do that would put you at ease? As a potential juror.

*It could be, if he presents to me all the facts, not just about what's positive for supporting his case – but if he could present all the facts and we could start off that way instead of saying, you know, this is what happened to my client. If they could give me the whole spectrum of the story before just kind of making it more secular to this is right and this is wrong. It would make me feel a sense of more honesty. And it would, I think, gain a little bit more of my ears, my willingness to try and see his point of view. You know, **a lot of lawyers, they're not concerned about the whole truth.** It's just like, I'm right, and this is why I'm right. Well, if you could just bring to us that situation and then start to break it down. Do you know what I'm saying?*

Yes, I do.

I think that would help me as a juror feel like, okay, he's being honest, so let's listen more. Because once you hit that point where, I don't believe that, everything from there is probably going to just not be as, well, it'd be kind of biased, I guess.

If you had a sense that the attorney wasn't being completely honest?

Like, everything he said, I would take it with a grain of salt. There would be a little bit of doubt, because why did he start off that way? **He started off too aggressive. I guess I'm trying to say, I want to hear more of the common ground. I want to hear more of just the truth, and then you start to give me your point of views. But don't start off and try to drag me to one side. Because we are here for, at the end of the day, honesty.**

Same question, only imagine that in this jury selection process, the lawyer's not supposed to tell you about the case but is supposed to learn about you as jurors to decide if you meet the requirements of the law to be fair and impartial.

To make me feel at ease initially?

What might a lawyer say to you in that initial jury selection where they're not talking about the case yet, but they're talking more about you and sometimes about the lawyer and him or herself, too.

Well, being a juror, that's heavy; it's a lot of weight. Because you know what you say means so much to both sides. So if he could say something, maybe lift that weight, to start off more light, like you just keep it light. I know that would help opposed to that weight being fully seen.

I understand. Something that maybe relaxes you a little bit more, takes some of that pressure?

Yes. Maybe if he talked to me about how many times he's dealt with people of the jury and make me feel like I have all the tools if I was picked.

So sharing something to you would - about the lawyer's experience?

Yes. About his experience and about just, as much as he's dealt with the jurors, for how many years, maybe, or how if we were picked, not to worry because we're going to give you all the tools you need. You're going to know the things you need to know to do what's right. It's not just on your shoulders. And it's a part of a big team, more than just you, right? I think I would just feel under a lot of pressure.

So whatever that could be done to make you feel a little less pressure?

Yes.

How about acknowledging the fact that there might be pressure, and talking about it?

I think, yeah, that's a wonderful – definitely. At least he knows that this is a big thing. Make me feel like, okay, we're all bearing the same kind of potential weight.

Do you have a sense that some of your fellow jurors might have personal agendas that would be contrary to the ends of justice?

It depends. There's a lot of people who, like you said, are biased. I would have to get a sense of a face, maybe the way they're presenting themselves, just look at it like that, I guess. I would hope not, but I would know that there's a huge possibility.

Would it surprise you if people spoke up or didn't speak up who had agendas for one side or the other?

No, it wouldn't surprise me because to be on a jury is an exciting thing, no matter what that ground or what mindset you're coming from. I can see people actually wanting to be there. It goes both ways. I feel like people don't generally like jury duty. But then again, I can see the attraction to it. So in general, there are going to be a population of people who, I do want to do it. I can tell my friends about this, I can call up mom and say guess what I did today, no matter what mindset. So it would not surprise me that there were people on the jury who were biased or had their own kind of thoughts of how they should, you know.

Everybody's entitled to their beliefs; my job is to find out what they are and get them to talk about it. Some people believe that under no circumstances should an injured person sue somebody that hurt them – that you don't sue your neighbor, for example. Other people feel very strongly that there's a lawsuit mentality that there will be too much abuse and doctors will leave the community and insurance rates will go up and things like that. What are your thoughts or feelings about just that in general?

*I have many feelings about it. First of all, I understand both ways, because one, as a Christian, which I am, the Bible says not to sue your brother. Morally, you're going to have this understanding that this is not acceptable. At the same time, this is 2015, and this is the way the world works. And there are many exceptions to that. For instance, if I was hurt because of you and it was obviously your fault – your company's fault and I had to take off days of work and miss out on opportunities or money to feed my family, shouldn't it be okay for me to expect you to reimburse me for that? I feel like, a multi-billion dollar corporation? And you know, I'm not asking for a million dollars, just maybe to replace those three or four days or whatever. I think that's acceptable. I think that as a corporation there is liability. **There are things that you are accountable for and you should be held accountable to that. Especially when we keep you going. We just have to make sure that it's fair. Each individual case deserves its own individual guideline and justice. So I see both ways, honestly.***

Every case is different.

Every case. Every case should be tried.

Is there anything that the lawyer getting up in front of you could say or do that would make you uncomfortable? What do you think might be – that the lawyer could avoid doing or saying?

What would make me uncomfortable? I don't know. I'd have to come back to that one. I mean, I would be uncomfortable if, this is probably pretty obvious, but if that person had a track record of suing people or if the company that was being sued was something that was like – it depends on the ideal of the company as far as – it makes you kind of feel bad, but it wouldn't – that wouldn't waver me any way or not, which some people may think that does just in itself, but – I guess to not focus on the facts, I guess?

To avoid talking about the facts of the case?

To speak about other things other than the specific facts of the case.

What could a lawyer do that would show that the lawyer is a human being?

*Talk about his feelings. Talk about how he feels that it wasn't right to do this or how this is not America's – this is not moral. Talk about his feelings, his morals. **Talk about the things that connect us as humans, what is right and what is wrong. Show outrage with this. Show a sense of humility and to show emotions of some sort. Not with just what he says, but with his body language. Because we're not just listening, we're watching.** So you have this power that you can either tap into or not. So just to show me that, I would be more – and I'm not trying to make it like a TV show, like the drama, but it's so real when you can just really feel what you're seeing. **To really care about that client and to really show that to the jury. I think that holds so much power,** than somebody just saying, this person, this victim is – but maybe to walk around the courtroom. Just look at the jury in the eye. Answer questions. Does this look like justice to you? That my client – to really feel it.*

There's a saying that caring in contagious. Do you think you can tell if a lawyer truly cares about his or her client?

Yes. I think you can. I'm not going to say in all instances, because some people are just not like that. But definitely, I think you would, when that is shown, I think it's easy to pick up on that. It's so important. Because a lot of times in the courtroom, it's not about who's right or wrong, but who has that most moxie and who gets their point across the best. And that's why I told you earlier, I'm not sure if I could be equipped to make the right decision. Because the court system is just amazing and atrocious at the same time.

What's amazing and what's atrocious about it in your mind?

Well, one of the things that is just atrocious is the mandatory minimum sentencing. In the criminal sense. It's ridiculous.

Doesn't take into account the individual.

No. You give so much power to the prosecutor. And no other place in the system gives that much power to one party. That's ridiculous. And it's unsupervised. There's no accountability. They're never penalized if the person that you put away for 30 years was deemed innocent from DNA after spending 20 years in prison. There's really no penalties for that. Like, court cases now, they don't go to trial, it's all about plea deals. Because prosecutors strong-arm through fear tactics. That's atrocious. And everyone knows it, I think. And then it's amazing, too, how we do a lot. How we supply a lot of people who don't have money with lawyers. And how we're moving towards somewhere. We're getting there. We have a strong sense of what's right and what's wrong. Now it's just about implicating that and making laws that show that. And so it goes two ways.

If you were in deliberations with your group of 12 people and were a dissenting or a minority voice, how would you feel you would stand up to that?

*Hundred percent. I would give it my all. I would try to be the voice of those who were silenced, as long as I believed it. As an African American, that touches me. Because I see so many African Americans going along with things because we're all black. So much that people don't take into account. They look at you and they say, yes or no. But you don't ever have to show what you're doing. **People will vote for people that are like them. And that's ignorance. I think that's just the easy way out.** I would try to be that voice. I would do research. I think that's the most important thing. Sorry, I talk a lot.*

The more you talk, the better for me. How can I comfortably ask a juror about their biases or prejudices that might make them not a very good juror in the case without hurting them or upsetting them or turning them against me?

Right. Like how to ask something?

How could I ask you, do you have any beliefs that may be better for a different kind of case?

I think it's more like how you ask. Like, your whole countenance, perfect. You're calm, attentive, and you're not like this stone, even though your question might be strong, you give them all this wiggle room. You're not even writing on the paper. I think it's how you ask. I think you've got it. But I would say that's such a general question. I think that helps, too. To start off general and then knock it down. How could you ask them? I think examples make people feel better. To know they're not the first ones. I would maybe say, in the case of, boom, boom, boom, this was shown, and what that did was that stopped him from doing the – and I understand that, but it's – I think examples. And then taking it straight back to them. So do you think if you had been, dut duh duh, do you think that you may have had, you know, some beliefs or maybe some emotional strain, you know, whatever?

If I were to, for example, share some particular bias or prejudice I have? Do you think I could do that without offending anybody?

Depending on what you say, yes. I think that's the best way. Because if they have to say yes or no and they feel like they're alone, I think people might be kind of reluctant to say the truth. But if you say, hey, you're not the only one. This happened; it happened. I feel this way. You know, I'm normal. We're all human. And there's nothing wrong with you having your feelings. I mean, some things are wrong. But what we're going to say is, there's nothing wrong with you having your own feelings. I don't know. The way you word it. But I think what you said, examples about your personal experiences would be great.

Some people say I will show mine if you'll show me yours, in terms of our beliefs and then it's – that way – I share, and then I invite you to share?

Right. It's like putting your hand out. Taking my hand instead of well, go first.

Is there anything in terms of sharing that you think would be off limits?

Well, there's some – I think that people are going to be reluctant – oh, as far as you? I would say, because you want them to talk about racism and things like that, right? That's what you want?

Well, if race is an issue in the case; it's not always an issue. It could be issues about people who just don't like lawsuits because of the McDonald's verdict, for example, where this lady got so much money because she spilled coffee in her lap. That's a popular case jurors like to talk about, saying there's something wrong with the system. We were talking about what could I disclose that would be about myself that would be not too much. I'll give an example. I do a lot of personal injury cases, and sometimes I sue doctors, I have my own personal experience where I sued a doctor. It was a serious case and a five-week trial. Is sharing that and also saying I understand the kind of pain they're suffering and injuries that a person who's gone through that has gone through, is that an appropriate share, or is that too personal and too much?

I think that gives me an idea that when I hear that, I hear that you're all for your client. I hear that you know which side you're on, and that you're serious. That's what that tells me. That you're going to fight. Now, does that make me uncomfortable? I think that speaks about the weight, but not in a way where too much. It just tells me this is real. It brings back the focus that these two are fighting. Does it make me more comfortable? It just tells me that you are about your business. That's what that makes me seem like, like you're serious.

Would it at all have the sense that you're being manipulated if you heard that?

Nope. Not in the way you just told me. It's just – you're very clear.

Thank you very much.

7

BE UNDERSTANDING

Caucasian female, age 24, single, Tutor/Non-Profit Management, Ph.D.

I wouldn't want to hear them asking questions that I felt like they were trying to figure out if I fit into a broad social category and then make assumptions about me. It would feel important to me that the lawyer eased into any really difficult or sensitive questions and was very understanding about like, if this may bring back traumatic memories or if this is a difficult topic for you, like empathize. Or just being understanding to the potential difficulty that you're actually going through in answering questions.

Recall that time you were called for jury service. You were brought into the courtroom, probably with 20 to 40 or more other potential jurors. Tune into that, because I'd like to talk to you in the "as if" mode, as you're sitting there, before anybody's spoken with you, other than the judge. What are the feelings you're having? What's going through your mind?

I felt really conflicted about whether or not I wanted to try to get on the jury, because on the one hand, I was really curious about the process and wanted to learn and have the experience of sitting in and listening to a case. But on the other hand, I felt like it's this huge kind of nervous responsibility of having a big impact on people's lives. And also just knowing the way that the judicial system can be very discriminatory and wrong-headed and feeling worried about being part of that process. So I had gone back and forth in my mind about whether I wanted to portray myself as someone that a lawyer wouldn't want to pick as being a juror or trying to come off as a little more moderate as a person to want to be selected.

Did you achieve that goal? Did you speak with the lawyer and articulate how you felt about that?

Well, I decided not to say anything about how I felt about the court being, you know, having a history of racial bias or anything like that.

Was this a racial issue? Was race involved in that case?

Yes. The person who was filing the suit was black. And the doctor was white, so I think race was definitely involved in the case. But they didn't ask about that specifically. So I ended up deciding that I couldn't figure out which way to portray myself, and just tried to answer as honestly as possible. Which I think resulted in – I was answering questions too many times. It seemed like the people who were chosen were often the people who didn't answer, didn't respond to a lot of the questions.

Do you feel that you were excluded by one side or the other when the challenges were made?

I think I probably was excluded by the doctor. And I think the reason that might have come up is – one question in particular I know they asked, how do you feel about doctors? Or do you go to a doctor regularly? At the time I preferred going to talk with a midwife who I thought was more trusting, and we had a more personal relationship. I think they perceived me as colored against doctors.

I heard you say, I think, that you ultimately felt the responsibility was great. You told the truth. So let me ask you this: when the lawyer for the plaintiff got up, what was your thought when that lawyer started asking questions of the panel? How did you feel about that?

I don't remember many of the questions the lawyer for the plaintiff asked. I guess they asked if we had family members or friends who had been injured. And I had, so I had to tell them the story; injured by a doctor's negligence.

So you've had firsthand experience as well.

I had a friend. I guess they did bring up race in the sense that there was an interracial couple. His partner was white. I thought it was strange that they brought that up, because it seemed like it wasn't at all relevant to the case, but they still asked us.

Forget for a moment the case you were in and think about a blank slate. What would make you comfortable when the lawyer for the injured person gets up and speaks to you? What could he or she say or do that would make the feeling of comfort?

During jury selection? I guess seeking questions that make me feel empathetic towards someone who's a victim. I think in that sense, asking a question about whether we had a family member that had a similar experience was smart, because it put me in the mindset of sharing empathy with that person.

How about connecting with the lawyer rather than the lawyer's client? What sort of things do you think you might want or need to hear? Or the opposite, would not want to hear from a lawyer who got up to talk to you in jury selection?

I wouldn't want to hear them asking questions that I felt like they were trying to figure out if I fit into a broad social category and then make assumptions about me. It would feel important to me that the lawyer eased into any really difficult or sensitive questions and was very understanding about like, if this may bring back traumatic memories or if this is a difficult topic for you, like empathize. Or just being understanding to the potential difficulty that you're actually going through in answering questions.

How about if the lawyer wants to share something about the lawyer personally as a way of gaining rapport or comfort with you? Maybe before asking you to share something, the lawyer shares something.

I didn't know that was allowed, but I certainly would feel better if that occurred.

Do you think so? Could you think of an example where something like that might fit in?

Well, if they said something like, my grandmother was dying because she couldn't afford medical care and the doctor refused to provide her medical care that was needed, and ultimately she died earlier than she needed to because – so recalling someone else's wrong, a family experience, and then like, that was really painful for me, and I know that that's maybe really painful for you as members of the jury, but since it is relevant to the case, I'd like to hear your stories.

Do you think there's a line that the lawyer could cross that's too much sharing?

Maybe if the lawyer comes off as trying too hard to get someone's emotion? I can imagine someone else responding negatively to that. Maybe someone who logic really matters to them. I imagine that they'd feel like the lawyer was obviously trying to persuade them one way or the other. But I think to me, an emotional appeal would be very convincing.

How did you feel about your prospective jury members in general? What was the sense you had about them?

Some people were obviously bored. Didn't answer almost any questions. There were other people, there was one woman who described an experience of losing someone to cancer and I think there was medical neglect involved in that story. She started crying. Some other juror there was comforting her. And in other circumstances people were just – I don't remember, but it seemed like a lot of people had really short answers and were trying to be honest without going into too much detail and telling that much about themselves.

Do you have a sense that some jurors more than others really wanted to be on the jury?

Oh, yeah. And it seemed like there were some people who were disqualifying themselves by being as honest and eager to participate in the process as they could.

Did you have a sense that anybody was terribly biased one way or another?

There was one woman who was really angry about an experience of medical neglect that happened. They ended up asking her to leave the room. They just said she could be excused from the jury process. Like I said, the people who seemed to be selected were the people who seemed most bored and disinterested and didn't answer questions, which, I don't know if that made me really confident about the jury as a judicial process, because I don't know if those were the people who were going to pay the most attention to the case and try to make the best decisions.

It's a difficult process, and we have very little time to talk to jurors. We may have two rounds of 30 minutes each, for example. What can a lawyer do in your mind to ensure that you can be open-minded to both sides? When the lawyer gets up and speaks with you and says we're really looking for people that can be open-minded and fair.

So looking at biases that jurors might already have?

Biases and prejudices that they may have and, in some cases, don't really want to talk about, or might not even know they have.

So asking about previous experiences, bad or good.

What I'm thinking is how can I have some confidence that a juror will be willing to give both sides a fair shake? That we'll all start from the same place without prejudgment?

Honestly, I find the jury hard to think about how a person would not already have some kind of predetermined judgment about how other people think about, for example, a police officer or doctors or someone professional.

What sort of questions do you think would be fair of jurors that may have those experiences? Is it fair to ask them directly about that and follow-up questions?

I kind of expected more direct questions about like, how do you feel about doctors? How do you feel about people who are seeking medical treatment?

How do you feel about people who bring lawsuits against people or corporations that have injured them and are seeking money for that?

I think it's really brave. I think it probably requires a lot of time and money and effort and vulnerability going on the stand. And then to stand up against people who have more money than you do.

Do you have a sense that's always the case? That when you're bringing a case, a person or a corporation that you're suing has more money?

If it's a corporation, I would probably assume that's true. If it's an individual doctor, I might think that maybe the financial playing field is a little more level.

So fundamentally, the concept of bringing a lawsuit, whether it's auto negligence, corporate negligence, medical negligence, products liability, those types of things – generally, how do you feel about the concept of that civil action?

I think certainly there can be cases of frivolity, like the media talks a lot about spilt coffee from McDonald's or whatever. But in general, I think that corporations don't have a whole lot of incentive to protect the rights of consumers unless consumers demand that their rights are protected. I think in general it's a positive thing for people to bring lawsuits in order to seek grievances but also to hold the corporations or the professionals accountable.

Do you think that opinion, attitude, belief is shared more or less among your demographic?

I'm not sure. My demographic as a young woman?

Your generation.

My generation? Maybe. I think probably more among young people than in older people, perhaps.

What do you think about engineers?

Really interesting. I'm going to say that engineers are more often well-educated, rich, and therefore, more likely to feel supported by institutions and corporations.

How do you feel about engineers as jurors? Do you think they make good jurors or might they not make good jurors, in general? In these kinds of cases that we're talking about.

Well, on the one hand, I would assume an engineer is more likely to be very detail-oriented and want to gather all the facts before coming to a conclusion. On the other hand, I might assume that an engineer would be more likely to support another professional and more likely to share that professional's fear of lawsuits.

Do you feel that the average individual in the jury pool with you here makes up their mind fairly quickly, before they've heard the evidence?

Probably.

How do you feel about that?

It's just that our legal system is such a hard thing. We pretend that it's about just the facts that are presented in the case, but there's so many things about the way people feel about the lawyers and the clients and that changed the way they make decisions.

Right. Part of the reason why I'm writing the book is to sort that out. How can a lawyer show you that he or she is human?

Maybe having an ability to see both sides. Like if it were x, y, and z circumstances, then I could understand the other side's case, but it's actually these circumstances, so therefore, we have to be prudent. On the side of the plaintiff or whatever.

Could you condense that into a couple shorter words?

By providing a counter-narrative in which the jury could make the opposite conclusion; in which the lawyer might be able to understand the other person's perspective.

Is that saying that if the lawyer is open-minded to both sides?

I don't know, I guess so.

When you were sitting in that jury and also as you think about it, in this hypothetical jury, what is your sense about the fact that both sides are taking different points of view?

Can you tell me more? What do you mean?

As lawyers, we take one side or another when we come to court. And it can be difficult to argue the other side when we're invested in the side we're on for our client's sake. What's your thought about the lawyer's role in having to represent one side?

I guess a good, honest lawyer would be wanting to stand on the side of justice, regardless of where it is and say, I've evaluated the case and given these facts, although I think it's clear that this is where it's necessary to decide, but – I guess just the lawyer being able to give a sense that they've considered both sides and would feel open to defending a doctor in another case if the circumstances were different.

Do you think you can tell if a lawyer is credible or genuine or honest or congruent when you're talking to them?

I definitely would get the sense of that. There's nothing factual that I can say or concrete that I can identify, but I've definitely described you know, that person feels slimy or that person feels really honest.

Do you have any special training in the behavioral sciences or social sciences that, in your case, helped you identify those kinds of impressions?

My work in social sciences is more around migration and mass incarceration.

You probably have some strong opinions about the legal system and criminal justice system.

Yes. Yes.

How do you feel about the fact that in most of these cases, the only remedy that the individual who is injured has is to get money from the party – the side that hurt them?

It's really tragic because it doesn't bring back a person's eye, doesn't repair the fact that their mother died of cancer or whatever. It doesn't solve the problem. And they have to go through this process of exposing themselves just to get money in the end. It doesn't really seem like it works out to being a fair conclusion.

Generally, the law allows money as compensation for actual costs, like medical bills and lost wages. But there's also a component for pain and suffering. There's no fixed standard for that. How do you feel is the best way for a lawyer to talk about that in jury selection? Which is to say, you know, we're here for money, but it's ultimately going to be you and your jurors who are going to make that decision of what the case value is to compensate.

Oh. Jurors decide how much money goes to the plaintiff?

Yes.

I didn't know that.

They decide whether or not there was negligence. And then they also decide, if there was, how much money will make the injured person whole - is one of the terms we use. But that our measure of justice is money.

Did you ask how I feel about that?

Right. How do you feel about that, and how might you go about making those calculations?

It seems like a very overwhelming question and task to take on. I guess that's the part where I might feel a little bit likely to be biased against a plaintiff if they're asking for an inordinate amount of pain and suffering money. Maybe if there's some explanation about how they were going to use the money and the way that money was going to compensate for – especially if it's emotional suffering.

Do you think there could be expert testimony that would help you with that?

Definitely. *If there was someone who was talking about a particular kind of treatment or – I guess just thinking about whatever the specific thing it was that they were going to use the money for would help me feel a lot better about it.*

One frustration we have is that every jury is different. So for the very same case, two juries can reach very different results, particularly with regard to the amounts of money that they may award. What do you think about that?

Even when the same facts are brought and the same experts are called?

When we're talking about those pain and suffering damages for which there's no fixed standard.

Right. I mean, because $1 to one person is $10 to another person. I think money is so relative. What do you do with that? I don't know.

That's what I'd like to know. How about the idea that sometimes an award of money for an individual can be a deterrent for the defendant doing this kind of thing again? How do you feel about deterrence?

That feels like a really powerful argument, especially if I felt like it was an institution, not as we're taking money away from a doctor and their family was somehow going to suffer financially, but if we were slapping the wrist on a hospital, say, then I would be much more inclined to –

Institution over an individual.

Yeah.

Let's go back to doctors for a moment - or professionals. When they're sued, do you believe if they're found to have committed wrong and money is assessed against them, it comes out of their pocket?

> *Maybe it comes out of insurance. I guess I assumed that it comes out of their pocket, but maybe it doesn't.*

If you had a stronger sense that it did come from an insurance company, would that change how you might determine the damages? The money part of the damages?

> *Yeah, because the part that makes me want to empathize with the doctor or the professional is feeling like they tried their best and they have a family, too.* **I don't want to make their family suffer because of this one individual's mistake, one time. But if it was coming out of an insurance company and it was more of resulting in institutional changes to the way that hospitals were, say – and less likely that there're going to be errors over the long run, then I'd be much more inclined to give large sums of money.**

Do you think that kind of deterrence does happen on a case by case basis if there's a finding of fault and an award is made? Do you think that the doctor or the institution do take steps to change down the road?

> *Probably, if it's a significant push on the institution's budget. Then they'd have a strong incentive to change their practices.*

Is there anything - speaking about you as a potential juror - we would need to know or would be helpful for the court to know?

> *I feel like the things I mentioned about being influenced by emotional appeals and being more inclined to side with the underdog, coming from a social justice kind of background, are things I would assume a lawyer would want to know, but I don't think I'd necessarily want lawyers to know.*

If an individual had a hidden agenda in the jury, for one side of the other, do you believe that needs to be addressed by the lawyers?

> *Probably the lawyers would want to address it.*

If, for example, somebody on the jury worked for an insurance company and the lawyer learned about it, do you feel that the lawyer should follow up?

> *Yeah, like to ask if you would always side with insurance companies or if you would be unlikely to allow a large fine going to an insurance company.*

Right.

> *Which is why it makes perfect sense that there's so many demographic questions that are asked. In the jury selection process I had, they asked me what bumper stickers I had on my car, which had no relevance to the case, but allowed them to –*

In some shortcut sense of who and what your values are. What bumper stickers do you have on your car?

Currently, I have none. At the time, I had one about migration and the other one was about a political conflict about an area of land on the Indian reservation land that was going to be developed.

Did you have the sense that the overwhelming number of jurors in your courtroom were conservative?

I got the sense most people in the courtroom didn't seem to have or didn't seem to express many personal opinions; maybe more moderate.

If you had an opinion about the case after it was all said and done and you were in a minority, do you feel that you would fight for your beliefs or would you just cave to get it over with and be done?

In my whole debate in my mind about how to approach the jury process, that was the one thing I felt clear about, that if I came to a conclusion and I felt in my heart that what I had concluded was true, I would try to stick it out and fight it out.

You would fight it out. To be heard? Even if you were voted –

Ultimately I would go against.

Because we're 10 to 2 here. So out of 12, 10 can override and carry the case. So, even if you were in that two, you would still speak up –

I hope that I would.

Is there anything you think that would be helpful that I haven't asked you or that you'd like to say about the process as you experienced it or as you envision it?

I guess I have a question for you. Is it necessary for them to ask questions of the jury with all the other jurors sitting there, or could they do it one-on-one?

There is such a congestion in the courts that they've moved to this group method, and limit our time. In some very sensitive cases, generally in criminal cases, that can happen. It almost never happens.

Because of court efficiency.

Because of court efficiency. It's not uncommon for there to be more than a hundred jurors brought in in a jury pool on a major case, because sometimes there will be multiple parties – several defendants, the doctor, the hospital, another doctor and their clinic, and the plaintiff, in a malpractice context. So they're all going to have to talk with them and these courts can't have trials lasting week upon month. Sometimes that happens, but by and large, it's moved along. Which is why it's important for me to learn how to get to some of these things efficiently, sensitively, and in a way that builds a connection with the jurors. I appreciate it. Thank you.

8

MANAGING BIASES

Caucasian male, age 51, married, Manager, B.A. Economics

It's not that you have biases, it's whether you can put them aside and how prevalent they really are.

Every trial requires that we select a jury from a large jury pool, which we don't get a lot of practice doing, because we don't try a lot of cases. The last case I tried was over two years ago. We have jurors who are over the age of 18 and either registered voters or have a driver's license or both – a broad cross-section of people. I'm trying to get a sense of what prevailing attitudes and beliefs are about jury service, about civil lawsuits, that is to say, suing people or corporations who have caused injury, for money. With that in mind and knowing that you haven't been called to a jury – you know what a courtroom looks like? You know what a jury box looks like?

Sure.

Imagine you've been called to jury service. There's a large group of people, 20 to 40 or more who have to be selected down to 12. The lawyers get very brief opportunities to elicit from that large group of people if they have biases, prejudices, or other things that may make them unsuitable for that case. In other words, are they going to be fair, first of all? Or, do they have some hidden agenda that wants to tank your case because they don't, for example, believe that you should sue people for pain and suffering or for injury.

Got it.

Imagine you're in the "as if" moment, in the courtroom and a lawyer, not necessarily me, but a lawyer who represents injured people for money, is going to get up and talk to you for about an hour. That's the scenario. The other side's lawyer will do the same thing. As you're sitting there taking all this in for the first time, what sense do you have? What's going on through your mind at that point? What are you thinking?

In this hypothetical I'd be more curious as to what the case was. What's the circumstances? I consider myself pretty fair-minded and there's no jumping to any conclusions, because there's no information at hand yet. If I had to put it into a word it'd be more inquisitive.

Let's assume it's a case where someone was injured as a result of a motor vehicle collision, and they're bringing a lawsuit against the owner of the vehicle. All the facts will be brought out later, but right now, we're here to determine your suitability for jury service. What are you thinking about the lawyer as he or she stands up to talk to you before they've even said anything?

Of which side?

It's the plaintiff's lawyer first, the one who represents the injured person, standing up and going to speak to you all. What are you thinking?

I have no predisposition to anything with him. It's completely neutral.

What might you expect to hear from that lawyer when they get up to talk?

The degree of the pain and suffering, what justification there was for trying to get some kind of damages from the person that caused it and inevitably, they're going to outline the severity of the injury to warrant such a thing. Because obviously, it has to have some size of impact to be standing in court. So I'm completely no predisposition to assume anything at this point.

If the lawyer's job is to elicit information from you and your fellow jurors, how do you think that lawyer can do that in a way that will best establish a connection with you?

I suspect if it's around this case, they're going to ask if I've ever known anyone that's been injured in a car accident or any motor vehicle accident of any kind. So motorcycle, I don't know if that would be relevant. I've been in a motorcycle accident; have a high regard for motorcycle accidents. I would imagine they would probably try to build some cadence with me on that level to understand where my sensibilities lie and what my experiences are with that, if it's going to conjure up any emotional reaction, or if I'm sympathetic already to somebody that might be on the receiving end of an accident.

Would you be okay with that, with questions about your experience having been in an accident?

Oh, yeah. And I would imagine they probably ask the alternate, and say, have you ever hit somebody or anything? Have you ever been on the protagonist side of causing an accident? And as much as I don't want to talk about it, I'd have to be transparent about that. It all seems like fair questions. It's nothing that feels icky or off bounds or intrusive if that's what the case is about.

What are your feelings in general about lawsuits where injured people are suing for money?

That in my head, they have to be substantiated, because I have been on the receiving end of a frivolous lawsuit, of a pedestrian lawsuit with a motor vehicle.

Were you brought to trial?

No, it was agreed out-of-court, through arbitration. The gentleman in question, the reason it got very exacerbated and in my head causes a sense of sourism, if there's such a word –

There is now.

– was that the person was arguably a homeless person. The police never initiated a ticket because they said, we ain't got nothing. The vehicle was backing up into a parking space, and as I'm backing into the parking space I hear a bang, and then I hear somebody screaming and saying, oh, you hit me, you hit me, and then a crowd of people all standing around and then people saying, he didn't hit you. And then other people saying, his friends, he did hit. And then the police come to issue a ticket, and I said, this is 99% cut and dried. You hit somebody, you get a ticket. I can't issue a ticket. So the police didn't do anything, and the guy ended up refusing medical attention and leaving. And then this just died as they tried to extract money which was apparently not his first time being "Fall Down Farley". It finally came to a head when it was about to go through its statute of limitation. I don't know how he got it through, but he got a lawyer that was able to make a case for it. And my insurance company was adamant about not paying, but they went through arbitration and apparently he did make something off of the transaction. It was kind of a cease and desist payment.

Given that you've been on that side and you've been on the other side, are you feeling that this is the kind of case that you'd be able to think of both sides?

I could be totally objective within that. If anything, there's no axe to grind. It gives me a sense of appreciation for the emotion that goes on both sides of the equation. Although, somebody may view it differently, I can be biased in either way.

Do you have concerns that lawsuits seeking money are driving up insurance? Or if there are cases against doctors, are causing doctors to leave? Or causing the price of products to go up as a result?

Wow. That's a much heftier question. So did I actually answer your first question, though? When you said –

Can you be –

Unbiased.

Can you give both sides a start from the same place?

I do have a perception that the amount of litigation is making it more complicated. I don't think it's unjust, but I think it does have repercussions that I still can't fully comprehend how much they're exacerbating cost of goods or things across the board. I don't compare medical, though, with this because medical, to me, is a whole different issue.

How's that?

I think anyone in the medical profession touching somebody's body should be totally accountable and know what they're doing, period.

People say, hey, accidents happen. How do you feel about that as a mitigator or – your thoughts?

I do think there's truth to the fact that if it is truly an accident that could have been caused by contributing factors, so if somebody was not doing anything and it literally was an accident, the road was icy, things happen. Something transpired that was really beyond anyone's control. I do believe there's huge truth to that in some form. At times people have a hard time accepting that and want to still lay blame. You can always deconstruct every situation to find something as an underlying contributor. So if the road was icy, you shouldn't have been driving fast. You shouldn't have been driving. You shouldn't have even been on the road. There's always something, right? But no, there is such a thing as accidents, in my head.

Getting back to the lawyer that's standing up in front of you who's trying to establish a connection, what might a lawyer say to you that would cause you to feel comfortable in that person's presence? Just right off the bat, what could they say or how could they be?

Having never been in it, I have no idea what the dialogue sounds like and what really does happen. I would imagine a little pre-frame. I would imagine whatever has been set up to pre-frame the situation. I don't know if there's any discussion from the judge or anyone prior to this.

Very brief.

Then I would imagine this lawyer would be appealing to the higher purpose of why sitting on a jury and being impartial and being transparent about whatever baggage you may have is important; that this is at the core of our political and judicial system and it's necessary. And at least try to level-set everyone so if you came in with any axe to grind or baggage or annoyance or, even distractions that, I'm missing a full day of work for this, I've got x, y. You've got to disengage from all that and really be present. So I'd imagine the first attorney has that responsibility, to try to make people present and engaged. That would be my guess.

Do you have a sense that your fellow jurors in that jury room – forgive me if I've asked this question – come in with a set of biases and prejudices of their own?

Oh, yeah. If it's a random calling, absolutely.

If you had such a bias or some biases – we don't have to talk about them yet – but how could a lawyer speak to you in such a way that you'd be willing to express your biases or prejudices in a given situation?

That's a tough one. It's funny because I love the expression "stereotyping just saves time." And there's actually some truth to that.

In a reptilian kind of a way.

*Yes, yes. Wow. **We all know there's huge generalities, no matter how much people want to believe that they're indifferent and take the higher road and don't play that way, everybody is, to some degree, subject to it. No one's***

impervious. If everyone would accept that, I think that might be the first premise, and then for an attorney to try to appeal to the fact that it's not that you have biases, it's whether you can put them aside and how prevalent they really are. *So it's one thing to have a rather comical interpretation of a group; it's another if that's truly going to inform the way you approach that group. Or is it just cocktail humor that is okay to kind of smirkishly say, my grandma's getting in the car and going for a drive – duck. Does that make you biased, or does that make you cognizant of the fact that there's challenges associated with elderly driving, you know, so on and so forth, with any other group. So I don't know how you would suss that out, but the ability to try to let people know that it's not that you don't have certain preconditionings; I mean if (expletive) television is doing it, everyone's doing it. The movies are doing it. There's nothing that you're not subject to that's trying to somehow pander to certain stereotypes and attitudes. It is too prevalent on every level, at every turn. It's just a matter of, can you subside that or suppress it enough? How much will that influence your thinking? So if someone was trying to get that out of me and come to a level,* **it would have to be a smart series of questions to start asking, first honoring the fact that it's there, so no one's trying to be puritanical or holier-than-thou thinking, I have no prejudice. Everyone has it to some degree.** *Even if you're just walking down the street with your loved one and you see somebody that looks a little odd and you just think, let's cross here. That's a prejudice. You just expose whether it's – there's no malice, there's nothing evil; why'd you do it? So if there was a way through* **some careful, loving, guided questions that feel unthreatening, to just try and help people assess that level if they can't necessarily articulate it.**

Do you think it would be appropriate for the attorney to share something of his or her own bias? As a way of saying, you know, I will share mine, and I'm going to ask you to share yours.

I don't know how much that makes the attorney vulnerable, but **I think it's very healthy to say, let's all start at the beginning.** *How many of you would wait before you pull out if you saw an older person in a huge vehicle trying to maneuver into a parking space? Are you doing it because you're being kind? Are you doing it because you're worried they're going dent your car? Are you doing it because you're worried about life and limb? That's being honest. Then you start working your way through, and by a show of hands, I'm sure you'd end up with 99% of the room with their hands raised over just about every one of those questions. And it may take the attorney saying, I'd be the first to admit I would. Some of it's a little scathing, but –*

Do you have a sense that an attorney who shows vulnerability has an advantage or a disadvantage in gaining connection with the jury?

I don't know. I think you're just the vessel representing the facts, and whether you sound incompetent or competent, whether they sound like a buffoon or not, the facts are what they are. They just add a much better spotlight to them, and somebody may, without the right kind of control and respect of the jurors, miss some of the statements, miss some of the germane points. So I think it's more of a huge amplifier and that's probably a bit naïve, because I know great attorneys can make or ruin a case on BS facts or great facts, right?

I don't really know.

I'd like to believe that the jurors, if they're paying attention to everything, can remove the – if it's around matters of likability, then you'd have to wonder because there's some who are pretty caustic and lame and very unappealing to look at. If that's the case, then only attorneys who would be successful are charming and suave and blah, blah, blah. And that's not the case either. If anything, it might be too distracting.

Going back to talking about the biases and the prejudices, as you're there in the courtroom, do you think your fellow jurors would answer those questions that we talked about? That they would come forward?

I think some people would. The ones I would be really suspicious about if I was going down that train of logic and reasoning or both, and I was trying to extract out of a jury their unspoken biases, it may not be profound, but they're there. Anyone that says no, I don't have any, I would immediately dive deeper and deeper. And the ones that still say no, I'd say, that's impossible, you're out. **It's impossible that you have these absolute white canvas saints walking around that have no filters.** It's impossible. So I think for some, they may be sanctimonious and try to play a role. And that's when, like in an interview, I would dive deeper with more grilling questions to the point where's there's nothing left.

In the amount of time that we have, limited as it is.

How long do you have? You have one hour with how many people? Twelve? You're asking them, all 12 the same thing?

Generally we can have as many as up to 80 in a room, from which we may have two rounds of 30 or two rounds of an hour to speak to the entire group, each lawyer.

But then how much interaction do they give back to you that you're like, him out, him out? It's in that two-hour period? Wow. You have to make it on the fly, don't you?

It's become a matter of judicial economy. How about honesty? What do you think an honest lawyer looks and sounds like? A credible lawyer. A congruent, genuine credible lawyer.

So that exactly is the case of bias. That actually proves the point. If you laugh at that and already in your head frame up a joke, then you're guilty of stereotyping and bias and that already implicates everyone in the room, right? If you're anyone that's giggling at that. There is a paradox of the statement. So, what do they look and sound like?

What might it sound like as you envision it, sitting in that "as if" space?

Having known a few lawyers and even dated one I think the part that resonated with me was this moment of full disclosure that quickly level-set all the images that you see on television where they're wearing slick suits and eating expensive meals and they work all the time, but they live in beautiful apartments, and all this other stuff; quickly dispelling it and saying, it's a very hard profession, you study all of these years, do all of this grunt work, you have huge bills. It's not a glamour business. You do it and the only reason you do it is because you love the clients, you love the work, you love the subject matter that you're working on. And the biggest one is to dispel all the other glamour-a-rama that seems to be swirling around it. Because that is maybe in reality one percent, if that. At best, it's more of a Hollywood portrayal. That, to me, was real sobering and helped me understand, wow, being an attorney is super tough. And then he gave me some of the statistics about burnout in that field and all those aspects. Again, humanizing it a lot gave me a huge degree of respect for what he was trying to do.

Do you think a credible attorney can wear an expensive suit?

Absolutely. As opposed to –

Well, you did use the word slick, so in my mind, I thought slick-dressed, for example. And overly dressed with lots of jewelry and those kinds of things.

Or they're in an impeccable stunning suit and you just know, at a glance, that's a really, really expensive suit, with gorgeous shoes. I mean, looking good is nice, but it's not the key.

Do you think it matters that a lawyer expresses genuine caring for his or her client?

No. I think it's cool.

That that person has gone to great lengths to bring that client's case this far?

I think it's very cool. It humanizes the whole thing and, to me, gives proof points that there's more there than meets the eye, if the attorney becomes a bit of a character witness by their mere span of influence and sphere of influence and authority. Being in the room saying, you know, yes, it's a client, but having blah, blah, blah and then giving some kind of implied testimonial support. I think it carries a lot of weight.

In most cases, you would hear from expert witnesses on both sides, and lay witnesses generally on the side of the injured person. How do you feel about testimony from paid expert witnesses and unpaid lay witnesses – that's generally friends and family.

Paid witnesses I struggle with because they are always for hire. Doesn't mean they change the authenticity of their message or – the credentials, not authenticity – the credentials of their message. So, I get it. It's a necessary evil. Never having been in court for a case, but having heard enough pieces of this, I'm always a little suspicious of how much they're applying their science to the situation and trying to deduce a laser fit when sometimes, it's not just, I'm a subject matter expert in this area, this is a topic that's related to this area, so I'm going to render an opinion. But between these two points is a (expletive) load of gray that no one actually can navigate. To me, it's just how accurate is this witness as the subject matter expert? How much leap of faith do you have to make to take their fact proof-points and apply it to the case?

Do you think that these experts also have biases and agendas?

*Other than compensation, I can't imagine what their biases or agendas are. If I'm an expert on hardwoods, and I'm not promoting anything by making a case that somehow this was implicated, I don't see a direct correlation. So they seem rather neutral except for the fact that **they're being compensated for their time, which is totally fine.** I have no issues with having paid witnesses, it's just, how much of a leap of faith you have to draw between their testimony and the subject matter.*

Do you have an issue with experts making tens and sometimes hundreds of thousands of dollars on a particular case?

I never thought about it. On some levels, I don't know if it's germane. If I had enough financial means to bring that kind of information forward and the information isn't tainted, if I paid a dollar for it or a million dollars for it, it's just a matter of there's an economic disparity for somebody with no financial means to have brought that kind of information to light. But that's a different matter. That's not the case, that's more about economic disparities.

In civil cases, we have money damages that are generally of two types. There are special damages, which are those kinds of things that have actually been spent or can be spent. For example, medical bills past, present, and future; wage loss past, present, and future. You also have this category for pain and suffering, for which there is no fixed standard to compensate. How do you feel about that, and how might you go about coming to a number to determine – when you decide ultimately – if you decide, as a jury, to give money to this plaintiff for pain and suffering?

*I have no idea how you do that. I'm always curious. I don't know if – pain and suffering. **So the calculable damages on economic loss and economic expenses seems pretty straightforward. Pain and suffering always feels like it cuts both ways. Sometimes it's more of a punishment to the defendant. Other times, it feels like a reward to the plaintiff. I never know which is which. It's hard to determine, because they do seem to be so flipping arbitrary.***

And there's no fixed standard. So, being that it's arbitrary and if you're chosen with 11 other people, how might you think about making those calculations?

*It's too abstract. **It really depends on who was hurt, who was at fault, what were the circumstances, what's their age, life? What's the long-term implications? I think pain and suffering sometimes is overused. It's one thing to get fair compensation for lost wages, for future wages, expenses.***

It's another to go for some untapped jugular that is more, at that point, opportunistic or punitive than it is fair. That's where I think it gets a little warped. So I'm conservative on that. Very conservative, until I understand the circumstances. If you said it was a young girl, a hugely different matter than if it was an older person who was already at end of life. Can they walk or not walk? All of that is super germane.

If I told you that the same facts, given two different juries, would have very different end results, would that surprise you?

*A little bit. **I do think juries are a lot of "groupthink" too.** And they follow – I mean, you have smart people in the room and dumb people in the room. And you can't control the IQ or the EQ. You can end up with a really savvy juror who's at least smart, and the others follow them, and they start helping mold people's opinion behind the scenes.*

If you were a juror, do you think you would be a leader, a follower, or somewhere in between?

I would naturally gravitate to a leader. I can't sit around the table and watch the melee and the stupidity happen for too long before I would want to – but I'm a collaborative leader. If there's a couple of other alpha dogs in the room, I would always play nice with them, but I'm not the type that would sit in the back and let someone else take the reins.

We require a majority of 10 out of 12 in order for a verdict to stand. If you were in the minority of two, or three, how strongly do you think you might fight for your opinion to be well-considered?

It really depends on what the stakes are because I'm also a realist. And once that case is over and we can finally all call it done and I can go back to my daily life or my life as it were, so I don't know how much sweat equity I would put into it, even though I don't want to see injustice, if I feel that strongly. But also it really depends on the situation. Are the other 10 really just a bunch of (expletive) heads that are all following their own – you know, they're lemmings and they're following each other? Or am I just, I see it differently and I can accept that.

Is there anything I should know about talking to gay jurors or having a gay client?

I never really thought about it.

I haven't either, but I mean –

It's a fair question.

I've had several gay people who've responded to me in these interviews. I'd like to talk about that a little bit because I would think there are biases and prejudicial issues there. So let's say I had a gay plaintiff and non-gay jury. Are there things that I would need to do to address that? Or, if I had a gay plaintiff and gay members of the jury, are there issues that I would need to be aware of?

You have a complicated job.

Generally, I'm not concerned about that issue in court.

If this were a different community, I'd say, yes. But if this was in a different community, I could see how people would secretly be recoiling and repulsed and possibly carrying baggage that is predisposing them to negative thoughts. But I can't imagine here.

I think I might prefer to have gay jurors, because they tend to be better educated.

There is that. There's a lot of stats that support that.

Although I don't know where the community fits in the issues of compensation and damages. Possibly a little conservative in the money way, I don't know.

But you can also play to that as a strength. All jurors know that it's not even a question of being judged by your peers. Sometimes it's who's your peers and what predispositions do you come with? That's really hard to find, people that you can peel back all the predispositions and truly make them appear to you. What would be considered a peer to a 50-year-old gay single man versus a young woman versus – so it's complicated.

I struggle with engineers as jurors. I was on a jury pool and an engineer was asked about whether he could decide objectively – I don't remember the exact question, but it had to do with his emotions. And he said, I can't possibly deal with this case emotionally because I'm a binary thinker. In my job, all day long, I deal with computers and numbers, and I can't possibly do anything but look at this case in a binary way. And that was very frustrating for me. That's not uncommon. This is a very conservative pool with a lot of aerospace engineers and software companies. People are making a lot of money; you think would be wanting to help your client; but generally are not there to help your client. They're generally against lawsuits, have very high standards of proof, and don't have great EQ. So how might I deal with those people?

That's a really interesting question. I don't know if you can. They're DNA and hard-coded that way. I worked with so many engineers for so many years, and I have kind of a secret love of them and loathe of them, because their linearity, while it's really refreshing and easy to navigate, it's also extraordinarily rigid and leaves very little expression or creativity. On some levels, I really value that, but – there's a classical joke – I'll speed it up and spare the time. A rabbi, a priest, a minister, and an engineer walk into a bar and go golfing as a foursome. The foursome in front of them is hitting a ball all over the place. They're driving the cart into the sand trap. They're driving it into the lake. They're not even really hitting the ball. And the foursome gets so frustrated they go back to the clubhouse, and say to the captain of the clubhouse, what the hell is with the foursome in front of us? They're acting like they're blind. And the guy goes, they are. We had a group of – that's the firemen. If you remember a few years ago, we had the horrible fire at the club and those are the firemen that raced in and saved everybody, but unfortunately, the smoke caused them to go blind. Well, the minister says, oh, I'm so sorry, of course my congregation will pray for them. And the rabbi, oh, I'm so sorry, well, of course the synagogue will pray for them. And the priest says, oh, we'll pray for them. And the engineer says, why don't they play at night? And in the joke, the guy says, we've given them unlimited rights to play whenever they want, and that's how – to understand that that's not even funny for them, an engineer normally won't laugh at that. They're like, why won't they play at night if they're blind? And you gotta love that, you gotta hate it at the same time. So I don't know how you work around that, because the whole idea of law is supposed to be, isn't something without reason or with reason? It's – law's without emotion? There's something about it –

Justice is blind, you know.

There's a lack of a sense of humanity in it.

For example, pity is a terrible motivator. The best motivator that we have is anger. If you can get the jury angry at the other side, you're far more likely to get an award than if they just pity your party.

Interesting. It's a hard emotion to elicit out of somebody that's very linear and logical.

Unless there's some rule that's been broken or some very bright line that's been ignored.

So is the defendant's lawyer typically trying to find engineers and people of that ilk, and you're trying to find people of more –

Yes.

Not compassionate, but a little bit more rounded in their emotional EQ.

For sure.

That's a tough one.

Thank you.

9

BE ACCEPTING

Caucasian female, age 38, single, one child, Fine Arts/Government Agency/Housecleaning, B.F.A., 2 years graduate school (Special Education)

Be accepting of however it is I'm going to react.

We were saying, imagine as if you're with up to 80 people in the courtroom, ready to go through the jury selection process.

A jury for a civil case?

Correct. At this point, the judge will say, ladies and gentlemen, please give your attention to the attorney for the plaintiff – that's the injured person – who's going to talk to you for approximately an hour about all sorts of things. But generally, he's going to ask you about bias, prejudice, prejudgment and things that weigh on your ability to judge the case fairly. The first question I have for you: as the judge says this and you're looking at the attorneys and their clients, what are you thinking and feeling, then and there?

Well, okay. The judge is looking at the clients, he's looking at the plaintiff.

The judge has just spoken to you and said, okay, one of the attorneys for the injured person is going to get up and talk to you. What are your thoughts?

My thoughts are it's really important to listen and not form any prejudgments. I've done this in jury research, and it can be a huge surprise once I hear both sides. I'll hear the first side in detail and I will swear that the plaintiff is guilty or is innocent. And then I hear the other side, and it's like the scales of justice. I have to hear what the laws are. Who is the most responsible party for the accident, because it was about an accident or bodily harm?

This is about some bodily harm. We won't necessarily talk specifically about what kind of bodily harm or how it happened, but just in general, when the lawyer stands up, your thoughts and impressions.

My thoughts would be, don't be scared. Don't be nervous, because that could impact my judgment, and because they're going to be asking for a lot of money, probably. It's pretty serious to not let it be an emotional – well, it should be emotional sometimes, but mostly like what are the laws and who's responsible for upholding the law? If it's a professional, it's important that they be held accountable. I just try to let everything else go and listen really closely. I try to be like a blank slate, like tabula rosa (sic) and have no impressions at all until I hear both sides because it could be a shocking turn around with the facts.

At this point of the case it's not about the facts; it's about the jury and learning

about the jury so that the lawyers can decide who is going to be on the jury. So from that large group of people, we're trying to get down to 12.

Well, they're going to want diversity, I'm sure. They're going to want male and female of all different economic backgrounds and different professions. Sometimes they'll ask, are you Democrat or Republican? I don't think that should be one of the – because you could make a decision based on law whether you're a Democrat or a Republican. But it wouldn't hurt to have both sides and I think all different races, cultures, so you get a comprehensive picture of what, in general, the public would want for the judge and the jury.

What would you like to hear from the lawyer who's going to talk to you? A lawyer will say, I'm going to learn about you. What would the lawyer want to ask you?

If I hear somebody's story, am I going to go by prejudices or am I going to be open to what actually happened or a myth and just be open to the actual facts. Am I going to be honest? Am I going to be open to new ideas from the team? Because I know juries break up into group sessions or, at least, open-minded. I've never had a lawyer actually talk to me about it.

If the lawyer talked to you to ask about you and your suitability for this particular case, how would you like the lawyer to ask you – how would you like the lawyer to approach you? What sort of questions would the lawyer want to ask to determine if you're, say, fair or neutral?

Well, under pressure, do I get nervous? Am I able to stay calm and absorb the facts? Usually if it's about somebody else I am. If it's about me, I get very nervous. But if it's about somebody else, I don't really mind. I'm sure the lawyer wants to make sure I'm not going to be deeply emotionally rerouted. Some people do get that way. But probably open to new ideas, too. I went to a case about a DUI and I thought this person was so guilty. You could do that math equation where they might go under, then I found out he refused the alcohol test, but I think that they had .113 or something. Then I found out the officer was supposed to issue a warrant, but they refused to take him to get a blood draw from the hospital. They just said, since he said no, they never took a breathalyzer. That changed my mind completely that they're innocent, just because the officer is responsible for making sure that there's a blood draw or some kind of factual proof of being over .08. So I guess if he refused it. That's the one where they refused it. They didn't have the blood draw, but they smelled, they reeked of alcohol. If I was emotionally inclined, I might say, no, it doesn't matter, they're guilty. But since I was logically inclined – and I think the lawyer wanted to make sure – but I don't know if that's how they proceed.

How can a lawyer who you never met, who's going to ask you and 79 other people, questions about a case you don't know, at this point, anything about – how can that lawyer establish a human connection with you?

Be accepting of however it is I'm going to react. I guess I'd have to think about it, but if there's pressure to be neutral and pressure to not show

emotion, I don't know what they do in that case, if it's better to just be accepting of who you are. I guess the lawyer would – I mean, if you get chosen for a jury, you're not going to get paid for it.

Ten dollars a day.

Okay.

Is that important to you to want to be on the jury or not want to be on the jury for a case?

I would probably not want to be on a jury. Maybe for the research, but not for the actual court case. If this case went either way, I'd like to stand up for what's just and what's right. And I'd be as honest as possible. Because I go to AA and part of the thing is to be rigorously honest. So when somebody gets justice that they deserve, I feel good about it. Because that's democracy. You know, I'd like to help.

You mentioned honesty. How are you able to determine if the lawyer is an honest and credible person?

I don't know. As far as I know, they gather facts and they present them to the judge. When it comes down to it, if they're dishonest, they might try to manipulate it this way or that way. But I would have good faith if they have the license, then I would trust that they are. I wouldn't have a bias. I've been in some focus groups where it seems like some of the male jurors were harder on the women plaintiffs. I don't think that has any place in a courtroom, but I could have been biased because I'm a female. So I know that's why they try to have male and female jurors.

If the lawyer wanted to ask you about biases that you might have, how would you feel about that question and how would you answer that?

My initial impressions usually are biased towards women being innocent until I hear the facts, when it comes to certain cases, like, domestic violence or things like that. That's usually the only time I'm biased. Because if she has dependents, like children with her, then it's extremely important that she gets the services she needs. Or if somebody's suing a doctor, I'd have to listen – if it's somebody trying to manipulate the system for a settlement or if the doctor actually screwed up really bad; in that case, I don't think the doctor needs to be enabled or – needs to be more cautious. Because I don't think they'd fire the doctor. I know that. But they need to be more – follow the itinerary closer.

The law allows people who are injured to bring cases against the people that have hurt them. How do you feel about that, in general?

If you hurt somebody you're held responsible?

Yes.

I think that's awesome. In some countries, it doesn't even exist. In America, we take the body and its health as a gift not to be abused and not to be taken lightly.

Whether or not the intent to abuse is there is one thing. But if somebody's going to be driving a car, making a surgery, it's best to be as aware of all the procedures as possible. Because that could be somebody's mom, somebody's son. It could be someone a lot of people are counting on, and I think that's our responsibility for the common good.

Are you okay with the notion of accountability being money to compensate the injured person?

I think so. Because they're going to have to pay for physical therapy, loss of wages. Sometimes they have to change a career, and then they have to have schooling. If they get depressed, or pain and suffering, from being put out – it could be excruciating pain, and I think they should be compensated for that. Because I think more people have to say, hey, maybe I'd better wake up a little bit right now, because somebody could seriously get hurt if I don't pay attention to what I'm doing.

Do you think that works as a check and a balance?

I think money is a good mode of reputation. It's a big motivator in our society. I think the less headache – who wants to get entangled in that huge of a – it's stressful, it's heartbreaking, it's very sad. I don't think anybody – what was your question? Is that a motivator? A check and balance?

Do you think that money going from the person that caused the injury to the person that's hurt is a good, effective way for the system to balance the scales and to do justice?

I think money is an appropriate way. I also think sometimes the person who committed it doesn't feel the effects because they might go to court, but they don't feel it on a deeper level because maybe they think they're innocent. But I don't think that has any place in deciding a jury. I think money is an awesome way to compensate somebody.

What do you think about the role of insurance in these kinds of cases?

I think it's very necessary. It's a way for people to come together and look out for each other. And it's not to be abused. As far as I know, it's not, but there are some people who might. I don't know. I think insurance is an awesome idea.

I want to come back to this idea that it's important to find a way to connect, as a human being, with the people that are going to be on that jury for days or weeks, sometimes longer. And I would like to hear more about how you would like an attorney to be so that you feel connected to that person.

I think they need to emphasize idealism, and emphasize that it's going to probably be emotional. And it's going to require taking in information and there might be emotion. Usually when I hear a story, I'll think of something from my past, and I get kind of emotional, but then I try to say, well. But I think from an attorney, they need to emphasize – and I love it when they say don't talk to anybody else.

Because then you know when you get in the focus group, that whatever I say there is going to be kept there. I like to hear that from the attorney. So it's like a sense of safeness, of not feeling pressure to lean this way or that way. Especially if there's money involved. And to be known that the people aren't going to know my name; I'm just the jury. I guess that's about it.

When you're in that hypothetical courtroom looking at these attorneys for the first time, do you have a sense that they're honest or not so honest?

I think they want to get to the bottom of things. I think they both have a set of evidence and they honestly want to find out what really happened. I think not one person can do that. So I think it's good to have two sides and get to the bottom. They're looking like, we're about to dig into something and it's going to be a little uncomfortable. But I think it's important so that justice comes. I don't think attorneys are bad. I think if we didn't have attorneys, this society would be a disaster. It would be chaos; just to have all things considered, like on NPR. I think it's important to consider all different sides.

Some people believe that trial lawyers are greedy and just trying to make a quick buck. How do you feel about that?

Well, it's a higher paid profession. I would hope my lawyer would be highly educated. And I would hope – quick buck? I don't know. I've heard that before. I don't agree with it at all.

What would you like to know about the lawyer when the lawyer gets up and starts talking to you?

If a lawyer started talking to me about a case?

About the lawyer or the case. If you had an opportunity to ask questions to the lawyer, what would you want to know?

I'd say, what type of people do you usually represent? I talked to a woman who helps people that get DUIs. She has an interesting spin on the law, and it kind of broke me out of the normal perspective. I'd say if somebody's a corporate lawyer, well, they have a lot of salaries they have to pay and they have to have liquid assets in case something happened to the company. I don't think they're greedy. But people always think, well, if you have big money behind a lawyer, they're going to abuse the common person because their vote, the corporation's vote is going to be bigger than just one person. And the common person gets lost in the sea of justice but where the people with money don't ever have to worry about getting in trouble. So I think that might be true. You look at OJ Simpson, and I think that was disgusting. And I just thought that whole case was really vulgar. It was really gross.

If I were the attorney in this civil case and was getting ready to learn about the jury, would you have any specific questions that you'd want to ask me before I started speaking to you? That you'd want to know about?

I don't know. I guess I'm not really wondering about you. I'm wondering about the case. I'm wondering what type of people you usually represent, because I'm already trusting you. I always think all lawyers are going to be – because you have to go to school, you have to get an education. I'm really concerned about the people that are afraid because they've lost something very important to them, their health. They've lost something. I'm afraid for them, that they're not going to get their needs met because somebody made a mistake. And maybe that person feels bad about it or not, I don't know. But I'm not really worried about the attorney.

If the lawyer, in an effort to connect, wanted to share something of his or her experience, how would you feel about that? At the outset?

I think it'd be very helpful. I think it would extremely helpful.

Can you think of an example of something you might like to hear or subject matter that would meaningful to you?

Maybe if they went through a similar situation and it caused them an intense emotion of fear or an intense emotion of anger, or if they've dealt with other cases. I think it would be nice to know they processed that situation in their mind and made a decision.

If the lawyer had been a juror, for example, how would you feel about the lawyer saying, I've been in your shoes in this jury panel. I know what it's like to be questioned.

***It'd be very helpful, because I'd feel more accepted for the process that I'm going to go through.** Because it is a process. It's like, first I have to hear this side. And then I have to hear this side. And then I have to talk to other people and it's draining. **It'd be nice to know they understand it's going to be draining.** And they might provide a longer break or they might provide refreshments or snacks or whatever to make it more tolerable.*

If the attorney said, I've been in the shoes of my client in a similar case where I've been the injured person. Would that be something you'd want to hear about?

I would want to hear about it. Well, maybe not, though. Because if they've been in the shoes of the client, I don't know – how much reform have they gone through? Unless they've been injured. If they've been injured, then I would want to hear it. If they broke a law, I don't want to know.

If the attorney had been seriously injured and had been in a case.

No. No. I'd feel like I was being pressured.

You'd feel like you're being pressured. Too much?

I'd feel like they're not supposed to pressure me to feel sorry for them. I think that's too close. There's enough distance to where there's, you're too close, you're just enough, and then there's too far. I just like to stay – even far is okay, but that's just too close.

As you're sitting there in this room – and I realize that this is all hypothetical – what is your sense of the people in the room around you who are also potential jurors?

I think they have an open mind at that point. They're generally interested in hearing both sides of the story. They know in America they're not going to be pressured at all. I know they were all randomly selected. I went to this movie about a Pakistani judge of women, and there's certain laws like, two women equals one man in a court. So they're going to be more pressured to listen to the man. But not in America.

Do you have a sense, one way or the other, that at least some of the potential jurors have agendas for one side or another?

I think they do have agendas. I definitely do. I don't think they're perfect at all. But that's democracy. Even I sometimes can be heavily biased, depending on the situation. Am I able to listen? Am I afraid at the time? Am I experiencing anxiety? Some people have a different routine. You don't know their routine. But they're definitely going to be biased.

How can the lawyer sensitively address the lawyer's concerns to people that may have biases or agendas?

Well, bias means, it's unfair, right? They're unfairly leaning? Or they're biased towards truth or –

They're not going to give both sides an equal opportunity from the start. In other words, they've prejudged; they've pre-decided.

Oh, really? Well, they're kind of leaning in towards – oh. How would you know that?

Sometimes, they will tell us. For example, you may have somebody who's profoundly religious who believes that you should never sue your neighbor. Or somebody who works for the insurance industry who clearly believes that – or may not want to say it – but whose bias is towards the insurer. Or people who are lawyers like me who represent injured people who may just have a bigger heart towards those kinds of people.

Right.

So if somebody were honest enough about it, how would the lawyer want to talk to them about it?

Well, I think – so you have a bias –

Or maybe you've been sued and you didn't like that experience, and so you want to –

I think it comes down to the evidence. How open to the evidence are you and putting your past behind? I can do that easily. But some people might not be able to. I would try to be open to the facts.

Do you think as you're in that room with these other people that you are more likely to be fair-minded than the average person? Just you.

Just me? Well, I don't know about average. It depends. I think we're all trying our best. How much that person is honest every day? I don't do it because I'm a good person; I just do it because I don't relapse. So I have to be honest with myself about my feelings. But some people are more gray area and they're probably luckier than me. But when it comes down to a case, maybe are they able to see the difference between – do they know when they're telling a white lie? I don't know.

What if the case is a relatively small case and say, instead of the case that the lawyer thinks is worth, say, a million dollars, it's a case where the lawyer thinks it's only worth $50,000. But it's going to take the same amount of time from your schedule to be on that jury. Is that case as significant to the individual as the other case?

Yes. Yes. I had a free lawyer but I felt like it put me at a disadvantage, because they say if you don't document it, it doesn't exist. And I can't do all the documenting myself. I think they're both equal because some people, all they have is a free lawyer, and it's just as equal for that person to be represented.

Even if the amount in controversy is –

Oh, for a bigger lawsuit. Well, even the smaller ones – it depends on what issue and how much it's going to change society. Because it might move up to the next court. I know they have district courts and then they have the next round and the next round. But yeah. I think it should be equally considered.

Do you think that there are such things as frivolous lawsuits?

***Definitely.** I know a couple of people who were always going to sue. I wasn't good friends with them, but I didn't even know people like that existed. I don't know how far they would go. Because the whole idea just seems so – I don't mean to use the word "stupid," but it just seems so not worth your time, to deliberately manipulate money out of a court.*

Do you think you'd be able to, for lack of a better term, sniff out if somebody were frivolous?

No. I'd never know. I'd never think somebody would do that. I'd always give them the benefit of the doubt. It's been a mental exercise I've had to develop.

Would you give the benefit of the doubt to both of the parties in the case that are on opposite sides?

I would have to see the facts. Because somebody could get a huge amount of money but it just depends.

Have you ever been hurt in an accident or a case where somebody's negligence injured you?

My car's been totaled.

Were you driving? Or were you in the car?

Yeah. But I wasn't hurt.

You weren't hurt.

I got the Blue Book *value of my car about three or four times. And I thought that was fair.*

If you had been hurt, would you have wanted to pursue some money claim to make you feel that justice was done?

Definitely.

Do you know anybody who's been seriously hurt in an accident or a medical case or something where they did bring a lawsuit?

Not to my knowledge, I've never known anybody. I mean, thank God, you know? Sometimes undisclosed information. If they would have had that information they might not have been as anxious. And that does cause psychological damage which can be detrimental.

Do you think that psychological injuries, which are things you can't really see, ought to be compensated for as well?

Yes. It depends on what level of psychological damage. It can't be random. It has to be very pinpointed. And if it's focused and pinpointed onto someone, and it's been deliberately planned and executed, I think that it's their responsibility to be honest and open about what they did and compensate the person so they can account for that and go on with their life.

We have two kinds of damages in injury cases. We have those where people have medical bills or lost wages, past and future. And those get paid – if the jury decides – sort of dollar for dollar. You can write them down on a chalkboard and add them up. But then there are these emotional damages where we can't do that. How would you go about putting a value on those kinds of injuries?

Well, for instance, I lost my son. I've lost over four years. There's no price tag that I can put on that. I'll never have those years back. If I was compensated for my art, I wouldn't be gung-ho about assuming a massive amount of money, because I think I'm talented enough where I don't need that. I know some people get into an accident and they can't go running any more. They've lost their job because they were a nurse and they can't stand for long periods. And they might have went to school for six years to be a nurse and now they can no longer be a nurse or be the mother that they'd like to be because they can't play ball with their kid. I think people need to be highly cautious about their behavior and how it impacts others, and be sensitive. Because it could cross the line where it breaks the law and we've decided as a society, people need to be able to function, their body needs to be treated with the utmost respect, and their psychological space needs to be treated with the utmost respect.

If I said to you that given the same facts, two different juries could reach very different conclusions in terms of the amount of money, how do you feel about that?

I think other people need to step in that are more neutral. There needs to be some hard looking at what really happened.

You've done focus group work, and having done that myself, I know you can bring in one group of people, give them this set of facts and they'll reach this number. Another group of people, different people, will reach a very different number.

That's very odd. Because the law is the law is the law. One way or another, it's cut and dried. If you have a driver's license it's a big responsibility. If somebody's not taking responsibility for their behavior and it hurts somebody, it should be easy for everybody to see that. I wonder if they're manipulating the system for money. Maybe the damages, how much they're going to award, if it's the difference between millions I think it needs to be taken into consideration, a lot of different things, areas of their life and for how much they should be awarded or compensated.

Is there anything that you'd like to say or mention that I haven't brought up that's on your mind? That might be helpful?

I like to see people in healthy relationships. I like to see people who've worked hard and are honest get things that they deserve. If somebody's dishonest or careless, it's not fair to the people who are honest and very careful. I think it's so important for everybody to be honest. Honesty is the best. Whether it's omission – is it omission or commission?

Omission.

Sometimes by not saying anything, you're still lying.

If you were in your jury deliberations, after hearing a case, and you were one of the lone voices, how strongly would you fight for the opinion that you have? Just in the context of the deliberation, if you know that you're out-voted, do you still think that you would be able to make sure that everybody understood your position?

I would.

You would stand up?

I would. Because I trust in my thoughts for what's just and not just. I would definitely make sure that they knew somebody on that day saw it from that perspective and that perspective was at least brought to the table. So maybe that's the only way justice was brought about, that somebody noticed. Not that any action was taken, but it didn't go unaccounted for.

Thank you very much.

10

FIRST THOUGHT, RIGHT THOUGHT

Caucasian female, age 32, single, Student, B.S.

If you start talking to someone about their biases and they say something that may or may not be appropriate and your first thought is I don't want that on my jury, don't keep asking the question. Please just dismiss the person. I mean, first thought, right thought, right?

The judge says, ladies and gentlemen, please give your attention to the attorney for the plaintiff. What's going through your head right then and there?

Probably let me think of all the ways that I can get out of this.

Get out of jury service?

Yeah. And let me think of all the ways that I either know too much about this already or that I've already served what I feel is my allotted amount of time.

Assuming you have to answer questions, honestly from the attorneys – and going through your head is, how am I going to get out of this, what are the impressions that you might have in general towards the lawyers and the clients, just going in?

I've done jury selection. I have family who are lawyers and who've been defense attorneys or DAs or whatever and so I always respect the situation that there are clients and there's something at stake for that person.

So going through your head is this sense that because I have family or friends who are lawyers, I understand that that's what they do, and so I want to honor them a little bit by –

Yeah, and I know people that have been significantly affected by court cases. I know there's skin in the game for those people, too. I'm just, on some very personal level, hoping that it's not my skin.

Your time?

Yeah. Either I have something or I've experienced something or I'm aware of something that would get me out of this, or I have an opinion that would get me out of this.

Sure. Skin in the game. That's a great expression. Do you think skin in the game applies to all of the participants?

Absolutely. Everyone in that courtroom. Even the people who are sitting there listening, right? They're sitting there, listening to a trial. They have something in it too, right? It's an investment. Whether it's your time, your money, your resources, your – for all I know, county government has an investment to the space. They want this stuff dealt with just as fast as everybody or as judiciously and as fast as everyone else does.

The lawyers? Do they have skin in the game, in your –

Yeah. Well, their intellectual property and also their time and commitments and money that they've put up for their services they've provided. Obviously their professional stake is important, right? I mean, it depends on the size of the case, but some people's entire careers hang in the balance based on how that type of case goes or doesn't go.

Do you think there are any entities or individuals behind the scenes who might have skin in the game?

Oh, sure. Well, there's everyone, right? There's the people who are the office assistants of the lawyers and their secretaries and the people who help – paralegals. And then all the people who serve the judge, right? So there's the bailiff, the plaintiff. And usually there's two police officers that sit in court all day and they don't care, but they're there too. That's money, time, and resources there. And there's all the clerical people and the schedulers and the IT people, because now all the cases are on the web and you can look up your case ID and figure out all this stuff, what's been filed, what's not been filed. So all that. All those people.

What about society's skin in the game?

I would agree there is that, too, right? We come at it from a personal standpoint, right? Every single one of us, when you license or you register to vote or something then you can serve jury duty. It's part of your civic duty.

Do you think that society has skin in the game with regard to the outcome and how the process is reached?

*Sure. **I think everybody is entitled to – every one of us, being American citizens, have our trials heard in court and a subset of our peers hear the trial and then make a decision about the verdict.** And it matters on some level, if there is evidence that somebody committed capital murder or whatever, that they're locked up and not just running around wielding swords.*

Do you think if you were a party in a case that you want a juror like you to hear the case?

That's a tough question. Actually I wouldn't want me to hear the case and the reason why is because I know too much. I'm too smart, I think. And I would probably be able to see through a lot of thinly-veiled cover-ups and I also think there are other people who feel much more strongly about serving on a jury and actually enjoy it and like it. Speaking from my own personal experience where I was sequestered for a week and half, I did not really enjoy it.

What do you think about people who gain something intrinsically by being on a jury, who really want to be on the jury? Do you think that desire can make a good juror?

No. I think there's a subset of the culture of people who desire to be on juries because they're interested in legal matters, not because they're aware of themselves in the moment. But I think it's happening where because of whatever school they went to or politics they're into and they want arbitrations in general and they like resolving arguments, there's a subset of the population that finds that to be very compelling. Not all people, but there is a subset. I think.

Changing gears, when the attorneys stand up to talk to you in the jury selection process, what can they do establish a connection with you? Or we can approach it the other way: what should they not do?

I would say my biggest don't do, and this is the last time I was in a jury, the DA was questioning jurors and I was like Juror No. 12, but from a selfish perspective, he gave away exactly what he was trying to fish out of the jury pool, so I just responded with the same thing they were dismissing everybody else for. I think you give it away too quickly if you do that. I don't know that much about jury selection, but in this one situation what I recall was it was very much a game of Clue. I don't know how else to describe it, and they had the answers and this set of, whatever, 40 people piled into the courtroom didn't have the answers and it feels like a really big mystery and they are trying to hold their cards close to themselves – you know, I gotta want to give up what I'm looking for, but at the same time, you give it up by automatically dismissing people who've already expressed a certain –

Expressed that opinion.

So I don't feel connected to them or the situation at all, because it's like, we have the answers and we're looking for who said that then, you know, if you answer this, you're gone.

Do you have a sense of what the purpose of jury selection is?

*In my mind, it's to get a set of 12 people that are your peers, that are not someone who either lives in the neighborhood that the case is heard in, goes to the same doctor, knows the people, knows the police officers, whatever. **The best pool of your peers.***

So if the judge gives the lawyer permission to explore biases and prejudices that the jurors might have, how do you feel about those questions being asked of you? What sort of biases or prejudices or prejudgments might you have going in?

I have a lot of judgments and a lot of biases.

How comfortable do you feel –

I have no problem expressing them, but that's why I have no problem straight shooting. I grew up in a very straight shooting environment. Say what you think.

Do you have a particular set of biases or prejudgments towards lawyers and the kinds of lawyers who do cases that represent people that are seeking money because they've been hurt?

I don't have any prejudgments about that. I've known trial lawyers who seek a ton of money for other things like, I don't know whether you'd call it tax and trust and will and durable power of attorney and corporate law, things like that. I have biases about that. I would say that I've thought about the fact that they gouge their client. Obviously, their services aren't necessarily rendering nearly as much as a large corporate settlement. I have personal opinions about things like the dumbest lawsuits that have ever existed, like the McDonald's hot cup of coffee lawsuit.

How do you feel about that one?

*That was stupid. I can't believe it went all the way to trial. But people who have been legitimately or are partially brain dead because of medical malpractice, I don't have a bias about that either. **Accidents happen, but you should be held accountable.***

How do you feel about people who use the courts to both get compensation for their injuries and to hold accountable the person that injured them or the entity that injured them?

I think that's fine.

Do you think there are more frivolous lawsuits than there are non-frivolous lawsuits on the civil personal injury side?

Yes. And the reason I say is because I, like you, watch television and find out that – those mesothelioma lawsuits and did you use vaginal mesh lawsuits and things like that; these people are spending time on that? I understand that someone along the way may have had a very severe complication, but if you're going to spend money on advertising, come on. Now you're just going out and culling to the public going how many of you have done this? And I feel like that bumps someone more against them.

Lawyers who advertise?

Yeah, but it's the ones they advertise about the stuff that, a lot of it's medical and they advertise about it and it almost becomes they're searching for these. But you get the wave-ish effect.

How can a lawyer establish credibility with you? In this environment that we're talking about.

***If it's a higher level of transparency or honesty, not about the case, but about what they're doing and why they're doing it,** not – I don't know if you can say why you're doing it, but what you're doing.*

Can you maybe elaborate on that a little bit? Maybe an example or –

Okay. A very good friend just finished law school. She worked for four years at a malpractice firm as a paralegal office assistant and was involved in a large case. We met, had dinner, the case had finished and they'd finally gotten out of jury selection and she said it was the most stressful situation ever. She was sitting in the office and her lawyer was texting her to look up people on the Internet and look for their social media or for whatever and try to see what else they could glean about those people. From a lawyering standpoint, I will tell you what you want to know; just ask me, even if it's personal. I find that sort of backhanded snooping leaves me with a bad taste in my mouth. Because I'm going to be honest, that I signed a thingy – waiver or whatever that I'm going to be honest as I know how to be.

So picture yourself in this room with 40 to 80 people. As you look around the room at the faces, do you have a sense they will do the same? That they will answer truthfully when they're asked about personal questions that have to do with their biases or their prejudices or their judgments?

*It's interesting you ask that question, because I don't honestly think about them. Not that it's only about me, but I don't care what they think. Everybody's too guarded because they're too worried about looking back. **Most people have this baggage where they don't want to look bad in front of anyone.** They don't want to seem not in a good space. And I'd say there's God-given America, grow the (expletive) up.*

Right. So accountability is an important theme in your life. Openness and accountability.

Exactly.

Do you have a strong sense of the connection between this civil system having the outcome that there is accountability for a wrongdoer and a victim?

*I do. I believe the reason why verdicts are handed down as they are and damages are given out as need be is because of people who have sat and deliberated in the room of a jury of people. **They are making the best decision they know how given the evidence they were provided and given the accounts they've been told or whatever.** Because personally, in my own experience, from being on a jury, that it was an arduous process just to come up with a verdict and everyone at that point had turned the cases inside out and was this the right verdict or was – whether it's right or wrong, it doesn't matter. Was it the best? Yes. And I think that's why people get caught up is that there's supposed to be some right or wrong, and it's like, no, it's the best. And that definition gets lost. The judge that was presiding over the case was very, very clear about that. That the case – moral things, not necessarily –*

Negligence or –

Yeah. And he was very clear that if you say that they're guilty of this, it's not representative of – is what they did bad and vice versa. If you say the person is not guilty of this, you're not saying, hey, every priest, please go out and molest all the little boys. That's not that. It's not a moral statement. Is this the best verdict given the information you've been provided? And he was really clear about that. And that was what we – every juror went right round on it.

Can I come back to the credibility issue? Because to me, it's very important that the jury perceive me as an honest, credible, transparent person representing my client. Sometimes I fall down and fail to the extent that I'd like to be more credible. What sorts of things do you think a juror is looking for or responds to?

I hate it, or, I did not like it, being asked the same question over and over again. They're the same question, over and over again, by that same lawyer, then by both lawyers. I really didn't appreciate that. And also, having a lawyer just ask the same question as me and Juror No. 11 and Juror No. 10 and Juror No. 7. I don't even want to answer your question now because you've asked the question five times. Please find another way to ask the question. And ask it using different vocabulary, different sentence structure. I know that sounds silly, but when I'm sitting there, just like everyone, time is money. I'm sitting there and I'm spending the day in your courthouse, can you please make this more entertaining? Use bigger words? Use smaller words? Use different for instances? So when you run through a hypothetical situation, I don't want the same hypothetical situation that they guy next to me got. Because it's not intellectually stimulating and that's like a professor at home, wah wah. And you just sound like the Peanuts mom in the background.

In your jury experiences, did you find the lawyers were talking down to the jurors or were struggling to find words to talk up to the juries?

Neither. Not talking down, not talking up. **My experience has just been that it's not interesting. And then words that come out of your mouth are not interesting to me because they ask five other people the same thing. I already have come up with my response, and I'm just sitting there waiting.**

Are there limits to what a lawyer can share with you about his or her own biases or prejudices when asking you about yours? In other words, sharing before asking?

This is going to sound awful. Quite frankly, I don't give a (expletive) about your biases or your prejudices or whatever. So are there limits to it? Less is more.

If the lawyer were to say, I'm going to ask you about your biases, but before I do that, it seems fair that I share something of my own experience, briefly, and then says that. Do you feel that eases whatever tension there might be in the natural moment there in the courtroom with that lawyer?

No. I don't think so at all.

What could ease the moment for you? What would make it better for you?

I'm not sure there's anything that can be said in the moment. You can call me jaded or whatever but I also came from a different region of the country where before you even go into jury selection, you have to sit down and watch a video about how it happens and why it happens and all that stuff and what the expectation is and they don't have that here, unfortunately or fortunately. So from my perspective, I'm not new to this. I don't need you to explain how – I don't need the lawyers – I wish they would show that video even if it's sort of patronizing. And if there was some way that they could flag it to be viewed by people who it was their first time serving, or first time being called; and I don't even know if you're familiar with the video I'm trying to speak of.

Sure.

*But I think that video is incredibly informational and also **it outlines expectation. It outlines how the process is going to go.** You're expected to share your biases and outlines, you know, the lawyers are going to ask you a question like this and you should answer how you feel. Or you should answer truthfully about your background or your whatever. And it's not like a mark against you or for you or whatever. I think it's probably unfortunate that you have to stand up and talk; it's the responsibility of the lawyers to educate the jurors or to give them a snapshot of this is what you should expect and here's a ton of questions I'm going to ask you and I'll talk a little bit about my biases and then you can talk about yours. I think that's unfortunate. It adds more burden to the lawyers and on some level, if you're sitting there and you're waiting in your pool of 40 and you're number 39, you're like, are we going to get there?*

Do you want to hear anything in jury selection about the parties that are having the dispute? Or are you just looking at them and forming your opinions, sort of on that basis?

So, the judge that presided over the trial that I – gave the synopsis, high level, not saying who was who, but gave enough background about what the dispute was, and I felt like that was all the information I needed to know. But then again, if it was civil, I'm not sure of the full nature of it, but it was clear that it was a man versus a woman and it was very clear, oh, there's a woman sitting over there and it's a woman.

Do you think the attorneys who are questioning jurors need to be aware that time is the most precious commodity jurors have? If they're being respectful of all of the jurors, as a group and individually, do you think that it's the jurors' time that is the most important thing to be respectful of? Or is there something else I'm not thinking about?

I'd say there's three things that are tied for me. I can't rank one above the other, but I can say time is important. The other thing, to me, that the lawyer has to respect is everyone's right to due process in a courtroom. And the third thing is probably the intellectual level of all the people that are there.

Talk about the second and the third of those a little bit more, the rights to due process and the intellectual level of the people.

*I put on the lawyer hat and use my imagination. Your job is to serve the people of this great state and country and city and town with your legal talents. "We" as a collective "we" all at some point need to tap that process whether it's for malpractice, road, DUI, you know? All the different reasons. And you must hold in high regard the fact that every single one of us could be entitled to this same level of trial fairness, hearing, whatever. So respecting that and understanding maybe more than the actual jurors, you know, things happen and life changes in an instant, and being able to hold that in a better place for that. Stand up for your profession and stand up for the whole arm of the government that is the justice arm of the government and say we're all entitled to this and so time is not the only thing that pushes you. What should push you in the same direction is the fact that you never know what's going to happen. I, very well, being a juror, could be on the flip side of the bench and need that same level of commitment from those other people in the room. And then intellect, I think, the two opportunities that I've had, I felt like – and maybe this is because I'm a younger person – but I felt like the lawyers would use simple words and would break things down again for me every single time they came to me. And granted, it was six days after I got my license. And yeah, he's got to abide by the law. **But just because I'm young doesn't mean I'm not smart.** And I wish very much that those lawyers could see that and then again, at the other trial, I was like, excuse me?*

To the lawyer?

*Yeah. I gave him a hard time. I said, I'm smarter than that. Try again. **Regardless of what your education background is, you can still be plenty smart and you can still understand plenty of things and you have different levels of emotional and intellectual intelligence and that's got to be respected by whoever is sitting on the other side.** Because they, too, can read your facial expressions and can hear the quiver in your voice, and can see the person tearing up over there just as well as I can.*

What's a lawyer to do when faced with an obviously biased juror who wants to be on that jury and wants to tank that lawyer's case because the bias is that they don't believe in lawsuits or they don't believe that lawsuits are good for the country or they think that doctors will be pushed out of the community or they think their insurance rates will go up or any number of reasons, what's the lawyer to do when faced with a juror like that?

If it was me? If I was the lawyer? I like a good challenge, so I'd be like, get on my case, buddy, I'll turn your opinion around.

Do you think those kinds of jurors I just described do exist?

Of course.

Do you think there are those who are less vocal about their biases? In other words, more stealthy? And how am I to find those jurors in this pool without asking difficult questions?

I have to ask you a question. If it's truly supposed to be a jury of your peers, there are all those people that exist in society, so how can you sleuth them out and say, I don't want this person on my jury given the fact that they truly do represent a portion of society? So, you tell me?

I don't know.

I think you just have to take whoever these people are and say, okay, this is a set of my peers. It's randomly selected. But if it's truly supposed to be a cross-section of your peers, there are those people.

I'm glad you brought that up, because that leads to something I've been thinking about which is, much of what they're teaching lawyers right now about jury selection has to do with – establish rapport, connection – and I'm wondering if I might want to break it down to simply asking the jury pool, if you think you can be fair and give both sides a fighting chance, equally, then I'm done here. I have no more questions. Raise your hand if you can; raise your hand if you can't. And I'm done.

I don't see why there would be any problem with that because in reality, if these people can go in with an open mind, or what they think is an open mind, then the best decision, as I said, will be made.

Will they be honest? Would you, as a juror, be honest? I guess that's the question I would say.

Oh, yeah.

All these people of all different backgrounds they come from and given that they're all over the age of 18 and are either registered voters or have a driver's license. And say, if you want to be here, or don't want to be here, I'll help you either way. And if you'll be honest with me – or, if you'll tell me that you can give each side –

A fair chance.

A fair start.

And listen with a blank slate, whatever.

That works for me. Do you think that approach is a credible approach to take?

I don't see why it wouldn't be. I think the judge might be like, what?

The judge would love it.

Oh, if he would love it, then at the same time, I'd be like, no questions, are you sure? Did you go to law school?

And that's it. Those people who may be honest enough to say they may have some biases, I'd like to talk to them a little bit more. But it would save the judge hours of time. And also –

Save the client money.

Well, the client – in our cases, we're contingent fees, so the only people that are going to give me heartburn are my peers who are saying, you're doing it all wrong.

Okay. No, no, no. What is the definition of insanity?

Right. Doing the same thing. Hitting your head against the wall and expecting a different result every time. My thought is, in this day and age, we're quick deciders. We're impressionistic from the get-go. We have lots of things competing for our time and attention, lots of talking doesn't really help. It may help to develop a relationship, that's the only thing. And some connection. Because if I talk to the jury for 50 minutes and the defense attorney talks to them for two or three hours and has all this time to connect, does it hurt me?

Right. I think the best way to test that approach would be if you were on the defense side, because it's the plaintiff that goes first, right? And it's the defense that goes second. So that would be a brilliant way from the defense too, you know? **I want to talk to you about biases. Would you think that there are biased people that are still on the jury? You encounter it from the perspective of I am going to be respectful of your time and realize that you have lives and rights and a family to go home to or dogs or whatever. I'm going to ask my questions, but I'm going to keep it short and let you go. Personally, I don't believe after being questioned for many hours that I had any connection with either side in the case.** *I had no connection to either the defense or the prosecution.*

By that token, do you think they learned anything more about you in those hours than learned in the first 15 minutes?

Nope.

If they were paying attention?

If they were paying attention, they would have learned whatever they asked me, like what newspapers do you read and where did you go to school? How much education have you had? Things like that. If they were truly invested, I think jury selection could be dropped down to like an hour.

It is that way now. We have a thing called the Golden Rule, which says we can't ask the jury to put themselves in the shoes of the party that is suing. How do you feel about that rule? That I can't say, folks, I'd like you to imagine that you were in my client's shoes when this happened with all of these things.

I'd feel, good or bad, actually. Everybody's going to respond differently when it's actually them. You would hope people would respond consistently, but not everyone.

Is there anything I haven't asked you that you'd like to mention before we conclude? Anything you think might be helpful that I didn't touch on?

I wish that lawyers who were interviewing jury selection stuff provided a little more humor. God. Someday –

A lot of seriousness.

It's so serious. And stop with your whispering. ***I wish people would go with first thought, right thought a little bit more.***

Can you give me an example of that? Because I've never heard that expression, though I think I know what it's referring to.

If you start talking to someone about their biases and they say something that may or may not be appropriate and your first thought is I don't want that on my jury, don't keep asking the question. Please just dismiss the person. I mean, first thought, right thought, right?

Right. Reptile thinking; go with the gut.

I strongly believe in the guy who wrote Tipping Point –

Malcolm Gladwell.

Malcolm Gladwell. And the story of the Getty kouros which was the statue that is very famous, a Greek statue which they found more of them in Greece. There was this one that came to the London museum of fine art or whatever and they had this expert come in. And the expert goes, that's not right. That's not from Greece, that's not authentic, that's a fake. And he spent like three years trying to figure out why it was fake and wouldn't let it go on its way. And when he had found all the imperfections and the reasons why it was fake, it was truly unearthed a fake.

He knew it at another level.

He knew it at another level, and I wish lawyers would start testing that a little bit more. You see people, you see the number of cases. You've built up enough acumen. You can begin to see the lurkers and the fakes and the people who are not being truthful and who came in to see the ulterior motive. I wish that you would just go, okay, that person's got ulterior motives. Let's dismiss or whatever. Go with that more. Because in general, I would think that by the time you've gotten through law school and you've seen enough cases and done it enough times, not that you're necessarily really good or better than anyone else, but you do have a lot of interactions with a random selection of people and are able to do a little more sorting a little more quickly.

All right.

First thought, right thought.

First thought, right thought. Thank you.

11

FAIRNESS

Caucasian male, age 51, married, one child, Police Officer (Retired)/Accident Investigation Expert, B.S.

I appreciate someone that says, hey, can you be fair in this case, wait to make up your mind until you've heard all of the facts, and then come up with a decision? If you can't do that, and you're going to let your prejudices, biases come in to it, at the start of the case or in the middle of the case, raise your hand. That's not the person we're looking for. If you think you can stay fair and impartial throughout the whole trial until you hear all of the facts and the closing arguments, that's the type of person I'm looking for. I think you would probably get the majority of the people to honestly raise their hand. You're going to get some to raise their hand just because they don't want to be there.

Give your attention to the attorney for the plaintiff who's going to conduct *voir dire*, his or her portion of the jury selection process. At that moment, what's going through your mind?

Here comes all the hard questions about your personal life and what you've experienced that you may or may not want to answer.

How do you feel about that? Do you feel that's an intrusion?

To some degree, yes. An intrusion in my life. I'm here to serve as a juror to try to figure out what happened in the case, if the plaintiff has truly been harmed or not, and my real history doesn't really play into your case.

Given you're feeling that way, what do you think a lawyer can do to put you at ease?

I'd have to say, you're not going to pry into your deep personal life. That you just need to know generic questions about your experience; your life experience, work experience, and past practice, so to speak, with this type of process.

Do you think that those types of questions would be adequate for the lawyer to get the information they really need to do a good job for their client?

Yes.

When you say "deep questions," what sorts of questions are you sort of referring to?

A lot of your family history, are you married, how many kids do you have, for the most part, have nothing to do with the civil or criminal trials that we go through. I could see knowing has that person ever been involved in crimes? What kind of character do they have? But their married life, things like that, I think are more personal and probably shouldn't be asked.

Do you think it's appropriate to ask if you have a family?

I don't think there's anything inappropriate for it, but I don't see the real need for it.

Explore further about the kinds of things you feel would be inappropriate for an attorney to ask. What kinds of questions would make you uncomfortable, or you feel wouldn't be helpful to the end result they're looking for, which is to find a fair juror?

Like I said, personally, married – marital status, I don't think, helps in any way. **Whether I have a family or not is really not about whether I can be a fair juror and determine if the plaintiff has been truly harmed by the defendant. My upbringing as a child, where I was raised, where I was born, really should not play into it. You're trying to figure out, okay, what kind of work do you do? Do you understand this is the type of case you're going to be listening to? Can you be fair and impartial? Those are the questions I would expect to be asked,** *not how many kids do I have, where were you born, do your mom and dad live in the area? I don't see any pertinent information that comes out of that to help the attorney decide if I'm a good person to be on the jury or not.*

If the attorney started asking you those kinds of questions, would it put you off on that lawyer?

To some degree, yes.

Do you think if that did happen and you were ultimately on the jury, you'd still be able to put that aside and be fair?

Absolutely. Because I'm there for the plaintiff and the defendant to determine what happened to the best of my ability.

When an attorney stands up before you in this context, at least for me, what I want to do is establish a connection and to show that I'm a human being who is doing meaningful work. What can I do to help you make that connection with me? Or, on the flip side, what must I not do so that I don't screw it up?

One of the things I see is, **if the attorney stays seated, they have no real respect for the people that they're talking to. They need to try their best to make eye contact with everyone in jury selection.**

Have you seen them remain seated in jury selection?

Yes, I have. To **try to open up with slight humor instead of just being rigid.**

We're here for this; here's the questions. You know, try to make small talk a little bit to make them feel comfortable.

Do you think that's okay?

*I do. **The ones that won't look at you, I have a hard time trusting them. If they can't make eye contact, I'm not sure I can associate with them and like them.** I still have to put that aside during the process, but it doesn't look good for the attorney.*

Opening up with a little bit of humor or lightheartedness can be a high wire act for some of us. Do you have any thoughts or suggestions on how to make that easier for the lawyers so that it doesn't backfire?

Obviously, if you're opening up with some type of humor, you have to stay away from any racial, sexual type jokes. I recently had an attorney I dealt with that opened up with – basically, he's an attorney, he's there to ask these experts and other people questions. He became an attorney because he didn't have anything else he could do, so he's at the bottom of the barrel. He made light of his job, and everyone laughed, and it seemed to work. He then apologized to the judge saying, no offense to you, Your Honor. But it seemed to get everyone at ease. And that was just last week. I was there to testify.

How about if a lawyer is going to start asking questions of potential jurors about things like their ability to be fair using words like prejudice or bias, but really, we're talking about fairness. Is it appropriate for the lawyer to make a sharing of their own prejudice or bias before or when they're talking to jurors about theirs? In other words, I'll show you mine, and then I'll ask you to show me yours.

*I don't see a major problem with it. There could be a backfire, where if you're showing you're prejudiced and it affects someone that's in that jury panel, you may turn that one or two people off. If your prejudice is against, say, Asians, or whatever, that may backfire. **Everyone has prejudice. And if they tell you they don't, they're a liar.***

Do you think all jurors in that jury pool are aware that they have prejudices and biases?

Not necessarily. I've seen some jurors in the process. A lot of people have prejudice against pedestrians and bicyclists in auto cases. And they may not realize that until they're sitting there and it's too late.

I'd be very grateful for the potential juror who would raise their hand and say, you know what? I really am prejudiced or biased or unable to be fair here. I would say, thank you. My concern probably is more for the juror that doesn't want to talk about that, who may be laying in the weeds, either intentionally to hurt the case or not really knowing, but still wanting to do that. How do you think I could go about finding those people if they're not forthcoming, in a way that's respectful to them and to the whole group?

*I'm not sure I have an answer for that one; that's tough. Because I know there are people like that. **Being able to pull them out during your very short time asking questions could be next to impossible. If they really want to be on the case, they're not going to be truthful. No matter what you ask.***

Or what I say. And the judge, as you know, can go a long way to rehabilitate just about any juror.

Right. They can try.

There are a lot of lawyers who have approaches toward jury selection that involve things other than just talking about fairness. I've been wondering if a better way to go about doing this is to get right up and say, you know, I'm only interested in whether you can be fair or not. And if you can, raise your hand. And if you can't, raise your hand. And I'm going to take your word for it and not waste anybody's time. What do you think about an approach like that? Do you think that I will get the information I ultimately need?

I believe you'll get it from about 99% of the people there. If you have that one that wants to sabotage your case, you probably won't.

I might lose them – and I might not find that person anyway.

*Right. But my philosophy throughout life is, I believe in being forward, blunt, and to the point. Sometimes it may not come across very nice. I don't sugar-coat much. But **I appreciate someone that says, hey, can you be fair in this case, wait to make up your mind until you've heard all of the facts, and then come up with a decision? If you can't do that, and you're going to let your prejudices, biases come in to it, at the start of the case or in the middle of the case, raise your hand. That's not the person we're looking for. If you think you can stay fair and impartial throughout the whole trial until you hear all of the facts and the closing arguments, that's the type of person I'm looking for. I think you would probably get the majority of the people to honestly raise their hand. You're going to get some to raise their hand just because they don't want to be there. Even though they could be fair and impartial, they don't have the time.***

That leads into the question of time. What do you think a juror such as yourself – potential juror – values the most when sitting in that potential jury panel? Your time? Your civic duty? What is of value to you there?

I'll have to answer this one honestly. I'm valuing my time. The civic duty, being in law enforcement, unfortunately, for the last almost 25 years, I think our process is extremely broken and not working appropriately. And a lot of time and money is wasted. How to fix it, I don't know.

Do you want to talk a little bit about what's broken about it? In your opinion?

Even the jury selection and sending out notices. I've known several people that have said, well, I just throw them away. You're not getting the people to show *up that's a sample of the population; you're only getting the people that was dumb enough to open it and show up and think they had to. Since we don't send it out certified mail, there's no way of proving that person got it or not. **Some of the trials are going for two, three, four, five, six weeks. Is that too much to ask of a person that maybe has a business or a job that they can't get the time off and they're going to lose income?** We pay jury members, I believe it's $10 or $15 a day. That's not adequate. I understand it's a civic duty, but it doesn't seem to come around fair. I know people that get hit every single year with a subpoena, and other people haven't been subpoenaed in 20 years. So in my opinion, fairness would be, you got a subpoena, we have a population of whatever it is. Once you've served, your name is off until they get through everybody else, and then your name is put back onto the list, and we start again. So not one person's getting pooled every year, where someone may never get pooled. I think my father's been pooled once; my mother's been pooled about 25 times. That's not quite the fairest system either. What else do I think is broken with the system? Not necessarily the jury selection part of it, but what is put into court and what's not, evidence-wise. As a police officer, obviously we have biases towards attorneys, at times, that they're smart and they've figured out a way to get true evidence of a crime excluded for, excuse my language, BS reasons. And that's not right. If you want a jury to make a valid decision, give them everything, let them know that, hey, they may not have collected the DNA by protocol, but it still shows it's 100% the defendant's blood. You make the determination. Did they screw up or not? If you truly want a jury to decide on the facts of the case, give them all the facts. And that's a bias as being a police officer.*

Right. There are issues with the process.

Yes.

What do you think it does to the integrity of the process and the ultimate outcome for society?

I think it's a more valid process of proving who's innocent and who's guilty; who harmed someone or who did not. When you have all the information instead of a good attorney that got, say, on a DUI crash, the blood sample thrown out for a technical reason; it's still a valid blood sample, but the attorney was smart enough to get it thrown out. Is that really showing the jury the evidence of the crime? No, it's not. And there's where I think our system is truly broken. And that's, like I say, coming from a police officer's experience.

How do you feel about the civil jury process functioning to make injured people whole and to create accountability for people or companies, entities, that are negligent or at fault?

With a civil case, it's still very similar to the criminal cases. Once again, some of the evidence is held out. I just had a civil case where some of my video, true video taken inside the same car, same driver, was excluded by the judge for who knows whatever reason? She really didn't explain herself, so I still don't know to this day, and I was sitting there as she explained it. She allowed one of five that we were asking to get in. She thought it would bias the jury because it's so visual. But it still was a like representation of what happened on the day of the crash. So once again, people were making decisions for a jury. That's their job to make the decision. Is that true evidence? How much do I weigh it? Not up to the judge or the attorneys, in my opinion. Let the jury make the decision. Another process that has some possible issues is, like the plaintiff being injured, how much do we award them? I'm not sure a whole bunch of jury members are extremely intelligent to give their proper award. I'm not sure if there's a way to say, we have this matrix. If you're injured to this extent, here's the average you should go through.

There's no standard. The jury instruction says there is no fixed standard. So as a juror, if I were to say, the group of people that come together in this trial could make an entirely different decision based on all the same evidence as a group of people that come in here in a week or two. How do you feel about that as a potential juror? And what can I do?

I don't know how to fix that. It's not a fair process, because one jury could say, we're going to award him ten million dollars. Then the next one may come in the next week and say, nah, we're going give him $150. We don't think it's worth what he's asking for. There has to be a happy medium somewhere. And leaving it up to a jury, you may get a highly educated jury that understands pain and suffering; you may get jury members that have no clue about pain and suffering and they've never been really injured in a collision or an accident falling off a curb or off a ladder or whatever. They don't appreciate how much pain that person may be suffering for the last three to five years as they go through this whole process. Six or seven years sometimes. And how do you balance that out? I don't know.

Do you believe that juries generally get it right?

I would say no. In my opinion, going through multiple injuries in my career as an officer and being injured, knowing the pain that you suffer just even tearing a tendon and having to battle it for two years to try to get back to where I could use my arm, they don't really appreciate what that person's going through. For the majority of them, I think the jury comes in a little too low. *There's been a few cases where I think the jury has been way overboard. The plaintiff's attorney has asked for ten million dollars on a fairly minor injury and the jury's now going, well, we have to give something. We find that the defendant did do it. Was the process tainted by asking for ten million for a broken leg?*

Do you think that the potential jurors you're sitting there with are going to be influenced in the amount they give by whether they like the lawyers? The plaintiff's lawyer, more or less?

I believe it will be influenced by that. By the plaintiff himself, if he's sitting at the table and the way he behaves at the table during the trial. *Talking to jury members in the civil cases, a lot of times they're looking at them to see are they still suffering? Or are they thinking this is more of a joke?* **How they present themselves during the trial can definitely affect the award. And how the attorney came across, especially during closing,** *it appears, from some of the jury members I've talked to, affected their decisions.*

Tell me a little bit more about that conversation about closing?

In one of the trials, I was able to sit through closing arguments for both sides. I'm on the plaintiff's side of that case. The defense attorney did a much better job in closing, was much more organized, well-prepared; kept it short, sweet, to the point. The plaintiff's attorney went well overboard, was not organized, stumbled through her closing, and was asking for an exorbitant amount of money that wasn't warranted in the type of case we had. Talking to four or five of the jurors afterwards, they picked up on that. They said the attorney was not prepared for her closing. She's asking for too much. She was trying to justify what she was doing but couldn't actually get there.

How do we attorneys, who represent the injured people, know what's enough to ask for or what's too much to ask for without turning a jury off or keeping them – to be credible? I don't want to ask for so much that I lose my credibility. At the same time, I've got a client to represent. How do I go about finding a way to stay in that sweet spot – that zone?

I'm not sure if there's any type of database that the attorneys can use that says, hey, our client got hit by a car, broke both his legs, took him a year to recover. Kind of put in the particulars of the case. What's the awards been over the last five years throughout the U.S.? And try to come up with an average, and then work in a range from there. Like I said, on this case, the attorney was asking for just over ten million dollars. One of the clients didn't even break any bones. It was a double head impact.

If you were told that I'm going to ask for an amount of money that's within a range, do you think that that's helpful?

I do.

If you heard that before there was any evidence, and I said, I'm going put this in a range because there's no possible way I could pick a number; I just think a range is fair.

Right. I believe that's more fair to the jury than saying, our client's been injured; we're asking for a ten million dollar award if you find that the plaintiff was injured due to the negligence of the defendant. I think if you put it more in a range, we feel that he's been injured, it took him this long to recover, if he's even recovered, everything he went through, and this is what we feel that he should be compensated for the negligence of the defendant. I think it'd be more fair. He's presented a brief synopsis of his client, what's wrong, and what they believe is fair. They're not asking for the moon. **I think asking for the moon turns off** *a lot of jury members. I know, working in the civil arena, sometimes it turns me off as an expert going, you're really asking for four or five million when you sprained a knee? I mean, some of the cases I've worked on have been close to that ridiculous, but not quite to that point.*

Do you think there are cases that ought not to be in trial?

Yes. I like the arbitration – mitigation process. It appears to be fairly fair. I've only been through a few of those, and the client usually comes out fairly decent, as long as the other side's willing to talk. I've had several cases I've started working on and actually turned down that said, no, your client could not have been injured the way they're saying. And what they're saying is against Newton's Laws of Motion, things like that; it's a fraudulent case. Some of the attorneys still continue with the case. To me, those cases shouldn't go forward, but that's not my decision.

You've had an opportunity to work with lawyers, observe lawyers and be in jury panels. What has stood out to you as having been helpful or decidedly not helpful to the process and to you as a juror?

What was helpful was the attorney, especially as I was sitting on a jury, giving me a brief synopsis of the case. *Having the attorney well-dressed. Sitting there watching some of these attorneys come in, they're not well-groomed, well-dressed – that could be one of my personal biases – is a turn off. You expect the attorney to argue a case to be in a suit and tie, be professional looking, and ready.* ***What's really helpful, like I said, was that short synopsis. This is the basis of what we're going to be telling you during the trial. Do you believe you can be fair and impartial knowing some of the facts?*** *When they beat around the bush during voir dire it's not very helpful to know about the case. I sat on one for eluding and they were very blunt but said, this case isn't an eluding case; it's a case where the officer's trying to stop our client. I want to know right then and there, is there evidence that the lights and sirens are warranted or not? The lights and sirens being activated. If they're not going to dance or they're going to dance around that until cross starts, I don't know if I can be fair and impartial or not. Those are some of the things. It's short, brief, facts of the case that's going to be presented. It's very helpful.*

When I ask a question about, do you think you can be fair, they say, well, I haven't heard the facts, so I can't tell you if I can be fair or not. So I encounter someone who's maybe a little hostile or a little resistant. In your mind, how do I best respond to that?

I would consider them not hostile or resistant. I think they're an educated person that doesn't want to answer the question until they know the facts of the case to some degree because they may have a prejudice against alcohol or a prejudice against whatever they know about. And unless they know if that's involved in the case or not, they can't tell you if they can be fair and impartial. So I think they're a highly educated person that understands they do have some issues and they want to know about the case before they can tell you, yes, I can be fair and impartial or I can't. Some people can't get past their prejudice.

This question's entirely unscientific, but if out of this group of 80 people, 12 people were chosen randomly, without a *voir dire* process, do you think I would end up with substantially the same result than if I were to go through this process of trying to determine biases and prejudices – whether people can be fair – with whatever tricks lawyers do to win their case then?

That's a tough one. I'd have to say probably, but with a caveat: as long as you understood everyone's limitations of time and how it's going to affect their life. If you take that into account and then you just pick 12 random people, I think you're going to come up with close to the same results if not the same results.

Let's say the judge gets rid of all the hardship people, so what we have left are people who, I can sit through this. The judge swears them to be fair and impartial. Do you think that people, by and large, the vast majority, are able to do that without me going through this sometimes uncomfortable and time-consuming process?

I do. And the reason I do is, they are there because they believe it's their civic duty. They showed up because they believe it's their civic duty. *That's very important. They've taken the steps to show up. They have the time, so it's not a major burden to their life and their business or their family. I think if you picked 12 random people, you'd probably get the same outcome out of that pool*

Do you think that if a case proceeds and somewhere along the way, probably in deliberation, it becomes clear to you that one of the jurors has a bias – they may not have been asked about it; they may not have volunteered it. How would you, as a juror, deal with that in the jury deliberation process?

If that occurs, I would definitely have to approach the bailiff and ask to talk to the judge and try to air it out. Obviously, most juries have alternates. If it's a consensus among the group that that person has definitely got a bias, it needs to be brought forward. It just taints the process if you don't step forward and be honest and say, hey, we have a problem, and here it is.

You've got more experience than the average person. Do you think the average person, in that same circumstance, would have the wherewithal to do what you're talking about?

No, but I believe if you have 12 jury members, you'll at least have one or two that would.

Especially if the biased juror is going against the tide.

Especially, yes.

And if the biased juror is going with the tide, then it probably isn't helping you a whole lot anyway, right?

Right. And it's probably not going to be as obvious. If they're obviously going with the tide, their prejudices are not going to come out as heavy as if they're going against the tide.

Tell me a little bit about frivolous lawsuits and what those look like to you in the civil context?

In the civil context, to me, frivolous lawsuits is someone that's been injured very minorly, is filing a huge lawsuit for damages and trying to sue everyone, not just the defendant – also the manufacturer of something. Maybe the person that sold that vehicle to the owner. It just goes down the line where they name five, six people throughout the lawsuit figuring if one or two drop out, they still have a chance to get more money somewhere. It looks like they're doing a shotgun approach. And when you're talking minor injury, I think it's a waste. You start naming five or six defendants, the costs associated with that to the courts and both sides are astronomical for all the depositions they take, everything else. It's a burden on the court system that's already overrun.

Do you think jurors have any sense of the costs and work that lawyers go through before putting a case to trial?

Absolutely not. Before I started my business as an expert, I had no clue what you guys went through. I thought you just went in, argued a case, tried to get the money, and walked out.

Do you think jurors believe that it's the plaintiff who proceeds in frivolous lawsuits or the lawyers that are the responsible parties, primarily, for advancing frivolous lawsuits?

I would have to answer, before I started my business, it was the lawyers. You have the ambulance chasers, as people call it. They go out looking for people to file a lawsuit so they can have a job and still make money. Being in the business, I see a lot more now it's the plaintiff trying to get an attorney to take his case. I've had several cases where the attorney's turned it down. The second attorney's turned it down. We're on the fourth attorney that's taken the case, and he thinks it's a great case and running forward. Somewhere the plaintiff has changed his story slightly and the facts get muddled a little bit, and the next thing you know, a case is going forward, and it's usually when it gets to me at that point, it's like, uh, no, that can't happen. So I see more it as the plaintiff filing the frivolous part than the attorneys.

Do you think you can tell when a plaintiff's lawyer truly believes in the case and the client? And when I say "truly believes," reasonably truly believes in it.

Yes. It's very obvious, to me at least, if the attorney truly believes in the case. If not, I'm not sure if they realize it or not – they have body mannerisms that are basically going, you know, we have this case, it's going to be a tough case, but it's a good case. And they try to sell it to their expert. And they try to sell their version of what they want you to prove instead of the attorney that says we have this case, we want you to look into all the facts and let us know what you see.

Be objective.

Instead of, this is what we want you to see; here's all the facts now. I get that a lot.

When you are sitting there with your peers of potential jurors and you're looking at the plaintiff's lawyer standing up and the defense lawyer, do you have a sense – there's a study that says the trial lawyer is the least credible professional next to maybe used-car dealers, but certainly in the courtroom, the plaintiff's trial lawyer is the least credible person, so he's definitely starting out from behind.

I would agree with that.

What can I do about that other than things we've already talked about? Can I acknowledge that? Bring it up to the jury?

*I think I would. Like I said, I don't like to sugar-coat anything. I like to be upfront, forward, kind of in-your-face type person that I understand you see me standing here. It's fairly well known that plaintiff's attorneys are considered some of the bottom-of-the-barrel people, right behind maybe a car dealer – now, you may offend a car dealer – or a used-car salesman. And then try to go, well, they've had bad raps. True, you could have the best used-car salesman that's as honest as the day is long, but he's going to get a bad rap because of all the bias. **I know I'm starting out at that level. I'm here for this reason. This is our case. I think I'll be able, by the end of the trial, to prove our client was truly injured and that you should come back with a verdict for the plaintiff. I think opening with that, that's kind of on that joke side, but still being honest.**

It's being honest. And with the hope that we're going to net 99% good jurors, most people will be honest and share.

Correct.

Is there anything I haven't touched on that you would like to comment on that you think might be helpful?

I'm not sure if it would be helpful, being in the business, so to speak. Not as an attorney, but just seeing the cases go forward on the civil side, is maybe letting the jury know how much effort's been put into the case – and I'm not sure it's legal to do – with the defense, trying to work it out, and we've come to an impasse, and that's why we're here. But we've done this, we've tried to settle it in arbitration or mediation, through the process. We've taken all these depositions now and unfortunately, we're at this point. We were hoping to resolve it, but we couldn't. And we're hoping that you can be fair, impartial, and resolve it for us. I think that would help the jury understand that you're not there just to waste their time and get money – that you tried to work it out.

Do you think that the jury's number one gripe is that their time is being wasted?

I would say yes.

And yet, there are some jurors – I can think of my dad – who couldn't wait. He just thought it was the greatest thing in the world to be called to jury service.

Right. My mother's the same way. She's loved every time she's went. There's only one time that she was a little resistant, because it was a domestic violence case she was sitting on and the people lived around the corner from where they live. And she felt maybe of retaliation if she was recognized. But other than that, she looks forward to it. Sitting on several jury panels of 40 to 60 of us in the room, I'm one of these people, I have the gift of gab. I love to talk. I'll strike up conversations with multiple people, and most of them are there and don't want to be, because they believe it's a fool waste of their time. And that's probably the majority of the people. Which is hard to get by.

A great trial lawyer I know and respect said, if a potential juror wants to be on my case, I probably don't want them. In other words, his belief was that if a person really wants to sit in judgment on another, then there's an agenda likely lurking behind that desire. What do you think about that?

*I would have to agree 100%. **If they really want to be there, you have to ask yourself, why?** And why do they want to judge somebody else? I don't think they're there for their civic duty. I think they're there for the personal agenda.*

So civic duty, the fact they showed up, and respectful of their time are key factors for you. And summing it up, you think that just broadly asking the group if they can be fair and impartial, if they can really, truly give each side the chance to start from the same place, is the way to go.

And not make a decision until they hear all the facts and give both sides their chance to present their case.

Thank you.

You're welcome.

12

KEEP IT LIGHTHEARTED

Caucasian male, age 43, married, two children, Realtor, B.A. Economics

Convey what you're trying to ask clearly and succinctly and be friendly to the jury. Jokes come up. That's a good thing. Keep it lighthearted even though it's always a very serious thing. If you can make it more lighthearted, that comes across well to most average Joes sitting in the jury wondering what the heck is going on.

With that framework, the judge says, please give your attention to the lawyer for the plaintiff who's going to talk to you for about an hour – ask you questions regarding your suitability to be a juror. What's going through your mind, right then and there, at that time? What are you thinking?

*What am I thinking? The first time I did it, it was just all new, it was kind of a new experience, so it's hard to – it was just more about the experience. **I didn't know what to expect.** If it was happening again, I guess I'd be paying attention, wanting to know what the questions are, what's being asked of me, what he's asking the other potential jurors, that sort of thing. Sometimes I can be a little bit, what's the word, not negative, but skeptical about what's going on. So maybe I want to hear what's behind the question. I'd be a little more curious about why is he asking that question.*

What kind of questions do you anticipate are going to be asked of you and your fellow jurors?

I don't know. Maybe lifestyle, habits, or I guess it'd be that kind of thing, not that I really care, but I'd just be kind of I guess divulging too much about myself to people I don't know. It's going to be like I'm being questioned in the case, being put on the spot for I've done something wrong. Or questioning what I'm going to say and that I might be caught for doing something. Or I don't know what it would be.

What do you think the lawyer is trying to learn by the questions you think or sense they may ask?

***I would think they are trying to find people who think along their same lines or have the same philosophy, be it about life or products or lifestyle.** It could be anything from religion to drug use or in this day and age, recreational drug use, that sort of thing. And I would think they would, depending on what the case is, want to know if you're more of down the straight and narrow kind* *of person or if you're more liberal in some of your thoughts and ideas and that sort of thing. So that's what I would think they'd be trying to get at is, **they want people with a certain philosophy that probably matches their client's** as opposed to – just as an example, they may not want a right-wing conservative Christian on a jury. Again, I don't know what kind of case it would be.*

Let's say this was an automobile accident case where the person who was hit is bringing a case against the person that was driving the car that hit them. This doesn't have to do with criminal acts, because we're talking about negligence. What do you think would be helpful to tell the attorneys about you that would let them determine if you would be suitable for that kind of case?

I think it's important to, when you're driving a car, you pay attention to the road. Distraction – you know, you don't want distracted driving, that sort of thing. So I would affirm that sort of philosophy if that question came up in that direction. I don't know what else. I don't know that I'd feel like I'd have to say anything in particular necessarily. I'd probably be guided by the questions, I suppose.

Let's say the lawyer says, the purpose of this is for the parties to be sure they have jurors who can be impartial and fair and unbiased and unprejudiced and haven't made judgments before the case has started or before the evidence has come in. Do you think you're the kind of person that can come into a case and be fair and impartial, or do you have, and many people do, we all really do have some personal beliefs that might make it so that one side might not get a fair trial.

I would say, yeah. I would want to be fair and impartial. I think I'm pretty good about seeing different sides of people's – listening to both sides of the story and trying to understand. I would definitely try to be fair and unbiased.

You've been on a jury. Did you feel that you were able to say whatever personal beliefs you have, you can put those aside, or at least make it so that you can view the case in a way that doesn't favor either party unfairly?

Sure.

Do you have a sense it could be difficult for some people more than others to be fair and unbiased?

I would think so. I think some people think they may be unbiased, but I think they have come from backgrounds or situations that they really aren't.

Can you share more about that? It sounds like given your dealing with the public, you might have some experiences or firsthand –

In my line of work, there's lots of fair housing laws and rules we have to abide by, so when we have clients that say things that aren't appropriate, you have to bring that up and say, you can't pick who you want to buy your house based on these, if they're in a protected class.

That's going to happen, especially with multiple offer situations, I'd bet.

Exactly. And people put in pretty pictures of their family and write a letter and that sort of thing, but sometimes, that backfires with certain sellers.

How do you feel when that happens, whether you represent the seller or the buyer, what is your thought process and reaction to that?

We have to look at just the facts of the contract and weigh the terms of the contract, and that's where you need to be making your decision. So it comes down to the facts of the case – the facts of the contract in my case – and you've got to put that other stuff aside and not use it to make a decision. But I know it's hard for some people to be dumb and explain it and sometimes they don't always agree. But for the most part, I think people do come around and are pretty logical in just looking at the facts and looking at the whole picture. I wouldn't say everybody is like that.

Not everyone. My experience, having been a lawyer for 30 years, is that it's important we develop a connection with the jurors during the trial. We want to be human and form a human connection with them. At the same time, we know from studies that jurors don't necessarily trust trial lawyers. How do you feel about trial lawyers? As a member of the general public.

*Evil. No, no, no. I actually have a friend, not very close, but he's an attorney, too. For the most part, lawyers I've met, they're pretty darned good people. Luckily, I've never been on the other side. So I don't know if I'd be more biased. But even in the one jury I was in, the lawyer was very good and seemed to talk slow and tried to make everything clear and then there was, I think, a young, straight-out-of-school public defender helping – and he was obviously not so good; a lot less skilled in that sense. **So I think that's very important in that situation, obviously, you have somebody who can convey what you're trying to ask clearly and succinctly and be friendly to the jury. Jokes come up. That's a good thing. Keep it lighthearted even though it's always a very serious thing. If you can make it more lighthearted, that comes across well to most average Joes sitting in the jury wondering what the heck is going on.** How long am I going to be here? That sort of thing. I'll back up and also say, **I wonder how long this is going to take? That would be one of my first things I'm thinking.***

Let's go back to that. Because as a potential juror, what are you valuing at that time? What is at the top of your value list? Is it your time? Is it your commitment to doing the right thing for the civil justice system? Is there something else that's very important to you in that moment?

***I would be happy to do the service, but hesitant on it being too much time. It's time. I don't get paid unless I'm working, right? Time is money.** But I understand the process, and it's a relatively good system, so I respect that, and therefore, I'm happy to spend a day or two. But I'd be scared of getting on a week long – sequestered and all that.*

I can't recall the last time I heard about a sequestration, but trials can go on for six, eight weeks or longer in major cases. And that's why the judge has hardship questioning. So certainly, time is an element of suitability, isn't it? I mean, would you want the lawyer to appreciate the demands of your personal life as well?

I hope they would. Because I would think the last thing you want is a bunch of grumpy jurors. You want people who it's not a huge hardship for them to be there. I would think that time aspect is very important to ferret out on the jurors what's doable, what's expected. I remember there being a raise your hand if you have a hardship type of thing. And there was another realtor. I'm a real estate agent, I don't get paid unless I am out there. So I think they let him go. But I was willing to do my time if it was a day or two, and it turned out to be a couple of days. But I was okay with that. So I think it's just expectations. That's how I am. I want to know what I'm getting into. I am willing to do some things as long as I know what I'm getting into and know the constraints and time commitments, whatever it is. Money commitment, if it's something, I just want to know. I don't want to be in the dark, have a question mark out there on time, energy. That's very important to me, anyway.

What can a lawyer do – or what should the lawyer definitely avoid – in attempting to establish a human bond or a connection with you? What would you respond to in that context? Or what would turn you off, which is maybe a better question?

Well, I think just being too grumpy or too much of an (expletive), frankly, to me or any of the other jurors. It would be like, this guy's a jerk. If he's treating us like that, I don't care what the case is about. If he's like that, his client's probably like that. The client's just trying to get money out of the – so my mind would start wandering and thinking things like that. I don't think you can ever go wrong just keeping it a little more lighthearted. Serious, but lighthearted, I think goes over pretty well with most people.

What you've said echoes pretty much what everybody has said in that way. If an attorney wanted to ask you about biases or prejudices, how would you want them to ask that question in a way that was inoffensive?

I think you'd have to be specific on what are you – do you go to church on Sundays? That's maybe some kind of question that – I don't know if that would come up.

Maybe a context for that might be – some people – and I'm not right and they're not wrong – don't believe in civil lawsuits. They don't believe you should sue your neighbor. So they have that bias. Where do you fit in that spectrum?

If somebody does something wrong, I think we have laws for that. I don't like hearing about frivolous, time-wasting, money-wasting type lawsuits, just to try to screw over that neighbor who really hasn't done – or it could have been – a lot of things can be worked out if people just talk. At least in my experience. So if it's a property – I'm taking it back to real estate – but property encroachment from the neighbors, and they're claiming adverse possession and things like that. If we just have the discussion as opposed to you throwing a lawsuit at them or something, usually things can get worked out pretty well just by talking. At the same time, if somebody's done something wrong, if there's a valid case, I don't have a problem with somebody suing somebody else.

What does a frivolous lawsuit look like to you? Or sound like to you?

What would it be? I don't know. I'm trying to think of an example.

A lot of people talk about McDonald's and the lady who had the hot coffee. That's a common one.

I guess I don't think you should be able to sue somebody else based on your own stupidity type of thing, if you're just a dumb ass. And accidents happen. Things do happen. Or if you get in a car accident, got whiplash, suing for damages and doctor bills and car repair and all that is one thing. But two million dollars for mental strain and stress and lack of work for those two weeks or whatever, things like that I would consider frivolous, over-the-top. I consider that something will undoubtedly get worked out, but it's how much time and energy and lawyer fees are involved to make that happen. I think that would be leaning towards the frivolous. It would depend on the case, but certain damages are, I think, logical.

What do you think was going on in the jurors' minds when they did that? When they reach those big numbers, what do you think is happening?

Well, and again, **some people are after corporate America.** They say, oh, they have big bucks, they can pay out. I would not have that opinion. I would say, coffee's hot. Don't be an idiot. I'm not against big corporate companies in that they have deep pockets because I understand that it's coming from somewhere and it's usually employees and that sort of thing. So I'd be skeptical on that person trying to get a bunch of money out of some company just because maybe they can.

Do you have a sense about whether the civil justice system works to do two things: to compensate the victim and to inform and deter similar conduct by the person or entity that caused the injury? Do you have a sense if the system works to both compensate the injured and to deter like conduct by the person or entity that caused that?

I think it probably does work if some damages are awarded and they have to put labels on their cup that says, caution, it's hot. I guess in that sense, it can work and does work. I just think it sometimes gets a little blown out of proportion. Our real estate contracts are now 25 pages long and it's more and more of that legal stuff to protect; everybody wants to protect themselves from everything. So it works to an extent, but I think it can go a little over-the-top, overboard.

Do you have a sense that the juries selected for each case, generally speaking, get it right? Both in their decision and in their award amount, if there is one?

I don't know. The one I was in, I think we got it right. But it wasn't a damages thing. It was pretty straightforward. So I don't know. Again, the jurors, that one experience, they all seem like pretty normal, logical people. I would think they would have been, but I don't know. That's a totally different kind of case, so I don't know how they would have necessarily reacted on that. I don't know how those come out.

What do you think lawyers like me are struggling with when we first stand up to talk to prospective jurors?

I think you're probably struggling to get that connection with them and try to first put them at ease, and then get to know them individually as best you can in a big group like that. It's a kind of interesting, delicate art. I mean, it's art, figuring those people out in such a relatively short amount of time for such an important issue. I don't know. I suspect it's kind of tough.

Do you have any thoughts as you're sitting there, taking in a sense of this other 40, 60, 80 people with you, that there are some folks who flat out don't like lawyers who represent injured people?

Oh, I'm sure. I have no doubt. You get the cross section of people who are mad that they're there, but a lot of those people are mad about everything anyway. And you get the people that are there just for the fun of it. And then you get the middle group. The middle group I would consider myself in. I'd rather be on the golf course, but I'll do what I need to do because it's important. I do feel it's important. But personally, that's what probably would interest me the most is that interaction with the other people and knowing the personalities of my fellow jurors. You can pick up on a lot of that stuff, especially with the questions that are asked. I think you can pick up on some of that stuff pretty quickly and know whether they're at one end or the other of a spectrum.

Do you have any thoughts about whether or not a lawyer like me could learn just as much about you in 15 minutes as in an hour and 15 minutes, say? In other words, do you think that all that I really need to know is whether you can be fair or not? I'm looking for a fair jury. Can I get away with asking jurors that question alone and accepting their answers, rather than having this time-consuming, somewhat uncomfortable dialogue for everybody? Do you think that you and your fellow jurors would give me an honest answer that I could rely on and say thank you and then just sit down? Or is there more I need to do?

*I don't know. **I think almost everybody would say, I can be fair and impartial. But can they? I don't know.** I would feel comfortable myself in saying that. Maybe I'm not, I don't know. I think I would be. But I think other people would say they'd be fair and impartial and I don't know that they would be, honestly.*

Do you think some people would raise their hands and say that they would have a hard time being impartial in a case like that? You think that there are people that would actually disclose bias or prejudice?

*I don't see why not. It would have to be a specific example. And yes. **Just a blanket statement, are you fair and impartial, I don't think anybody's going to say – yeah. But if it's in some context, I think, you'll get some that – absolutely.** I think it could be a little bold.*

How would feel if the lawyer shared something of his or her own bias to get the ball rolling? Say, you know what, I struggle with bicyclists, for example. I don't like them. I'm angry. I don't think I could be fair in a bicyclist case. So by sharing, do you think that encourages the jurors to share a little bit of their own?

It could. Some kind of example, I think you've got to have some scenario, some context that a juror can think about. Well, I don't mind bicycles, but this bugs the heck out of me. So, I think that could.

Like if you were an insurance adjuster, you might be biased for the insurance companies that you work for. You want people to talk about that. What would be off-limits areas or questions? Places where an attorney should not go in questioning you or your fellow jurors?

It may almost come down to the protected classes questions. Are you gay? Lesbian? Disability? Things like that would probably be crossing the line for a lot of people. But other than that, I can't really think of anything.

If you were a plaintiff in a civil lawsuit or you'd been hit in a car, let's say, and you were physically injured and unable to work and support your family, what kind of a juror would you like to have on your jury who's determining your case? Would you like it to be someone like you, or is there a different set of qualities that you'd like to see?

Well, then I want that bleeding heart liberal on my case that will get all the damages I can.

Is that your perception?

Well, that's an interesting question. I want people on my side. I don't know how I'd feel about my attorney – are they in the room when you ask the questions?

Generally. If the person is very seriously injured, they may not be in the courtroom ever. But for the most part, yes.

So they're there.

You want them there because they may sense a connection or no connection with a juror and you want that input.

So I don't know. If I'm in that situation, I may want my attorney to find the – maybe, lean it in my favor.

How's the lawyer going to do that in a way that doesn't offend anybody?

*I don't know. **You want people who've been in similar situations or felt they've been wronged and didn't get their due justice and that sort of thing.***

But that's a whole lot more questions and trying to get that out of people and they probably aren't going to divulge that in a situation like that. Some may. I don't know.

I think that lawyers who do the kind of work I do are more interested in spotting those jurors who are likely to hurt us than identifying those who are more likely to help us.

*That's true. And it kind of comes down to, you're looking for that fair – **you're trying to find that middle group of fair, impartial people. And when the bells and whistles go off on the outliers, one side, you definitely are trying to get rid of. So I think – but I don't know how much – I don't know if that can be answered in a simple question or not.***

Case by case, I think. What's your sense or feeling or impression about insurance in civil lawsuits? The role of insurance and how it might affect you and your fellow jurors?

Well, it kind of does come back to if I, as a juror, feel something's too frivolous against an insurance company, just like a corporation or insurance company, but if they win, my insurance rates are going to go up. I mean, the money's coming from somewhere kind of idea. So I would lump that in the same as a company or if they do something wrong, the person should get compensated. In the same case, an insurance company is probably not much different other than the insurance company isn't being sued, they're just the ones paying out, right?

Is that your general sense, that in most instances, when somebody sues somebody else, it's an insurance company that's defending them and paying out?

I would think so, unless they're uninsured. But then they don't have any money anyway, so I don't think I have an opinion whether it's an insurance company paying, a company paying, I would still look at the facts of the case and see if it merits what they're asking for.

Do you think civil trials and judgments cause insurance rates to go up or cause the prices of goods and services to increase or chase doctors out of the community as the premiums become too high? Do you have any particular thoughts about that?

I think that doesn't help. It does make it harder for a very good dentist friend of mine. I have to deal with ever-increasing insurance premiums.

You probably have E and O as well?

I have to pay all that. So yeah, now that you mention that. I think that helps to increase which makes me mad.

Makes you mad about –

Just if it's a blurry line, but I don't want to cross into that frivolous – well, getting into politics – but in my opinion, it's similar to the government paying for too much or people getting dependent on government aid which raises all of our taxes. Kind of the same idea that it's, I think, inflationary. **People need to rely on themselves to get through life and not do stupid things.** *Actually work for a living, all that kind of stuff. Not get hooked on – all kinds of things – and rely on other people who are trying to get it out of other people and they don't deserve it.*

How about personal responsibility or corporate responsibility? Do you feel that civil courts are a good place for safety laws and rules to enforce responsibility on the part of the public or the business entities?

I think yes and no. Yes, I think again, there's always within reason. **People, companies do things wrong and it falls into that honest mistake kind of category.** *Honest mistake; here's damages. Here's your refund. I'm talking very basic. And then, I won't do that again. So I do think that the courts and the laws, sometimes they obviously do help that process, because some people don't change without a threat of something like that, right? So you can have a bunch of negative Yelp reviews but that may only do so much until they actually sue you for it. But it kind of is that, not everybody – some bad people get away with things. Some good people get stuck with frivolous lawsuits. And there's a balance in there somewhere, and sometimes the bad ones do get set right and the good ones obviously, a lot of good ones make it through fine. So it's not a horrible checks and balances kind of thing. I think it's there and it's the best we've got. I would like to see less of it. The unnecessary frivolous stuff.*

Is there a range of money in your mind that distinguishes between a frivolous and a non-frivolous lawsuit? One lawyer says, this case is worth $50,000, and you're going to be here for the better part of a week to decide it. Whereas another lawyer in a different case might say, well, this is a case that is a million or five million, and you're going to be here for a week or two. Do you think that smaller money cases are frivolous just by virtue of the amount being sought?

No.

Okay. Why?

I would say that the bigger one would probably be almost a higher potential of being frivolous in that – I think it all depends what – did the person lose a leg? Are they really damaged for life type of thing? Or if it's just the medical bills and the other side isn't paying. It's really only $50,000. I think it would be more important if – I would not consider that to be frivolous unless it really is – I scratch my ear a little when – on that accident and they're fine, up walking around. But if they're out of work for a few weeks and they have medical bills; personally, **it's all about the context of the case, what the issues are. It's not just about the money.**

Medical bills, lost wages, and those out-of-pocket costs are generally pretty easy to prove and show to a jury on a chart. But what's hard to prove or to ask a jury to do is to make an award for what we call general damages, which is pain and suffering, disability, loss of enjoyment of life, which have no fixed standard for determination,

which means that every single person can approach it every single different way. How do you think about that? And how might you go about putting value on those kinds of things that you can't see or touch or put on a spreadsheet?

> Well, it'd have to be, **I would probably look at what is the injury? And if it's something for life, a lost limb or disabled for life somehow or something like that, I'd put a pretty high value on damages for that.** And I'd probably look at it, personally, if that were me, there's always a number that I can live with. So I'd probably try to view it though, as if it were if I was in that position, what would I be looking for? That's a hard one. Obviously there's no clear cut answer. I think everybody's going to have – everybody has different income potential and income. So you add the income part, but it's really more the pain and suffering idea.

Does Russell Wilson's or Bill Gates' pain and suffering have any more value than the person sitting at the other table?

> That's a good point. I don't know. And no, they obviously don't, but I don't know. That's a tough one.

Is there anything not covered that you think might be helpful for me to know in this context about your thoughts or what you think your fellow jurors are coming to the courtroom with in today's world? Anything you think that might help me in engaging with these people and helping make their experience better for them and to help them engage and connect with me and my client in a way that's overall better for me, the client and the system in general? That's really what I'd like, is a fair trial. And for people to share if they can be fair.

> **Right. Just going back, I think it's about putting people at ease at the beginning. Establishing what's going to happen, what is happening, what's going to happen and just having a little road map. I like schedules. I like checklists,** that sort of thing, but that's me. And then again, putting people at ease in the sense that they don't have to divulge anything they don't want to about their life and –

Respect their privacy?

> Exactly. That sort of thing.

Honor their opinions and sharings.

> And just **make it clear that there's no wrong answer,** whatever you say or bring up. It's interesting. I would think some people, they almost view it as a little bit of a game and it's like a test. I want to pass, so I'm going to answer the way I think he wants me to answer. I bet there's a lot of that. And probably you have to figure out with your questions, are you guiding them towards a certain answer and are you trying to, or is it, it just happens? And some people are going to be taking this so it can go the opposite just to be opposite.

If they're giving me the business and it's clear that I didn't deserve it, do you think the fellow jurors are going to know that it's that person and not me?

I think so.

How do you think I ought to respond to the person who's giving me the business?

Just probably smile and nod and move on. Thank you for your opinion, then move onto somebody else. You probably have your answer of whether you want that person, you're interested in having that person on the jury.

In your profession, and you deal with people from a lot of different backgrounds, do you get a sense that the first impression is generally the right impression for you?

***Most of the time. Not always.** And that's what you can't predict. A house can be a high stress thing. I've had personalities change on me. It's like divorcing. I don't know where this is coming from, but now they're just being stubborn to be stubborn, and I thought everything was groovy. But for the most part, I do think first impressions are pretty accurate.*

Do you think it's important that I address with the jury or that they understand we're all in a fairly stressful, what you might say artificial situation? That we're all going through this kind of nervous, uncomfortable place? Acknowledge that? Without pandering.

That's what I do with a lot of. I deal with a lot of older elderly people that are living in houses for 50, 60 years and it's a big emotional deal, so you've got to take it at their pace and tell them you understand this is a big deal. And while I do it every day, I understand you don't. So I want to go at your pace and keep you informed of the process and ask me questions as you have them and that sort of thing.

People have to process at their own rate or they're going to be unhappy. They may be unhappy anyway.

They may. If we're trying to force – people, I don't think, like to be told what to do. If you guide them in the right direction, most of the time they'll follow along. But if you just tell them what to do, people are naturally, I think, kind of resistant to that.

Change, emotions.

Change, yep. Or thinking a certain way or this, that, or the other, so – a lot of it just comes down to listening.

Thank you.

13

ACKNOWLEDGE THEM

Caucasian male, age 34, single, Real Estate, B.S. Business

I think in general, the way people tend to warm up, on an average they'll warm up to someone who is at least acknowledging them and their value, acknowledging the fact that I don't know where you've come from or what your opinions are, but I value your opinion and I value you. I'm thankful that you're here. If you're viewing jurors as your competition or something that could very well change the dynamics of what's going to happen.

With this background, when the judge says, give your attention to the lawyers who are going to start asking you questions about jury service, what's going through your mind right then at that time?

*Probably a little bit of tension, a little bit of unfamiliarity in my case, being that I haven't encountered that before. I have never been in a courtroom in the form of on the stand or any form in that regard, so it would be nerve-racking for me, I think, being that it would be a first time experience. In terms of the questioning and all that, I think I'd just want to be as open and as letting it all soak it in and just letting it all happen as it naturally needs to. I wouldn't want to go in there with any preconceived notions or go in there with any sort of idea that I have to perform or anything like that. For the most part, I would think going and doing that as a service, in some cases, **it can be a major distraction from your overall goals and what you're doing on a daily basis within your work life.** I think a lot of people view jury duty as an obligation, and it's often something that they don't want to do. I used to view it – and in some way I can see that, I can view it as that – but I now realize that there's an element of service there, too. I think there's an element of duty for all of us in our society to help and be a part of society. So I think that now that I'm at this point in my life, I understand that if that is my calling and if I have to do that, I think I'm in a position where I'd be willing to do it and able to do it without any feeling of, oh, this is just something I'm obligated to do and I don't want to do it at all.*

Thank you for that. It's not something we hear from everybody.

I think the majority of people I've talked to when they get that letter in the mail and they say that they've got to do it, it's usually a feeling of, oh, great, I'm not excited about this at all, and I'm going to have to miss work, and I'll have to take vacation or whatever it may be, so yeah.

What sort of inquiries or questions from the lawyers do you anticipate you're going to get? They're going to ask?

That's actually a great question. I wouldn't know exactly what to expect. I would imagine it depends on the situation. It depends on what kind of questioning comes up throughout the process of whatever it is that this person may – whoever's on the stand or whoever it is you're defending, those kind of things, would be highly dictating what happens in that regard.

What I'm looking for are jurors who can be fair. And by fair, I mean who are willing to acknowledge if they have unfairnesses or biases or prejudgments and are willing to put those aside, or who can say that both sides are going to start from the same place. How do you feel about that?

*I would like to think I could go in there with an unbiased ability to see both sides and open my mind to what's going on. I can't imagine why anybody who is just a random selection going into a courtroom and needing to serve that purpose would ever feel as though they're supposed to create some sort of notion of, oh, I should side with this party immediately. I'm hoping that as somebody, if I'm in those shoes, that I'm the type of person that can see both sides and be as open and taking in anything and everything that's coming my way. However, **I think that there's also an element of "groupthink" that can happen in any type of room.** If you've got multiple minds around you and you're observing what's going on and you may even observe body language of whoever it is that the defendant is, whoever you're representing, those folks can probably give you a feeling that maybe you develop your opinions on pretty quickly. **I think that as a human being, I think people will often, despite trying to be as open and trying to be as determined to focus on one thing, as soon as you start observing and you start hearing people's opinions and then you start seeing the jurors all kind of put their minds together, "groupthink" is a very prevalent – I've always seen in groups that get together. There's usually a couple people that give opinions and they're very strong-minded and then the rest of the people around them start to follow.***

Where do you fit in that? Are you a leader or a follower?

I'm definitely a leader. I tend to be the type of person that plays devil's advocate a lot. I tend to be very unaccepting of what people tell me just right off the bat. I like to question as much as I possibly can.

Challenge?

I like to push the boundaries. I recognize personalities very easily in my profession. I identify people and can figure out what their MO is in terms of where they're going in life and what they're trying to communicate. Some people are very forceful; others are a little bit more sheepish, and they tend to follow what others tell them. So it's just identifying those personalities. My personality is the type of personality to not buy into anything just because somebody says it.

I recognize, probably from the same sources we've studied, is that people do tend to make judgments. Or, I shouldn't say judgments, but they make determinations and decisions fairly quickly and then maybe rationalize that down the road somewhat and I get the sense you're pretty much a balanced person in your evaluations. What do you think might be some prejudgments that you have with regards to the civil justice system, and people who are plaintiffs in personal injury lawsuits? And their lawyers that represent them?

I'll admit I've got a little bit of a preconceived notion as to what I think of medical malpractice issues and those kinds of things. Because my father is a dentist, I've been exposed to the medical field a lot. I hear my father and everyone in the medical field constantly complaining about how many lawsuits come up and how much they have to pay for insurance just to protect themselves in that regard and just how ridiculous the nature is of the business these days and how often they're having to spend time in a courtroom dealing with these kinds of things. So I do probably have an initial siding with the medical field and understanding that there's an element of ridiculousness in our society of lawsuits just constantly popping up. In some cases, totally legitimate, there's 100% reason for those things to come up. In other cases, I think maybe it's a little extreme, and I think that the insurance industry and how they control things and dictate things is probably a little extreme, too.

Given that exposure, if you were a juror in one of those medical or dental cases, do you think, even though you've heard this from your dad and his colleagues, that if the case facts were such you could put that aside and still make a decision, if the facts were such that the fairest thing was to find for the injured person, you could do that?

Absolutely.

You wouldn't hold them to an impossible burden?

No, I would not. Or at least, I would think I would not, because I haven't done it. For the most part, I would say that every person and every situation is entirely different, especially in the medical field. It's so complex. It's an unbelievably challenging area to practice your business. Also, it's an incredibly complex element of solving health issues, because everybody reacts differently to different things, different medications, different surgeries. It's limitless in terms of where I think that can happen and what can happen in that business.

Has your dad had this experience personally?

No. He's been fortunate. He's never had to deal with any lawsuits. I'd consider him more on the side of due diligence. He was always very concentrated on each individual client and not necessarily the element of churning and burning to make a profit. But I know that he knows, and there was a lot of talk between him and friends, about how certain dentists were getting into trouble because they were trying to rush things through and just quick procedure was the solution and get it done and send them out the door type of thing.

Do you think your dad, or maybe he told you or shared with you, that in some cases, those individuals had it coming?

I never heard that, but anything in life, I can see where certain people may rub people the wrong way and may not get themselves into the right situation because they're not allowing themselves to get the right reputation and the right kind of rapport with whoever it is that you're dealing with, regardless of whether it's business or it's friendship. Those, I think, personalities and emotions, are involved in anything in life.

Do you have insurance in the business that you're in?

I have liability. I primarily have it related to the driving of my vehicle and taking clients around and that kind of thing. And I have an umbrella policy related to anything that may transpire in my field of work, so injuries that I may incur or clients may incur. That kind of thing.

Are you sensitive to the fact that you could need protection someday?

Absolutely. I have disability insurance. For me, in my line of work, if I'm not protecting the back end of what's the worst-case scenario, it could be a quick fall from the top, that's for sure.

Not only to protect yourself, but it's there to protect others as well.

Absolutely.

Which in a sense is also protecting you. How do you perceive insurance in these kinds of cases? Where do you fall on the side of, it's okay that people are sued and their insurance may take care of that?

I think the reality is that nobody wants to go through those struggles. Nobody wants to deal with the fact that they've been hurt or lost a family member or lost something as a result of malpractice or whatever it may be. Nobody wants that, regardless of what the situation is. And I think there's a very small percentage of people that would ever want to go through the process of going through the courtroom and dealing with all those costs and expenses related to it. Very few people would even make the initial thought or effort to do that unless they really felt passionate and really felt as though it was justified.

Where do you suppose the role of the attorney fits in there? In terms of that decision making process to pursue a case?

I have an uncle who is the Appeals judge in Denver, Colorado. In terms of where his perceptions are, I've talked to him a little bit. But for the most part, I think lawyers, just as much as anyone, have choice in who they take on and what they do. Unless you're someone who's just grabbing anything and everything they can for the sake of making money, then I suppose there are some of those money-grubbing individuals out there that would take on anything just because it's there in front of them. But I'm pretty sure the majority of the attorneys out there are representing a client because they think they really can do justice for that client.

Thank you. Going back to that moment when the lawyer stands up, and he's getting ready to talk to you, what are you thinking about that lawyer when you're seeing that person for the first time? What is your feeling toward that lawyer?

Number one, I know it's 100% in their interest to represent their client and to represent their opinions and convince people that their opinions are right. So of course, I'm going to play my role of devil's advocate a little bit. I'm going to sit there and think, well, is what this person is saying entirely true? Do I really buy into – I want to dig into the elements of what I'm seeing and I want to dig into both opinions and both sides.

Is that the same for both sets of lawyers?

Absolutely. I don't want to take what anyone says at face value, so if anybody's trying to convince me of anything in life, I'd like to be able to think I could see that they're trying to convince me of that because it's in their interest to do it.

Looking at this attorney and being somewhat skeptical, do you have a sense that – well, let me ask you this: do you share the opinion that plaintiff's trial lawyers have low credibility?

I do not. I don't necessarily think that's true. I think in some cases, there's probably some justified examples of where that is the case. I think that's the case with anything in life. You can create a perception just based on stereotypes, and a few people can give many people a bad name. So if there's extreme cases that pop up, more often than not those get more attention and where people create their initial opinions is off of what they've seen in the news or what's been publicized, and usually, that's in the form of something really shocking or something really public.

Anything in particular that comes to mind? Any particular example?

Well, a lot of cases have been published. For me, in my formative years, is the OJ case. All these things were happening and this whole idea that everybody thought OJ was guilty, of course. I thought so too. I was like, this guy definitely did it. No question in my mind. And I felt as though there was an element of money taking precedent and there was an element of misleading people. You could tell there was definitely corruption in what was happening there. I was in middle school at the time, so I was 12, 13, years old.

And you probably have heard about the McDonald's case, too.

Yep.

Tell me how you feel about that.

I've actually read into what the background was on that, so I have a more formulated idea as to what happened. It was actually pretty extreme. It was a situation where, once again, it goes back to what I was saying. She was not filing that lawsuit because she wanted to go in and expose all of these things that majorly changed her physical being and composition. That's not something anybody would ever want to go through or desire to go through and humiliate themselves in the process.

Thank you for that. I will share that in my entire career, since that case came up, every person that I've spoken to about the McDonald's case, you're the only person who has ever told me that they've gone beyond the news story. That's so rare. I really appreciate it on a personal level as well as a professional level. There's – we've been unable to convince juries that that case wasn't as extreme as the public perception of it is. Even with the movie, *Black Coffee*; even with the exposés about it. So I really appreciate that you would have taken the time to learn about that.

Sure. Absolutely.

How can I as a lawyer, or the lawyer who's standing there in front of you – this is a two-part question – how can they manage to create a connection with you, or on the flip side, what can they do to avoid ruining their opportunity to connect with you?

*What it goes to for me is, **if I feel as though there is a heavy element at the outset happening, as though there is a lot of exaggeration and this over-flamboyant kind of approach to how they're trying to sell what they're doing, to me that's a sign of being a little bit disingenuous, maybe forcing things down people's throats.** As an attorney, if you're seeing both sides of the coin and acknowledging that certain things may have happened, but then putting the spin on it, trying to think that jurors are stupid in what they're doing, if you come up there essentially trying to say, I think I've got you guys, I think I can convince you of what it is that I believe in, then I think most people will see through that. But if you're taking both sides and at least taking it into consideration, maybe there is something going on here, let's think about this, too. Let's dig into this. Now what happened here? If you're pushing it to a different limit but also acknowledging that things did happen, that can gain a little bit more trust from anything in life. **If you're able to see both sides and acknowledge and be humble, I think those are traits that generally help people warm up to what it is you're doing.***

How do you think the 40 to 60 other people in that room with you, who are all together for the first time in this situation, are thinking about that lawyer?

People are unbelievably complex. People will come in every form, especially if it's entirely random. You're going to get people of various educational backgrounds. You're going to get anything and everything in that room. Some will, I'm sure, be very emotionally reactive to things; others may be more pragmatic about it. It really just depends.

On the luck of the draw?

Exactly. I think that's true.

You mentioned "groupthink" earlier. Do you have a strong conviction that when the evidence is heard, regardless of the group of individuals, they'll do the right thing?

Yes, I do. I believe in the human belief that overall goodwill reigns supreme. I believe that considering the majority of the people who are a jurors' base, they're going to be the type of people that are not incentivized to believe one thing or the other; that's the whole purpose of it, obviously, to be random for it to be unbiased. I think as a whole, jurors are going to make decisions that they believe are right and whether they are right or not, that's how they perceive it. Overall, when the decisions are made, they are made in true interest of what they think is right.

Suppose there was a juror who was a lifelong employee of an insurance company and absolutely had an agenda to either cause the plaintiff to lose or to minimize the amount that the plaintiff would get? How do you think a jury would handle that when it came time to deliberate?

*Going back to that "groupthink", **if you get one person in the room that's supposedly an expert in this field or supposedly brings more to the table in their knowledge base and then shares that knowledge base with everybody else, it could influence the way everybody around is thinking.** If you get some folks in the room who don't have an educational background of what is being talked about in the case or what exactly is going on, and you get one person who's saying, this is what's going on, and this is what I believe is right, then I think those that may not know much are going to say, well, he knows more than me, so I think maybe he's right.*

So disproportionate influence.

Exactly.

It's pretty easy for a person who expresses a bias to remain on a jury as long as they answer the judge's question that if they've heard all the evidence, they can be fair and impartial and follow the judge's instructions, regardless of the bias that they admit, because we all bring biases. So those people can slip on. Not every bias is relevant to the case. But we do need to ask jurors about their biases and do it in a way that's not offensive to them. How do you think the lawyer can best do that? Asking those questions, initially, where we don't really know each other yet?

I think in general, the way people tend to warm up, on an average they'll warm up to someone who is at least acknowledging them and their value, acknowledging the fact that I don't know where you've come from or what your opinions are, but I value your opinion and I value you. I'm thankful that you're here. If you're viewing jurors as your competition or something that could very well change the dynamics of what's going to happen. I think that will come through in the way you approach people in any form. In my line of work, I always approach people with the knowledge that nobody's the same, and I need to understand they're coming from a different place than anybody else I've encountered. I deal with divorces, I deal with the full gamut of emotions that happen.

What's more emotional than a house, right?

Absolutely. You never know what kind of mental state someone might be in, even if they're coming to a situation that seems unbiased and they don't have a reason to construe things. There's probably a guarantee that every person in that room is going through something different in their life and they've dealt with things and to devalue them or to give them any impression that they're not right in what they're thinking, I think that's the quickest way to get somebody to withdraw from anything you're saying if you give any sort of impression that they're not valued.

Invalidate them? Or not acknowledge them?

Exactly.

As a potential juror, what do you value? A lot of people say, we value our time, more than anything else.

*Absolutely. I agree. **I think that is one element of jury duty that is a little bit scary, the idea of it running on and on and on and your time being consumed to an extent that you didn't budget for.** I think that could be a pretty heavy influence on how a jury gets through things and how they approach things. If they're getting exhausted by the process, I think there's definitely an element of at some point, everybody values their time enough that they may try to get through the process just to get it done. And they might take shortcuts, depending on the group, depending on the people that are there.*

Like a lot of verdicts that come in on Friday afternoon?

There you go. They've got their boat trip over the weekend and they gotta get it done.

It used to be that jury selection could take days. Lawyers liked it, because it gave them an opportunity to take their time, settle in and get to know jurors. Our civil justice system now is suffering from backlog, so judges have adopted this new approach that says, lawyers have an hour to two hours for the entire panel - maybe more with the judge's discretion - which makes it hard to get to know 80 or more people and see what we think is a fair jury.

So you get to know the jurors a bit more? You get to know their backgrounds?

Given that we have a restricted time limit, one of the ideas for my book is that we may be spending more time in jury selection than we need, given that it's been reduced to an hour. Maybe all I need to do is ask the jurors if they can be fair and then accept their answer. What do you think about that? Or do I need to go deeper?

No, I think that's a fair way to approach it. I think giving people a reality check in any form is a good thing. I do that often in my line of work. I'll say, where do you stand? What can I do to help? I think it's just that opening up of, you can tell me whatever it is you need to tell me and you can be receptive and be fair to me in any form. If that open communication or open feeling of what you're doing isn't there, then it usually doesn't work well as a reciprocation in a relationship of any form. I think at any point you can just state, are you evaluating this from an unbiased standpoint? Just giving that reality check to people.

Right. Before they've heard any of the evidence. All they know is the short one or two sentence statement that it's a case where a person's been injured and they're suing somebody. My thought is, can I just get up there, respect everybody's time, which they value, and accept that, in this day and age, people will be honest? They'll say, yes, either I am an appropriate juror for this case or I'm not. I'm curious if you think that people will give me enough information – will be honest enough for me to take that at face value?

I would like to think so. Once again, I'm coming from a standpoint of, I haven't seen what you've seen. I would like to think that as a whole, if you're taking the approach of what the role of a juror is and what their duty is in that role, then you would hope they would respect the fact that you're acknowledging that's their role. I think reassuring that and getting to the point that, we're not here to create any sort of manifesto or false perceptions; it's about getting to the problem and solving the problem.

Do you have any sense one way or the other if it's appropriate for the lawyer to share a little bit about him or herself before asking the jurors to share something about themselves?

I think that that's a fair thing to do. From a strategical standpoint, I think most lawyers would probably want to try to warm up to the people in the room and to present themselves in a manner that creates a validation that they're not just some random guy coming off the streets; that you have legitimacy behind you to show that you're coming from somewhere.

How do we do that without appearing manipulative and untrustworthy?

I think it comes down to presenting the facts rather than trying to exaggerate whatever it is you're trying to accomplish. Just presenting the facts. *Thank you, I'm David Crump, here's my history and experience as an attorney, just essentially presenting as it's almost like your little résumé as an introduction type of thing.*

Got it. Do you have any concerns that jury awards are too high?

I do think it's very biased. I do think that it is very negligible at times, too, in terms of how those numbers are determined and where they come from. I think it's the incentive of whoever it is you're representing to just shoot high. I think that's anything in life. You shoot for whatever you can, and if you get it, great. If not, then maybe you adjust as you need to get to that reasonable. I think there's certain cases where maybe it is a little bit outrageous, maybe a little bit extreme.

But in other cases, I think there are large corporations paying out a chunk of money that's nothing to them just to get it out of their hair. They'll just resolve it. Here's our offer. If you take it, we'll just throw this case out the door and move on.

Mentioning corporations leads me to this question: there are a couple goals of money awards or judgments. One is compensation. Do you have a sense that awards also deter similar conduct in the future?

I think so. I think there's a certain element that supposedly money resolves everything, when in reality people need to own up to whatever it is that has happened and it needs to be done in a form of time. It needs to be done in the form of community service. It needs to be done in manners that show they're a human being like anyone else and that they need to pay their services and own up to what they've done instead of just paying a dollar amount and saying, all right, we're done with that. Out the door. That's where money is a huge influence on a lot of cases that have taken place. Guys that have a lot of money, they get the best lawyers and get the best ability to navigate the situation and may not serve time. They may just serve money instead.

If the defendant in a civil case is a corporation, how do you feel about the corporation having to disgorge profits?

I'm in the real estate business. Look back on 2008 to 2009 and why we were in that situation, and it was a lot of money-grubbing people that essentially represented the banks, and the banks essentially walked about scotch (sic) free and essentially ruined thousands of people's lives that now may be struggling just to live, maybe in situations where they've done desperate things and as a result have ended up in bad places. I think there's a trickle-down effect when you destroy people's livelihoods with their financials. You should pay the price for what you've done. You should be held just as responsible as anybody, and you should be putting in your time the same way.

I think we've covered it.

Okay.

Really helpful. Thank you.

14

DATA

Caucasian male, age 51, divorced, three children, Consulting, M.S.

They're going to want data.

After the judge says, please give your attention to the attorney, what are you feeling in that moment?

Probably curiosity. Just wondering what's going to happen during that process.

Do you have any concerns about the process and how it might affect you? What you might value in the process?

Not personally, no. Doing what I do as a consultant and a coach and dealing with people and process all the time, I'd just be curious about how it all works. So I would probably analyze what's going on.

How do you feel about being there in the first place?

I have an attitude of a civil servant. It's a responsibility to be there if I'm selected. That's my attitude. It's okay, and it's part of the responsibility to society. That's how I would feel about it.

I appreciate that. There are many people who would rather not do it. It sounds like you're happy to be there. If you're called.

Yeah, and I may not feel that way if it were two or three times, but the first time, right, it would be really cool.

As you're looking at the parties and their attorneys, what are you feeling about the parties? You said curious, but can you elaborate on that a little bit more about the lawyers and the litigants?

Being in a professional service where people hire me to help them as well, I look at it as, from the attorneys' point of view, they've gone through a lot of training. And they've got a lot of experience, so it's more an attitude of respect afforded to what they do. Having done something similar, being a consultant, I look at the legal profession as consultants for legal matters. That's really all I'm thinking about in that moment.

That's very refreshing, because it's not uncommon for people to have an opinion of lawyers that's a lesser one. That they're not credible. Or that their clients are not deserving or worthy. How do you feel about that?

I think in our society those are probably – I'm going to be a little judgmental now – they're just not really aware or in tune with what's really going on and what the training happens to be or how hard it is to get to that place in their life, in the legal profession point of view. I think that's a society thing, because there's always jokes about lawyers, too, right? You don't find a whole lot of jokes about doctors, necessarily, but you do find a lot of jokes about lawyers. So that's a societal impression, maybe a quote/unquote "societal norm".

How do you feel about that? That some of your cohorts in that group have those opinions and attitudes?

At that moment, being a corporate coach, coaching leadership and coaching teams, I'm feeling like I'm probably going to have to do a lot of coaching about this, if I'm part of the jury selection process, getting people to let go of their biases around the whole thing. That's probably what's going through my mind. How much am I going to have to coach these people to let go of that crap?

Do you think that's possible to do?

I always believe it's possible, you know? You don't really know until you're in the moment with someone about how coachable they're going to be or how much they're going to be cooperative and set aside their personal biases and serve. It's interesting.

The attorney's job is to determine whether or not there are jurors that can give a fair trial. And fairness – I think everybody has a different metric about what that is. The court may define that some, but what we're looking for are attitudes, beliefs, prejudices, and biases that may make a juror unsuitable for that case. How would you like to be asked? How would you best feel about being asked about your particular prejudices or biases?

Probably through presenting scenarios. Maybe these are real-world scenarios, prior cases that have occurred or life scenario-based questions, being presented with something and then being asked what my opinion might be on that in order to understand what this person is thinking. It's almost like – well, it is like an interview.

Can you give me give a concrete example from real life?

In my profession when I'm looking at another coach, I'm trying to judge how dogmatic versus pragmatic they are in their thinking around something. I'm presenting them with scenarios for, if they're working with a businessperson and they're trying to get this businessperson to understand the importance of creating – and again, this is the software world that I work in. So that's the primary case of getting them to work in a fashion that gets clear business understanding and where the product direction, the vision is. Giving them scenarios of me being an (expletive), essentially. It's like, how would you coach me? So that, and seeing how they react. If I give them a scenario where they're trying to get me to give them software requirements or whatever, and just being stubborn, to see how they react to that, to me being stubborn, and how they would coach me to elicit a yes, I'll help you through the process. That's what I mean by scenario based, where I maybe take on a persona or I present them with a scenario and ask how they might do that. And it can be third party as well, so I would say, here's a person that shows up in this way, they show up stubborn or they had a fight with their wife that morning. How are you going to coach them to get to a place? And just see how they respond.

I think I understand. How would an attorney fail in that regard, asking you to elicit your own biases or prejudices? What would be something that would make you very uncomfortable?

Wow, that's a good question.

Because sometimes we learn better by learning what not to do. Rather than what to do.

In my own experience, I've done that, and maybe there's a mindfulness. That's a really good question, and I think, if you're a brand new attorney, this is your first time and maybe there's coursework that they go through to help get to this process, part of the three-year journey of your training.

Not much.

*It's similar to my profession; you learn it as you go. I was pretty crappy at it when I first started being a coach. I would say really understand. I think there's a lot of this; there's probably overlap. There's understanding what coaching questions are, which are what and how questions versus accusatory questions, instead of pointing out someone's failings, because it creates a lot less defensiveness. **Then you're really listening and you're not directing.** I think the failing would show up as to fail to understand the defensive mechanisms of people when they go to defensiveness because they're being accused of something. Or they're being accused of being wrong about an opinion or wrong about something. **The cool thing about what and how questions is there's no wrong. You're just asking for an opinion. I think the failure of understanding that dynamic, of what would set someone off from a defensiveness mechanism, because humans get defensive all the time.** What does it really mean to ask, you know, coaching-based questions or elicitation-based questions, **open-ended based questions that don't create defensiveness?** That would be ideal training for the legal profession in general. So they could feel that way, I suppose, by not understanding that.*

Do you feel if you're asked directly, do you have any prejudices or biases that you think might compromise your ability to be a juror in this case, that you would respond in a way that was authentic or credible or genuine?

Personally, I would. But that's my profession. I have my own training around authenticity and showing up in the world. I fully recognize, given the profession I'm in, there's a lot of people that don't do that. When I'm working with someone, I get to see them over a period of time. And what the legal profession is doing is, you have this really short window to make a quick call and it's like an interview.

*It's really difficult, and the advantage I have is I can actually see people over time. I joke around with people, there's – **humans have two tongues. There's the one in their mouth and one in their shoes, right? So the shoes tell me what they're really doing versus what they're saying, if that makes sense.***

Their actions rather than their words.

Yep. And I have time to see that. In the juror selection process, there's probably not a whole lot of time. So you're making the best judgment as possible. Weeding those people out, I think, would be difficult.

That's right. Or selecting you. You deal with people. If you were asked, do you think you could give each side a fair start – here's an example: if somebody worked for an insurance company, they might have been indoctrinated into the insurance business to be distrustful of lawyers who represent injured people because it's ultimately the insurance company that's paying. So they may have a bias toward their insurance company if the attorney were to say, hey, do you have any reasons why you may have a difficult time giving each side a fair start, an even start?

Because there's a built-in bias. Let's say I worked at some insurance company. Maybe there's a built-in bias because I'm working at the insurance company.

Sure, or it could be race, it could be sex, it could be any number of things. How do you think it's best to approach those kinds of issues with people that you don't know anything about when you want them to answer honestly?

I would probably fall back on the what-based questions around what their profession is or who they know in that field. Wouldn't it be great if people would just be authentic and honest? Perfect? But they're not. So then it's whatever those right set of questions are to get very specific, you know, in the in-ambiguity of language to just be – I would hope they would be truthful. Maybe there's more direct questions like what affiliation do they have with something or someone. I imagine it's very difficult.

It is, because it's on the fly. When you're sitting there looking at these attorneys, how are you judging which attorney is credible or more credible than another?

*My own personal bias on that is how well they articulate. If they're going to stumble, if they're not prepared to ask the questions, then I'm self-aware enough to know. But at the same time, I'm going to give them the benefit of the doubt. Maybe they're just new. Who knows? But, knowing myself well enough, **there's going to be how professional they show up. I'm going to tune into that.***

What about their clients? In general, what sort of things are you looking at?

*As much as I would like to say I've risen above all that, I'm still human. I'm probably looking at how they're dressed and what their demeanor is or what their attitude is and if they've got an attitude of entitlement, whether I can judge that or not. You don't really know that until you start speaking to them. I'd probably be looking for that, because that's a big deal for me, personally, **the*** *whole entitlement attitude.*

What do you think that says about a party in court vis-à-vis you? And would you be able to get past that?

Given my coaching profession, I would say yes. Where that comes from personally is because how I grew up, by growing up on welfare and working my way through university and joining the Army to get money for college so that I can change my own life and not have an entitlement attitude. That's where the personal history comes from. But being in the profession I've been in for 27 years, I don't really know until they show up. So I would like to say it would be, I'm just going to fall back on give everyone a fair chance and rely on my own self-awareness to say, you know, this is my own game I'm playing in my head, and the story I'm telling about this person, but I have no idea who they are.

How do you think – and you apparently can do it, because of your background and training, but –

And most people, I don't think, can.

I'm willing to accept that people have biases, but I would like them to at least be self-aware of it when they're on a jury. How do you think I could broach that subject with them? You're a juror, potentially, and these are your people. I want to be able to say, I'm willing to accept that you may have things that are of some concern, but if you're willing to be aware of this.

I think it's directing that. It's creating, during the questioning and answering process, an environment of authenticity. I know personally I would appreciate if either the judge instructed us or the lawyers went through a process of just calling it out. Seems like we all have biases, and just bringing it on the table.

And we can do that. In that run up to that, do you think it would be effective for you or your fellow jurors for me, the attorney, to share something about my own bias – as a can opener?

Totally. Yes. Because it creates a vulnerability. As a coach I can tell you, and you see it too, right, in your profession, that works with people. I'm going to create some vulnerability so that it makes it a safe environment for them to be vulnerable.

So the question is, would you be concerned that you're being manipulated if the attorney shared something?

I personally wouldn't take it that way because I do the same thing in my profession. It's a guided conversation. I look at it as a process where it's necessary in order to get what you're after, and that is fair and unbiased people. That's hard. The way to do that is to go through a structured process that at least calls that out. And if that means, you, as a lawyer, tell the same story over and over, great. That's part of – if I look at that as a checklist process, okay, I need to do this so I can get people to be open. I think that's probably training, right, how someone presents that? It could be seen as fake, or they could present it in a way of just being authentic, saying look, guys, we all have biases, so I'm just going to tell you what some of my own are in all fairness so that, you know, we can get to the bottom of this so that we do the best thing by both sides. I think if someone showed up that authentic, say look, let's just put it on the table. We have them, so let's talk about them.

My understanding is that you work in the tech industry primarily. And have for a long time. Tech jurors are a new phenomenon. It used to be aerospace jurors, or the engineers, that we were worried about. Now, with the influx of tech, we've got more binary thinkers than we had before. And it presents some challenges.

Very black and white.

Very black and white. How do you think it's best to approach those kinds of jurors? They're generally younger people who want things to be, as you say, black and white. How do we address them? How do we get to them? You're a juror and some of them are with you.

*Typically, I'm going to start here. If it's a software engineer, that's the one if I'm in your position, **I'd want to know what they actually do in the tech industry. Are they an engineer? Are they a tester? Are they a program manager? Are they an executive? Because that's going to influence how they show up.** Engineers tend to be it's either right or wrong; that's their life. It's either one or zero. That's the way they live. They're data-driven. Program managers are more in the gray space of, it could be this or it could be this. They're always looking at options. And a manager is looking at people and depending if they're a tech manager or a program manager, you know, that's going to be their bias. They're somewhere in the middle. So, it depends on what you're after. If you want a black and white person that it's either right or wrong –*

If you have a data-driven case that could be helpful.

That could be helpful. If you've got a case where you want someone to be thinking, you know, so – there's a distinguishment between thought, right? As humans, we react out of our thought a lot, and that's how I see engineers. There's the distinction of thinking, and that's where a manager and a program manager have to work in, because it's not just this or that, it's this and that. It can be. An engineer's "or" thinking and a manager or a program manager's "and" thinking, so they can go broader.

Often in injury cases it's not so much whether negligence happened. Generally, by the time we've gotten that far, it's more a question of what is the value, what is the injury, what are the damages. And those are not easily established because we have no fixed standards for those things like pain and suffering, disability, loss of enjoyment of life. So with those particular kinds of jurors who are used to being non-empathetic and more ones and zeroes, how are they going to understand our situation best? How am I going to get them to think about injury and damages in a human way?

Data.

Data.

They're going to want data.

Got it.

It's interesting. An interesting question would be depending on the organization. For instance one company sends most of their people through Insights for Learning education. That teaches them what type of person – how they show up at work. There's generally four personality types. There's the person that shows up as the cheerleader, rallying the troops and getting them to do things, making it a fun environment. There's the helpers that are constantly helping things. And then there's the people that are more data-driven and they don't want you to push them. They want me to present information to them, and then they want to go think about it. Then there is the, hey, (snapping fingers) be brief, give me really short answers so I can make a decision now, types of people. That's the variety of people that exist like that. So it's getting to that understanding of what type of person is this? When I'm interviewing people, there's a little test I do to get them to tell me what – give them a scenario like – if you're in the Army and you're on the obstacle course, you come to the really tall wall. How would they approach that with other people? That gives me an idea of how they show up. It's a really fast test that I put someone through in the interview. What type of person are you? Those types of questions. I think that would help to understand, is this an empathetic person? Is this a data person? Is this a pushy person? Is this a cheerleader person?

We do have some data metrics. For example, when we're talking about disability that could be measured under tolerances of the individual's strength or grip or range of motion – things like that. Those are the kinds of things that data-driven people are going to want to look at?

*Right. **They would probably want to look at scales.** Like, on a scale of 1 to 10, where are you on that?*

I guess it doesn't really matter, but we need to translate that to some human way of understanding.

*They want to know **how much is the suffering related to what?***

Related to what. That's the question.

Yeah. So for them, a scale would be good. Like if the average human full range of motion is 10 and this person has a 2, for a data-driven person, that's very meaningful to them.

How do you feel, in general, about personal injury cases? Good, bad, or indifferent – and their role in society?

Having been involved in personal injury rights – I was in a car accident when I was 14 – someone hit us from behind, I've been a recipient of that. There's that aspect of my life history, but also, I show up in the world as responsible. I would love it if we had society where people would naturally be responsible for what they say and do. But we're not. German culture, you have more of that attitude. American culture, not so much.

Yet we have a system that is set up to ultimately get accountability.

Right. And it's because we're not.

Good point. Do you feel that our civil justice system for personal injury cases works to balance the scales of justice or to get accountability for people?

Personally, I do, and I think it's a mix of who's accountable and who's not accountable. It's just the society we live in. So having a system that creates accountability, it's just necessary. It's needed. I would love it if we lived in a society where it wasn't necessary. But reality is, we need it.

Some people would say that it's out of control, that we're having a crisis, that there are too many lawsuits, that there are not only too many lawsuits, but there are bogus lawsuits and people are seeking lottery justice. How do you feel about that? Do you think that's happening?

I don't know. Having lived in a foreign country and how they approach it differently – this is in Germany – a lot of it's pushed to solve it on your own and you really need to solve it on your own. We don't live in that society. You know, people, they're going to look for mediation and whether it's we've been trained that way or that's just the way our society evolved, I don't know. It is what it is, is how I look at it. It's just reality. I don't look at it as manipulative. It's just a necessary part of the system in which we live. Could we change the system over time? Sure. But that would mean we'd need to push accountability down to, you know, if you go to court and it's frivolous, it's going to cost you and whoever defines frivolous, that's for the court system to define. We don't necessarily do that, right? Or maybe we've started to do that. I don't know. The only way to change systems is to change the reward and the pain aspect with it. Especially on a societal level.

Do you think we have too many frivolous lawsuits in this country?

I don't know. I can't judge that.

Are there any particular cases you've heard of that society tends to think are frivolous? Well-known cases that –

Only the McDonald's coffee thing, right?

How do you feel about that case?

I don't know all the details around it. It's just at this point, it's like the societal story, so I don't really know. What I would like to say, if I spill coffee on myself, I'm responsible for spilling coffee on myself. It's like, what? There's no way I would think you didn't tell me it was hot. Wait, what?

Do you think given a set of facts that you've listened to as a juror with your fellow jurors, regardless of the composition of the people that are selected, you are going to get it right? Are you going to get to the right outcome?

We're going to get to the right outcome based on the data and the people we have. **Right is relative.**

In your group process.

Right is relative, meaning if you could change one juror, the outcomes might be slightly different. It's a reality thing. Those people with the data and the facts presented, it's the right outcome. That's just what it is.

Do you have a sense that the other 60 people in the room with you take it seriously and want to do the right thing?

I would hope so, but I don't believe that's always the case. I think that's part of the process to understand that about someone, how responsible they feel about society or themselves and ensuring that they listen and create an environment of fairness. I'm sure some people just don't care. You're going to have a wide selection of people. I was going to say I would hope the foreman would be strong enough to call people on their (expletive).

Or the group.

Yeah. The group. And make sure that happens.

If you were a party in a civil lawsuit, plaintiff or defendant, what kind of a juror would you want on your jury?

The first thing that comes to mind is really a self-aware, like who they are as a person, even to the level of recusing themselves if they feel like I can't be impartial on this; I just can't do it and explain why, instead of out to get something or out to prove something. **I would just want them to be people that have lived life; they've seen a lot of things in life to really give them a bigger picture.**

You think broad experience is helpful?

Yeah, broad experience, a bigger picture of what's going on in life and society and not necessarily have tunnel vision. *Would I want the introvert dev that just plays video games all the time? No. Definitely not.*

A dev meaning developer?

Developer. I wouldn't want him on the jury, because he's so myopic in his views, he's just right here. And he doesn't have the broad experience of life.

Does that equate to selfishness or entitlement?

Those words don't come to mind when I think about that, someone that's just narrowly viewed in life versus broader view in life, of really having an understanding of what happens.

Interesting. I'm glad I asked you that question.

I think a person that has a broader view in life – in my profession, when I'm looking at coaches and consultants, I'm looking at people that have a lot of variety, because it makes them a better coach.

As a general rule, do you find that those people we were talking about, the data-driven people, generally do not have broad life experience, even though many of them may come from halfway around the world and have had significant levels of education and have interacted with many people on difficult projects?

Oh, yeah. They can still have – I work with a lot of Indian culture people. A lot of them, especially engineers, they're very black and white. And it's helping them see different perspectives that I've always found interesting and a challenge, in a good way of, you could think that, or you could think y. It's not always x, you know; sometimes it's y.

You're saying that you can get to that?

Yeah. But I have to call it out like, hey, you're stuck in this thinking so let's – but in a juror selection process, you don't really have time to do that.

It's very, very short. The judge may give us a little time to develop the theme of our case, but primarily, it's about finding out who can be fair and at least is willing to –

Explore possibilities.

– be impartial to the extent they can be. Almost any juror can be rehabilitated by the judge by simply asking them, can you follow the judge's instructions to be fair and impartial? And if they say yes, they're in.

Got it.

What can the attorney do to establish a human connection with you? Right off the bat.

I'm probably going to walk up to the pew, if I'm the attorney, to establish a personal connection and just get to know people. I don't know if there's time to get to like, hey, what do you do? What's your life? Tell me a story about yourself. If I'm getting to know someone, it's like, tell me a favorite childhood memory that you have, or whatever. But I think earlier you talked about allowing yourself to be vulnerable and saying, hey, you know, here's – I think just calling it out, just like that. It's like, some of you don't want to be here, I get that, and I'll share some things about what this process looks like, maybe some of my own vulnerability. If you have to do it in such a fast way, it's kind of like speed dating. What's your approach for speed dating of allowing yourself to be authentic and vulnerable at the same time? So I think it's just being up close, physically close to them, but then also sharing a little bit about who you are as a person. Here I am, here's my name, this is what I do, here's some things that I think about when I'm in your position. Here's my own biases, like you mentioned earlier, as quickly as possible, because you don't have that much time.

You mentioned physical space. What is an appropriate physical space? What's the zone of comfort?

*If they're in the pews, there's already a separation because they've got the furniture right there. So I think not being too distant, not being across the room, but just talking to them and just **looking them in the eye.***

Talking to one juror at a time?

And making eye contact with everybody, if that's allowed.

Suppose that one of the people in this group of potential jurors is being very difficult. How do I best handle that situation so as to not turn the group against me?

How's difficult look like? What does that look like?

They won't answer softball questions easily; it's very clear they're resistant to me or my client or my purpose or any number of things. And I'm trying to get enough information so that I can get them off of the jury in a polite way. But that's a difficult thing to do because they're a group member, and I'm trying to get information from them that they may not want to give. And I don't want to poison the rest of the well.

When I'm in my own profession, coaching, I have an opportunity to notice that happening and I'll call it out. So, again, it goes to non-defensive questions like, hey, here's what I'm noticing. You're noticing the environment about this person. Here's what I'm noticing. What's going on for you right now? In a non-confrontational way, you're just calling out what's happening. This is happening, and everyone else knows it's happening too.

It's the gorilla or elephant in the room.

Yes. And to diffuse it is you're just putting it on the table. This is what I'm noticing, and you can say, I'm really concerned about this, and I want to give an opportunity to say, hey, what's going on for you?

I may lose that juror regardless, but the other jurors have perceived it as inappropriate as well.

It diffuses it, and now they're looking at you as oh, this person is really caring. What they're noticing is we're noticing it too, and it's a respect thing. When I do that as a coach, I get instant respect (snaps fingers) for one, handling it, and two, it's not making the person defensive because you're just concerned. Like hey, there's something going on. We all know there's something going on. Let's talk about what's going on. And you're just asking them, how is this – so I'll say, this appears to be landing funny. How is this landing for you? What's going on for you right now? That's it. And then they get a chance to speak. If they don't, that's also telling. It's like, all right –

If I ignored it, would that be –

That's worse.

That's worse.

Of course. In any coaching situation I've been in, that's one of the worst things to do is ignore it.

Thank you very much.

15

SPILLED COFFEE

Caucasian male, age 37, married, one child, Sales, B.A.

Are millions of dollars of pain and suffering worth it for a guy who spills the McDonald's coffee cup in his lap?

You just said that you had been called for jury service, but weren't able to go because your employer wasn't able to let you at that time.

Exactly. Due to the lack of employees in the showroom and a busy time, I couldn't leave. Especially if it were something that was going to be weeks and weeks. It just couldn't happen at that time.

Did the county ever send you another summons to come back at another time?

I don't believe so, no.

Here's what I'd like: imagine you've been called for jury duty service. You've been marched with about 40 other people up to a courtroom. There's going to be a trial. The judge has told you this is a civil case, not a criminal case, and it's the kind of case where a person has been injured and they are suing a person or a company that they claim hurt them and they're suing for money. It doesn't matter what kind of injury or what kind of incident it was. You're in this courtroom with about 40 other people. The judge explains very briefly the type of case it is and says, this is jury selection. It will take between two to three hours. Each lawyer is going to have an opportunity to ask you questions about whether or not you're suitable to be a juror in a case like this. When the judge says, please give your attention to the attorney for the plaintiff, that's the injured person, what are your thoughts as you sit there in that moment? What are you thinking? What comes to you right away?

I don't know if I'm thinking anything. I'm just ready to hear what the attorney's going to say.

Are you feeling any specific emotions about the jury system or your role in it or the parties or the lawyers?

Not necessarily. I think I'm more interested in the case and just wondering what it's all about.

Are you excited to be there?

Probably. Excited might be a little extreme. Interested is probably more like it.

Some people have an aversion to wanting to be jurors because it takes time from their work or their lives. How do you feel about that?

Don't get me wrong, **I don't want to be in a case that's going to be eight weeks long and have to use all my vacation, and then my employer will not pay me for the days that I'm gone. I don't want to be in a situation like that.**

Right. So, at this point, you're not feeling any strong emotions? You're not thinking anything other than – you're just waiting for things to happen?

Right. Exactly.

When you see the lawyer stand up, do you have any sense, in general, how you feel about lawyers or their clients and these kinds of cases?

No. Maybe after I figure out what the case is, I might have some preconceived notions, but just going into it, it's just a lawyer.

What would trigger preconceived notions you might have in a case like that? Or what sort of notions might you later have?

I don't know exactly what it would be. I'd have to think about it. And it might be too long thinking for today's time. It could be anything from, well, this person's really hurt to now, what is this person up to? It could be the whole spectrum. I just don't know.

What's the sense of credibility that the attorney has in your mind? Or is that also the same? You just have no leaning one way or another?

I have no leaning one way or the other. If anything, 51% credible, 49% not credible. I don't go into it thinking, this is foul play.

Sure. Some people will readily admit they come into these cases and lean a little more toward the side that says the lawyers are greedy and their clients are greedy or up to no good. How do you feel about that? How do you feel just about hearing that?

There's always instances that people will hear about of greedy lawyers. But I don't feel anything about that. It's the U.S., we can sue over anything. I just don't think anything about it though.

The job of the lawyers in this jury selection process is first and foremost to find jurors who can be fair and impartial. What does that mean to you in this context?

Probably going in, not having any preconceived notions. *Just going in there, finding out about the case, and not thinking either way.*

Do you as a person feel that you're pretty good about being able to temper preconceived notions?

For sure.

Is there something about your personality or background that gives you that confidence?

I don't know about my background, but I know this is a job I'm supposed to do, and I'm going to do it correctly. That's just what I'm supposed to do.

When the attorneys are looking for people who can be fair and give everybody a fair start, there needs to be asked of the jurors if they have any bias or prejudice towards these kinds of cases or towards anything. Do you share that?

For me? Do I agree with that?

Do you agree that in order to be fair, you have to put aside biases and prejudices?

I'd have to have a situation come up where I'd have to put it on the plate, but I do agree. I have a – yes.

Lawyers hope to ask jurors, if they have a bias or a preconceived notion, to share that with us, if they're willing to. How would you like to be asked that question? If a lawyer had never spoken with you, but needed to know about you, what would be the best way for the lawyer to ask you if you had any biases or prejudices?

Just about – this is the first question he's asking me?

Well, not the first question. There's a lot of people in this room and we can't get to everybody, and at this point, there's really nothing that you can be told about the case. The lawyers are just trying to learn about you. And how would a lawyer go about establishing a rapport with you?

I don't know. I haven't been in a situation yet, so I don't know. I feel like I could better answer that question if I'd had this happen already.

If you could go into the imagination of "as if" you were in that setting, in the courtroom with your fellow jurors around you and a lawyer asking you, let's say, do you think you have any biases or prejudices just in your own life?

I mean, it's a fair question.

Without sharing what they are, do you think you might have some – or let me put it another way. Do you think that everybody has some biases or prejudices?

Absolutely. I think – asking that question is so vague, but leading, I think that's a fair question. Yep.

Doesn't turn you off to have that question asked? Is there a better way to ask it?

*No, I don't think so, because **that's the question that you want to know.** And we're there to do, essentially, we're there to do the job.*

If you said you had something, and the lawyer said to you, do you think, no matter what it is, that you could put that aside in this case? How would you feel about that question?

I think it's a fair question. I don't agree or disagree with it. It depends – that's really hard. It depends on what situation that comes up. That would be the toughest question, probably, to be asked.

Can you give me a more open-ended answer about why that would be the toughest question for you so far?

Well, what if the case was about a police officer getting shot and your family's in law enforcement? Could you put that aside?

It would be helpful for us to know if there's anything in your personal background that deals with something specific like that.

I think there would have to be questions asked – are we still at the point of, you can't talk about the case?

That's right. We've only been able to give you a small synopsis of the case. We can't give testimony at this point. We're just taking questions and answers here.

Wow, that's difficult. **How do you figure out questions to ask that have to do with the case without talking about the case?**

They have to do with the jurors themselves and how they feel about jury service and how they feel about cases, personal injury cases, lawsuits against other people for money. How do you feel about lawsuits against people or corporations where money is the remedy?

If that was the first thing the person suing wanted to go for, I don't think I feel anything, I'm just – I wonder, is that the only way that the problem could be solved?

Can you think of some other ways that a problem might be solved before it got to court? And if it wasn't, would that cause you to have problems being open to the trial? In other words, if it hadn't been solved, are you holding that against the parties because they're there?

Do you have an example?

Well, there was an automobile accident and somebody was hurt or claims they're hurt. There's no dispute that the defendant caused the accident, but there is a dispute as to how much injury the person had. So they couldn't come to an agreement on that; they had to go court to have a jury decide what's fair in that case. So that's the best example I can give you.

Makes sense. Well, there's no hard and fast rule in a book that says, this is what happened, flip open to that page and this is what you get. So there has to be a case. If you can't come to the conclusion together on your own, privately, on what's fair, then what other avenue can anyone take? Is there another avenue? I don't think there is.

None that I'm aware of, short of all the steps that take you there.

Right. Exactly.

Do you have a sense that the parties want to be there? Or that their lawyers want to be there trying that case?

I would say, overall, no. Because nobody wanted to get in said car accident. I would say absolutely not. I would hope that the person isn't just greedy and wants to go for money or was convinced by a lawyer that they should go for money. But everyone doesn't think the way that I think, and I know that's just part of human nature.

Would you describe yourself on a spectrum as being conservative, being liberal, or somewhere in the middle? Where would you put yourself?

Probably in the middle. I'm not extreme in any direction.

If you were a plaintiff in a case like this, what kind of a juror would you want?

I'd want a bunch of jurors, probably like me, how they go into it with just no notions, no bias, no preconceived notion – any of that. There's a job to be done. Do it in the fairest way possible.

If you wanted to know if a juror might have some preconception or some notion that would hurt you, how would you want to know about that? Would you want them to just come straight out and say, I can't be fair in this case?

Probably. Or tell somebody. They don't have to tell me.

How would you feel if they said, I don't like personal injury cases overall. I think we have a crisis with too many lawsuits, but if the judge tells me to put that aside, I will do it. How do you feel about that answer in that case?

I'm a fairly trustworthy person, and I would trust that they are telling the truth.

I know you haven't been in a trial or you haven't been on a jury, but do you have a sense that a jury of 12 people generally get it right given the evidence that they hear?

I think in general, probably. I guess it's up to the lawyer. I don't know. I think you're right. I'd have to be there, being part of that environment. But I would like to think that it's probably all right. But I don't know. I'm not around cases. I know lawyers, lots of them. I just don't talk to them about their work.

How could an attorney create a positive impression with you? Or on the flip side, what could an attorney do that would create a negative impression fairly quickly with you?

I don't know if I could describe it, but I feel like I can pick out the sleazy lawyer versus the one who's not. But I have a fairly good sense of character. Though, also, lawyers are good at what they do, so could they present themselves a different way? I don't know. I'm so far removed from the court scene, lawyers and –

Sure. And most people are.

And shows and things. I just don't watch them.

That may be a good thing. Many people have almost their entire legal education

from American television courtroom drama. Is there anything at the outset you'd like to know about the lawyer who's getting up to talk to you?

No. Not necessarily.

No? Okay. If the lawyer were wanting to ask some questions about your or your fellow jurors' biases or preconceived notions, do you think it's appropriate if the lawyer shares something of his or her own experience of having some bias or preconceived notion or prejudice of their own?

Maybe. If the example that they come up with has no leading consequences on how this specific case is – yeah. They're not leading the jury into anything that has to do with the case.

Not manipulation?

Yep. Exactly.

So stay away from the case.

Yeah.

Can you be any more specific or add to that?

I don't know. Possibly the case is about a car accident and he's coming up and he's going to tell you about his bias about a previous car accident or even a case that he worked on or something like that. I don't need to know that. The question can be asked, possibly. But probably not the right opportunity to anything that I think could make me steer one way or another. Towards him or not towards him.

If the lawyer were attempting to persuade you and you felt that, that would make you feel how?

If it was before, trying to get my bias out, I'd probably roll my eyes and say, this person's doing it the wrong way. I don't know how I'd feel until it's happening to me if I think – if I'm actually going to then just dismiss it in the back of my head. But I would probably initially think, ugh, this isn't the way you're supposed to be doing it, but I'm not sure where I would go after that.

What's your feeling about the fact that when those two sides come into the courtroom, their positions are in opposition to each other and how that affects the job the lawyers have to do for their clients? In the context of being a juror and knowing these people haven't been able to agree. So considering that you're going to be hearing them talk to you and that each side has a specific point of view, what are you looking for to determine what side or the other you are going to ultimately land on?

I guess the one that sticks with me the most, I mean, that's the job. They couldn't come to an agreement, so now it comes into the court and now it's the attorneys' jobs to prove, better than the other one, that they're correct. Or that the other person's incorrect.

When you're looking for proof, do you consider yourself a person who's more on the data side or more on the side of emotion?

Data side, for sure. I would try to not have any emotion involved in any way. I mean, that could be impossible for any typical case or any specific case, but I would go data.

Do you have an engineering-type background or has your life been data-centric as opposed to say, emotion or empathy-centric, or is that an equal balance?

Towards the middle of the spectrum, but probably a couple points towards data.

Where do you think that came from in your life?

I don't know. Must have inherited it.

Your educational background take you into sciences or into mathematics fields?

No, not at all. My mom was a decision sciences major – she's a very analytical person, so maybe it came from her. Thinking logically versus –

Do you tend to approach problems in a more logical way, to start?

Generally, yes.

Not all the time? What sort of situations occur that bring the emotional side in for you?

Just things that I guess I'd be more interested in personally.

Coming back to the same theme a little bit, is there anything that an attorney can say or do to be sure that you would be open-minded in a case? Other than just you're saying, I think I can be open-minded and I truly believe I can be.

What could they do more? I'm not sure. Probably nothing.

Just to question you or go down that road with you a little bit. Or if not you, the people around you as you might sense they would be given the composition coming from the community.

I don't know. I don't know how that would work, because I speak for myself, and I have no idea how others are going to take it.

How do you feel about being asked to make a determination for an amount of money as a remedy in a case?

Overall, I would like to think that problem conflicts can be resolved without money. That's how I'd prefer it to be, but if it can't always be like that, if that's what the next step is, that's what the next step is.

If the Court instructs that you and your fellow jurors are to come to a money amount as a remedy, but also tells you there are no fixed standards for which to come to those amounts, how do you think you might approach that? Given that you're on the data side of things?

Good question. **Probably start low.** *I don't know. We were talking about it, I would try to get money out of the discussion and then figure out what the problems are together and then bring them in later. I mean, that's how I would be, imagine going well for me. Money, I don't know.* **Problems shouldn't be solved with money.**

If a person is injured and they lose time from work, is it okay to compensate them for that?

I think so. Depending if I thought it was legitimate. If the injury was legitimate and there was a fault at play, and they couldn't go to work for those days, I think so. **Some people need that money.**

What if that injury caused them to lose a limb? And they couldn't work going forward in the future because their way of life is impacted? Would you listen to experts, perhaps, who are talking about what the person would be able or not be able to do?

I think so.

If there were things like pain and suffering and the judge says, you must consider this, you must award it, but I can't tell you how –

Pain and suffering, that's a very hard one. Are millions of dollars of pain and suffering worth it for a guy who spills the McDonald's coffee cup in his lap? *I don't know. That's stuff when I start rolling my eyes, going are we getting real here? If the jury decides it, then the jury just decided it. But for me, that's when I start getting into, okay, now we're getting a little overboard.*

Do you have a sense about why the jury got where they got in that case? Do you know anything about it?

I have no idea. Well, I know the guy – so it was a woman who did it. A woman spilled it. And then the guy sued because he couldn't have relations with her because her paunch was hurting, and so he sued for millions of dollars or whatever it was. I don't know how they got to that number. It's an astronomical number.

You are in the vast majority of people who feel the same way about that case. But if it's an itemized thing, and there are receipts and you can show their cause, then how do you feel about that?

I think that's proof I can see and data that I can put together.

If I said that given the exact same set of facts presented to two different groups of 12 people, that they might reach very different bottom line figures, how would you feel about that and what thoughts do you have about it?

Well, that's 24 people. Everyone's a little bit different. And I know in juries there's persuasive people in the jury and they're talking to each other that might be able to persuade or dissuade somebody who doesn't care or needs someone to tell them what to think. You know, those types of personality traits could come in there. And that's 24 different people and there are millions of different types of personality traits, so it wouldn't surprise me, how about that?

Do you consider that you're one of the persuader - dissuader types, or do you think you're a different part of that spectrum?

I would say I'm towards there; I'm not that person. But just through the leadership roles I have at work and in life, I know – to answer that question, I would have to be. I'd have to answer towards persuader or dissuader because I've been told –

You've been told that about you? And you mentioned the word "leader." You see yourself as a person who has leadership quality?

It's definitely more leader than follower.

Did you have a background with leadership? Groups or scouting or anything that developed that when you were younger?

Scouting for sure. I was a scout. And just captains of sports teams, those types of things.

You're from Nebraska. Is there anything in your geographic background that you think has developed you in a way that we've been talking about as far as these cases go?

Could be. I mean, there's the quote/unquote "Midwestern work ethic". That's a thing that exists that may not be so much on the West Coast. West Coasts are laid back – as a general rule. General categories, assumptions, would be more laid-back and go with the flow on the West Coast, especially like Southern California. Go with the flow types of people. Midwests aren't really go with the flow type of people. It's work hard, get things done.

If a potential juror said, because of my religious beliefs, I don't believe in lawsuits, period; I don't believe that brother should sue his brother. And the judge says, okay, but if I tell you that you have to follow the law in this case, will you do it? And the person says, yes, I will, how do you feel about that?

I'd hope that they would.

You've got a sense of the kinds of things we're trying to learn through this interview. I've been working through a model that pays respect to the time that many people say is their great value. In other words, they don't want to be there. Their time is being used. They don't want to sit and listen to all these questions. I'm almost to a point where I'm willing to get up in front of a group of potential jurors and say, if you can be fair, please tell me. If you can't, please tell me. I'll respect your decision, and I'll sit down. Do you think that will get me the same result that people would stand up and share without fielding questions and those kinds of things?

I think so. For types of people like me, for sure.

What do you think about the role of insurance in these cases? Do you think insurance is behind or underneath all of these personal injury cases?

I have no idea. That's never even crossed my mind. How about that? But by now, no. I don't know. I'd like to think not.

Why would you like to think not?

Because that's not the way it's supposed to be.

Tell me more.

I feel that sounds malicious of an insurance company.

Oh, on the insurance company's part? Okay.

So I was thinking of an example of one insurance company – well, what would be the example?

Here's the example. The vast majority of injuries that happen, that go to trial, generally have the at-fault person who's insured. Their insurance company generally pays for their lawyer and ultimately is the entity that's ultimately paying the damages. So even though the person who caused the accident is sitting there, it's really their insurance company that's paying. Along the way, the insurance company and the plaintiff had a dispute as to how the damage was done to begin with or how much the damage is. That's how it works in the real world. We aren't allowed to talk about that in the context of the jury selection. What is your thought about that?

We pay for insurance, so –

It should be there?

Pay up. It's not an automatic – just kidding. We pay for insurance and that's what it's all about. Again, the – now coming back around in a circle, I wouldn't find, even if being the plaintiff, I wouldn't find any fault to the other person. I do realize that it is insurance company versus insurance company. So it's not really about the person. I guess the person can say, I don't want to do it. I mean, could they do that? Or does insurance always –

Yes. Generally speaking. How do you feel about the role of these cases in deterring future negligent conduct?

I'm pro that.

Do you think that happens?

I have no idea. Do I think that that happens?

Do you think that in addition to compensating an individual for their injuries that the purpose of the trial and the result is so next time the defendant will be more careful? Let's say we're talking about corporate defendants.

Sure, sure. I don't think it'll happen, or that'd be great. But I don't think that'll happen. When it's done, it's done. It's forgotten.

Thank you.

16

DOG AND PONY SHOW

Caucasian male, age 56, married, five children, two grandchildren, Accountant, College degree

I'm getting $10 a day to sit here for their dog and pony show, that they're going to make a third if they win. They can't do it without us, but yet we have to give up our day or a week or a month.

You're being called into a courtroom for jury service, and the judge explains – all he can tell you is, it's a personal injury case where somebody has been injured, is suing someone or something for money damages because of negligence. It doesn't matter what kind of case it is, car wreck or medical malpractice. The judge then says, would you give your attention to the attorney for the plaintiff who's going to conduct their portion of the jury selection process. At that moment, what are your thoughts? What's going through your mind at that point?

I'm curious about the case. I'm looking over the jury pool, sizing them up. Nothing in particular. Just looking. Seeing what – are these my peers? Or aren't they? And making that judgment. That's probably not fair, but.

Asking yourself if these are people you'd want to sit in judgment of you?

Exactly. Is this a jury of my peers?

What are you thinking about the lawyer and the lawyers?

A little contempt. Because I'm getting $10 a day to sit here for their dog and pony show, that they're going to make a third if they win. They can't do it without us, but yet we have to give up our day or a week or a month. *Depending on how big the case is. So it's a little bitterness there.*

As you're sitting there, what is it that you value about the process or what are you most valuing in that situation? Is it your time? Is it integrity of the process?

My time. *Truly.*

How can the attorney acknowledge that in an effective way?

I don't know if it's possible. If I was retired, that wouldn't be a problem at all. I wouldn't mind sitting there and I'd do a better job, probably, instead of spending all my time thinking of how am I going to get out of this if I get picked? Seriously. **I do not want to be any part of that process.**

A colleagues of mine jokes that a jury is nothing more than 12 people who weren't smart enough to get out of jury service.

I don't think it's a joke. I mean, it depends. *If you work at a place like*

government where they encourage you to take that time and they pay you for it and it's not a big deal if you get selected for a long trial, heck yeah, I'd do it. And feel good about it. But where I work, if it was more than a week, it's going to cost me my vacation pay. I'm not going to be happy about that. The last one I was selected for was going to be a three-week trial, so I did my best to get out of it.

Sure. You explain to the Court that you have some conflicts with time and they're generally pretty good about that.

They were. And they let me go.

So you feel contempt, but are you thinking or feeling anything else about the lawyers or their clients at that point?

*I'm curious about the case at that point, too. And probably prejudging them a little bit for the merits if – if the person's sitting over there saying, you know, I've got millions of dollars' worth of damage to myself and they're doing handsprings, I'm kind of going, wait a second. If they're in a wheelchair and all beat up, that's another thing. So **I think you start prejudging before you even hear anything.** Just as a human, sitting there looking at it and listening to what he has to say. It probably depends on the attorney's demeanor, too.*

What are you looking for there? What would be good or what would be bad in demeanor?

I think Hollywood has set the bar for sleaze versus non-sleaze, but just looking at the guy, you know. Maybe just the attorney's appearance might have something to do with – is it a shiny suit, or a scruffy looking guy or a good-looking gal? We're all prejudiced that way, to a certain extent. It'd be hard not to be.

Do you have a sense one way or the other that attorneys doing personal injury work are more or less sleazy? That there are more of them that are sleazy than not?

You know, that I don't know. Just from the term PI, we all jump to that conclusion real quick, but I've known a lot of PIs – good people. We live in an era right now of tort reform ideas and how much is a person really worth. I get kind of contemptuous on that, too, when I look at somebody and I say well, this person is worth more than that person if they get maimed? I don't know how I feel about that one. I think we're all kind of equal. A juror sits there and he looks at, you know, this guy was the president of the warehouse when he got killed, well, he's worth twenty million dollars and this person was a derelict on the street, we're going to award $50 for the burial.

How do you feel about money that's compensation based on earning capacities or past earning history?

That's probably what a lot of it's based on is if you're not able to continue to make the big money you did. You're going to get a bigger award. Which, maybe that is a fair mark, I don't know. Maybe they were worth a little more because of what they did. And I guess that's how the process probably works.

What can the attorney do to develop a kinship or relationship or rapport with you right away? Or conversely, what could they do that would damage their ability to make a connection with you?

Might be language. **You start throwing around a lot of legal terms that are Latin-type words and stuff, and I'm going to get turned off pretty quick. If you come across as a common guy, like, you know, you're my guy. I'm going to like you better, I think. Just simple language, not being talked down to or feeling like I'm being talked down to.** *Like, I'm a superior guy because I'm up here trying this in court and you're just there for me.*

Can you think of an example where you feel like you were manipulated or turned off by the lawyer in some way? If you got a sense that you were being manipulated, I guess, how would –

Well, if I did have a sense I was being manipulated, I'd be kind of angry about that.

Would you speak up?

Probably not. I'd just wait until I voted.

Do you have a sense that the lawyer's personality or demeanor would influence the result you would have for this individual that's –

You mean like swaying the evidence? If I thought it was really guilty but if I didn't like the guy that I would change my idea? Just to get –

– you didn't like the lawyer, but there was a worthwhile case for the plaintiff.

I would hope that I didn't do that. But I guess, until you're in the box – no, I would hope that I would be fair and impartial that way.

The jury selection process is designed, first and foremost, to determine who can be fair, impartial, unbiased, and non-prejudiced. And that's what our ultimate goal is there. How do you think you'd like to be approached about whether you have any biases or prejudice or partialities that would affect your sitting on that jury?

Maybe just a simple explanation of some of the facts in the case or what the case is about. And then I could answer, do I have experience in this area? Have I been affected in this area? Or do I even care about this area? *And then I suppose if I had gone down in a Ponzi scheme and there was a Ponzi guy, you know, I'm going to be pissed. So I think just pertinent questions about the case without getting too deep into it.*

If it was an auto case, just, have you ever been in an auto accident?

That would be a fair thing. And then, did the cop cite you? Did the cop cite the other person? Did the insurance company run you through the wringer? Were you compensated if it wasn't your fault? That kind of thing.

Do you think that there are any biases or prejudices or beliefs that would sway you at the start for one side or another?

I don't think so. Not in a traffic case.

How about in a medical case?

Probably not. In the PI end of things, I think I could pretty impartial. In the criminal end, it's probably the opposite. A lot different, I think. The one I was selected for was a rape case. I just told the judge, I've got four daughters and wife. And all I said was, the prosecutor's brought it this far, I think he's probably guilty. He goes, you're kidding? And I said, no. I don't think she'd have wasted her time, or the county's money.

Where do you fit in the scale of say, being a conservative? Are you more conservative about the legal system than, say, you are progressive or liberal?

I'd say I'm pretty conservative.

Okay. What does that mean to you?

That the law is written and needs to be followed. I realize there is a gray area, but I think a lot of it's pretty black and white by 2015.

Do you think we have a tort crisis or a jury crisis or a personal injury crisis right now?

Crisis isn't the word I'd use. I'd say not a level playing field.

How so?

Well, some awards are a lot bigger than other awards for maybe the same mishap.

What do you think is behind that or underlies that?

*Skill of the attorney and the pockets of the one that's being sued. If they've got really deep pockets, I think that a jury pool would – and you know, **it depends, too, on the person who got injured.** She's a grandmother taking care of her foster kids. Oh, man, she needs money, you know?*

How about the composition of the jury themselves?

I think that could make a big difference, too.

Would you be surprised if I suggested that given the very same set of facts presented in the exact same way that two different juries would reach very different results?

Absolutely. It wouldn't surprise me a bit. Especially when – maybe not so much on the guilt, but on the compensation. I can see that being huge. I can see a Rush Limbaugh listener with tort reform in their mind saying, this isn't worth more than $200,000 and somebody else who watches MSNBC saying, this is worth three million.

How do you think the lawyer who's representing the injured person can best approach that with a jury – with a group of 40-some odd people that he's never met before and has a very short period of time to get to know?

*I think **showing how much the person needs.** Their expected life is going to be this. They're going to need this much per year, and my fee's a third of it, so we need to add that on. What goes through my mind first is, I know the attorney, if he wins, is going to get a third of it. So I'm thinking, okay, if they're awarding three million dollars, we're really awarding two million.*

Do you think the average juror thinks about that?

I have no idea. I don't think they're clued in on that, to tell you the truth.

I agree with you. Do you think the average juror is clued in that often there is insurance underlying who's going to pay the award?

You know, I don't know if they know that or not. I bet they don't. Unless they're either medical professionals, attorneys themselves or accountants. Or actuaries. I doubt if they really have much of a clue on that one.

How do you think your accountant background would influence or affect your being a juror?

*I don't think that it'd affect me being a juror, **but it would affect the way I think about the compensation.***

How so?

Well, going through so many x amount of returns in a year and seeing what the average person makes. And let's say the average person that comes across my desk makes $170,000. And we're saying that this person gets $300,000 a year to live on before any medical type – I'm thinking that's on the high end, you know? So I might not agree with that.

So you have a sense of what people are earning.

Yes. And I don't know how that would affect me if I knew this person was a radiologist versus an airline pilot versus – because I know what those professions all make. And would that sway me? Do I think that they should get more?

Would you listen to expert testimony, the vocational experts and economist experts that have data that can explain what they were earning and likely to earn or not earn in the future?

I'd listen to that. And depending on how they came across, I would say, that's BS or I agree with them. It'd be hard until you're sitting in there listening to that.

If you were presented with conflicting evidence from experts on different sides, what might you use to resolve the conflict?

My own experience.

You think you have more experience in that area than the average person, right?

Oh, absolutely.

Do you think that would make you a leader in the jury on some of these money issues?

I probably wouldn't say anything unless the jury was having a lot of trouble with it. If they were all coming pretty well down the road to the same conclusion, I probably wouldn't say anything. But if we had one – a lot of times there's one person on the jury that's got their foot stuck right in the – they're just not going to budge from their beliefs. Then I might try to explain why they're thinking wrong if I could sway them or not.

In a civil jury, it only has to be 10 to 2. So if there's a budger, they often don't –

Don't factor into it at all.

Right. There are different kinds of damages in injury cases. You've got special damages, which are those that can be itemized, based on actual damage. Medical bills, wage loss, past and future, things like that. Out-of-pocket expenses. There are another kind of damages called general damages, which are pain, suffering, disability, loss of enjoyment of life –

Punitive?

– also consortium. We don't have punitives here.

Oh, okay. But that's what it would be right? Or compensatory?

Compensatory, right. Pain, suffering, disability - those are things that have no fixed standard to determine.

Right. And that's the gray area.

That's the gray area. How would you go about putting a value on those things that have no fixed standard?

Just listening to the case, I guess, and trying to figure out what happened. If the really rich person's kid takes the Mercedes out and drives 200 miles an hour and kills somebody, I'm going to be a little more angry and want to punish him than something that's purely an accident that just happened.

If the Court says we don't have punitives, you're not to allow punishment to factor into your evaluation, how would you resolve that at that point? Do you think you could put that aside?

It would be hard. It would be in the back of my mind.

Do you think the average person can never truly be impartial?

I think if you have any life experience at all, it's going to influence you somehow.

I'm coming around to an idea that lawyers are trying to do too much in jury selection.

Well, they're trying to favor their side. Why wouldn't they?

Right. And they're trying to put a spin on their case. But I also think that some lawyers, unless they're very skilled, are doing themselves and their clients a disservice because they're getting too invasive with the jurors. My thought is, given that time is such an important element in jury service for most people, I'm almost ready to simply ask the entire group, who can be partial, who thinks they can be partial, or impartial? Raise their hand, and whatever answer they give me, I will accept. And leave it at that, rather than go on and do these kinds of questions that may turn some people off. What do you think about that?

*I don't disagree with that. **If I'm sitting there at the jury pool, and I see a demographic being eliminated pretty quick that kind of angers me a little bit,** too.*

I've seen black people eliminated routinely.

Yes. That would make me mad.

It makes me mad.

It would make me mad. Or Chinese – anybody.

Although I will tell you I'm not mad to see insurance people go, because they generally –

No. Because they're going to be very biased on that award. They're going to be your tort reformers.

Tend to be.

Totally, not tend. I think totally. Unless they're the one that got damaged, and then they're going to want to go the other way because they've seen things across their desk.

If I'm stuck with tort reformers and people of that kind, how do you think a plaintiff's attorney can best get them to acknowledge that they might have a difficult time being unbiased? In a respectful way?

How would you know you had that kind of a problem as the attorney?

Well, They brought it up. They said, we don't believe in these kinds of cases very much.

*I suppose then you just come back to your economist and lay it out that, hey, we're not trying to screw anybody here. **This person really is going to need this much money for this many years.** And you just have to hope that you swayed them or convinced them. I don't think you can do anything after that, can you?*

I think it's pretty difficult.

So if you're sitting there through trial, you win, you're awarded a pretty low-ball figure, does the judge have discretion to come back and change that award?

Not really. There could be a motion for *additur*, but it's unlikely that the judge, unless it's a very egregious case, is going to add anything and substitute the judge's judgment for the jury's, who are after all, ten people. Twelve people.

And at that point, that's going to be appealed pretty quickly by the other side.

It's difficult to appeal a number.

If the judge changes the number?

It's pretty unlikely that would happen. There are some cases where juries come back with zero, and then the judge says, well, you can't do that. If you found that there was an injury, if you found that there was an event, you can't give zero.

You can't give zero compensation. It just doesn't add up.

For pain and suffering, the general damages. So going back to that early part of jury selection, what could a lawyer do to make you feel comfortable with the process, so that you're more likely to participate?

When I did it, they show you a movie on voir dire, a little thing. And the person who came in was one of the judges who explains it and says, I was on a jury just recently. And then I think she explained also that she was kicked off the jury pool almost instantly when the judge said, you can go, you're one of my colleagues and you're too involved with the process here. So I don't know anybody else. I was comfortable. I kind of knew what the process was and what was going to happen. It just – you sit around and you wait a long time. You'd better bring a book or something to pass the time.

Can you think of something a lawyer would do, in the jury selection time, that would be useless or valueless to the process as you see it? In the process of getting fair and impartial jurors?

Not really. It's been a while since I've sat there. I'm trying to think of what went on.

Are there certain questions they might ask that would be, in your mind, just not very helpful?

I'd have to hear the question, I think, before I could say that.

When a lawyer is asking you about whether you have any preconceived notions or judgments that might affect your ability to be fair, do you think it's appropriate for the lawyer to share something of his or her own personal experience, say a bias they might have?

No. Because I don't care. You know.

Some people say, well, show me yours and I'll show you mine, as a kind of a courtesy, a psychological way to open people up. Like to say, I have a bias. I really don't like bicyclists when I'm driving. I really just don't. And I think I'd be a poor juror on a bicycle case. How do you feel? Do you have any biases? What do you think about something like an exchange like that?

That'd be okay.

Would it tend to turn you off or would it –

Well, if it was on common ground, I might like him a little better. But I hate the bicyclists, too, when they pull out in front of me. If they stay in their lane, they're okay. If they stop at the red lights they're okay. Which they don't.

That's the problem. That's what upsets me so much about them.

If I'm sitting on a bicycle injury case and the driver says, the bicyclist ran the red light and I hit him, I'm not going to listen to anything else. I'm done. That bicyclist will get nothing from me. And I don't care what the circumstances were because I've seen it too many times.

If you were picked for that jury, would you hear the evidence and weigh the evidence?

Yes, I would.

And if the evidence were contrary to that?

I would have to weigh the evidence.

If you were later convinced that the bicyclist didn't run, for whatever – maybe there was an independent witness or something?

If the guy swerved over and hit the bicyclist and clipped him, I would not have a bias at that. But if it was proven that that bicyclist did something to endanger himself –

Sure. Do you think you might still have a bias that would carry over to the damages part of the case?

Absolutely. It would go hand in hand.

You'd find for the bicyclist, but because it's a bicyclist, you might give less money?

No. If I found for the bicyclist, I'd be okay with it. If I could establish in my mind who was the guilty party or what really happened, I don't think that would affect me. Getting me there would be the hard part.

You've been an accountant for a long time. You know a lot of accountants. Do you think accountants, as a general rule, tend to be more or less conservative?

More. Just by the nature of us.

What do you think it is about being an accountant that leads to the conservatism? I mean, why can't there be aggressive accountants –

Oh, there are some.

– or liberal accountants?

There's some, I'm sure. I think the profession leads that type of person into it. It's like an actuary. I think they're probably way more conservative than we are, as a group. And attorneys, I think, are probably a 50/50 split. You're going to have both sides of that aisle.

Do you think it's because you're working more with numbers or data than with people?

Oh, that wouldn't surprise me.

Are you, comfortable with data more than, say, emotions?

No. I can handle both.

You can. What about your peers? Colleagues?

Probably not.

One of the things you're going to be asked to look at as a juror is the emotional impact of this event on a person. How do you look at that? How do you think about emotion as opposed to – in a monetary sense, putting a value on an emotional impact?

I might be a little cold on that one.

Even though the law recognizes that as a genuine, legitimate element of damage?

*Again, **it would come back to the severity of the case. How bad was the person injured in my mind?** If you can determine that at the moment. Some back injuries may not show up for a couple years. And that kind of thing. **If I could see it, it would affect me differently than if I couldn't see it.***

If you can't see emotional damages very well, like, post-traumatic stress or some sort of anxiety or depression that was caused by an injury, how do we prove that to you? Other than expert testimony?

Maybe just looking at –

– lay witnesses.

– just looking at the person that's there and – you know, you're going to be watching them for however long that case lasts and probably forming some kind of an opinion, from what I've seen. If that person is sitting there and they look like they're in pain and they're all bandaged up versus the guy that's sitting there all relaxed and just waiting for his payday, it's going to affect me. How I see that person. Because you get to sit there and stare at them the whole time.

How do you feel about hearing from lay witnesses, non-expert people, friends and family and co-workers about the effect or impact of this incident on a person?

I might put more weight on that than I did the expert, because I know the expert's paid to say what they were told to say. And that same expert might say something different depending on who hired him.

Do you think experts can be objective even though they've been paid?

I think if they're experts and they're objective and it's the wrong way, they're not going to be asked to do it again, so yes. I think that their future income stream depends on what they say, how they say it.

Would you feel that way about a treating doctor?

It depends. If he's a chiropractor doing back work on a whiplash, I'm going to feel a lot different than I am about a surgeon who got in there and said, this back is screwed up.

Chiropractors, generally speaking, have a lower level of credibility for you?

Absolutely. I don't know if there's one chiropractor out there that would say, you only need this one visit. It's never happened, I'm sure, in the history of chiropractic.

There actually are some watchdogs for the profession out there, who can be more objective than others. But you're right that it is true, they seem to want to continue on with maintenance therapy.

Yes. So you see D.C. behind that name and you get turned off the second you see it.

Do you do chiropractor returns?

We've done a few in the past. They're strange ducks to deal with.

What's the worst way a lawyer could ask about your feelings about personal injury cases or biases you might have?

It would depend on how they asked it. If they were leading me into something, I'd be really angry; just blatantly asked it and I said, I don't think I know right now, I would want to just let it go at that point. And not try to lead me down some path. Because then I'm going to dig my heels in and become very resistant. Because I don't want to be told what to think.

You don't want questions to be suggested?

Not at all.

If you're given an open-ended question, do you think that you would tend to take it and run with it?

Depends what it is.

What would be an off-limits area for you?

Be a hard one to answer. I don't know. I don't know until it was asked. And who it was asked in front of.

Going back to the attorney establishing a human connection with you, what can an attorney do to show that he or she is a human being who's doing meaningful, good work for this client?

Presentation. Plain language. Maybe not strutting around. Sitting on the bench – sitting on the table, your desk. Relaxing, acting very calm about the whole thing.

Is good or bad?

Good. Good.

You like to see the lawyer be calm?

Calm, and just explain what's going on. In plain language.

Is it important to you if the attorney articulates in some way how much he or she cares about this client they're representing?

That would depend on the attorney's demeanor if I truly bought it or just thought they were saying it. I would have to make that judgment at that point. It would definitely depend. You've seen a lot of people you wouldn't give much credibility to. Especially if they mis-said your name.

Speaking of names, if the lawyer was very good at learning people's names in a hurry and called you by name, how would you feel about that if you were referred to as your name instead of Juror No. 14?

My first opinion was, this guy's pretty intelligent. Of course, he made it through law school, so he's not stupid in the first place. But to do that, that's a unique gift to have. I don't think I would put much into except that, this guy's pretty smart. Or he's got a good memory.

It's my belief that the lawyer needs to establish trust and credibility.

Absolutely.

Off the bat. What can the lawyer do to establish trust and credibility? Or conversely, what's the worst thing they can do to have that go away, in your mind?

I don't like people who act like they're superior. So if he's out there acting like we're there to service him, basically. I'm going to get turned off pretty quick by the whole process.

Can you think of an example how that might play out?

In ordinary words, if I feel like I'm being spoken down to, that's going to turn me off pretty quick.

What happens if you see two lawyers arguing in front of the judge? Emotionally getting involved in it?

I could care less about that. You're probably not going to hear it. They're going to be in muffled voices. Somebody's trying to bring up a point and the other one is objecting to it, and I'm not privy to – I don't care.

If you saw that the judge was playing favorites to one side or the other, because we're all human, how would you feel about that?

That might sway me the other way. I'm going to protect the one who's getting whacked, maybe. Depending again on the case.

On the case or how you feel about it.

If the judge doesn't like the bicyclist either, I don't know, I may have to go buy him lunch.

Do you think that some cases are too small to be brought in Superior Court if they haven't settled? Do you think there's a number of a case that -

Seems like a waste of time? If they're only looking for a little bit of money or they're looking for a little bit of –

Let's say they're looking for $50,000 instead of a million?

I would hope that wouldn't be the case, that justice should be blind to the dollars. But the cost of court, the cost to the taxpayers, maybe the small claims court should be raised. So it does distract – detract. Because that's valuable time, I think. The judges, the bailiffs, the whole system is expensive.

Sure. How do you feel about the civil justice system and its role in both compensating victims and deterring future bad conduct? Do you think it accomplishes its goal?

It'd probably be hit and miss. It probably does both. Some people get what they should; some people get less and some people get more. As far as swaying what happens out there in the real world, I doubt it.

Do you think in some extreme cases there might be a deterrent factor but for the most part, in the civil justice system, deterrence isn't really the end goal.

I think the deterrents happen from other sources. Your insurance company will say, here's five different breeds of dog you cannot own or we won't insure you because these things cost us a lot of money in the past. I think insurance companies look at civil cases and determine what happens. Automobile manufacturers change things because they've been sued because this didn't work. Things like that, more so than the public saying, oh, I'm not going to do that again.

It sounds like deterrence works with corporate entities and businesses, but generally speaking, is not going to happen much with individuals?

Yes. You just buy more insurance. And that's the insurance company's problem then. Civil matters might be a little – or criminal, I think, is different.

There are some pretty interesting studies about deterrence and criminal cases, too.

I'll bet there are. If you're going to kill somebody, you don't do it in Florida or Texas, but they do it.

But they do it.

But they do it anyway. So those are crimes of passion, I guess, that don't go into a lot of thought into the consequences.

Can you think of anything I haven't asked that would be helpful to me or my peers who would be reading this?

> *A lot of it just comes down to their demeanor. Just the way they present themselves is important.* To dress nice, but not too sharp. If I have to look at that Armani suit that I know cost a fortune, eh, you're overdressed for this occasion. The court must have a standard, don't they, for the attorneys? There's no standard?

There probably are standards, but I don't think hard and fast rules.

> Oh, really? I always just figured there was a professional standard or professional look that needed to be attained.

Thank you.

17

JUST ASK

Black male, age 62, divorced, Warehouse Shipping and Receiving, B.S.

The shortest route between two distances is from point to point, a straight line. If you got something you want to ask me, don't go all the way around the freaking corner. Just come right on out and ask. I'm going to tell you one way or the other.

The judge says, ladies and gentlemen, please give your attention to the attorney for the plaintiff. At that point, what thoughts and feelings are going through your head as you're sitting there in the courtroom?

Probably the first thought running through my mind is what this case is all about. Second of all, do I have anything positive to add to this case? If I don't, then I would deem myself not a suitable participant as a juror. Because if I don't know and didn't say anything, how can I give a positive point of view? Because this person's life or lifestyle or whatever it is may be on the line. And I don't want to do anything to damage it.

Do you feel there is anything in a case like that, as you think about it that would make you uncomfortable about serving on a jury?

Yes, if I had a biased opinion.

Let's talk about that. One of the things lawyers want to find out is, do prospective jurors have bias or prejudgment? How would you like an attorney to go about asking you about any biases or prejudgments you might have?

First of all, the shortest route between two distances is from point to point, a straight line. If you got something you want to ask me, don't go all the way around the freaking corner. Just come right on out and ask. I'm going to tell you one way or the other. So a direct approach would be my opinion.

Then, being direct, are there any biases or prejudices or prejudgments you might have in a civil injury case like that that would make it difficult for you to serve?

Once again, it depends on what the case is all about.

Okay. In an injury case.

In an injury case? I don't know if I would have a bias. I mean, my approach to these types of things – I'm seeking the truth. I'm out to help the person who's not at fault. So if I know you and I know your character to be shady or anything negative, no, I wouldn't be a suitable juror. Because more than likely, if I know your background and if I know your character, I would either be more for you or more against you, depending on what kind of person you are.

What do you look for when you're trying to determine if a person is credible or truthful or honest?

Honesty.

When you look at the lawyer standing before you, what are you thinking about lawyers in general?

Okay. Let me tell you how I'd approach it. First of all, I've had Psychology 101 and 102. **I judge a person by their responses, their body posture, their demeanor; I look at the whole spectrum and if it doesn't look right and I got a red flag that comes up, that tells me something's wrong.**

Do you have any particular feelings one way or another about whether or not people should be able to sue for injuries that happen to them?

Absolutely. Because first of all – let's take this crosswalk right here. Now, the light turns green. I'm in the right; I'm walking within that crosswalk. I'm walking across the street, and you come hit me. Now, I'm following the rules. You only cross when the light tells you, and you stay within the crosswalk. If you follow those rules and you still get injured, then somebody else was not following the rules or not paying attention. So now, if I'm a working person and I got a job, now you injure me, I can't go to work; I can't support myself. Can't pay the doctor bill. None of that stuff. Somebody's responsible. So yes, a person should be able to. But you have to be in the right. I know there's a lot of cases that are fraudulent lawsuits.

How do you feel about fraudulent lawsuits?

That hurts everybody. That drives everything up. First of all, if I come into a large coffee chain and I'm thinking that they're a pretty profitable company, let me go ahead and try and make a slip here, see if I can't get some money. I don't know. I'm not that type of person. I'm not geared like that. And I think that a person who does that is an opportunist. But on the flip side, sometimes, survival out here will make you turn to do things like that. But I feel that it's really unnecessary.

You've talked about following the rules.

Yes.

And if somebody doesn't follow the rules and they hurt somebody, there should be accountability?

Absolutely. Unequivocally.

Right. And in our system of civil justice, that is most often in the form of money to compensate for injuries and the harms that have happened. You talked about not being able to work. How would you go about calculating the loss, the value of the harms that were –

Okay. First of all, if the person that's working has a job, how much money per day does this person stand to lose, number one. Number two, if an ambulance comes and picks you up and takes you to the hospital, do you know how much that's going to cost? Just for the ambulance pick up alone? Then, if you ain't got insurance, if they take you to the hospital, I'm not going to tell you how the medical bills are going to start piling up. All right. You also have to think now the injury that I have suffered, is it a short-term injury? Will I be well? Back to normal, in a short time? Or am I going to be disabled for the rest of my life? That's a big impact. So I would look at all aspects of the case, of the injury, how it happened, and make my judgment there. But I would make an educational decision. Get all the facts together, weigh them, then make a decision.

You can determine what people's incomes are, what their medical bills are, but for things like pain and suffering or disability, where there's no fixed standard, how do you go about calculating those?

That's a hard calculation, because my threshold for pain may be different from yours. *You may stand to lose more through pain and suffering than I will. I don't know.* ***You have to weigh it individually, case by case.***

Do you think that some people are more deserving of money for pain and suffering than others?

Yes.

Why?

Depending on their situation. Or the situation that the accident has caused. It wasn't there before, now you have caused something, pain and suffering or whatever. But you're the main reason that they are going through this now. So I'd take that into account.

Have you ever had an injury of any kind caused by some other person?

No.

Know anybody close in that regard? Anybody close to you that – friend or family – that's –

Yes.

How has that impacted them?

Well, it was a low impact. All they wanted to do was be compensated for their time off from work and pay their medical bills. I don't know if they got anything for pain and suffering. I don't know if they were even looking for that. All they wanted was to get back to ground zero, make me well and healthy again so I can go back to work, pay me for the time this injury has caused me to lose from work. That's about as far as it went.

If you were called for jury service, would you want to go? Given that you have to take time, travel down there, spend possibly a week or more?

If I'm compensated and if I can help the person – let me say, the right person. I don't know who – which party is right or whatever, but I'm there to help the right party.

When you say compensated, do you know that jury service only pays $10 a day?

No, I didn't. I'm not going to no jury service. Because any job, even a minimum wage job a day pays you more than $10. **Something's wrong with that picture.**

Would you not go because of that?

I don't know. I don't want to think of myself as a capitalist pig, but it seems a little bit unfair. **You're going make me come to a jury, and I'm going to lose $150 a day from being away from work? That's not a balance.**

Even if someone called it a civic duty?

Okay, **I believe in doing my civic duty, don't get me wrong. But if I'm going to do my civic duty, at least compensate for doing my duty.** *But you know, nine times out of ten, a lot of people would do it out of the goodness of their heart. And I can understand that. So some jobs, there're rules about jury duty, I guess – I don't know.*

Do you think the civil justice system works well? Not the criminal system, but the civil system.

I don't know much about the civil system. I know a lot about the criminal system, and if the criminal system is anything like the civil system, it needs a lot of work.

Have you got any opinions one way or the other about whether or not there are too many frivolous lawsuits?

That's a yes. Let me tell you something. This is America. This is what we do here. We sue each other. Everybody is climbing that money ladder, trying to get some cash. Just like I told you, if I was downtrodden, broke, no job, and homeless, and if I thought I could come in here and slip on this floor and get $10,000 – so yes, there is a lot of – and there are people out there who set up to do things like this. And I would say over half of them profit from it.

Do you think those cases make it to a courtroom?

I don't know the statistics, if it's more than half or less than half. But I would say about 50/50, most of them don't make it to court; they settle out of court. And the reason they do that is because if I can pay you $10 to drop this BS rather than go to court and pay a half a million dollars to settle it, I'll give you $10. Why take it to court? Lawyers' fees, court fees, blah blah blah blah. No, here. Take this $10 and get up out of my face.

Is there anything that the lawyer standing before you can do to show that he or she is human and make you comfortable in their presence?

Be direct, be informative. Don't make me feel uncomfortable by your actions. Because like I said, body posture and your demeanor, you know,

if you make me uncomfortable and I think you're lying about something –

Is there anything in particular you're imagining a person doing that could make you uncomfortable by their demeanor or posture?

Talking to me and not looking me directly in my face. See when people talk to you and don't look at you, they're hiding something.

They're hiding something.

Oh, yeah. See, it was a prerequisite of mine in college to take Psych 101 and 102. And they teach you things to look for in a person's character to determine whether they're either on the up and up or on the down low.

Can I ask you a difficult question?

Sure.

How do you feel about race and the fact that you would be a minority on the jury and your personal experience?

Okay, first of all, let me explain to you about race. I have a mulatto daughter. And the second thing you need to know is this: I have a problem with color vision. I can't tell colors. I don't know one color from the other. I'm being facetious.

Of course.

Second of all, you know what? I served in the military and if me and you are fighting in a war, I don't give a (expletive) what color you are. As long as you've got my back, I don't give a (expletive) what color you are. To me, that's very shallow thinking. Second of all, an experiment was conducted. If you put two infants, no matter where they're from, Oriental, black, green, white, blue, purple. If you put them together as infants and leave them alone to grow, they will never know what racism is. It's a taught thing. You learn it. So my thing about me – now, if I was in a jury and I'm the only black person there, say man, I'm a people person. I can get along with anybody, if you get along with me. And color has nothing to do with it. But some people let color – use it as a determining factor, but it shouldn't.

If one of the parties in the case or one of the lawyers were black, would that affect you?

No. Because there's good and bad in every race. Just because you black, that don't make you – and I'm black – that doesn't make you okay or all right. I might fear you more than I fear the white guy. Uh-uh, I'm from the hood. And I know there's some black people in there you don't want to – just like I wouldn't go to Atlanta. I mean, that's a chocolate city. Washington, D.C. And I'm black. I love black people. But you know, I want to see something else other than black. And I know my people, my race. I know how they can be sometimes and – but once again, don't get it twisted. I love the black race, but there's bad in everybody. Come on, now.

There is a perception, right or wrong, that black jurors are more generous than white jurors. Do you have any thoughts about that?

Yes.

What are those?

Okay. Traditionally, most black people – not all – are downtrodden. They're trying to climb up whatever it is they're trying to climb up out of. And a lot of times, they might – you know, like I say – it goes from case to case. They may deserve it and they may not. If I feel in my heart with all the given information about what's going on, if I determine in my heart that you deserve it, once again, I don't care if you're black or white; compensate that person. And if it so happens to be a black person, once again, the rules apply the same to them. If you're in the right, I'm for you. If you're in the wrong, tough cookies.

Okay, I want to make it clear that when I said the perception is that black people are more generous, I mean to everybody, not just to their own race, but to white parties as well.

Yes. I understand you. Generous.

In terms of the amount of money they're willing to award.

It's my perception, and I'm not always right, that most black people look at things in a monetary standpoint, whereas a lot of white people would say, okay, well, I got injured. I can pay my own bills. But a lot of black people feel that when I'm not working, I'm low-income, I can't pay all this stuff. So I think I deserve this much instead of this much. A lot of black people would be more than generous.

What would you like to know, if anything, about the lawyer himself or herself when they're talking to you early in the –

Their character. What kind of lawyer is he? Because some people are ambulance chasers. Some lawyers are ambulance chasing. They don't care about you; they care about how much they can make off your case. Because the more they make off your case, the more they're going to get. They could care less about you. And if he's that kind of lawyer, I don't want him.

If a potential juror was asked if they have a bias or a prejudice and they say they don't have any biases or prejudices, would you believe them? You've got 40 or so other people around you and they're all being asked, as you are, do you folks have any biases or prejudices that might affect your ability to sit in this case? Some people don't raise their hands. They don't think they have any prejudices. Do you believe that?

No. Everybody has some type of prejudice. It may not be any prejudice toward that particular case, but everybody has a prejudice. Because your prejudice is what makes you an individual. And you can't like everything. On the flip side, you can't hate every damn thing either. But your prejudice is part of your character make up.

How can the lawyer find who can be fair, just fair, in the least amount of time? I'll give you an example. I could ask, can you be fair in a case like this? And a person might say yes, but they could have a hidden agenda and I wouldn't know it.

Okay. I would think that if a lawyer was smart, he'd set up five questions to ask each juror and determine from their answer if they, in general, can be fair. **You can learn a lot from a person from what they say; also, you can learn a lot from what they don't say.**

Anything that you think would, in terms of those questions that you just mentioned, be more effective than another to find out if a person really would be fair?

I would ask them a simple question about how they feel about race, diversity, or something that has to do with race. I would say eight times out of ten, if a person is biased or prejudiced, and you ask them about a race question and watch their reaction, you can generally gauge – not all the time – you can generally gauge if a person is a bigot or is prejudiced by their responses. It doesn't always work. But I would say nine times out of ten you can ask some general questions and you can get a feel for a person from their responses.

Would that be helpful in a civil case? Where race isn't an issue in the case?

Absolutely. Absolutely. Absolutely. Because say you walk out of there and you got hit, and you were in the right, but because you white, people say, he was wrong, I'm against you. Not because you are correct and you follow all the rules, I'm going to get you because of your skin color. And no, I don't want you to get paid.

What's the best way I can ask people if they can be fair and get a reliable answer?

I don't know what thing you would use to gauge a person's response to a race question, because some people do a good job of hiding it. There's no 100% effective way to gauge a person if they're a racist or not.

If a person says, you know what, I do have some prejudices and biases, but I think I can put them aside in this case, how do you feel about that?

I don't know if I would believe them.

What kind of a juror would you like in a case if you were a civil injury victim?

An open-minded juror. *Not only open-minded, but also if they were a person that's an advocate of doing the right thing.*

Got it. Even if the right thing is something that might be different in their mind from one another?

Even – if it's the right thing, but you have a different opinion, then that means your opinion is wrong. Because you're going to try to do the right thing.

Going back to open-minded, tell me a little bit more about what the open-minded person looks like. I don't mean physically, but what their –

An open-minded person is one who don't shut off, that won't close their mind or thought patterns to any idea that might come across the table. Entertain any thought. Investigate anything and everything. And the main focus of that is deriving to the right answer. So if you've got a closed mind, I don't know how you can get to the right answer, because you're not an accepting person. If I tell you that something happened to me and I'm telling you the truth, but you don't believe me, you've got a closed mind. I'm screwed.

Do you think the average person who shows up for jury service is open-minded?

No.

Do you think the average person is closed-minded?

I think that the average person that goes through jury – you pick these people randomly?

Yes.

And they don't know what the case is about. Nine times out of ten, they come there out of their obligation to the State. You may have found one or two that's really interested in what's going on, what the case is all about. But those other people, they just want to get in there, get this over with, and get out. They're not concerned about the case. They're there because you forced them to come.

How do I get them to feel comfortable with me as a human being, as an attorney, knowing that they don't want to be there and that they may be closed-minded?

First of all, you come to them in a direct manner. You explain to them what the case is about. And you give them an overview of both sides of the case. And then you wait to judge their response.

What are your thoughts if I said that given the same set of facts, if they were presented to two different juries, we would have different results? In other words, the same case presented to two random groups of people will have a different result? Does that feel like justice to you?

I don't know. One group of people may think differently than another group of people. I think that's why – who does the jury selection? The defense? Or the –

Both sides.

Okay. Well, that's why they ask these questions, to pick people who have like-minded thoughts. Why would you pick a jury that doesn't think the same way you think? Because if you do, then he's going to go against you. That's why they ask questions and pick jurors who have like-minded opinions.

Not necessarily open-minded, but like-minded?

Yeah. Not necessarily open-minded. Because if you're a shady lawyer, then you're going to pick somebody with a closed mind that when the trial comes, he's going to go against the person that's probably in the right?

What does a shady lawyer look like? And I don't mean just physically, but –

Well, he wears a $1,500 suit. He's not interested in your opinion. And he's going to try to lead you, steer you the way he wants you to go. And I could be wrong about all this.

How do you feel about the other jurors? What are your general thoughts about those other 40 people there?

Okay. Well, I wouldn't have a thought about them. I would perceive that they're there for the same reason I'm there. I don't know what thoughts they're carrying in their head about the case, and you know what? I respect everybody's individual decisions and thought patterns. I would more or less worry about me, about the people around me. You know what, I may not agree with you, but I do respect your opinion.

If the lawyer asks a question to one of the jurors and the juror gets upset or jumps all over the lawyer, how do you think that affects you and your relationship with the lawyer if somebody else is giving the lawyer a hard time?

Okay. I would pay close attention, and I would try to reason out why that person is mad at that lawyer. Did that lawyer do something to them? Did that lawyer say something out of line? Or is that person just a straight (expletive)? You gotta make judgments, you know? Before I make a decision, I weigh things. I don't just make a snap decision.

Is there anything – any thoughts that have been brought up by this interview that you think would be helpful to share that I would need to know about?

I would have say that I'm not much versed on civil law cases or even jury duty. Before a person is coming to jury duty, it should be explained to them what they're involved in, why they have been chosen, and above all, give an honest, unbiased opinion of what you're being asked.

That's pretty direct.

You know, I love my country, but our judicial system needs to be worked on, because some things carry more weight than others, and it's out of whack. Some of the laws that are in place now and rules are there to keep chaos in order. But also, rules are made to be changed.

Sometimes when an attorney is talking to jurors and is asking them to share something, the attorney himself might share something about their life. So in other words, if I'm going to ask you to share a bias or a prejudice, I should share something of my own. Do you think that's appropriate or fair to do?

It's not appropriate, because they're using that as a ploy, as a tool to get you to come to their side. *Case in point. I'm the lawyer, but I'm trying to sway your opinion to my side. I find out that maybe you have a son or a child that goes to the same school my child goes. And I start talking to you about my son and in* *relations to your son, oh, they go to the same school? Blah blah blah, trying to, you know, slowly reel you in to view things my way.*

Is it okay, though, to seek common ground with somebody?

Yes. It is. But be very careful, because like I said, some lawyers are smart enough to use that as a weapon.

It's clear that you don't want to be used or manipulated.

Hell, no. Does anybody like being manipulated? Especially against their will? I don't like being manipulated.

So the coming back to it, the shortest distance is –

Is a straight line. You can't beat it.

Even if it deals with sensitive –

Issues? Look here. Honesty is always – no. Okay, me and you are two different people. I don't know what you think or how you believe, but the way I was taught, my parents taught me honesty, no matter if it hurts, it's always the best policy. Because if you tell one lie, you have to tell two to cover up that one. So that's a lot of wasted time. Just tell the truth. Come on, man. I have no patience.

In addition to trying to find a juror who can be open-minded, it's my job to establish trust. How do I do that? Or maybe the better question is, what can I do to screw that up?

*Okay. Say you were trying to recruit me as a juror. **The best thing you can do is look me in my eye and be straight and direct forth.** Lay all the cards on the table, tell it like it is, and hope that I can make a sound decision.*

There's a lot on the line.

I understand that part. Listen to me. Let me tell you something. I'm an educated person, and I look at things in an educated way, I hope, or a logical way. I like people to think that I'm a logical thinker. If I have to make a judgment about someone, give me as much of the facts and the information that you can give me. Let me cipher through it, and all things being equal and normal, then I will try to make an educated decision. That's as much as you can ask of me.

Thank you.

18

DRAMA

Asian male, age 37, single, Marketing, B.A. Communications

I know that I wanted to be in a trial that had some drama; that had some sensation to it.

The judge says, ladies and gentlemen of the jury, please give your attention to the attorney for the plaintiff who's going to conduct jury selection. At that point, what are your thoughts? What are your feelings at that time before anybody's said anything? As you're in that "as if" moment.

It was all new to me. I've never been through a process like that. I'm not that familiar with the court system. I don't watch courtroom drama TV. I really didn't know what to expect. I was just going along with what was happening. There was no instruction. You're learning what you're supposed to be doing as it's happening.

Did you get a sense the attorneys were attempting to get information from you and about you in that process?

*Yes. It was definitely a process where they wanted to find out more information about you as a potential juror. They asked us how we would approach making a decision in a case such as what we might be facing, what our thought process is. What our prior experience is with going through anything similar to what the court case is about. They asked a lot of medical questions, particularly if you knew someone or had someone who went through a traumatic illness or some type of injury. They tried to figure out a little bit more about what you did for a living, and I think they wanted to gauge maybe what your interest in participating as a juror was. It was opened up to questions and comments. I thought it got a lot more emotional than I expected from some of the potential jurors when they started talking about experiences they went through in terms of illness or injury that they had close family members go through or whatever. It got emotional. And that was surprising to me. **They asked me specifically how do you go about making a decision.** And I gave them basically, you know, I make a decision, I try to look at both sides, and I make a decision based on facts, also rationality, and I try not to make a decision that's based on emotions.*

Did they ask about things like your ability to be fair, as you see what fairness is?

I don't remember specifically if that question was raised using the word fair. I don't remember that being brought up.

We might use bias or prejudice or prejudgment or favoring one side or the other.

I remember them talking about and using the word bias. I think they were trying to figure out if any of these potential jurors had any bias.

How did you feel about that part of the process?

I had no issue with that. I understood what they were going for. **They want a person who's neutral and doesn't have their mind made up in terms of whatever the issue may be regarding the case.**

Did you have a sense that your fellow jurors were more or less neutral as a group?

I'd say most of them were neutral. There were a few that had strong opinions. I know one person in particular didn't want to be a jurist.

It's not uncommon.

Right. Mainly because he worked as a salesperson. If he doesn't work, he doesn't make money. He was one of the top five people they wanted. But he kept fighting his way to get off the pool. I think he intentionally was very biased on one end so that they wouldn't select him. He understood what they didn't want to hear, so he told them that. But for the most part, most people were neutral. There were a few people who did have strong opinions and it did come across. And they were very emotional opinions.

How did you feel about the way the lawyers handled those people with emotional opinions, or opinions that maybe the attorneys didn't want to hear?

I thought it was handled fine. I didn't see anything wrong with what they did or anything necessarily right. I just saw it as, they looked for someone they thought would be a good fit for them, for whatever side. They wanted someone who would side with them, but in the most neutral manner as possible.

Did you have the feeling you were being selected or picked by one side or the other?

No. I was only questioned by the defense side. I did not get any questions from the plaintiff side. I remember specifically the lawyer asking me, how would you handle that case or how do you make decisions?

You said some people were asked how they go about making decisions. How do you go about making decisions when you're dealing with conflicting evidence?

What I mentioned earlier. I look at the facts. I try to make a rational decision. I try to see things from both sides. And I try not to base that decision on emotion.

Did you feel during deliberation and after deliberation that this case was not a close call?

I thought it was a close call for most of the time I was there. It became a little more clear to me toward the end of the trial.

Did you sense that any of your prospective jury pool were biased for one side or the other, either in things they said or in ways they behaved or didn't?

There might have been a couple. It wasn't a strong sense of that. It was more a strong sense of what their experience was, not necessarily for which side.

When the attorney got up to speak with you, did you feel any emotions toward the lawyers or the parties at the outset?

No. I know some people give lawyers a bad rap, but I'm not one of those people.

How did you feel about the way the judge handled the proceedings?

I thought she was great. She is now in the State Supreme Court, I believe.

Going back to asking questions of the jurors, what I think most lawyers are looking for are jurors who can be open-minded. How do you think it's best to approach that, either with you or with the people in your jury pool?

I think the lawyers did what they could – ask questions. I don't see any other way they can figure out.

Anything they could have done better?

I don't see. No, I don't.

Do you think they were successful in getting the information needed that made a difference in that case? What I'm getting at here is, do you think the efforts they put forth yielded any different result than a random selection might have gotten?

Basically, they got the information off the sheet that we filled out.

There's that, sure. And the time spent questioning.

I felt like most of the information they got was from the sheet as far as what happened at voir dire. It didn't feel very intensive. There was questioning; there was good questioning. I didn't get a sense of whether or not they based it on the questions or on the sheets that we filled out. I didn't know if one was better than the other or that one helped the other. I didn't get a sense of that.

Did anything that either side did in the jury selection process stand out to you as having been especially good or especially bad?

No. I didn't feel that way at all.

Did any of your fellow jurors remark on the demeanor or the ability of the attorneys in anything that was done that was satisfactory or unsatisfactory?

During voir dire? No comments were made about that. Later on, yeah. During the trial, people picked up on some things the lawyers did that stood out. But not during voir dire.

Anything stand out that was negatively impacting?

Not to my memory. Nothing stood out.

I'm certain the attorneys were fairy professional.

I definitely got a sense they were professional.

And their presentations were good on both sides, most likely.

During the trial? Or during voir dire?

During the trial.

One was better than the other.

Got it. How about during *voir dire*?

Made no difference.

When you say that one was better than the other, do you mean better as a lawyer or better by virtue of what they had to work with?

Right, right, right. I would say on the defense side, the lawyers made a better presentation. **The reason they made a better presentation was it felt more focused.** *And the way that they presented information, whether it was on the screen or the format, it was so much clearer. The simple act of using bullet points to lay out what they're trying to accomplish, what they want you to understand, breaking it down like that, made it so much easier. And their explanations, I thought, were better. Maybe it's because they had a stronger case. It crossed my mind.*

Did you have a sense in jury selection that one side's presentation was any better – and I may have asked you this already – any better than the other?

I didn't feel it, no.

Did the attorneys talk about the facts or details of the case in jury selection?

No. I don't remember any facts about the case specifically. I don't remember. What happened was, the plaintiff was going through a gallbladder surgery. I don't remember them talking about a gallbladder surgery.

Did you just know it was an injury case where medical negligence was alleged and that there was a suit seeking money damages?

Yes. It was at a very high level.

How did you feel knowing only that information during the jury selection process? Did that hamper you or would you have liked to know more? Would it have made a difference?

It wouldn't have made a difference to me.

Your fellow jurors, do you think they needed anything more?

I never got the sense they wanted more. I think we all knew what we needed to know.

For yourself and your fellow jurors, what do you think was most valued? Their

commitment to the civil justice system, their desire to do the right thing, or their time? I'm just picking those three things. There could be other things, but what do you sense was most valued by the jury? Their commitment to the civil justice system because they've been called in, their desire to do the right thing, their desire to advance their own agenda, or their time being there?

> *So you're asking me what one of those three factors influenced their decision to be there the most?*

What I'm getting at is, in interviews in the past, jurors have told me they don't feel their time is being recognized. They're being asked to give up a lot of time. They feel like lawyers are talking and using a lot more time than is necessary. Time has become a currency I'm picking up as a theme among people who have done jury service and who may say, it's really hard for me to be here. And if I'm going to be here, I don't want it to be unnecessarily long. At the same time, there are people who say, what's most important to me is getting it right and staying longer. Or what's most important is my commitment to the civil justice system and doing my civic duty. So there are those things – or advancing their own agenda. There are people who become jurors and have their own agenda and want to advance that. For example, you get somebody who's what they call a tort reformer – who doesn't believe in personal injury lawsuits. They may get on a jury and try to persuade the other jurors that there shouldn't be a case. You have all sorts of people and all kinds of opinions. I'm curious if you have a sense of the prevailing Zeitgeist of your juror pool, or you own self, for that matter.

> *Personally, I was always curious what it would be like to be a juror, so I embraced the experience. I was open to it. I wanted to be part of it. And I was glad to do that. **I think out of the three that you mentioned, I would say maybe a sense of doing the right thing, a civic duty, is what propelled them to be there and to stay there.***

Did you feel they were genuine in that commitment?

> *I think so.*

You're talking about those jurors who sat through the trial or those in the jury pool?

> *Right. And I think first in my mind was, I thought about the people who got selected.*

Right. A fair amount of those in the jury pool probably got excused for hardship.

> *Quite a lot did.*

Because of the length of the trial probably more than anything.

> *Right. They told you up front how long it might last. And that crossed off a lot of people. If I were to generalize things, I got a sense that people were there to do their civic duty and there was a minority there that really dreaded the thought of doing that, of being a juror, who really didn't want to be there.*

Thank you for saying that you wanted to be there, because that's a minority opinion.

I agree. That's what I hear.

You indicated that you wanted to be there. Did you want to be selected for that jury?

Not necessarily. I just wanted to be a part of a jury. I always thought, well, if I want to be in a jury, I want to be in something that's exciting, like a murder trial or something like that. And looking back, I know how difficult this process is and I totally understand. If I knew I was going into a murder case for three months, I don't know how I'd feel about that. **But I know that I wanted to be in a trial that had some drama; that had some sensation to it.**

You had it. And good lawyering. I'll tell you why I asked this question. You mentioned that jury duty was something you were looking forward to doing and wanted to do. I imagine there were folks like you that wanted to be there. There were an equal number of people that probably didn't want to be there, as you know, from those who were excused and others who maybe didn't get excused. It has been said, generally speaking, that those who want to be jurors in a case need to be looked at carefully because of their desire to sit in judgment on another person. How do you respond or how do you feel about that?

I can understand why someone would say that. That's not the reason why I wanted to be selected. I wanted to be selected out of, again, this curiosity, what it would be like to be a jurist, not because I felt I had an important judgment to make or something important to say about the case. It was just out of pure curiosity. I just like going through different experiences.

Did you feel your age, vis-à-vis, your fellow jurors was a factor in the way your decision was arrived at? Did you see things differently than other members of the jury by virtue of being younger?

We had a really good mix.

Good. That's important.

We had two alternates, so we had fourteen people. It was pretty split between male and female. There were a few older people and maybe a couple of younger people. But for the most part, I probably fell in the middle.

Do you feel that the attorney for the plaintiff should have talked to you in jury selection? Do you think that would have helped bond you to that lawyer?

No. They had a male and a female. During voir dire, it was the female. She was pretty much the lead.

As I said, we're looking for who can be impartial, who can give both sides a fair start and also looking to build credibility and connection with the jury at the beginning. How can that be done without manipulating a juror? And did you get a sense at all that you were being manipulated in the jury selection?

I didn't get a sense at all that I was being manipulated. I saw it for what it was. The lawyers were looking for people they felt would work for them and made their decisions based on what they saw on paper. Then if they felt like they wanted to learn more about that prospective juror, they asked that juror questions. And if they didn't hear what they wanted to hear, then they didn't want them.

Do you have a sense the lawyers tended to focus more on the people that were saying things they didn't want to hear? To get a discussion going about that topic?

*The topic they talked about most was – **they really wanted to find people who had experience with someone they either knew or experience they had of their own of an illness or injury that was traumatic.** They really focused on talking to those people. That was from both sides. They wanted to get a sense if they were going to be biased one way or the other, is what I felt.*

Did you feel that your prospective juror group were more or less receptive to all those questions? Nobody took offense to any line of questioning?

I don't remember anyone taking offense to any of the questions. I was surprised at how open and public it was. Again, people got emotional. It was so wide open. There's so many people there. You're thrust into this room; you know nobody; and here you are about to possibly embark on this major case. I just went with it, not even trying to examine what was happening, but just going along with what they were doing and asking us to do.

What made this a major case?

What do you mean?

You referred to it as a major case, and we do talk about those. What about this case made it a major case?

I guess I just threw that word out, major. I didn't think of it necessarily as a major case, more as a –

Significant case?

As something – not that it's a significant case, but it was something of significance. Not that that case was bigger than any other case, it was just the significance of what we're doing today. We're going to be asked to judge, to make a decision on this person. There's lawyers involved and laws and the court and the judge and it just made things feel like, wow, this is for real, you know?

And the parties themselves, too, right? The plaintiff and the defendant. And what happens to them?

I just felt the gravity of the situation is where I was going with that.

Was the injury very significant?

It affected his life. It still continues to affect his life, I'm assuming.

Is there anything, in hindsight or going forward, that you'd want to know about the lawyers themselves? Would you want them to share any of their experience when they're asking you to share yours?

Not one time while I was there did I even want to know whether or not – or what their background was. It didn't matter to me.

Do you feel that's a sentiment shared by most people that were there with you?

*I think so. **No one asked any questions about the lawyers. And I didn't feel it was relevant. It probably isn't relevant. It's probably better that we don't know.***

Was there any sense of time wasting by the lawyers who were asking questions in jury selection?

No. The process started in the morning. We had to come back after lunch. I didn't feel like they wasted any time.

You didn't get to the damages phase of the verdict because the jury found there was either no negligence or no causation.

Right.

Was it a no negligence case?

No negligence.

Did you talk about damages at all?

The foreman, she wanted us to complete the rest of the jury instructions, but one of the jurors blew up. He like – well, we already have a decision; why even go there? He didn't want to waste time doing that. But I can see from the foreman's standpoint that she didn't want to leave any stone unturned. She saw this as a serious process. She didn't want to walk away without doing everything first. I saw it from her vantage point.

Did the lawyers talk about money or the gravity of the case in terms of value in jury selection?

Not in jury selection. They didn't talk about money.

Did you know about the gravity of the injury in jury selection?

I don't remember knowing that.

Nobody threw out an anchor number of any kind?

No. I don't remember that.

Did you have a sense there was a role of insurance underlying that case? Even though you were instructed not to consider it?

Insurance in terms of –

Insurance representing the defendant.

Right. **I think we all understood that insurance is involved in some way.** *During the trial, clearly that was discussed. They had expert witnesses from one either insurance company or hospital that detailed what some of those costs were. But I think everyone understood that insurance companies are there.*

If you were a plaintiff in a similar case, or a defendant, what kind of a juror would you like to have?

I would want someone who is **open-minded** *to see both sides of the argument.*

To consider both sides or to understand both sides?

To understand both sides, not just to consider.

Tell me about what open-minded means to you.

It means to come in with a blank slate and not base your knowledge of the trial on experiences that you have; not even allowing what your experience was like to influence your decision.

How realistic is that?

Not 100% realistic, no. **I think everyone comes in with a certain amount of bias. But they should also see past or have the ability to see past their bias so they can make an unbiased decision.**

How do you get a juror to be vigilant about keeping their bias in the corral?

I don't know if you can do that. It's up to the juror how much they want to disclose of what their bias may be.

If a juror does disclose a bias, do you feel that act of disclosure will make them more likely to at least be aware of it when they're in the decision-making process later? And perhaps work a little harder?

If they were open about it. I think it would be better that they put it out there rather than to have a hidden agenda.

Is there anything I haven't talked about that you think would be helpful for me or my readers, recognizing that you're unique because you've had this experience.

Just some of my thoughts: as a juror, I didn't do it for the money, but there should be more compensation. For what you go through – $10 a day and a bus pass. At least parking. And maybe $20 a day. I know some places pay more, but $10 a day – you're paying for lunch, is what they're doing. I understand that's taxpayer money.

And some say our civic duty, we should do it for free, *et cetera*. Who can do that though?

Just having the option of being able to drive myself in and have a place to park is at least something that should be –

You live fairly close to the courthouse. Imagine those people across the water or in the outer parts of the County.

Exactly. Right. I ended up taking the bus, which I don't mind. It's when I have to take transfers and that, things take too long. I would rather have driven in myself and been able to park, not worry about where I need to park and stuff like that. So compensation for jurors is one thing that should be considered more. From my standpoint, the jurors that I was a part of, if I were going to court on either side, I would want those people to be in the jury. I had a great group. I didn't know what to expect. I figured there would be at least one or two people who would be really difficult and would be bullheaded and try to dominate a conversation or whatnot. But I found this group to be – I was impressed. Everyone was competent. And I felt good about what happened. I felt like it worked.

And that's what we want. Because you get to live with that decision for the rest of your life. It's nice that the jury feels like they got it right. I think for the most part if they feel that way, they probably have. I'm sure the plaintiff was disappointed. How long were your deliberations?

It was quick. Deliberation was no more than an hour.

Given that, did you feel that case never should have seen the light of day? Or do you feel that it was a legitimate dispute that a jury needed to –

I felt it was legitimate. A lot happened there. I didn't feel it was frivolous at all, even though – I started out probably siding with the plaintiff. And as the case grew, that eroded. And that turned to favoring the defendant.

That's very interesting. Anything else you want to –

No.

Thank you.

19

THEY DON'T WANT TO BE THERE

Black male, age 48, single, Accountant, B.A. Accounting

I think the lawyer should remember that they're dealing with people that, one, don't want to be there and people that are growing contentious. I'm sure they're used to it, but if it's a new lawyer that's pretty green, they'd need to understand and put themselves in the situation of the jury.

The judge says, ladies and gentlemen of the jury, give your attention to the attorney for the plaintiff who's going to ask *voir dire* or jury selection questions. What are you thinking and feeling about the attorneys and the process at that time? What's going through your head?

I'm looking at the attorney that is prosecuting the case, the DA, to see what information they're trying to glean, what information they may have, and if they have a strong case. I'm thinking that if they have a strong case, then it's not going to be a long jury trial. If they don't, then it will be. I think that's what a lot of the others are also thinking. How strong is the evidence? Is it going to be a long case or is not going to be a long case?

Are you thinking of a criminal case in particular have you sat as a juror in a civil case where injury's at issue?

No.

But mock jury you've done.

Yes, I've done mock jury.

In a civil case, the lawyers need to ask questions to find out if you're going to be open-minded. How can they best go about that?

With me and staying within the guidelines of what they can ask and can't ask? **I would ask an example of something I would do in my professional life that would allow me to be open-minded.** *A lot of the questions they ask, you can tell, are kind of cookie cutter, reading off of a card. And of course, they do that because that's the process; that's what they have to do. But there should be some leeway where they can ask questions that – and not necessarily pertaining to the case.*

Can you think of a question, an example like you bring up? Something that pertains to being an accountant or a CPA that would go to open-mindedness?

Okay. How would you handle a prospective client that would come to your door and you have a certain mindset against that type of person. Would you accept them or would you not accept them?

Open-mindedness, I think, is another way of talking about fairness.

Yes.

Do other terms come to mind when we talk about open-mindedness or fairness?

Open-mindedness and fairness; judgmental and non-judgmental. What's the other word I'm thinking? Someone who is experienced and is going to be more open – I mean, we know the person is going to be more focused – they're going to ask more questions. Whereas a younger person, I believe, from what I've seen, tends to take things at face value. They don't really look behind the questions or see that there might be something else behind it.

Life experience.

Yes. That's why an older person would use their life experiences and they would ask more questions.

What about bias and prejudice? As an impediment to open-mindedness?

Definitely there. Especially if somebody – myself – that's a person of color, as you can see – there's going to be a certain bias that you can't help. It's human nature.

What would be a sensitive way to deal with you or your fellow jurors to ask questions about bias and prejudice?

That's tough. Mainly because you can ask a question to ten different people and get ten different answers and each one of them can be offended. It's not a question that is meant to be offending, it's just a question that –

Right. In a case where color or race is not an issue, that wouldn't be a bias or prejudice to talk about to the jury. But suppose there are other things that could affect them that have to do with civil cases. Can you think of any other things that would prevent people from being open-minded in a personal injury case?

*The age of the victim, of the person that's pursuing the case. **In my opinion younger people are not as responsible.** And they might want to go after a quick buck in a civil case, whereas an older person would probably not go into a civil case unless they have more reason to do it.*

That thought process – let me try to repeat that – is that you might tend to think that a younger plaintiff is less credible because they're more likely to advance a case that had less basis?

Well, I wouldn't say credible, because they may have a legitimate case. But a younger person is more susceptible to people and outer forces saying, you should do this, you should do that, and they're more willing to respond to that. Whereas an older person is going to be more, okay, let me think about this before I actually do it. They're not going to be looking at the settlement at the end. They're going to be looking at the long range, where, okay, I'm going to go to court. It's not just the money that's going to be coming up. There's things about myself, my personal life that's going to be out there. Whereas I think a younger person's not going to care as much. You know, they just want what they want at the end. That's my opinion.

That's your opinion. And if you've got it, you can be sure other people have that as well. Thank you, by the way, for sharing that. That's illuminating. Every interview, something is said I'd never thought of before. You mentioned that somebody or something might be behind the scenes pushing them to do the case? Who are we talking about?

Well, you have your ambulance-chasing lawyers. You have the media. You have family members. I'll give you an example. Let's say identity theft. If it's an extreme case of it and that person feels they've been wronged, they've lost their job and whatever, then why not sue the people they feel are responsible for it? Like their employers. Or an example would be that large retailer. A lot of people, their information was exposed, and now they've got these blemishes on their credit reports.

They've suffered some damage.

Exactly.

So, class action lawyers, or as you said, the ambulance-chasing lawyers; tell me about what the ambulance-chasing lawyer looks like to you?

Some of them are necessary. I mean, they do a service because sometimes a person does have to be pushed to know, hey, you have rights. You don't have to take this. But at the same time, you have someone that might be unscrupulous and say, hey, I see this. I could really make a killing off of this person if I get them into a courtroom.

How do you perceive a lawyer who takes the client as they are? Client's had an injury. The harm may not be great, but they've come to the lawyer. Is a lawyer an ambulance chaser because he or she takes that case? Even though the damage is small?

*In my opinion, no. I think they're being responsible, and their job is to win the case for the client. **Sometimes, you have to take facts and amplify them, but not over-embellish the facts of the case.** You know, you can't make a direct lie, but you can make something look like, okay, the coffee was hot. It didn't burn metal, but it burned me.*

So the ambulance-chaser is more likely to oversell and overstate and go for more than what's fair and reasonable?

Possibly, yes.

Instead of talking about the ambulance chaser, tell me how we distinguish between a credible lawyer who genuinely cares for the client and is motivated to do good for the person and the system versus this person that the public has a bad perception of?

*Well, outside of fiction, I can't think of any way of finding a lawyer in that vein, but it's like with any professional. **You have to go with your gut feeling.** When people come to me and want me to do their tax returns, there's a level of trust. There's references to a lot of businesses, checking the background of the person, and then they have to trust the person is going to do what they actually say. That really comes into play, to me, first. The questions are designed to help you form an opinion and not tools that will actually say, okay, this is the person that I should select. It helps you to form an opinion.*

It helps me to form opinions. Is there anything that the lawyer who represents the injured person - or any lawyer in the courtroom - can do to establish a genuine connection with you without being manipulative?

*Like I say, outside of fiction, I can't think of a way, especially today. **People just have a natural view of lawyers as being oily and slippery and they're in it for the money.** And that could be a good thing if you want to win a case.*

Do you think if you held that point of view or maybe your other jurors did that they would put that view aside when it came time to decide the case that's going to impact this injured person?

*That's a tough question. Because – and from my own experience, **people do make personal connections where they shouldn't. They should look at the facts and focus on what's tangible and what you can actually see.** I like this lawyer because she's well-dressed, she's articulate, and she carries herself well in the courtroom. It doesn't matter if the case is correct or if the case is viable, if they like the lawyer, that can be a factor that would basically hurt justice, but there's so many different ways of saying what I'd like to say. You know, you have a justice system that is not exactly perfect, and the public knows it, and so do the lawyers. And people use that to their advantage.*

Do you think in the end the jury most likely gets it right?

I think in the end, the jury has to follow the instructions of the court. And whether they get it right or not, it's basically what the court, the judge and everyone that's involved has agreed is what we're going to go by. Whether the jury gets it right – most of the times, I think they do.

As I said, we're looking for jurors who can be open-minded. Some training tries to teach lawyers to win the case in jury selection maybe go too far. I'm learning that jurors' time is very important to them. I want to know what I can do to respect the potential jurors' time in jury selection. Do you think the same result will happen, more or less, with any 12 people that are selected out of that group?

There's other factors you have to consider, because it's not just how you're trying to respect their time. There's also the environment that you're in, the courtroom itself. The judge, the players that are involved. They're also going to have an effect that you can help with their time by being as open and upfront – if they ask for something, you know, say, hey, we'd like to see this to clarify it while they're deliberating, I would say give it to them right away without question.

So don't hide anything?

Exactly.

When you come into this courtroom as a potential juror, do you have a perception that both sides have extremely different opposite positions? That they're not in agreement on much of anything?

Sometimes. But from my own experience and my own opinion, I believe because they have to work together to put the case together, any disagreements they have when they get to the courtroom is going to be put together professionally. They may both agree with the case that, hey, this is what is happening, but they have to do their jobs. That's the key. Opposing counsel has to fight for the company, and the other side has to fight for their side. So, they may, in the beginning, come together and say, this is wrong. But in the courtroom, they have to fight tooth and nail to win their side. That's how I see it.

What would turn you off if a lawyer had questions to ask in jury selection and started asking them of you?

That's another tough question, because I don't think any question is bad. I think you should ask everything, but there are guidelines that you can't ask these questions.

Do you have any particular perspectives about civil cases by virtue of your profession? The way you come to it?

In a civil case, more than likely, it's going to be corporate against the consumer. I think they should leave out the corporation's earnings and the corporation's financial picture. That should not be a motive for either side. Which usually it is, because, hey, this company – Google is a multi-billion dollar company, so they want a piece of those profits. But that should not be brought up. They should be focusing on, this is the actual event. It actually happened, and who's at fault? Who are we assigning blame to? We're not assigning blame to Google, the company, the corporation, because they're this large company and they should be held responsible.

When it comes to assigning blame, it's often not so hard to establish right and wrong. What can be very difficult for jurors is coming to that place where they have to decide what amount of money is going to be the right amount of money to serve the ends of justice. There are different kinds of damages. There are damages for things like lost wages and medical bills. Those you can put on a blackboard and add them up. But there is also what we call general damages, which are pain and suffering and disability. These are things for which there is no fixed standard. How would you go about determining the value of an injury to a person?

*We had that come up as one of the cases. Compensatory and punitive damages. Compensatory damages are pretty much straightforward. It's going to be based on the wages that were lost, based on the time period that the person was out of work, and if they're able to return to work or whatever the case may be. That part is simple. **But the damages that are based upon emotional – it's tough to say. Because you're putting a dollar value on a person's feelings and the injury if they lost an arm or a limb.***

As an accountant, you're dealing with dollars all the time, and you know what earnings relatively are. Do you think that's helpful to you?

Yes. Because you want to make sure they get what they would have earned had the event not happened. That's the focus of compensatory.

Does it help or hinder you in your evaluation of the emotional pain and suffering type damages?

No. Because they have to be separate.

Would you have a difficult time with the notion of awarding pain and suffering damages and emotional damages?

It is difficult, yes. Because it's hard to put a dollar value on somebody's suffering.

What would help you do that?

Well, you look at precedents, you know, did this happen before? Like with the air bags. Many years ago, when the SUV first came out, you had a lot of them that were flipping, especially in the south. Certain parties sued the companies and were awarded damages. So you would look at what happened and how much were they given as far as the punitive or the pain and suffering. That would be a guideline.

Past results.

Past results. Correct.

Are there other metrics or data we could use when we're talking about these difficult to quantify damages for emotional pain and physical pain and suffering? Some attorneys suggest a certain amount of money each day for the projected duration of that person's life, assuming they have the injury, or however long they have or may have had it. Can you think of anything?

I see what you're saying. I've heard that before, where compensatory is more backwards and this is more forwards. How much should we pay them based upon – according to the event, they've lost.

Sure. You can pay a person for the loss of an arm based on whether they can do their job or not, and what jobs might be available to them with re-training. But there is an emotional cost to losing an arm. How do we put a dollar a value on that? What metrics could we use? And guidelines?

*It's difficult. When you're talking about the loss of a limb, that's something you would have to sit down and all the jurors would have to decide how important that arm is to that person, especially if that person is, say, somebody who uses their arm quite a bit, like a plumber or a trade person. That's what I would go with. I would say **it would be something you would have to do case by case,** and the jurors would have to decide.*

Do you lean more toward or against the notion that there are too many lawsuits or too many frivolous lawsuits in this country right now?

*Based on what I've read, **yes there are definitely too many frivolous lawsuits. But sometimes, the lawsuits serve a purpose.** When it brings attention to something that needs to be fixed. Maybe too many frivolous lawsuits bring attention to the fact that, hey, maybe we need to look at this and prevent this from happening again. Where nobody's going to be found at fault, some law could be passed or something can be brought up to say, hey, let's stop this now.*

Like a deterrent or a teaching of some sort.

Exactly. Exactly.

How do you feel about the law both as a compensatory vehicle and as a vehicle for change?

Well, that's kind of the purpose of the law.

To enforce the rules.

Right. To enforce, protect, but also, as society evolves, you're going to have to have these cases that are going to help evolve the law with it. The law is not technically static. It should evolve with society. It should evolve with people. It doesn't always happen, but that's how it should be.

Do you think your profession tends to be more or less conservative in money awards in civil cases?

Well, accounting has to be conservative, because there is property that it's protecting on the client behalf – but at the same time, there's some leeway. And some openness. There's a lot more trust now where a consumer would trust an accountant more now than they did 50 years ago. There are things I'm doing for clients today that would not be allowed years and years ago.

In your profession, and for yourself, do you think you'd be able to let both sides start from the same starting line?

Yes. I can definitely do that.

Being an accountant wouldn't sway you one way or another at the start? Or, maybe give the other side a push along the way somehow?

No. Because that setting is designed for it to happen exactly the way you describe. It has to be that way. Otherwise, you're going have the loser coming back saying, hey, the trial was not the way it should be, so we should have a new trial.

If they can get one.

Exactly.

You deal in a world of numbers; you probably see some big ones. Does that anger you? If lawyers start talking about big numbers, does that close you off or open you up or neither? Let's say they start talking about – now, this might be a million dollar case. You know what a million dollars is more than some people might.

Yes. Whether they actually get the million dollars is a different story, because they may put that out there as an incentive for the other side to settle. No, I don't see it as a problem, because I believe if you're found guilty of something and that penalty is that dollar value, the purpose of that dollar value is punishment, and it's to make you pay a price you can't afford.

Sure. Even though we call it something other than punishment in the civil context. If you were a plaintiff or a defendant in a civil case, what kind of a jury would you like on your case?

Obviously somebody that's going to work on my behalf, but I would love to see people who are more experienced in the situation I was in. For instance, let's say I'm part of a class action suit or I'm suing because of something that other people use every day. I'm suing because Google is too open-source. Well, I would like a set of jurors who actually have that same mindset and understand that. Not that they're going to vote for me or against me. I'm going to trust that they're going to make the right decision, but they would have an understanding of the situation; that's the key.

How do they get that? Do they come to the trial with that, or do they learn it through the evidence?

It would help if they came to trial with it rather than through the evidence. Because the evidence can be tainted and it can be misrepresentative. It would work on my behalf, of course, or against me as well, but it's not good to look at evidence for that reason. I think they should have experience with what the rule is.

Given all that's required here to be a juror is that you're either a registered voter or have a license to drive and it's selected randomly, do you think those are the kind of people that are going to show up at jury service?

Yes. And that's how it should be. You should keep it like that because you want a jury of your peers, people that are just like you. Then you wheedle them down and the lawyers will determine who would best fit that case. It doesn't mean they're bad. It doesn't mean they're not competent, it just means these people best fit this situation. The others that didn't work in this case may work in another case.

If a lawyer had the sense he wasn't getting along with you, what would he or she need to do to make it right? To get that on the table and explore that without losing the case early on with you?

You have to look at it as the profession. If the behavior is professional or if it's just personal. If it's personal, then it should be brought up to the other lawyer as well as to the judge. If it's unprofessional behavior, that definitely should be brought up then and there. Because it can affect the case afterwards.

If one of the prospective jurors was going off on the lawyer for no good reason, how would you feel about that? This is part of your group having a dialogue that's not going so well. What can the lawyer do to not lose the rest of this group?

I think the lawyer should remember that they're dealing with people that, one, don't want to be there and people that are growing contentious. *I'm sure they're used to it, but if it's a new lawyer that's pretty green, they'd need to understand and put themselves in the situation of the jury. Why is this person so aggravated and contentious with me? That would help them soften the blow.*

No matter how much we do of this, it never gets easy. Because it's always a different group.

They never want to be there, but it's duty; it's service.

Nobody's getting paid very well. How do you feel about tort reform?

I don't know. It's kind of like you fix one problem but you cause two others to pop up. It's necessary; it's part of the process. That's how I see it.

I've heard say that black jurors tend to be more generous than white jurors. Do you have any feedback or thoughts on that, when they give an award to a plaintiff, they tend to give more money than white people do?

The cases I've been in, I've only been one of two African Americans and most of them were white or Asian. So I couldn't draw it from experience. But based on what I've seen and heard, there's definitely truth to that. Many of them feel, I think, that the justice system is so skewed and biased against minorities that they feel this is their way of making up for it. That's an opinion; I can't state that as natural fact, but that's how I see it.

I've been frustrated seeing defense attorneys excuse the black jurors from trials. Everybody's allowed to excuse *x* number of jurors for no cause. Thank you for the answer and your honesty. Was that an inappropriate question?

No, it isn't.

I wouldn't ask you in jury selection. This is strictly here.

And that's exactly what I was thinking.

I interviewed an African American gentleman this morning, asked that question and he was fine with it, too. His answer was almost the same, identical.

And based on my experience, I think it should be asked. That's my opinion.

What can the lawyer do to develop trust and credibility from the onset?

*I think the credibility of the lawyer starts with how they deal with the judge and with their opposing counsel. **You can tell if a lawyer has integrity by how they deal with other people. If they seem dismissive or seem like they would rather run the show, then you tend to not like them. But if the lawyer is more gregarious and more allowing the other person to talk and being respectful of other people's opinions, you tend to like them a little bit more.***

Is there anything we haven't talked about that you think might be helpful for me to know or think about?

The jury selection process, it's necessary and there's a lot that could be done better, but at the same time, you have to look at the fact it's done for a reason, and if it's not done right in the beginning, it could have problems down the road. So I don't know if this is a part of, you know, you're going to make a change.

I want to be better, and pass this information on to my colleagues. I'm looking to find some universal truths from and "a-ha" moments. I've had a few. Primarily, I'm looking for two things: a truly open-minded person; and if people have biases and they're willing to admit it and tell me they're willing to work to overcome them or deal with them at least – it's good enough for me. The other is to make sure I'm establishing a human connection, and that's probably the most difficult part, and what I'd be curious to know what your thoughts are. What a lawyer can do to be real.

I think bias is a human emotion. It's a judgmental emotion and it's necessary to the person. It's how that person handles the bias. You can not like somebody but still be professional and courteous towards them. That's the key. It's how you express your bias. A consumer is discriminating, whether they pick product A, B, or C. If I pick A, that doesn't mean I'm discriminating against B or C because I don't like them. I'm picking A because it's the one that appeals to me the most.

So discrimination in that context isn't necessarily a bad thing.

Right, but at the same time, in jury selection, it's going to be there. It's how those people put that aside and keep it professional as possible. The law system does not specifically state you have to have an exact mix of men, women, minorities in a jury. You have to pool them, but whether you put them on there or not is not by law.

As a person of color, are there any truths about white people that would be helpful for me to know, from your perspective? In other words, things that I ought to know about white people.

I'm 57 years old. I've learned from the past. I don't see people the way I did when I was 25. And society does help form those opinions and you find out things that, you know, this is not true. And I thought this all these years. Then you find out things, oh, well, it is true. And I've ignored it all these years. As far as the question you asked, I don't see anything that you could say in a general sense. It's really the same on both sides. I think that whites do not have a lot of knowledge of other minorities. And it's not their fault. It's just the way things are. The same goes on the other side. People of color may not have the knowledge of whites in general.

I'm trying to zero in on in the context of a courtroom setting, if there have been things you've observed about white people in general, traits or tendencies that might apply in those settings that will be truths that would be important to know. And if not, I mean, that's okay, too.

I think sometimes many of them feel like they have a sense of entitlement.

Tell me what that means? What you mean by entitlement? And I think I know what you're talking about.

There's the expectation, well, I'm here and this is what I expect. And if they don't get that, then that's when the problems start. It depends upon the person. Some people can handle it and brush it off. I can say, right then and there, no, that's not how it's going be. I want this, I want it now. So there is that sense of entitlement. I think with people of color, minorities, there's that sense of expectation, well, they're not going to pick me. I'm just going to show up anyway. So, that's kind of both sides.

Do you feel other minorities like Asians feel the same way?

Yes. When I was in several focus groups, that's one of the things we talked about. A lot of them feel that way. And feel like, well I'm going to say it – it's just the way it is. I mean, what can you do? How can you change that? You can educate people, but we have more information now than we've ever had at any point in history, and yet people still behave more barbaric than ever. How do you change that? You can't.

It's still the caveman in a mechanized society.

Exactly. And it seems the more information we get, the less courteous and the more barbaric we become.

This has been helpful. Anything else at all you want to share?

I don't know. I can't think of anything. I'm just basically saying my experience.

Thank you.

20

WHAT-IFS AND DOUBTS

Caucasian female, age 31, married, one child, Technical Recruiter, B.S.

Developers are very black and whites and tend to deal with the facts that are in front of them and not all of them can deal with the what-ifs or doubts or things like that. And that's mostly because you can't have doubt when you're shipping to billions of people.

The judge says ladies and gentlemen, please give your attention to the attorney for the plaintiff – that's the injured party's attorney – who will ask you some questions in jury selection. At that moment, what are your thoughts and feelings, before anything else is said?

*My personal thoughts, putting myself in that spot, would be **hoping it would be a short case.** That would be something I'd be worried about. Also, I'd probably be surveying the room, looking at the other people, trying to figure out how I fit into this. Because I haven't been there, are there, in this group of 40 or so, is everybody being asked questions at the same time?*

They can be. It's completely free-flowing on who the attorney wants to talk to. Generally, they're concentrating on the earlier numbers, because those are the people most likely to be on the jury. Everybody's numbered. The people at the end are less likely to be on the jury.

I'd probably be listening to how people are answering their questions. Unfortunately, I'm one of those that sometimes I stop paying attention and think about how I would answer that question and then miss out on other things being said. I might miss out on some pertinent things. I tend to think too much about how I answer questions instead of letting them be completely in free-flow, most of the time. And that might be because of my job. I pre-think about the best answer instead of the most natural answer and how I truly feel. That's probably what I'd be doing, having this internal struggle about how to answer questions in this case.

Is the feeling you have one of comfort? Are you happy to be there? Are you not happy to be there? Would you rather be somewhere else?

I'd definitely rather be somewhere else. I'm that personality that when I'm starting to do things or see things on my calendar or I know I have to be somewhere, I'm like, I hate it and this internal struggle. But once I get involved with it, I tend to enjoy the experience. If it's something on TV, I'll think about like, oh, being on a jury would be great and I want to do my civil duty and am very interested in the law and things like that. So I think it would be something that I would not enjoy, but be proud to do. But probably at first, not be too happy to be there.

This is a case where somebody's been injured and they want to money from some other person or entity because of the harm caused. You've got connections to the legal profession and the medical profession. Is there anything about those connections that gives you a feeling in general about this kind of case?

To be honest, no. I have connections to those people in the field, but we don't ever talk too much about what they do or what I do. They're family members, so we try not to talk about work, so I've never heard them comment on cases like this. My friend that is a judge, it's usually dads who don't pay child support and domestic violence and things like that.

You are from Texas. Is there anything about being a Texan that makes you think about jury service in any unique way?

No, I don't think so. We left Texas for a reason, so we're not your typical Texans when you think of that cliché Texan. So no, I can't think of anything there that would influence my thought process.

Or your upbringing there? Nothing that gives you a cause to be more or less conservative or liberal about these kinds of cases?

Not anymore. Maybe my 18-year-old self, when I first registered to vote, had a lot of my parents' influence. I would have been a lot more conservative and probably a lot more doubtful and had less empathy for people and probably assumed guilt either way right away.

When you say doubtful, what does that mean?

Thinking about personal injury or workers' comp or things like that, I probably wouldn't have sided with the victim right away.

Would you have been able to keep an open mind?

Back then, no. No. If I'm honest with myself, I don't think so.

Well, thank you. And how about now?

Definitely now. Now, I am totally innocent until proven guilty, two sides to the story, and really try and understand people and what's going on with them. Very different now.

You work for a large software engineering company. Is there anything that has changed in you since you've worked there that's helped you be more open-minded or look at these cases differently?

Absolutely. The culture there is global, and it's not just people from here, it's people from all over the world. We even have recruiters who are based in our global dev centers in India. Everything is vastly different, and everybody's got a different point of view. We need all those different points of view to function and be well-rounded. My role is recruiting college kids from all over the world. So I need to know about different cultures and ways that things are done and how even female and male developers think. There's just too much greatness to not consider everybody's point of view and individual story.

You talked about developers, male and female, and how they think. Tell me about your perceptions of how developers think?

It really depends. It's very different. Some are truly antisocial and shine when they're alone and not functioning in a team environment. And there's those developers who sit in dark offices with their windows closed and five or six computer screens going; three have their Minecraft game and the other three have the code they're working on. Then there's those who are independent and individual contributors, but they thrive off a team environment, so they're much more inclusive and walk around the offices checking in on people and just more social. So it's hard to say how they think, but they tend to be very one-track mind. Sometimes I think they just want us to put a screen in front of them and they push the button and everything works. Sometimes they have to be reminded that they are paid to solve these big issues. And sometimes it's terrible and code doesn't work. So I can't pinpoint exactly how they think. **But developers are very curious people who have the problem of fixing the world's issues on their plates and doing it with computers and software.** *I think a lot of them are aware that a lot of people are afraid of "AI" and having too much technology and trying to educate the world slowly on the benefits. I find them to be, most of the time, very warm-hearted and considerate. Then you've got what we call the "brogrammer" who is not so considerate. Good person, but cares mostly about themselves.*

How do you think a developer might approach deciding a jury case differently than you might?

I'm going to get them confused. I don't know if I'm left-brained or right-brained, but they'd be the opposite of what I am. I'm more of a humanities background and more of holistic thinking and I consider all things. I can deal with a black – white, and I can deal in the gray area. **Developers are very black and whites and tend to deal with the facts that are in front of them and not all of them can deal with the what-ifs or doubts or things like that. And that's mostly because you can't have doubt when you're shipping to billions of people.** *I assume that a developer facing jury duty would be, these are the facts. I've seen on TV lots of times attorneys paint the picture of doubt or try and poke holes. If there's not substantial evidence behind that, I can see someone with a science or tech background having issue with that. But making that general statement is also dangerous because a lot of computer science people have doubted along the way. Not everything we do is based in fact. But those that I know tend to be very black or white; can't handle gray.*

What kind of information do developers like to have when they're making decisions?

In the developer world?

Yes. Say you're working with them, you're having communications and they need information. What ways do you approach or – do they have a specific way of getting information from you?

I think first they want to know what the problem is. What's the problem they're solving for. How much time do they have to solve this problem? What are their resources? Who are the other people they're solving the problem with? In some cases, who is the customer? Not necessarily what is the problem, but who's the customer?

What about information they're being given to solve the problem?

Right. Developers also have a team member called a program manager who's a sort of developer. That program manager would be the one to say, this is your information, and they do all the pre-research. The developer would heavily rely on their PM team to provide them that info. That's where a lot of that is coming from. Then once you get into the actual solving of the problem is when you realize, oh, we're missing this information and the PM will go back, do the research and figure out where it is. So they heavily rely on someone to provide that info to them.

Do you think developer-types are on the entire spectrum of open-mindedness from closed to open, or do they tend to fall more one way or another?

I think they are on the entire spectrum, especially those that I know. And because I am in recruiting, most of my day-to-day interactions are with those who are very passionate about getting great college talent. They are extremely open-minded, very empathetic people. But, some of the schools I work with, they're very top-tier schools, and those that I come across are not so open-minded. But I don't think they're missing something inside them, I just think it's lack of exposure and constantly being in a computer lab and lacking human interaction and things like that. So I feel like there's probably a big circle on the other side of the spectrum.

What does open-mindedness mean to you?

Going into something not having your mind made up and being willing to hear people out or, to me, going in thinking, I don't really have an opinion on this and I just want to help. Or curious to learn and accept the fact that you don't know right away what the answer or the end of the story is.

Do you think there are any parts of you, starting off, that are less open-minded than in other areas? Do you have any beliefs, strongly one way or another, that might lead you to be less open-minded in some things than in others?

I'm sure there are. I tend to be on the more liberal side of things now. When I hear something that's more conservative, I tend to think poorly of that person and definitely – I'm going to say yes. I'm sure there are. I'm trying to think of a situation where that's happened recently. I'm sure when we get more into the presidential race, I'll start dealing with those things again.

When you are in a situation and you recognize some part of yourself that's closed-minded or less open-minded than you ordinarily are, what do you do to remind yourself to be aware of and deal with that when you're trying to make a decision?

I usually am not able to realize that I've been closed-minded or not a nice person until I've been away from the situation for 30 minutes. Once the frustration or anger subsides and my conscience takes over, I realize I messed up there and I have the opportunity to help somebody. Or also, somebody could have been having a bad day, because I have terrible days, and sometimes people think poorly of me. So it usually takes me a while. It's just remembering human nature and humans are humans. But it does take me a while.

What led to this shift in being more on the conservative side to more on the liberal side?

*It was college. I did go to school in Texas, which, I think when people hear, they're like, what? My school was Texas A&M and we've been in the headlines in the past for pretty racist, pretty conservative things, but after thinking about it, because I wanted to defend my school, I realized that was a very small outspoken population. And it was a conservative school, but it was college. So most everybody was really happy to be with other people and getting through college together. That was my first experience. And I right away joined a mentorship club. It was so diverse with people from all over the world, even international students. That was my first taste. I moved from El Paso to College Station so I'd always been exposed to the Hispanic culture and going across to the Mexico border was a weekly thing for us. But anything, people from the Middle East, Africa – that was new to me. Just hearing about all the different things that were going on, **it's kind of eye-opening that the way you've always done things is not the way the rest of the world works.** But truth be told, the change for me was a professor who was head of the communications department. I took one of his courses, and from then on I took all of his courses. The final straw for me was hearing him talk in the course called Rhetoric of the Civil Rights Movement, listening to how those leaders used the power of persuasion to open the minds of many Americans. I was never that bad. I was never racist or anything like that. But listening to these people who constantly were being degraded by other humans and how they got through that with patience and kindness. I decided that – not that my parents were bad people – but I think they were only exposed to very limited things. They grew up in the Civil Rights Movement in the south. So it was hearing the story from different sides and realizing that humans came together. I decided I wanted to be that kind of human. That was really it. He was an amazing speaker and presented history and rhetoric in a way I'd never heard before.*

That's neat that it had that effect on you personally, and probably others, too.

Oh, I'm sure. He has a very strong following of former students, who I think credit him and his ability to reach the 20-year-old crowd when we think we're invincible.

Let's transition to talking about personal injury cases. There are all sorts of opinions about lawyers who do that kind of work, personal injury cases. Do you have any beliefs about that?

I do.

Can you share?

I'll say I'm 50/50. I know that people do get injured. I have had friends who have been severely injured and minorly injured in personal injury cases. I think the naysayer in me comes from social media and pop culture and how sometimes personal injury lawyers are personified as ambulance chasers or – what comes to mind is Denzel Washington's character in the movie Philadelphia. He's in the hospital, he's in the elevator, and he's handing his business cards out to those who are obviously really injured. I've never personally had that experience, but that's how my knowledge has been shaped.

Given that, how do you think you might approach being a juror in a personal injury case and you have that part of you?

*I would be pretty open in the beginning, honestly, just because I have had friends that have been pretty injured. Sometimes the stories when you hear them are just like, what? How did you even get to that situation? **In one case, someone got hit at 15 miles an hour. Seems super slow to me,** but was really just – I don't know. Something snapped in her back, and it was really strange. I had a hard time believing that, but then I see the after-effects still, many years later.*

Did she have a trial or a settlement in that case where she received some money?

She did have a trial date, and then it ended in settlement. She did receive some money.

Talk about this perception of the ambulance chasers and do you think that's representative of the kind of people that do civil injury work in general?

The intelligent person in me says no, that can't be. I just don't know very many. My experience has been those that I have known that have had this kind of attorney, it's been beneficial for them, and so very appreciative that they had help. I'd say probably 75% of me would be open to this, and then there'd be that little devil on my shoulder reminding me of Denzel in that movie.

Without trying to put words in your mouth, would you say that's something like a healthy skepticism?

I would call it healthy. I don't think it would cause me to not want to hear something out in all honesty.

So less rigid and unbending, and willing to – if evidence is presented that causes

you to think differently about ambulance chasers or civil cases, you would be able to process that?

I believe so. I would hope so.

When you're approaching a decision, are you more on the emotional side or more on the data side?

I think initially it would be more on the emotional side, especially if we were looking at somebody who was really injured, I think the human side of me – I've been more emotional since I've had my son, to be honest. Everything makes me super emotional and just value life that much more.

Having a child has?

*Having a child, yeah. I definitely valued humans before, but now I see how quickly it could be taken away and how devastated I would be if it was my son or my husband. **I just value the human life a lot more than I did before, because it's a different way to think about it when you have your own.***

Definitely a life-changing experience.

It is.

Can you tell me more? I'd like to know what that experience is like in the way that it's changed a person.

*Sure. Initially, before my son, we'd been married almost ten years, and very happy. I would be sad if I lost my husband for sure, but I think like most people, you would eventually move on. It would be crushing. **I don't know how I'd go on if I lost my son.** It's just very different. Even when I was pregnant, I felt a connection to him, but it really changed once I held him. You are essentially responsible for this person in their life and protecting them until they're at least 18 when they can walk out on you. That was really just it. And right now when he's young – he's almost two – everything in his life, he fully relies on us. He has no idea if he's safe or not. If we do the seatbelt wrong or his car seat wrong, if something happened in the car, it could either end his life or save his life. **So just having that responsibility at all times has made me appreciate all the little things and my attention to detail.** We're not helicopter parents. Right now he's got a stitch across his forehead and that was devastating enough to see that I don't want any further. It's all the cliché things that have been said before in movies. There are no words. **The connection I feel to my husband is strong, but the connection I feel to my son is almost all-encompassing in my body.** I can fully understand how people cannot move past that grief, truly. **So everybody is somebody's child is how I look at things now.** I rolled my eyes a lot at my parents when I was growing up, like, oh, God. And they always said, oh, you won't understand until you have your own. I now understand.*

Having had a child, being a mother, I gather you're also in a community of other women who are mothers and have children. Do you think their experience is very similar to yours in their emotions and feelings?

That's a very interesting question. I am in two different moms groups; one in our neighborhood and one is a PEPS (Program for Early Parent Support) group I joined when my son was six weeks old and there were other parents who had similar aged children. It was a support group because you're sleep deprived and everything's going wrong. I had my fun group and my support group. The support group, they've been able to put into words what I just did, that this is their life now. And even though I went back to work, everything I do, I'm now working to provide for my son kind of thing. And my fun play date group, I feel there are some moms that are lacking that compassionship, that see the play dates more as a break. Sometimes I see or feel that the parents are just relieved there's 20 other moms around and they're now off mom duty and can sit to the side and maybe gossip. I have met a few that I feel resent that they're moms. They feel like too much freedom has been taken away, things like that. So I'm not going to lie; myself and some of the other moms have voiced concern and chatted with each other about, should we bring this up to this mom? Maybe it could be like postpartum depression. Should we get her help? Does she truly not want to be a mom and is pressured into starting a family or what? I do sense and feel, even though they have not outright said I don't, that sometimes they wish they could send their child away, wish they weren't a mom, kind of thing.

One of the things the lawyers need to know is if a person has any bias or prejudice or prejudgments that will make a juror immediately side with one or the other. How do you think a lawyer should best approach whether or not a person like you has a bias or a prejudice that would make them not the right juror for that case?

That's a great question. I actually have no idea.

If a lawyer were to ask you, is there anything that might make you predetermine a case or use the word biased against one side or the other, how would you feel about answering that?

I would be fine answering it. My first instinct right now is, nothing off the top of my mind. I would have to say that. Because there's nothing even in the back of my head that I'm even thinking about – afraid to suggest.

No experiences that have impacted you either very negatively or very positively that would color the decision that you might make? And we all have them.

I would agree with that. I'm very fortunate in the fact I've never felt targeted or there's not anyone that I've felt targeted by or would have a personal bias against. I can't think of anything off the top of my head.

That's okay. If you can't find it off the top of your head, then it's probably not a lot there to be too concerned about. How do you think an attorney can best develop a human connection with you? Somebody you've never met before is representing one side and has to learn about you in a very short period of time. What can the attorney do to establish a connection and be credible and genuine?

To me as a juror?

Yes.

As a recruiter, I have to do the same thing with these students that have 10, 15 offers to our competitors. So how do I stand out and make myself credible? This might not translate, because I don't know the day-to-day of an attorney, but for me, I know everything about them by the time we're ready to give them an offer. So to gain their trust, I let them know everything about me, or at least be open to they can ask me anything.

Are you comfortable sharing about yourself?

I am. Because essentially, I am that person recruiting that 21-, 22-year-old to move from the other side of the country, a different country. Through a lot of that, I get to know their family members. Sometimes I meet them as freshmen and don't get them to us until they're seniors, so it's a four-year long relationship. By then, they've been to my house for dinner. They know my husband. We're friends on social media. I know that can't happen with, probably attorneys and jurors; there's just no way to do that.

Not at least at that time, right.

*But that's how I do it. **If I'm going to know about you, ask me what you need to know about me to make this a comfortable transaction** so that I don't come off as a car salesman, that I'm just trying to convince them to come to work for us, and when you get here it's not going to be terrible. They need to know a lot about me and why I'm with who I'm with and why I'm choosing to do this job and why I choose to do this job for this company.*

Do they want to know if you believe in the company that you work for and the job you're doing?

Absolutely. That's one of the first questions I always get. Why are you there? Have you had other offers? How did you think through the process? What were big factors for you? Then a lot of times, too, people are aware that I relocated from Texas, and express concerns about leaving their friends behind and establishing community and support in a new place.

Do you find those questions challenging?

I do. Fortunately I've been answering those questions for six years, so I feel pretty comfortable. Where they challenge me is, why have I chosen to stay here? Because in tech, it's pretty normal to bounce around every two years, regardless of the role. It's not one of those places you stay until retirement.

Not a lot of brand loyalty, even among the employees, is there?

It's very rare. There's those who've stayed for 25, 30 years; with this younger Generation Y, two to three years max or they feel like they're a little bit stale. What we see is they stay for two or three years, leave, and then come back and do ten years. Then they leave and do a start-up and sell it to a big company and come back. There's a lot of going back and forth. But it's more what companies are solving what problems and what problem do I want to solve, then bouncing around like that. It's interesting, because the old company took it personally. The new company is very on board with –

That kind of change?

Yeah. We're totally off topic.

Actually, very on topic, and leads me to a question. Talk to me about 21-, 22-, 23-, 24-year-old people.

I find they're pretty evenly split between those who are very self-involved and all about the money and all about what we can do for them and not necessarily what they can do for the company or the good of the world. And then I find – I'm 31, so as I start talking to 21-year-olds, I start thinking about, aren't you worried about 401k's and don't you want to go to a company that right away you can have a 401k and health insurance and an entire team that can help you find a house and get settled? And they're like, absolutely not. They still think living with ten people in a small studio in San Francisco sounds great, so there is a little bit of a disconnect between, that makes no sense to me and this is what they want to do in the tech bubble. Then there are those who are very thoughtful, who would prioritize job content and career growth over money, even though our offers are insane. It's insane to think what a 21-year-old can make with a four-year degree. And they're like, that's great, but what can I do? What am I going to learn there and what am I going to contribute in my first year? Where will I be in five years? So I feel like it's very evenly split almost every year between the 200 or so that I recruit. There's that half that it's all about them and what are they going to get out of this transaction? Then there's the other half that are very concerned about, what is our stance on philanthropy? What does – if we make a bad political move, then we've automatically alienated a good portion of our student body. So we need to be seen as very encompassing, which it actually is, and we do have those people who aren't perfect and are not as encompassing. But the culture is very welcoming, and we're very aware of that. The students are as well. We have those who want to know immediately, how much of my paycheck goes back to the community? How can I get involved? Are there mentorship groups? And then you get down into the smaller population of, are there support groups for females there since it's well-known there are vastly more males than females. If they're aware of issues – sometimes, it's even come down to the company matches me dollar-for-dollar in my giving to a certain place, and some people will only match up to $10,000, but it has to be one of these ten charities they've preapproved. So there are those that are that thoughtful about the world and those around them and not necessarily what goes directly into their pocket. Those are the ones, obviously, that every recruiter loves.

Do you think that a 21-, 22-, 23-, 24-year-old has enough life experience to sit in a jury and deal with questions that involve a person's life?

The schools I have worked with and the 21- and 22-year-olds that I have worked come – I've worked with the University of Washington, Harvard, and MIT exclusively for six years. All fantastic people. The kids from Harvard, the ones I meet and see us or come to Harvard to do tech – which you think of Harvard, you think of a humanities type school – when I meet them, I'm always floored. There's one kid we recently hired. He lived in Cleveland, homeless all through high school, but continued to go. He couch surfed, slept in bus terminals, did his application to Harvard in a bathroom stall in the middle of winter in Cleveland. There's another kid at Harvard I had the opportunity to meet who grew up in a dump in Rwanda and is now living as a teenager with a missionary that found him. Then you have stories of these kids that lived through political revolution in refugee tents and have seen things I will never see in my life, from childhood all the way until they were able to get to Harvard. So in my experience, these kids have seen things that I will never see and their thought process is so different.

Do you find that that's more of an exception than the rule?

That's what I'm afraid of, is the schools I work with are so competitive and the admissions process so thorough and these three schools so particular about having a very inclusive environment that when they're picking these people, they are very conscious of the backgrounds. These kids are not what you think of Harvard, the Prime Minister's child or a legacy. I'm sure that happens but in tech, it's a very different level. The schools have been really conscious about how they create these communities. So for sure. My limited view is that I have been exposed to the most thoughtful, most brilliant students in tech, for sure.

What about your peers? Your friends or folks that you know? You think at that age that there's enough life experience to understand when a person is hurt and how that's going to affect them for their lifetime?

When I think of myself as a 21-, 22-year-old I had mostly changed completely to the other side, but I was still figuring out who I was, still in a bubble because I was in college. I was in the real world but not, still figuring out who I was and how to make it on my own. It wasn't until my mid-20s, until my first job that I finally realized, oh, this is the real world, and interesting things happen. So in most cases, no. I think the person who has the average American upbringing has not been exposed to what these international students have, who probably can't be on a jury, now that I think about it, because they're not citizens.

If you were in the situation of the friend that you talked earlier who was hurt, what kind of a juror would you want on your case? If that were a question that had to be decided in court?

Honestly, I would want someone near my age, late 20s to mid-30s. Sometimes I feel like the older you get into the generations, the more set they are in their ways and would be less open-minded to a story. I'm thinking about my grandparents, some of the things I hear them say. That would be the first sign of comfort I would look for. The younger generations who are tending to be conscientious about – I know that's a bit of a random comment, because you have the Millennials who are being perceived as self-involved and never off their phones. So that's why I'm saying –

The Millennials are what age?

I'd say 25 and younger is how I would consider them in recruiting. So that mid-20 to mid-40s, I would feel comfortable with. I would be looking in their faces, probably trying to guess their ages. I'd say like the average American who's not in that 1% – feels like you can connect more with a human who's –

More like you?

Right. More like me. I know that's hard to guess; you don't know if anybody in this coffee shop is a billionaire because people, you know. I would definitely look for, not necessarily someone else who is white, but just – I don't know. Someone who I feel I could walk up to in a bar, sit next to and have a drink with. If that makes sense.

That might understand you. As a woman, would you feel more or less comfortable with a woman juror in that age range, that 25 to 40?

*Tricky question. **I feel like women are harder on other women.***

Do you think there's a reason for that?

That's something I've tried to figure out, because I've noticed just throughout life that women are very hard on themselves naturally, but also equally as hard on other women. It doesn't make any sense because we're fighting the same fight, right?

Would you consider that to be a prejudgment or bias issue?

I would.

Do you have that yourself? If you were to think about it? Do you feel that you're harder on women?

Actually, no. Because I'm so conscious about feeling that from other women.

You're aware of that.

I try and be supportive. I am that girl, and most of my girlfriends, we have more guy friends. And that's an unfair statement to make, but sometimes, I think I gravitate more towards males at work because there is a little bit less drama. Even my husband's friends are not as gossipy as when they first come to the house, they're not like, guess what so-and-so did at work today. It's just about the friendship and let's go do something fun. So I feel like that is definitely a bias, because that is not true of all women and I know that.

What would you look for to see that? Or ask to find it out if a person had that judging part of their self?

I don't know if it's something I'd ask. I think it'd be more of a behavior to watch for and see. It usually comes out when it's just a group of women, how they interact with each other. That's honestly how I assess that's definitely not someone I'm going to go to after work and tell about my bad day because it'll turn into gossip or something like that. I don't know if it's a trait I can initially pinpoint.

What kinds of things do you look for when you're trying to assess the credibility of that person, right off the bat? What can they do – or maybe the better question is, what should they not do?

I think credibility comes from someone's ability to listen and to be empathetic. Sometimes if you're telling a story and someone tries to jump in and trump your experience or someone tries to tell you your feelings or thoughts are null, it's very typical for a conversation with a woman; oh, this happened to me today and then jumping right in and saying, oh, well that's nothing, because this happened to me. And it's like, okay, so my thoughts and experiences have no credit.

So being listened to and heard?

That's so cliché, but yes. Being listened to.

How do you feel about the fact that civil cases both compensate an injured victim but also may serve a purpose of teaching lessons to the community or deterring similar wrongful conduct in the future. Do you think that works?

In my case, absolutely. I know that's a hard lesson to learn and almost like a sacrificing of someone, but I always appreciate the lessons learned. It's scary when you hear about things people go through and it could have been you because you were often in those situations or you do those things. So yes, I think they're beneficial to the community at a cost. I think the issue is oftentimes, I don't think we hear about these outcomes of the civil cases very much. We hear a lot about the criminal cases, obviously. And we tend to only hear about the community issues or the civil issues when something explodes, and not necessarily early enough on where it could be caught. So I think that's the main issue; I feel more people would be cognizant of it if we knew about it or how the outcomes were or things like that. But I don't read much about civil cases in the papers.

These kinds of cases rarely make it to – unless it's a very large award. How do you feel, one way or another, along the spectrum that lawsuits make things more expensive or drive doctors out of the community or cause corporations to have to shut down. Do you have any thoughts about that?

I'm fine with that. I generally feel that if it's driving a doctor or a corporation out of business, it's probably for the best. If it's gone the way to someone losing a licensing or a company no longer existing, then that company or doctor probably should have been done away with a long time ago. Who knows? I know there's a lot of injustice in the world, and a lot times people don't have the money to take it to court or don't have the know-how to get it recognized, which I think is a problem in the U.S. But I'm fine with that. **I'd rather that doctor lose their license than continue to mess up.** I have heard of cases along the way where I wasn't exactly convinced that the doctor was bad, some of those malpractice suits, and it could have just been a one-time slip-up. **And the human in me is like, so much pressure on being a doctor. They could have completely not done that intentionally or thought they were doing the right thing.** So I feel in those cases, there's probably been enough doubt painted for me to think like that. But the ones that – there's bad people everywhere.

What do you think the role of insurance is in these kinds of cases?

That's tricky. Insurance is a necessary evil and I am very glad to have insurance for sure, absolutely thrilled to have health and auto and home insurance and all that, but.

You work for a big company, so you probably have workers' comp too.

Oh, workers' comp, life insurance, disability. All kinds of things I am extremely grateful for.

That you hope you never need.

Exactly. I have had co-workers who needed to rely on some of these bigger insurances. Most of the time, and I think it's because these insurance companies don't want to lose the big company contract, we are treated very well. Very, very well. Things happen quickly when the name is behind it. I can't imagine working for a small company. I've heard this before – I had a friend from El Paso lamenting about how hard it's been to get a workers' comp case processed and they're suffering and can't work. She's posting pictures of her injury and she's got kids and I'm just, why is it so hard? So I am extremely grateful for it. And I think my personal experiences definitely affect my thought on insurance, but I do see the struggle from friends and when I hear people complain the insurance will only cover x amount of dollars on the whole thing. So, it's a necessary evil. Everybody needs insurance. But I think you're definitely treated differently.

If?

I think you're treated differently by your income level. Definitely the company name packs a lot of punch with these people, and at the end of the line, it's probably someone's top account. So we're treated very well in all cases. In auto insurance, we have a company and my mom's been a lifelong member because she's military. So my husband and I are treated as legacy and they are very quick to respond. We're a gold-level account; it says so on our thing. And they have a commitment to get back to us within an hour every time we contact them. I know other people don't have that luxury.

In civil cases the jury determines, first of all, if somebody was at fault; if they caused injury negligently or wrongfully. If you get over that hurdle, then we talk about, what are the amount of money damages for the harms that the person has suffered? There are things like lost wages, damages to the car, medical bills. Those are things

that can be pretty easily put down on a spreadsheet. But there's another category called general damages, which are pain and suffering, disability, loss of enjoyment of life. There's no fixed standard for figuring out how much an injury is worth to one person than to another. What kinds of things would you think about when you're trying to make an award of damages for pain and suffering?

*In any point in these cases **is the previous life before the injury painted?** Say, for example, this is a typical week in this person's life, and these are all the things they did and were able to do even with their kids versus now that they have this injury, they can't leave the house and their kids watch TV all day. **Is there any comparison between what the life was and what it is now?***

Before and after.

*That would help me. If it was somebody who wasn't doing much, that would definitely affect my decision, especially if it was someone who lost ability to use limbs and could no longer go on family vacations or – **now that I am a parent, I am aware of all these things that are important to expose them to and get out and do, even if it's just going to a park to let them run.** So if a parent's unable to do that, I think that would definitely affect how I think about compensation. I know the expense of childcare and if it's that the parent is in a wheelchair or even in a wheelchair temporarily or lost limbs, they'd probably have to hire somebody to not only take care of them, but someone to take their child to the park and give the child those experiences.*

Is there any kind of a metric that you might want to apply, like a *per diem* or per week or some way that you would think to go about calculating?

Sure. I would think of it as a weekly cost; that's how we pay for our nanny. We have a pre-contract that says we will at least give her 40 hours of employment per week and not on the weekends. Then if we need her, we'll pay x amount over for every hour we need her longer than the 40 hours. We also pay the nanny taxes and guarantee her sick time and at least two weeks of vacation a year and prepay that in advance. I would definitely think about all that. The weekly per diem and then the caretaker also needs to have the ability to have a life. I can tell my employer I'm taking a vacation day, and they automatically pay me because I've earned that vacation day. So considering things like that and then considering we also provide health insurance for this person because she is an employee, there's a lot to factor into the caretakers. It's not cheap. Definitely you want to make sure they're taken care of, and that statement is especially true in this area, because there is a lot of wealth. If you don't take care of your nanny or caretaker, somebody else will pay them $20 more an hour and that's a better quality of life for that nanny, because they now can do more things on the weekends. So I'd say the per diem and even a competitive per diem is important around here if you want good care for yourself and for your child.

Is there anything that has come up in the conversation that you think would be helpful for me to know?

That's a great question. I've not spent any time thinking about jury selection so I can't think of anything off the top of my head. This was very eye-opening to have to dig down and think how I would react to situations I haven't been in.

You've been so forthcoming and communicative.

Humans are very interesting people, sure.

Thank you.

21

IT'S SCARY

Caucasian male, age 30, single, Freelance Web and Graphic Design/Barista, B.A., partial Masters

I think it's scary for a lot of people. They believe the things that make them feel safe.

The judge will say, ladies and gentlemen, please give your attention to the attorney for the plaintiff, that's the injured person, who's going to conduct the jury selection. What are your thoughts and feelings? What are you thinking about in that moment?

I'm just giving them my attention, probably.

Do you have any thoughts about courts or lawsuits or lawyers in general?

I tend to assume, based on what I hear, that somebody who's suing a company is probably just trying to take advantage of the system.

That's the default starting point for you?

Yeah because it seems like it happens a lot. Like somebody spills hot coffee on themselves and sues. That's retarded. It's coffee. Don't put it on your lap. But because companies have lots of money, then they try and get it. I'm not stuck to that. I tend to be someone who's pretty good at – **I mean, we all have judgments. We have to have judgments to be able to adapt to what we don't know.** *If you're in a dark alley and there's a black guy coming towards you, it's a safe judgment to assume you're in danger. It's not necessarily accurate, but you've got to have some information to act on. I'm open to discovering that he's a really cool dude and then going and getting coffee with him. It's not like I'm held onto my judgments; I just have to fill in the gaps. So that's where I start; that's my assumptions in that kind of case.*

What would help you get over that gap?

Meeting the actual person and hearing their story. I feel I'm pretty intuitive in terms of judging people's character and intention; just seeing how genuine, I guess, where they were coming from. Are they trying to cover the cost of medical expenses? Are they trying to sue for a hundred million dollars? Punitive damages for getting a burn?

Do you think that every case is different?

Of course.

So that on a scale, some cases will be more worthy than others? Or less frivolous.

Yeah. I feel I would be somewhat concerned that it might be a waste of my time

to be there. But I wouldn't know until I started hearing more about what was going on.

If the money were a little better, would you be more interested wanting to be there and participating for some time?

*Sure. That's what I'm trying to do with my daytime, right, is meet my basic needs. I don't have any issues volunteering for things that are meaningful to me. **But if it's some stupid case, and I'm making $10 a day, then that feels like a waste of my time.***

What's meaningful to you? What sort of things are meaningful to you and your time?

Well, in general, justice is valuable. If I'm a part of supporting something that's really significant, then that would be valuable. In general, the things I lean towards are usually in terms of education, working with kids. I've done a lot of different things with kids and sometimes underprivileged kids or kids from bad parts of town.

How did you come to that?

I had a similar situation and I got through it. But I feel like not everybody does. Not everybody is able to shift their paradigm to get out of that victim mentality and find the things they need and find the surrogacy to fill in the gaps of things they didn't get developmentally.

Got it. On the scale open-minded or closed-minded, where do you think you fit?

I'm open-minded. Who says they're closed-minded? I am open-minded, though, in that I'm willing to challenge my assumptions.

If you know you've got some kind of a belief or prejudice or bias, you tend to be aware of it?

I'm aware that I'm making judgments. I'm aware that, ultimately, I know very little.

Does that awareness help you if it comes to having to overcome that a little bit?

Yeah. Because this is the default information I have. This is what I believe right now. I'm always gathering information, always gathering more data. I'm almost always changing my opinions about things because I don't take them that seriously.

Are you more data driven or more heartfelt and intuitive?

Intuitive.

Tell me more about how that works for you.

Well, I studied philosophy, and from a rhetorical standpoint, you can make anything make sense. I'm fairly intellectually sharp, and I can make anything make sense. I've studied all these different philosophers and they're all saying different things, contrary things. But when you're reading them, you're like, this is it. This is the system. If you're smart, you can make something make sense. So at the end of the day, there had to be more than logic to determine –

Or rhetoric.

Or rhetoric, right. And logic and rhetoric, they're hard to separate. So I value that; it has a place. But I don't rely solely on that. I see a balance of the two. I'm not just wishy-washy emotional. I get information but I don't necessarily know where it comes from. But in my experience, when I test it, it's been accurate, so I've learned to rely on that.

What do you think about, in that moment in the courtroom with all those other people, when you're looking at the lawyers, what are you thinking about them and the job they have to do?

I'm thinking I don't trust them, because they're essentially hired hands that are going to do the bidding of whoever pays them and not really necessarily coming from a place of integrity – like, pay enough money to a good lawyer, they'll try and get you off a murder. To me, if they know you did it, they should just be, he did it. Put him in jail.

How do the lawyers in the courtroom get over that perception with you? What can they do to develop a human connection that's credible?

I don't know. I feel like it would probably happen once I decided what I believed about it. Then I would give credibility to whoever was on their side. Just being honest. I don't know. That's probably not the best way to do it.

Do you think the attorneys on both sides share that same lack of credibility at the start or do you think it's one type of attorney? So if you have plaintiff attorney and defense attorney – the plaintiff attorney is the one who represents the injured person, and the defense attorney represents the –

Well, it does seem much easier to beat up on the defense attorney.

Why is that?

Because you generally assume the plaintiff is the victim and the defense attorney is defending the antagonist. These are assumptions going on, right? Now, if I get there and find out the victim is the idiot who spilled coffee on themselves and wants to sue for it, then I think their lawyer is an idiot. Not an idiot, but just lacking integrity for being like, I'm going to get you money even though you don't deserve it.

With that, as the evidence comes in and you hear from the people about what happened and what injuries are there, your open-mindedness can transcend?

Always. I'm sure everything I'm saying now, if I had been through the experience, I would have completely different answers.

How do you know that you could transcend that experience?

Just because I've done it in every situation in my life. When I go into something, I don't know what I'm going into. I'm going to come out with all sorts of different – yeah.

Do you think that's true of the rest of the people sitting around you?

No.

Why's that?

*I mean, certainly a number of them, but not everyone. To me, that's what real bias or real discrimination or racism is; a lot of religious systems, that's what it is. **You've decided that you believe something, and now you're going to squeeze all of your experience; bend, twist and break it, to make it fit what you believe.** It's retarded. I was raised really Christian, and that's why, because I was really in that mindset. I had to work out of that and study philosophy and become much more pragmatic about developing the skills of really being comfortable in challenging what I believe. Because **I think it's scary for a lot of people. They believe the things that make them feel safe.***

You're comfortable challenging your beliefs?

Yeah. Because I've learned to feel safe based on something that's larger than just what I think that I know.

So faced with something that challenges a long-held belief – you've had experiences where you've overcome and actually –

Yeah. I used to believe that if I didn't do certain things I was going to go to hell; I was terrified. I feel if somebody can get over that, you can challenge any belief. And I have – then I was just afraid. I believed the things that I believed because I was afraid. I'm not now, and I trust that whatever I don't know, learning that is only going to make me more empowered.

On the scale of self-awareness and no self-awareness, where do you think you fit?

Pretty self-aware.

Does that involve empathy, too? Where do you think empathy fits?

I'm overly empathetic.

What does that mean?

I feel what other people are feeling, whether I want to or not. I walk into a room and I'll feel all the different energies in that room. I'm always trying to build boundaries energetically so I don't feel all that stuff, but for a lot of my life, I'm just kind of running away from it.

Is that from training you've had, or is that something that's come to you naturally?

No, it's something that happens to people who are raised the way that I was raised. It's a coping mechanism.

I understand empathy and I've read Goleman's books on empathy and EQ – emotional awareness. So I can talk the talk with you and share and relate to that. Here's the question: where does sympathy fall? You can feel and appreciate being in other people's shoes, but what about sympathy?

It's different. Right now I tend to be annoyed at everybody because I don't want to feel. I feel what they're feeling and then I'm agitated at them. Because they're feeling, it's causing me – obviously, I know that's dumb. They get to feel what they're feeling. But I don't have as much space to be sympathetic, because I'm constantly trying to get people out of my space.

Is that in your professional life? Or in your personal life? Both?

In my personal life. It's easier in my professional life to have clearer boundaries with people.

What have you learned in your professional life that would impact your experience as a juror?

I've learned a lot about working with people. I've learned a lot about dealing with emotions, and I've done lots of different things. I've been a teacher. I've worked with preschool teachers at the Waldorf education, which is all about working with emotions. I've done lots of that myself because I had to learn how to deal with that because I wasn't taught how to deal with emotions. I think that's huge as humans being both emotional and intellectual. I think a lot of our downfalls come from an imbalance of the two in one direction or the other. When people get too emotional, they lose all sense of logic and rational.

They sure do.

When people are so cut off from themselves they're just sue-like; I'm like an atheist, and I know everything.

Rigid and dogmatic.

Rigid and dogmatic. And not feeling. That also can lead them to that.

So you feel that empathy and sympathy are different things?

Yeah.

Let's talk about a little bit more about empathy. What does that involve for you? What's the process? Let's say you're in a courtroom and you see these parties and lawyers. Are you putting yourself in their shoes?

Judgment is an obstacle to empathy. *So I tend to assume for most people that I don't know anything about them. I don't know why – you know, they're flipping somebody off; they're honking in traffic. You don't know. Maybe their dad just died. It doesn't excuse the behavior, but you don't know.*

Is there anything the attorney could do that would turn you off right away?

I don't know necessarily, like, what he does as much as his attitude or his demeanor. Vibe, I guess. For example, I was downtown when Obama got re-elected, and then the new governor got elected. He was trying to give his speech, and we were all – we're waiting for Obama to give his speech. The dude finally decided to give his speech, and when Obama came on, he didn't stop. Everybody in the room was shouting, stop, stop. We could see it, we just couldn't hear it. And I could sense there was so much ego, like he wanted to assert himself and whatever. He didn't have the humility to say, oh, I'll come back to my speech. And I was like – I don't know.

Rude behavior.

*Yeah. **Humility is big. It takes humility to challenge your judgments. It takes humility to be honest, to admit mistakes, to learn new things, to think that you don't know everything.***

You were saying one of the things that an attorney would do that would turn you off would be –

To seem not genuine.

To seem not genuine. What does that look like? Other examples?

In general, you can tell people that look you in the eye, usually they're not trying to hide anything. People that can laugh a little bit. I know it's strange in a courtroom, but there's a general levity you can still have that's not so locked down that lends itself to communicating.

Do you think you'd want to know anything about the lawyer, him or herself, in the process?

Like what? I mean, I'd love to know all sorts of things about them, but…

For example, we've asked you to share things about yourself. Would you want to know if the lawyer had some closed-mindedness on issues? Or prejudice or bias?

Yeah.

And you wouldn't feel manipulated by that? If the lawyer were to get up and share something?

I wouldn't feel manipulated; I would feel like it maybe wouldn't serve the case. Say the lawyer is defending somebody who is not guilty and he gets up and says he's a douche bag – not in so many words, but he says something that triggers me to pass a judgment on the lawyer, right? It's totally non-related. He's defending somebody, and for whatever reason, he decides to get up and say he does not support gay marriage. Then I'm like, he's clearly, in my opinion, closed-minded. Then I'm going to be less likely to trust him, even if he's defending somebody that's innocent or whatever.

You indicated family members or close friends in both the legal profession and medical profession. What was that?

I took care of the kids of two lawyers. They were cool.

Do you know what kind of work they did? Civil or criminal?

I think criminal.

How about in the medical?

I started to training medicine, and I've got a bunch of friends who are naturopaths.

With those exposures to the law and medicine, is there anything about those exposures that would impact your decision-making process in a court?

I don't know. I tend to trust alternative healthcare professionals. And I tend to strongly distrust mainstream medical, Western healthcare practitioners.

If an individual who's injured has been seeking care from both the mainstream and the alternative, would you have a problem with that?

No. What they're seeking care for – I mean, it depends. If they cut their leg open, they need to see a Western doctor. So how they're approaching care really doesn't affect – you know, if the company caused them to get cancer and they're doing treatments that I don't think are the most effective, that has no bearing on whether the company's responsible for that.

How about whether or not the company should pay for the medical bills?

Still no bearing. It's their choice how they want to get treated, and it's the company's responsibility.

Do you have any peers or people you know who've been injured and have had lawsuits or cases?

I have one –

Workers' comp or personal injury?

I didn't know her that well, but she was a fellow student in my class. She got hit by a taxi crossing in a crosswalk. He wasn't looking. He just went. He was stopped, and then he started driving and she was in front of him. That was huge, huge for her. In my opinion, it's terrible that she even has to go to court to fight that, because she's got the medical bills and she can't work.

Do you think that impacted her ability to be a student?

She was graduated at that point.

How did it affect her life?

Definitely adversely. It's going to slow everything down. Everything that she's trying to move forward with is going to slow down. Maybe it takes her a year

to get back to a point where she can pick up things again.

Do you think she would be fairly entitled to lost wages or medical bills, things like that?

Definitely.

So that's one part of damages; another part of damages is pain and suffering and disability and loss of enjoyment of life that we can't, with any degree of reliability, put a money number on. There's no fixed standard. How would you go about putting a money figure on something like that?

*I don't know. **It seems pretty arbitrary because it's so relative.** This isn't what necessarily would happen, but if it were me, and I, say, was working something out with somebody and of course, I would want to be like, well, what is it worth to you? What would make you feel better? I mean, that's what I would do in a situation that isn't monetary. If I'm in a fight with my partner and I do something dumb, I'm going to be like, what can I do? I'm not going to be like, okay, here's what I'll offer you because I did that dumb thing. I'm going to be like, what do you need to feel better about this? But when it comes to money, obviously, anybody'll just say ten billion dollars or whatever. So it's hard to –*

And you're going to have a jury of 11 other people who are going to come at it from a different point of view. How would you go about discussing that with them?

*I guess I would choose a number that felt good to me. **Can't I really use logic in that case. Then I would think about why it felt good to me and make a case for it.** And I would explain – I would break it down, all the different things it's covering. I would think how that person can use that money to do things. Maybe I would think they deserve a vacation; how much is that going to cost them? Things that would help support them and what those things would cost.*

What you just said is so obvious; I hadn't really thought about it this way, but you can't use logic in that situation. Which makes it very difficult for those of us who have to make arguments and pleas for money. Can you give me help there?

What do you mean?

Well, I've got to talk to 12 very different people and get them to give what I call maximum justice, because I want the most for the client. Without losing my credibility.

*Right. Well, that's where you use rhetoric. You come up with something; there's a very creative element. As humans, we're always being creative. Even science is creative; we're making interpretations. We're always interpreting data. As a philosopher, I was really interested in epistemology. What's knowable? How we know what we know. Ultimately, at the end of the day, we don't know anything. None of us. Everything that we believe is based on a presupposition. If you cut it down to that, that's based on a presupposition. We all believe everything that we think we know. So we're choosing and we're making meaning. **We're choosing***

what to believe in, what makes sense, and what works for us in our lives. So I think there's a place to be creative. Creative doesn't just mean on doing a painting. It means you're deciding this feels good to me, and now I'm going to create a case for that based on what feels good to me.

Do you think the attorney should get up and say that there's no logic here but this is what feels right to me?

No. Because – people, you can't tell them there's no logic. You have to make them believe there's logic. And ultimately there is. You're using logic; you're just using logic to support a decision that you've made. I think there's times when that's appropriate and times when it's not appropriate. In this case, you're not just making a decision to believe something and ignoring all the data and then trying to force it to be something. You're making a decision that's creative. And you're using logic to defend why that makes sense. Even if it isn't something that you could find under a microscope.

We were talking about general damages for things like pain and suffering, that there's no fixed standard for it and how you had made that point that it is entirely illogical. Yet, we need to create a fiction there's logic by being creative.

Well, lots of things aren't logical in the sense that – is there logic in something like marriage equality? Is there logic in race equality? I mean, it makes sense to us emotionally, right? How would you reason that, though? You're reasoning based on what it feels – you're reasoning based on empathy. This would hurt me if you treated me like this, so it doesn't make sense to treat them like that. But it's not.

Are you saying that you would default to what would work for you?

I mean, what else do we have?

If you'd been hurt on the job, in a car accident or medical malpractice, what kind of a juror would you want?

An empathetic one. I would want someone who was able to make decisions with a balance of reasoning and feeling. And with absolutely zero bias that they couldn't transcend using reason and –

How do you think an attorney should reach engineers and tech-type people who are in their 20s?

You mean because they're very technical and logic-driven?

Sure.

You mean reach them to make a case?

To get them to become empathetic.

Oh. You mean because they tend to be more left-brained?

More analytical, more binary, more black and white.

> *Right. Well, I think if you're using a balance with skill then you can –* **so if you're empathic, then you're able to get yourself inside their shoes and figure out what they need to hear to understand what you're saying.** *And if what you're saying is true, then you can say it in a million different ways, right? If you're not making something up – if I'm describing something that I'm seeing, I can describe it in this way you'll understand it, and I can describe in that way you'll understand it. Because I'm just looking at it, and I'm like, okay, I'm going to give this part to them and this part to them. If you're making stuff up, it takes a lot more skill to figure out how to say it in different ways.*

Absolute brutal honesty at all costs? Would that be something you think would be helpful for a lawyer in a courtroom?

> *It would be helpful for me; it wouldn't be helpful for the client.*

But would it help the lawyer be more credible with you?

> *Of course. But a lot of times the defense lawyer knows if their client is guilty, right?*

Sometimes cases turn on the question of what is the value of the case. Many cases are not about whether the right or wrong happened, but what is going to be the resolution, what is justice going to give that person for their harms? The money part.

> *Yeah.* **Anytime when I see somebody being honest to a point of vulnerability, I'm going to trust them.**

What philosophers, modern day or ancient, have been of real impression on you?

> *For me it wasn't so much about picking certain philosophers and philosophies to go with, it was more about serving all the different ways we thought about the world, getting a firm sense of the fickleness of our reasoning. And understanding the creativity that is inherent and necessary in making life make sense and building paradigms and learning how to think critically. And learning how to create my own paradigms. So there's pieces of all those different philosophers that resonated with me that work for me. I'm very pragmatic at the end of the day. It's got to work. I don't care if you're Christian or Buddhist or whatever. If you're a Christian and you're developing compassion and empathy, what you're doing is right. If you're a Christian and you're developing judgment, your path is (expletive). It doesn't matter what the belief is, ultimately, it's about who we're becoming. We're the truth. We're what matters; who we are. Everything else is just a tool. And either it works or it doesn't. Either the hammer hits the nail or it doesn't.*

Right. It is pretty easy, isn't it? Is there anything that's come up in the conversation that you think might be helpful?

> *Not necessarily. At the beginning, I was thinking about the movie Runaway Jury.*

Have you seen that movie?

Sure.

It's a good movie. I'm wondering if that really happens? If people really stack juries?

Unlikely. Not in that way.

Well, I'm sure it's never that dramatic.

Not to say that a lot isn't known about jurors. In long trials you have an opportunity to investigate. Have jurors been tampered with? Absolutely. I don't think it would ever happen in my practice, because the cases I have aren't that significant. But if we're talking some monstrous corporate behemoth versus behemoth kind of thing that lasts for 15 years, maybe. I don't know. Thank you.

22

INTEGRITY

Caucasian female, age 66, married, one son, two grandchildren, Writer/Photographer, B.A.

I think it all comes down to is, the lawyer who steps out there either is a person of substance and integrity or he isn't. And I don't know that you can make a lawyer have integrity who doesn't.

The judge will say, ladies and gentlemen, please give your attention to the attorney for the plaintiff. The plaintiff is the injured party. They go first. The attorney will stand up and have 30 minutes to an hour to address all of you. Some people may not be given an opportunity to talk just because of the numbers. Can you share with me what you're feeling in that moment?

I think the first thing I'm thinking is, I'm going to pay very close attention to what he has to say.

How do you feel about being there in the first place?

I think it's a civic duty. It's the same that I feel about voting. I feel like we're privileged to live in a country where we can vote and that it's a right and a privilege and that everyone should vote. And the same thing with jury duty, that it's our justice system and we should participate, that we live in a country where we're lucky we can participate. So I feel it's a duty and it's a privilege.

How do you feel about the time commitment that may be asked of you?

That's hard for me, because we have a small business and there's just the two of us. *If it were months at a time, it would be a real hardship on our business. If it was a criminal case that was very extensive and I was gone for a month or two, I don't think I could do that. If I were a regular employee and my employer was okay, I wouldn't think twice about it. But when you run a small business, that's difficult. So I'm torn about that.*

How do you feel about the fact they're paying only $10 a day plus a bus pass?

That doesn't bother me. Because we live in a society that gives us so much, we should be able to give back.

How do you feel about these kinds of cases where somebody's injured and is suing someone for some money compensation?

I have an ability to put myself in both people's shoes. I can visualize someone who's hurt, who's been wrongfully hurt, who has been treated poorly, has not been given what they need to be given in order to compensate them for pain and suffering that has not only occurred on the spot but will occur on a long-term basis. Because I've been in a car accident, and I've had problems over the 30 years since then. In some ways, worse 20 years later than it was on the spot. So I can relate to that. At the same time, I can see from the other side where they're trying to fairly compensate this person. They feel like what they've offered or what they've done is right. And this person may be seeing this as, oh boy, I can hit this insurance company or I can hit this person and I can make myself on easy street by this thing. So I'm very middle of the road. I can see it from both sides.

Do you have any opinions one way or the other about whether or not there's a litigation crisis or too many frivolous lawsuits?

It's like with people in general, there's people that take advantage and people that are victimized. I don't think I'm the person to say without knowing what the circumstances are whether it's frivolous or not frivolous. I read some of these things where someone goes to McDonald's and gets a million dollars because they spill themselves with hot coffee, and I think, this is ridiculous. But at the same time, I don't know all the details. And I don't think the reports necessarily in the news – they're slanted. So I'm not very judgmental.

Is it fair to say you would want to know more?

I'd want to know more.

About any given case?

Yes. I know there are people that take advantage. But I also know there's – and that's people on both side. I know that insurance companies, the first thing they say is no.

When the attorney stands up in front of you, what's your thought about that individual, the lawyer or lawyers in that moment?

I suppose I have thoughts on the law profession in general. Individually when that person, male or female, stands up, **I think every person judges people when they see them. The way they carry themselves, the way they speak. Even though you don't want to make a judgment on people, you do.** I wouldn't make any judgment until I saw the person. Lawyers in general – **again, we're back to human nature.** There are really horrible lawyers and there are really wonderful lawyers and then there's real average lawyers. I've dealt with and seen on a wide spectrum. So I think lawyers – they're better educated in some ways; that does not mean they're smarter. They should have a level of competency; it doesn't always mean that they have it.

The purpose of *voir dire* is primarily to determine if a juror has some sort of bias or prejudice or prejudgment or is just unable to be fair in a given circumstance. How would you like this attorney to ask about whether or not you can be fair or impartial or unbiased from the start?

I think this would be really difficult for an attorney. I really do. I put myself in his place and think, on paper, I would probably not be a good choice for a *jury because I've got an ex-judge on one side, a retired judge who was a retired attorney. I've got a deputy sheriff that's a nephew. I come from a very conservative background. I'm Alaskan. I got my first gun when I was 10. I've been involved in different legal things. I've got a nephew who owns his own insurance company or a branch of it. So I would not look like – if I were the defense attorney for the person who was doing this – like I would be a fair juror.*

Let me make sure I understand that. You would be fair or not fair for which side?

Well, I'm thinking if I were the person that was defending –

Who was being sued?

If I represented the insurance company, I would think, oh, she's for me. And I would think the other attorney that's defending whoever is suing would think, oh boy, we don't want her. Two law enforcement, two insurance – and in reality, I am a very fair and open person. But I don't know how you would determine that unless you sat down and really talked with me. And when you have 60 people, I think I would be eliminated. My husband has been eliminated from every jury that they ever called because all he has to do is say that his brother is a retired judge and that he was military and his background – we get eliminated which I think, in a lot of cases, is really unfortunate for the defense who is – I mean, not the defense but for the plaintiff. Because I think both of us would be very fair. But I think that's getting to know the individual. I don't know how, when you've got 60 people, you make that determination. That's the thing that would be really difficult if I were picking a jury is, how do you have time to sit down and individually talk to each one of these people? You really don't.

We don't. And we tend to focus on the earlier numbers. The attorney has to bring up these issues with folks about whether or not they believe they can be fair or impartial. Can you think of a way for the lawyer to address that sensitively so that nobody's offended or so that you're not offended by it? And is it fair for the lawyer to just say, we're here to find out if anybody may be biased or prejudiced. And if you have those that may interfere with this case, would you raise your hand?

*I don't think that's out of line at all. I'm not sure that necessarily people will be truthful. **People's perception of their own character lots of times is not correct.** But no, I wouldn't be offended at all if somebody said that. And if I really felt that way, if I felt like – for instance, I was hurt in a car accident and we did not get really compensated and we never went after that. That was my decision. That was my choice. I was young enough to not realize that there might be some long-term consequences to that, and that's being uneducated on our part. We never thought about going to a lawyer. We never thought about pursuing that. Still probably wouldn't, even though I've had some problems with it. It's just part of life. But that gave me the perspective on both sides, which I think gave me an openness to these kind of things where I feel like, you'd have to be hurt more than I was. But I know from the minimal amount that I was – and I have repercussions. I can only imagine if someone has substantial injuries that it* would be something they needed to be compensated for long-term, so that leaves me open. But at the same time, I've known people who have barely been hurt who've gone out and gotten a lawyer and gone after this stuff to try and, I think, milk the system. So I've seen both.

Do you think that juries, after they've had a trial and observe the parties and listen to the evidence, can sniff out if somebody's trying to game the system?

That goes back to everybody's personal perception. I think I'm pretty good at that, but that's because I've run my own business for 40 years and been tried to be taken advantage on. **When you run your own business you get a discernment about people.** *I've found over the years a lot of people don't have that discernment. I feel that I have a lot of common sense. Not maybe blessed with a lot of extreme intelligence, but I have good, common sense. And I treasure that, because I've known over the years a lot of people do not have a grasp on common sense. So I don't know.*

If you were selected to be part of a jury of 12 people and there was a deliberation, what role do you think you would fit in in the group? Would you be a leader? Would you be a follower? Would you be somebody more middle of the road, weighing all the options? Where would you lean?

As far as making the decision, I could be middle of the road. I would be taking notes through the whole trial on what I felt the important points were. For example, like on the OJ Simpson trial, I felt he was totally guilty. But I felt like, if I were on the jury, I could not have found him guilty because I thought the prosecution made such a poor case, that the evidence was not presented in a way that you could make a guilty verdict. I would have had to say I can't on this evidence. In my mind, he's guilty.

The prosecution hadn't met their burden of proof?

I found them to be shockingly incompetent on a national stage. It was a real education because you expect when you see a televised case that's in the world – we saw that televised in Saigon and I'm thinking, it's all over the world. And my opinion was, it was poorly done. And I was shocked by the judge. I thought he was unprofessional in so many ways. I thought both Marcia Clark and –

Darden?

— were unprofessional in their behavior. I thought they set the legal profession back. But if I were on that jury, I would have wanted to find him guilty.

But you were able to understand the difference between the burden of proof and the feelings that you have?

Yes. You can't make a judgment on feelings. I thought the jury were more professional than any of the lawyers. They were much more professional. It made me believe – I had the admiration for them. And I didn't like the decision, but I respected the decision.

When this lawyer stands up before you for the first time and says that he or she represents this plaintiff in a lawsuit who is suing somebody, what's your instant opinion about the credibility of lawyers who do that kind of work?

*I think that work is necessary. I think without the best of the law profession – and **I know that there are a lot of sleazeball lawyers – but I'd like to believe they're a very small minority out there.** I would think people go into law because they are contributing to the right of our society. That without a lawyer, without someone standing up for a person that's been hurt, a person that's been wronged, a person who wants their freedom back. I would find it difficult to be a lawyer in a lot of ways because you're always dealing with people who are in trouble. I would think personally, it could drag you down. I think a person that goes into the legal profession and keeps their own sense of right and wrong and keeps their personal life and their personal integrity is someone I admire greatly because they're there representing – they're saving the people who are taken advantage of.*

Sure. One person at a time.

One person at a time.

There is a perception, and it's been written about, that plaintiff's trial lawyers are perceived as having a lack of credibility second only to used-car salesmen. Do you agree or disagree with that? Where do you fall on that continuum?

That's another one of those individual basis things. I mean, you see some ads on TV – which lawyers never used to advertise on TV but you see them now. I would think if you were a law firm you'd almost be forced to do them because your competitors are. It is a business, after all. But it's that fine line of being able to say, I'm here for you and – hey, if you're in an accident, give me a call because – call 1-800-ACCIDENT. Being a used-car salesman. I think there's an example – I think it's called the Advocates or something that does a really nice commercial on TV and gives you the feeling in what they present that they are there to help and to make a wrong right without being slick used-car salesman which a lot of them are call something – I'm the lawyer for you. It's a fine line that lawyers walk, because you want to get your name out there and if you keep yourself too pristine or too superior, then you're unapproachable. It's like the lawmakers who did the – this is the place for the Sport of Kings, and people stopped going because they want to go there to drink beer and gamble. It's a fine line, because you're educating yourself to know the law, to be a champion of people and of the law, and yet you've got to advertise your services.

How are you able to determine if that lawyer is more likely or less likely credible from the start?

I suppose it's the way they present themselves and the way they talk to the jury, as well as – probably the way they present their case more than anything. And the way they present themselves.

We're looking for people to be open-minded.

Absolutely.

We recognize that everybody comes with their own life experience and baggage, bias, prejudice, whatever you want to call it. In an ideal world, we would love if people who had things that would be clearly obstructing our goals let us know about it, but we don't think everybody would. How do I talk to you and your group about finding out if you're all open-minded? Giving everybody a fair start?

That's a tough one. I have, in some ways, a problem with the whole jury studying because it's supposed to be a trial by your peers. So we should, in an ideal world, pick out the jury from whoever comes in there, whoever we don't know their backgrounds, and they're supposed to be our peers. Unfortunately, we live in a society that that's really not fair.

Our peers are defined as 18 years old, voter registered or driver licensed.

Exactly. So would that be my peers? No. If I were to go to court, would I want a group of 18-year-old gangbangers – if they were the first ones that walked in, would that be a fair representation of what I felt my peers were? No. I think it's sad that we've come to the place where to just have a fair chance you have to do this jury selection and this jury qualification.

Before the courts became so crowded we had a longer time to do this process. Now it's condensed. We have very little time. What I want is to learn how to not lose my case in jury selection. Because lawyers are getting up absolutely cold in a somewhat hostile environment. A lot of people don't want to be there; a lot of people have opinions against these kinds of cases; a lot of people are cynical; and some are friendly. But our job is to show that we're credible, that we care, and that we're looking for the open-minded juror.

Well, it would be kind of a shocking way to do it, but walk in there and say, okay, how many people think that my defendant should get a butt load of money and be set for life? And see how many people raise their hands. They would be the people that would be instantly eliminated by the other side. They'd never make it in there. I mean, there's some really blunt, shocking questions that people will answer. I think sometimes the subtle things that you go around and try and find out how people – that works with people like me, but a lot of people that come into the jury – I wouldn't raise my hand to any of these things. And the people who probably won't raise their hand are going to be the people who are going to really – the people who don't respond to either question, how many people think that all these lawsuits are frivolous? And you'll get people who'll raise their hand. So you know you want them on your side. The other side wants them. But that takes care of both. The ones who would instantly give you money, the ones that would instantly think you're wrong. And you want those people gone. Then you get down to the people who are not going to react to either one of those things, and you've got a smaller pool of people to deal with. Then you've got to work on the experiences each one of them has had, whether or not they're law enforcement-minded, whether or not they're insurance-minded. And like I say, unfortunately mine, I would be eliminated. And that's too bad, because I'd be fair. But on the other hand on paper, I'm not a good risk.

How about the way the lawyer and the client dress? Is there anything about –

It makes a difference to me.

What would you like to see that helps inspire you to think the attorney is credible or caring or worthy of being given a fair chance?

I think in order to be respectful to the Court, and I'm no fashion person, so it has nothing to do with design or whatever. They need to be clean; they need to wear a suit. They need to walk in and look more presentable. Both the defense and the plaintiff lawyers need to look like they're professional.

Do you think it matters if the lawyer cares for his or her client? If so, how would that best be shown to you?

I want to see that both lawyers care about their profession, that they care about what they're doing, that they have a personal set of standards for themselves, and I would like to look at the lawyer who's taking care of the plaintiff and feel like he has respect for his client. He has respect for himself. He has respect for the Court. I think you can see that in how a person carries themselves. That to me would be what I would want in a lawyer. Sure, I'd like my lawyer, to really care about me, but I'm hiring him and wanting him to take me through the legal process and to know enough about that legal process to defend me or to navigate it in my favor. So I want someone who stands up there and shows everyone not only that they have a respect for their profession, but they have a real knowledge of their profession, that they know what they're doing, that they understand the law, and they understand how to use it for the client in the very best way that they can.

Getting back to the issues of bias and fairness, do you think it would be appropriate for the lawyer, before asking jurors to share about themselves, to share something of him or herself to show – I'll show you mine and ask you to show me yours?

Yes and no. That's kind of a strange thing, for me. This is just for me. I want the lawyer to be professional. So I don't know how much I want to know about him personally. I don't think you have to know about me personally to have me be – I mean, I know it colors what jurors do. I'm an exception to probably who you're talking about. I would think of myself, if I went into the jury, as being professional in my position in the court which would be, I would want to be the best juror I could be, to be there on time, take notes, be attentive through the whole thing, and be totally fair on what is presented, regardless of what I felt about I liked you as an attorney because you have a dog and it's really wonderful. I would try and not let that color the decision I was making. Unfortunately, that's not the norm.

Some advocates are suggesting that lawyers share a fear if it's pertinent to the case.

I think most jurors, if you went out and said, okay, I have gone through where I had medical neglect personally. I am here representing the plaintiff because I know even when I go in, and I'm a malpractice attorney, and I go into the hospital and to this doctor and they're negligent to me, who, of all people, should be treated – not that I expect to be treated better, but I expect them to know they're dealing with a malpractice attorney and yet I had problems. So these things happen. In a lot of ways, that instantly makes you more human. It makes you more sympathetic. It makes them think you're going to be a better champion. Because you're going to come with your life experience – and so you're in the perfect place. It would be hard for you to be representing the insurance company and have the same background and try and be the champion on that side. So you – they instantly know that you are all in.

How does an attorney do that without having it sound of manipulation which would then breed distrust?

***I think you have to be really careful on details. You don't have to give details on what it is. You say, I know what it's like to be** – you have to give them a little bit without, oh, and then I went through this and then this was like this and I was like down and I was beaten and I was whatever and now I'm back. I think you could make it schmaltzy or you could make it professional. I think it's in the way you present it. I don't think a lot has to be said, but enough just in a very short amount that, I know what I'm talking about because I have first-hand knowledge of this. **And it's also not even the words that you say, it's in the demeanor that you say them with** and – not hey, let's have this fireside chat together. There's that fine line between I don't know you; I'm just here. Who are you? You're trying to be chummy with me and I don't know who you are and this is just manipulation by the lawyer. But if you're standing there as a lawyer, looking professional, speaking professional, you maintain the position as the lawyer and yet you've given them the sense that you're personally committed.*

What can a lawyer do to establish a human connection with you? Or what might they do that would completely destroy any chance of establishing a human connection with you? You can look at it either way. What would be helpful to establish a human connection and what would be hurtful in that?

*I think what would be hurtful for me if they were really unprofessional. If they came in looking sloppy, if they were putting out their cigarette when they walked in the door, if they were crude in their language, if they were – I don't want to hear profanity coming out of a – we're going to get those whatever whatever. Or if they were too trying to buddy-buddy or were too condescending, too superior. It's a fine line. They figure that the jury is dumb, so they're talking down to them. There's that. **I want the lawyer to treat the jury with some respect. If a lawyer walks in, he makes things easy to understand. He speaks to you. He looks each person in the eye or tries to. He stands up straight, looks good*** *and says, I'm here to represent. He can say, I've got a personal tie to this. I've got to ask a few questions of you in order to* – we're not trying to preselect to the point where we feel like you've already made your decision before; **we're trying to find people who are open.**

Do you think they will believe a lawyer that says that, rather than think to themselves, oh, he's full of it, because he just really wants to win for his side?

What I think it all comes down to is, the lawyer who steps out there either is a person of substance and integrity or he isn't. And I don't know that you can make a lawyer have integrity who doesn't have it. So I think that this all – it's going to come through the person, because that person works on being the best he can be for himself. He sets his own standards of his own professional behavior and his own personal behavior. And that shines through. And phoniness shines through, too. When he's putting himself in a position where he wants to sell that, but really he is not that. So some of these things; I think you can train yourself to be better and to make a better presentation. But I think ultimately, what you have to do is work on being – being, not just acting – some of the things that you need to be.

Right. Being a real person.

Being a real person.

Being credible.

Yep.

And that really is – my training has come down to, you have to be the most credible person in the courtroom.

Yes.

In order to bond with that jury and to make that jury your jury.

Yes.

Often I find that the best way to learn about how to be is to know what not to be.

True. I would want a lawyer who is really committed to the case, who has really done their homework and it's obvious, has a clear program of how he's going to come in there and defend this person. He's going to go down all the – I mean, I was flabbergasted with the OJ Simpson case in that I felt like there was no organization in their presentation. They didn't make all their marks and they were all there to make. I felt like I, from the outside, could have given a better prosecution of that. But who comes in and doesn't waste the Court's time, their time, the defendant's time by being unprepared, unprofessional, or just plain not confident. You want someone who walks in and they own that courtroom. And regardless of what anybody else says or whatever, you don't deviate from your goal which is proving all – I mean, even if you lose, you walk away knowing that you have made the best defense on this, that you have believed in this, that you have done an excellent job for this client regardless of the outcome. And sometimes – sometimes, you can have the best in the world and it doesn't – for whatever reason, it doesn't work.

There's a lot of information I'm trying to get from a lot of people. The lawyer really can't. Do you think the group could be selected at random just as well as the same group after we've gone through all of this? In other words is this much ado about nothing?

No, I don't think it's a total waste. I do think that there's things – it's sort of like that Chief Justice that gets placed in there because he's conservative and then he votes the liberal, right? Sometimes. But you can do all this and be shocked by the decision that someone would make at the end because I think people will say sometimes the things that they think you want to hear. And then they'll turn around to the other attorney and say the things he wants to hear so that they can get in there because, oh, won't this be fun? It'll be really interesting. That said, maybe those are the ones who would be fair, because they're open either way. But I think if you randomly took people off the street and the first number that came in, you put in the jury, it could be blatantly unfair. I understand the necessity for this. I wish there wasn't a necessity for this. I wish that people felt it was their civic duty and that they need to be fair and they would step up. If I went into a jury, I would probably end up being a juror because I would be saying, okay, we all have to be fair. Here are my notes. Here are my reasons for this. These are the things we have to consider. I'm not sure how many people on the jury would be doing that. It's like my husband and I, we always say we have to be careful about joining anything because we end up having them wanting us to be the leaders. Probably if I got on a jury, I'd end up being the leader of the jury just because I have a set of standards I think should be met.

Right. And you're probably not afraid to stand up and show people that you have those standards.

*No. I don't expect other people to have my standards, and I don't expect other people to adhere to those standards, **but in something like a jury, I would expect that the overriding standard would be fairness.** So I wouldn't be tolerating, hey, let's all believe he's guilty. Let's hang the guy. Right? Or let's whatever. I would be saying, we have to do this in a fair and appropriate and lawful manner. People have to be held to the standard. It's like in the courtroom, the lawyers have to be held to their standard. The judge should be held to a standard. I find it distressing when judges get away with unfairness in their court. Or lawyers. I hold lawyers and doctors to a higher standard. And it's a huge disappointment to me, and I'd be harder on that lawyer than I would be on a normal person because you've studied the law, you know better. You know what's right and wrong. I would be more judgmental of you than I would be a normal person off the street because I know that you know better. If I were into a murder case and it was a lawyer, I would be – I'd have to see the evidence, because maybe they would be innocent. But if they weren't innocent, I'd be harder on them because they know better.*

Right. They know better. The ultimate outcome in these cases, unfortunately, is money to make a person whole for the harms they've suffered. There are kinds of damages we call special damages. Those are things you can put on a blackboard that have receipts: medical bills, lost wages – past and future – they will incur down the road because the doctors say they'll need this kind of treatment. Things to fix whatever has been damaged. But there are other damages that are called general damages and those are pain and suffering and disability and they have no fixed standard for people to determine. Now, you've come together with a group of people, how do you go about determining a way of making a person whole for those damages?

> *That's a tough one. I do think people should be compensated for pain and suffering. And I do think that there are long-term consequences to real damages.* *And I do know that things are expensive in the long term. And I do know that there's things that cost money to make a person whole again, whether that's counseling, whether that's retrofitting a home or an office place or a car or whatever.*

Those are special damages, because we can have experts talk about what that will cost. But when you talk about something like emotional damage, loss of enjoyment of life, somebody may have a limb removed or some other injury so they have to have their life colored by that.

> *Right. Absolutely.*

The challenge is to explain to juries what we think is fair. Is it just guesswork? We give a number, we don't give a number. How do you think you would –

> *I would want you to say to me okay, I've come up with this number, not out of the clear blue sky but for A, B, C, D.* *I would want that because I don't think the normal person out there would say, well, pain and suffering, let's give him a million bucks, or should we give him ten million? Or should we give him $500,000?* *So I would expect you, who is more knowledgeable on this to say to me, these are the reasons why ten million or these are the reasons why,* *and I'm sure that most jurors are going to say, well, how much out of that ten million do you get? And you needed to be compensated for that. But a normal person saying, I just made the lawyer and the plaintiff a zillionaire and I got $10 a day. Right? So I know that falls in there. Okay, I'm getting $10 a day. Well, I'm not going to let him get wealthy when it's my decision. I mean, there's some of that stuff. I think that's one reason why* *if I were a plaintiff's lawyer, I'd be looking for a jury that was healthy financially themselves, that was satisfied in their own work and in their own life. Because I think people who are happy in their own life financially, physically, emotionally, whatever, they're more generous. They're much more giving.*

What kinds of questions would elicit a response to find out if they're happy or satisfied in their place in life?

> *Just some of the simple things you do here on the form. How long have I lived in the place? I've lived in it for 15 years. I could say I've lived in the neighborhood*

for 40-some. I've been married; I'm not divorced. I have worked in my business for a long time. You might ask someone questions on employment. I don't know about – how long have you been in this profession. I think that shows a sense of stability or non-stability. I think if you've got a single mom who's supporting a child who's working at the K-Mart, in some ways they say, give them a lot of money because they project themselves on that, but at the same time, they're saying, hey, they're getting all this money and I'm getting $10 a day. I don't know. Where someone making $200,000 – they're going to be more generous. I mean, just that they're sitting on the jury when they make that kind of money and have all kinds of professions say that they are motivated by civic duty and they are also successful, they're also stable, they've also built up something that's successful, and they might be more generous. Just in general. But that question of, how much money? You'd have to guide them on that. I really do think that. I feel like I'm a stable person. I'm happily married. I love what I do. I get up every morning and thank God for the day. I am a happy person.

Some approaches are to more or less suggest a dollar figure a day for the rest of their life. Is it worth a dollar a day, for example, to deal with chronic neck pain or back pain or loss of a limb or something? Otherwise, it's really guesswork.

Otherwise it's guesswork.

Any number. I have to be careful I don't oversell and lose credibility. At the same time, I need to ask for enough that nobody's offended and that I believe is fair.

I think that's really good, especially with a young person. They've got a projected – the actuarial charts say that they're going to live to be 85. So that's how many days?

How many more years?

That's how many more years? That's how many more days? And we're talking a dollar a day.

Right. And how do we reconcile that with a very elderly person who may say their remaining days are more valuable to them?

*That's true. And you can say, this person only has ten years, but their expenses in those ten years are going to be substantial. Because just nursing care for someone who's sick 24 hours a day is $360 a day. So at $360 a day times whatever – and that's just for the basic nurse; that doesn't count for any of the medications, and nothing for the pain and suffering. What can we do for this person to bring a sense of comfort? And also to the family? Because the family is dealing with this and so aren't we, in a case of an elderly, compensating not only him, but giving some compensation to the family who's having to deal with this? Because we're going to be probably shortening this person's life. So then you're talking funeral. Then you get into the whole thing. I think in either case, the young or the old. **With the young, I like the how many dollars a day? With the old, it's like, you've got a chance to make the last part of this person's life meaningful and to comfort the family.** So you've got – there's a justification either way.*

Without any feeling like you're beating up or taking advantage of the insurance company – and I think most people want the insurance companies to step up to their obligations. They don't want them to be taken, you know, they don't want to be wrongfully cheated, but they want – because insurance companies don't want to step up. They don't want to pay out. They're all about profit. I think you have to remind juries that insurance companies are all about profit and that that's one reason why you're in court because their first response to this person is no. And if they say no and people take the no when they say it, they keep their profit. If people stand up for themselves and stand up for their rights and ask for compensation rightfully – rightful compensation for the pain and suffering that they've gone through, then that hurts their bottom line a little bit. It doesn't hurt them substantially, but they don't give out their bonuses this year or they don't buy their Lamborghini. That was a good line you can use. Because people saw her, the director of Planned Parenthood, standing there saying, I want a Lamborghini. It's that whole sense of greed. She wants something frivolous and foolish and in-your-face arrogant. And that's sort of what that stands for. She's a gal like my age sitting there, I want a Lamborghini while I'm selling body parts of fetuses. That was pretty bad. What are you thinking that you would even in jest say – I mean, sometimes stupidity of people is astonishing. But anyway. It's a good one for you.

Stupidity and greed.

And greed. Total greed. And that's what that stood for. Total greed. And no moral compass whatsoever.

We're in a jurisdiction that tends to be pretty conservative.

Really? I was going to say, because we're in a liberal state and a liberal city.

We're in a liberal three counties.

Yeah, three counties, right.

But they are still blue-collar conservative, for the most part. One of the challenges we're having is getting juries to award sums of money that are commonly awarded in other parts of the country.

*Really? Okay. I'm surprised at that. But I think of myself as more conservative. I would have no qualms about well-compensating someone because I think they need – and maybe it's because **I've gone through so many medical things with both of the parents and everything, I know how expensive this is and how emotionally draining this is. How physically draining this is. How that pain and suffering is in it and extends to the family because I've been the extended family of someone – the family caretaker.** So I understand that better. I know what that's worth . I won't say that it's worth five hundred million, but a million dollars is not what it used to be.*

What is a shocking number to you?

I suppose five hundred million is a shocking number to me. That would be a shock. That would be nothing to Bill Gates, right?

Because you brought Bill Gates up: all other things being equal, let's say Bill Gates and another person had the same injury. Their medical bills are absolutely identical. They didn't miss any work. But they have pain and suffering. Does Bill Gates get compensated any differently for his pain and suffering than the other person?

As far as I'm concerned, he shouldn't. If he was saying my lost wages are – I get paid this much per day; that would be a different story than someone who works at K-Mart that gets less than this. So if you gave someone like that $50,000, they'd think they'd died and gone to heaven. I don't know why I'm saying $50,000. Five hundred million, $50,000. They would think that was a substantial difference in their life. To Bill Gates, that's pocket change. But if you would compensate percentage-wise equally, then he would get five hundred million dollars and she would get $50,000 because it's the percentage of what each of them makes. I don't know. That would be another one of those things where I would want someone to counsel me on the reasons why. I think that would be scary. It's like, I don't understand the award out of McDonald's when they burned themselves. I think it was like ten million dollars. I did not understand that. The damages to that person were not substantial.

Some states allow punitive damages, where the jury may assess a punishment to the defendant as a deterrent. We don't have punitive damages here. That is one of the reasons our damages can be lower here than others because we're not allowed to punish. Only to compensate.

I see that. It's like a death penalty thing. Is it a deterrent? I don't think it's necessarily a deterrent. I don't think you put people to death as a deterrent, but I think you stop that person from ever –

– doing it again. Assuming that the crime is proved.

Oh, absolutely. I think in order to have the death penalty, there should be absolutely no question.

You talked about burden of proof. In criminal cases and civil cases there are two different standards for burden of proof. Criminal, obviously it's beyond a reasonable doubt. In a civil case, it's a preponderance, or as they say, more likely than not. What does that mean to you? More likely than not?

More likely than not means that you've made a case that there was negligence, that you have shown me why you are saying that this doctor, this hospital, this emergency care thing, why their job was poorly done.

Do you think that more likely than not or to a reasonable degree of certainty is just whatever tips the scales a little bit more than the other? Or does it have to be something more substantial?

I would feel like if it just barely goes over the scale, then I would probably say it still went over the scale. I'm not sure in the compensation stage that they wouldn't go for a lower compensation because I would feel like you just – barely. I mean, they were wrong, but they weren't – but if you show me a preponderance of reasons why I should – I see that this person was – they misdiagnosed, they – I mean, look at that doctor who told people they had cancer. Of course, he should be fried. He should never see the light of day. And most people, I don't think there's enough money out there to compensate those people. I don't think any insurance company or that doctor – but every single thing that doctor owns and anything that he has should be sold and split up between those 500 patients. And he should be found guilty criminally. That he got 13 years is a gift, right? If I had been on the jury, I'd put him away for the rest of his life. That man was a monster. So what would I vote for those people to an insurance company?

Do you think that an insurance company is always behind who's paying?

Not necessarily, no. And in his case, I don't know that it would be an insurance company. I think the insurance company was as victimized by that doctor, every bit. And if I were an insurance company, I'd go after him, too. I think that's very, very rare, I would like to believe. I think there's incompetent doctors. A really evil doctor like that I would like to think is rare. But I think they should so throw the book at him to keep other people – I mean, use him as a – string him up and throw eggs at him. I mean, you know, he had no humanity.

No good reason, no nothing.

It was greed. It was totally selfish. And he cried. He stood before them and cried. He didn't cry because of what he did for them, he cried because he got caught. He cried because his gravy train was at an end. And he'd been doing this for years. We had a dentist that was sexually molesting the patients that came in. He shouldn't see the light of day.

Those are extreme cases.

They are extreme cases, but they happen. I would be really tough on them because I would want them to be an example.

More often than not the cases we're taking to trial are the least extreme cases. People who are jurors may feel that their time is being wasted because this is only a $50,000 case or why are we here for this little automobile –

But $50,000 is a lot of money. *I know one guy advertises on TV, oh, everybody said this was worth nothing but he got me a million dollars. See, I know his name because he advertises. Would I call him? No. But would a lot of people, yes. Because hey, I'm going to get a bunch. She looks fine. She's a hot babe and she looks perfectly fine but she got a million dollars out of it, so I'm going after the insurance company because I can get a million dollars, too.*

If you were on a jury and the judge said, don't read anything about this case. Stay away from the news, would you be tempted to Google the lawyers to learn about them?

Not if I were on the jury, no.

Do you think that jurors would do it anyway?

Some of them, absolutely. But the same ones who would Google the lawyers will also Google the headlines on the case. I mean, there are people that are going to read online. You'd almost have to take the phones away from the juries.

That doesn't happen. Nobody gets sequestered anymore, or at least it's very rare.

I was going to say, you'd have to sequester them to keep them from doing it. I think you have to assume –

You can assume they're going on their cell phones during a break and looking up the lawyers on their phones.

And some of them are not going to be educated enough to do that. They're not going to be curious enough. They're not going to care in general. So some of them will do that not just because they're going to be honest, but because they're just not that knowledgeable.

Thank you.

23

REASSURANCE

Caucasian female, age 51, single, Marketing/Community Relations, B.S. Psychology

There's not a right or a wrong answer. Reassure people of that.

At that moment, the judge says, please give your attention to the attorney for the plaintiff who's going to conduct jury selection. What are you thinking and feeling?

Curiosity, probably.

What would you be curious about?

What are the questions going to be?

Is there anything of a questioning nature that you would expect to hear or not hear?

On a civil case? Have you been in an accident? Have you been in court yourself? Has a family member been in court? How do you feel about insurance companies, maybe? Ever worked for one?

Do you think those are fair questions?

Yeah.

Do you think there are any questions that would be unfair to ask of you or your group?

Maybe stuff that wouldn't have any bearing, like religious beliefs, sexual orientation, race. Stuff that would mean they're narrowing down for – it's not a true jury of peers, where it's a select jury group.

What are your thoughts, feelings and impressions about the potential jurors you're seated with? This group?

It's hard to say without seeing them. I don't know. Probably impressions would be, how many women? How many older people? How many kids – well, I won't say kids, they're all over 21. That sort of thing.

What are your feelings about the lawyer who's standing up to talk to you and the fact this is a personal injury lawyer representing an injured person?

Doing his job. I probably have a more realistic view of attorneys than maybe some of the people on the jury.

Because of your background. Tell me a little bit about your views about attorneys.

I think most of them are nice guys and gals with sucky jobs. I wouldn't want to do it.

Why do you think they have sucky jobs?

I think of the perceptions, you know, the stereotype. They work long hours.

What do you think the perceptions of these kinds of lawyers are to the public?

Ambulance chasers. That's probably the stereotype that comes to mind.

Do you think that ambulance-chasers are representative of the profession?

No. I don't.

Do you think the general public does?

Yes.

What do you think can be done in this instance, for the lawyer standing up before you to show the group that this lawyer isn't that type?

*Something to personalize it a bit. I don't know what the rules are for that, whether they can or not, but **something to make him or herself look human in the eyes of these average people on the jury.***

That's one of the questions I have: how can this attorney present him or herself as a human and establish a human connection with you and your group, without being manipulative?

*Just an off-chance like – I want to say small talk, but for lack of a better – oh, wow, it's raining outside – you know. How was your guys' commute in this rain or something like that. **If there's a way to work a little bit of humor in, that tends to put people at ease.***

What would an attorney need to avoid doing to ruin this potential connection they're trying to establish?

*For me? **Coming off as condescending. I do not like being treated like I'm stupid. It's a pet peeve. I think that's probably true for most people.***

Can you give me an example of what a question like that or a comment to you would be?

It's more tone of voice. Defining something that doesn't need to be defined, you know? Assuming that people don't know things. Some people probably don't, but you can always preface it with, well, in case you didn't know this, here's an interesting fact or something like that.

Do you think your level of education is representative of the average juror?

I wonder, because so many people do their damnedest to get out of jury duty, how representative it is.

Is there anything else the attorney might do that could help make you comfortable in that setting? You said humanize it a little bit. Do you mean to learn something about the attorney, him or herself?

Yeah, maybe something like that.

Sometimes, people will say, I will share something of myself first in hope that will invite the other person to share something of themselves. Do you think that that's an appropriate or fair way to go?

Depending on what they're sharing, you know. I mean, that's human nature, the reciprocity.

Right. What do you think would feel manipulative to you that you wouldn't feel comfortable hearing or being asked?

I think it's almost more non-verbal than what you actually say. At least for me. But it's more tone of voice. It's just sort of feeling.

Would you want to know about the attorney at the outset?

I would. I like to know about people. I'm curious. But I don't know what the rules are as far as what attorneys can and can't do. I had a professor who came across as really intimidating – huge guy. But he always had like a cap pin or something little that made him seem like a real person as opposed to this big scary guy trying to teach me statistics.

Right. Something that you noticed that –

That meant he had a background.

And the pin was something that reflected a genuine interest in that person's life?

Yeah.

Not something like a patriotic flag to maybe tell people something that wasn't true.

Yeah. Because that I can see being used as more manipulative. I suppose anything could. But something that like represents a hobby or something.

What if the attorney wore a ribbon or something? Would that be manipulative? To share anything like that?

That would honestly depend on the case. If it were a lawsuit about drug side effects, that'd be manipulative.

Many people end up doing jury service for all kinds of reasons. How do you feel, having received your jury summons knowing that you're possibly going to be a juror in a case?

I think it's something everyone should do.

Thank you.

I find it a little scary because you don't know what kind of case you're going to get on. If I walked into it knowing it was going to be a civil case or even a non-injury DUI, it would be a different feeling than knowing I was walking into a murder case. So that uncertainty. Especially the first time I did it.

Are there cases that you personally would not want to be a juror on? Or that you might say to yourself, I'm not the right juror for this case?

Probably any child abuse case. Of which, I'm sure, most people say. It's pretty hard to be objective there. Although, honestly, even then, I could still be rational about it. I wouldn't like it, but I could be.

So you feel that although you have strong feelings about it, in the end, you could do the right thing.

I could be fair. But that's probably my exposure and working in the public defender's office. It changes your outlook a bit.

Many people who are called to jury service, for reasons that are valid, don't want to be there because of the time commitment, they have other important things in their life, or because the money isn't enough to make up for the money they might lose. How do you feel about that?

I was fortunate. First time I was a college student, didn't matter. Second time, the company I worked for paid me normal wages. It's tough. Because, you know, people with newborn babies, they're not going to do it. When I got jury duty the first time, I got the summons the exact week I was going to be in Disneyworld, and I'm like, uh, guys?

Hardship, please.

They let you defer it for up to six months. So that was good.

How important is it that the attorney is mindful of your time?

I think that's important although the whole process is better than it used to be. When I first did it, you went in, and you sat for two weeks, not knowing if you're going to be called. There wasn't the call in or the go in – you can go home now. When I did it, I was there half a day. They have improved on that.

It's my experience that most people would rather not have to do it if they could avoid it.

The one jury I did get called for that I didn't get to complete, they were doing the voir dire, and he asked the guy sitting next to me what he does. The guy got a big grin and he says, I'm a public defender. And the attorney's like, get out of here.

Is there anything in your background having a psychology degree that would color your experience or your attitudes or beliefs about jury service or the case? What I'm asking is, what does that bring to the table for you?

Possibly, because I do tend to look at motivations a lot.

The motivation being the why?

The why. Assuming we're talking about a criminal case, does this person have mental illness? Are they on drugs? That sort of thing. I know not everybody does.

I don't think it's an excuse, but there are reasons.

What would be a motivation in a civil case? What would we be looking at there?

*Somebody just out trying to get money. I mean, **there's some pretty frivolous stuff out there.***

Talk to me about frivolous lawsuits. People mention that, and I'm wondering what comes to mind when you hear the words "frivolous lawsuit"?

When people sue manufacturers for something they should have been aware of. I mean, granted, the McDonald's lady, I know that was a much more severe burn than it should have been, but there's a reason they all have wordings on the cups. You look at a warning on a product and say, somebody was dumb enough that they had to put that there. I think people sue over things that should be just handled with like, hey, I screwed up. And an apology. Somebody falls on your sidewalk, you know, accidents happen.

What is your feeling about responsibility and duty on the part of both the injured person and the person that's claimed to be negligent?

*Obviously, to be truthful about what happened and not try to tell a story to prove a point. **I think people need to be responsible for themselves.** Honestly, accidents happen, but if it's because somebody has a crack in the sidewalk that's all broken and they've been told by the city to fix it and they didn't, that's different than just somebody slipping on wet leaves. I guess it's point of degree in some ways.*

Do you think that frivolous is a matter of the degree of injury? Or some other factor?

*In some cases, it could be. In some cases it's just people trying to make a quick buck off of what they see as a rich corporation. People at Disney who stand up on rides and then sue Disney because they fell out. Hello? They tell you to sit down. Don't take off the seatbelt, you can fall. Stuff like that. **People are not following the rules.***

There are rules. Do you have any perspectives about human nature with your background that would be relevant in this setting?

Possibly. Again, looking for why did somebody do it?

How do you feel about the role of civil lawsuits in America?

I think they're important.

Why?

Because otherwise, I don't think corporations would ever admit to doing something wrong.

Do you think that admission – that there's accountability as a result?

Yeah. Because again, larger corporations, I think they're more likely to sweep something under the rug unless it becomes public. And sometimes the only way it becomes public is if there's a lawsuit.

What's your feeling about the role of civil courts to change that behavior?

On the part of the corporations?

Or individuals. Wrongful behavior. Harmful behavior.

Well, if you've got somebody who's in a civil suit because this is their third time they've run into somebody – not because of DUI or anything where it's not quite criminal, but they're just stupid and can't drive – or something like that, maybe it'll make them think twice. Although most people have insurance to cover it.

You've talked about that a number of times. I'll share that I'm unsure what the general public thinks and feels about the role of insurance in these kinds of cases. What is your sense of the role of insurance?

In some ways, insurance probably makes people ask for and payout more than if there weren't insurance. But on the other hand, we'd have a whole lot of people going bankrupt if there weren't insurance for home owner injury or whatever. I know. It's a Catch-22, like most things in life.

Do you think the person who's being sued, if it's an individual, is going to have to pay some damage award out of their own pocket as opposed to an insurance company paying whatever the damages are?

I would assume so, because there are some things you just don't have insurance for. I mean, you've got car owner, home owner, that sort of thing. But if you're somebody who's taking care of a child, babysitting or whatever, and you're negligent and let them run out in the street, climb on the roof, whatever, you'd be done. Especially if they want hospital bills for the kid, that sort of thing.

How do you feel about professional negligence? Do you think that's something that happens?

I think it does happen, definitely.

What do you think the remedy should be if there's negligence on the part of the professional, say in your field, that harms a patient or person?

Because there's gotta be accountability. Doctors are wonderful – most of them. They're not perfect. You've gotta draw that line between an innocent mistake and somebody not being as careful as they should have been.

The real reason for *voir dire*, in my opinion, is to find people who are open-minded and to find those who can be. How do you think a lawyer can best address that question to you and to your group?

Open-ended questions.

Can you think of questions that would be more or less appropriate than others? Or should one just come out and say, you know, folks, I'm looking for open-minded people?

*I wouldn't do that, because **everybody thinks they're open-minded. And they aren't.** Maybe ask opinions, obviously, not on the case, but something half on a tangent but that's still related. If you're personal injury, ask about some personal injury case in the news. Then you'd get an idea of people who said – okay, people are just stupid. They screw up all the time, they don't follow directions, it's all their own fault.*

Do you think the profession a person is in is relevant to or will have some predictive effect on where they might go in their decision?

I think so. Because there are some professionals that are and should be held to a higher standard. People in positions of – teachers.

Positions of trust.

Over kids. A teacher who abuses a kid? They ought to have whatever can be done.

What I mean is, as potential jurors, do you think it's helpful to know what they do when I'm looking at what their approach might be to how they're going to look at this case?

Oh, yeah.

Tell me what might be helpful to know.

If you've got a case where somebody's suing a cop for alleged abuse or rough treatment, if you've got a cop on the jury, they're probably going to side with the cop. So, there is some of that, having your co-worker's back, so to speak.

Let's say I can't determine for sure if a person is biased or prejudiced. What if I was willing to accept that they had a bias and prejudice, but all I wanted them to do was to be aware of it when they ultimately made a decision? In other words, at least make room for the possibility they've got something that could color their opinion one way or the other.

*Honestly, that depends on the person. **Some people are not self-aware to realize, even when it's pointed out to them, there's a bias.***

Thank you. That enlightens me. How do we identify individuals who fall into the category of not aware or not enlightened enough to know that they have bias, prejudice, or aren't open-minded?

Part of it you're going to see when you're talking to them if you bring up the possibility and they get defensive. It comes back to behavior.

If I bring up something that causes a member of your group, our group, to become defensive, how will the rest of the group treat me?

That's a good question. That depends on how well you've established rapport at the beginning. Because if the potential juror who's becoming defensive is rude about it, people are likely to side against them.

People will tend to know what's fair and what isn't fair.

Yeah.

What do you think would be the best can opener question I could ask? If I had only one question to ask every juror and I ask them to raise their hand yes or no, what do you think would be such a question?

Is the world black and white? Because that'll get you some close-minded people right there.

Okay. That question is a yes or no question, but that's fair to ask a yes or no question in that context?

I think so. Yes, it's a yes or no question, but boy, does it reveal a whole lot about a person. Because it's, how do you view the world?

So engineers, for example, they tend to think in terms of zeroes and ones and there's one way that's better than another way. There tend to not be gray areas, whereas maybe in the social sciences there can be lots of different –

I wasn't thinking of it as profession. Maybe the view is – in your life view, which would encompass everything, is the world black or white or shades of gray?

Is there another way to phrase that that might be, for lack of a better word, more accessible or friendlier to the average group? Do you think we could brainstorm that?

What about, do you view – and this is a line from a science fiction book – is the universe a friendly place or an unfriendly place?

Do you feel that those questions would be taken in a non-defensive or non-manipulative way? Would the group accept that question without feeling like, what the hell does this have to do with anything?

*You might have to preface it with, well, just to begin with, **we're looking at general attitudes.***

Okay. We're just looking for general attitudes and would like to know –

There's not a right or a wrong answer. Reassure people of that.

Right. And that way, at least there's some lead-in; it gives them a context?

Yeah.

That helps. What about how the attorney physically presents and looks? What does a credible attorney look like?

If they're in court, they should be dressed for it, you know, professional. *Even if they're just meeting a client informally, sort of professional, you know, not jeans and t-shirt. Much as I hate to say it, probably very conformist in hairstyle and piercings and things. It's not right, but that is how people judge people.*

I've had some people in interviews say they would be distrustful of somebody in a $1,500 suit. What's your thought on that?

Possibly. It depends on what kind of attorney. I'm so used to dealing with public defenders. Trust me, they're not wearing –

Plenty of earrings and ponytails.

Definitely the ponytails. I'm not real good at judging whether something's a $1,500 suit, so I'm not sure I'd notice.

All right. How about the client? What would draw you towards or away from the client?

Again, **it's not fair, but appearance, because people make snap judgments.** *If they come in looking reasonably professional, they will probably be judged different than if they come in – it's Saturday; I'm in jeans and a t-shirt. I wouldn't wear it to work if there were going to be people in the office besides my usual work.* **They need to dress to fit the occasion.**

Let's talk about the money part of the case. When these cases happen, there are a couple parts. There's, was there negligence? Did the negligence cause harm? Okay, now we're talking about the harm itself. Things like lost wages and medical bills can be pretty easily shown on a spreadsheet, because there are bills for those and receipts. But there's another element called pain and suffering, disability, loss of enjoyment of life, what we call general damages for which there are no fixed standards. How would you go compensating for that part of harm?

Part of it is **I would want to know what their life was like before the accident** *or whatever. Somebody who enjoys computer gaming and isn't really physically active would be less impacted by that than a mountain climber. So it would depend on the context.*

Depends entirely on the context and the individual.

Yeah.

So the kinds of things that you'd like to know about would be...?

What was your life like before? What do you miss the most? *That would be a good one. And then what effects do you feel it's had on your life, stress-wise?*

Do you think you and the potential jurors view that different people experience the same injury but have different emotional responses to it?

Oh, yeah.

Do you think that it's fair to compensate a person more if their emotional response is genuinely greater than another?

Yeah. Genuinely is definitely the key word there. If they've incurred extra expenses because of it, I would say – if they're doing therapy that wouldn't necessarily be covered as part of the medical expense, although that happens less often now. Maybe something like that would make a difference. If they have to put their children in therapy because of it. **Because something like that doesn't just affect the individual, it affects their whole circle.**

Would you want to know exhaustively all the ways this has affected a person's life, or would you just want to know about one or two or three main things?

I'd probably say give me the top five.

If you were a plaintiff in an injury lawsuit, what kind of jury would you like to have in your case?

Somebody who's fair and somebody who will think it through and not just jump to a knee-jerk reaction.

How would you go about asking or finding that out?

That's a good question. **Ask them if they or somebody close to them has been under a similar circumstance,** *because that's more likely to cause a knee-jerk reaction.*

Is there a type of juror that you would not want to be on your case?

Somebody who thinks they're always right. Somebody – and I don't know how to put this in a politically correct way – who has the intelligence to look at it objectively. There is a correlation with IQ and open-mindedness. At least according to some of what I've read.

What about empathy and the ability to put yourself in the other person's shoes?

I think that's important.

How do we go about identifying someone who may be more empathetic – not sympathetic, but empathetic for another person?

Again, asking if they've been in similar situations because they're more likely to at least understand it which would lead to more empathy. Some people are naturally empathetic. That's a little harder to tease out without spending time with them. I'm not sure what kind of question you'd ask to obtain that.

Would it be helpful to know how they've dealt with other situations in the past?

Possibly.

You mentioned that there's a correlation with IQ and open-mindedness. Is that the work of Daniel Goleman, or is there somebody else that you can think of on that?

I don't remember where I read it. I probably came across it as a link in a news article and then followed it out of curiosity. You know, chasing rabbit trails down the Internet. I do that a lot.

If you were on a jury, would you be tempted to look at the web pages of the lawyers?

Of the actual attorneys? Probably.

Are there any kinds of things that would be of importance to you on those web pages?

Maybe years of experience. It's funny that this is coming up because what I'm doing right now at work is, I help people find senior housing. Specifically, we help them find dementia care and assisted living. And we are ramping up a Q and A section on our website so people can ask care-giving questions, legal questions. Right now, I am recruiting attorneys for that website, so I've been looking at a lot of attorney websites.

So you've had a sense of some are better than others in your mind?

Yeah.

Tell me what doesn't work.

Well, people that don't answer my emails. Probably, because I'm just going through emails these days. I'm not talking to anybody. It's a little different situation, because you want somebody to be nice to a client who's asking questions on your website. If the email comes back as condescending and rude, I probably won't follow up that closely.

How about first impressions when you click onto the page? Are you looking for pictures or experience or –

The feel of a good website. Because I work in SEO, so I do a lot of website analysis – Search Engine Optimization. How do you rank according to Google and how do you improve that? Part of it is looking at how the website looks. Part of it's looking at their domain authority, which is a rough idea of how Google ranks them. If you've got a domain authority of one versus 70 – big difference. I think Google and some of the government websites are the only ones that are at 100, to give you a comparison. It's all general impressions of what their area of expertise is. We want somebody who's strong in elder law, probate, estate, that sort of thing.

Do you think you can get a sense of credibility of the lawyer by looking at a website?

Possibly. A lot of them list all of their credentials, their memberships of this organization, this other part of the Bar Association, that sort of thing. Knowing a little bit about the legal field, I can. Whether the average person who has not had contact with it other than through episodes of Law & Order, maybe, maybe not.

Every person I meet walks in and I think to myself, this is going to be an interesting interview, comes up with unique and valuable ideas. Every person has given me something valuable. To recap, do you think a question about open-mindedness would encompass the issues of bias and prejudice? In other words, if I use the words bias and prejudice, am I more likely to cause people to become defensive?

They're loaded words. I suppose even open-mindedness is to an extent, but I don't think it is to the extent, especially of the word prejudice.

Sure. Because who's going to admit to being close-minded, right? What about the word fair?

I don't think that has as much of a negative connotation because everybody likes to think they're fair. That's a neutral to positive word.

It's my belief that because of the limited time we're given in jury selection, that there's not much I can learn about the group or the individuals, unless I focus on only a couple of them. I wonder if it may not matter. In other words, with the exception of one or two individuals who may be there to do wrong or harm to my case because of a personal agenda, for the most part, the jury I get will be as fair as I could ask.

Kind of averages out.

I wonder that it may be all I really need to do is stand up and say, if there's anyone here who thinks they're not the right kind of juror for this case, please let me know. Otherwise, I accept the panel. It saves everybody time and from what I've understood, time being so important to most jurors, they would be appreciative of that.

Mm-hmm. Get a more positive reaction to you personally and are more likely to pay attention to you.

Because I'm not wasting their time.

Especially if the other side was incredibly annoying with all the questions.

Which they would be in most cases.

Absolutely. That makes total sense to me.

In other words, my goal being to just identify the very worst jurors, those who may be potentially close-minded from the very get-go and cannot ever be open-minded.

I would probably, if you're standing in front of everybody, take a look at everybody's facial expressions, especially what they call the micro expressions. Because anybody who's really angry, you probably don't want them in the jury.

Right. Hostile. Talking about the micro expressions, do you think having somebody who's skilled in reading facial language or body language would be helpful in that setting or do you think that's too soft of a science, given the constraints and undertones that are happening?

It's a pretty soft science. I wouldn't use it as the sole determiner, but it would be a piece of the puzzle.

Any other profiles you can think of or things that I haven't brought up that would be helpful for me to think about or know in this context?

Maybe somehow to put people at ease. Most people find the whole legal system pretty intense. And totally out of their norm. Personally, I think it's fascinating. I used to, when I was a student, sneak in the back of the courtroom and listen to cases. That was more of a curiosity thing.

Do you think people in the social sciences, psychologists, students of psychology or sociology, would tend to be more open-minded than other professions?

Possibly. Just because they're used to looking at multiple possibilities for behavior.

Ranges of human behavior.

Yeah. But on the other hand, they might be more fair too, because they're looking at options as opposed to, like you said, an engineer. This is very – there's no other way.

When we talk about the significance of each case, some cases may be viewed as more significant than others because of the issues. Maybe they're of first impression or maybe because the amount in controversy is so great. What can I do in small cases to have the jury understand that it's significant to this person here?

Point out that it's a person, not just a number. *They're not just a face over there. They're a human with children or whatever, career.*

What's your sense of being able to tell if the lawyer is truly engaged and involved in the relationship with the client? In other words, the notion that caring is contagious. True caring. Do you think that comes through?

*I think so. Again, **it really does come down to all the non-verbal stuff.** As a die-hard introvert, I tend to notice that probably more than somebody who's more extroverted and takes things at face value.*

You think that extroverts tend to take things at face value and introverts tend to what?

I think introverts tend to be much more hyper-aware of people's moods, because as everything's been saying lately, interaction tends to suck energy from an introvert, so they're very hyper-aware of, how am I going to relate to this person. Whereas extroverts are like, oh, hi, what's up?

Well, one more question, and that is, who is someone you admire and why?

Lots of people.

What sort of traits do they have that –

Open-mindedness.

Anybody in particular that you can think of? Living or dead; famous or not?

George Takei. Partially because he stands up for what he believes in.

Has a great Facebook page, right?

He keeps me amused. He does it with a sense of humor, even when people are nasty to him in comments, he comes back very polite and thoughtful.

Do you think that question I just asked would be an appropriate question in a *voir dire* setting?

I don't see why not. It would probably be good, because it would kind of break the ice.

Sure. Get people thinking a little bit?

Get people thinking, get people to feel a little more comfortable with the people around them. Because if they end up on something that's got a lot of deliberation, it kind of helps if you're not hating the person next to you.

Right. Well, that's great. Thank you.

24

DIGGING

Caucasian male, age 60, married, 8 children, 2 grandchildren, Land Acquisition, Real Estate and Records/City Government, B.A. English, Teaching Certificate

It's one thing to ask someone how they feel about something, but to continue digging, trying to find out why they feel the way they do and if they would ever change their mind or something, I'm not so sure that's comfortable for me.

The judge will then say, each side has approximately 30 minutes to an hour to conduct the jury selection process, and the plaintiff's side will go first. You went through that?

Yes.

Ladies and gentlemen, please give your attention to the lawyer for the plaintiff who's going to conduct jury selection. At that point, what are you feeling and thinking?

I don't know if it's common, but I think most people would prefer not to have to serve. I'm just thinking, geez, I hope I don't get called.

Can you explain why you were feeling that way?

*It's a lot of time you spend on the jury. And **from past experience, I know it's pretty monotonous, listening to the same testimony over and over again.***

You value your time?

Yeah.

How do you feel about jury service as a civic duty or a civic responsibility?

I totally believe in it. I'm just telling you my honest feelings are I wish I wasn't there being grilled.

Did you feel like you were being grilled?

For the jury selection you do. After that, you're kind of on your own.

What happened that led you to feel being grilled? Were there any specific questions or the manner that they were being asked that made you feel that way?

*I can't remember the questions at this point, but **anything that shows you might be prejudiced or have unsubstantiated views in front of a group of other people. It's kind of embarrassing, you know? To be put on the hot spot.***

With that being said, how do you feel about the necessity of that? On the scale of those questions being important or needed or not, how do you feel about that?

Well, I know why they're doing it, and I understand. ***I'm not sure that honesty is always forthcoming because you are in front of a group of people,*** *whereas you might be more honest if it were a smaller group or just you and the attorney. And I know that's not how it works.*

Do you think it's okay for lawyers to ask about things like bias or prejudice or closed-mindedness on issues?

I think that's the only way they're going to be able to guess how you might perform in a jury.

For your own self, and maybe for the group with you, do you have a sense you're getting at least reasonably honest answers?

For the most part, I think so. I know there are people that don't tell the truth. I don't know how you'd be able to weed them out.

Are there any ways you would be most comfortable being asked about things like open- or closed-mindedness? Or maybe the better way – to flip it over and say, what would not work for you? That would turn you off that way?

I'm just wondering if written questions might be more revealing.

Explain to me a little bit more about that.

The same questions that are asked verbally might be asked on a written questionnaire and you might be able to say what you think without the fear of ridicule from your peers.

What is it about answering questions about things like personal opinions about these kinds of issues that you think would submit somebody to ridicule?

Just lack of knowledge in an area might show your ignorance.

If you were being asked about your personal beliefs, would that be a different thing?

I kind of think it is a little bit.

So if the approach here is to learn about the personal beliefs and attitudes of each individual juror, how would you think it's best to ask those kinds of questions?

Personally. Not in a group.

Right. Okay. But given that we're in the group –

Without making it too difficult, maybe a numbered system, 1 to 10, how do you feel about this? Strongly or less strongly.

Would you ask people to raise their hands or – I like what you've said about the ranges. That resonates with me. Tell me a more what you're thinking about.

I'd have to have more of a specific question like, how do you feel about drinking and driving? Or something like that. And are you strongly against or there might be occasions where it's permissible if you're not going very far. I'm just trying to guess.

Right. Do you feel more strongly one way or another in that?

Yeah.

Okay. Do you think then it's permissible to follow up and say, if somebody says, I feel pretty strongly about that, to ask them to talk about it? Or should that just be left alone?

Well, once again, you're trying to establish someone's state of mind, and I guess a follow-up is totally understandable.

What if you're just being asked to raise your hand if you felt a certain way?

I think some of my questioning when I was on the jury pool that occurred. And that's not so hard.

Did you feel that the lawyers did or said anything that worked particularly well?

That's hard to say. I know I probably did at the time, but it's been over ten years at least.

A long time.

Humor is always helpful. And keeping the questions simple is always helpful.

When the attorney stands up and you know that's an attorney for the plaintiff, what are your thoughts about the attorney and attorneys in general that do the kind of work that's going on in the courtroom then? How do you feel about lawyers that are doing those kinds of cases?

I never experienced it except on TV. So the reality is a lot different. They seem genuine and friendly for the most part, and I didn't have any negative feelings.

Do you have any feelings, strongly one way or another, about the civil justice system that allows people to seek a money compensation for injuries caused by negligence?

I don't know how else you could compensate someone for an injury aside from money or repair, medical assistance.

Do you feel strongly one way or another that there's a litigation crisis or that there are too many frivolous lawsuits?

I'm not sure I believe that's the case. I don't really see that. The news plays up a lot of these things and makes the frivolous stuff come to the top, but I don't think that's the way the system generally works.

Is there anything that you might want to have the attorney say or do at the outset to make you feel more comfortable?

I have no idea.

Would you be interested in knowing anything about the lawyer before you're being asked to share a little bit about yourself?

It's human nature to wonder where they came from and – I may have been naïve. I didn't realize that the first person doing the questioning was for the plaintiff. Maybe they, at the time, told me. I don't remember. But would I need to know anything about the attorneys? I'm not so sure it's relevant, as long as they're doing their jobs.

What, to you, would be an example of something that would feel manipulative by the attorney in that setting?

Usually I think that happens when they continue to dig down on different questions. Multiple deep questions, trying to get you to identify where in your life or whatever it is makes you feel a certain way. It's one thing to ask someone how they feel about something, but to continue digging, trying to find out why they feel the way they do and if they would ever change their mind or something, *I'm not so sure that's comfortable for me.*

How has the education you have and the career you have, if at all, what has it done for your world view when you go into a courtroom in this setting as a potential juror?

I'm sure it's colored a lot, because – well, I work with governmental officials and even law enforcement at times. I see them as a positive force. I really don't have any negative dealings with the legal profession.

Do you think lawyers are able to tell when people are being truthful with them?

You'd imagine if they've had enough experience, they've picked up on certain keys. I think that's where people generally assume, and I would tend to think that myself.

It's important for a lawyer to establish a level of credibility and trust with you. How do you think a lawyer can best show the lawyer's human and very reputable and credible?

I'm just thinking, **a lot of it is appearances, being well-presented, clean. We all respond to outward appearances on the first part. Then just being well spoken, using proper language rather than slang. And maybe some witty humor along with it helps also breaking the ice.**

Are there any particular things that stand out that would lead you to think a lawyer was not very credible?

Being disorganized, late, ruffled. Not remembering what the answers were to questions. Just being a bumbling person.

Would there be any other physical traits that you would be affected by?

Well, dressing poorly. **Not looking at the jurors.** *Any of the classic – I can't think of anything in particular.*

If I say the words "sleazy lawyer," what comes to mind, and do you think they exist?

I'm sure they do. I've seen a few of them go in and out of the courthouse, and they try to fit that description of being snarkily dressed and speaking more in a vernacular.

Do you think a lawyer can be folksy and down-home and still be professional and credible?

Sure.

So that's not what you were talking about when you said the vernacular?

No. Just slang and poor language. Curse words, that kind of stuff.

Right. So knowing it's a civil case, that there's going to be a play for a determination of a money damage award at the end – and we have two kinds of damages – special damages, which are like wages and medical bills that are easily determined, relatively – and general damages, which are pain, suffering, loss of enjoyment of life and disability that we can't have a fixed standard for – how do you think about compensating or awarding money damages?

You would hope that the experts will have a scale, but I suppose there isn't one. But whatever would make someone as close to whole as possible would make sense to me.

Since you're one of the decision makers, what are you looking for to help you make that decision?

The case I was on, we really didn't have any guidance as to what anything was worth. It was just a final number. It would have been helpful to see what generally is awarded for different types of things. I don't know if that's possible. We also weren't able to ask questions as many jurors are able to do now.

If it was the case that there are no fixed standards or guidelines that can be given to you as a juror, what sort of things do you think you'd want to know or think about when you're determining what would make a person whole economically, beyond just recovering out-of-pockets?

I would tend to look at percentages of time and that kind of thing, spent doing what normally they would do, and what percent of time or cost was taken away from them by not being able to continue doing or having whatever it was they were deprived of. So percentages probably.

Right. So you're looking at a percentage, like a metric of some kind, some comparison?

Yeah. Like how many hours a day did you kayak and now that you can't do that, what percentage of your life is missing – is that missing from?

So then you can say, well, this is a fixed amount of time and then you would put some money to that, right? Or something like that?

Some intrinsic value. Money, level of enjoyment, that kind of thing.

Who would you want to hear from to help you learn about those facts?

Well, from the plaintiff. I mean, how are you going to get it from the defendant?

Would you feel that testimony from friends and co-workers would be more credible than from the plaintiff?

I think both are important. Ultimately, it's the person who's been injured that knows best.

Do you describe yourself as generally more trusting than untrusting?

Probably more trusting.

How about empathetic? Do you tend to be more empathetic or more, let's say, linear?

Skeptical.

Sure. Do you consider yourself a very empathetic person, or where on the scale do you fit?

I'm probably more empathetic, probably like a six or seven.

When you make decisions, are you more empathetic or are you using more reason and logic?

When I have to make a decision, I hopefully have been using reason and logic.

When you make decisions, do you use both your emotion and your reason?

Yeah, that would be what I would hope.

Do you feel you use one more than any other?

I would think in the final course of things it would be logic.

Do you think the rest of the people in that room with you are more like you or less like you in that way?

I originally thought they were more like me, but I was pretty surprised that they're less like me.

How did you find that out?

In the deliberations.

Can you share with me what the differences were?

At least in my instance, people were not really interested in awarding anything. They had no empathy.

Do you think your view was colored by virtue of the fact that you know a lawyer who does that kind of work?

*Probably a little bit, but not really. **I guess the question would be more, do you believe that seeking compensation for an injury is something that we should do?** And I do think that's right.*

In the case you sat on, there were many jurors that felt otherwise?

Yeah.

Do you think in the *voir dire* in that case the attorney or the attorneys didn't get to the heart of the matter with those people?

That's a good question. I think many of them presented themselves differently.

Do you think there's anything that could have been done to get them to present more authentically?

I'm sure there probably is. I'm not an expert, so I'm not really sure where – if you had drilled down more and asked what their personal beliefs are about our litigious society or – some people just don't like to see anyone awarded anything.

Right. Do you think those people were reacting to the system, to the lawyer, or to the person who was claiming injury or some part of all three?

I think they were reacting more to the person claiming injury and to the system, not necessarily the lawyer. I don't know if this matters or not, but we weren't given all the information, that this had been a drunk driving accident and the guy had pled guilty on it. So that was not allowed. And to me, that was huge.

How do you feel knowing that kind of a fact is typically excluded in a case to avoid inflaming jurors?

It seems to defeat the whole purpose of the litigation.

How's that?

Well, if someone has caused an accident and has been negligent causing it, they should be responsible for the reduced pleasure in life the other person experiences beyond just fixing the vehicle or fixing the medical injury.

Right. So the jury in the case you sat on was okay with awarding things like medical bills and wage losses, but not comfortable with awarding pain and suffering?

Not at all. They didn't see it all.

Do you think jurors like yourself think about insurance during the jury selection process?

We're told not to. But as soon as we got into the deliberations, it came up immediately.

How was it dealt with?

It had an effect on how much they were willing to award. I may have even mentioned that we weren't supposed to consider insurance. And people just went right around it.

Do you think they were concerned about causing financial harm to the defendant?

You know, it may have been even more than that, just setting a precedent or giving in to the system.

How so?

By awarding anything to someone who goes through the system essentially proves that someone can complain and get what they want.

I see. And that sets a precedent and then –

And they continue to have these high awards and that kind of thing.

Do you think in that case the jury was reacting to anything else?

It was a multitude of things.

Sure. Other than what we've talked about?

I don't think they had any other considerations.

As a potential juror, sitting there in the jury selection process, are you thinking about the significance of the case as being important or of any consequence to you?

I think if something is highly advertised or – I think that does have an effect.

Okay. If the lawyer said at some point in the jury selection process that this was a case where the injuries to the person were catastrophic, what's going through your head at that point?

How bad is it, and what's it going to be worth to this person?

You've worked for over 25 years in local and municipal government, do you feel that the views and attitudes about juries and this system we're talking about are similar to yours or that your views are more unique or more liberal than the general type of person you work with?

I'm probably more liberal.

So you think more of the people you work with would be more conservative when it came to things like money awards?

Slightly.

If you were the plaintiff, the person who brought the case, what kind of a juror would you like to have?

Someone who's open-minded and empathetic. Someone who believes in the system and justice.

Do you think jury selection is not very helpful, given the way it's done with the amount of time the lawyers are reduced to? Do you think it makes a difference at all in getting a fair jury?

I don't really have a good way of comparing that. Our system's set up to be a trial by peers; I'm not so sure that's the greatest way. Maybe professional jurors might have a better understanding than lay people.

They might have a better understanding of what?

Of what they're hearing if they're being given evidence, than lay people.

Do you think you and your fellow potential jurors will possess enough intelligence to arrive at a reasonable and just outcome?

Well, that's the question. I'm not so sure that we are.

When you were in deliberations, and it was clear that your opinion was in the minority, how vocal were you and did it move the needle?

I wasn't that vocal. And it may have slowed things down a little bit and had people reconsider some of their positions, but I think ultimately, the majority just does what they want.

Is there anything that's come up that I haven't asked about that might be helpful for me to know or think about?

No. It's not really my field.

Is there anything you can think of that a lawyer who does this kind of work ought to be mindful of to help make the process better for the system and for you?

It almost seems like a moderator or someone in the jury, a professional who could keep the group on track, would be helpful. But I don't know that our system's set up that way.

In the constraints of the system, can you think of anything a lawyer could do that would make this process better for everyone? I know you've talked about keeping it shorter and not asking questions over and over again.

Voir dire – or you mean the actual trial itself?

In the jury selection, but also in the trial if you want to talk about that.

The length of it, of course, it's stress on a lot of people because they're not getting paid. I don't know if recordings of the actual trial are permissible to cut back to what's been said already, to keep things clear.

Right. Anything else?

Not really.

Thank you.

25

IS THERE SOMETHING WE SHOULD KNOW?

Caucasian female, age 62, married, two children, four grandchildren, Licensed Mental Health Counselor/ CPG, Masters Counseling, Masters Human Resource Management

Just put it out there. Is there something you think we should know about you that would interfere with your ability to be open-minded about this case?

The judge will say, ladies and gentlemen, please give your attention to the lawyer for the plaintiff who's going to conduct jury selection. At that moment, what are you thinking and feeling?

I'm thinking, I wonder what question they're going to ask of me and what my response will be.

Do you have a sense of what questions may be asked of you?

I'm guessing they might ask if I've ever been awarded compensation for a civil case.

Sure. Similar situations.

Or if somebody in my family has ever been injured and awarded compensation, or anybody else I might know.

As you look at the lawyer and the lawyer's client, what are you thinking and feeling about them?

It would depend. I'm not sure. I'm thinking that I'm probably going to overcompensate to try and give this person – that he or she is innocent until proven guilty. I probably will overcompensate in that way, because I think I might have a tendency to think that most of the times when you convict people they're correct. Or that when they come to trial the prosecutors know what they're doing.

We're talking about – those are criminal cases, and we're talking about civil cases – where a person is suing because they've been hurt – for money, rather than losing their liberty. Do you have any strong feelings about the civil justice system and the fact that people can sue for compensation?

What else could we do? If a wrong's been done to us, what else do we have to remedy that with?

Have you had any personal experiences where you've been –

I have.

Can you share?

I was in a car accident, and a person ran a stop sign; totaled our truck. I was the driver and injured my arm, and I did receive compensation for that.

Was that an out-of-court settlement?

Yes. It was filed but it didn't go any further than that. It was settled during the deposition process.

Was that a satisfying resolution for you?

It was. I was kind of shocked. I didn't expect to get any kind of monetary value. I'd never been through anything like that. But as soon as the insurance company started getting involved and it started getting muddled and murky – and I started to not trust my own insurance company – I went for a consult with an attorney. He ended up taking my case and did get me a sizable amount. Sizable for me, at that time.

Good. You felt you were made whole? You were compensated for your injuries to the extent that you felt it was a fair and just amount to restore you, to the extent you could be, to pre-accident status.

Yes. It paid for my medical bills and that, too.

Safe to say you had a good rapport with your lawyer?

Yes.

When somebody uses the words "sleazy lawyer," what do you think of?

The one that will keep things going to get monetary benefits for himself. An ambulance chaser.

Given what you've said, I'm going to leap that your attorney, in your mind, was not a sleazy lawyer.

No.

What made that lawyer not a sleazy lawyer?

He didn't call us a lot. His paralegal did a lot of emails and calling. They kept us apprised of everything. I felt that he was telling me the truth. If I asked for anything, he would give us an answer; we would get a communication right away.

Professional?

Yes. Very. I think so.

How did you hear about your lawyer?

I can't even remember.

That's fine. As you're looking at the plaintiff who's in that situation where the case didn't settle and they're now in court, how do you feel about what they must be going through?

I'm thinking they're probably nervous. I'm hopeful that they have insurance. I have some empathy for them; that I hope something like that never happens to me because sometimes you can't get insurance payment unless you do a suit against the individual first, right?

Given that sense of empathy and the fact you've been through something similar, how would that affect your ability to be fair to both sides?

I would probably end up overcompensating. I honestly probably would. How do you really – what is fair? Just because the jury says it's fair doesn't really mean to the people that are being compensated or not that it's fair.

To one side or the other, right?

Uh-huh.

We're looking for jurors that can be, first and foremost, open-minded, or at least not closed-minded. Or if they have biases, as we all do, are willing to at least recognize that when they're considering. As you said, that's kind of like overcompensation. How do you think the attorney should go about asking you and your fellow jurors whether they have anything that might make them more closed-minded than would be beneficial or helpful to the process?

Just to overtly ask that. Just put it out there. Is there something you think we should know about you that would interfere with your ability to be open-minded about this case?

Do you believe that question is one most people would be able to hear and take without feeling their privacy was being infringed on or that would make them too uncomfortable?

I think so. Because there's just the people there.

That being said, do you think, for yourself and also for your fellow potential jurors, that they would answer truthfully?

I would say probably. I think about 75 - 80% would. I think people that really want to get out of the jury process are not going to answer that truthfully. So if they really don't want to be there, they probably shouldn't be there.

Is there anything in your professional background, education, or experience that colors your ability to be a juror? Or that helps you; that would make you a good juror in a case?

I think I'm a good listener. I'm pretty open-minded, especially about different cultures and races, and it's probably because I was in the Navy for ten years. Everybody was there and it was really eye-opening that we're all the same. And I do believe that. I grew up in an environment that was all Caucasian. But I think I have pretty much gone beyond that. I really do think that we are all the same. We're all struggling in the same way.

I was thinking because of your counseling background that you may have a sense that you understand people are very different and that everybody's situation is unique. That's what I'm getting at. Does that define you or your –

No, not so much. No.

I asked you that question about how might the attorney elicit bias or closed-minded or open-minded tendencies in a way that might be comfortable. What would be an inappropriate or uncomfortable way to ask that question? In other words, I want to avoid doing that, so it's often good to know how to do something, but it's often good to know how not to do something.

How not to do it. I think it would make people really uncomfortable to be really, really specific and to ask them to share a specific example in their lives.

That might be intrusive?

Yeah.

Do you believe that you and your juror group would respond well if the lawyer shared something about his or her own closed-mindedness on some issue before asking?

Yes. I do.

Would that feel like a manipulation to you in any way? How could that be done so that it was well-handled?

By prefacing it with, I'm going to tell you this about myself so you can understand what I'm trying to get at with you. This is my personal story about my closed-mindedness and I'm wondering if this triggers anything about yours.

Does it have to relate specifically to the kind of case?

I think it would probably be better if it didn't relate. To me, it would be less manipulative.

In your experience during the jury selection process or at any time, did you feel you were being manipulated by one of the attorneys or another?

Never.

Good. Is there anything you'd like to know personally about the lawyers and their clients as you're sitting there in the jury selection process?

There's probably things I don't want to know.

Is there anything you'd like to know about that person and also about the client?

Probably lots. There probably is, but I don't know if I have a right to know that and if I ever will know that, but I'm probably very, very curious about many things. How did we get this far along? Why aren't they settling? And then wondering if the person has a family, where they came from.

How about the lawyer? Is there anything you'd like to know about the lawyer as a person?

Maybe about their record, and I don't even think that's important to me. No. Not so much about the lawyer. I'm just more inquisitive about the person.

If a lawyer encounters somebody who's obviously closed-minded, who may or may not be open and honest about it, but it's clear to the lawyer and everyone else that there's some resistance, how do you think the lawyer should best handle that interaction without losing trust with the rest of the group?

Probably to do nothing. To just have that be one of the ones you just don't choose. I don't think I would address it there. It would be obvious to most people there that this person really doesn't belong on the jury. So I don't think I would address it in front of everybody or push it or anything like that.

Do you have a sense that there are frivolous lawsuits in this country? Or too many? Some people think there's a litigation crisis.

I know that.

What do you think about that?

I don't know enough about the numbers. And having, like I said, having my own experience, I don't think that it's necessarily frivolous. I think it's a lack of understanding on everybody's parts. **If you're injured or wronged, you have this right, and it is our right, to get something for our damages.**

Do you believe the civil justice system both compensates and can deter future similar wrongful conduct?

I'm not sure it deters. You mean, just by having the case that it's going to stop somebody from doing another wrong?

That it may teach a wrong-doer to not do that?

Oh, I don't think so. Not necessarily. As a general rule, I don't think so. But that's not going happen anyway.

Unless maybe some business is being fined a tremendous amount –

Yes. In something like that, maybe in a business, but individual –

Individual behavior?

No.

Having caused an accident and then being sued wouldn't make you less likely to cause one in the future?

It might me, but most people, I don't think so. I really don't believe that.

What do you think a lawyer in jury selection can do to establish a human connection with you and create trust?

Through their non-verbal behavior. Looking at everybody in the eye and trying to make everybody relaxed. Making sure they know what this trial is about, how long it might take, this is the jury selection, and this is how we do it. I'm going to ask you questions, and so is the other party, and we want you to answer truthfully. To really educate them.

Given that many people don't want to be there because their time is very important to them, or they can't be because they have children or jobs that make it very difficult, do you have a sense that lawyers should be very short - brief in their questions and take into account the time considerations?

No. For me, the importance of the case overrides that.

If there are say, 40 or 60 jurors in the room, and a very limited amount of time for the lawyer to get to know everybody, many people will not have an opportunity to participate. If that were you, because of where you were seated or some other, how would you feel?

If I didn't want to be selected, I'd probably feel relieved and think I'm going to sit in the last row from now on. If I felt it was my duty and I believe in the system, I would probably feel disappointed that I didn't get questioned and didn't get an opportunity. But it's not something I would dwell on. That's just part of the – what happens.

We talked about establishing a human connection. Similar to that is this issue of trust and credibility. You talked about non-verbal behavior. What can a lawyer do non-verbally to show that person is trustworthy?

Be professional, make good eye contact, listen to the potential juror and clarify if there's something they don't understand and you'll let the juror know you're hearing them. Ask the potential juror if they have any questions.

When eye contact is made, how can the lawyer be certain to do it in a way that is relaxed and doesn't make the juror nervous?

Probably from a distance, not to get right in their face or in their personal space.

You were in the military for ten years. Did that experience lead you to be more of a rules-based person than you were before that?

Good question. I've never thought about that. Because I came from a really strict family. I think it probably did.

When you make decisions, do you tend to make them more on the emotional side or more on the rational, linear side?

Oh, God, I just got asked this the other day. Emotional. Right or wrong, that's what I probably do.

Right. But that's a leaning; do you still use the rational?

Oh, definitely.

Jumping back to the experience when you were a juror, what was the jury deliberation experience like for you?

It was like – I was just in awe. Like I say, I had never done it before, and I was amazed that we came from listening to everything, going into there, and suddenly we had a lead juror and he said, well, let's vote. And I was like, oh my God.

Already?

That's right. It's like, we can't do this. It was about half and half. And I was absolutely amazed.

It was a disparate –

It was.

Was the group respectful to one another?

Yes. Yes. Very much so.

Why do you think the group got along so well and was respectful? Were there any currents that ran through everybody?

I think it was because it had to do with a developmentally disabled man being punched by a gang member. That made all of us bring in some TLC. The whole thing was kind of about that.

Maybe, just throwing a word out there, the humanity? There was some humanity there?

That's what it was.

And the group, even those who were on different sides, were still respectful of the other?

Yes. Yes, they were.

How long was the trial?

It lasted three days.

You said there was a guilty finding?

There was.

And everybody felt okay with that?

I think so, yes.

Prior to the Sexual Assault Center, where had you worked or what were you doing?

I was a certified professional guardian. Still am. And a GAL.

You know lawyers and the legal system.

I do, yes.

How do you feel about this question of having to make a money damages decision?

I think it's difficult.

You've been through it, so you know the difference between special damages, which are like wages and medical bills, and general damages, which is pain and suffering and loss of enjoyment of life, where we don't have a way to – a fixed standard.

Yeah. You just kind of pick something out and they kind of go for it. Although I understand they kind of have a standard. If you had a broken arm, you might get this.

In Labor and Industries workers' comp they have it, a standard. But in these kinds of cases, any juror can come up with any amount. I'm wondering what things might you want to know to help you arrive at a number?

I would want to know the age of the person that was injured. Will they be able to work again? What kind of medical bills they had, what kind of pain and suffering they had. Do they have a family and what was their lifestyle, what was the income?

Do you make room for the notion that two different people with the same injury might experience it very differently in an emotional sense?

Yes.

If one person was more stoic and wasn't affected as much, and another person was, would you award more because it affected that person more than the other person in the same instance?

I would like to think not. I would try and keep that out of it.

So no matter how the person responds – let's say a person is more fragile or tender emotionally than another, and they suffer an injury that causes them to have a greater negative reaction to it – do you think their damages and harms are greater than the other?

I think they might show it, but I don't know that's necessarily a fact. That might be what I could see, but there might be other things going on with the other person who's stoic that I just can't see.

How might you go about thinking about compensating each person differently or the same? What would you be looking to do there? If two people are in an automobile accident; one is strong physically; one is weak physically and emotionally and they have a cascading of emotional events because they're previously fragile.

Previously? Before the accident as well?

Right.

Okay. So that makes a difference. I would consider that.

If the judge says, they may be compensated for pain and suffering, do you believe their pain and suffering may be greater than somebody who was in the identical collision but was not showing it, or didn't experience it as much.

I think it's something we don't really know, especially if they were fragile before the accident, and if that could be proven to us. We had people telling us, gosh, he comes from this dysfunctional family and this happened, and blah blah blah, and then he's very fragile now, maybe he's a little bit more fragile.

Say somebody was badly in a depression and the accident caused them to relapse into a deeper depression. Would that be something you'd consider compensable?

Yes, but I would want to see the records, not just that they felt depressed, but they were seeing a therapist and a doctor and had antidepressants and whatever.

So you want to hear from the experts.

Yes.

Generally in these cases both sides present experts that tend to have conflicting points of view. How would you go about resolving that?

Oh, wow. That's just a hard one. That really is. I would look for fault with all of them.

Fault being?

Perhaps they're not telling the truth. And then sometimes just their presentation. I'm just not trusting this person. I would be looking for fault for everybody.

Keeping a keen eye to the whole process and trying to see what stacks up as the most believable and credible to you?

Yeah.

In criminal cases, as you know, the burden of proof is beyond a reasonable doubt. I think everybody knows that from TV. Civil cases have a different burden of proof, and it's called a preponderance of the evidence. What does that mean to you?

Not that – there can be some doubt, but greater than not being guilty, it points to that. They should be determined to be guilty or there should be some compensation. So there can be some doubt, but more that it's looking like they're guilty.

So Lady Justice wears a blindfold and holds scales. If the scales are tipped ever-so-slightly, 49% to 51%, is that a preponderance in your mind?

Wow. I think it is. I think it is. That to me means, yeah.

Do you have any personal feelings about professional negligence cases; cases against medical providers as opposed to automobile accident cases; where a doctor or a hospital is being sued for some accountability or claimed negligence? Do you feel that there is a different standard or that they –

There should be a different standard or that?

Well, how do you feel about cases in general against medical professionals?

That is more of a trigger point for me.

Why?

I want those people – they're in this profession. They've been trained to take care of lives, and by God, that'd better be what they're doing. That is the one thing that is infuriating to me is, when I read about those kinds of cases, I'm kind of amazed. Like the one that was the doctor telling people they had cancer and they didn't. It is very sad that we hear about the bad eggs instead of the good eggs. Those are the ones that I probably really, really take more seriously than somebody that was, like myself, just injured in a car accident.

Do you feel that doctors or lawyers or any credentialed professional ought to be held to an accountability standard for any negligence in the course of their professional duties?

Yes.

If I represented to you that doctors who are sued win approximately nine out of ten times, would you be surprised?

Yeah. Is that true?

Approximately.

Wow. It's really hard to sue them, huh?

They can be sued; it's hard to win.

But to win. Huh. Okay.

Do you think you'd want to know the amount of money in controversy that's been asked for by the plaintiff; would you want to know what that amount is during jury selection?

No. I don't know a reason to.

If later on you were told that the case was worth one amount of money that was much more than another amount of money, would you feel the case was more significant because of that? Or might you have a knee-jerk reaction away from that? In other words, that maybe they were asking for too much?

Without knowing about it, all about the case? That they just told me the amount?

Right. This is how much they were going to be asking for during the trial.

I probably would. If there was an exorbitant amount, I'd be like, wow.

What's an exorbitant amount?

In the millions.

Is there anything that has come up that you think would be helpful for me?

About serving on a jury?

Serving on a jury, or your thoughts or experiences.

Maybe what the judge did during the jury process, during the jury selection. What kind of an influence would a judge have?

They do have some influence.

I think they do.

Often, it comes down to the lawyer trying to get a juror excused because of good cause. In other words, a juror is clearly exhibiting some bias and the lawyer will appeal to the judge to remove that juror.

For the judge to remove instead of it be one of –

It can be one of the peremptory challenges. Sometimes the judges won't do it, and then the lawyer and the judge get into a dynamic. The juror is involved as well, so there can be some tension.

Okay. What I do remember is the judge made everybody feel at ease. He was very nice and handled us like, thank you so much for coming and we really need you to be here, telling us how important it was. He was appealing to us.

It sounded like you had a good experience all the way around from the judge, the lawyers, your group, the length of time of service. Was your group diverse and representative of the community?

Yes. It was. We had three people on the jury that were black.

Anything else that would be helpful for me to know as a lawyer doing jury selection, primarily with two goals: getting people to share if they're closed-minded and can't be fair; and maybe more important, being credible and being perceived as credible.

Are you allowed to ask them to put anything in writing? If they're uncomfortable sharing it in front of everybody?

We can ask judges to give written questionnaires before cases, but generally all of this interaction is in a large group and it's brought up verbally, not privately.

Okay. And do you ask a blanket statement of everybody? Does anyone have any –

We can do that, or we can speak individually to any juror. You can talk to anybody. You can try and get people talking; you can get them to raise their hands. There's no one way to do it.

Do you have some information about them? It seems like I remember they had some information –

This is about it, in the written questionnaire.

That's it? Okay. But that's a lot. I think it is.

It can be, with the exception that we don't want to make decisions just based on the data, because we could be wrong.

Yes. Yes.

Just because a person works for an insurance company doesn't necessarily mean they'll be unfavorably disposed toward our case, but a good chance. Because a person is an engineer, we may have more difficulties. What about your own demographic, do you think, is important?

That I'm a therapist, that I'm a counselor. I think people will come up with ideas about how I might go and it would give you some idea of what questions to ask me.

I feel very comfortable because I understand the nomenclature and tend to think that people in the social sciences are probably more open-minded towards behavior, and probably willing to acknowledge their own biases and prejudices.

Yes. But I think that gives you a lot to go on, a lot to start asking questions off of.

Right. And as you said, what you might tend to do is err on the side of caution.

Yeah.

Thank you.

26

SHARE

Caucasian female, age 34, married, one child, Stay-at-Home Mom/Student, B.A. Graphic Design/Art History

I definitely think that when people tell you more about themselves, you are, whether you realize it or not, more willing to open up and share about yourself.

Ladies and gentlemen, please give your attention to the lawyer for the plaintiff who's going to conduct jury selection. What's going through your mind in that moment?

Probably not a whole lot, other than wondering how interesting this is going to be and are they going to pick me or not.

Are you looking forward to the experience?

Probably so, just as a novel experience.

Many people would rather be somewhere else? How do you feel on that, wanting to be there or wanting or needing to be somewhere else?

Scale of 1 to 10, probably closer to 7 as far as wanting to be there.

People who have children, in particular, claim hardship because they can't get away. Would that be something you'd be able to handle?

It would be a hardship, because I am a stay-at-home mom. However, my husband does have a fairly flexible schedule, so unless the case went on for several weeks, you know. If it were a few days, it wouldn't be an issue.

Somewhere between a few days and couple weeks you'd probably be interested and able to do it?

Sure.

Thank you for that, because many people would rather not do it at all. Many of them talk about their time as a value. So you're curious to know what sort of things are going to happen.

Yes.

What do you think is going to happen? What do you think you might be asked?

You know, I don't know. I can imagine a whole range of questions may, in some random way, pertain to the case. Some of the questions on the questionnaire are ones that I would expect to be asked, you know, have I been involved in a lawsuit. Other than that, I have no idea what they may ask.

Jury selection is about determining if jurors are potentially biased or prejudiced in a way that would cause them to not be fair to one side or the other. The lawyer's job is to ask questions that find out about you. How would a lawyer best ask if you were open-minded or less open-minded in a case like this?

I don't know how they would ask me that.

How would you feel comfortable being asked about your potential biases or prejudices?

I would be very open. I don't have any secrets. I feel that I'm a pretty fair and just person, so I don't think I have anything that would make me not that way. I would certainly answer to the best of my ability and wouldn't have a problem with whatever questions they asked.

How about in the manner they might ask them? Do you think there's a way that would make you feel more comfortable?

*I think as long as they were polite and genuine – or seem genuine. I think, definitely, lawyers have a bad reputation, and may come off as abrupt or rude, especially from all the TV dramas. **I think if they were just polite and treated me with some form of respect that that would make me very willing to answer whatever.***

If they were to ask do you have any life experiences that would tend you to lean more toward one side or another, would you have any response to that?

I definitely would say, yes or no, and then whatever life experience it may be.

Anything come to mind that would cause you to think you might side with one side more than another as you're starting out?

No. I had colleagues that I worked with for a very short period of time who sued a company I worked for, a whole fiasco. I definitely saw it from both viewpoints, where I could very much see where the company wasn't necessarily at fault, but at the same time, the employees did have a little bit of a case there. So I definitely try to keep an open mind and look at both viewpoints. I'm glad I wasn't on that jury, because I don't know what I would have decided. One bias I probably have, and this may be getting totally off topic, is just the way the legal system in civil court is set up, where the only reward is a monetary value. Because a lot of times, that's not what people are necessarily searching for, but that's the way the system is set up.

So the bias there, how does that affect you?

Well, I don't feel that the monetary issue is the best way to reward someone or the best way to penalize someone. I don't know in the workings of an actual case how much effect it would have, because I realize that's the way the system is and that's the best we have.

What's your sense of why the system is set up, in civil cases, to make a determination first of whether or not a wrong occurred and then how much to compensate a person for that harm? What do you think about that?

I don't know all the specific details with how everything works, but I think you can learn a lot from looking at how the 9/11 money was doled out, and several other lawsuits, as far as determining how much money everybody got paid?

So there's an award pool and then it's going to go to the different –

Right, right. And basically, he looked at things like life expectancies for the person – this is in case someone died, but also how much they made while working. So I think there are things like that where you might be able to figure out if someone's no longer able to work, well, how much would they have earned working? **The thing that gets tricky, though, is the whole emotional distress. I think lawyers play a big role in that, where if you have a good lawyer, then you may be more likely to get more money.**

For things like the emotional distress, the pain and suffering.

Right, that are very gray areas, or if you're the plaintiff and you're really sympathetic and pull at everybody's heartstrings whether you may not deserve it, but you're a very sympathetic person.

Do you feel that money awards compensating for pain, suffering, disability or loss of enjoyment of life are not appropriate in these kinds of cases; that they shouldn't have that?

No. As I said earlier, I definitely feel there's a big issue with monetary awards in general, but that's the way the system is set up. And honestly, I don't know of an alternative. So I do feel like people should be awarded for that because certainly, there are dramatic events that may have happened that do affect you. Just because you're not physically harmed doesn't mean that you don't necessarily have on-going issues that you should be possibly compensated for.

If they're physically injured, as well as emotionally injured, would it be easier for you to consider the emotional damage?

Definitely. It's the way the medical system is, too. A physical issue is a lot easier to treat and diagnose as opposed to a mental issue.

Would expert testimony – how would that help you?

That would definitely pull very strongly in favor or against, depending on the testimony. I'm a believer in science, and if there's an expert that has some background in whatever and can give me hard data, then that's going to help a lot.

Do you think that monetary awards in civil injury cases are too high in this country or that there's a civil litigation crisis or runaway jury verdicts?

I definitely think there are some cases that have gone too far and that I definitely know from personal experience having former employees that talked about suing their former companies or whatever when they very much stated to me, I'm out for the money. There are definite issues there.

Did you think they were out for money that was more than they deserved?

In one particular case, I don't know for a fact, but I'm pretty sure that everything was fabricated. They got a good lawyer and very much played the hurt victim even though they didn't have any ongoing issues. It was a minor fender-bender, and then they take someone to court saying they've got all this ongoing back injury stuff.

Did that case go to trial?

Yeah. It was a former employee who got a pretty good settlement out of it.

So the jury, after having heard all the testimony on both sides, made a determination, and how did you feel about that amount, that outcome?

*I can't necessarily fault the jury, because they don't have all the information. You don't know – in this case, this is a very nice, likable person, and the only reason I knew everything wasn't legit is because she flat out told me. I think that jaded me a little bit because I'm pretty innocent and want to take people at their face value. **But there are people like that out there, and I do think they take advantage of the system.***

Do you think they're representative of the greater pool?

No.

You mentioned the word "data" earlier, which is a word that sometimes comes up and it's very important to me, because more and more we're seeing data-driven jurors, people who work in data-driven fields, who see things a little more right and wrong, black and white, rather than people who tend to see things more emotionally. You also said that you're very open-minded. What that suggests to me is that you're very well-balanced in terms of your ability, when you make decisions that you take in all kinds of information. Is that right? Is that fair?

I think so. I have a degree in art, but right now I'm working on a degree in accounting. So I very much have the hippie-dippy and the analytical side.

How is that affecting your life view, right now, as you study accounting? You probably have some experience in your background with it, too.

I have a little bit of basic bookkeeping experience. How it's affecting my life is just, I'm a stay-at-home mom who's juggling going back to school. So as far as the specific subject matter, it's more just juggling life circumstances.

Does your immersion in the accounting field tend to have you be more focused on specific correct right and wrong answers or less in that way?

You think of the accounting world as being very black and white, but there are certainly gray areas. And there are people who may think of accounting as, you know, you have cash and how's that cash disbursed, but when you actually know the inner workings of accounting, it's not cash, it's assets, which can include a number of things. And just because a company is valued at some certain amount doesn't mean that they might not be a successful company just because they have that value. So, yeah. You would think accounting is very black and white, but the more I get into it, it's got a lot of gray. And there are certain rules, of course, but still.

We touched on how a lawyer can ask you whether or not you are open-minded and likely to be fair. The other question is, what can that lawyer do to establish a human connection with you? To be perceived as credible?

I think humor, within reason, professional humor, if that's a thing. I think that's a great way to establish rapport with a person and some sort of connection.

If the parties, who are very serious in a conflicting role against each other, are in a courtroom with a lot at stake and there's 60 strangers who are potential jurors and a lawyer there, how in that setting do you think a lawyer can be humorous, in that moment, enough to break the ice?

I don't know if they do some first speech to all the jurors, but even if there's just some corny lawyer joke or something they can throw out there that wouldn't be inappropriate, somehow related. I speak to humor a lot, so that might just be me personally, I think that would help.

What must a lawyer avoid doing to hurt his or her chances of establishing that connection?

*Especially in this part, **I would say antagonizing a potential juror. If you come off and start questioning me really heartily and I feel like you're judging me, then I'm not going to have a good relationship with you. Also, I think professionalism is a big thing. You're a lawyer, people expect a certain level of professionalism. So if you come off looking like an idiot I'm not going to treat you very well.***

If that did happen, do you think by the time the trial was over you would be focusing more on the facts of the case, or would that initial interaction with the lawyer carry through?

*I think it would depend on how the lawyer progresses through the case. If the lawyer comes off as an idiot on that first encounter and they continue to do idiotic things, then it's like, okay, you're an idiot; you don't know what you're doing. That's going to sway my opinion. **But I don't think first impressions are the only factor. Certainly we'll still look at the actual case.** Sometimes, if you have a really bad lawyer, you may be more sympathetic to that person, because it's like, oh man, this is all they could afford, you know?*

What is an idiot? Just throw a little description at me. What sort of behaviors would that encompass?

If they're constantly fumbling around and trying to remember what they were going to ask or they just don't seem put together; like they don't know what's going on. Or they ask some question that you're like, why would you ask?

What's your perception of the group around you? I realize this is a fiction, but as you're in that moment, what do you sense is going on with your group of potential jurors?

I feel like most people probably don't want to be there. So there's probably a lot of built-up tension and antagonism from the get-go; people looking at their clocks, questioning, why are we here? How long is this going to take? I feel like it's definitely going to be a mixed group of all socioeconomic, race, you know, whatever. So especially when you're living in a neighborhood that's a very contained bubble that is definitely an experience to see all walks of life in one setting.

How would you feel if the attorney shared something about the attorney's own bias or prejudice? How would that play with you?

I would be pretty sympathetic to that. The attorney's trying to come across as a real person, and that definitely speaks to people and myself included.

Is there a limit to what that could be? Is there something that's too personal or not germane to the case that would turn you off?

Certainly. If it were some civil lawsuit for a sexual harassment case and the attorney shared that he was sued and this is what happened, I'd be like, you know what, I don't need to know that you were sued for sexual harassment, because it's not going to make me feel better for you. There are definitely things that might turn me off; if it's a little too personal.

If the objective is to – as they say – if I show you mine, I invite you to share some of yours, how do you think about that?

I definitely think that when people tell you more about themselves, you are, whether you realize it or not, more willing to open up and share about yourself.

What can the attorney do to ensure that it doesn't come off as a manipulation?

It's just an overall demeanor. If from the beginning you've been polite and respectful, then that, for a lot people, it's hard to teach. It's something that someone automatically has. It's like customer service. I worked in customer service for many years, and some people are excellent at customer service; some people, it doesn't matter how many training sessions they go to, they're just bad.

Right. Different wiring. Part of the reason I'm doing this project is, we don't try very many cases, especially if we're doing very difficult cases, because they take a long

time. I may not try a case for a year or two years. I don't get a lot of experience doing jury selection. I'm trying to learn about what jurors are thinking.

That's interesting. I never really thought about it. That makes sense, though, that you don't get a lot of –

Some lawyers do. They're in court a lot. So we've talked about establishing a human connection - restate what the lawyer can do or must avoid doing in to establish a connection with you that's genuine and credible so that lawyer will be the jury's leader?

I definitely think, as I've stated, a polite demeanor and tone, treating people as if you respect them, and not belittling people. So eye contact. Just like you have now. A pleasant expression on your face. A pleasant tone of voice. You see on TV the lawyers, and they're grilling someone on the stand – didn't you do this? You definitely don't want that at jury selection. Maybe that's what you need during the course of the trial.

If it happened that one of the potential jurors became openly antagonistic with the lawyer through questioning, how would you feel about that, and how would you like to see it resolved?

I would be very uncomfortable. I am very much a person for avoiding conflicts. I would be thinking in my head, oh my God, I hope, I hope, I hope I'm not on a jury with this person. And there would come a point where, I don't know how the process works, but I'd think to myself, okay, the judge needs to get this person out of here because this is not conducive for anybody.

If you were on a jury, what do you think your role in the group would be? Do you think you'd be on the side of outspoken or more on the side of quiet and weighing everything from that point of view?

In general, I would be the quiet, weighing everything from that point of view. There definitely comes a point, if people are so far outside the scope of where I think it makes sense, that I'm going to speak up and be like, wait, wait, wait. This is what I believe and this is why.

What's your comfort level expressing yourself in a group when you feel something needs to be said?

I'm definitely not going to be the first one to say anything, but if something continues that I disagree with, I'm not going to just sit on my hands indefinitely. There will be a point where I will say, okay, guys. I'm not going to be the person who automatically comes in saying, this is what I believe and this is how we should do this. I definitely am a sit back and wait approach.

Do you think you would be a foreperson, or that somebody else would likely be a foreperson?

I think someone else would likely be a foreperson.

Okay. Burden of proof. In criminal cases, everybody knows, the burden of proof is beyond a reasonable doubt. In a civil case, we have a preponderance of the evidence or more likely than not. What does that mean to you?

To me, that means if you are 51% sure that whatever occurred, then that's the way this case should go or you should vote. If you're on a scale and you're just even slightly tipped in one way – I don't know if that's how it should be or not, but.

Most lawyers would say that's exactly what we're looking for. Tell me how you've arrived at that, because that is not the response I most often get.

Really? I don't know.

And yet, it is the response I am most often looking for.

I've always understood the difference between criminal and civil with the burden of proof, and I don't know how I came to that conclusion.

If the case were a professional liability case where a doctor was being sued because of negligence, and the standard is also a preponderance of the evidence, do you feel that it would be the same, that 51/49%?

I do. I feel like regardless, if it's a civil case, that's the way you judge it.

There are many people who lean more towards the side that in cases with doctors, the standard should be clear and convincing evidence, which tends to raise the standard higher for the plaintiff, for the person who has the burden of proof. How do you feel about that?

Maybe people think of doctors more as strict scientists and maybe they think there's going to be some clear – the world is round, so the world is round. But I definitely think of doctors as more artists that scientists. I think there's a much more gray area in medicine than maybe some people realize.

Some people say that these lawsuits drive doctors away or drive insurance rates up and make it harder to get medical care. How do you feel about that statement?

*I definitely agree that the lawsuits do – whether it's an insurance scheme issue – the insurance companies are like, ha ha, we're going to make lots of money. I don't necessarily think there's something quite that scheming, **but I do think it increases premiums for doctors' insurance.** Having had a child and going through the childbirth experience, I definitely heard stories of some doctors refusing to go into obstetrics because the potential for lawsuits was too high. But also, it kind of levels the playing field a little more where the people who want to be doctors are really there because they want to be doctors and not because of just the potential of making money. Whereas teachers, teachers want to be teachers. They don't go into teaching to make money. So whether it's right or wrong, maybe the high cost of lawsuits and insurance weeds out some people who may decide to be stockbrokers instead.*

Tell me about your generation, people that you know, your contemporaries, your friends that you've gone to school with – how do they talk about lawsuits and civil cases and how do they view and feel about them?

I don't really know that I've ever had a conversation with a friend of my age about civil suits or lawsuits.

Ambulance chasers or greedy lawyers or things like that ever come up?

I think in general, all generations tend to think of lawyers negatively. I think that's across the board, no offense. I think especially at this point in my life, my generation, everybody's too busy having babies. We're all in these little bubbles of raising a kid.

And buying houses and –

Right. It's like my teenage niece was visiting and she turned on the radio and was singing along to all these songs, and I'm like, I don't know what any of this is, because I don't have time to turn on the radio. I was in a college and high school, and even then you don't think about civil cases unless it's in some law class. So I don't know what everybody else's opinions are.

How do you feel about the demographic of your generation from Ohio as opposed to what you've encountered here?

I grew up in South Carolina and lived in Ohio for ten years, and now I'm here. I was raised very liberally and very much identify as a liberal, even though I don't necessarily like the current connotations of that word. But I definitely grew up in a very conservative, very racist, closeted racism, area. As I moved farther west, it's gotten progressively more to how I'm most comfortable. Ohio is very much a big mixture. There's a reason they do product testing in Ohio, because it is a melting pot where I had very conservative friends that were very similar to how I grew up and I had very liberal friends. Now that I'm here, it's almost funny, I don't even know if I have met anybody that I would consider super-conservative. I see stickers, and I'm like, oh, that's so awesome. That would never fly in South Carolina. Your car would get keyed, you know?

How do you think your husband would be as a juror?

He's very analytical, so he would, even more so than me, want specific facts.

Is he a developer?

He is. He's an engineer, so he's got that mindset. He would not openly be antagonistic; he's very passive as well. But he definitely would, because he's very intelligent, be thinking of the best way to get out of this without causing some sort of harm to himself. He's not going to lie, but what can he say that will get him out of this?

I was called for jury service and one of the potential jurors was a software engineer who, in responding to a question about emotion or empathy or something, said

how can I possibly answer any of your questions or decide this case? I am a binary thinker, and I sit with a computer all day long that is only right and wrong. I thought that was a very polarizing way of looking at things. Since then I've been wondering how can I get to this juror if I had that juror on a case.

That's interesting. I wouldn't consider my husband to be to that extent. He, like myself, is fairly balanced. I'm so not a black and white person. I find people like that intriguing and – I don't know how you get to those people.

If you were the plaintiff in a case, what kind of a juror would you like to have?

*I think, because I'm a woman, and I'm a mom, I definitely would feel a connection with other women, especially moms. **I definitely would prefer, honestly, people who have open minds. Extremism, one way or another, is bad in my opinion.** So I'd want the crazy extremists thrown out whether it was an extremism that I could get behind more so or not. And I think I'd definitely want people who are educated.*

I have heard that women as jurors may tend to be harder on women who are plaintiffs. Can you speak to that?

I can definitely see that. You know, there's definitely, and it's more evident now that I have a kid, a women shaming women culture. When you have a kid that becomes very obvious, because it doesn't matter how you raise your child, someone is going to come out against that.

Against the way you're raising them?

*Right. And there again, I think very much as it relates to weight. It doesn't matter if you're extremely thin, other women will come out and say, oh, she's anorexic. She needs to eat. If you are slightly overweight or more overweight, as I tend to be, then you've got the opposite. Oh, she's having another piece of chocolate, you know? And I think all women tend to judge women that way. **Becoming a mom has made me realize that I'm going to try my hardest not to judge in that manner.** Because it's hard.*

Helped you to be more aware of potential judgments?

Definitely.

Tell me what you think the role of insurance is in these kinds of cases?

I think the role of insurance anywhere is to protect the insurance holder from going bankrupt. Without that liability insurance, then every doctor out there would probably be bankrupt and destitute. Or in the case of large companies, the same is true. You have insurance to protect yourself, just like I have car insurance, because if something happens to my car, I'm going to need another car to continue my existence.

When it comes to the jury making a damages award, who do you think pays that in an auto case to the person who's being compensated?

The insurance company. Or, I don't even know if insurance companies have insurance companies?

Re-insurers, actually.

I would expect whoever is actually getting sued, unless, for whatever reason, they don't have insurance which, in that case, sorry.

Is there anything that's come up that would be helpful for me to know?

I don't think so.

Thank you.

27

IDEALS

Maybe you tell them, we all come into any given situation with biases. And for this system to work right, it's incumbent on everybody coming into this situation to acknowledge what their biases are with respect to this situation. So if they're asked a question, don't measure yourself against some ideal that you think you should be.

Caucasian male, age 71, married, three children, five grandchildren, Biotech Project Management Registered Patent Agent/Retired, Ph.D. Medical Physiology

The judge will say, ladies and gentlemen, please direct your attention to the attorney for the plaintiff who is going to conduct jury selection, or *voir dire*. What are you thinking and feeling, right then and there?

I'm thinking this is something I've never experienced before, so the whole process, the gravity of it, becomes pretty apparent pretty quickly. You know this is a serious thing and it's done with every intent to make it as serious as possible. It's not something you just take lightly, the gravity of the situation.

And that's without knowing what the facts of the case are.

Right. Because you're in this courtroom with a lot of other potential jurors, all of whom have been drawn at random. And you've got the judge on the bench, and all the staff. It's unlike any situation I have ever been in before.

It is a unique environment.

*It is. And it's a serious environment, and part of it, at least in my case, was going into the courthouse for your scan. **From the moment you walk into the building, it's unlike most things you've ever experienced.***

And feeling that, does that change the way you view the courts in that way?

No. I've generally had a pretty good, pretty high respect for the courts. I may not always have a high respect for the legal profession in all regards. You do read about the variety of judges and they don't always get a good rap, and maybe they're not positively spoken of in all cases, and maybe they deserve that, but I felt like it was a positive experience. Certainly the gravity of the situation and the way it's handled by the particular judge makes you realize this is being handled professionally. This is not something that just happens. This is something that is very intentional and it's done very seriously.

Do you think the average potential juror has a similar point of view in terms of taking it that seriously?

*No. Because **I think people go into it bringing everything they have in their past with them.** Or even, what have I gotten myself into? I have this project at work and what's going to happen? Am I actually going to end up on a jury where I have to get away from my normal life for some period of time? And to be honest, I think some people are thinking, how am I going to get out of this?*

With that perspective, how are you feeling about the lawyer who's going to speak to this group of people and elicit from them whether they might be open-minded to what's going to happen?

Well, my actual feeling was, this is an overwhelming task because this is a group of people that they only know by a piece of paper. I don't know how long they've had that, but we filled it out fairly close to when we were actually chosen as the group that was going to be questioned.

We generally get it as soon as you're coming up.

So at least in this case, there were a hundred. Because they expected to lose a bunch.

Through hardships and other –

Or through not being able to consider the case fairly. I don't envy you.

The purpose of jury selection is to determine whether jurors have biases or prejudices or judgments that would make them unsuitable for either side of the case. How do you think the attorney can best learn from you and your group in a way that makes the group feel good about it? Are there any ways of asking a question or lead-ins to the question that you think are more fair or more right than others?

***One thing that does make a difference is if the attorney somehow communicates to the potential juror that there's a trust that they are going to be honest in their answers, and that it's a difficult situation for the potential juror as well as you.** Because, this is only my feeling, but people who I observed around me, they come into it from so many different points of view that they don't really think about what's it like for you. You have to be careful, of course, because you have to keep it kind of flat, so to speak.*

Well, I don't want to be perceived as manipulating.

No, right.

So that's the goal is how do I get people to open up, express their prejudices if they have them, without feeling intruded upon unfairly or without feeling manipulated?

*The judge says upfront that your answers are just for information, so don't think about what the questioner wants to hear; be honest. Just be honest. Because that's the only requirement. The only requirement is for you to think about your own personal situation and to give an honest answer. Don't go outside of that. I think that was really good advice. I think **anything you can do to emphasize*** *that you're not judging them; you're trying to pick a fair jury. Because that's how our system is based. It requires that people have a jury that's unbiased going into it.*

That being the ideal, what do you think about the notion of there being an unbiased juror? Assume we all come to the table with biases, prejudices and inabilities to be open-minded. How do we get people to at least acknowledge that within themselves?

*Maybe you tell them, we all come into any given situation with biases. For this system to work right, it's incumbent on everybody coming into this situation to acknowledge what their biases are with respect to this situation. So if asked a question, don't measure yourself against some ideal that you think you should be. In our case, it was, do you have a bias against the use of guns? Because guns were used. Then if the answer is, I do have a bias against guns, **then the next question almost always is, would that prevent you from making an unbiased judgment in this case? That's where it gets difficult because you don't know yourself necessarily what the answer is. But you do your best.** Then you have to remember, I said this, and regardless of the way I feel, this is how I have to handle it. In a death penalty case, you may go into it knowing that you have a bias and saying, but it's not going to affect me, but then you can't turn around during the deliberations say, but I don't believe in this.*

A person may say, well, I have this bias and it might affect me from being fair. Then the attorney has to dig in a little deeper in order to get the judge to excuse that individual for bias. That then becomes a difficult dynamic, because suddenly you're antagonistic with a juror, and you've got the rest of this juror's group looking at you. How does a lawyer ask that next question fairly and without losing the group?

Interesting. I don't think I saw that.

You can be in the "as if"; you don't have to necessarily resort to your own experience.

But I'm affected by what I saw or what I experienced.

It's hard. Of course you are.

*You're in a situation where you have to voice. Maybe you have to be pretty blunt about saying, you know, you acknowledged that you have a bias, and I really have to figure out whether this will affect you. I'm going to help you through this process so you can give an answer you may not even recognize yet, because you've never really thought about this. This is new for you, too; you, the potential juror. They're thinking on their feet as well. **And that question, would this affect you, would this prevent you from being unbiased in reaching a decision, is a difficult question to answer for the potential juror if they're taking the question seriously because it's projecting yourself into a situation that you're not in yet.** Maybe you can acknowledge this is not a simple situation, or it's not easy to come to a conclusion for any individual in a hypothetical case.*

Right. Especially when they can't learn the details of the case before it's happened.

So you're going to help them through this; and not to take it personally, but this is part of the process. And the judge should help by giving that broader instruction. In our case, he was very good about doing that.

It's been shown, people who represent plaintiffs have the least amount of credibility going into the courtroom. I realize you've had some experience with lawyers, but how does a lawyer earn the trust and show that he or she is credible and human, in front of a jury who probably doesn't respect that person or their profession from the get-go?

*I don't know how much leeway you have, but **anything you can do to educate the potential jurors as to how valuable this is to any individual and that anybody can find themselves in a situation where they're going to need somebody to like you.** I don't know exactly how you get that message through, but it's true. We can all have something happen to us that was unexpected and affected us and made us lose something. And when that happens or we're being accused of something, you're our best hope to make sure the system works for us.*

Right. Do you think it's appropriate for the attorney to share something about him or herself; perhaps a personal anecdote or even a bias as a way of saying, hey, people, it's okay, because I'm sharing something here.

*I do. **Anything that can make you be like one of us helps** because the fact is, neither attorney or the judge are like any of us normal people. There's a fine line because you don't want to be manipulative or viewed as being manipulative.*

Exactly, because my belief is that resistance will just beget more resistance.

I'm a little bit idealistic. I go into situations like that with the feeling that people will treat every situation reasonably fairly and not judge you as being manipulative. If you come into it saying, you know, I just want to show you I'm human too; maybe not in those words, but except for the fact that I have this role I have now, I have the same difficulties as all of you do. And so, I know the things I have to try to overcome to make sure I can get the best response from you, or the most accurate. I think that's important, too, that they know you're trying to get an honest answer from them in a situation that's difficult for them to come up with the honest answer on-the-fly.

With their peers listening to them and probably trying to decide if they want to answer honestly and whether they want to be on the jury or they don't want to be on the jury.

Right.

If you were a plaintiff in a civil suit, what are the qualities you would look for in a juror, that you would feel comfortable as you're looking at the jury?

I would like to see a jury that doesn't prejudge. I don't really care too much what their background is. I want to know who they are now. So I guess I'd like to know I have a jury where every member of the jury is going to be willing to listen to the facts of the case, whatever those are, and will not make a prejudgment until that happens. Because you really can't. I don't know how to figure that out either, necessarily, for any given juror. How do you know that's going to be the case? But I think it's incumbent upon the system, the judge and you, to make sure they know that's the requirement of the system. And for the system to work right, they're going to have to come into it with that attitude. And if they can't, then they have to say, I can't do that.

Do you feel strongly one way or the other about a juror, if you were a plaintiff, having a higher education or a particular professional background or sex or race or religion?

I don't care about gender; it doesn't matter to me. Or race. That doesn't. *Where they're from, I could see that being important, because our system is somewhat unique to us.* If they've come from Africa or South America or Mexico – I mean – they have a different view.

Different world view.

And depending on how long they've been here, I'm not sure how long it takes to get repositioned. I never thought about this before, but maybe race is a little bit like that, but to me, it's abhorrent to say I wouldn't pick somebody because they're a different race. Because my race can be just as biased, against me. Did that make any sense?

It absolutely does. When you said you were looking for someone who doesn't prejudge, is there a term of art? Or maybe that is the term of art when the lawyer is asking jurors, these are the kinds of people we're looking for here. And being honest with them that sure, I'd love people that prejudged my side just as the defense lawyer would love people that prejudged his or her side. But to be best for the system, we're looking for people that don't prejudge, that they're open-minded. Using the word bias or prejudice can, at least to me, those are emotional words, and I don't want people to feel they're bad if they hear those words. So I'm looking for something more innocuous.

Maybe coming into it saying, one comes into a situation with particular views that you've developed over your lifetime. You want to be able to understand – each one wants to understand what views they come into this with. I mean, maybe you can use something like that. You're still saying biased, you're not saying biased in those terms.

And it may be that's an okay word to use. And it may be this is not all that relevant. I'm testing whether I only need to ask folks to raise their hand if they think they can be fair. And if they think they can't, I'll –

Let's talk about it.

And if people say they can be, that's good enough for me.

I was surprised in our situation that people ended up on the jury who admitted that they had bias. That could have been problematic, like the gun views. But, I think we were fairly highly educated as a group. And so when you asked about the selection of a jury, what would I like my jurors to be; at some educational level, well certainly scientists are, at least in theory, unbiased because they look at the data. I think it looked like as the defense was questioning jurors, they were trying to figure out, are these people that will make a decision based on the data? Or not?

Or perhaps more emotionally, or something in the middle.

Because it looked like the people that were eliminated by the defense had a more emotional response to some of the questions. And, you know, I understand.

Let me put this to you: I'll suggest that trials are emotional experiences for everybody. Given that, do you have any sense how a data-driven juror can be reached? Sure, there's times when data in the case is important, but what about those emotional parts? How do you get a data person, a software developer or scientist, somebody like that, to access parts of themselves they might not be used to?

I think data-driven people aren't always non-emotional. I think you need both. You need to pick people that have both sides.

These are people that have to be reached, because they come onto juries. So I was curious. You mentioned data and scientists, so I wondered if you had any thoughts there.

I can see a difference between criminal and civil in that regard. Because criminal is, is the data there? Does the data say the person's guilty or not? And if you have any question whether the data proves the case, you have to find them not guilty. So in a criminal case, I'm not sure there's room for a lot of emotion. In a civil case, I don't think that's necessarily as cut and dried. Maybe in that kind of a situation you don't necessarily want somebody to be just a data-driven person. I've never thought of it like that.

The old saying is that we never wanted aerospace engineers on our cases. Burden of proof: as you know, a criminal case, the burden of proof is beyond a reasonable doubt. In a civil case it's what we call a preponderance of the evidence or more likely than not. What is your understanding of what more likely than not means?

To me, more likely than not probably means if you take a group of people and you give them this information, will they find that conclusion that the person did it or not? Or will you find the situation – what side will you fall on? So preponderance kind of depends on what a group of normal people would find in a given case.

Let's come back to more likely than not, and tell me what those words suggest to you as the burden in a civil case?

More likely than not means to me that there's better than 50% chance that it's going to go one way. The more likely –

Better than 50% chance.

Yeah. Because that is more likely than not. It is 50%, so.

If you were presented with a case where just more than 50% was the burden that you felt was reached, would you then stand your ground and fight for that, even if other jurors had a different weighting?

I could be swayed, even in a criminal case. I think when you have deliberations, everybody has to go into that being willing to listen to everybody else. In either kind of case. So it's kind of arrogant to think I have the answer and I know what's right.

If you felt strongly, though, that it was proved, even by that small amount –

But then I have to convince the others. What happens then? I guess that's a question too? What happens in a civil case? Is it –

It's ten to two. Any – nine to three would be –

So it doesn't have to be unanimous.

No. Nine to three would be a hung jury. Ten to two, the burden – the case is decided at that point.

If I felt really strongly, then in either case, the burden's on me as a juror to convince the ones who – and we had that situation in our case as well.

You had that situation?

In hindsight, we think what happened was, there's at least a small group who said, I want to question this just to make sure that we're doing the right thing. It was just to be overly cautious.

Absolutely. And the stakes are very high. You're looking at the loss of liberty there.

That's right. So I think in any case, if I felt strongly, it's incumbent upon me to articulate that well enough to bring people over to my side until it gets to whatever that bar is.

If you can.

If I can. And if I can't, then maybe I'm wrong. Or they're wrong. But that's the way the system works. I guess there's another side. The extension to that is, it's probably worse in a criminal case, if you make the wrong decision it has a big impact on somebody wrongly. So you have to be pretty careful. So again, it'd be arrogant of me to say, I know and the rest of them don't.

Well, you have to trust your judgment.

Right.

Civil cases, we essentially have to prove three elements. We have to prove negligence; we have to prove harm; we have to prove that the negligence caused harm to that individual. Negligence, causation and damages. Negligence, in many cases we can be less concerned about. Causation, often, similar kind of thing. What I'm more concerned about are money damages. How do you feel about money being the medium of exchange for these cases ultimately?

What's an alternative?

Right. What is an alternative? We have two kinds of damages. We have special damages which are those kinds of damages – money, wages, medical bills, other kinds of out-of-pocket costs that can be calculated fairly well.

You can figure that out, right.

Then we have general damages for pain, suffering, and loss of enjoyment of life, which have no fixed standard. What would be your approach to figuring that out, recognizing everyone else may have a different idea.

I don't know the answer to that. The easy answer is, you look at similar cases and try to figure out what's happened in other situations that have a related fact pattern.

And if you couldn't?

And if you couldn't? **Then you have to think about what a person's potential is. Because that's really what you're compensating for** *is –*

Their potential.

I don't know about the pain and suffering. That one is really difficult to put a number value on; *but at least the potential loss of livelihood.*

We can have experts talk about those kinds of questions, because they can look at past earnings and –

Right. You can actually put numbers on those.

Right. You can have people vocationally tested and aptitude tested and then experts can opine on that. But when it comes to these general damages, where there's no fixed standard –

That touchy-feely stuff.

Would you think you're on the more conservative side when it comes to a money damage award, or are you on the more liberal side?

*I'm probably a little conservative, because I know a little bit about the medical malpractice thing. I have a daughter who is a physician. When those things come up, I can see what she does and how she does it, and say, **there's a lot of pressure on a physician to make the right decision,** but they don't always. Then the flip side is, you've got a person to whom something has happened and it'll affect them the rest of their lives.*

If ten people came to agreement one way or the other that there was negligence or there was causation or there were damages or there weren't, do you think they're more likely than not right; just by virtue of the fact that ten of them made that decision?

Yes, provided you've done your job; provided the way the case was presented put out all the information that was prudent to making the decision that the jury made.

In the case you sat on, do you feel you had too much information, not enough information, or just enough information? The reason I'm asking is, so many jurors have said, we had to hear this over and over and over again. And others have said, we feel like there was a lot of important information we didn't get to hear.

Both. For our situation, the defendant had these hard drives containing huge amounts of information. And a lot of it could be incriminating information, but was not exactly pertinent to the case. In the long run, yes, it was there, and yes, it portrayed a scary person. In hindsight, talking afterwards to the prosecutors, there was a lot more that was not shared because the judge ruled, this can't be shared.

Might be prejudicial or inflammatory. We talked about two different ways; you have too much information, not enough information, or –

*So in that case, they kept emphasizing, there's all this information, talking about what megabytes of information are and how many pages that is. And like I said, we were all pretty highly educated, so at some point, in fact, we were joking about it in the jury room, **we just thought, enough already.** But then there were other cases and for me this was mostly on the prosecution side, they're asking questions of the witnesses and they stop at some point and you think, yeah, but you should ask this. You wanted to be able to say, I have a question.*

Weren't you allowed to ask questions?

No. In hindsight, they may not have had, or couldn't ask the question because they didn't know what the answer was going to be. You don't want to throw something out and have it come back and hit you in the face.

Sure. You talked about your daughter being a doctor. What sort of doctor is she?

Family practice. The worst possible situation; somebody who needs to know everything because anything can walk in the door. It's not a specialty. You know everything. And it's pressure on her.

When you hear about doctors being sued, do you have any feelings one way or another about those kinds of cases and whether maybe doctors should have immunity or should not have immunity? Or whether damages should be limited or capped?

I don't think they should have immunity, and I'm not even sure about the question of capping damages. I know that's part of tort reform that gets talked about. There's some situations where there's just no justifiable reason why they should be protected. Yes, they're all human, but some are not doing the job they needed to do or that they could do, and I don't think they should be protected. I also have an attorney son.

You're doing well as a parent.

But he's a trademark attorney.

If I shared that approximately nine out of ten times at trial, doctors win medical malpractice cases, would that surprise you?

It doesn't surprise me because I think our society raises them on a pedestal. I think the bar to prove negligence is higher than the bar to prove they weren't negligent.

Right. The vast majority of civil cases that work their way through the courts, are cases where the amount in controversy or the amount being sought is relatively small, to the point that some may feel the case isn't significant enough or their time isn't justified hearing it. What can a lawyer do to get a group of jurors to understand that even if the amount in controversy is small, the case is still important? In criminal cases, we have liberty issues. But we're talking about small amounts of money, something under $100,000 for example.

Look at the poverty level; what's the poverty level? So if it's a relatively small amount, that's measured against something that's not the poverty level.

It's measured against something. So *x* amount of dollars to one person's metric may be different than somebody else's metric.

Yeah. Because to a large number of people, that small amount of money is a lot. And it's their right. It may not be a liberty issue, but it certainly is a right issue. There's nothing in our description of rights that says there's a lower limit below which rights are not important.

Would you as a potential juror want to know before the case started how much is being sought?

That's an interesting question. My initial reaction was no, it shouldn't matter. Then the question that popped into my mind was, when I found out what it was, would I feel blindsided by having spent the time we spent on something so trivial? But I think I'd still come back to the original, and that is, no, I would rather not know.

You'd rather not know at the time of jury selection.

Because that's not prudent. The question is, it should not be money related. How the jury determines should not be money related. Whether the jury determines – how the jury comes up with damages, of course, isn't related.

Some attorneys like to give the jurors, maybe not in jury selection, but in opening statement, a preview that they're going to ask for a large sum of money. They may even give them an amount which is intended to anchor them. What do you think about that? Do you think that's more likely to result in a loss of credibility, or do you think that's an effective way of doing it, since none of us can really say what's fair or right or not anyway?

So they want to give them a value going into it?

Yes.

So that they actually have a view.

So they have a view that this is what we're talking about. It's up to the lawyer to get that number right or risk the consequences; a backlash.

That's tough, because some potential jurors, I think, are going to say, that's ridiculous. That has the potential to bias the jury, or at least, a juror. I don't know if it's true or not.

Or elicit a bias, maybe?

It might.

If you feel biased because this is the amount that's being sought in this case.

It might. So in a civil case, you go negligence –

Causation.

– causation, and then damages. And it goes like that.

And harm. That's the way you have to prove it. First negligence, then causation, then the damages, the elements.

I think giving a number for the damages first is misleading. It's throwing it out of whack.

Understood.

I understand what you're saying, but you have the potential of affecting the way the jury hears the rest of it, out of sync. To me that feels wrong.

This jurisdiction tends to be conservative in terms of the actual money awards the juries end up giving, especially compared to some other jurisdictions. Why do you suppose that is and what do you think could be done to get jurors to award larger sums of money, particularly when we have so many wealthy people in the community.

So awards are lower. I don't know.

Neither do I. I have some theories: maybe fewer minorities; more engineer types; blue-collar conservatism. Those tend to be my thoughts on that.

I could see the makeup of the area being less liberal, generally, and if it's less liberal, generally, that would show up in that area as well. I would not have guessed that.

I think the lack of minorities on juries is probably the biggest driver of that.

I can see that.

I haven't had a civil case that I've been a plaintiff's attorney on where a black person made it.

We didn't on ours.

Is there anything I haven't asked that would be helpful for me to consider?

Well, I have a question for you.

Sure.

It's interesting to me this whole concept of a fair and impartial jury of your peers.

Well, it's an ideal.

It is an ideal. With the practical limitations of who can actually serve on a jury that goes anywhere beyond one or two or three days; it seems to me that, as I'm going through the ones who were selected, or who were excused, that the ones who were excused tended to be people who were working multiple jobs or who were at a lower level financially than others because they're the ones for whom there was a true financial hardship, and they're working for places that won't give them the time off without pay. So those things all very much affect who ends up on the jury.

To say nothing of those who never show up when they receive a summons.

The interesting thing for us is that we all got along. We started with 14 and you lose two just before deliberations. And even when we disagreed during deliberations, we ultimately ended up wanting to get together sometime down the road, all of us.

You felt good about the decision?

It didn't happen though. So somebody took the bull by the horns and said, let's get together. I think we all responded, but it never happened. But we did get along together. So the night we finished serving, I went home and watched Twelve Angry Men.

There you go.

Which I'd never seen before.

Thank you.

28

OPEN-ENDED QUESTIONS

Caucasian female, age 35, married, two children, Homemaker/Advertising and Marketing/Journalism, Masters Broadcast Journalism

I think asking questions is really important; open-ended questions that make people think. Because if you are choosing and you're talking and teaching and teaching, people zone out quickly. They just do. But if you're asking questions that are open-ended, even if you don't expect a response, questions allow people to process and think. It keeps their brains alive.

At this point, the judge says, ladies and gentlemen, please give your attention to the lawyer for the plaintiff who's going to conduct jury selection. Right then and there, what are you feeling and what are your thoughts?

I think I would feel a little nervous, because you want to do your very best. I know it's not a criminal case, it's a civil case, but you want justice to be done. I and my husband are both high justice people as far as wanting to see it gets right. And just not necessarily hoping to be chosen or not chosen, but just that strong desire to make the right decisions. I hope I'm alert if I'm picked. That's what would be going through my head.

Do you feel that you'd confidently be able to do that?

I think so.

You said both you and your husband are strong justice people. What in your background has led you to that?

I think for us, because we are Christian, and we follow the Bible. We use it as our guide book. So based on that, that system of belief, it does have a moral absolute for us, for our family. We believe in that. And so we have been shaped by that so strongly that we want to see good win, you know what I mean? As far as that goes.

Do you have a belief about individuals suing other individuals and whether that's appropriate, fair, or right?

As far as our belief system and what we believe about the Bible? I think yes, the Bible teaches that as far as it is up to us, we are to live at peace with all people. The first thing we would pursue personally would be going to that person, obviously, and trying to resolve it outside of court. However, I believe there's a place for suing, because you want justice done. I think that supersedes not the good and bad of the suing, but it supersedes like, oh, you should sue because you should pursue peace individually, on your own time, in that regard.

What is your sense of what degree the parties have tried to resolve a dispute before they've actually gotten to trial?

I think if you go one on one and you try – well, it's hard. You can proceed up to like going and talking to the people, maybe pulling in external sources, other family members or friends or people who are in law who could give helpful guidance as a mediator. Try to pursue those avenues first just because in my mind, from what I've seen, the small benefit I've seen, it's very costly to sue someone. So I would try to skirt around – in our background, my older sister has brain damage from birth. It happened because of the fault of a doctor who wasn't there for the birth. My parents decided not to sue. So we want to forgive. Even though it's causing grave damage to our family, this is a hard thing to deal with that came from the fault of somebody else. It's hard, because it's in your faith, like, we want to forgive also.

Was that doctor part of your faith group or somebody outside of that?

He was a part of our faith group.

If the doctor had not been, do you think it would have been a different decision about suing?

No. I don't think so. It wouldn't have mattered. I think it's an individual decision. I can't say that, oh, if it was all done over again, my parents would have decided the same thing. I can't say that about them. Or that my husband and I would have followed the same track. But we pray, you know, and then try to listen to the Holy Spirit, like, what is He telling? What are we sensing that we should do, based on what we know of the Bible and what we follow? And we act on what we feel we receive from the Holy Spirit and what we know about the Bible.

As far as people who are participating in the legal and your beliefs, would you hold it against somebody for –

Oh, right. No. We moved here to start a church and we wanted to do it differently, where we still follow the Bible, top to bottom. But we wanted to love and serve the community, and we've found that is a lot different than how it might be in the south where there are dividing lines between denominations or types of people. We are trying to break down stereotypes of judging. It's a fine line, but no, we wouldn't base our decision – you know what I mean?

Wouldn't hold it against somebody for bringing a lawsuit.

Right.

We're looking for people who are not biased or prejudiced in such a manner that they can be open-minded and allow both sides to start out from an equal footing. Is that something you think you could do?

Yes.

What about the rest of your group; imagining these people around you, what do you think their ability – their capacity is to be open-minded in this context?

When you think about your own self, and you think, I'm objective, I'm open-minded, and I would be fair, if you balloon that to include everybody, maybe everybody in the room is thinking that. Like, I am open-minded; I am unbiased; and I have the ability to be fair. **However, I know because of our shaping, our upbringing, and how our brains are put together, we all have biases. We always fight against them.** *That's what I did in the news industry. It was always checking and re-checking and asking other people, what do you see? Is this story clean? Is it unbiased? Suppressing some of the things that would rise up in you, anger sometimes, reporting.*

Because in journalism you are taught to report the news.

Yes. Just the facts.

How have you been able to do that, and be able to report news and facts without your own personal shapings?

I've really tried to. I can't say I've always done it perfectly, because I know I'm human and I'm not infallible. But as far as it has been up to me, I've really tried to do it in a way that's fair to all sides. Because like after a murder case for instance, we would interview both the victims of that murder and the family members of the person who had been convicted. In doing that and reporting that story, you wanted to give both sides an equal voice. So I think that in a jury selection type of thing, whether it's the beginning stage or the very end of it when you're trying to decide, you want to bring both sides to light as much as possible to give fair weight. I think it would be very difficult though, if there's a big group of people and they're all speaking.

When you talk about interviewing the family members and victims, I would imagine there's a lot of emotion.

Yes.

How do you deal with emotion as opposed to dealing with facts when you're weighing a question where there's emotional aspects and factual aspects?

I'll just go by the cases I've seen. The judge is making the decisions. We haven't been there for the deliberations in the room. We don't know, but we hear the facts that the judge is stating about this person who has maybe killed another person or rape or whatever it is. And that's what you lean on, because you must; those are the facts. Afterwards, when you're interviewing the people, my heart may be broken for both sides; the compassion extends to both sides, because both sides are very much hurting. Does that make sense?

It sounds like you're very good at being able to put yourself in the shoes of all of the parties.

Right. But it doesn't mean I don't think that was very wrong for this to happen.

If you put yourself in the shoes of all the different parties, you're still able, even though you have great empathy, to be objective? Is that what you're saying?

*Yes. Because **I value justice over emotion. I think that's very important.***

If the lawyer is addressing this group for the first time, potential jurors, including you, what would be the best way for the lawyer to ask about whether there are potential biases or prejudices or things that might make people closed-minded? What could get them to talk about that; things they might not want to talk about, in a way that doesn't make anybody too uncomfortable or cause the lawyer to lose credibility?

*Well, marketing, you know, that mindset. Something like, **if you think there is anything in your past you have experienced that would cause you to have a stronger emotional response or a stronger feeling of – not judgment, but maybe a stronger feeling favorable or unfavorable towards this person, would you mind admitting that or stepping aside or stepping up?***

I appreciate that because I'm always looking for ways to ask that question in a way that inspires people to be truthful and willing to come forward.

Yes. I think that's very challenging.

It can be, because people come from so many different communication styles and places. Even in this community, which is a fairly homogenous community, we still have lots of diversity.

Right. Oh, yes.

Everybody I've learned from in these interviews is very, very different.

Right. And you want to get across what you're trying to say. You don't want to be so general that they don't understand what you're –

That they don't understand. At the same time, I need to do it in a way that's sensitive and respectful to everyone. That's why I ask what thoughts you have about that. What do you think the attorney needs to do to be perceived as credible and genuine and human?

*For me, it's not being overly emotional. If an attorney is trying to hook into the jurors through emotion, like, I know what you feel, I know you must – or everyone feels this way, don't they? You know, this kind of thing. But if it's more factually based, to me that's more helpful, because **the jurors are going to be scrambling for facts.** And some people may be swayed by emotion, right? But to me, emotive behavior from attorneys is more of a façade because they're doing their job. Emotion comes from this innate place of, I can't restrain myself from showing these things. But if it's a speech he's giving and emotion is placed in there, as a form he needs to gain trust, it almost works against itself, for me. **But if it's just factual, for me, that's more persuasive.***

If we turn that question upside down, what must the attorney avoid doing to impair his or her credibility? What's the thing that the attorney must not do?

Probably the obvious things, like avoiding racial slurs and those kind of things.

But to avoid being perceived as manipulative?

*That's a very hard question, because each case is so different and all the facts are so different. I do think, again, playing to people's emotions. That would really get to me when I did sit in on cases. At the same time, I could tell it affected some of the jurors in a strong way. Like, some of the women would cry. And it's like, I can't believe they're falling for that. And not necessarily that what he was saying was true or untrue, but just the way it was done. **It was so like a performance, like an actor. So I think the most important thing is for an attorney to be himself or herself because hopefully, people are good at seeing the truth of a person.** Like, this is who this person is. Because then it clears the air; you're not focusing on the attorney and on their affect or their mannerisms. You're just focusing on the truth behind what they're saying; like diminish the person so that the story can come to life.*

What does a credible attorney look like in your mind's eye?

That's very hard, again, because I've known brilliant people who are very disheveled.

And it may be there is no answer there. I just was wondering. You may or you may not have a response to that based on some experience.

Right. That's a tough one. Stereotypically, it would be a person who's probably neat, his or her hygiene is taken care of, because an attorney looks for details and is a researcher. I think that his details are in order as far as – hair combed. But it's hard, because maybe they've been working really hard for weeks on end and are not, you know. So it's really a tough call to make. I don't want to say it's like this or like this.

Many people don't want to do jury service for valid reasons. In some cases, they're not able to put the time to doing it or they can't afford to because they're only being paid $10 a day. You're a mother of two.

Right.

You're busy building your church. How do you feel about having to give your time? Would you be able to do that, given all that you have, or would you ask for hardship?

You know, I think I would want to do it, just because the whole system is important. It goes with what we like our country set up to be, as far as we have the freedom to do it. For me, it'd be very much an honor to serve in that way.

Thank you.

You're welcome.

One of the end goals of a case for a plaintiff's lawyer is to get the jury to make an award of money. We have different kinds of damages like lost wages, medical bills, out-of-pocket expenses that can be fairly easily proved and calculated. You can add them up and you have a bottom line. But there are also damages for pain and suffering, loss of enjoyment of life, disability, things like that, where there's no fixed standard. What are your thoughts about how you go about determining what amount should be awarded for those kind of general damages, where everybody may have a different point of view? First of all, how do you feel about just doing that in general? Because some people don't feel it's appropriate.

Right. I feel like it would be an appropriate thing, but it's so general.

Do you tend to be more conservative or more liberal, say generous, on where you might award money for somebody who's been physically and emotionally injured?

I think it would depend on the case. Like with my sister, we didn't pursue that. So it's like money is not the end goal of pain as it doesn't make you happy; it really doesn't. But some people might feel like we really need this money. We feel we are entitled to it, or maybe they are entitled to it; it's not a feeling. So that's another call that's really hard to make as an individual, outside of both circumstances of people coming together. What I would do probably is take the median, or try to find some middle ground or, based on the case at hand, how much can this company afford, you know what I mean? Is it a gigantic company and a little more might be appropriate for them so they understand the impact of what they're doing versus – it's hard to say, how much has this family suffered; based on not even ever interacting with the family or – do you know what I mean?

How do you perceive the defendant's ability to pay an award as factoring into your decision? And the follow-up is, what if the judge told you that's not to be considered?

Oh. Like if it's a small company and they can't afford –

Or a person.

– right. They can't afford a million and half dollars, however –

This is what the damage is. How would you reconcile that in your mind?

That's hard. I think by law, it would be in the best interest to award what is just, even if it was not – you know what I mean? If they were not able to pay, I don't want to say, too bad, but I want to say, well, what happened? And each case will be different. What happened here? Then pay here. What happened here? Pay much more; pay much less. But I have never been in that situation before, so I don't know.

A stereotypical example might be, you have a schoolteacher who's a defendant, and you have a plaintiff who is paralyzed. One would think that the schoolteacher probably doesn't have the kind of money that it would take to compensate the paralyzed person. Then you're in a situation of, well, what do you do?

That's true.

What would you do?

As far as the options, I don't know what the options are by law; if this schoolteacher would have to take a loan, a gigantic loan, and be paying off over time, almost like an enslaved kind of lifestyle for the rest of their life; or would some other type of compensation do, you know what I mean? We would rather see this teacher go and volunteer at this facility or – because yes, a person can't make a million dollars to pay back out of the blue.

What is your understanding of the role of insurance in civil cases where people have been injured and they're suing somebody?

I don't know. If they have pursued all the avenues of insurance, and the insurance company is saying, it's not our fault, it's maybe, say, this teacher's fault because they're an internal entity inside our company. We don't have jurisdiction over them. They're acting of their own accord. We don't have anything to do with it. If that's the rub, then if I was on the jury and they're saying, okay, you decide; what is the rub? What are you going to do? I would say, maybe the school is entitled to take some responsibility. The teacher – what is the full load that person can handle? Okay, that's what the jury will award. What is the full load that the school could handle? Probably that's what needs to happen. And then it seems like the insurance company should be found responsible through the school, because they have all those systems set up. They should.

In the real world the jurors are instructed to not consider whether one side has insurance or not. Generally, there's an instruction from the judge that says, make your determination without any reference or thought as to whether there is insurance on any side.

I guess it would come down to what happened? And if it was intentional *or – because I don't know. If it was an accidental – like a big accident that happened, well, what then?*

That's right. And most of these cases are what we call negligent, which in a sense is an accident.

Civil.

There are many people who believe accidents happen and they shouldn't have to pay if there's an accident, because they didn't intend the harm.

Right. It makes sense. It's hard. I mean, you can see – that's why we go to court, because there are both sides, and people think, I think this way. No, I think this way.

Have you been in a situation where you felt you might need to bring a case to prove some wrong has happened?

Not me personally.

Your family certainly has gone through that. I'm sure that was a lot of anguish for them.

Yes.

Let's talk about what we call the burden of proof. Everybody knows in criminal cases it's beyond a reasonable doubt. In civil cases, we have what's called a preponderance of the evidence. What does that suggest to you?

I don't know.

If you heard that it was a preponderance or, "more likely than not" is the instruction, what does that suggest to you is the burden of proof?

In a civil case?

Yes.

It still seems not weighty enough. *I don't know.*

When you say not weighty enough, what is that? What is a preponderance, in your mind?

What would be a way to say it?

How do you define or describe that for yourself?

You mean in my own life?

Well, the judge will say to the jury, the burden of proof is more probable than not or more likely than not. One side has to prove their case simply by a preponderance. To what degree, in your mind, is a preponderance of evidence? In a criminal case, it's beyond a reasonable doubt. What does a preponderance mean to you?

I don't know. That's a good question.

If it's then further defined as, more likely than not, to a reasonable degree of certainty, does that help you get a sense of what preponderance is?

Mm-hmm. Yes. I mean, more likely than not this happened, and there are facts to back that up. That's what we have to go on. That would be what you'd have to trust.

Sure. Often a lawyer will say, if you've got the scales of justice, starting out on an equal level, can you determine what a preponderance would be using the scales as an example?

Like, if one side is 51% versus 49%?

Right.

Is that enough of a tilt, shift, to –

In your mind, yes. Would that be enough for you?

I don't think so. *My dad used to be a chaplain for men on death row at this big prison in Florida. He would talk to a lot of men, and yes, a lot of them were definitely there for a reason. But once in a while, he had pause – like, I just wonder; I just wonder. And we've read stories before about people being wrongly convicted and things like that. So I think even in a civil case, it would have to be – **because people lie. Not everybody tells the truth, so it would have to be more than a little more than wishy-washy.** But you have to have some facts, you know? I can't put a percentage on it, like 65% or 70%, but I would have to have a pretty strong feeling of, this is what happened and this is not right and this needs to happen. I can imagine, though, being in a situation where all 12 people, everyone on the jury, is trying to decide together, what is that?*

What is that? Trying to get, in a civil case, ten people to agree.

Right. I don't know.

If you were an injured person, a plaintiff in a civil case, what kind of juror would you want to hear your case fairly; to give you the most fair chance of winning? I don't mean someone who would certainly side with you in every case. What sort of qualities would they have?

Man, that's another, it's hard again, because it goes by stereotypes or what we perceive a person to be. We know a guy who is a street person, and he has crazy colored hair and wears make up and is very dirty, but he's very brilliant, and very fair and does a lot for the community. But first glance, people are terrified of him. So if he was on a jury, I would be very happy to see him there. But perception-wise, I'm sure you want people that are normal looking as far as clean-cut, average, awake, not falling asleep. There aren't many fat people here, but there are a lot of really obese people in the south. In the south, sometimes I think that obesity connotes laziness. It's not our stereotype, but I think that's a stereotype some people have.

Do you feel more one way or more the other that women may tend to be more hard on women; a woman juror may be more judgmental about a woman plaintiff? Do you have a sense about that? Experience?

I have never thought about that before. I don't know. More critical, you mean?

Yes. Critical is probably better than judgmental.

In all of my experience, I haven't noticed that or thought about that. But I've read articles online that talk about this way of thinking. And it delineates, like, women are very critical of other women. Or judgmental. So I think it exists. It's definitely out there. This is just my own observation but I think it's coming up. It's more and more becoming that way because I've seen it in young girls in schools. It wasn't like that when I was in school. But girls are very mean, very mean now. I don't know if it's because of bullying or cyber or social, but I think it's going to be a challenge in the future with the next generation of young women. It's almost like a cutthroat.

Is there anything about your education and experience that has shaped your world view in any specific way you think would be helpful for me to know about in this context – jury selection? How have you been shaped in such a way that would make you more or less open-minded for a case?

> *I really value people. Being a reporter, I got to talk to many different kinds of people. It didn't matter what they looked like or if they were a trash collector or a mayor. There were people that had very terrible motives, high up in government, and then people that were – where people may stereotypically look down on them, like a garbage collector. They were amazing, gold-hearted, hard-working folks. So I think the main thrust of choosing a jury should be the inside of a person; what's going on inside them? Do they have a clear mind? Are they stable?* **Do they have a lot of anger? Because I think the anger really roots out. It causes a lot of other external affects or external problems.**

How can we identify people that have a lot of anger? Do you have a thought about that? A question or an observation? Things that you did?

> *Yes. If a person is deeply angry about something, they may be very kind and sweet, but if you touch the nerve of what makes them angry, they will become very passionate about that particular answer. It's not necessarily that they become angry, but they might get shaky and nervous and loud and talk very quickly. They get really, really excited and very passionate. I don't know any other way to say it, but usually, in my understanding and experience, something's happened that causes that reaction. I'd be careful of people that have that. Even if they claim, no, I have no ties; I have no bias about this. You can psychologically ask questions that lead and just feel, you know, like feel the water. Oh, there's an eel. It's an electric eel. That's a red flag.*

Feel the current there. Do you think there are sleazy trial lawyers and a crisis in the courts today where there are runaway juries?

> *I think there could be. But it does help that there are multiple people on a jury because you will have this election. It's just not 12 random people, it's selected randomness. I think over time, lawyers gain a great deal of insight into the inner workings of people and can pick up subliminal messages or can pick up unconscious things in a person's makeup that give them pause.* **I think you should listen to those internal warning flags because more than often, those are correct.** *I was doing an interview with someone, and I just felt like something was off, even though there was nothing said that was false. Later, we would find out all these things were going on under the surface.*

In your gut, you picked that up.

> *Yes. Yes. Yes. So it's hard, because you don't want to judge people, but at the same time, you need to listen to what's going on inside when you choose because it can tell you a lot. My mom used to say, when you're taking a test, your first impression is usually right, and that can be transferred to people and selection of juries, I think.*

I agree with you. Is there anything you think would be helpful about what a lawyer needs to know about people in that context of asking questions that are personal or intrusive?

In the selection process? **I think asking questions is really important; open-ended questions that make people think. Because if you are choosing and you're talking and teaching and teaching, people zone out quickly. They just do. But if you're asking questions that are open-ended, even if you don't expect a response, questions allow people to process and think. It keeps their brains alive,** *if that makes sense.*

In a group of 40 people, how does the attorney know who to start with, or should the questions be addressed to the whole group?

I think the whole group is a first because when you get up, maybe people are like, what is this, what are we doing here, what's going to be expected of me?

Do you think a show of hands is the better way to ask of the whole group? You have to get their responses, and what's the best way to get that?

I think so. It's harder though, if they're delicate questions, or if somebody may not want to let the rest of the group know this is who I am. I don't know if it would be easier to pass something around and they sign or if that just takes too long.

Sometimes there are written questionnaires the lawyers have a chance to see without that information being made public.

What about digitally? Like what if you had an iPad and you said, I'm going to ask a set of questions? Everybody pick up your iPhones and ask that they download this little app, just temporarily.

That's brilliant. That's technologically advanced. We don't have that yet. But that would be interesting. In a sense, focus groups do that, where they're asking people to judge how they feel as the case is going along. But no such luck for juries at this point. In journalism and marketing, do you think of those as more liberal than conservative professions? Journalists tend to be perceived as liberal. Nowadays, it's a lot different, because we have the 24-hour news cycle and agenda-driven news.

Yes. When I was working in the news, everybody talked about marketing as the dark side; advertising: the dark side. It's like, we're a part of this group; this is good, you know? We laughed about it, because it's not true. But that's how many people in news perceived advertising and marketing agencies. I can't remember why that was. I think because many people eventually did go over to marketing, and they perceived people in marketing as con men or – you know, not black and white. They have an agenda. They're trying to sell. They're trying to get people to believe these things. You're working very hard for your client. You want to let the general public see them in the best light as possible, and when crisis happens, you want to handle that as – diminish crisis management. It's very interesting.

Sounds like what lawyers do.

Yes, I know.

We take our client and do the best for the client that we can.

Right. Right. While justice is served. But I guess I wouldn't say marketing is seen as conservative, though. Not from my experience.

Not from your point of view. Thank you.

29

NEEDS-BASED JUSTICE

Caucasian male, age 33, married, two children, Pastor, B.A. Speech Communications, Masters Divinity

It goes back to the justice part of are they suing out of need and out of a real injustice done to them? I understand and I accept that, even though I wouldn't choose that. Maybe I would. I'm okay with them doing that if the situation warrants it as a big injustice being done.

The judge says, please give your attention, ladies and gentlemen, to the lawyer for the plaintiff, who will conduct jury selection. At that moment what's going through your mind?

Do I have time to do this? Probably. Is this going to be interesting or is this going to be a very boring couple of days that are going to take me away from something, from things that I really need to be doing?

That said, will you ask to get out of it because of hardship for time?

No, If there's no real reason for me not to do it, then that's a part of it, right, of doing it.

Many people say family or their jobs won't allow them to do it or the $10 a day just isn't enough. How do you feel about that?

I didn't know it was $10 a day. That sounds pretty cheap to me. So that doesn't sound like a fair compensation, but most jobs, don't they let you off for jury duty, for the most part?

There are no rules. Some do and some don't.

It seems like the compensation would need to be a little greater than $10.

As you're sitting there, do you have any leaning one way or another about this system of civil justice? How do you feel about these kinds of cases?

I think it's a good way to do it, bringing people in that don't know the situation and giving them the facts and letting them decide as a group.

How about the fact that people are suing or somebody's suing another person? How do you feel about that?

Generally, I wouldn't sue, for the most part. I think that's abused in some ways, but I think there's corporations that abuse, too. Just have to see what the situation is.

There are people who believe that a person should not ever sue another person. Do you lean one way or another in that?

Personally, I lean towards not suing. I think it's a situation by situation basis.

If you were a juror, how would you feel about your ability to be objective?

I think I'd be able to be pretty objective, because I see abuses on both sides, and I'd be pretty open to hearing the facts before I decided.

In your background, educationally and professionally, do you feel that is more or less likely to make you open-minded?

I know a lot of pastors get out of jury duty or are dismissed because people don't want their religious views to be put in with that.

One way or another.

Right. I think for me it helps to come from a justice standpoint because I see that a lot in the Bible, right? Justice being served and truth being said and shared. I don't know if that would make me more biased or not. Maybe a little bit.

What, in your mind, if any, is the difference between the justice that the Bible talks about and the justice that our civil justice system in America is?

I think they're similar. As Christians, we're called to go above and beyond in our forgiveness, where maybe we have a legal right to sue, but we choose not to for good. That's really what scripture talks about. I think that's where the difference would be.

As a juror, looking at these parties who are involved, how do you keep your own personal feelings about that from being put out to them?

*Right. **I think, one, I understand that not everybody has the same belief as I do, and they're not going to come from that standpoint. And two, it goes back to the justice part of are they suing out of need and out of a real injustice done to them? I understand and I accept that, even though I wouldn't choose that, maybe I would. I'm okay with them doing that if the situation warrants it as a big injustice being done.***

You talked about need. What would be a motive for a suit that would make you uncomfortable?

*I think some of the, what do they call it, **punitive damages or emotional harm or things like that; that's where the line blurs a little bit in my opinion. If it's medical needs, that's very clear. I understand that. But if it's emotional damage or things like that, I might be a little more biased, I guess, in that.***

Got it. We have what are known as compensatory damages. We're a State that does not have punitive damages. Compensatory damages are, as you talked about, medical bills, past or future; wages, past and future; any kind of out-of-pocket costs. But we have this other element called general damages where people are entitled to be compensated, to the extent they can prove it, for emotional suffering and pain, disability, loss of enjoyment of life. How do you feel about that?

> *I think that's a case by case basis. I think there are legitimate things where people have gone through a lot of emotional pain or something like that* because of a situation that could have been handled better; or a boss that treated someone wrongly.

How about if they're injured in an accident? Given that scenario, what kind of proof or evidence or testimony would you like to hear?

> *You know, I don't know; **maybe people close to them that have experienced or seen that.** I don't know if they went to a counselor or pastor or a psychologist or something that heard their experience to help them through that and could testify to the fact this was legitimate emotional –*

As their profession would be able to offer some opinion about?

> *Yeah.*

As a pastor, do you think you would rely on the testimony of a psychological expert that you have kind of a common viewpoint with? You help people.

> *Yeah. We do. There's different approaches. For me, ultimately, psychology, there's a great wealth in that – a value for that. I think that's a valid practice. There's some pastors that would say that's not. For me, I know the ultimate need is a spiritual need, right? That's what is ultimately going to heal people. But I think there's value in it and psychology as well.*

Would you be willing to consider compensatory damage if a person's spiritual being was harmed because of what they went through? Maybe they were in a significant accident and their life was changed and their faiths, maybe their beliefs were challenged. Would that be compensable to you?

> *I don't think so. Because, ultimately, there's been people that have gone through very drastic terrible challenges and their faith was strengthened through it instead of injured. So I don't think that would be a valid thing. Because that's up to them, choosing to trust God or whoever, or go against him. Do you know what I mean?*

I do. Now, if part of the compensation they were asking for was, say, money to pursue counseling, would that be something that –

> *I think that's valid. Like I said, I think that psychology has a value. I would hope they would be in some kind of community that would help with that as well.*

What's your opinion of lawyers who do these kinds of lawsuits?

> *Honestly, I think it's abused a lot in some ways. But I think, like I said, there's legitimate things, too.*

We hear the words sleazy lawyers or litigation crisis or runaway juries. How do you feel? What comes to mind when you hear those?

What do you mean "runaway jury"?

Cases where the money that's been awarded seems so excessive compared to what people have heard about the injuries. There are one or two cases that come to mind quite often.

I think that – and I don't know if you're talking about the lady spilling hot coffee on her lap. Some of those things sound so ridiculous, and in my opinion kind of are, but I wasn't a part of hearing the facts or any of that. So I can't legitimately give a definitive answer on that.

That being said, has it shaped your opinion?

*Yeah. I think a balance of both. **I think there are legitimate things where you see, man, this person was really wronged or this company really should have thought through this or done this in a better way. I think there are some where people are just greedy and trying to take advantage of the system.** I think that's a lot with the spiritual walk, and walking with Christ is having a balance of – a lot of life is about balancing; trusting in Christ as you go through it and measuring the extremes and finding the best way.*

When you talk about balance, and you look at the scales of justice, that's –

Right. That's where I wonder sometimes if it's tipped just to make a point or to set a precedent for something when it shouldn't be. But, I don't know, because I wasn't a part of that jury.

Abuse is in all systems.

Yeah.

One of the things lawyers are trying to do in jury selection, that the judges would like them to do, is to find out who's open-minded. Who's going to be fair? If people have biases, what are they? How can the lawyer best get that information from a group of people he or she's never met before, who may not want to be there and who could potentially be hostile or don't want to share it?

Right. I think just an interview like this would probably be your only bet. Either that or getting opinions from people that know that person well. I think that's another alley. But of course, that's a huge time –

Our constraint is basically an hour to the group of people.

Not to each individual person?

That's right. To the whole group.

So I think having an hour, or at least 30 minutes with each individual person would tell you a lot.

But we don't. We just have the hour with the whole entire group.

Right. So I'm saying if you were asking me what would be the best, I'd say at least 30 minutes to an hour with each person.

Right. That said, if the lawyer has to ask this whole group, you being part of that, how would you best be asked about your personal beliefs that make you more or less suitable to be a juror? Fair?

*I think it's a really tough spot, because if you blanket stereotype people, you're going to have that. I mean, there are some religious people that are very biased, right, against suing, like you said. I feel I could have a fairly balanced view based on the facts. **Everybody has some sort of bias.** So it's not like we see the law as bad or against what I think – there's a big way that Christians have pulled out of the law and politics, and because of that, they've lost a lot of their voice to society. So I don't think it's a bad thing.*

If the lawyer's going ask, how can I trust you to be fair and open-minded, what's the best way to ask you that?

Let me ask you, how much can the lawyer present about the case before?

Really nothing other than what's already been said. He can't say much about the facts, because they haven't been proved.

So I think if you can tell the situation enough and say –

This is the kind of case it is.

***I think you have to just ask, does anybody have a bias against someone suing a company? Does anybody have a religious or personal conviction against suing?** I think you just have to ask those.*

Just ask the question. What about suing – we've talked about suing companies, but in most instances, it's individuals suing individuals. Is that a different situation for you?

I think it's a little bit. But again, I think it just depends on – you can't blanket it, because there are – there's sin in the world, so people do really bad things to people. So there are situations where that might be warranted.

When what might be warranted?

Suing another individual.

In civil cases, the only remedy is a money verdict. How important in your mind is it whether or not the defendant can pay it? And would you factor that into your decision when you make the money determination?

I think it plays some factor in it, but depending on what they did, justice has to be served, so ultimately, a just compensation should be weighed out, whether the person can pay it or not.

When you think of justice and the scales and having the blindfold on, does that evoke any images or thoughts?

It's not judging a person, discriminatory, based on who the person is or –

How does that apply to both of the sides?

Well, it goes both ways. There's – in what sense do you mean?

When we're looking at plaintiffs in lawsuits, the injured people have to prove the case. And if there's going to be a money verdict, that verdict is going to be assessed against the defendant who may be a person of insignificant means. You're not supposed to consider that, but we're humans, and we probably do. How would you reconcile?

That might be something where as a believer, personally, I would say, okay – like I wouldn't sue someone with insignificant means if I was able to be okay without suing them, or if I felt like it was an injustice to sue this person. But I think a part of it, they're civil cases, so it's more like accidental – negligence. I think that plays a role in it, too. **If it's something that's maliciously done or heinous, then I think that makes a big difference.**

Do you have any feelings or beliefs about the Catholic Church issue where they're being sued for many, many millions of dollars for physical abuse and emotional abuse?

Like what kind of opinions were you thinking?

How do you feel about that? Do you feel that those lawsuits are appropriate and helpful and will they change –

I think so. I think it's a part of justice. They did something that's against the law. Whether it's a priest or it's a guy over here, either way, they did something wrong, and they did something very wrong to a minor. It doesn't matter what they did, it's against the law, so they need to come to justice for it. That's how I view it. If I did it, I should be brought to justice for it.

We're talking primarily about professional negligence. I'm a lawyer; I think lawyers need to be accountable to the rules of our profession. And doctors need to be accountable under the rules and that being said, are you comfortable more one way or more the other way about the fact that anyone can be negligent or make mistakes and needs to be accountable for that? Do you think accountability is for accidents as well as intentional or malicious behavior?

Yes. I think there are accidental – that's a tricky line, too.

How so?

It's situational, on the nature of what they did. Is this some obscure law or situation where they cross the line and, okay, it might be understandable that they didn't know that law or were not aware or – you know what I mean? Or is it something that's pretty blatant and they just stepped across it?

Like running a red light?

Right, or something like that. I would see that as different, a little bit.

Let's throw a hypothetical out. Running a red light is clearly against the rules. What if somebody daydreamed? Didn't intend to run the red light, but they did and caused the same kind of harm. How do you feel justice should treat those two separate instances, given that the same injury happened in both cases?

I think it'd be the same result.

You mean the end result, the verdict amount?

Right, because they know running a red light is wrong. So if they daydreamed or were driving while they were too tired or – like I got hit. I got t-boned by a guy head-on. I was going through a green light and he hit me. He says, hey, I'm sorry, I was golfing all day and I'm really tired. It's like, well, okay, I appreciate that. I understand that.

You gotta pay for that.

You nailed me. I didn't sue him, but –

Did you make an insurance claim?

I made an insurance claim. So there's that or there's, I parked here and I didn't know this was a no parking zone or something like that and so you couldn't get out of your house. Something like that. That's what I'm talking about. Total difference.

Do you feel one way strongly or another that these kinds of lawsuits compensate but also can teach accountability to people or companies that have engaged in some wrongful or negligent behavior?

I think there's some value in that.

Beyond punitive.

Right. Is it good that they had a warning on the cup saying it's this amount of degrees? Should McDonald's be careful not to overheat their coffee? Yeah. But there's a limit to that, where it goes beyond lesson and to just rewarding for the sake of rewarding or making too much of a point, if that makes sense.

It does. In a criminal case, the burden of proof is beyond a reasonable doubt. In a civil case, it's called a preponderance of the evidence. What does that mean to you?

That maybe it appears to be based on what you've heard and seen. That's what that sounds like to me, but I don't know.

It's also further described as more likely than not or more probable than not. Does that help you?

In what way?

Well, the judge would give an instruction at the end of the case. You've heard this evidence, now it's the plaintiff's burden to prove –

That it's more likely that this happened.

That it's more likely than not that this happened, these are the injuries, and this is the compensation that they're seeking. What is that weight to you?

*That doesn't seem as solid, right, as beyond a reasonable doubt. That seems more – **that sounds more like based on your opinion than on the facts.***

How do you feel about that? Being that is the law the judge would instruct?

I wouldn't feel as good about it, honestly. Just because sometimes people do bring crazy stuff. Or sometimes it's he said, she said.

Well, there may genuinely be situations where nothing's been proved, it's totally 50/50, but doing this kind of work, often it is a thin line. How would the lawyer in jury selection talk to you about burden of proof and say, you know, it may not be a lot, but it's still more likely than not. How do you feel about that being it might be a thin line?

*I think it would be good to say, here's the situation. It may come up to where it could go either way. **Do you feel comfortable making these decisions about this person's life based on that?***

Based on that. It might not be that level of beyond a reasonable doubt, but – so if you were looking at the scales of justice, do you have a sense how much would have to go one way or the other to get to a preponderance?

*I don't know what percentage you would need to say. **Sixty/forty; seventy/thirty; something like that.***

If the lawyer said it's whatever tips the scales, what would be your response internally? If you were arguing or debating with your jurors and said well, this is all it was, and one juror said, that's enough for me, how would you respond?

I think situationally, so going back to if it's a person of means or no means; so if it's this close, is this guy going to be okay without suing this person? Is this going to ruin this person's life? That's where that would weigh in, I think more so.

How do you think an attorney can earn your trust, be credible, and establish a human connection with you early on?

*Presenting facts clearly, which obviously, what's that? Because how they present it, how does that show it's clear or not? It's a challenge. But I think **just being as honest and authentic as possible; not mincing words. The smooth talk, or what would appear as smooth talk, would dissuade me from trusting a lawyer.***

If you were to distrust the lawyer, would that affect your ability to look at the client fairly?

*Maybe. **If I felt like that lawyer was twisting the facts in a certain direction that would definitely not help the person's case.***

What do you think the role of insurance is, once it's gotten to this level? People have not been able to settle or resolve it so they're in court. What do you think the role of insurance is underlying, if at all?

In the situation of an accident or something?

Sure, or any kind of a negligent situation; auto accident or professional negligence or house negligence.

They should be held accountable to it. If it's on company property or – they should definitely factor into that.

When you're thinking of the defendant who may be this individual person who's being sued, is it factoring into your mind they may have insurance that hasn't been brought into the trial?

When you said that, it was factored into my mind, but I think before that, I'd want to know, were they under that insurance? I think that's one of the facts that needs to be told. Did it happen with company property? Do they have personal insurance that covers this? And the plaintiff, what happens with their insurance? Are they going above and beyond that? Or were they compensated fairly by their insurance company?

The instruction the judge gives is that jurors are not to consider whether either side has insurance.

Oh, really? Okay.

The belief behind that is, you don't want jurors to award too much just because somebody does have insurance. But you also don't want them to not award if they don't. But people do.

Right. Yes.

If you were a plaintiff, you'd been injured, like you talked about your case, if it didn't settle through insurance and you did decide to sue, what kind of a juror would you want? What sort of personality traits or thought processes would be important?

Obviously a fair and balanced view; someone who is not strong one way or the other but was able to be objective about it.

If you were to help your lawyer pick a jury, what would be a question you would ask people?

I think a good question would be, if you're in this situation, how will you view this? Let me see, how to ask that question? Basically putting them in the place; so if you were put in the situation of these two people, do you think you would be able to be the person that you would want to be on your jury or do you think you're going to be too slanted one way or the other?

Let me make this a little more difficult for you. We have a thing called the Golden Rule. We're not allowed to ask jurors to put themselves in the shoes of any side.

Really? What the heck?

Exactly. And the theory is that they become –

They will get too emotionally invested. I see that.

That being said, can you think of a way to – if you were ministering to your church, how do you know that any of them would be fair? Fair being open-minded.

I might start it out by saying, at the outset, do any of you have a very strong opinion or emotion about this case now?

Or about this kind of case?

Right. Having not heard the facts, do you have any strong emotion or opinion right now? And then say, okay, do you think this is going to push you one way or the other in being able to listen to these facts objectively and make an appropriate response, knowing that it might come close and your decision is going to significantly affect someone's lifestyle.

Would you tend, more or less, to believe the answers you get?

Working with people, as I know you have, we both know that people have bias. If they say they have no bias, they're lying.

Would you be more concerned about those individuals than those who acknowledged a bias?

It seems like many people see jury duty as a challenge unless the case is exciting or something, right? So it seems like people would be more likely to say, I have some kind of bias, to get off, than they would to be honest and say I have no bias. So I think I would trust those people a little more because of that.

A very successful attorney on a national scale said, any juror who says they want to be a juror is somebody I don't want on my case. Does that resonate with you?

It makes sense. I could see it; if somebody just wants to get in on the action and – overzealous.

He followed it up by saying, anyone who wants to sit in judgment of another is someone I would be cautious of. Do you have any further thoughts to add?

I think that's true. It's like in ministry, I don't desire to address conflict, but I will, because I see the value and the health in addressing that conflict and resolving it. There are people who thrive on conflict and there are people who avoid it. There's got to be a balance of that, right? I think it's the same way. It's like, maybe they're not gung-ho about it, they don't thrive on it, they don't try and background it, but they're willing to do it and be balanced in it, in their response.

Are there any stereotypes you've come across in your encounters with many people that you think, in a knee-jerk way, you could share would not be good juror types?

I've experienced people that are strongly religious and would be very biased to see things as ridiculous, you know what I mean? Their first opinion would be, oh, that's ridiculous that they would sue that person. There's those stereotypes, and there's those who are very sympathetic and yet don't care about the facts. I feel like there's a lot of people here that are very anti-corporate, and that would be a type of person I would be careful about.

What about socioeconomic? Any particular socioeconomic classes that would be less fair jurors in your mind?

I think maybe, but you can't –

No thoughts on that?

I just don't think you can put a cap on that. Anything I would say would be a stereotype and wouldn't be fair. It seems like the general trend would be the more poor would be in favor of rewarding more, just as from a justice, stick it to the man kind of mentality. But then again, it goes back to, who is the person they're suing? So you could flip completely the other way.

Thank you.

30

SAY WHY

Caucasian male, age 45, married, two children, Sales Specialist, B.F.A. Photography

If you're volunteering the information to say, I want to be on the case, you should be willing to say why. I want to be on the case because this sounds really interesting to me.

The judge says, ladies and gentleman, please give your attention to the attorney for the plaintiff who will conduct *voir dire* or jury selection. Having been through that process, tell me what you're feeling and thinking.

> *I don't have any preconceived – sometimes when the judge reads what is going on, you're like, this seems pretty cut and dry but we'll find out, because that's what the jury process is about. When you see certain things like that and they open up the floor, it's like, okay, so what are you going to say? Why should I believe you over the defense?*

We're trying to determine, first and foremost, who can be fair? What could the attorney do to ask about whether or not you could be a fair and impartial juror in a case?

> ***Ask questions about what your past experiences are.*** *For instance, if it is a wrongful injury, somebody was injured due to negligence of somebody else, if that occurred to me in the past, obviously, the plaintiff is going to prefer me staying on the jury. So asking that kind of question. Or if I'm this staunch anti-corporate person and the defense is a corporation thats negligence caused injury, they're going to want to know that I have that bias, and they'll ask one of those questions. My experience with jury selection is, the defense is automatically like, Juror No. 9, he's outta here, because clearly, he's going to not favor us.*

How can the lawyer do it in such a way that they respect the juror and they're sensitive to the jurors' privacy? If a juror had a bias or a prejudice and didn't want to talk about it, what would be a way for the lawyer to do it that's fair and doesn't cause that juror to resent the lawyer?

> *It has to be asked in a non-demeaning fashion. You're trying to find out if they have a bias for that, but maybe you ask a question like the famous coffee spill McDonald's thing. **Ask a question related to that and see how the person feels. A lot of what the attorneys do is watch people and see how they're body language-ing.** I noticed when I was on the jury, somebody who hadn't even been spoken to yet would get tossed by one party or the other, because they must have been exasperated when they heard a question some other juror was – you know? I wasn't paying attention, but it's like, wait, they didn't even talk to that*

guy and they're letting him go? Was he falling asleep? Was he getting angry at some question?

Or was there something in their profile maybe, their questionnaire that –

Right. Maybe that was it, too. I think part of it is the watching and seeing what they find.

Do you think that non-verbal communication you're sort of talking about is a reliable; that lawyers in those situations can rely on that?

I think so to some degree. Especially in this day and age. I know you're not supposed to be on your phones, but if you saw somebody doing this, right? Like, that guy's not paying attention.

Looking at their phone.

Am I going to trust him to be impartial and listen to all the facts? There's too much involved there to keep that person on. Of course, that might be somebody you want to toss later, because he's better than this other person I talked to that's – whether he's going to have a bias against my case.

Right. The lesser of evils.

Yeah.

What, as you're projecting in this "as if" moment, would be something an attorney must avoid doing to cause some resentment against him or her?

Getting personal would definitely be a thing. *In the one case somebody volunteered information about the disease of alcoholism. But you don't want to force somebody to play that hand, because that might be something somebody's not comfortable speaking about. And maybe somebody was, say, beaten up by somebody else, or if you bought a product that hurt you from a company that is the defendant here and you didn't like it for whatever reason, digging that deep to make somebody tell a personal story to say, I didn't like the medication Merck made that my doctor put me on because I felt like it made me sick or crazy.*

Sure. Or maybe they didn't even want to admit they'd been on that medication.

Right. Exactly. ***So digging into that personal bit is probably something that's going to make somebody resentful.***

Is there a way to preface that those are important issues and perhaps the attorney could open that up more?

*They say something to that effect, but **I think there's going to be some people that are more sensitive than other people.** I personally understand what's at stake here. I'm willing to answer questions as truthfully as possible without having to reveal something I don't need to reveal to the rest of the court.*

If something was very sensitive, people could ask to do it in private, if they felt that was important, too, right?

I guess that would be an option. I don't recall if that was something said at the very beginning. It might have been.

It's up to the individual judge. Do you think people are forthcoming with their judgments to the lawyers when they're being asked if they can be fair and impartial?

*It's hard to say. **I feel like everybody I talk to, it seems like jury duty is like going to the dentist for most people.** It's kind of funny, because I'm the opposite of most people in both cases. I like going to the dentist, and I like the idea of jury duty.*

You probably like going to the dentist because you have no cavities, right?

Yes.

Exactly. I know that type.

A lot of people, when they hear you have jury duty – I talked to a neighbor when it happened, and they're like, oh, we just threw ours out. We just threw our jury duty away.

Summons away. Didn't even respond.

We didn't even respond. We just threw it out. And it was like, wow, that sounds extreme and illegal. People are all telling you all these strategies of how to get out of it; what you have to do, you just say that your brother's a cop or whatever.

Or you can't follow the instructions.

Or you're just like, aren't they all guilty? So I feel like American society is so biased towards that, to being forthcoming with information that might not be 100% truthful. Most people probably don't want to get selected. But sometimes it's hard to know, unless you've been called to jury duty a lot. It's probably hard to know, if I answer yes to this question, am I going to get kicked; or am I answering no and going to get kicked? So it's probably fairly close to the truthful, forthcoming, because if you're answering in a way you think you're going to get kicked off, you might be held on. You might think people don't really know that nuance. But I think there's probably a certain aspect of, I'm going to try and favor looking biased.

In order to?

To get kicked off.

How would you feel as a juror if the attorney asked the group, who would like to be here for this trial, and who would rather not be? Do you think that that's a fair question?

***I think it's a fair question,** but for my experience last year, I would love to serve on a jury. It's just that it would wreak havoc on my real life.*

Do you think there's a way to frame the question so those who would like to be here

can be here, and those who, for whatever reason for this trial, can't – or maybe think they're not right for this case, let me know, and maybe I can help you?

I think that's a way to phrase it. But I think the problem with that is, there's a bias in that question.

How's that?

Let's say because, before they start asking the jury all these questions, the judge explains the charges and explains the case. Maybe you don't know what corporation it is, but you're that person that has bias against corporations. The corporation is defendant, and you're like, I want to be on this case because I want to stick it to McDonald's for that hot coffee. Asking that question could bring a lot of those people into saying, I do want to be here because I want to make a political action by being on this jury.

That leads to my follow-up question, which is, do you lean more one way or the other that if a person says they really want to be on this jury, that person ought to be looked at more carefully?

*I would say that's true because, for me, I would like to be on a jury. **Some cases are probably more interesting than others.** The case I was on was multiple drug selling charges. It was reasonably interesting. I don't know how I'd feel about a murder case. That's pretty heavy stuff. I'm not saying I wouldn't want to be on it if I got chosen.*

Time-consuming.

If I got called for it and it was financially feasible with the rest of my life, I'd be like, this is pretty interesting. This is a big deal. But you're making a decision about something very heavy.

With consequences.

Yeah. Not that there wasn't consequences in the drug case when we found people guilty and they were definitely going to jail, but there's definitely heavier charges with a murder case; there's victims at stake where in a drug selling case, it's like –

Society is the victim.

Society is the victim. So it's not like you have, say, the widow or something in the courtroom.

If somebody volunteered and said, I'd like to be on the jury, would it be okay to follow up and ask why, or what is it about the case that? Is that fair?

*I think that's totally fair. **Because if you're volunteering the information to say, I want to be on the case, you should be willing to say why. I want to be on the case because this sounds really interesting to me.** Or I don't know anything about business law, and I want to know about counterfeit cigarettes.*

What do you think about civil lawsuits; our civil justice system in general? Do you feel it serves its purpose or it's a necessary evil or that we have too many lawsuits?

I probably lean towards there's too many lawsuits. I always bring up this: my wife and I were in Quebec City for New Year's over a decade ago. It's one of the oldest cities in America. And the Promenade about the St. Lawrence in the winter is all snowed up and they have a toboggan run up they build. Everything on the Promenade was solid ice. We're walking around like, this would never fly in the U.S. because too many people would be like, I fell, I broke my tail-bone, and I'm going to sue. It's refreshing to see that hey, leave yourself to your own devices, kind of thing.

A little more personal responsibility.

A little bit more personal responsibility. **There's definitely a lot of frivolous lawsuits,** *but until you know the merits of the case, you can't really – like to go back to the example I've been citing, the McDonald's hot coffee thing. I think that one is kind of frivolous. It says caution, hot. You know coffee is hot. You spill it on yourself. If you made it at home and spilled it on yourself, what, are you going to sue yourself? It's your fault for spilling hot coffee on yourself, not McDonald's fault for making hot coffee.*

Sure. When you're in the courtroom in that moment, what are your thoughts about the lawyers that do that kind of work for people who are injured and are claiming money damages?

It's gotta be taken at individual merit. John Edwards ran for president. I think the other side tried to paint him as an ambulance chaser. There's definitely guys on the back of the phone book that probably qualify for that definition; when you get those spam emails that are like, have you been injured by this or that? But you could legitimately have a reason to be suing, like malpractice or what have you.

Do you have a sense of the credibility of the attorney for the plaintiff? Do you think they're more credible or less credible?

I don't think I would pass judgment until I saw what was going on. In the case that I was in, there was one of the witnesses the defense attorney brought up and it was the most comical thing. This is the best you could do for a defense witness? They brought up a guy who was citing the time of day to try and say that the police were stating the wrong time of day. He knew what time of day it was because he was drinking on the corner in front of the general store and they don't start selling liquor until 10 a.m. So he knew it was after 10 a.m. and the police were saying it was 8 a.m. or 9 a.m. I'm like, first of all, a guy that drinks on the corner at 10 a.m. is not a credible witness and this is the best you've got? I understand you're a public defender and this really is the best you have. But did I think he was a bad attorney? I would say no. He's dealing with what he works with. You hear sometimes that an attorney leaves a case because they're not happy with the client or they've decided this is not the case they want to pursue.

So as the case unfolds, you might get an idea of like, this case really doesn't have much merit, so I don't have much of an opinion of this attorney for taking the case. In the beginning, you can't really make that claim. Maybe you can make some prejudices on visual appearance, like if they're not coming in the nice suit; the guy's innocent because he's wearing a suit; this guy is guilty because he's in a DOC jumper.

Because it seems there's a perception or, according to some studies that somebody's done, that trial lawyers rank almost dead last on a credibility scale of professions, right just above –

Used-car salesman.

Used-car dealers. Nurses, your wife will love to hear this, are the most credible witnesses. Given that, and if there's some validity to that, what can the lawyer do to at least come to equal in the jury's eyes before this trial's even started?

On a personal level, I don't know if there is. I think on a group level, I think this is a prejudice. **People see that ambulance chaser thing and they think, everybody's an ambulance chaser. How do you cure that perception as a whole? You can't really. I mean, you do it one attorney at a time, but it's not going to eliminate that prejudice going into jury selection. You can only eliminate that prejudice through the course of the trial.**

In that instance, is there anything the lawyer could do or say right off the bat or early in the proceedings to gain the trust of the jury, to show the lawyer's human and establish a connection?

There's probably something. I'm going to use a reference from last night. We went out to dinner and my wife told the server, the food is great. And he was like, but the service, kind of shoddy? It's this self-deprecating thing that you're like, his service was actually very good. He played it off like he wasn't that good, but we're definitely going to tip him well. And something like, maybe a joke or something light-hearted because, he is human, he just made a joke. It could backfire, because people might be like, this guy's joking about this serious matter. But if it's done well; and what I've found, having worked in a law firm for four years, is that attorneys are very good with words. They're very creative people with words. It's not far-fetched to come up with something, even if it's like, I use this line every time because it's a new jury group; a few lines like that you use every week because it's a new jury selection pool; something that kind of breaks the ice. Then it's like, oh, this guy's human. He golfs just like I do.

What can the attorney do so it doesn't appear as a manipulation?

I don't know. It may be that it just has to come off as natural and not, this is my canned line to open the thing with to make you laugh and make me seem human.

How about if the attorney shared something of the attorney's own bias, or say, I'm asking these personal questions, let me share something personal about myself that's relevant to the case.

I think that would completely work. I don't know how many attorneys will have relative information to every case they're working but it's something that – hey, watch as I open up here. I'm going to tell you something that's private.

Show you mine if you'll show me yours.

Exactly.

It's a contract.

Maybe that'll open up the door a little more to not be biased against me or what have you.

How do you feel about the term "open-minded" as a catch-all for words like bias and prejudice or judgments? Do you think open-minded is really the kind of juror that is best for any given case?

As opposed to bias or whatever, yeah, I would say. I've been training to do something that I kind of already knew how to do. I came home and told my wife, I'm sure it's some kind of Zen thing, but it's like, assume the mind of the student, where I don't know anything.

A heightened sense of awareness that you're able to see it from another point of view.

Right. And I don't know how many people can go in like that. After I said I had known the prosecutor and got kicked out, I was like, would that really bias me? I could be totally conscious of knowing that. But realistically, this is a person that I know, that I've had personal conversations with, that I trust. That automatically gives me a bias to trusting them more than the defense attorney. There's no way I can eliminate that from my being.

No. You can only be aware of it.

I can only be aware of it. But that might also make me try and swing too far against; to be like, oh, you know what? She's just saying that. Like I'm going to have to believe him more because I'm biased towards her. That's just complicated as a juror. I'm not going to do that. It's easier to say, I am going to be biased, because there's too much going on in your head in a case anyway to have the ability to try and mitigate knowledge of one of the parties.

Social scientists are arguing pretty credibly that we're making up our minds long before we've considered the evidence, at a subconscious level. Do you have any thoughts about that?

The case I was in, I don't know if my mind was made up in the beginning, but definitely, before the jury got the case, I was pretty confident. There was no "ah-ha" moment from the defense that was like, they're going to have something.

Nothing to change the scales.

Yeah. And when you listen to the police testifying you're like, you're supposed to believe the police because they're the police. But realistically, I'm a little skeptical of the police. I don't 100% believe them, but I don't 100% believe the other guys, and they're making a better story over here than – the story that we didn't do it, it's very piecemeal. This is a little bit more organized. It still could be the organized machine of the prosecuting attorney, but I think the whole thing is, you made your case. It's not, are they really guilty? The prosecutor made a better case than the defense. And throughout, I'm swinging that way, to the prosecutors, because nothing is happening on the defense side that's really engaging me.

Or challenging you?

Yeah. So that's where I end up. In that same thing, the guy who wanted to believe the younger defendant was innocent; they were both African American, and I think that played into it. I could imagine going in and thinking, this guy who is of central European heritage couldn't have done it because I'm just like him. I could see where that bias could come in very early on. It's like when they read that description at the beginning; I don't remember any of the descriptions from last year when I did it, but they read that description and it sounds like, oh, this is pretty cut and dry. Sometimes the judge even says, you'll probably be here for the week; sometimes they're like, you're probably going to be here into next week. Then you're like, whoa, this is some big stuff because if we have that much evidence to go through, it's hard to make any decision right off the bat. Clearly there's going to be a lot of stuff. Or maybe you do make a decision off the bat and then the proverbial smoking gun comes out, and you're like, holy cow, I have to rethink everything that just happened because I am wrong because they just blew my mind.

Do you think it's good or not so good to have a healthy dose of skepticism as a juror going in and throughout the case?

I think it's probably good for the legal system to have a healthy dose of skepticism. From a personal standpoint, I found it stressful.

How's that?

Like when I left after saying I knew the prosecutor, and I'm like, well, would it have biased me? I didn't 100% believe the police in the criminal case I sat on; I'm skeptical, but you keep thinking over, like, what else? There's a lot more going on in your head. If I was not as skeptical, I would be, yeah, the police are telling the truth. It's very easy to say these guys are guilty; the police are telling the truth. But now I have this kind of like, you tell a decent story, but it's not 100% convincing to me because I'm skeptical. But your story is still better than their story and that's what I'm going on. You guys found him on the corner selling drugs, chased him, caught him –

Right. Found drugs on him, probably.

Found drugs on him. But it's not 100% clear.

By nature, as humans, it's hard to have absolutes. Let's talk about burden of proof. We're all familiar with this burden of proof, which is beyond a reasonable doubt. That doesn't have to imply certainty; it's who proves the case to whatever beyond a reasonable doubt is to your mind, right? But in a civil case, the burden of proof is a preponderance of the evidence. What does that suggest to you? What is a preponderance of the evidence?

I guess a majority of it. To put it in simple numbers, you showed me six things; you showed me four things. I'm going with six things because the preponderance of the evidence is over here for your case, not your side. It's weighted here.

If the instruction went on to say, a preponderance means more likely than not, to a reasonable degree of certainty, does that help you narrow your definition?

To me that's still like you're 51%, you're 49%.

You're comfortable with that?

I think so. If that's what the law says, I'm comfortable with it. It might not be the easiest thing to determine, is it? Civil cases, there's probably two biases. There's the bias of stick it to the man, the person who's being sued; or the bias of ambulance chaser, right? So you're swinging near the middle or what have you. In a criminal case I think a lot of people are probably depending on how they go in, you know, innocent until proven guilty or guilty until proven guilty.

If somebody had that wrong in the deliberation process, how comfortable would you feel trying to explain to them what the law really was?

I think I'd feel pretty comfortable.

Speaking up?

Yeah. In the deliberation we had, there was me and this other guy, and we felt pretty confident about the charges. We really were like, one hold-out, what needs to happen so we don't spend another week in here?

Or possibly have a hung jury.

We actually tried to say we did.

The judge wouldn't let you?

The judge was like, you haven't been doing it long enough. That's when we realized it was like Friday afternoon and then we came back on Monday and we're like, we have to have a different strategy. What can we do so that we're not here for the rest of the week or winding up with a hung jury? I was one of the people in the deliberation that's like, something has not happened here. Either I'm going to have to break and say, they're not guilty on all charges or you're going to have to break and say, they are guilty on all charges. Or we're going to have to meet somewhere in between.

You felt they reached a compromise verdict?

At least with one defendant, there was a compromised verdict. I feel comfortable he was found guilty on something.

Some accountability.

There was some accountability, and if it was true what this one hold-out was saying, that he might have been innocent and just got swept up into this, he's a young guy and whatever, that if it's his first offense, he's probably going to spend some time in County and get released. If it turns out, because we don't know his background, this is like his third offense for selling drugs, he's probably going to go away for a while.

What was your educational degree?

Photography.

Is there anything in your educational or professional background you bring to the table as a potential juror, or that leads you to look at things one way or another? Somebody could be an engineer, for example, and they're very specific about things needing to be black and white and having a right or a not right answer.

Since you used that example, I studied architecture for four years. Architecture is like being an engineer, but it's more artsy. There's still an attention to detail kind of thing. I'm kind of a detail-oriented person, so for me, very like, oh, hey, the defense just admitted this detail, right? Or if you're bringing up details, I was drinking on the corner at 10 a.m., that's how come I know it was 10 a.m. That's maybe not the best thing. That's a detail I feel you would have been better off leaving out. It was credible; as credible as somebody that drinks on the corner at 10 a.m.

It maybe created a little backlash for you.

Finding those details; I think maybe a lot more people aren't that interested in that. I know my wife is not as detail-oriented when it comes to say, not her job, but –

She's probably very detail-oriented about her job, right?

*Yes. She's very detail-oriented about her job, but then certain things like washing the dishes might not be as detail-oriented for her. She might not take in that kind of evidence the same way as I would, but **I think everybody brings something different to the table.** I don't think any attorney would want a jury full of engineers or artists. It's better to have the spectrum between engineers and artists.*

It sounds like you have a very well-balanced world view, given both that attention to detail and artistic bent.

I try, I guess.

Is there anything in your growth just as a human being, beyond the training, that has shaped your world view; being from the east coast, for example?

There's probably some of that. It's interesting to move from the New York metro area to here where there isn't as much diversity. This city prides itself as being a liberal city and such, but it isn't necessarily displayed in the ethnic diversity or in say, better compassion or anything like that. My wife is from New Jersey, and grew up in a town that is predominately Jewish. There's like three synagogues here. It's interesting to swing from this diversity to here where it is mostly northern European descent.

Right. I'm observant to that. Damages. When we have these civil cases, ultimately, we're seeking money for the injured person. How do you feel about that as a remedy?

It depends. You don't see it that often, but I know there's situations where they're, we find for the plaintiff for $1. Sometimes that makes a lot of sense. You made your case. They are wrong, and I'm willing to say they are wrong, but you're not damaged enough to deserve compensation. I think that's an interesting, say, political statement to make. I could see being a party to a jury that would do something like that, but I could also see, holy cow, you died and you shouldn't have. I have a bias for – I am trained to race-car drive, and did that for a while at an amateur level. The whole 90's thing with the Ford Explorers and the Firestone tires; Road & Track *basically dispelled there was no faults in –*

There was no rollover problem, or no problem with the tires, if I remember correctly.

There's really no problem with the tires. If you look at the data, all of it happened in the southeast where it's hotter. People weren't checking tire pressures. When they were coming in for the recall, that left rear tire was often at almost single-digit PSI, 30% of normal inflation. When you ride it on the highway in the heat in summer in the southeast, it pops because it'll overheat. Most people in this country don't have great driving skills. They only have to pass a legal test, not a physics test of how to drive a car. And so – oh, my gosh, something just happened, and let's make herky-jerky movements, then I'm slamming on the brakes and turning the wheel to get off the road –

They're not trained how to deal with that.

They're not trained how to deal with that, and they roll the vehicle and are injured or die, or not injured at all. But I'd be hard-pressed to say Firestone or Ford was in the wrong because you were driving a car with low tire pressure. I can't forgive you for that. Do I think you deserve money? No. But maybe somewhere I would say, oh, the airbag didn't go off and it would've saved your life; or the airbag went off when it wasn't supposed to and broke your nose and you had to have reconstructive face surgery. You might have gotten into a motor vehicle collision and that's a bummer and probably your fault, but that shouldn't have happened that way; they're in the wrong.

As a motorcycle rider, do you have any biases toward or against motorcyclists? If you were on a case where a motorcyclist was claiming injury, how would you look at that? I see a lot of really dumb motorcyclists out there. Bicyclists, too, I'm kind of biased against, to be quite honest, yet I'm a part of that motorcycle community.

There's a guy who – the New York City Bike Snob. He does a blog. He's lives in Brooklyn, rides a bike, commutes to work and wrote a book about the road to enlightenment on bike commuting. He thinks cyclists are the chosen ones. He ignores motorcycles, which is funny, because I'm a bicyclist and motorcyclist and a pedestrian and a car driver. I do all of them. He thinks bicyclists are the chosen because they're in-between pedestrian and a car. Well, there's two spots in the middle. Motorcycles and bicycles are in the middle between cars and pedestrians. I see people on bicycles and motorcycles do stupid things. The event at the Big Four Ice Caves; there's a sign stating it's dangerous, you shouldn't go in. I don't have any sympathy for the families involved. It's the same thing if you were riding a motorcycle without a helmet on. I don't lane split. It's tempting sometimes, but it's just not something I'm willing to do. I know it's legal in California, but you could definitely get injured doing it. As a cyclist, I feel if you get doored while riding close to parked cars you are partially responsible because you were maybe riding too fast to see there was a person in that car that was going to open the door. So if you were suing because you broke your neck or collarbone because you got doored, I'm not going to feel like – but do I have a bias for or against it? I have very good knowledge of what it's like to ride a bicycle.

Sure. You have a good sense of responsibility.

In an urban environment. So maybe I do have a bias, because it's your responsibility to ride at a speed that allows you to see that a car door could open or that there's somebody in a car that you see that the brake lights are on. When you do race-car training, you're supposed to be ten seconds ahead of the car.

Ten seconds is a long time.

Ten seconds is a long time. So if you're on a bicycle, let's say, because the speeds are slow, you're just doing five seconds, right? That's still –

Still longer than the two they train us.

Right. You should still be seeing a door or a person getting into a car or getting out of a car or stopping; brake lights on or somebody about to step out. They should have looked out their window as well, but if you were traveling at a speed you could avoid it, or see the person. If a car has tinted windows, you don't see that person in the seat. It's hard.

You can't make eye contact with them.

Right. You don't know if somebody's in that seat. I could go really slow and then if I get doored I'm just going to bonk into it and not go flying over. I make that decision myself. That's acceptable risk I'm willing to make.

Coming back to damages, we have special damages, which are things that can be readily calculated, like wage losses, medical bills and car damage. People have receipts and bills, and experts can say the treatment was reasonable and necessary. We also have this element of damages called general damages. People are entitled

to compensation for pain and suffering and disability and loss of enjoyment of life. How do you feel about that, and how would you go about calculating what that value is or the worth of somebody's injury?

I would hope, as far as calculating is concerned, that I would be coached by the attorneys or at least somebody in the courtroom regarding that. I think it's kind of impossible. You lose your life in an accident – not lose your life – lose your leg. That is definitely going to decrease your enjoyment of life. And yes, let's say you're found in the right and there's a negligent party and **yes, you're definitely entitled to all the medical bills, no doubt about it. That's easy to understand. The rest of that other stuff is impossible to calculate.** I mean, did you lose your foot and you're a runner? Can you get a prosthetic? Maybe part of the damages has to cover something that makes you be able to run again. **I don't feel like you need to have "you're set for life" money.** I would think somebody that has more courtroom experience, like the plaintiff's attorney, could suggest how that works.

If the instruction says, there's no fixed standard for that, what would you think the attorney could do, given that there is nothing other than the attorney's suggestion to help you get to an amount you'd feel right awarding as damages? Especially given that the attorney wants as much money as he can possibly get, not only for the client, but because the attorney is getting –

A percentage.

A percentage of that. How can you trust that?

I think you're skeptical about everything in there until you get an idea of, well, the truth is somewhere in between here and here. Maybe a million dollars is what they're asking and the other side says that's way too high. And you say, well, why is it too high? How much does a prosthetic foot cost; and rehab involved with that? It falls somewhere in between, you know?

Do you think you would be more generous or more conservative when it came to those damages for which there's no fixed standard?

I'd probably be more conservative, but it's hard to know without having gone down that road.

How do you feel about the suggestion of a multiple of those actual damages as a benchmark for the total award? Let's say the medical bills and wage losses are, for example, $100,000. What if the attorney were to suggest, okay, how about three times that as a guideline; or maybe saying, how about x dollars a day for that person's foreseeable future or life, if that's how long they're —

I like the concreteness of the three times. I don't know if it would be easy to apply in every scenario. To use my example of the, you lost your foot and you're a runner. Were you 18 and about to have a scholarship to college with that; or are you 55 and retired? That's going to play differently for me, because here's *somebody that has most of their life left who lost a foot versus somebody who has less of their life left.*

So the longer period of time, the more days they're going to experience this loss, is perhaps more compensable than for someone who's older?

Right. If those two cases were everything else equal, I'm much more likely to reward somebody who's 18 than somebody who's 55 more money. So that three times guideline wouldn't work because maybe I'd give three times to the 18-year-old, but maybe one and a half times for the 55-year-old.

If you were a plaintiff, an injured person, is there any kind of juror you would like to have, or someone you would definitely not like to have on your case; or traits of those people?

A compassionate person would be a person to have on; *a prejudiced person not so much. Even if they are prejudiced towards me, I don't think that's good to have somebody like that. I'd rather – a compassionate person, I think, would be what I'd feel rapport.*

Is there anything you think might be helpful for lawyers to know about jury selection or jurors?

Back to the dentist reference. I read an article about the lion poacher dentist from Minnesota, an opinion piece from a dentist who was like, we're already vilified enough that people don't like to go to the dentist; why do they keep repeating that he's a dentist?

Yeah. What does that matter?

Because they just want to further emphasize he's some type of sadist, right? They never say things like, the trumpet factory worker who killed 17 people. And he's like, you didn't know Jeffrey Dahmer had a job, did you? I think it's probably being used to show that he's affluent and not that he's a sadist. I think attorneys are in that boat where they are vilified, like dentists. I think jury duty is like a visit to the dentist, having that knowledge going in as an attorney, kind of the walk a mile in your shoes kind of thing. I have an idea why you don't want to be here. What makes you uncomfortable? This is like going to get a root canal. How can we make it more pleasant? And no, I can't give you nitrous oxide. I think that's the helpful thing.

Not only that, it's not like going for a root canal; the pain lasts a lot longer.

Yeah.

Thank you.

31

YOU DON'T GET THEM BACK

Caucasian male, age 61, married, Architectural Designer

People size you up almost as words are spilling out of your mouth. You can turn people off from the beginning and you don't win them back. You don't get them back.

The judge says, ladies and gentlemen of the jury, please give your attention to the attorney for the plaintiff. The plaintiff is the party claiming injury and seeking compensation. What are you thinking and how are you feeling at that moment?

At that moment, maybe they've said what the injury is. Sometimes you put yourself in that situation, you know, if I was injured this way, is this how I would do this? Would I sue? Would I move on? And then be ready to listen.

Do you have any strong feelings one way or another about the process in general; that it's a good process or a bad process or a process we shouldn't have in America or that we should have in America? How do you feel about civil lawsuits in general?

I think there's abuse. I do. I think they're overdone. I think in some cases they're frivolous. But there are other cases where they're very warranted. There are lots of cases where something was wrong, whether it be the car manufacturer or something you use. Any number of things can be faultily made or whatever. So sure, there are. But I also think people will sue people at the drop of a hat sometimes.

How would you approach going in and not knowing anything about a case? How would you deal with this feeling that there are abuses and too many lawsuits? How would you reconcile that?

I have an open mind. So until I heard all the facts, I'd be open. Is this person – are they injured? Do they look injured? Did they lose an arm? There's going to be things to steer you to thinking, wow, this person maybe really has a case or is this person looking like me and really, what is their injury? None of that you're going to know until you hear it. I certainly wouldn't have any preconceived prejudices as I was sitting there trying to be selected or not. I know people who will answer a question the way they know they don't want it to be answered just to get out of jury duty. There's that, too. That's not me. I enjoy the process.

When you're there, how do you feel about being a part of the process? Because many people, time is very important. They would rather not be there. Are you more okay being there or more you'd rather not be there?

I'm okay being there, because at some point, maybe I'm going to be that person.

I would like to have an intelligent jury and not all the people who've got nothing better to do except be on a jury. Most of the people who want to get out of it are the people you'd probably want on it.

Is that sense informed by anything that happened in that criminal case you saw?

No, we sat a pretty good jury. I was excited to do it. It was real obvious this person just wasn't truthful in their testimony. We all saw it and the judge saw it and that was that.

And then you got dismissed. Thank you for your service. Do you have a sense that there are more frivolous cases than cases that have merit?

No. I don't think it tips in that favor, no.

If it doesn't tip in that favor, do you have a sense that frivolous cases are more the exception than the rule, or closer to the middle? Where do you think you'd fall?

My gut would say 70/30, frivolous being 30.

How do you look at the lawyers when you're sitting there at this very first moment? What's going through your mind? I realize we're talking about a fictional situation, but this goes to your feelings about lawyers who are doing civil cases, trial lawyers. Do the words trial lawyers give you any thoughts and feelings?

There's always, what's the joke, kill the lawyers first.

That's an old joke, back to the 1600s.

But I really don't – no. I find the use of the law very interesting.

How so?

There's fine lines there, and sometimes those lines blur. For instance, if I was a trial attorney defending somebody who was accused of murder; if I'm videotaping it and this person pleads not guilty, I don't know how you do that. I don't know how you stand there and try and get somebody off that you know is guilty. But we have this system set up that says, this person is entitled to a fair trial. Civil cases like you're doing, I'm ready to listen to whatever's coming out.

Some people feel that trial lawyers, especially plaintiff's trial lawyers, are inherently not trustworthy or don't have credibility. How do you feel about that?

As a generalization? No, I don't believe that at all.

There have been studies that say trial lawyers, among the professions, are second only to used-car salesman in terms of credibility.

I think that is media-driven, socially-driven. I don't think people necessarily, if you pinned them down and said, why do you think that? I don't know that they have any experience with that or it's like a prejudice almost. I think there have been examples of bad attorneys, and all it takes is a bad attorney to take what you think about all attorneys. It's like the one bad cop the situations going on now; one bad cop makes them all bad cops. They might be one in a hundred who's the bad cop. But that takes people and makes everybody think they're all bad. I think the same thing happens with attorneys. It takes a good one, a big shining example out there. It's like stockbrokers. You get a Bernie Madoff and suddenly, God, I'm not investing my money with anybody; they're just there to steal it.

How do you think an attorney coming into court to talk to a group of people to find out if they're open-minded can learn whether or not some people have that bias and can't let go of it? How do you ask the group?

That's a good question; I suppose just the way you asked me. **Do you have any kind of preconceived notions about attorneys? Good, bad, or indifferent? Usually, the straightforward approach is the best approach. Sometimes when people think you're trying to work around something, then they're cautious or suspect. I have found that bluntness works better than beating around the bush.**

Pussy footing and dancing around.

Exactly. Just off the subject a little bit, I think that's the appeal right now going on with some of the people, with Donald Trump, that the guy is saying what so many people want to say and everybody else is, you know, can't say anything like that. But good, bad or indifferent, when he says PC is killing us – was it him? Or it might have been Dr. Carson, said PC is killing us. And it is. People have gotten, good God. I saw something today, 2015, the year something offends everyone.

The year something offends everyone.

Look at the movie, you're old enough to have seen it, Blazing Saddles. *Good God, could you make that movie today? I don't know. But that movie is classic and there's nothing about it that's serious, but people can't see the humor anymore.*

You mentioned earlier that you're fairly open-minded as you perceive. What is it about your background, either growing up or education-wise or professionally, that's helped you become open-minded as the person you are? Anything shaped that?

Growing up in the '60s and the '70s, and the Vietnam War; my dad went to Vietnam. I will admit that my views have gone from liberal to more conservative as I got older and it started to be my money. But I think just life in general. I've been (expletive) on. I've been rewarded. I've been married. I've been divorced. I've been cheated on. Too many people get bogged without moving on. Somebody said to me the other day, God, how did you go from a woman's cheating on you, having to sell your house, to getting married and moving on? That's exactly how I did it. This is no longer relevant; this is. This is what you do; you move on. Staying back here does nothing. Wallowing in the why did she do that or pity me, oh God, I can't live my life that way.

Or turning it around and framing it into a positive; thank God I learned now rather than –

> *Than later or anything else. So, no. I went to six elementary schools, three junior high schools. My dad was in the service, so I've lived all over the world. I've been to all 50 states. **I've seen it. I've done it. All those things, they just make you a well-rounded person.***

Do you think that part is just, you've had a lot of different experiences that have helped you –

> *Yeah. I come from a big family. I've got six brothers and sisters. There isn't one of us that has a bad thing to say about the other, which is very unusual. We still like our parents. We still have family gatherings.*

Where are you all from?

> *Well, that's another good one.*

I know you moved around a lot.

> *My dad was born in Pennsylvania. He went to England as a young enlisted man in the Air Force; met my mother, went on four dates, got married. Within a year, literally five days after their first anniversary, I was born. I'm the oldest, and off life went. He went to OCS and became a helicopter pilot and we lived all over the place. Like I said, all those different schools. We lived on Okinawa for a while. He went to Vietnam in '69, '70. I have an adopted sister. She's from Taiwan. We adopted her at two and a half years old. She's now a colonel in the Army and she will be a general before she retires. She's a full-bird colonel right now. We went back to Washington, D.C., to go to her promotion, and I'd never seen more generals in my life, but they were there to support her because she worked at the Pentagon. She's an up-and-comer. I have a brother who, him and his wife just opened a bed and breakfast. My other brother, he's a project manager for a big construction company. My sister works for the lottery. Another sister is in Texas where there's more of Mexico north than is south; way down, the very tip of Texas. Her husband is the Superintendent of Public Schools. He has his Ph.D. His school district sends 93% of their high school graduates – well, first of all, over 95% graduate from high school; 93% of them go to college. Unbelievable. He has turned that whole thing around down there. So we have a varied family. Both my parents are still alive. They live independently. They're past the midway in their 80s. He went to Vietnam late; it was the last year of his service, which I thought was a real crock. He went as a captain, got shot down, didn't get captured, retired as a major.*

That explains the well-roundedness, I think. It certainly does. One of the things a lawyer has to do when talking to this large group in a short period of time is to find out who has biases that are going to make them unfair jurors. One way is to say, who can be open-minded? But what we're really looking for is, who's closed-minded? Who has bias or prejudice or prejudgment? How do you think the lawyer needs to go about talking to this large group of people in a short period of time without offending them, trying to learn about personal things they may not want to talk about?

> *That's just tailored questions, I think. How do you tailor your questions to bring that out in somebody? Every question would depend on what your case is about. If your case is about negligent firearms, let's say, if you have a preconceived, I hate guns, that might not be somebody you might want, because, oh my God, I hate guns and this gun injured this person. Or it might be the person you don't want because for whatever.* **I would have to say all the questions could only be tailored to whatever the case was; but again, direct questions.**

Direct questions. For the most part, we have either auto cases or lawsuits against physicians or hospitals for some negligence. You suggest tailoring questions that have to do with aspects of those kinds of cases?

> *Well, sure.* **Certainly if it's a hospital case, has anyone had a bad experience in a hospital? Has anyone had family members that have had that kind of thing; or a good experience?**

Right.

> *The medical malpractice ones sometimes are the toughest unless it's gross, like you didn't mark the right leg you were going to operate on, you know? And you put a knee in the good knee.*

Cut off the wrong leg.

> *And that has happened, so let's not make light of it, it's happened. And that's gross negligence. But at the same time, inherently, God, if you're in the hospital for an operation to save your life and there are unforeseen circumstances, contingencies that, while you may have planned for, happened, Is that anyone's fault or is that what happens? Is it any different than, I'm going to drive down a neighborhood and I don't plan to hit a pedestrian or run into the lake or anything, but by God, somebody could run out in front of me? I could veer off the road? Did I plan that? No. Am I negligent? I'm not negligent. But I might get blamed for that; avoiding this person and hitting that person. Which am I really at fault for, you know? Should I have hit the first person because they were in my way, or did I avoid them and as a result did something else?* **The medical ones would be really tough for me. I would really want to know, was this a real case of mismanagement and gross negligence or was this a consequence of, gee, we were in your gut and we were doing all these things and it didn't turn out as well as we thought.**

Do you have experience in that area, good or bad, with regard to hospitals or surgeries?

> *No. Fortunately, I have all my parts. I am probably looking at that in that I'm going to have a knee replaced. But, no. And I don't have anybody in my family either that's come out of a situation like that wrongly.*

You used the words gross negligence. That is a term talked about in the law in special applications. What is your definition of gross negligence? If you could give me some example other than saying, you know, in medical cases, you think it maybe needs to be gross negligence.

I'll give you a personal example; it's so long ago. My father's an only child because when he was born, my grandmother's doctor was drunk and he didn't get all the afterbirth out; huge infection. My grandmother, at the age of 23, has a hysterectomy because of the infection. That's gross negligence. At the time, there was no such thing as medical malpractice. She just went on with her life. Who knows whether that doctor did any more or felt sorry for her or whatever. I guess that's an example of gross negligence. I mean, hell, being drunk in the operating room would be a bad thing. But gross negligence; interview the patient, mark the leg, and take the other one off.

Let me ask it this way: in criminal cases the burden of proof is beyond a reasonable doubt. I think everybody has a sense, personally, what that means. It's different for every person, because we're all different. Civil cases have what's called a preponderance of the evidence standard. What does that mean to you?

Preponderance. That always bugged me. It's like when you get a speeding ticket, you go to fight it and the judge tells you the preponderance of evidence is that the police clocked you doing this. What am I here for then? You've already told me I'm guilty. I find that a hard one to swallow in that a preponderance of the evidence seems to be weighted against the person who's defending themselves. I've never really understood that term. I mean, I understand the term, but I don't like the way it's applied, I guess.

At the end of a civil case, when the judge gives instructions and says the burden of proof is a preponderance, there's an additional sentence which says, means more likely true than not true or more likely to have happened than not to have happened. So more likely than not is what a preponderance means. Does that help you further?

Sure.

How does that help you? What would that do for you?

Well, like when you have a speeding ticket. I was speeding, but I'd like to tell you I wasn't. So has what you heard led you to believe what we're saying is true? And if it has, even if you have little doubts but we've turned you in that direction, then yes, you need to find for whoever we're finding for. So, yes. I understand that.

Would you have a difficult time applying in a medical malpractice case when you feel more strongly the burden might need to be a recklessness standard or a gross negligence standard? For example, a medical malpractice case, that would be a civil lawsuit. The standard that applies would be a preponderance or more likely than not. What was interesting about the conversation we've been having is, there are maybe more jurors than not who apply a higher standard when doctors are defendants.

A higher standard against them or they hold them to a higher standard?

They give them the benefit of the doubt to a higher standard. So when we were talking about the burden being a preponderance or more likely than not, which is the civil standard, we'll often talk to jurors who later say, you know, it just didn't seem like gross negligence to me, or it didn't seem like they really intended it, even if the scale was tipped.

Wow. I couldn't say that would do that to me, because I know – good gracious. I don't give the doctor any more credence than anybody else in a situation if they are in fact – if something they did resulted in somebody not coming out of there the way they thought they were coming out. Just because it was a doctor, I don't give that any more credence that – no. No, not to me.

Looking at the scales of justice, the statue of the blindfolded lady, tell me what you think a preponderance is just based on the scales?

Which way it's weighted?

How far would the scale have to tip in order for a preponderance to be had?

I would have to put myself in the position of the person suing the doctor and saying, okay, it doesn't happen to be acceptable or did this doctor really screw up?

We don't have to limit this to medical cases. It could be any civil case.

It would always still be, how harmed was I? Obviously, I was fairly harmed because I've hired an attorney and I've done this. But as somebody on the outside looking, I would still put myself in that same position. Geez, if this had happened to me, what's the outcome I would want to have happen? I certainly wouldn't give more credence to the professional, if you will, versus the poor layman who this happened to. No. I would tend to keep that fairly balanced until I got that – and sometimes it's going to – and I even think I would be good at persuading others in that same direction to find for this poor person who is suing not to just take the fact that the gee, it was a doctor so how did he do wrong? We're all fallible. Or infallible.

One or the other or both? What do you think a lawyer can do - a lawyer who has come into this courtroom with 40 to 60 people who have never been introduced to the lawyer? What can the lawyer do to establish a human connection with that group and be credible; to say, look, I'm human here and I want to form a tribe, without it feeling like a manipulation?

That's an interesting point because people size you up almost as words are spilling out of your mouth.

If not sooner.

Yeah. Who is this guy? Is he pompous? Is he friendly? Is he in a $1,000 suit? I've always found that looking you in the eye, speaking, addressing each one of those people. I've done this when I've given speeches or teaching a class. If *you're focused and they think you're reading from a script or they're – you don't feel like this person's really talking to me, man that shuts people down real quickly when you're addressing somebody and you're talking to them and your eyes are shifting.* Even though they're an attorney and they're the jury and you don't know these people from Adam, there still has to be that little bit of they feel like they've connected with you. **Because as I said, you can turn people off from the beginning and you don't win them back. You don't get them back.**

Right. No matter what the evidence is.

Sometimes that happens; you just don't get them back. That can happen with the other side, too. If that guy's more charming, they can be swayed to listen more to the other side.

Pay more attention.

I don't envy that part of the job at all.

It's real hard.

It would be, no matter how good your case is.

Very different. Everything's serious although these interviews are teaching me to be a little more human.

So here's the deal. Attorneys tend to be – what do you want to call them? Well, it depends. We just had an attorney because we updated our will. All she does is family law kind of thing. That person was as friendly as your best friend.

Sure. She's not fighting anyone else.

Exactly. So my whole outlook on attorneys with her was completely different than somebody I might be adversarial with or that I'm going to be adversarial with. The more you can break that wall down and not put yourself up there on that box and you know, I'm the attorney and you need to listen to me because I'm right. Even though you are maybe in the particular case. There's a whole lot to getting the jury to like you.

Is there anything the lawyer could say to build rapport quickly with a large group of people? Because in the short time we have, it's very probable that a large group of people will not have been spoken to, the ones in the back, for the most part. We're focusing on who's up front and likely to fit into the box. How do we make time for everybody?

Don't you still get to interview each individual person?

No. It's all done in a group where the lawyer gets a limited amount of time to speak to the entire group. When that clock ends, the judge says, sit down.

And then you randomly just pick people? There's no dismiss for cause or any of that?

There's cause. If a person says, I can't be fair, then that's a ground for cause. They can be rehabilitated by the judge if the judge says, can you follow the law as I give it? The person says, well, I really hate bicyclists, but in this case, I'll follow the law. The judge will say, okay, that's good enough. Then we have challenges for no reason whatsoever; we can just exercise. We don't like the way somebody feels to us or there's something on their –

So is it different in a higher profile case then?

For the most part, you'll get in a higher profile case a little bit more time.

Okay. Then I think it would be the same thing. It would almost be like, God, I know you're all here and you don't necessarily want to be here, but this is part of our country; this is part of how we do things. Imagine yourself in this chair and wondering, who are going to be the people either judging against me or judging for me? And this is what we need to do here; we need to do this and we need to be impartial and we need to listen to everything and I'm here and yes, you're not all going to get selected. Some of you are.

Some clearly don't want to be.

And if you don't want to be, now's your chance to speak up. Because we don't want people who don't want to be here; maybe giving those people the out.

What about the juror who is laying in wait to take your case down? There are people that have an agenda. How do we find them? For example, someone in the insurance business may tend to think auto cases are overcompensated or there's too many of them or they shouldn't have them. They're just more conservative about them than others might be. I've had experiences where they tend to not want to talk about what they do or their connection to it. They will very clearly come in at the end if they're let on and advance their own agenda. Everybody has an agenda. How do we get people who have agendas that are harmful to the case to speak up? Again, that's talking about biases.

You just threw something at me that I wouldn't think happened.

You're in the construction business. Suppose the victim was injured in a construction site. Would you feel more strongly one way than another for that person? Or for the defendant, maybe, that's the contractor?

I understand that. We have never had one of those, because we are way up on all the OSHA requirements. In fact, my boss, if he sees a roofer on the roof who's not roped off, he shuts that job down right now; tells everybody to go home, calls their boss and says, this is what I did. You guys need to figure –

Your boss is the general –

My boss is the president in charge of construction something. We hire subs for everybody.

So most things, the general contractor is responsible for whatever happens.

Right, to the whole thing. So would I feel one way more or the other? Boy, you know, that's a good example. I might, depending on knowing the circumstances or – God, how do you get that out in the beginning? Man, that's crazy, because you don't know.

Just hope they'll talk.

Because they fill out something like this, right?

It's not much more than this.

So I mean, if somebody worked in insurance, you might want to –

Might have a sense.

And if it was a suit against an insurance company, that person might not want to – you might want to move them along for no other reason than that. In that short amount of time, that's tough to weed that kind of thing out.

Right. And we only get these questionnaires as you're walking into the courtroom. It's a lot happening in a very short period of time. What if the lawyer, to get people to share some personal things, shared something about him or herself? Like, I'm going to show you mine if you'll show me yours? Can that be done without it being a manipulation?

I don't know. I might feel kind of weird with the lawyer, especially if it was a personal thing, going, really? TMI, you know? I don't even know you; why are you telling me these things? Maybe too soon. Once the trial starts, I don't think you can share that then. Maybe you can, but then it tends to be, stick to the case.

Well, a lawyer could say, we're going to talk about bias. A famous lawyer likes to say, I don't like bankers and golfers. Hopefully, that inspires people to talk about what their biases are. Just curious to know what your thought was.

Do you personally have any, I don't likes? Man, I rode bikes for years, I can't stand bicyclists.

I don't like bicyclists.

Right? Because they feel above the – it'd be one thing if they come to a stop sign and stop with me, but when they blow on through, I hate that.

In a bicycle case, I'd be harder on the bicyclist, I think.

Exactly. I don't know. Maybe you have a couple you could throw out that way. Depends on the place. If it's bicycle-friendly you could say, I hate bicyclists and have half the jury turn on you, or you could have some go, dude, I'm with you. I don't know in this town how you could find common ground with things that everybody dislikes.

We are pretty diverse that way. If you were an injured person in a civil case, let's

say it was a construction case, what would be the traits of a juror you would feel comfortable hearing your case? Would it be somebody like you or somebody with different traits and qualities?

In a case like that, you would want that blue-collar kind of guy who's come up against unsafe work environments. You might not want the office worker who has absolutely no idea what goes on in the field. In a company like ours, we're small enough that we all get out in the field. We're not stuck in the office all day, so you see those different things. You might not want the code writer for a software company because he ain't going to know what the heck you're talking about. If you're trying to get a jury in your favor, get that person who might do the same kind of work.

What about somebody who has a sense of rules? How do you feel about civil lawsuits as a way to enforce rules so that the world is a safer place?

My wife has this saying, she goes, rules are meant to be followed until they're not. She constantly tells me, you're such a rule follower. Well, because –

It's part of your background? Military?

Certainly growing up in a military family; even as kids, when a woman came to the table, the men stood up. When your little sister got up to go to the bathroom, you stood up. When she came back, you stood up. I still open the door for people. I get my wife's chair when we go out. She goes, whoa, what are you doing? I said, I don't know, it's what I know. So without rules, there's chaos. But do I break rules? Sure I do. There are rules I think are not good rules. But by breaking them, I'm not causing harm to others. We're supposed to throw all our compostables in the bin. Every once in a while I throw stuff down the garbage disposal, and I go (expletive) you, just to do it. The idea that some guy's going through my garbage to see if I've thrown my napkins in the right bin absolutely is against my grain.

We're talking safety rules for the most part.

Sure, like I said, without rules, there's chaos. I'm all for rules. Rules are good and the laws are written because if there is no law, what is there? There has to be laws and rules. You know what the problem with laws are? My God, we have more laws than people know what to do with, and making more doesn't solve the problem. Gun laws; my God, we have more gun laws than we know what to do with, and making more of them doesn't change anything. Enforce the laws we have, you know? We've done a good job of writing laws and done a good job of coming up with rules, but making more of them doesn't solve a problem.

Do you think that jurors, when they make a decision on a case, are helping to enforce laws? In other words, somebody ran a stop sign and injured a pedestrian. The law says, you can't run a stop sign. Is the jury then serving a purpose by helping us follow the law and possibly deter future conduct?

I think so, sure. I know every ticket I've ever gotten and I make sure I don't do that particular thing again. One of the first tickets I ever got was on a motorcycle entering the freeway. I went from the on-ramp to the speed lane in one fell swoop. You can't do that. You have to travel in your lane and go. Well, I travel in my lane and go now.

Sure. Takes once.

But yes, I think you do enforce the law. If somebody runs a stop sign and hits somebody; one, I bet they never run a stop sign again, hopefully. That's more than likely the outcome of that.

So hopefully that conduct is deterred in that individual; it is a teaching moment there?

I think so.

What about why we're really there, which is to get money for the injured person. How do you feel about that?

If somebody runs a stop sign, hits me, breaks my legs, I'm out of work – there's some compensation there. I was not at fault. How much is that compensation worth? It's not worth two million dollars.

How would you figure that out? How would you decide what it is?

There's something to be said for pain and injury. I might have pain for the rest of my life from those broken legs.

Generally with damages we tell juries that there are special damages. Those are wages, medical bills, specific out-of-pocket costs that we can put on a spreadsheet, add up and get a total pretty easily; anything that has a receipt attached to it. Lost wages, too, can be calculated by economists and vocational people. General damages are what you said, pain and suffering, disability, loss of enjoyment of life. The judge will explain there are no fixed standards for coming up with that, what's fair. Every person is going to have a different feeling about that. What do you think? How would you go about determining what's fair in a pain and suffering instance?

I would put myself in the situation and say what I expect that it is. We have become a greedy society, you know? And a real gimme society; and I deserve. There's a lot of that out there. So that's a tough one, because somebody might say, if I was in this situation, this is what I'd want. I've seen those where they seem grossly excessive. Really? Really? You got that much money from this?

You've got a specific example or two that you've seen?

I mean, I've seen them. I can't cite one, but I've seen them. I remember hearing about them, specific cases where they were awarded a dollar for this and then ten million dollars for this, and I'm like what?

A lot of people talk about the McDonald's case.

That woman putting coffee in her lap. For God's sake, really? Seriously? Now they have to put warnings on the cup this is hot liquid? That was

obscene, and it was obscene that the person thought that it was McDonald's'
fault that they put a hot cup of coffee in their crotch.

How do we reconcile that a jury sat through that trial and came up with that result;
that that case was tried, had a jury, and a jury of 12 people came up with that. How
can we respect that? Do we have to, or is it just an anomaly? What is your thought
about that?

I'm hoping that was an anomaly, seriously. Because when did common sense go
out the window? And when did personal responsibility go out the window? You
know, you might want me as a great jury person, because I believe in personal
responsibility. And it seems like it's just non-existent any more. So I don't know
how. That's the problem. You send that jury off and you have no idea. You've
done your best to do it. Which side are you typically on?

I represent the plaintiff, the injured side.

Okay. Probably a verdict like that is great for you, right? Because you get a
percentage of that?

I've never had a verdict like that. But I do know the lawyer.

That would be an interesting conundrum because at the same time you're going,
holy crap, that didn't go the way I thought it would, but holy crap, that benefited
me. But at the same time, it's like, does that set a precedent? Does that make
other juries remember this and go, well, that's what this person got; we should
give it to this person? After all, it's not our money; it's the insurance company's
money. Which is another whole – seriously? That's not your money? Well, sure
it is. Because somewhere down the line, that insurance company, they just don't
make that money up. That's what people fail to see is that money comes from
somewhere.

If you were on the jury, looking at the plaintiff and looking at the defendant; the
defendant's an individual, not a business, just an individual who's being sued for,
say, a car accident, would you assume that person has insurance?

I don't like to use the word assume, because you know what that means, but I
would presume they did and that responsible people have insurance. In order to
have a license in this state, you're supposed to have insurance. But just as easily,
you can go down, get your license, show them proof of insurance, cancel your
insurance the next day, they don't know about it for four years. What a scam that
is. But I would make the presumption that yes, they had insurance.

The judge would say you are not to consider whether the person has insurance
or not. If you were in a position where you felt a large sum of money would be
fair to the plaintiff but you had a sense the defendant didn't have any money,
keeping insurance out of it, would you still make that large award for the plaintiff?
Some people say, I don't want to do this because it might put the defendant into
bankruptcy; she's a teacher, for example, or a little old lady. So they're reluctant to

do what they might think is fair, because they're not sure who's going to pay it or if the person would suffer some significant hardship.

There's another tough one. You might have sympathy for an individual over somebody that has a table full of lawyers sitting there and thinking, well, there comes that, they can afford it. I don't know that you can take that out of the equation because I think people, for the most part, are sympathetic. In other words, God, if I do this to an excess, have I ruined that person's life for something they didn't do on purpose?

Sure. It was an accident.

Yeah. A drunk driving case?

Different story.

You're not getting anything. You're not getting one bit of sympathy from me. You're driving drunk and you hit somebody, kill somebody, whatever; throw away the key.

Then there's a punitive motive there.

But for somebody who was driving along and – I don't know. It would have to be, is this a person who's a chronic texter and has – now, you can't even introduce that evidence to say, they had 10 tickets for texting while driving.

You can't introduce DUI. You generally can't introduce that they were intoxicated at the time of the accident, because the theory is that will inflame the jury.

Good Lord, are you kidding me?

We can only talk about whether the driving was negligent. We can't say about the underlying alcohol part.

Oh, good Lord.

That doesn't come in. The judges have wide discretion about keeping information out so the trial is quote/unquote "fair" because if the jury heard that the guy was a drunk driver and had a blood alcohol level twice the legal limit, they'd say, any amount of money, we'll sign the check. Judges and the courts don't think that's fair. We don't have punitive damages in our State, just compensatory.

Wow, you're just working against a wall all the time, huh?

It's difficult. Is there anything you think would be a helpful for me to consider?

No, you've just left me with more questions. Seriously. Because there's some things I didn't know about how tough your job can be.

I appreciate that.

Wow. I had my eyes opened there at the end. That seems wrong.

Excluding prejudicial evidence?

Yeah. I think I've heard that before, but I don't think I've had it put in that context like that.

It is often the case where jurors will walk out and they'll go, we just don't feel like we heard everything. They know something's missing, because it just leaks out, but they don't know what. It frustrates them to have to make a decision when they don't have everything they think they need. But that's the law.

Do you do interviews? Do you typically try and interview jurors afterward?

Try to. We question whether or not what we get from jurors is accurate. Social scientists will tell you it takes a long interview before you can be convinced that what the person is telling you is what they really feel rather than what they think you want to hear. Generally speaking, we don't rely on what we hear from jurors, win or lose, immediately after a trial. You'd have to spend a lot of time with them. I think, and many who do this kind of work think, that most of us come in with the baggage that we have. We make really quick decisions based on whatever, and then we look for whatever we can to support that decision that we've made, early, early on. It's called the Reptile Theory; we're all looking to preserve our safety. First and foremost is, is how can I protect myself? Some people protect themselves by not liking lawyers. Some people protect themselves by - you know, everybody has a different strategy.

Huh. Interesting.

Thank you.

32

ORDINARY LANGUAGE

Caucasian female, age 66, single, one child, one grandchild, Statistical Reporting/Administration/ Demographic Analysis, B.A. General Studies

If I hear a legal term I've never heard before, I turn off. So I would concentrate on using ordinary language as much as possible.

At that point, the judge says please begin. What is it that you're primarily thinking and feeling about this process and the people that are there?

I want to make sure I understand what's being said.

Being said by the judge and the lawyers?

Yeah. And the questions they ask, I want to make sure I understand them when they ask. **If they ask me a question, I want to make sure I understand it and give them a useful answer.**

Had you been questioned in the past?

Yes.

Did you have any difficulty then with the questions that were asked? Understanding them in a way that was meaningful?

No.

Is there any way of communicating you feel the attorney can provide that would help you understand the question and make it better for you, or to make it serve that need?

Gosh. I don't know. I haven't had any trouble understanding the questions, but that's always my first thing when I'm in an atmosphere where questions are going to be asked is, I want to make sure I understand them and give a clear answer.

Got it. When you give the answer, in this context we're talking about here, in the "as if" moment at jury selection, other than understand the question, is there anything you wish to communicate about yourself in that moment?

I want them to know I'm telling the truth.

Okay, and thank you. That's appreciated, because it isn't always the case, as you might imagine. A group of people have different agendas. What the lawyers are trying to accomplish in jury selection is to determine who can be open-minded. How do you think a lawyer can best explore that with this group of people in a fairly short amount of time?

Maybe ask them about something they've read in the newspaper, or a news item that's current and just ask them what they think about it. That's just off the top of my head.

Something that's not necessarily pertinent to the case, but about something that's current.

Yeah.

Can you think of something that, on the flip side, an attorney must definitely not do to avoid alienating the jury or turning them against the attorney?

I would say the body language; showing – having a respectful body language.

What would that look like?

*I keep thinking of one time I was really insulted by someone's body language, and it mostly had to do with their grooming. It was a doctor, and I was a patient. I go to a clinic, so sometimes I see my regular doctor, and sometimes I see somebody else. This guy came in and he was all sloppy. I didn't like that at all. I expect a certain level of proper appearance. **Another way that a person's body language can be offensive is if they look down their nose at people or they act like they don't care what you're saying. It's just paying attention and giving a certain basic level of respect.***

Is respect for you a very strong issue where you really demand or need that from people in interactions where you expect it from them?

I expect it to be like a basic. I respect other people, and I expect a certain basic level of respect from them.

The lawyer is trying to determine who can be open-minded, to get people to say if they have bias or prejudice. People may not want to admit their biases or prejudices, or may not know they have them. What's the best strategy for a lawyer to explore that with people in the jury pool?

In one of the panels I was in, and I didn't get picked, it was a DUI or something, the lawyer asked, would you take a policeman's word over a civilian's word every time? And I said yes. At the time I was working weekends at a 7-11, and the police were my best friends. I've learned, especially in the last few years, that there's a lot more bad police out there than I thought. I always knew there were some bad ones, but if somebody asked me that question now, I would say no. But either way, I wouldn't care about admitting it, because I respect the justice system and if the lawyer asked me that, I figure the lawyer has a reason, and I'm going to tell him how I feel.

If a lawyer were to ask you how you feel about the civil justice system and lawsuits, how do you feel about civil lawsuits? Some people, for various reasons, religious reasons, don't believe it's okay to sue your neighbor. Other people think there's a litigation crisis and this thing is out of control and there are frivolous suits. How do you feel?

*I would say that I'm willing to listen. I don't see it in terms of all lawsuits are bad or anything like that. I don't have a religious objection. **I would look at each case as it's presented.***

How would you weigh and listen to the evidence with an open mind?

Can I give another example? The juveniles that were being tried as adults in the case I was on were Cambodian. Most of their witnesses were Cambodian. I listened to them very carefully and it was very clear to me they didn't tell time the same way that Americans do. Their concept of time was not, oh, I remember it was 3:15 when such and such happened. They would say, oh, it happened in the morning. Then later on, this same person would say, oh, it happened in the afternoon. I realized that anything they would say concerning time, from my point of view, was unreliable.

Probably for others on the jury, too, I would guess.

*It's something I noticed, but I don't know if everybody else did or not. There was another instance where this guy was an eyewitness to the assault that happened. Other people on the jury noticed he was very nervous. But I didn't notice that. It didn't change the way I looked at the case. I realized there's some things I don't notice, but I like to listen to what people have to say and their tone of voice and, again, their body language as I perceive it. I don't consider myself the kind of person that just looks at somebody and figures out whether they're a liar or not. **I listen and try to get the best impression I can.***

Do you feel, even with the willingness to listen, that you tend to make decisions fairly quickly, based on what you see or what happens in the earlier parts of the interaction?

I might make a decision, but I'm willing to change it if I figure that I'm not correct.

Is there anything significant in your background, upbringing, education or career that's helped you become open-minded in these kinds of instances?

In my childhood, I was surrounded by people who were perfect examples of prejudice about this and that and the other thing.

So you saw it from that side.

Yeah. And I was like, nope, I'm not going to be that way. I'm going to fight it. I've had computer jobs most of my life and you have to be willing to try something over again if something doesn't work, and not to be crushed by failure.

You have the great benefit of awareness at an early age of something you thought needed to be different. That's what I'm always hoping for with jurors. I will accept that people have the background they have, if they're just willing to acknowledge, that they try to be aware of it when they're making their decisions, in good faith. Do you work with data in your job?

Yeah.

Is your data job one of those where, what we call binary thinkers, where there is absolute right and wrong?

Well, in math, yes. Math is always absolute.

You've got a math background?

Yeah.

As a person with a math background, do you tend to arrive at decisions in a more logical way or in a more emotional way or somewhere in the middle? Where do you land?

My job requires the mathematical, logical approach. But my life in general, I go by my intuition more. So I would say it's more intuitive than logical.

How do you do that? Because those I've come across in the data world tend to be more data-driven in their decision making.

Are they accountants by any chance?

Accountants and developers.

Accountants are different than computer people. When I was going to college, I was studying data processing and accounting. I found the accounting people just weren't very friendly. They weren't very nice. They didn't laugh very much. And computer people, they're not like that. They laugh. Of course, I guess accountants have to work together, too. But I just felt more comfortable around the computer people. They were looser, I guess.

When you say computer people, do you mean developers?

Programmers, because my job is part data processing and part program.

Did you feel the programmers had the ability to be both emotional and data-driven in their decision making? They could balance?

That's my impression.

It's been said that the youthful web developers and types today, in order for them to determine in court proceedings, need lots and lots of data. They tend to not go in the emotional way. I'm wondering how to reach them.

I wouldn't know, because I'm a dinosaur. I'm 66, and one of the people that was in my office for a while was born after I started working there, you know? So I wouldn't know. My daughter is 43, so she's an older person, too. So in terms of the much younger people, you gotta ask somebody else.

Well, and they tend to find ways to get off of jury service, too.

My boss at the time told me all the stuff he did to get out of jury service. I'm like, wait a minute, I'm a citizen, and I got called, so I'm going.

How did you feel about jury service? Because many people do everything they can to not be there.

I thought it was very interesting. I'd rather not be on another criminal trial but if I got put on one, I'd do it. It's like voting and all that other stuff, you know? It's just something that you do.

Are there any formative experiences working at a university with youthful contingents that have shaped you in ways that might be helpful for a trial lawyer to know about in jury selection? The various generations.

It is very clear to me that the older a person gets, the more familiar they become with compromise and seeing things in shades of gray rather than black and white. I know that a lot of the younger people are real black and white types. When I was younger, I thought that seeing things in shades of gray was copping out. But the older I get, the more I see that I pretty much have to do it because if I don't understand something completely, how can I possibly see it in black and white? But my job doesn't bring me in that much contact with students. I like the student newspaper, I read the editorials and like to listen to what they have to say.

I'm sure it's fascinating. In addition to finding out first and foremost who is open- or closed-minded and who's fit to be a juror on the particular case, the lawyer really needs to establish a human connection and trust with the jurors, right off the bat. Given that there's 40 to 60 people in a courtroom, with serious lawyer types and their clients with lots to worry about, how can a lawyer do that; become human; establish a human connection with a group of people, or yourself, in such a short period of time?

*I'd say using ordinary conversation, like you are now. **I know for me, if I hear a legal term I've never heard before, I turn off. So I would concentrate on using ordinary language as much as possible.** And again, with body language, showing that you're interested in the people. That kind of thing.*

What could be done to ensure that whatever the lawyer's doing does not come off as a manipulation; so that the lawyer appears genuine?

Well, I mean part of it is a manipulation, because you're presenting your side. That's something that I know, and so, for me, it wouldn't be a problem unless you looked right at me and said something that was just blatant or whatever. But that's me. I'm a very easy person to manipulate, so I just kind of assume I'm going to get manipulated.

You're at least aware? You're on guard?

Well, I'm paying attention. I try to.

The lawyer in these kinds of cases gets maybe an hour to talk to this group of people, standing up. You and I are sitting face-to-face in a comfortable place. Standing up, when you're farther away, becomes a different dynamic. What would you think if a lawyer sat in a chair and talked to you? Would you think that was offensive? Would you feel disrespected if the lawyer sat down rather than stood up and talked?

No. It wouldn't bother me at all.

Okay. Jurors, when they come to us, have names and numbers. Some lawyers are very good at a device that allows them to remember people's names; others have to rely on numbers. If a lawyer went to the trouble to remember your name, would that hold any special sway to you?

No. Not me. I'm sure everybody has their own feelings, but I don't care.

I had an experience where I asked a juror if – I said, Juror No. 12 may I have your name please? And she said, no you may not.

Well, she got struck off the list.

The problem is, that contaminates the rest of the jury. Whenever the dynamic with one changes, it changes with all.

I'll give you an example of something I said one time. I got called to drug court. I ended up talking with a judge about this in front of everybody. I said, I can't be on this court, because I used drugs recreationally when I was younger, and when I look at that person in that chair, it looks like it's me sitting there, and I can't be on this jury. One of the other jurors turned around and looked at me and says, what about jury nullification? And I'm like, that's not what I'm here for. So the judge said, that's fine. Go away. I might have contaminated the rest of the jury by saying that, but I had to. I didn't just volunteer it, but somebody asked me a question that led me to that, and I couldn't keep my mouth shut about it, because it was something I felt very strongly about.

That's the beauty of the integrity and spontaneity of the system. It's all valid. Whatever happens is part of the process. Is there anything you would want to know about the attorney at the outset, about the attorney as a person? The attorney would get up and say hello, ladies and gentlemen. My name is, and by the way, I, fill in the blank. Is there anything that occurs to you?

No.

Okay. Wouldn't help humanize or make a connection in that way?

I don't think that's important; not in that situation.

I get the sense you just want to focus on what they're there for?

Yeah.

I hear this a lot from jurors who've been in trials, boy, we heard it two and three and four times, and we just didn't need to hear over and over again the same facts. Did you have that experience?

No. I needed to pay attention to everything.

About the lawyer sharing a little bit, if a lawyer is going to ask the panel or individuals to share their biases or prejudices, things that may lead them to judgment, do you think it's appropriate or not or maybe it depends, for the lawyer to share something about his or her bias, if he or she has one?

No. If you've only got an hour, I don't think it would be a good use of time. That's just my opinion again.

It's helpful. It's valid. The burden of proof in criminal cases is beyond a reasonable doubt. In a civil case, the burden is different, because liberty is not at stake; only money is at stake. We have what's called the preponderance of the evidence. That's the standard in a civil case. What does that mean to you; the preponderance of the evidence?

I would have to be more than 50%. That's what it would mean to me.

Right. And the law then defines it as more likely than not or more probable than not. When you say more than 50%, if the scales are tipped ever so slightly, how comfortable are you in making that decision if the scales are only a little bit tipped?

I don't remember being in a situation like that.

If you were; if the law says it's a preponderance of the evidence and to you that means more than 50%, what would your thought process be?

I take a lot of surveys, just because I think it's fun. I very rarely mark right in the middle. I like to mark on one end or the other. So I would be observing from that point of view, and if I were allowed to stay with the case the whole time, I would not have any problem tiptoeing around the middle. I think it'd be real clear to me. I also like to listen to what the other jurors have to say, but I don't know what I'd do if I couldn't get there.

If it was a close call, and in your mind and heart, you did feel it was, say, 49% versus 51%; let's say the plaintiff proved it 51%. You felt that. Would you be able to find for the plaintiff if that's how you felt?

Yeah.

If it was just that thin?

Yeah.

Okay. A lot of people have difficulty with that, particularly given who the defendant might be. If the defendant's a doctor, for example, many people think the doctor should be given the benefit of – that the standard should be recklessness, for example, or gross negligence, rather than just negligence. How do you feel about that?

I'd have to study up on it. I never really thought about it.

If you were in a situation where the defendant was a doctor, do you have any difficulties or concerns knowing that the defendant is someone who comes from a medical profession rather than any other profession?

*In terms of doctors, I only know one. She's very intelligent and has very high standards. But I wouldn't have any trouble figuring that it's possible for a doctor not to be intelligent and not to have high standards. I don't know if it's still this way, but there used to be some that, they were like legacies, so they slid through medical school or whatever. I don't know. **I'm inclined to respect a doctor, but I'm not inclined to consider that they're more than human.***

Sure. And that's something that all of us who do the work I do would love to hear more jurors say. Do you have any feelings about what's called tort reform or that there should be caps on damages; that there should be limits on how much any jury can award in a given case?

I've read about that and usually I'm inclined not to support it because I think there's some really bad circumstances where the person who hurt the other person needs to get the book thrown at them. So I would be inclined not to support a limit on monetary damages.

You come from a highly educational background and work in the educational realm. Do you find that educators tend to be more liberal than conservative?

No. Well, the school where I work is a private Christian school, and a lot of the people, they're not all conservative, but a lot of them are. I wouldn't naturally assume just because somebody's on the faculty they would be a liberal. Although, if I didn't work at a school, I might not feel the same way.

Are there any departments or areas that tend to be more conservative than others in that part of academia you observe? You can't draw any generalizations that sociologists tend to be more liberal than accounting professors or something?

No, I can't. Just on the basis of my own experience, I couldn't say that.

In civil cases there are questions that call for testimony by non-lay people, by experts. We often rely on people from academia or from the field of expertise. How do you think you would listen and compare conflicting testimony if each side had an expert and they said somewhat different things? How would you reconcile that?

That's where I'd go on my intuition, because I have a pretty good ear for somebody who's trying to BS me. I would listen very carefully and then make sure that my BS meter was moving.

I think most jurors feel that everything that's happening is BS in the courtroom, at least in civil cases.

I never – I would not – that wouldn't be my attitude. I might change, but I wouldn't go into it with that assumption. Because you miss stuff if you go into some place with an assumption like that.

The reason I think that may be the case is because each side is advocating an opposite position. There's no attempt by the parties to find a middle ground. The jury has to reach the decision. When you come into a forum where both sides have completely different positions, it's pretty hard to say there's not a lot of slinging going on, you know?

Well, people can still have good manners and they can still –

Be civil.

Yeah. I mean, a basic thing I expect in any situation is that people are going to be civil to each other and they're going to have good manners, I guess. But I'm kind of an isolated – I don't get out much. I don't jump into social situations that much.

But you would answer a jury summons, and you may very well be on a jury.

Yeah.

That's why what you have to say is so valuable to me. So after the jury has to determine if there was negligence and if the negligence caused harm, then we get to this ultimate question of, what is the jury going to determine is the right amount of compensation? There are two kinds of damages. There are special damages, which are things like medical bills and lost wages that can be put onto a spreadsheet and added up with receipts to prove. There's also this element of damages called general damages, which are pain and suffering and disability and loss of enjoyment of life, for which there is no fixed standard for each juror to determine, ultimately, what is the right amount of money. How would you go about determining and calculating what is the fair amount of money for an injury that a person may experience differently than another person?

So this isn't the kind where you add up the bills, right? This is the other kind.

Right. This is the emotional pain and suffering, disability, loss of enjoyment of life; things that – a person could become severely depressed or have a limp for the rest of their life or have a medical device or who knows what. How would you go about determining what is a value on something that can't be valued under a fixed standard?

I guess one thing a jury can do, they can ask the judge for information. I would do that. And I would also ask if there was anything I could read that could help me understand the process.

The process of getting to a dollar figure or the process of what the person is going through?

*Getting to the dollar figure. Because if you plunked me down right now and told me I had to do it, I would have no clue. I know that sometimes juries award a dollar when they find there was harm done but they think the person is just okay aside from the bills and stuff like that. **But anything other than a dollar, I would be flummoxed. I wouldn't know what to do.** I would ask the judge.*

Nothing in your experience that would help you that you can think of? That would help guide you to that?

Nothing at all.

Are there amounts of money that, when you think about them, shock good conscience; like what amount of money would begin to shock good conscience, or would that be totally dependent on every case?

It'd depend on the situation. The only time I really get mad about dollar amounts is when I find out about some boss somewhere that's making like a thousand times what the average worker in their company makes?

And he's probably not adding that kind of value to the company either.

That's the kind of thing that makes me mad. But other than that, it's either a dollar amount I can kind of understand or it's a great big huge one like how much it costs to build a submarine or whatever. I feel completely disconnected from that. I just go to work. I get paid. I pay my bills, and that's all.

It's a very difficult area. Every juror approaches it differently and often they're driven by such things as, it's Friday afternoon, we need to come up with a number. Let's get done with this. It's frustrating. And there are lots of cases that jurors don't feel are that meaningful, depending on the injuries. How would an attorney convince you that a case is meaningful even if the amounts at stake were small?

Well, it's always meaningful. I wouldn't have to be convinced. If it's gotten as far as a case that's being heard by a judge and a jury, I would consider it meaningful.

Would you have any sympathy for a defendant if you thought the defendant didn't have any money to pay whatever judgment the jury might award? Would that influence you? For example, if the defendant were a school teacher and that's all you knew about the defendant, and yet it looked as if the plaintiff suffered very significant injuries in the hundreds of thousands, how would you be able to get over that hump where whatever you award may do something to hurt the life, at least, the monetary life, of the defendant?

Well, if they did it, I wouldn't care.

Would the question of insurance enter your mind at all?

Well, I thought that would all be explicit. Isn't it?

No. The instructions are, no one is to consider whether any side has insurance. It's not to enter the conversation.

Wow. I didn't know that.

I think as a practical matter, almost everybody kind of thinks about that, but nobody knows how much insurance the individual may have. They may just have minimum limits; different, generally, with entities, large companies that are being sued. I think everybody knows that they have big earnings and insurance. But with individuals, it's often very tough for an attorney doing the work I do to get juries to avoid sympathy on both sides. We don't want sympathy for the defendant. We just want what's right. How do you think that can be communicated?

I think by being very clear and again, with the body language, showing respect to people and using a good tone of voice. A person can do things with their tone of voice. **If I were sitting listening to an attorney, I'd like that person to use a normal tone of voice and very clear language.**

How important to you is it or would it be that the attorney genuinely cares for his client or her client?

I can't see that it would matter to me, unless the attorney was, like, if they hated their client and always looking at them funny. Other than that, I would assume that if it's their client that they would have a basic level of respect for the person and value.

Some lawyers that have gone through some wonderful training have learned how to become very good at putting themselves in the shoes of their client and become connected to and passionate about their client's case. We say, caring is contagious. I wonder if you have any thoughts about that.

No. If I were a person that had to have a lawyer, it wouldn't matter to me if they cared about me or not. I just would want them to do a good job.

Just that level of competence.

Yeah.

Okay. If you were a plaintiff who'd been injured and you were in a civil case, what kind of a juror do you think you would feel most comfortable with? What sort of traits would that person have?

They'd be a good listener. They'd have some intelligence in their eyes when you looked at them. I don't know. I guess that's about it. I'm trying to think of the jury I was on. There were all kinds of different people on it, but all of them – well, one of them was a little flaky, but the rest of them were all people who listened and thought about what was going on.

Are there any stereotypes that you would not want on your jury?

I doubt this person would show up, but I wouldn't want the women you see with those big ol' platform shoes and the pink hair and the slapped on make-up. That tells me that person, there's not much there; that once you scrape off all the junk, there's nothing there.

So they're wearing a mask?

Yeah, and somebody who shows with their body language that they don't care; you know, they're sitting there trying to look cool or something like that. I wouldn't want that. I just want an ordinary person who was paying attention.

How can a lawyer tell who's wearing a mask and who isn't?

I have no idea. I can't do that myself. Sometimes I can and sometimes I can't, but then again, most of my interactions are on a level where it doesn't matter.

We talked about traits and the kinds of people that we wouldn't want. I'm not sure this advances the discussion, but I tend to be avoidant of people who talk a lot and want to monopolize the jury selection process.

Jurors who do?

Yeah. People who want to make it all about them.

I never encountered that. But I wouldn't like that either.

You're sitting there with your group, whoever these people are, and the question is asked, do you want to be on this jury? Raise your hand. How would you feel, in general, about those people who raise their hand who say they want to be on the jury? Do you think they have ulterior motives?

No. I don't. I don't tend to assign an ulterior motive to a person. I have to pretty much be hit by a sledgehammer.

Until you have it. It's put in front of you. Is there anything you think would be helpful that I haven't touched on?

One thing I did want to say was that at the end of the trial that I was on, the jury members were grouped in the hall and the defense attorneys came out.

Sure. They want to know what's behind your decision.

One of us, I can't remember which one it was, asked them, how did you guys pick us for this jury? And he said, you were the ones that were left over after we got rid of the ones we really wanted to get rid of.

That's right. That's the way it kind of works.

I thought, in a way, I was like, gosh, that was a very honest answer. That was great. But on the other hand, I was like, I'm left over?

Sure. Because there are challenges for cause, the cause being that you get the judge to dismiss them because they can't be fair; which is very difficult to make. And then there are peremptory challenges, where each side gets x number of challenges for any reason. Then as you say, it becomes a little bit of a chess game. Part of this book has been to explore whether much of what's happening in jury selection really doesn't matter, that the most important thing is to ask people if they can be fair, trust their answer, respect their time and move on to the evidence gathering phase; unless there's some very, very obvious situation. It's going to do more harm for me to try and explore people's biases and find cause to get them off than it is if I just respect everybody's answers and proceed. I hope that's correct. I really do, because it'll make it a lot easier for all of us.

There was one question they asked, again, this was a criminal case and there had been injuries involved; they asked, would you have any trouble looking at a photo of some injuries?

Depending on what they might be.

I said no. But I could hear, there was this one woman that she made a sound, so there's some things that bother some people that don't bother other people.

Sure. I can look at books of cadavers for hours because I love the anatomy. To me, it's intriguing. But other people are just like, ugh, I can't look at that.

Even the idea of looking at it really upset her.

Thank you.

33

INVEST THAT TIME

Caucasian male, age 51, married, one child, one grandchild, FAA Analyst, Multiple 2-year degrees

I need you to be digesting what I'm saying to you, and don't take an hour digesting it, just don't take a microsecond. If I were to tell an attorney something that would help them engage, that would be the most important thing. Invest that time.

The judge says, ladies and gentlemen, please give your attention to the attorney for the plaintiff who's going to conduct jury selection. Having been in that position and imagining that, what is going through your mind and what are you thinking and feeling in that moment?

*My experience, on the prior case was they almost start arguing their case subliminally to you. So I just watch the attorney. **I watch their demeanor, their posture, their non-verbal cues.** I just start trying to prepare myself to being more attentive to them, wondering what direction they're coming from. **I want to make sure I answer the questions truthfully, that I don't misunderstand the questions. I have to really tune in.** It's the moment among moments where you have to be listening. You have to be on your A game. Those are the things that go through my mind.*

What are your motivations to be on your A game in that moment?

Because there are legal consequences. You have to scour the breadth of your life to make sure that if anybody asks you a question that you're truthful and don't forget something that happened in your childhood or that something happened 20 years ago. It takes a while. A lot of us don't spend time in the past, so when somebody asks you, have you ever been a victim of or known a victim of a crime or in a similar situation, you can't just say, oh, no, doesn't seem to be. And then you wake up five minutes later and you're like, oh, my God, I forgot about Joe Bob or whoever. So what goes through my mind is, okay, is there any chance that I know anything having to do with this and who was it? Do I have name? So if they ask, I'm not searching and feeling pressure to blurt something out. I'm going to make sure I have the answer forefront so I can answer truthfully and not take ten minutes to get to it.

Are you feeling comfortable with the notion of jury service itself? Some people feel very strongly they don't want to be there and will do all they can to not be there, whereas others embrace the notion of serving, even though it's only $10 a day for this right or privilege that we have. How do you feel?

I feel honored to serve. I don't feel it's appropriate to have it both ways. You

*can't argue out of one side of your mouth that you're being inconvenienced as a citizen and then complain that you're serving and gripe about the amount of money you make. The alternative is to have one or two people, maybe a very small percentage of your populace, making all the decisions about the case. **You have to be involved, and that doesn't mean you need to like it.** So, I'm very for that. I willingly accept that I may be paid pennies on the dollar. But I feel honored to do it.*

Thank you. That's appreciated, because there are many people who don't feel that way.

I know. I heard from many of them when I was in jury selection.

When you are in that moment, do you have any suspicions or criticisms or things you're tuning into that really matter to you right then; that you're expecting to hear or don't want to hear?

*Like I said, **I watch the attorneys just to watch their non-vocal cues, all of that stuff. I look for how much eye contact they make to get a sense of the sincerity of the conviction** of their – a lot of it's just making mental notes. If I've got an attorney and they're engaging me, but their dodging me, I start asking myself – I just follow the way.*

What's a dodge?

A dodge is where you're asking the question, but you're not giving me direct eye contact, you're not squaring up on me, you may be just going through the motions for your client. The notion of an engaging attorney, somebody that I'm making a mental note that seems to have a lot of interest in their case and conviction is somebody that approaches me, looks me in the eye, and just watches me as I answer the question. I try to collect as much intelligence as I can from the attorneys, if nothing else, to kind of get an idea of the full scope of the experience. Because I don't know anything about the case, my main thing is, okay, who's presenting the case and what do I know about them? If I see them and they're talking about it, did they have this tic that I observe before long or did they start to tic when they started talking about their case?

You're tuning into non-verbal communication, a large part of that. Do you have any special training in reading of non-verbal cues?

I don't; not beyond the run of the mill CSI type thing. I don't have any formal training in it. It's just an instinct.

I think we all have this. Pretty much right away we're being very critical, making decisions. I've come to the position, as we talked about earlier before the recording that I'm trying to find people who are open-minded, really open-minded. Granted, I would like people who are the most open-minded for my point of view, my case. I'm trying to even get away from ownership of that. How would you like to be asked about things, say, whether you're open-minded or not? Do you have biases or prejudices that might affect you in a given case? In a way that's respectful.

I don't have a protocol that I insist that people follow. Here's why: when you insist upon a protocol, you cut out large swaths of the communication process. If I can count on you and we have a close relationship, you should be able to ask me, are you biased? And I should be able to say, I'm biased. If, on the other hand, you have to toe a very fine line and check in with me, not only are there things you'd like to use as communication tools that might not get to me, but I may be cutting things out responding to you, so we're reduced to like 20% of the communication process.

Right. Not being completely genuine.

Yeah. You should be able to engage me and say, are you biased? Do you have these, and where do you think they come – anything like that. You certainly won't offend me.

That said, do you have any biases or prejudices in the civil context, with regard to civil injury cases? Have you had experiences or anything in your professional career where you think, I really don't like those?

Absolutely. I was a union local vice president for three and half years for a very large government union. In that capacity, I had a lot of people approach me for remedies of various kinds. Some of them extended to run of the mill grievances, but ranging into areas where they may have been physically harmed. In that capacity, you don't want to talk about the details out of respect for them, but you do form habits in your mind. You begin to profile, if you will, individuals, to the extent where you can almost by how they walk, what they say, it almost follows – it's eerie, in my experience. I can't speak for anybody else. But for me, it became almost like they were following a template. So when somebody comes in, would I have biases? Absolutely. Things you have to be aware of and say, is this person beginning to overlay with this template you've seen and how are you going to manage that?

It sounds like you have the awareness of your preconceived notions or biases.

I do. It's not fun being aware of them, because it's a lot of work testing them. When you're in a capacity, when you have to make a decision that's very important for a person, you don't want to be the guy that made the wrong decision because you chose to ignore critical information because of a bias you have. So you're always scrubbing. Are you being fair or unfair? Are you giving them too much latitude because you're terrified about being unfair?

Do you think the best we can hope for of people is that they have a bias and we just want them to at least, as you say, constantly be scrubbing?

I think it is. I don't know any person on the face of the planet in my 51 years that has demonstrated objectivity. I've never seen it proven. It's all relative to your personal paradigm. Somebody that you meet, they're completely objective, well yeah, they're of your political party. They grew up in your neighborhood, knew the same people, had the same biases, speak the same language.

Sure. Just more like you.

I've never seen that happen.

I will want to get to your work, because I think there may be an opportunity in your work where you are dealing with objective criteria. But before I do that, there's one question that came to mind. If we were in the courtroom for the first time and your turn came up and it was for me to ask you, how would I get to know who you are? What makes you tick as a potential juror?

I don't know that you can do that in a moment.

I'd have a lot less than that with you. I've got a room of 60 people.

Here's the challenge: when you fight biases, the advantage biases give you is making very fast decisions about things.

Right. Reptile decisions.

Reptile decisions. *You're fighting an inclination to ask them maybe their top three questions that'll get you an 80 percentile of their type, and then we're done here; moving on to the next client.*

Do you have a sense of what those questions might be?

I've never had anybody ask those questions of me, and I haven't asked them of myself. But if somebody were to ask me, name three questions that might get me close to understanding you, one of them would be akin to, and the wording would vary, **what is your concept of personal responsibility?** *I say that because I believe the individual bears the responsibility. I will happily admit there are times when things happen to you, but* **I think a person bears a lot of responsibility for the things that happen to them and for the things they do in life, so that's one. Another one is what is your obligation to grow, to evolve, as a human being?** *Which would be an odd question, probably not something you'd find comfortable asking in a courtroom. The reason I think that's a relevant question, though, is it promotes the notion that you have a responsibility to make things known that you don't know.*

Can you rephrase that question for me more concretely, so I understand it better?

Sure. In very simple terms, **do you have a personal obligation to learn?** *That's probably the simplest way I can put that. They'll either say, nope, or they'll say yeah. If they say no, then well, those are both different rides, but that's probably the simplest way I can phrase that question.*

Do you have a personal obligation to learn? If I ask you that question, what would be your response?

I'd say yes, for multiple reasons. As a juror, I'd say, I have an obligation to learn because I'm born into a culture and I'm obligated to learn that culture, to know the rules of the culture. I do not have the latitude to be born into a culture and remain willfully ignorant of its constraints.

So in a sense, we're trying to find out are people comfortable with being ignorant?

That's a true statement. That is certainly another way to phrase it. I think it still hits the mark. Is it acceptable for you to remain ignorant? Personally, I don't believe it is.

Okay. And there was a third?

The third thing would probably have something to do with the ability to make decisions in groups. How to phrase that question, I'm not entirely sure about, but it would have something to do with, **have you had to make tough decisions in groups?**

Stand up for yourself in a group?

Stand up for yourself in the middle of a group; a social experiment over time to find out how well you operate in the mix.

It also tells you what that person is willing to do to stand up for their –

Their convictions. Absolutely. I think those three questions would do a fair job of exposing, without purporting to kind of peg you, kind of get to a nucleus of a jury and see where your risk factors are, if you have any.

Do you have a sense if those are the same questions you would use or if there's a different set to find out if people can be open-minded? If they think they're open-minded, could I just say, hey, do you think you're open-minded, in general? Because everybody will have a different view of that.

I'm not comfortable – if I may, I'd like to lay aside the term open-minded and say I would ask a question akin to, **have you ever changed your decision based on new information?** *That won't capture everything, because you can dance around that one, too. But I think you made a great point.* **Open-minded is all relative. But if you ask a person, have you and how many times, or something; have you changed your decision based on new information, you might get a sense of their ability to be quote/unquote "open-minded." Flexible.**

Open-minded. Not dogmatic.

Not dogmatic. Not positional.

And then follow up if one really wants to. Like, can you tell me what that was?

Something that flows from that would be having a few words to describe, and I'm just going to pull this because I have a sense of what the question would need to be without a good feel for how, but it's the concept of intra-spaced versus positional bargaining. Are you the type of person that climbs on a hill and they have to knock you off, or will you walk up the hill with other people and negotiate how to climb the hill as you go, step by step? What type of person are you if you had a sense of your own being?

Interesting. I'm envisioning that; having fun in my mind with that question.

Are you the king of the hill type of guy?

On your own and you have to be knocked off, or do you negotiate? Positional versus bargaining.

Yeah, you didn't negotiate the terrain as you encounter it.

Researchers and the public weighed in and scale the most credible and least credible professions. Plaintiff's trial lawyers are second only to used-car salesmen in the public's perception. I'm walking in already having to catch up. How can I explore a juror's – your point of view; your perceptions; and your biases against civil trial lawyers? How can I learn whether you've got them, and are you at least willing to be aware of them during your process?

Here's the challenge. I don't purport to speak for the jurors involved here – just personally speaking, I'm fully aware you have to be an advocate for your client. They don't hire you so you can make the appropriate call. That is what judges and juries are for. They hire you to be an advocate for them. As a juror, I know that.

Do you think the other 40 – 60 jurors know that?

No, and that's just the law of averages. I know full well I can point to several people at random and safely assume they have some sort of bias against lawyers, because of what they've read in the paper, because of personal experience or whatever it is. They're advocates. If they're not advocates for you, they are an enemy. So it doesn't impact me being confronted by a trial lawyer. Now, to the question about how might you be able to expose some biases against trial lawyers –

Or just get people to share that they have them.

My personal techniques to confront very difficult topics are to use humor. To answer your question, hypothetically speaking, I would maybe use the old, there were 20 trial lawyers at the bottom of a – a joke-type thing, just to see –

What do you call it when a bus goes over –

*A good start or whatever. Just something. I just pull that out of thin air, because I have no experience trying to extract that. My personal experience in other difficult things is floating that and reading how people react. **The people that are looking through you and trying to burn a hole in the back of your head, you know, well, they're sending you a different message than those that are having a good old time with it.** I'm not quite sure. I wish I had a clean way to answer that. If they want to serve, and they have biases and they* *want opportunity for those biases to manifest, they'll find a way. That's hard to confront.*

What if I were to honor that?

How do you mean?

Judo. Somehow embrace that bias, if I knew about it.

Turn it to your advantage.

Any thoughts about that?

I think it is, and here's why. I'll return to a similar conversation having to do with how you reach jurors that may not be sympathetic to a plaintiff that's been injured; and there are people. My answer in that conversation had to do with making sure society realized they were trying to contribute; they were trying to plug into that culture; contribute to that culture. You're not looking for an opportunity to take the first free ride that shows up on an E Ticket attraction from Disneyworld, they're trying to contribute. Something happened to them to keep them from contributing. And everything then flows from that. That is a way, if a person were biased, if I came in and –

Show why this one is different?

Yeah. I'm never going to be qualified to tell you I'm not biased. That's what other people observe of me, right? But somebody would reach me, if I had a bias against people that were plaintiffs being harmed, that would be a way into me to say, you know, they're trying to contribute. Because my experience, if I'm biased against them, isn't that they were trying to do something for the organization, they were looking for a meal ticket, they got it, or some sort of something and there's experiences accumulated, crystallized into a bias, and the only way you break it is by taking it off another degree or two.

In criminal cases the burden of proof is beyond a reasonable doubt. In a civil case, the burden is defined differently. The burden of proof is a preponderance of the evidence. What does a preponderance mean to you?

*To put it in terms of statistics, **I would probably translate to mean, in my head, there's 70% plus more evidence in favor of one or the other. It's not a simple majority.***

70/30 is what a preponderance means for you. The definition goes on further: preponderance means more likely true than not true. Does that change your –

***Yes. That takes me to 51%.** Because all I need is a percentage point.*

If you got that, how comfortable are you in a close call making that at 51%?

I'm very comfortable. That's assuming all of the unanswered questions are capable of being answered, the totality. For example, if I was perched at 51% and I need more information from the judge or from somewhere else, I would need to get it. If I'm at 51%, and the judge said, sorry Charlie, you've got what you've got, then uncomfortable. Because I can say, you know what, all I have is all I have. There's no other information about this that I can get.

The 70/30 that you talked about, in my experience, tends to be more of gross negligence. Often, with medical negligence cases, jurors tend to apply a stricter standard, or impose a stricter burden of proof for the plaintiff when they're suing a doctor rather than, say, in the auto case. Any thoughts about that?

No. Let me ask you to state that one more time.

Sure. We were talking about the burden of proof and the preponderance being more likely than not. In medical malpractice cases, we find that jurors tend to require more instead of just that 51%, even though that is still the burden, the standard. They tend to need more. Do you have any thoughts about that?

*I do and I can see why, **because that 1% is easily absorbed by you second guessing yourself.** I liken it to these terms: it is like watching an almost stationary object and needing to see it move beyond one mile per hour to two so you're sure it's moving; or to hear something go up by a decibel or enough where you're like, you know what, I know that tone changed. When you're at 51%, you're still in that threshold where you're like, am I interpreting this correctly?*

Because we're talking subjectively, right?

Yes. That's why when I talk about terms of 70/30, which I know if we're talking in terms of 70/30, more likely than not, we're not even going to be in a courtroom or some situation where you actually have to make a case. But as a juror, where my life is impacted by making this decision, I need to be as crystal clear about the evidence as I can be. And in my mind, while it's not practical perhaps, I will argue for more than that 1% where I'm still in my head wondering, is that enough? Did you see them move or did you hear that sound?

Right. The eyes on the prize for us is almost always going to be, how much money is the jury going to award the client. A defense attorney is asking the same question; they just want it to be a lot less. We have two measures of damages: special damages, which are lost wages, medical bills, out-of-pockets; anything you can have a receipt for and add up to a fairly concrete number, even if it takes expert testimony to get there. We also have a second category called general damages. Those are pain, suffering, disability, loss of enjoyment of life. Those are entirely subjective, and there's no fixed standard for a juror to determine what amount of money should be awarded. All 12 jurors are going to have a different idea. How would you approach making that decision? What things would you want to consider? What information would you need?

What I need to make that decision is some sense of the life they led up to the accident. I'm going to tell you what I would need, that doesn't mean I have a realistic expectation of getting it. In the hypothetical world where I feel like I've been fed every piece of information I need, I know exactly what their spending habits were up until the moment they were injured; that way, it's simple math for me. In a data-driven world, as a binary thinker, I'm propagating that logic to say, well, they were averaging 30k a year, they weren't in school; they weren't developing. More than likely, adding for inflation, all of that stuff, they're on this trajectory.

And those are special damages, things like wages and medical bills that experts can come in and agree or disagree on to some extent. We're talking about those unseen damages; the pain and suffering and disability everybody experiences differently. If you lost an arm and I lost an arm, we might deal with things differently.

Okay. Thank you for clarifying that for me.

I didn't ask it very well. There's no fixed standard to make an award of money. The plaintiff proved they've been injured because of negligence. You penciled out these other damages, the actual monetary losses. How do you get to what's fair for the pain and suffering and disability that the law allows?

*The thought process there would be trying to bring the unknown into a known, which means, if I know you're in pain, I know you're suffering, I would try to reach for something getting back to what sort of data and information I would need. What is the average rate for a therapist of this kind or a doctor of this kind? I don't mean to imply I'm just looking for simple math, because you're dealing with a person's impact. **But to be perfectly frank, I'm not going to give somebody millions of dollars just to make them feel better. You have to do something with that.** Now to do something with that, you need to convert that into therapy or something and get on that path. This isn't a meal ticket.*

Potentially others would argue with you in the jury room at deliberations that no, we think this person's been hurt and no amount of money is ever going to restore them to the life they had before. How do you –

How would I engage in that argument? My approach would be this: I would say, thank you, you're making my point for me. No amount of money. So if it's not money, what is it? Were they fishing with the arm before it was broken? What were they doing with the arm? Is there a rehab clinic we can bring into the fold that can replace that function; not necessarily give them a brand new arm, but can restore that life? Can they still go fishing with their son? You can't reconstruct their life, but the next best thing you can do is reason through their depiction of their life and the realistic depiction of their life to try to put it back together and restore it the best way you can.

The average person's life is pretty boring and the lawyer has to show the jurors what the life was like before the injury. Either it's going to be an exhaustive list or story of lots of little things like, well, she used to tend her roses or she used to make doilies or – what meaningful information would you need to hear about the individual, and who would you need to hear it from about how their life's been impacted?

No, I get it.

Emotionally and physically.

> As a juror, I'm fully aware that one side of the argument is getting somebody that's so close to them they're going to give you every little thing. They used to read two or three books a day, they were tending garden while they were doing needlepoint; to the cold hard doctor or somebody that's like, well, they've demonstrated this or they're capable of doing that. I know they're somewhere in between that scale. I don't know that there is a way to pick one person that has the credibility I'm looking for because that would like, okay, they can be a relative, but they can't be more than one step closer to them. Just to play this out, I wouldn't need to conduct exhaustive interviews to see what they did with their daily schedule as much as, say, **give me a general sense of what they would do. You should be able to depict to me in ten minutes what your life is, whether it's vigorous or not. If it's boring, okay, two minutes. But you should be able to get to the point.** I like doing gardening and reading, and that tells me, okay, then you can't be color blind, more than likely, or you can have some sort of work around with that. You need to have these functions. You should be able to get there fairly quickly and without telling me it takes exactly two hours to do this. That is de minimis.

Here's an example: two people, very different; one's strong, one frail; one young, one old. They each lose a non-dominant arm. Should they be compensated equally, all other things, medical bills, wage losses, being equal? For that pain and suffering and disability and loss of enjoyment of life that one would expect with the loss of a limb, should they be compensated equally for that, or are there to be different considerations?

> When you say equally, do you mean literally the same dollar figure?

Right.

> I would say no, because when you're talking about youth or the lack thereof, youth or wisdom, okay – the equation takes on a different form. You have a number that's either larger or smaller that plays in that equation. Time. I can't see giving an individual a certain amount of money and then somebody that's older than them precisely the same amount, because they're not going to be around long enough to enjoy the same benefits.

Could you apply the same multiplier, let's say, only to a different time frame?

> Yes.

Something to that extent? An attorney could argue, how about $5 a day for every day they have in their average life?

> Absolutely. Because you can have a philosophical argument and a decision made that's meaningful to people. You have to be able to quantify that. So if you know what the multiplier is, then it becomes, okay, well, what dollar figure are you going to associate with this? It's just – it's math again. Is it $5 a day, what is it?

What state are you in?

Some would argue that the older person's time is every bit as valuable because that's all the time they have left. In other words –

No, I'm totally tracking with you. I totally get that. I would understand their line of argument if they're suddenly waking up one day and realizing, oh, (expletive), I need to make twice as much value per day. So I'm doing twice as much and almost negating the advantage the younger person has.

The argument that I've reached my golden years; I've put in all that time and now I've got to deal with – I only have ten years left, and those ten years are going to be impaired. I'm just curious what your response to that would be.

My response would be, well, lucky you that it took this incident for you to have that awakening moment and suddenly do things with your life that you weren't doing up until the moment you got injured.

In addition to finding who is a credible, non-biased or at least learning about what biases people have on a jury, what can the attorney do to establish a human connection with you in that period of time, in that environment?

I would say the same techniques as if I just met you in a bar or a coffee shop or some other location; the same standard applies. There is a slight disadvantage in that, personally, I'm tactile. I like to shake hands. Depending on the nature of the relationship, I will wrap my arms around you. You don't have the luxury of that in the courtroom without making a lot of people very uncomfortable. **But what you can do are engage somebody, direct eye contact, the same things we're taught; using your tone, responding with – how shall I say this – considering my responses before moving on to the next question. If I sense your cadence is a little too flip, a little too fast, I'll know you're not engaging with me. If, on the other hand, you listen to me for a minute and I give you an answer, you don't need to take ten minutes to ponder what I said to you, but take more than a microsecond.** *That way I know, okay, because if you don't, then I know you're fishing. You were looking for a key word or two in what I said and you didn't find it, so you're moving to the next thing.*

Truly honor the communication.

Yeah. I'd watch that. It's very important. If you do those things, the chance that I'll make a human connection to you increases dramatically.

Do you think that would change how you view the evidence?

It may, but you're not operating in a vacuum. You have another person that may connect with me, too. So the challenge becomes, which one of you connected better and is there a trust relationship? I can form a human connection to you and not trust you.

I need to be the most credible person in the courtroom. How do you think a lawyer can do that? Do you think brutal honesty is the way to do it? Is there some other –

Brutal honesty helps, but you need to take a tack where it puts emotion in its proper place. *I say that as a binary thinker, as somebody in a data-driven occupation, because the flip side of the argument is where you've come in and you talk about how this organization injured this person and the first thing you're trying to do is make me very angry and sympathetic for that individual. The way you reach me is this individual had maybe ten years on the job without an incident. They're very productive. They spent so many years and they were at the top of their game. They were in the top three producers of their organization. After this incident, they weren't in the top ten, assuming for a moment they had ten. You build a track record of success through statistics, to me.*

Sure. You need the dance.

Now, **emotion does have its place, just not a big place. Because if you come at me with emotion, then I know you're weak on evidence.** *I can't say it any other way than that.*

In almost every civil case, a large part of is played by experts on both sides, of all degree of pedigree and of ability to communicate and likability. It doesn't seem to matter; you can have a Harvard-trained expert and you can have paid experts of questionable motive. Jurors, for the most part, don't seem to –

Discern?

– make much of a distinction between one or the other. How would you view differing expert testimony?

The first thing I look for, and same thing most people would tell you, I look for the package first. If you walk in, you could have no credibility, but if you dress well, you make the first cut. If you are the Rainman, but you're wearing a burlap sack, you may not make the first cut, even though you should have. You need to prove to me you're taking my time up if you walk into that courtroom; you need to dress like you're about to explain something very important.

You need to see something?

I need to see something from you. I don't need you to act, I need to see the package first. After that comes the next part, which is how you come across as being trustworthy. That falls back into eye contact and all of those other signals. But you have to walk in with a package first. That doesn't mean the package is supposed to be any particular way, but this is a very important process. If I'm a juror, I shouldn't be walking in with flip flops. If I'm not walking in flip flops, you shouldn't be either. Walk in like you're taking it seriously.

If one expert was making $50,000 for their time and opinions and the other was making $10,000, would you feel there is an inherent bias there? Or would you feel that's just the way it is? Would you be more swayed for or against the one who earns more because they've been paid more or do you have any thoughts?

I have some thoughts. Me, personally, I say to the guy that's not getting the best bang for his buck, you need to market yourself better. If you're making money, that's fine. You making money in and of itself doesn't tell me there's anything wrong with the process.

Some would say, they're getting paid more, therefore, they're more inherently biased for the side –

Which is a logical fallacy, because the only thing you know is they're being paid more for the same evidence they're giving. That doesn't extend to any wrongdoing. Perhaps, but perhaps not. Are you going to be the guy that banks on that and they're wrong? Maybe I'm just a very credible witness. Maybe I do my homework. Maybe I can articulate my way out of a paper bag. Should I be punished because I can do that when Joe Bob over here can tell you the same thing, take twice as long to say it, and in a language I may or may not understand? That's not my problem.

When you first look at the plaintiff, what are you looking to see, one way or the other? Given that we all come from very different backgrounds.

That is very difficult for me to answer. I'll take a stab at it. Because I'm not sure, in the final analysis. I'll tell you what I'm not looking for. That's probably better. **I need to see that the plaintiff takes the process seriously. So they need to be engaged as well, same standard for everybody else.** *If they're slouching, if they're texting or they're doing something, just sort of, you're wasting my time, I'm just kind of here, that doesn't indicate to me that they're engaged in the process. I don't know that I'm particularly impressioned by their wardrobe. I would probably expect them to be groomed. I think that's a reasonable expectation. Even if you're of modest means and you got injured in a case, in this day and age, you can find a way to dress yourself up. You can run down to the Goodwill or whatever and look pretty good. I need you to look decent when you come in. I need you to be engaged, I need your posture to communicate to me, I'm focused, I'm trying to make my case here. I feel like I am wronged and I need you to be listening to me. I don't want to see reactions to the opposing attorney's arguments that I perceive to be childish. Now, I need to be fair, because if I were wronged and some attorney made an outlandish claim, I can't say I'd be stoic. I also wouldn't be a child and smirking and very exacerbated type of –*

Decorum, I think.

I would use decorum. I think some people may not fully understand what decorum means. Actually, I think I'd be okay with slight breaches of decorum based upon how important the case was. We're talking about multi-million dollars and you're lying, if I perceive lying, I might permit you to shake your head or that type.

Sure. Situational.

Just don't blurt and do handstands in the courtroom.

If you were a plaintiff in a civil suit, what kind of juror would you be most comfortable with? What traits would you be looking for in a jury?

That is very difficult for me to answer, because I'm personally very uncomfortable making a case to anybody that I don't know; total strangers. I need to have some sort of connection with somebody. It's hard for me to say what type of juror. You know what? Okay. Let me modify that. I would prefer females, because they're more sympathetic to emotional responses, generally speaking. If I had males, well, let me pause for a moment. If I could cherry pick, it would really be based on the merit of my case. If I know there weren't a lot of stats, there wasn't any database that could chronicle my epic performance as an employee, I would know there's nothing that says how good or bad a job I could point to. My performance appraisals, if I could, I'd be comfortable with people that comprehended stats. So geek types, I'd be okay with. The extent of my injury, I would want to pitch to females, generally, because I could look them in the eye and say, you know, I've been – and know there's, statistically speaking, a greater likelihood they'll be sympathetic than that cold stats guy I need because of my performance appraisals. So as a plaintiff, I need to be able to hit both and target them depending on what my case looks like.

Do you have any personal reservations if you were ever a victim to having to be a plaintiff in a lawsuit?

I have a lot of pride. It would have to be egregious, it would have to dramatically alter the course of my life. There are a lot of things, you know nickel and dime stuff, they do, but man, I – yeah.

When you say nickel and dime, does that suggest any monetary limit to you?

*I place a very, very high value on my time. What I mean by that, just to quantify, a hundred or so dollars an hour, not in terms of some sort of business arrangement, it's just when I do things, they are either important or they're setting up important things that need to be done to include building relationships, maintaining relationships. If I'm in court to argue something that's been done because I mashed my hand and I'll be back in the fight, so to speak, in about a month; the cost of me correcting the issue with my hand is more than offset by the time I need to spend thinking about the court case, hiring an attorney. When I say nickel and dime, that's what I mean. **If, on the other hand, it takes me out of the fight for a year, I have to change jobs, is something that doesn't thrill me, that's a different conversation.***

Do you make room for the notion that different people make different amounts of money and so different amounts of money are more or less meaningful; or the same amount of money may be more or less meaningful to different people?

*I absolutely do. One of the reasons for that is because I'm experiencing that right now. For the first time in my life I know full well that a dollar means far more to me at this moment in time than it did before. I'm careful. I pinch pennies now far more than I did before. And I did it before that. I know other people have walked similar paths. So **I'm absolutely aware that a dollar will mean far more to some people than others.***

Is there anything that has come up that might be helpful for me to hear or think about?

> The only thing I'll mention will have to do with, interpersonal content, I think it goes a long way. It certainly doesn't trump trust. Many people will love it. I'm fully aware of that. But I'm also fully aware that somebody that has all the credibility in the world and no interpersonal skills will sometimes get shafted just by virtue of the fact they don't have interpersonal skills. Some people, it takes a while for them to cultivate. **My advice to people that are wanting to reach out to jurors is, you need to invest the time in them. They may be a foregone conclusion in your mind or they're a necessary evil, however you want to quantify it, and I get all of those rationale. I don't begrudge them feeling that way. But do not take them for granted, because they will detect it, and they'll detect it quickly.** It's very important that an attorney be tuned in and detect that. When I make statements I'll watch how you digest what I say to you, and if you move onto the next question before it's out of my – before the answer to the previous one's out of my mouth, I'll know that. I've got a clock in my head, and I can tell the cadence that you're marching to.

Which suggests the attorney's not really engaging, investing in you personally?

> Yes. And the reason they're not engaging with me is because they're – I'll put it in terms, again, in a computer world, digitized world – they are looking through my stream of data that I'm transmitting to them, right? They're searching for a pattern. If they don't detect the pattern, they're moving on to the next question. **If you're engaging with me, you don't listen until I say something having to do with money or sympathy. You were listening to everything I had to say to you, and you're giving it all due regard.** If I'm watching you and you're just kind of bobbing your head and you're off in your analytical mind, just searching through that byte stream as I'm emitting it, I'll know what you're doing. **I need you to be digesting what I'm saying to you, and don't take an hour digesting it, just don't take a microsecond. If I were to tell an attorney something that would help them engage, that would be the most important thing. Invest that time.** You may not think it's worth a lot. You may think, well, for the microsecond I invest in you, I could be off on the other juror and we can move this case along. It's like, well, you have a higher likelihood of losing because you were turning people off like switches as you interview them just because you're not dwelling for a minute, taking a step closer to them. I don't mean to go on about it, but I will for just a minute, because it's very important to me. I watched Bill Clinton in the first presidential race and his ability to do that. There was one forum in particular where he did a remarkable job of getting out behind the podium and getting into the audience; not running up into there, but engaging and stepping toward them. The media made a lot out of it and said it was a very effective technique, and I agree because when he did it, I was moved. He took three steps, four steps, but I was moved because he was trying to come out to me. He was – what people perceived as, he's coming out to me. It's small, but when you factor that in to how you're packaged, whether you're coming out,

you're stepping toward me, whether you're taking just a minute to ponder what I'm saying, it adds up. It's all math.

With all that, is there a way to avoid the notion that the attorney is just selling a bill of goods? Doing a job? I'm just here because. A lot of people are frustrated that when they walk into a courtroom, they can't trust anybody because both sides are coming from completely different points of view. So they say, I don't trust either one of them. They're both trying to sell me a bill of goods. What are your thoughts?

Well, that is not the attorneys' fault. That is the process. They have to understand and respect the process.

Should the attorney talk about that?

If the Court permits you to, I would. I would stand in front of the jurors and say, you're going to hear me make a case for my client. That is what I do. I make a case for my client. It is up to you, the jury, and to the extent the judge is involved in the process, collectively, to make a decision and assess damages in the course of it. I am not here to tell you which one of us is right or wrong; I'm here to be an advocate for my case, so I'm going to present all the facts and all of the evidence to you pertaining to my client. That doesn't mean the opposing counsel is a bad person. It just means I'm not here to represent their interest, I'm here to represent his or hers. I understand you may have concerns about me not presenting the full breadth and scope of the case, but this process involves me presenting a piece of it. And collectively, we present a 360-degree perspective.

Thank you.

34

FAIR QUESTIONS

Caucasian female, age 25, single, Admissions Counselor, B.A. Liberal Arts

I think as long as you have the option not to answer any questions, it's a fair question.

Ladies and gentlemen, please give your attention to the lawyers who are going to conduct jury selection. In Washington, that's a pretty short process. We have about an hour each to get a fair jury. When the judge says that and you're in the courtroom with your potential jury peers, what are you thinking and what are you feeling?

I would be pretty interested or excited to be a part of it, honestly. I would probably find it pretty fascinating. I've heard that it's really dull from parents of friends who had to do it, but I would probably be pretty interested. It's a part of the legal system I know very little about. It's interesting that people who know very little about it get to be participants in it. That's pretty unique. Like when you get to vote, you don't have to be educated about it. It's interesting that they smoosh you together and that – there isn't a lot that I would know about going in. My own education and learning about the judicial system a little bit more would be really interesting to me. Day off work.

It'd be more than a day. Many people feel they'd rather not be there. Have you heard that from friends of yours?

My dad will do anything to get out of it. He's not a great candidate for a jury because of his occupation. He's in journalism. I'm sure the second time is a lot less interesting than the first. It would be novel to me. So I would be like, oh, interesting.

It's not a liberty issue like a criminal case but it's a money issue; how do you feel about sitting in judgment on these parties that are having a dispute?

I feel okay about that. I feel very trusting of people and try to see the best in everybody. We live in a culture, especially in America, where any little thing happens and immediately someone threatens to sue somebody, which I think is a little extreme. But I feel really confident in my own moral compass. A complication there would be from feeling like I don't really know what I'm talking about or what I'm doing and wanting to make an educated decision rather than like a gut feeling. But I think the part of it that's just listening and evaluating and paying attention to detail. I would feel confident. I don't think I would be somebody who could go home with a guilty conscience at the end of the day. I would have to feel really good about my decision.

A trial is essentially the sides educating the jurors about the facts of the case. It is the lawyer's job to give you the information you need to feel good about your decision. But again, sitting in judgment, how do you feel about the notion that your decision may require someone to pay sums of money to another person because of an injury they caused negligently or wrongfully?

It's hard because if you're negligent, that doesn't mean you're intentionally hurting somebody, but I think we should be responsible for our actions. Someone almost hit me in the crosswalk with my dog when I was walking here; was looking at their phone.

That's living in the city every day, right?

Yeah. We were paying attention so we didn't get hit by the car. But if I were blind, I would have been hit by that car because I had to jump away. If that happened to a blind person walking across the road or a deaf person, I would – I feel like people should be responsible for their actions. I think negligence is still a mistake. If you hit somebody because you were texting while driving, even though you weren't driving off the road to hit them, still, for me, you have to take responsibility for your behavior.

How do you feel about the system set up to, not punish, but compensate? Not punish the offender, but compensate the person who's been injured? Do you think that is a workable –

I still think it seems really, really extreme. Sometimes I hear people getting millions of dollars for really minor injuries. I think it should be within reason. If you break your leg, and you get all this extra compensation, extra compensation, extra compensation because you have a smarter lawyer or a more manipulative lawyer, I think that's kind of tricky. I've definitely learned not to sign any contract at a job that I didn't read and give to somebody who was willing to take a look at it; a lawyer to look at it and tell me what I'm getting into. But, again, I'm naïve and have a lot of blind faith in – I don't know. I probably like the court system more than any other branch, the judicial branch more than other branches. I probably have more faith in it than the other branches.*

Why do you suppose that is?

I think probably because it's the one I know the least about. Maybe the other branches are more on my radar. Big court cases affect me, obviously. But that little minutiae, I've never been in a position where I was being sued or suing somebody, so I don't know very much about it. I guess the circumstances I hear of are extreme. This person got millions of dollars. On this smaller scale, I don't hear about those trials.

Those cases that you hear about, the extreme ones, do you place a lot of validity in what you hear about those?

*I think a lot of times the victims are – **sometimes I think victims are taking*** *advantage of the system. I definitely know people. I used to work at a local grocery store. I definitely know people in environments like that, like grocery store environments, they're eager to get injured and take some time off. Not in a big way, but they would milk that.*

You mean employees?

*Yeah. Like an employee would – if you trip and fall, all of sudden you're getting sick comp days. Even on a little scale like that I definitely felt like, if so-and-so broke their leg at work, they would really milk that. I don't necessarily think those places treat employees very well or make them want to work there or – you know, a lot of times those places, people are not working in the right conditions and they have every right to feel disgruntled, but I still think there's a little bit of that that happens. If a city bus hits me when I'm crossing the crosswalk, I'm going to want a lot of money from the city even if I just stubbed my toe or broke my toe or whatever and couldn't go to work. **I think people take advantage of that because it's so normal now to sue somebody for all they're worth.***

When you hear about somebody suing, how often do you think the jury hears the evidence and does something reasonable as opposed to something that's –

Extravagant?

Extreme.

I don't know. I think the cases I hear about are usually the cases that are extreme.

McDonald's, for example?

*Right. It would be this big blown out thing, and usually, in my experience, I hear about corporations versus individuals where I'm like, sure, sue me. I don't care. That seems reasonable. But if someone sued my mom for any reason, it would be devastating. We don't have a lot of money, so it would be a huge deal. Any amount. Again, I tend to side with – like **if someone injures you, the person that injures you should be responsible for making that right in some way;** just like hitting someone's car.*

When we have trials and get jurors together, one of the things the system wants is a fair trial. I'm trying to get jurors who can be open-minded. How do you think a lawyer can find out who is and isn't open-minded in a group of people like that?

Do you do it by profession? I've heard that there are certain professions that you tend to stay away from.

There can be rules of thought that, you know, software developers may tend to be more data-driven, less sympathetic or empathetic. What I'm getting at is, how can the lawyer ask you, for example, if you have any biases or prejudices or preconceptions that might make it hard for you to be fair and give each side an even start?

That's a really hard question. I don't know. I don't even know how anybody could *be unbiased. **Maybe it's more about bringing in people with different biases and just being upfront about what those biases are.** Like writing a paper, an essay, in college, you always have to state that you have some kind of bias going and you have to disclaim, okay, I'm writing about this political system, but just so you know, I'm really hard right or hard left or I don't vote or something. You have to disclose that. I'm writing this paper about the fallacies of something; but you have to say. Then maybe you can look and like, this jury is all super, super liberal and maybe we need some more conservative or – you know? Or all these people are bosses at big corporations and we need some little guys in there. Whatever it is. Maybe that puts too much trust on people to disclose that information when they don't want to.*

That's the difficulty. How does this lawyer dealing with a group of strangers get people to be honest about their abilities to be the right juror on that case?

You put them all on like the airplane in the exit aisle, are you capable? Do you need to be reassigned?

That's a good point; and some really do.

It's probably hard, too, because a lot of people don't want to be there like you said.

A lot of people don't want to be there. The ones that don't want to be there often will speak up and say they've got a hardship or just can't be there.

Or make up a reason; to not be there?

Do you think it's fair to ask if you have any biases or prejudices or preconceived notions that might make it difficult to give each side a fair start? Is that a fair question?

I think it's a fair question. I think as long as you have the option not to answer any questions, it's a fair question. *When people ask me questions, as long as they're not upset when I'm like, I don't want to answer that question, then I'm not that easily offended.*

Does that question elicit anything that would be uncomfortable for you without going into it now?

No. I don't think so. Maybe people who aren't willing to answer that question aren't comfortable about their biases. I think we all have them. I've always wondered how those selections are made. It doesn't feel random to me when – like my mom gets asked to be on juries all the time and my dad's never been. They're like, we don't want you.

I've heard those stories.

They're like, we don't want you because they know he's biased. My mom's pretty biased too, but she gets asked all the time. And I'm like why do you? On paper, she must look more impartial, I'm assuming, because of her job or something about her. She gets asked to go on juries all the time.

Here?

No. My parents live in Colorado. They could write a movie about her called The Constant Juror because she's always on a jury or doing something. She works with school boards and stuff like that, so I think they just think she's going to be dynamic in that way. But she's got her own biases, too.

When the attorney begins to inquire to you and the group about things like open-mindedness, is there anything that an attorney must absolutely avoid doing to turn you off to the process or that individual?

There are certain types of bias that I think someone might say like – because I'm pretty broke. So that affects certain ways that I might interact with the world. But I don't necessarily think of that as a bias. I'm not biased against wealth.

Just your experience.

It's like who I am, or like being a woman or being white; I think those inherently make you biased a certain way. But I think my biases are more personal to me. They're not categorical like that. They're not like, I'm a lady so I think this, or I'm white, so I think this. I think those sort of questions get really tricky to me, especially right now. There's a lot of feminist tension and a lot of black and white tension. I think there's a lot of minority tension; political tension. I think it's good to give people space to express other parts of themselves that might be more dynamic than just like, oh, you're this way, so you must be biased in this direction or you're this way so you must be biased against –

Because of the category that you're in.

*Right. And **I think people are surprisingly dynamic in that way, where they're just not categorical like that.** I'm always like a little bit offended when someone implies that I might think or do or be a certain way because of my gender or something. Does it really matter?*

What we're getting at in the context of these trials when I talk about bias, race is generally not an issue; sex is generally not an issue in the kinds of cases we're talking about. The big bias that we are facing, that we like people to talk about, is a bias against jury trials or against compensating people who have been injured - people who are against lawsuits against doctors, for example, because they don't believe a doctor should be sued. All of these legitimate beliefs. It's just helpful to learn -

Is that what this is about?

Yes. For example, if you're close to people in the medical profession, you may have strong feelings about that, and same if you're in the legal profession.

Do the people on the jury get information about the trial beforehand; like, it's against a doctor?

At the time of jury selection, you would know the names of the parties. So it could be -

So you could be like that's my brother, I can't be on.

John Doe versus So-And-So, M.D. and Such-And-Such hospital or clinic. The judge would explain this is a case where there was negligence caused - allegedly caused - by the doctor or the hospital or the clinic.

And then the question is like, do you ask specifically, do you have any biases against –

That's what we're trying to learn when I'm asking you how these questions could be asked of you in a sensitive way, especially where you're not feeling manipulated somehow; where you're feeling open and trusting enough to answer the questions honestly.

I think I always feel better asking. I'm also really not sensitive to stuff like, what race are you? What gender are you? And check off the box questions, because I took the SATs and all of those college applications or job applications are really fresh in my mind where I'm just like check the boxes. I love when people let you fill in the answer yourself. So you can say, my dad is a doctor, but I don't have any problem with it or whatever. But I think when people ask you, it feels like you're getting an opportunity to say whatever you need to say about it, rather than being like, these are you two choices and neither of these apply. A lot of times I feel like – other.

Like when you're doing a survey for something you've bought.

It's always other when I need help with something. There's never a help box that's helpful to me. But I like when there's an opportunity to just as a person be like, will this help me? I might support and care about doctors, but it doesn't mean that I want a negligent doctor to not be in trouble. But maybe that's misleading on the form if I'm like, yes, my mom's a doctor. That doesn't mean I don't think doctors should be sued if the situation was correct.

That gives the opportunity to ask further questions about it. Oh, I see you've got a close friend in the medical profession, how close is that and has that shaped your opinion? If so, would you be willing to share? That's kind of how it –

*I just feel more honest, too. It's nice to be asked. Or if it's sensitive, I think people are more willing to be forthcoming about things about them. **I feel like most people are pretty willing to talk about their experience of the world if you ask them. But it's different if you're just like, these are your three choices and none of them apply to you.***

Right. How do you feel about cases where doctors could be sued, for example, as opposed to just automobile cases? Many people feel that doctors should have immunity. How do you feel about that?

I think it would depend on the case. If you entered or your mom or someone entered a risky surgery and you knew there was a chance – I mean, a risk of life is dying or having complications from complicated surgeries. For the most part, medical professionals want their patients to be healthy – and as long as the doctor's doing everything in their power – **but I also think in any job there can be someone who abuses that power.** I hate when you read about cases of doctors administering drugs incorrectly, intentionally or unintentionally. **That's a really important field to know what you're doing. And if you don't know what you're doing, you shouldn't be a doctor.** So I kind of feel like if there's nothing they can do for you or they did what was in their power and you didn't listen or it didn't work out, it's not their fault. It's a complicated surgery. People are different. People react to things differently. I'm sure that's just part of the job for them is losing patients.

If rules aren't followed, does that cause you to think any differently? For example, a doctor who doesn't administer a correct dose on a proper schedule. Or – I got a little afield on the doctors, and that's my fault. But, for example, a person who's texting when driving. The rule is, you can't do that. People do it. We all probably do it. I've done it. And then somebody's hurt. They didn't intend to cause hurt.

I guess if you are texting and driving and you hit someone with your car then, I mean, you didn't have to be texting. You just hit someone with your car. There's always a way, especially automobiles I feel are so black and white. Some way eventually they find cause or they don't. It was everybody's fault or it was your fault. I feel like with a doctor, it's kind of like dropping a baby. If I found out someone was prescribing me medication incorrectly, I would be really upset, because it's money, it's a lot of money; it's really expensive to be a patient. And your health is so important. You can't trust the person responsible who's supposed to be an expert and know more and take care of you. I would understand wanting to sue for that.

Do you feel that your generation, generally speaking, has the same views as you've been expressing to me about the court system?

I don't want to speak for everybody, but I definitely think my generation is fairly fed up with a lot of the ways that things are done. **I think my generation is in favor of justice, whether that's against a police officer or a judge or a doctor. I feel like my generation is way more obsessed with protecting little people, because most of us are little people that don't make a lot of money and are really struggling – and the economy – and are educated and have very little power. I think a lot of us feel that way; like the system doesn't necessarily protect or serve us.**

So accountability is important?

For sure, but not in an unreasonable way. I don't feel oh, I want to ruin someone's life for an exorbitant amount of money so I can be rich and well off. **I think people want to feel safe and taken care of by the systems that are supposed to keep them safe and take care of them.** Anybody, and I definitely think doctors and law enforcement –

Any profession.

*Any profession where you're like, this is the person I turn to when I need help and you damage instead of helping me. Or your employer; anything. It's like, **those are the people that my generation really turns to and we're like, guide us,** and then you don't always have that.*

If I didn't know you to the extent that I do here in this interview, what would be the one or two best questions to find out who you are and what your values are?

I think I would ask me like what I'm doing, not for work, but what I'm passionate about and what my work is in the world. I work in admissions, but I'm a musician; that's my thing. And I travel. I have to have jobs that enable me to travel and make art, and that's the core thing about me. When I talk to other people, a lot of times I'm like, how are you? What have you been up to? And they're like, this is my job. And I'm like, I know, but what are you doing? What drives you? I think for a lot of young people especially, we're not doing jobs in our field. We're doing other jobs getting to our field. I think it opens more doors – what kind of lifestyle you have.

What's your passion?

***How do you classify yourself?** I always say that I'm a musician, even though that's not how I make money.*

How do you classify yourself?

That's how I describe myself and what I put my time and energy into. And that's a hard question.

If you were asked that same question but with the word label instead of classification, does it have the same effect or would it be –

Yeah, but I think label is a negative word.

Negative word. So classification. Okay. I'm just wondering if I asked somebody how they classify themselves, they might –

How do you describe – I don't know. It's such a hard thing. I know very few people under 30 who are in my bracket that are doing what they want to be doing and love what they're doing. People a little bit older, hopefully, they're on a career path that's meaningful to them. But a lot of us are not at all, and are still figuring it out or know what we want to do and are doing it for no money. It's a hard question. How do you spend your day, your time?

So I would learn about you if I asked that question that your musicianship and your art, your creativity are very important to you? Is that what I would learn?

Yeah. And you would probably also learn I am somebody that works a lot of really long hours and multiple jobs. This is my first real grown-up job. I was teaching music part-time. I was waitressing. I was working at a grocery store, and touring, *all at the same time. So I'm not really in one community. I think it also says in a way that maybe my political leaning is like, this isn't working, a little bit. I don't feel steadily employed. I don't feel employable in my field, even though I have a high education for my age. There's definitely some dissatisfaction there that I am a little biased towards big corporations or systems that I feel have not served me well, which I feel in those kind of lawsuits that you're talking about are important, because if I was on a jury, if it was a big chain grocery store, I would probably be not the person to ask, because I would be like, down with grocery stores. (Expletive) grocery stores, even the nice ones. Whereas if you put me on something about school, I'd be school's great, you know? Or **maybe a better way to phrase is it is, what systems do you feel are serving you and what systems do you feel are not serving you?** Maybe that's too sophisticated of a question.*

That's helpful.

There are certain systems that really serve me well.

Such as?

Such as my insurance is amazing.

You mean your health insurance?

Yeah. On every job I've had now because I had the Obamacare option, I feel really satisfied with that. I feel like it's a little different living here. My voice is heard a lot more here in terms of voting and local government. I really like the park systems. There's some governmental things that I feel very pro. And then there are other things where I'm like, you're not working for me.

Bicycle lanes aren't working for me.

Right.

There have been studies that say on the scale of credibility, profession-wise, nurses are the most credible; second to the bottom are trial lawyers.

Oh, interesting.

Next to used-car salesmen. How do you feel about that? Do you think that's true? Do you have any strong feelings or leanings one way or another?

You know, I don't. I have met nurses that I don't trust. My fiancé's dad is a lawyer. Her whole family is lawyers. I'm not close with them, but I trust him. I give him all my things to read. Tell me what to do. But that's such a hard statistic. I feel like that can't possibly be true. How do you test someone's credibility? I don't know.

What do you look for? What can the lawyer do to establish a genuine human connection with you?

Like in a group of people?

In the group that we're talking about, in this context where they have to learn about things like biases and open-mindedness and closed-mindedness.

Is it possible to have a discussion about the case? You're briefing them, right? A little bit? Or do they not get briefed at all about, this is what you're getting into.

The judge doesn't let us talk about the specifics because that's what the evidence phase is about. Here, it's all about you.

If someone looked me in the eye and was like, do you have any biases in favor of or against doctors it would be really hard for me to be like, no, if I did. I guess when I think of bias, too, I usually think of being biased against something, not in favor.

There's that flip side.

*It would help in person to be like, I really am pro-biking and anti-car and so I don't know if I'm – what do you think? A lot of times I get intimidated when it's cut and dried. Like not being able to pencil it in and being, well, I'm not sure if this counts as a bias, but – and I think asking people is why they do it on the airplanes because it's where they're, can you sit here? And you're, yes or no, but not really thinking, are you physically and mentally capable of doing this or are you going to be tripping over a Snuggie trying to get – you know. **So asking people verbally, do you feel like you can be fair and impartial in this case; I just think people are more honest.***

I'm testing that that may be all I need to do. Many lawyers are trying to do too much and trying to learn too much and, I think, invading the space and privacy and taking time away from jurors. I'm trying to learn, is that question alone enough?

***I think for me it would, and I think for most people.** I hope that people aren't so manipulative that they weasel their way into or out of that. I'm sure it's going to happen either way.*

We see what we call snakes in the grass.

Right. I think people are more honest. I would answer that question honestly on a piece of paper. But sometimes when you're unsure, you're like, it's not applicable. Then when someone really takes a moment to ask you in person, you might realize that you do or don't, depending on how that is phrased. I think I'm someone who has a lot more positive biases than negative biases.

Coming back to that, given the negative perception of trial lawyers, how can the lawyer overcome that and show that the lawyer's a credible person and a human, establishing that credible connection with you? What needs to happen or what definitely should not happen? Either way you want to answer that.

I don't know. I would probably want it to be like a pretty concise thing with rules and information. I like to have a lot of information. I was not able to get on the bus four times yesterday trying to get home. I'd been there, other people were coming and I just want some kind of line. I want some kind of regulation. I want to know what time I'm going to get home. I feel so out of control. All these things are happening and nobody's telling me. I do really well with structure. I tend to trust people who are like, this is how the day's going to go. Here's some coffee. This is where the things are.

A road map.

Right. **I just need to know how things are going to happen. This is the information you need; this is what we expect of you.** *I'm definitely someone that thrives when I know what the expectations are. And I'm someone that panics or feels really uncomfortable or unsure if I don't know what I'm doing. I don't know when I'm going to get on the bus. I don't know how long this is going to take. I know trials, you never know a lot of that. So I feel like any information is probably comforting and would make people be like, oh, okay, I can settle into it. I love an itinerary. I love going into like a meeting and, these are the things we're going to cover, this is how the day's going to go. Especially because I've never done something like that before. That also empowers me to share and contribute. Otherwise I would just be a fly on the wall; I don't really want to contribute to this conversation. I would probably feel intimidated by more aggressive personalities.*

Do you think you'd be someone that would participate willingly in a group situation like that if the lawyer said, raise your hand if you have something that would make it hard for you to be on this case, or make it easy for you to be on this case?

I would if I was asked. If I was not asked I would probably be like, I hope so; not in a malicious or intentional way. Hopefully.

How are you in groups when you are making decisions?

Depends on the group. I'm young. I also appear really young. I was really nervous in my job interview, a lot of older people and you have to rise to the occasion. I look like I'm 14, so I have to present myself differently.

Nobody ever looks their age.

I know. If I'm comfortable with a group of people, I'm very open and have a lot to share and a lot to contribute. But if someone was really aggressive or had a really strong voice, I could go either way. If someone's really butting heads with me, I could rise to that occasion, too, if I strongly disagree. But if someone else is carrying my opinion, then I'll just be oh, they're expressing what I would have expressed; unless I really feel I have something to contribute.

If you're in a group, in a jury selection setting, would you consider yourself a leader or a follower or more in the middle? And maybe that depends on how strong you would feel.

It would depend on how strong I was feeling and it would depend on if I felt there was leadership coming from – I quickly assert myself into leadership positions. A lot of the times it's because I perceive there to be an apathy or a lack of desire to be in those positions. I'm always that person that will go and do this thing because no one –

The fact that you answered the ad and came here shows that you're someone who will –

Right. And people are, I don't know what movie to see. And I'm, this movie because I don't want to spend time talking about it. If I know how I feel, I'll share that expression. But there have been times where I've been in other groups of people who are expressing their opinion and if I feel like my opinion is being expressed in a clear way, then I don't feel the need to. I don't have to do this. But when everyone's just oh, I don't know, what do you think? I don't know, then I'm definitely like, this is what I think. Let's start talking about it.

Assertive. I don't want to beat it to death, but the whole notion of credibility is so important. Is there anything you can think of that the lawyer must absolutely avoid doing to break trust with you?

I think obviously being really professional; not being sleazy or weird. That's really important in how you present yourself. *I'm comfortable with anybody that's clean and normal looking and not talking to me in a weird way or – like when people stand too close. There's social cues like that. It's really basic. Are you homeless? What's going on? Sometimes professional people are like that and they don't understand.* ***You have to have professional boundaries.***

Dress codes are an interesting issue these days.

Just be on your game a little bit. This is what's going on and I'm here and I'm clean and I'm prepared and I'm talking to you in a professional way and making you feel like you're supposed to be here. You are here. We're part of a team and a system. Okay, great. Thank you. Nice to meet you.

Do you have any inherent cynicism, being a juror, about the process that will happen in the trial as it unfolds?

I'd probably initially be excited and then I'd be – fear of boredom more than anything. ***Trying to pay attention would be the hard part for me.*** *I don't have a negative connotation associated with lawyers necessarily. I know they have a reputation. That hasn't been my experience.*

Some people say the lawyers are representing their own sides and have opposite opinions, so it's adversarial. It's hard to believe what either one says because it's win at all cost.

I'm more swayed by evidence than arguing. When people are arguing about something, I'm like, well, who has proof? That would be more important to me than showmanship or words. *It's a trust thing where I understand that's a lawyer's job to make a point, whether or not that's completely backed up. But isn't it up to the jury to be smart enough to know the difference? I have to trust that on some level. I hope it comes down to evidence and facts as much as possible. That would be what I would be looking for.*

You've told me about your interesting background. Is there anything in your academic or professional vocational part of your life that shaped you more than any other in terms of how you might be a juror?

I've always gone to very intimate schools, and I do better in a small group than in a sea of people. For me, that's a comfort thing. I like environments that are more creative and flexible where you can talk about issues not in an indirect way, but just allowing for there to be a discussion. I don't do well in environments that are black and white and cut and dried. A jury, I imagine, is a weird combination of both of those things where there's a lot of discussion but eventually you have to reach some kind of consensus. Part of what would be interesting to me about it would be like, it's a really weird group of people and an interesting dynamic to navigate. I'm not used to that. I'm used being with like-minded people through better and worse. I don't have a lot of experience with balancing really different viewpoints, which I'm sure, isn't an asset on a jury to have people attempting to balance those different viewpoints.

It's good to have intelligent points of view. When you're deciding an issue are you more on the scale of deciding emotionally and by instinct or more by data and hard evidence?

I think initially, I always have a strong gut reaction, and then I have to question that.

Does it serve you right most of the time?

I think so. I always try to question a really strong feeling; negative feelings.

Jurors don't want long trials. They want to hear it and they've pretty much made their mind up quickly and get this thing underway please, we want to go. That's the culture we're in now, I think. We know what we want; we know what we know. I want to talk to you about what's called the burden of proof. In a criminal case, the burden of proof is beyond a reasonable doubt. Everybody knows that. In a civil case, it's a preponderance of the evidence. So if I told you it was a preponderance –

I like that word.

– what does that mean to you?

I'm assuming it means pondering in some way. Is that related? Preponderance of evidence? More evidence? I don't know.

Preponderance is then defined as more likely than not.

More likely than not.

What does more likely than not mean to you?

That's really tricky. I would definitely prefer it to be more black and white.

Beyond a reasonable doubt? Sure.

Yeah, of course. That's really tough. That adds a whole other layer because I definitely like to feel sure before condemning somebody.

We're not talking about liberty issues. This is civil where money –

Right. But still, money. If the evidence is more likely than not, then I guess it does kind of come down to did you convince me in a way where it's like this seemed really compelling and it seemed so possible that it happened this way and it seems so un-possible that it happened this other way. The evidence doesn't really tend to lean that way, you know.

How would you feel if the evidence were only a tip?

Like 60/40?

51/49.

__I probably would not like that at all. I would probably want to not have a say in it.__ Can you do that? Can you be like, no, I don't want to participate. I feel unsure.

Well, the process of jury deliberation would get you around somewhere.

You can kind of opt out, in that deliberation?

In a civil case, we have 12 jurors, and ten of them have to agree. Two jurors can disagree. If three jurors disagree, then it's a hung jury. The case might then be retried to a different jury. So it takes ten but there's all kinds of compromising that goes on in there.

Yeah. I definitely feel if it were really that, like a hair, I wouldn't feel comfortable going in.

Even if the judge's instructions to you were that if it was proved by just that preponderance, that it's your duty to find for that party?

I don't think I would be able to – no. __I think I would have to opt out unless I felt really confident in my vote.__ If I was like, oh, maybe it's only 51% of the evidence, but I feel really strongly that this is the case –

You feel really strongly that it is more than the other.

Right. I think that's where my bias probably would come in really strongly for me where I would try not to weigh in because I'd be like, oh, if it's McDonald's, they can afford it. That would be hard to stay impartial. Would I do that if it was a different kind of company? That would be really, really tricky, because I would struggle with that morally.

Right. Is it any more or less fair just because it's a multi-billion dollar corporate –

And of course it's not. It's very much unfair.

What's your sense of the role that insurance plays in these kinds of injury cases?

Insurance is one of those things that doesn't make much sense to me, in terms of my own experience of the world. But I think it's important to have it. It's important to be protected. I had my car rear-ended parked with no information left and you're like, great. But I'm glad I am protected from people being bad or whatever. My insurance isn't very good, so it doesn't cover very much for me, my auto insurance. I don't have life insurance. At work, I have really good health insurance, but I don't have that kind of insurance where you get compensated for short-term disability. I have long-term disability but not short-term disability. So if I broke a hand or something – I don't know really. I always forget. Or they have dismemberment insurance.

That's death and dismemberment.

Cut off these two fingers. It's really interesting, because the language is too complicated. I don't even know what's covered. And I especially don't know how to take advantage of it. We have rental insurance. Our house flooded, and we didn't even claim for anything because we weren't smart enough to be like, our instruments got ruined. We could have bought new instruments, but by the time we figured it out and made all those calls, which was not that much longer after it happened, it was too late. We couldn't prove that was why they were damaged at that point. Like you have to call mid-flood.

I'm sorry for the instruments.

It wasn't too bad, but I could have gotten some money to replace an instrument.

An instrument being damaged is a hard loss to feel.

It's part of the game. I'm trying to be better since all that stuff has happened, knowing what rights I have and in what ways I am protected. But it's very hard. It's not intuitive. **I don't feel like my insurance companies want to take care of me when something happens.** *That's not the sense I get or, we feel really bad that this happened. They're like, we want to give you as little as possible for that. I'm always just sort of like okay, well, I hope nothing bad happens to me because it's not going to be good.*

Do you have any sense one way or the other that people who are being sued in cases like the one we're pretending is happening more likely than not have insurance or don't have insurance?

I wouldn't know. I guess it depends on what kind of insurance, too. I feel like most people I know have health insurance and auto insurance but that's about it.

Like an auto case; would you feel better about making a larger award if you knew that person had insurance?

Probably. But I don't think that should be part of the decision. I wouldn't really want to know that information. It would be easier for me to be unbiased, whereas this person they're suing is really wealthy or this person that is suing is really poor or really sick or whatever. I don't feel like that should play into it at all. **It** *would be hard to ignore that information, so I just would hope I wouldn't have it.*

Generally, the Court won't let you have that.

I wouldn't want that information.

The concern is, if the defendant is, let's say, a likable little old lady school teacher and the plaintiff is, whatever, a 20-something young man who was hurt by the lady, how can you as a juror award the right amount of damages she can't pay? Does that factor into your thought process?

I think it should be the same for everybody. I think it's really inflated. I don't understand why it's so much that a normal individual can't correctly compensate for their actions. I don't get that. If I did something wrong, I would want to make it right. It would be terrible if that were my life, because it's so exorbitant.

As a general rule, people who are sued almost always have insurance. If their insurance limits are low, they're almost never required to pay more than just what their insurance limits are. Rarely is anyone bankrupted in injury cases.

That's interesting.

If you were a plaintiff, had been injured and were bringing a lawsuit, what kind of a juror would you want hearing your case and deciding it?

Impartial, and paying attention. I would definitely want somebody, I want to say educated, but that's not necessarily the right – like focused on what's happened, processing the information in a logical, clear way. *They're not just going on gut instinct or we don't like blonde ladies, so we hate you and you don't get any money. Not that anyone would do that, but I'm pretty lucky. I'm not a black guy or something. I feel that way a lot where I'm not going to be treated in the same way. I would definitely want somebody to look at factual evidence and decide fairly; probably what everyone wants.*

Women have told me that women can be harder as jurors on women who are plaintiffs.

I'm sure that's true.

Why would that be? I like women jurors, but if I have a woman client, that might not serve the purpose.

I think women are really competitive and hard on women. *I don't think it's right. I try not to be that way. Women really notch each other down on purpose because, I think, you're competing with women. But you're competing with everybody, that's the truth. Women should raise each other up and help each other, but I don't think they do a lot of the times. I think they feel like they're pitted against each other instead of like, we're on a team; let's work together.*

How could I determine if I was in that situation where I had a female client, there were a predominant group of women on the jury and I wanted to learn if there was some potential –

I don't think you could. I don't think that's a question to ask because I don't think you want to be like, do you hate women? Women are afraid of and intimidated by other, especially intelligent –

I certainly wouldn't ask the question because I'd be afraid of the backlash.

I'm sure there would be. I think most modern women are not feeling that way as much. But I understand that attitude; it's been really prevalent. I think women are starting to be like, oh, this is a bad attitude that's bringing us all down.

How old are you?

Twenty-four. Twenty-five in November.

Your generation, there seem to be quite a few of your age that are tech-driven. Tell me, if you have any thoughts in general about that age group, temperament and mindset.

*Just started working downtown, and I don't really like being around that so much. My fiancé, we've agreed we like to have the resources of the city and be away. **I don't really like the tech people because they inflate everything and that makes it really hard to live here.** Judging by all the neighborhoods, I think it makes it hard to be artistic. Making it really hard to live here makes me want to move. I have friends in that industry who are wonderful and very smart and very kind. It's like everyone I meet is in the tech industry and I'm kind of bored of it.*

As potential jurors, just general rule, broad brush?

I think they're probably fine jurors. I think they're a little judged by it. I think they're very wealthy.

I've heard entitled is a word.

Very entitled. They make a lot more money than other people their age and spend exorbitantly and are smart but in a very specific kind of way. Not in a creative, problem-solving kind of way; more in a thought, like straightforward kind of way which I think in some ways it'd be great.

Binary.

*Yeah. That's why **I think you'd want a balance of different types.** I wouldn't want a whole jury of them, but I think they could be very useful as well.*

Part of the well-rounded group?

Exactly.

If they're willing to take the time off to be there. Is there anything you want to add that you think would be helpful?

No, it's been really interesting.

Thank you.

35

IT'S ABOUT THE CLIENT

Caucasian female, age 35, divorced, IT Professional, MS

It's not about me. Yes, the jury selection process is about me, but ultimately, the trial isn't about me and it's not about you; it's about the client. So if you're going to stand up and during your juror selection process make it about you, the lawyer, versus me, the juror, or you're going to stand up and talk like it's about you the lawyer and not the client, then I'm going to be like, well, hey, you missed the entire boat of what this process is supposed to be about, and I won't want to be a part of it.

The judge says, ladies and gentlemen, please give your attention to the attorney for the plaintiff who will conduct jury selection, what they call *voir dire*. What are your feelings and thoughts at that moment?

When I went through it, I remember feeling a certain amount of anxiety because you don't know what's going to happen. You don't know what they're going to ask. You have mixed feelings about whether you want to be a juror or not, so you're trying to come up with like, do I say something. I remember people being like, if you don't want to be a juror, here's what you say. I remember thinking, I feel like I want to be one, because I want to have that experience of understanding. God help me, I hope I'm never on the other side of that, of watching the process happen. I remember the main feeling I had was a conflict of, do I actually want to be a juror or not and that anxiety of what's going to happen?

What was the value question you had about wanting to be a juror or not? Was it time or was it compensation or –

Well, it was time, right? You're taking time away from work to be and watch the process. It does feel like a big imposition in your life because you're having to take time out, but I thought at least once. I'm positive it's probably going to happen again, but you know, at least once. It's one of those things, you do your civic duty.

In terms of having an overwhelming feeling like, I've gotta get out of here, you felt it was okay? On the side of, yes, I can be here versus I've got to get out of here.

I was more on the side of, yes, I can be here, which is why I was really honest and figured that the process would – being a process person, I was like, the process will either weed me out or it will select me. If it selects me, I'm meant to be here. I'm meant to experience this.

Did you have a strong feeling one way or another that you wanted to be or didn't want to be on the jury? Going through the process is one thing, but actually being selected –

I didn't have a super big passion one way or the other. But I am naïve enough to believe in the process, so if the process tells me I'm supposed to be here, then I look at it as kind of a cool opportunity to serve and see the jury process because I had never been inside of a courtroom aside from watching it on TV, which I feel like isn't real.

You had a criminal case; how would you have felt if it's a civil case instead?

I would feel the same way, because I don't think I remember knowing whether it was civil or criminal. I just knew it was a thing. It might have been to the point where I didn't pay attention, didn't really care what kind of case it was, just as long as I got to be either part of the process or not. I don't think it would have mattered for me.

How do you feel in general about that part of the civil justice system, that part of the court system where people can sue for money if they are injured and can prove the injury was caused by somebody's negligence?

I have mixed feelings about it. **There's always going to be scenarios where somebody made a mistake. No one's perfect, so there's that.** *If you're the person who has been wronged, whether it be by somebody else or by a doctor or by a corporation or by – to me, there's a personal belief of, I'm trying to think of the right word, I don't know. It's like that ethical honor of,* **are you taking advantage of somebody else because you can and that person just made an honest mistake, or did they really do something that was purposefully negligent?** *I recognize that's that fine line. I don't like when people are unethical. I also don't like when people take advantage of other people because they can. That to me is just being an (expletive).* **My feeling would probably depend on the scenario.** *I wouldn't necessarily sit firmly on one side or the other. It probably depended on the scenario of, is this person just being a jerk? And this person truly made a mistake? I don't know. If I was that person, and a doctor did something wrong or if somebody did something wrong to me, I might feel something very different. There are a lot of people who take advantage of the system because they can, and that to me doesn't set well. Doctors make mistakes. They do. Or whoever. They make honest mistakes. They're not perfect. They're people. It's not my job to know, but there is a fine line between them actually having messed up and them just making an honest mistake. If they're willing to rectify it, then is there really a problem? I don't know.*

What would rectify the – when you use that word?

I've seen scenarios where a doctor did something wrong, and they were willing to go in and correct it, and it's correctable. That to me is being willing to rectify the situation, versus a doctor did something wrong because they didn't sleep enough.

Whereas they're making an honest – and they can't, because it's irreparable. If there's due reason why they couldn't – to me, that's a different – I don't know. I feel like they've been in different buckets.

If the mistake was shown to be because a rule wasn't followed or some rules, either rules of law or rules of good practice in a profession, would you feel differently about that?

Yes, I would. **To me, if a rule wasn't followed, then that wasn't an honest mistake,** *it was a mistake based on your profession. To me then, there's good reason that somebody might want some sort of payment or, I don't know, rectification for that.*

How do you feel, when you're in that courtroom, at the very beginning, looking at the lawyers, and you see this lawyer who's representing the injured person. What are your senses about that individual and what they do and their credibility?

I'm not a person who makes assumptions about people based on their appearances. *I might not be the best person to make that – I'm not going to judge them. This is their profession. It's their chosen profession. It doesn't imply that they're a good person or a bad person, in my opinion. I see people like that who just want to do right by others. I don't see them as, you're just that person who's trying to get money from other people. To me,* **you're trying to do right by your client, and there's honor in that, too.**

How do you feel about lawyers in general with regards to things like credibility and honesty? Some people have used the words "greedy trial lawyers" or "sleazy lawyers."

I have only known people in that profession who have been good people. I don't necessarily have a negative impression about them. The lawyer I've worked with, any of my friends who are lawyers, they've always been good people who just want to do right for their clients. I don't have a negative impression. I know there are people out there that do, but I don't have a negative impression.

Do you have any family or friends who have a negative impression about lawyers, especially in the civil case context? Who have had bad experiences or, in general because of their politics or their religion or some other experience?

No. I really don't think I do.

For example, very conservative people, business people, tend to think there are too many trial lawyers and that the system is not working because –

I don't. I know one person who's had a somewhat so-so experience with a lawyer in a civil case, and I'm not entirely sure that was due to negligence or anything. It was more due to their capacity to lawyer, be a lawyer, lawyering. I don't know the scenario. I can't off the top of my head think of anyone who's had that, or at least been outwardly expressive about that. Do I buck the trend?

I don't know. In your professional experience, you've met a lot of people, you've done a lot of technical work. Tell me about the people you've met that are in your age group, your cohorts, your intellectual equals. What do they generally think about the civil justice system and access to the courts for people who've been injured and want some compensation?

Sure. The people that I generally work with, I'm going to approach this from two different angles. There are two ways I've seen them access that type of court system. One is through a company supplied lawyer network, pre-paid legal services, which for those few people that I have remote relationships with, I haven't heard very positive things in terms of their being able to support them. They've moved away from that system to a more well-known lawyer. From the few people that have really easy access to lawyers, they generally are people who make a good deal of money. To be perfectly honest, they generally spend their time in front of a computer, so it's not like they're out doing something in terms of an occupation that might warrant them to have that on a regular basis from their job.

I was thinking more in general about the notion that people are going to the courts when they're injured. You've got one side and you've got the other. Some people think you never should sue, because it's clogging up the court system and it's frivolous. Then other people say, we need access to the courts because that's how we get accountability and compensation and justice.

In my experience, either my friends or my parents' friends I've seen have some sort of problem to where they either could or should have or did, which has been few and far between, they generally lie on the spectrum of don't. I look at one of my parents' really good friends who has had a variety of different – is now on the fourth surgery of the same surgery that should have been done once, and they haven't done anything about it. They're just continuing to have surgery versus saying, hey, I'm going to sue you for negligence because you left cement in my joint, which is bad. So they generally sit on the spectrum of don't sue because they can afford it or they have insurance to go and do it again. I don't know if that's because they're more conservative or because they're more financially well off. It might be. If I were to think about a trend, that's probably where they would sit. The few people that I know who have sued are in more of a monetary risky situation to where they're seeking something for it because they have a family and they support their family and they couldn't afford to get it re-fixed.

More like need-based.

It was needs-based. And the other person that I can think about just has that mentality. But that's few and far between of the people I either work with or spend time with. Generally they sit on the spectrum of don't, or maybe they recognize they should, but then they're like, eh, it's fine. I'll just go get it fixed.

In those early moments when the lawyer's talking to this group of people, what can the lawyer do to show you that the lawyer is human and credible?

Smile. Look people in the eye. I'm one of those people – smile. Act like you can relate to me as a person. I think the biggest asset a lawyer could have in trying to explain or relate something that is unfamiliar, because it's going to be unfamiliar to me, is don't use big fancy words, because I'm not going to understand what they are, and I'm going to be put off. Use words that are relatable. I hesitate to say dumb it down, but dumb it down so the average person can understand what you're talking about. The other thing is, the way I felt when I was in the scenario is, don't paint me into a corner. Don't try and box me into a type, because it will put me off. Do you understand what I mean? I'm looking for a female, age 35, who has this occupation, who is this. I'm more than that, so if you're going to select me based on that, at least don't make me feel like you are.

Or deselect you.

Or deselect me, right? Anybody over the age of 35, go. It's not a very nice thing to do. So maybe be nice. Be thoughtful to the fact that you're in a room with a variety of different experiences. But make eye contact, smile. Make a joke. Make it so that people want to be here. Because there's a majority of them that probably don't; so if you can at least make it worth their while or try. Making a joke would be funny. Those would be the four things that would make me more relate to the person who is talking to me.

What's your sense of what the purpose of jury selection is; what the process is designed to do?

I think what lawyers are trying to do is find people who will vote in their general direction. I recognize it's not a voting process. But I think jury selection is trying to come up with a set of people who will either evenly vote A or B, or is in the general population of somebody who you don't know but you think might vote your direction. It's, I'm going to put an even split of people who might vote Jury A and Jury B, and then there's going to be those unknowns that you're saying, okay, this person might because they're in the general demographics of somebody who I feel like might be able to relate to my side of the story; I think is what the process is intended to do. In part, that provides a very fair assessment. If I'm Lawyer A, I want people who're going to vote my way. If I'm Lawyer B, I'm going to want people to vote my way. In the jury selection process, you're going to end up with a mix of both. What you're going to end up trying to hit are those unknown people that, based on their demographic, you might be able to get them to vote one way or the other. I think that's the intended process, but I don't know. And it's all about voting.

It is a vote. There's no question about that. I think the framers of the Constitution, people that created the core process, one of the things they're trying to do is to ensure that whatever the trial is, it's fair. The courts say that a fair trial is one generally, where the jurors are unbiased to one side or the other to the extent that that's humanly possible.

Right.

One of the things lawyers try to do in that jury selection process is determine who has biases? Some people, for example, are very biased against these kinds of cases. Other people are okay with them. Some people are more liberal with the amount of money they want to give the person if the case is proved, and others are very much not so. In medical cases, for example, some people think doctors should have immunity. There are all sorts of beliefs and attitudes, and they're all valid. So given that one of the things we're trying to do is find out who can be unbiased, to the extent they can be, or open-minded, What's the best way for the lawyer to ask that question and get reliable information from a person such as yourself?

Oh, man, that's a hard question.

We could turn it on its head and say, what's the thing the lawyer should not do in order to –

Right. I don't know. I think understanding whether somebody's either been through a case or been a juror on a case might be telling. If you've been through a case, if you've actually been a participant, it's going to show that there's a bias in some way, shape or form.

These are the kinds of questions the lawyer might want to ask?

Right.

Part of the question is, how can the lawyer ask in such a way that it doesn't offend you to speak about any particular beliefs you might have? That it's okay to express a negative bias as well as a positive bias.

This might be a really weird way of coming at this problem or coming at this question; I think ascertaining how somebody feels about going to the doctor is a really good way of understanding whether they have a bias towards or against the medical profession.

In medical cases.

I'm not going to say I love going to the doctor, but I like going to the doctor, because the doctor serves a purpose, right? I can see if somebody doesn't – you're going to get a certain feeling about somebody depending on how they answer that question. So if you can look at do they like going to the doctor; or how do you feel about your doctor?

Do you like powerful people doing good things? That can be a good feeling.

Well, right? And the way somebody responds, if you pay attention to the way they respond, if they respond super negatively, there's a negative thing there that you can catch; but it's not an insulting question, like, how do you feel about malpractice cases?

How do you feel going to the doctor?

How do you feel going to the doctor? How is your relationship with your doctor? I don't know how you ask that question, but it's a really open-ended question where you can get some really heavy feelings out. If somebody says, oh my God, I hate it, because blah blah blah, that's going to be a telling thing.

What if it was not a medical case? Auto cases, for example, or a product liability case or a construction site injury case where we're not talking about doctors.

That's fair. This is a really tough answer for me. I don't know. I think generally, asking about what you know versus what you feel is more powerful and telling. If you're trying to assess how somebody feels about it without insulting them, asking them how they feel about it is going to be less insulting than how much they know. I don't know how much of a can of worms that opens in a courtroom.

We can pretty much ask any question. We only have short period of time to do it.

I think if you continually ask different types of questions around the same thing, but ask how somebody feels about something, it's going to be a lot more telling than how much do you know about a malpractice case. They may say, I don't feel anything, because I don't know anything. I would be the first person to claim complete innocence and naïveté around this stuff. I'm not going to make any assumptions, because I don't know anything about it. That's just who I am. It's a hard question for me to answer.

The lawyer doesn't know you, and you know this is some kind of an injury case, is there anything about you that the parties need to know that would help them decide if you could be fair and open-minded to that case?

Asking if I had ever been injured before so I can empathize with somebody who has been injured and been through that is obviously a really good way of assessing somebody's feelings about it, depending how I'd been injured, understanding not only whether I had but how that injury happened. If somebody were to ask me, have you been injured before, I say yes. Well, how? Walking down the street. That's not going to provide any sort of anything other than I've been injured and I know how it feels and it sucks. Whether I sought any sort of care; if I was in some sort of work environment when that happened; understanding all of that will better inform those decisions. That would be where you start.

Everybody comes with some bias or other. We all have our belief systems that help us approach things differently. I'm coming around to accepting people if they are willing to acknowledge their biases when they're deliberating in the process; to be fairly comfortable with them even if they have a negative bias from my perspective. How do you think I could communicate that to the jury? In other words, if you're willing to share something I may not want to hear about this case, I'm willing to trust you, as long as you're open enough to talk about it. If you tell me, I don't like these kinds of cases, I'll say, I accept that, as long as you keep in the back of your mind that we're trying to make sure everybody gets a fair start. How do you think that can be best brought up to you and this group of people with you?

I think you acknowledging that you don't know everything, and just saying, hey, I just want to let you know that I'm not painting you into a box; I'm not putting you in a corner. I'm really open to perspectives. Because that's going to help me; it's going to help the case. You know, all that jazz. Providing information or data around people that you have or haven't taken on that have been positive or negative could, for me anyway, be meaningful. Or acknowledging up front that you're not necessarily looking for a specific type or bias or something to say, look I'm not looking for people who are necessarily on my side or I don't know how you say that, but –

Do you think jurors will believe me when I say that? Given that I have a self-interest and my client's interest is different from the other side's interest? That they'll believe me and not feel that's a manipulation?

Some will, some won't. I think it depends on how you present it, right? If I were to acknowledge my own bias, I am one that believes that people are, innocent and naïve or not, in the world to do right by others and be good people. That would mean I would believe that you're just there to do your job. And your job is to represent your person, and you're going to do your job correctly. For other people, you're right. I recognize there will be people that walk in the door that say – and maybe that's a really good question to them. I don't know if you can ask that, but, do you believe by me saying this that I'm trying to manipulate you into believing my side? And if somebody says, yeah, then you're like, I'm out. That's telling, too, right?

Thank you for that.

I believe people don't ask enough questions in this world and people aren't honest about things. If you can say that, and be like, okay, who actually in this room believes me? And these people say yes, you make everyone else go. Because what you want is immaterial of whether they have a positive or negative view. If you can be honest about it, then those are the people you want, or might not want, I don't know, depends on the case maybe. If you ask them those people that don't want to be there are going to recognize that that's their out, too. They're like, I'm out. I don't believe you. They raise their hand and you dismiss them.

I try to help people who don't want to be there. Although oftentimes, some of the people that don't want to be there are people that should be there.

Right?

I'm more suspicious of people that really want to be there; they may have an agenda. And also looking for the snake in the grass. Really, that's the biggest question here is, without turning the group against the lawyer, how can I identify who's the snake in the grass? Who's the person that really has an agenda that wants to, one way or the other, make this case about them?

If I were standing in your shoes, I would look at how people answer my questions. ***To me, it's a body language issue, a body language problem. Who's showing***

the body language of I'm sitting, I'm watching, I'm giving eye contact to you.
I'm being assertive, or I'm at least paying attention versus those people that
are slouching or trying not to make eye contact, which are the people that
probably don't want to be there. They're avoiding your eye contact because
they don't want you to pick them. Or they're doing whatever they're doing to
show that body language to where they're not interested or they don't want to be
there. To me, it's just as much of a social experiment in body language as it is in
how are people answering your questions? I don't know if that's a class that you
take to be a lawyer, but it maybe should.

Some people are hired for that purpose. In worthy cases. You're a project manager?
Is that how you would describe your –

IT Professional Project Manager, sure.

You work with a lot of IT people, probably most of them in their 20s and 30s, right?

And now probably 40s, but yeah.

Is there anything I need to know about that group of people in the context of trying
a case; of what they need to hear and how they need to hear it?

Yep. Most of the people I work with are super analytical. They're very data-
focused. They're socially awkward.

Do you think they have empathy, as a general rule?

No. I don't. I don't think they know how to communicate in general. I think many
of them know a lot of stuff, so they will know and probably be interested in what
you're telling them, but they're not going to have necessarily the same body
language and the same signals that everyone else does.

Probably pretty confident, I would guess. They're making a lot of money.

I don't think that would be the general trend of they're confident or not. I know a
lot of people that aren't. They're super confident in what they do, they call it book
smart versus street smart. They're really book smart, and the minute they get on
the street and actually have to, this is going to sound really negative, but exist in
normal society, they don't do that very well. They are not somebody that I would
necessarily walk out the door and be like, you are confident in yourself. They are
defined by their jobs. Most. Or their occupation or –

Or whatever project they're on at the time.

Exactly. I don't necessarily see that changes necessarily when they have a family.
Most of them are men and have a family, but most of them still define their lives
by their jobs.

Empathy is something that maybe tends to be lacking a little bit more, what do they
need, and how do they need it presented to understand if there's an injury, the law
says a person should be compensated and made whole? How would they approach

that? Assuming we've proven the negligence happened, there was an injury, and it was caused by this other party. Now we get to compensating them.

I generally come at that type of problem in two ways. Data, data, data, data, data. Show them data. Show them the actual material goods, whether that's data or something that can explain facts. And make sure they are being heard, if you can.

Who's being heard? The juror or the injured person?

The juror, if they can actually speak.

They can ask questions now. So emphasize they can be a part of that process if they want to be.

Yes. I generally find that many of them just want to be heard or validated or both in that they are whole in what they are doing. They are a part of it. They are contributing. They are purposeful. They are being used for a purpose.

There's some meaning.

Yeah. Because they have other stuff to do, and I generally find in my occupation that those people, if they don't see a purpose in what they do, they're doing, they're out.

Right. Because they're moving on –

– to something they can contribute to and can feel a part of.

A lot of potential jurors who come from tech, even though they can personally afford the financial hardship that comes from only getting $10 a day, will use the excuse that I have a big project I can't get away from. To some extent, we respect that. Well, we always respect it, but at the same time, if the judge doesn't excuse them for hardship, how can I keep them there without them being resentful? And maybe you answered that question by give them some meaning and purpose to this.

I think that is universally going to be something you have to battle against; I'll be the first to acknowledge that.

I will do everything I can to help them get off if they need it.

I can tell you the challenge. The challenge is if they do serve on the jury, the first thing they're going to do is go home and work because they can't get four days behind on their project, even though they can, really; so understanding the capacity at which they are going to be needed, which I recognize is not necessarily something you can say, you're only going to be out of work for five days. But being able to contain it to –

Some trials can go weeks and months.

I know. So a certain time box, if it's possible, would be a wise –

Generally the judge will say, this is a trial that's expected to last three days, five days, two weeks.

> *So reiterating that is probably a good thing; providing them the reasoning for their being there.* **It would be really good to have you on this jury because – or, we're really looking for this type of person because –**

We value your analytical skills, for example.

> *Exactly. Again, getting them to really and actually feel like what they're going to provide is something that's useful.* **In my experience, there will be few people, few and far between, that feel an actual passion around a malpractice case of some sort.**

It's even worse because the garden variety case is an auto case.

> *Right. So unless they've been directly a part of a case like that, or have a friend or some sort of emotional tie to that ethical dilemma or that scenario, it's going to be hard. But that's pretty common, right? People come in and they always have other things to do. To me, right or wrong, it's probably a failing on the judge's part to say, hey, I'm going to dismiss you for hardship. Because it's not right. That's not hardship for them.*

Different judges have a different personal standard.

> *Definition, right.*

It depends on how many jurors you have and what kind of case it is.

> *Right. So to me the hardship is where a different conversation needs to happen. I recognize you can't necessarily control that, but maybe you can.*

I can certainly ask people about their hardships and, tell me about it and what can I do to help you?

> *Right. Though you run a risk if you're also having to quantify somebody else's hardship, which is –*

Maybe turns the other juror off. Hey, you didn't help me.

> *Exactly. So making them feel like they can relate to having an impact and the outcome.*

That set a light bulb off for me.

> *The other thing is, having a personal impact and outcome to your juror, right? You are changing somebody else's life. You are helping, potentially helping, somebody else. There's an emotional heartstring you can pull that, yes, is a skosh manipulative, but that's your job, right? Your job is to help your client. So there is a little bit of that that comes with your job.* **If you're guilt-tripping me into wanting to be there, you're going to fail. But if you're just pulling at, like, my job is to be here and help my client, you can help be a part of that,**

yes, it's manipulative. But it's not manipulative out of your controlled job. That's, be a part of what I'm trying to do. This is my job and I want to do it in a fair way and I want both positive and negative people in terms of what I'm doing to be here. I want it to be a fair, stressing that you just want it to be a fair trial. **You can only do so much in the position you're in, so using the words fair and listening to people and making them want to feel like they're going to be part of that impact and that outcome, I think is, in my opinion, probably one of the biggest things you can do.**

What would turn you off in this process? What would cause you to turn away from the message?

Trying to sell me on wanting to be there. That would paint you in the bucket of smarmy sales guy. Trying to sell me on, like, oh my God, this is going to be so awesome or whatever that fake smarmy thing is would turn me off; not showing your sincerity of wanting to help your client would turn me off. Those are the two things that, not coming out of a place of, I'm really just trying to be here for my client and wanting a fair assessment. But being like, oh my God, I'm so badass, I'm going to win this case. Making it about you rather than about them is a big –

Making it about the juror rather than about the client?

No, making it about you, the lawyer –

Oh, the lawyer.

– versus making it about your client.

Got it.

It's not about me. Yes, the jury selection process is about me, but ultimately, the trial isn't about me and it's not about you; it's about the client. So if you're going to stand up and during your juror selection process make it about you, the lawyer, versus me, the juror, or you're going to stand up and talk like it's about you the lawyer and not the client, then I'm going to be like, well, hey, you missed the entire boat of what this process is supposed to be about, and I won't want to be a part of it.

Right. Some really good lawyers espouse that caring is contagious, and they get so involved in who their client is that there's kind of a transference in a way, so passionate, and the jury picks up on that. Do you think a person can take that too far?

Well, yeah.

I've seen lawyers cry in closing arguments over the injuries their clients have had, genuine tears. But I've also seen jurors say, you took it too far.

I think there is a taking it too far. A part of this is your job, and you can care a lot. You can almost care too much. But if you're showing outward caring in an unprofessional way, I think that is taking it too far because it's unprofessional for your work environment, right? I mean, you can care to the moon and back about the things you do, and there is a transference of caring, right? This is what your job is, to care enough about your client to where you're willing to go up and represent their injuries; you absolutely should care. **If you're caring enough to where you're overly involved in your client's life or you're showing up in an emotional way, your job isn't to be their therapist. It's not to be emotional. It's to care enough to where you can actually show up and present their arguments and their side of the story in a way that feels empathetic and in a way that feels like you have passion around their problem. But not in a way to where, if you care too much, it can show up as manipulating the jury. Let the client cry; it's the client's problem.** *Your job is to care enough, but not to care so much that you are going to show up in a way to where – to me, if a lawyer is crying in court, I'd be like, why are you crying? This is not your problem. This is not your injury. It's like somebody showing up and you talking to them as a friend and they'll be like, I totally know how you feel. Do ya? Because my life is different than yours, and you might have gone through a break up, but do you really know how I feel?*

Have you been in my shoes?

You've never been in my shoes. It's that same idea. You don't know. To me, that is the worst thing anybody can ever tell me is, I know how you feel. Do you? Do you really? You don't. You're not me. So yes, to answer your question, I think there is over-caring.

We talked about getting people to open up about their judgments and biases. How would you feel if the lawyer wanted to disclose something personal about him or herself to get that process rolling? He says, I'm here to learn about whether you have any biases, and I have to be honest with you, I can't stand bicyclists, for example. They really bug me. I've had experiences where bicyclists have frustrated me when I drive. I'd be a bad juror on a bicycle case.

I am going to give you the consultant answer and say, it depends. I think as a lawyer if you're trying to seek biases, the best thing that you can do is get them to talk about themselves, right? Everyone wants to talk about themselves. It is innately a human condition of, I just want to talk about what's going on in my life. It's a human condition to just want to talk about yourself. That opening line in terms of sharing something that you're biased is a trigger for that.

Because some people say, I'll show you mine and then you show me yours. That's part of this.

And what you're trying to do is say, I have the same feeling about bicyclists or not. Or I am a bicyclist or whatever. To me, if somebody were doing that, what they're trying to do is get the other person to trigger on the fact that I just opened up to you, which can go one of two ways. It can go, I'm going to listen and I recognize you're putting yourself out there, so I'm going to put myself out there. Or it can go, I'm now focused on something else; I'm focused on your bias about bicyclists.

What do you really want them to focus on? I'm wondering if something were re-framed to me and saying, I recognize everyone has a bias. I have my own biases. I'm wondering what yours are in terms of this thing? It's an open-ended question they can then respond to. You're not directing their conversation. That to me would be a better way of presenting something like that because you're still opening up, you're just not opening up about a specific bias.

Right. I've got them. We've all got them. I'd like to hear about yours. Without being –

Directive. But you also have to be open to the fact that some people won't have a bias.

Or won't express it or don't know they have it.

Exactly. Or won't have a bias about a certain topic, right? You asked me, do you have a bias about malpractice cases, and my answer was, I don't know, maybe. Yes, no. Well, I just think people are good people. So it's obvious that I don't. And it might be a case-by-case thing. You have to be open to that, too and recognize, in advance, what your thoughts are around each bias. Yes, no, or I really don't know.

It's interesting. In that dialogue, it made me think, maybe bias isn't the word. Maybe agenda is a better word.

Or opinion.

Opinions. Strong opinions.

Do you have an opinion? *Because I think agenda can come off as a negative word.*

Right. As I think bias does.

I think it can, too. Agenda can come off as a negative word, because it will sit on that line of people who have agendas are generally bad, because they're generally bad agendas. You don't call something positive as an agenda, you call it a plan, or you call it a –

I think opinion – or belief, I suppose – but even beliefs get –

Thoughts, maybe? Even thoughts. Do you have thoughts around –

Some people use the word feelings. I've come to the sense that people go, are you trying to psychoanalyze me?

Right.

I like that language, but in the jury context, you know, how do you feel? I'm not sure that's appreciated.

Their feelings at the moment are not about the thing you want them to feel something about. Their feelings at the moment are about the fact that

they're sitting there, they have to go through this process, they have to take time off of work.

They're feeling lots of things.

So at the moment, they're not feeling the thing you want them to feel. They're not going to feel that until you start presenting the case, in my opinion. Because they're going to have to process the fact they're now not working and they're going to have to deal with that another time. They're now listening to the case that's been presented. What they're feeling at the moment has nothing to do – you can ask them, how do you feel about being here? Which is what they're feeling at the moment. Versus, what are your thoughts around this specific topic? You can gauge their feeling about it by them talking through, oh, I'm thinking about this and this and this. You can gauge their feeling about it because really, what they're feeling at the moment is, I don't want to be here or I do want to be here or something about the thing, the being here, or having to sit there.

I want to honor their time and have them know that. So stick with the topic; what are your thoughts and opinions about lawsuits in general?

Which, they'll talk. They will talk. Because what you're doing is given them an open-ended answer which is always a super important thing in this case to let them just talk. Some people will be like, I don't have a thought and feeling. That's just as telling as somebody going on for five minutes about, you know, blah, blah, blah.

I get this answer sometimes. The resistant one will say, how can I have a thought or an opinion about it if I haven't heard the evidence? They're negative from the get-go. It's really tough.

Which is just as telling. But that's just as telling, right?

Sometimes I don't know what it's telling, that's the thing.

But it's the behavior, right? If they sit back and they're trying to lawyer you just as much as you're trying to lawyer them –

Right. They're antagonistic.

And the person you're looking for is somebody who's open to the process and all that stuff, that's not them. So, okay, you're not going to be as open, you're trying to be antagonistic, that to me is a human behavior just as telling as somebody who's like, oh my God, I have all these thoughts and feelings, and here are my thoughts and feelings and blah blah blah.

There will be those who monopolize.

I'm sure.

What are your thoughts and opinions about women versus men as open-minded, more or less, juror-wise? Who do you think would be more open-minded?

I don't think there's necessarily one versus the other about being open-minded. I think women will be more expressive than men will, generally.

In what way?

In what they say and how they communicate. Which is, again, that's just women versus men in general, right?

Do you think they'll reach – men and women will get to the same place?

I don't know if you have to ask everyone the same questions, but if you have a conversation with women, the type of questions that you ask, they might need to be different than the ones with men, right? **Very rarely are you going to find somebody who's a woman who's super analytical who wants the data. Those are few and far between. And very rarely do you find a man who's super sensitive who wants to have a conversation about their feelings.** *You're putting people in buckets, I recognize that, but in general, men are really analytical. They want the facts. Just the way you ask questions might be different. The way they answer might be different, and that's okay. A woman might be like, oh my God, blah blah blah versus a man's like, yep. That's just as much a fundamental problem in dating as it is in jury selection.*

How about in the way they approach an injury and how they might look at the end result? Do you think women might tend to be more generous than men?

Yes.

When it comes to determining an amount of money?

I think so. Because women are known as being more empathetic and more sympathetic than men are, just in human nature.

You think that's a fairly valid –

I do. I think that goes back to that motherly caring versus men who stand on principle a little bit more. And now thinking about it, it might depend on their demographic, right? So if a woman is a mom and somebody who maybe does work in an analytical space or is a mom and maybe works in daycares or a teacher or something, they might have a more caring attitude towards the human nature than a man who's worked in a corporation who's single, who doesn't necessarily show in their demographic that they have to care. And some say they don't, but that's their lifestyle demographic.

They're not using those skills probably as much.

Right.

And developing that.

And in their occupation; I recognize their occupation might show the same thing.

Some people like to draw conclusions based on the jobs people have. I'm not sure

I can do that or not, although we didn't want aerospace engineers and didn't want nurses, generally speaking. Now it's not just aerospace engineers; it's software engineers. I'm not sure about nurses in general. I like them, because they understand the medicine, so it's easy to let them teach the other jurors about that. How about, if my client, the plaintiff, is a woman, do you feel that woman jurors tend to be more critical of women in that position?

I think they can be. Women versus women, that whole dynamic is a really tough one. I am not somebody who generally sits on that women versus women thing. I probably sit more in the dude space than the girl space. I think if you're presenting a case, regardless of whether it's a woman or a man, women are bound to be more empathetic. I do agree with you in terms of profession. I am not one that has a female profession. I have a male profession. But that doesn't mean that my female traits don't come out. My job is to be a good communicator, and my job is to be empathetic and understand why things are happening. But it's also to drive work to getting it done. It's also to be the hard ass when I need to be. So I have a profession where some traits need to sit more on the side of a woman, and some traits need to sit more on the side of a man.

Really well-rounded.

Which is why I'm good at my job. I'm going to paint a picture. Women that get to know each other that don't like other women generally get really catty. They get catty and girly and they fight over stupid crap and they get all, whatever, stupid. I don't think if a woman is a juror that they're going to have enough time for that female thing to come out for it to be a negative thing.

You don't think they'll judge instantly?

Everyone judges instantly. That's not a man versus woman thing, it's just a matter of what they're judging, right? I'm going to judge a guy who's wearing socks with sandals. I'm just going to. It doesn't necessarily mean I judge him negatively, but I'm going to judge a woman who has a different color hair or – everyone judges everyone. It's like finding somebody attractive versus not attractive. You make a judgment call. I'm not sure that's something you can control. Because everyone's going to judge. It's just human nature.

Two more topics here. You were on a criminal case and know the burden of proof is beyond a reasonable doubt. In the civil arena, we have a different burden of proof, it's called a preponderance of the evidence. What does that suggest to you?

Why do you guys always use big words?

I'll give you another definition of it, but what does a preponderance suggest to you?

A preponderance?

A preponderance of the evidence is the burden of proof. So if you find, by a preponderance of the evidence, that the plaintiff has proved their case or not, then –

They've shown enough evidence that they can prove they have the injury and they did enough –

What does a preponderance mean to you?

I have no – a preponderance. I have – pre – I don't know.

Let's say that the definition in the instruction the judge will give you further goes on to say, a preponderance simply means more likely than not.

Why can't they just say that?

Because some lawyer got paid –

Back to my thing about making things relatable.

Right. The judge is going to give that. So, more likely than not, what does that suggest to you? What is more likely than not? How much evidence is a more likely than not standard to you?

The way my brain processes that information is, I look at it in terms of numbers. Is there more than a 50% chance that – have they presented more than 50% of the evidence? Is there 50% of what I need to understand this case? So I look at it very 50%/50% and there's that middle. That line in the middle would be the way I would look at it.

That's exactly what I like to hear people say.

A plus.

You have the scales of justice. The scales are balanced. We like people to say that if it's just tipped a little bit in favor, that's a preponderance. That's more likely than not; 49/51 or whatever.

Right.

Are you comfortable with that as a burden of proof; if you're making a decision where lots of money is at stake where there's a question, but it tipped, just ever so slightly.

*Probably not. Again, for me and my work, **I have to say it probably depends on who it's being tipped against.** If it's being tipped against somebody who was a drunk driver, where there was some sort of negligence because somebody was being an idiot, I'm going to feel a lot more okay with it than if it was against a doctor who made a mistake, and it was a human mistake. There's going to be a scale to where – there's an okay-ness scale for me. It does go against that ethical human nature. Did somebody just make an honest mistake or was it somebody really being negligent?*

Or reckless.

Or reckless, yes.

Beyond negligence.

> *Exactly. So it would come down – I would have to add another dimension of where's the morality and the ethics around the two parties? You can provide me all the facts in the world, but that doesn't necessarily mean I'm going to not feel for that other person. If that person was completely wasted and they did something, like, you're just being an idiot, I'm not going to feel very bad for you; versus somebody where I might make a conscious choice differently. You're having to battle the personal ethics between somebody who sits in the bucket of, I'm never going to drive drunk; I always get a cab versus the juror next to you say, well, I sometimes drive drunk, or have. The morality of that is different, right? That's kind of that uphill battle of what do you do with that. So there is going to be another dimension of morality of how much am I going to feel? That's probably the case the other party is trying to make; how much do you feel for that doctor or that person or that car accident or even that company? Certain people might feel really bad for that company, because you may be bankrupting them. I have no idea. But there is an added dimensionality in that I can't answer that question. I would have to consider that.*

The consequences to the defendant as well as the plaintiff?

> *Yeah.*

And the degree of negligence, the degree of recklessness, that would factor in?

> *I think the other thing that would be helpful is, is there a scale for awardship? What I mean by that is, there's been these many cases in the past of the same nature, so you look at similar cases, and this is the amount of money that has been awarded, so you're awarding something that's fair. And what they're asking for is fair. So those numbers that you're saying – in these types of cases, there's been ten in the past, and they have awarded anything from one million to ten million. I don't know. I'm making it up. Awarding fifty million wouldn't be fair; it would actually be really crappy; versus all the other stuff that has happened in the past.*

If you had some kind of a scale based on –

> *Some sort of comparative scale and numbers to say, of these cases, this has generally been the –*

A range of some sort.

> *I don't know if that's reasonable, but at least I know what I'm doing is fair based on other cases that have happened in the past. It's not just this one case where this person's asking for an exorbitant amount of money and we're going to give to him because we don't know any better, right? **Allow us to know better.***

That brings us to this question of damages and money, which is the end result, the only thing that civil courts can do. Can't make the person better; all we can do is make them whole. There are two kinds of damages: special damages, which

are those kinds of things you can have a receipt for; medical bills; wage losses; personal property; things that experts can weigh in on. People can talk about what that number is going to be. There may be disputes, but by and large, you can put them on a spreadsheet and add them up. The other part, general damages, are pain, suffering, disability, loss of enjoyment of life. There's no fixed standard the law can apply. Every juror can apply a different number to how they value that kind of damage. So a person comes in, they've proven they've been hurt, they've proven it was caused by somebody else. Now it comes time for you as a juror to put a dollar figure on their injury. We're talking about emotional injuries and physical pain; suffering and pain, things you can't put on a spreadsheet, because it's different for every person. How would you go about determining what's a fair figure? What are the kinds of things you'd want to think about, look at and hear to get there?

> *That goes back to the empathy you're trying to gauge from people, right? Your jurors, no doubt.*

Recognizing that jurors may have empathy for the other side as well.

> *Right.*

One's a rural school teacher. She can't afford to pay all of these damages. What do we do then?

> *I think it depends on the level of injury. How long were you out of commission of your life, whatever that looks like? What kind of out did it put you in? Were you in a hospital for six months versus at home with a broken leg? Those differences are important. I believe in life people need to suck it up. People have become soft. This is probably the only bias in terms of people that I have is that people become soft. Like antibacterial, why do people use – I ate dirt when I was four. Come on, people. I think people have become soft in life and people need to suck it up. Just suck it up and go live life. Yes, there's emotional damage, but how do you gauge – that's trying to gauge how much therapy one needs to deal with the same situation. You can't. I don't understand that concept. I don't understand personal suffering. Everyone's personal suffering is different. It's not my responsibility to gauge how much your personal – maybe you're making it my responsibility, but it shouldn't be my responsibility to gauge how much it's going to cost to make that suffering go away, because it's not monetary.*

Well, you can't make it go away.

> *But that's it, right? You're asking me to come up with a monetary figure to make it okay.*

You and your fellow jurors.

> *If I'm looking at it from a personal responsibility, I can't do that.*

And you need to feel good about it.

I can't. **How do you put a monetary value on the fact that this person is suffering more or less than this person? You can't, right?** *Let's say you're a doctor and you're going to make your practice go out of business because you made an honest mistake and this person's going to win. I can guarantee you, this person, the defendant doctor person, is going to suffer more in the long term than you, Mr. Blah Blah Blah, who maybe broke a leg and then got – like this person did something wrong, right?* **So I actually feel negative about the fact that it's my responsibility to grant any of that money because it's not my job to gauge your suffering. It shouldn't be.**

How do you feel about your job doing the special damages part?

I think that's fine because there is an assessment that is, hey, I need to pay my bills while I'm out and hey, I need to blah blah blah. Gauging that part, especially against a scale of some other form of this has all happened and blah blah blah, I think that's okay. If you can prove some sort of negligence to where I need to be able to reimburse and pay for my things and my life, I feel like that's okay, but if I'm trying to gauge some sort of monetary assessment for somebody's suffering, unless it's for therapy, which by the way, comes with a bill – does that make sense?

Absolutely. Let's say an individual is in a car wreck. The person that hit them was texting or – no, we'll take that out of it, they just were inattentive. There was a bad car wreck. A person was injured as a result. They have a significant back condition. They've had a couple of surgeries, but they're going to always be in chronic pain. That's the part we'd be asking compensation for, chronic pain for life. Would you still feel that's a suck up thing?

I don't. I have a friend who's in that condition. She was in a car accident. She has chronic pain. And she goes to Pilates and does the acupuncture stuff that creeps me out. She does all this other stuff to say, you know what? I have to deal with this. But I can either let it rule my life or I can try tackle it face on. And I think that's an attitude, and that's dealing with the suffering. I can't put monetary – I don't think it's right. I think that's – everyone suffers from something.

If the Court's instructions were that if you find –

If I had to.

– if you find there was this kind of pain and suffering that you must reach some figure; the jury must provide some award, some compensation. Would you weigh in?

Probably not. I wouldn't. Because it's not my place. I recognize in being a juror, you're asking for it to be my place. And there is that obligation. But again, I would want to go back and say, what is the average figure? What is the number that have been awarded? Because then you're normalizing it, right? Then you're saying, your pain and suffering is not more than anyone else's, it's just average and this is the general number that we're going to grant.

Can you think of something where it goes beyond the ability of a person to suck it up? It could be the loss of a child or an amputation of a limb –

No.

– or some horrible quadriplegia type of a thing?

Maybe. If you're in a situation where you're going to have to pay medical bills for life because of somebody else that would probably be the only reason. But I really don't. I think it's a life choice. What you're being asked to assess is, can this person deal with life? Versus something else, right? If somebody can come to me and present the fact that this person feels like they're going to need therapy for the next five years and that's the figure I'm asking for, and they're showing me they're going to deal with their suffering and they're not just – I have pain and suffering. I'm not getting any money. And it was caused by other people. I'm not a quadriplegic and I haven't been in a car accident or anything like that, but that doesn't necessarily discount that my pain and suffering is worse or better than somebody else's. Because I can tell you, mine sucks. But it doesn't mean that I might be stuck in a wheelchair but have the most amazing husband and have two kids. It's perspective. So if you can come to me and say, really, what we're assessing and what we're asking for is this figure, because of five years of therapy or ten years of therapy and this person needs to go shopping with $400 a month because that's how they feel good about themselves, whatever, I would feel better about granting a number than just saying, we're asking $100,000 for pain and suffering when you can't actually prove to me what it's going to do. I want $100,000 for my pain and suffering.

It's hard for us to come up with some number, look the jury in the eye and say, we think this is reasonable because.

*What would help me make that decision is, we think it's reasonable because. Here's what we're assessing it against. Whether it's like all the other pain and suffering in similar cases or we've come up with this figure because we're looking at ten years of meeting with a therapist. Whatever those figures end up being. Shopping money. I don't care what it is, **as long as I can say, okay, it's being granted towards something and not just a monetary figure.***

So a specific purpose, not just a blank check.

***The reason why is because it shows it's going towards something. It shows that person is willing to face their pain and suffering and it's something they're willing to do versus, I have pain and suffering. Well, everyone has pain and suffering. What makes you special?** Aside from the fact you're sitting in this courthouse.*

And somebody else caused it and it wasn't your fault, let's say. Tell me this: has your upbringing or your education or your profession informed you on that part of what we've been talking about that makes you have that fairly strong attitude – not attitude, but belief? Is it the way you were raised? You have a family where the family says, we just suck it up and move on?

*I think part of it was the way I was raised. **Part of it was growing up as an athlete. You don't get to wallow in your pain and suffering; you deal with it. You rehab. You get back in the game.** Some of that is empathy towards people who are willing to face their problems versus – not a judgment against, but there is a – I'm going to use the word bias – there's a bias towards people who are willing to face their challenges and who are willing to look at life in a positive perspective and not wallow. I think that's because as an athlete, that's what you're forced to do. I was an athlete for 25 years and still consider myself an athlete. Part of that comes from my upbringing. My family is very work-focused. They're types of people who, you figure it out. You figure out a solution and then move on, almost to a fault; almost to a place where my family, though fun and awesome, they are most un-empathetic. We're Italian. You just hit it over the head with a slice of cheese and call it a day, pretty much. There is a certain aspect of my upbringing where I did a lot of things in my life first compared to my friends. A lot of the relationship-y things that happen, I did first. And my friends came to me a lot. And I learned, because of my family, I'm the quiet one in my family, I learned how to listen really well. And what ends up happening when you're a listener is you end up listening, and you can choose to either offer advice or you choose to offer – you can choose how to respond. When you hear somebody over and over and over say, I want to do this, I want to do this, I want to do this, the question then becomes, okay, when are you going to do it? And if you don't do it, it actually says just as much as it does.*

You want to see actions.

Yeah. I've become more introverted as I've grown older. I've become more inwardly thoughtful, in part because in a way, I've become a therapist to a lot of people, like a friends' therapist-y person.

It comes with being a listener.

It does. So you combine all of that with somebody who's like, I really do feel like I've just had to survive in a lot of things. I wasn't super in love with my sport, so you make decisions and you understand trade-offs and if you have any ounce of perspective, you recognize what you're doing. I've been in therapy myself. I've suffered through a lot. A lot of it comes from being in a place of suffering and understanding and being somebody who has come out at the other end as a really happy person with myself, and it was really a personal struggle; you actually become more biased towards the people who do that versus the people who just sit there and complain about it. Because you recognize that despite the hopeless feeling of the situation you were in, you know you can come out the other side. And I think if you're willing to do it –

Willing to do the therapy.

Yeah. It not only makes you more empathetic towards the people who are willing to take action, it also makes you a little more critical to those that aren't. I'm not somebody who will judge somebody who isn't, because I don't know their life situation. But I will always be an encourager towards it. I think that's why I have that attitude of, you know what? If you're just wanting money because you want money, not a good enough reason. It's just not.

What if an expert said, we don't think therapy will make a difference at this point? This person's reached maximum medical improvement.

What is it your place to judge? I don't care if you are a medical expert and you can tell me they've reached their medical –

Because these cases are often battles of experts.

Well, it is, and I recognize that. But if the expert comes in and tells me as a therapist, they've reached their potential in terms of their pain and suffering, I would have almost a vapid negative reaction towards that –

Even if they're credentialed?

It doesn't even matter. Because who are you to judge? It's not my job; it's not your job. Your job, especially as a therapist, your job is not to judge. Your job is – that is the anti-your job.

Do you have a sense that experts are hired guns in these cases?

No. I think it depends on who you are, right? And what judgment you're trying to make or what case you're trying to present. If you're coming in as the medical expert to say, this doctor could have done nothing more, okay. That might be the case. And that's probably true. But if you're coming in as the opposing side of a therapist and that therapist is trying to make a judgment about this person's pain and suffering, screw you man. I'm sorry, but you have no right to judge this person. Unless it is your therapist and that person's therapist, which might be the case. I've been at that wits' end of my therapist telling me, there's nothing else you can do. There was more I could do. There's always more you can do. And it is no right of anybody else's to judge somebody's mental health. You can judge a negative, like, hey dude, you really need help. I don't know what kind of help that looks like, but it's not yours to judge how that person needs help or what help that person needs or whether that person's ready for help. It's a personal thing.

That's very helpful. That's created a whole dimension that I won't get into explaining, but you have given me a lot to think about in terms of dealing with how can I get the jury to think about compensation. It's got to be something with a purpose. Just giving money isn't going to do anything, but if it's money for something that will make their life better in a demonstrable way, or reasonably demonstrable way, that's a really good thing for me to think about.

If I was in your position as the lawyer of your client, wouldn't you want to know that this person isn't just coming forth, I mean from an ethical mental perspective, saying, I need two million because I'm suffering? If you care about that, and you can show you care about that, to me, that shows that I should *care about it. Because you're that person's lifeline. If it were me, and I recognize money is money, but if that person comes to me saying, I need two million for pain and suffering, my job would be to ask why do you feel like this is your pain and suffering? And if they can't explain it, this might be a judgmental thing to say, but would you really want them as a client?*

Case selection is everything. What do you think the role of insurance is in these cases?

To me, their job is, unless they don't pay, unless it's insurance negligence, I'm not sure there is a role other than just them paying for insurance. I'm not sure I know enough. Unless it's insurance negligence, like insurance isn't willing to pay, but it's a thing which might be a whole different kind of case, I don't know.

What I mean is, do you think there's insurance standing behind the person who's being sued; or the doctor or the corporation?

Probably. I don't know about the doctor or the person, but in terms of a corporation, probably. I might be the best kind of juror, because I still don't believe it's right to use that to your advantage.

We can't talk about it in trial. It's not allowed to be considered, unless it's a case where we've sued an insurance company for bad faith or something like that.

Right.

Last question: is there anything you think would be helpful; kind of open-ended?

*No. **I feel like part of the challenge you would have as the lawyer is just to build a connection between you and the jurors, right? A lot of that is done through how you relate to your client, but also how you relate to them and your body language and looking at them and understanding who they are and trying to trigger that, because that's going to be the way that you relate to people.** And you do that really well. But there's other ways of looking at people. A lot of this is just behavioral science and understanding. What's that profession? What's the people degree that people get? Not Philosophy – Psychology and Anthropology. Right? Isn't that Anthropology? I don't know. Anyway, a lot of it's just understanding how people behave and how people –*

What I'm finding is that everybody behaves differently.

Oh, sure. But there are tells, right? It's one of those things I thought about when I was there, I almost would be on the sidelines to look at people's body language, and be a consultant as to, here's maybe who, and it's always a guessing game, right? But here's maybe who you should have chosen because this person did this and you didn't notice.

Right. Thank you.

36

EXPLAIN THE PROCESS

Caucasian male, 57, divorced, two children, Attorney, J.D.

It's important to put folks at ease. Explain the process and that it's necessary to come up with an unbiased jury, an open-minded jury.

Ladies and gentlemen, please give your attention to the lawyer for the plaintiff who's going to conduct jury selection. Given your background, as you're in that moment, what are you thinking? And what's important to you?

I'm in the panel in the courtroom? And the questioning's going to start. Different things are going to go through my mind. One is, does this attorney know what he's doing? My profession is an attorney, and I'm probably going to take a look at him or her and see if he's doing it, she's doing it, like I do or substandard or an excellent job. I'll probably try to stay anonymous, too, just kind of hide back there. I don't think I'd be raising my hand much to answer questions. I'm kind of an introvert, so I think I'd be quiet.

On that same question, given your experience, what do you think the rest of the jury pool is thinking at that moment? Or feeling?

There's going to be some of them that don't want to be there. They're going to think, why am I here, why do I have listen to this, why do I have to go through this? I've got better things to do. Some are going to be, I imagine, happy to do their civic duty and contribute their time and effort toward hearing the case. They judge attorneys, too. They'll be looking at what they're wearing. I had a case once, a two-week trial, and the attorney wore the same suit every day. We talked to the jury afterwards, and they didn't think that was too cool. They think about how the attorneys present, too.

Is there anything the attorney could say or do at the outset that would influence you, either positively or more negatively? Right then at the outset?

*I don't know if I'm answering your question here, but **I think it's important to put folks at ease. Explain the process and that it's necessary to come up with an unbiased jury, an open-minded jury.** The better a lawyer's able to present that from the start, to get it comfortable from the start, because it is nerve-wracking, you know, the better. If I'm asked questions as a juror, my voice might be shaking, even though I've tried 250 cases. So, putting me at ease. There's the what not to do, too. Not sure I answered it.*

If you have thoughts on what not to do, I'd love to hear that. And we're talking about what not to do to interfere with your ability to be a fair juror, to not be turned off.

Be organized. It's important not to waste my time in court; for the attorney to have a plan of action, to follow the plan, to have their questions written out. To follow some sense of order. To perhaps ask intelligent questions, not what's your favorite book? I don't ask that one. I wouldn't want to be asked that one. I think the meaningful questions are tying the questions into your case somehow, just to make it meaningful.

When you talk about the lawyer explaining the process, how much should go into that, and how much is needed to be said?

It's pretty preliminary, just a short, brief statement; less than five minutes. Less than that probably. It's a preamble.

As a juror, what is your sense of how plaintiff's lawyers, but it can be defense lawyers, too, what can they do to establish a human connection with their jury and to be credible; to have credibility with that jury?

They need to have humility. They should not be condescending, not preach to.

Do you think that applies to the rest of the jury pool as well, that they have the same feelings and thoughts about that?

I think so.

Have you seen exceptions where maybe there has been some preaching to or somebody has been a little less humble and yet it's worked?

I've never seen it work. I've talked to juries afterwards, and they don't like the attorney. It affects the case in chief sometimes, sometimes to a great extent. If they stop listening to the person because they've been put off by him, there's a problem.

What's the number one thing you've seen a plaintiff's lawyer do that's put off a jury?

The things I just said. Another is being unorganized; shuffling papers, having books stacked on your desk and knocking them over.

What about a genuine caring for the client? For you as a potential juror, you see a lawyer who seems to exude a real sense of caring and investment and involvement in his or her client. What does that do for you?

That's critical. It helps me understand the lawyer cares for his client. I have seen lawyers who call their client the plaintiff, and that's not humanizing them. You call them by their name.

Have you seen it backfire where somebody's exhibited too much caring; a little too much transference or something?

I have.

Tell me about that.

It eventually appears to be a dog and pony show. It's like a show without the heart behind it. It's superficial.

Somebody told me they thought it became too much about the lawyer and not about the client; have you seen that?

True. I have.

Let's talk a little bit about bias and prejudice, or what I've lately been talking about, which is open-mindedness. As a potential juror, how would you like to be asked the question about your ability to be open-minded and fair?

Notwithstanding what we talked about earlier –

Why don't you cover that ground again?

You've suggested the possibility of an abbreviated voir dire where you just say, do you believe you can keep an open mind? I believe in that, what you said, and I may incorporate that to a certain extent.

Just don't give me attribution.

The problem with it is, with me, that's kind of a general question.

You as a potential juror?

Yeah. What do you mean? I'm open-minded about what? What are you talking about? *You talking about the neck surgery? Are you talking about whether I believe medical bills should be paid; am I open-minded about that? Or general damages or –*

How could the question be phrased better, so that there's a meaningful response?

*The way I would like to see that brought up potentially is when, say you're asked about being a victim of a crime. And you do have hurt feelings about it. You may have a bias and a grudge and be revenge-minded. So the question then posed, do you think you can have an open mind **even though this case involves** –*

Given that it's happened to you. What I'm taking from that is that you need to tie it into something that's personal to that person's experience.

Agreed.

Rather than just general questioning like, can you be open-minded or not? Can you be open-minded about this particular thing, given your experience?

I have asked that question in a general manner, and juries go dead silent when you ask that question. You have to call on them, and even when you call on them, they don't like tackling that question. So it's good to tie in.

Tie it in. Do you have any sense as a potential juror, and also as a lawyer who's done many of these cases, that the words bias and prejudice are hot words that need to be avoided with jurors, or can they be used?

Yeah, those are labels. If there are softer words to use, that's probably good.

Have you got any experience with that, or is that –

You had them earlier. What were they?

Open-mindedness?

Open-mindedness.

Maybe leaning more one way than another?

Yeah.

Ability to be fair.

That's it.

Have you ever asked the question, or as a potential juror how would you feel if you were asked the question, what do you think fairness is in, say, a case where somebody is claiming to be compensated for injuries? How would that work with you?

Fairness in my mind would be giving both parties the benefit of the doubt, listening to all of the evidence, not deciding until you've heard it all; how it all ties in at the end with closing and doing the best you can to be fair after all that.

If the lawyer is asking you, what is it I need to know about you as a juror relevant to this particular case, to you as a juror that would be important to know? What would that be? And is that a good question for you?

It is. There's two parts to it. One, as a lawyer – important for you to know about me.

What would be a way to find out who you are as a person? Or what do I need to know in this context that would be important and helpful for everybody and for a fair trial?

I guess it's really hard for me to separate the lawyer and the juror with that case.

You mean you as a lawyer and juror?

Yeah.

That's okay, because that's who you are.

Yeah, okay. So what would you like to know about me? How to approach me?

What would be good for all of us to know about you?

Just where I may falter; where I may not be helpful for your case. What hot buttons are there from my experience growing up, as a lawyer? One of them is, what do you think about treatment? Should a plaintiff receive treatment beyond that which is curative? Should they be entitled to maintenance treatment? I've been doing this such a long time, I'm biased, a little bit biased, maybe not fair, about how long a person should treat. I think an attorney would want to know that because that could hurt their case.

And that's about you.

Yeah. In a positive aspect, I'm really good at reading people. I think that could be elicited. I fancy that I have this magical power to judge who's going to be good on my case and who's not. I've had plaintiff's lawyers where I can predict their next move, their next peremptory challenge. I know who it's going to be. And they know who mine are going to be. You know you're both doing it right there, probably. But then you get one stricken that you were going to strike, too, and you start thinking, could they have hurt my case? Or both of our cases? These stereotypes don't always fit.

One of the things that may be the biggest thing I need to know is, who's the snake in the grass in the jury pool? How would we find that person? Do they let us know?

You can judge that by looking at them. If I'm in a panel of prospective jurors, and there's an ass, just a crabby, unpleasant person, you're not going to want that. I sure wouldn't want that for my case. So that's one of them. People you're looking for are anti-insurance industry. You don't like managers of small businesses; you don't like HR people. You don't like people with relatable experiences but had it worse. You're coming into court with a whiplash, with no damage to the cars, and you've got someone on the panel of prospective jurors that had low back surgery, neck or back, from a real significant accident. I think the plaintiff's lawyer is going to want to bump that person. You want to stay away from people that are fiscally conservative; dislike frivolous lawsuits.

Tell me how that question would be best asked?

You know how that comes up? It's the McDonald's question. That was really helpful to get that out to the panel that there are frivolous suits. There are suits that ask for way too much money. Over the years, the plaintiff's bar has had a very nice softening of that McDonald's case. I forget what they do, but it takes the punch out of it.

Number one is, we don't try to persuade the juror that their thinking may be based on inaccurate reading of what actually happened.

Yeah.

A short story: Stella Liebeck was an old lady, right? Well, somebody said to me, just not long ago, you know, that case was all about her boyfriend suing for loss of consortium. There's a lot of bad information out there.

People who favor tort reform, you don't want those.

How do we get them to talk about that in a meaningful way without being threatened?

It depends on what the area is. If it's tort reform, you ask the question in general.

Have them raise their hand and then get to them little by little. If it's a more general question, to get to bias, let's say frivolous lawsuits, that's kind of the same thing. Another thing I do is loop the jurors. I'll ask the question of one and then the neighbor, and then the neighbor and then the neighbor, so you get a full picture.

Do you think as a potential juror, or in your experience as a lawyer doing these cases, that there's anything in an audio or visual way that can be helpful in *voir dire*?

What you're saying makes two impressions to me: how the attorney presents; and what he may have as far as electronics.

Right. Electronics or boards or anything.

Juries don't like boards anymore; they like electronics. They like the projector with medical records up. As far as a presentation of the lawyer himself, just have good posture and be confident. Be professional. Have humility. Dress well. Smile. Know they're looking at you all the time.

As a potential juror, do you have the sense, as many people do, that the plaintiff's trial lawyer is at the bottom of the scale of credibility as far as professions go?

Not me. No.

Do you think that's true of your fellow jurors? As a general proposition?

I don't. I do run into that sometimes when I say I'm a lawyer. What do you do? Personal injury. Oh, you –

Ambulance chaser.

Then the insult comes.

Sleazy lawyer.

No, I'm on the defense side.

Do you come in thinking that the plaintiff's lawyer is a sleazy lawyer, ambulance chaser, or just generally not credible?

No. That lawyer has every possibility to impress me beyond imagine.

The plaintiff's lawyer is earning a fee and often there is insurance underlying these cases, as the lawyer, how does that affect your evaluation of the case?

It doesn't. I mean, if my client is the person that was in the accident, it's not the insurance company.

As a juror, though. And you know these things.

So do jurors. They know there's insurance.

Do they know that the lawyer is generally getting a contingent fee on the plaintiff's side?

I think so.

Do you think that's factored in when they make their award?

I would say at least half the time. I have talked to juries directly, and they factored it in.

How can a plaintiff's lawyer make sure they know that without falling afoul of the rules? In a fair way? Because it kind of is fair.

I think plaintiff's attorneys should build the case up and take the value for what it's worth.

Got it. As a potential juror, would you be tempted to go to the website of the plaintiff's lawyer or the defense lawyer and see who and what they're all about?

I don't think so. I never checked on my Christmas presents early. I never looked in anyone's iPhone. I would not research them. Now, if the question's about a technical medical term or injury, I probably would. Some of these injuries, you can't even pronounce them. I would probably research that a little bit.

Do you think the average or majority of jurors are checking out the lawyers?

I don't know how snoopy they are. I just wouldn't be able to guess. Depends on the person, personality. What do you think?

I think they do. And I think that really creative lawyers are tailoring their websites for that very reason, so that the first thing jurors see is extreme competence and philanthropy; doing good without greed. That's a personal belief. It's never been informed by anything anyone's ever said to me. I just have that sense.

As long as you're not putting up photocopies of million dollar settlement checks on your web page, you're probably okay.

Or celebrities of the moment.

That's good.

Well, you know there are very fine lawyers putting up the numbers they've had in their cases, and those numbers can be ten figures.

You've got a point there. That's data, and if they helped them, that many people doing that, well, they're going to help me, too.

Just shows they know what they're doing.

Well, it's like you're going to go to a Thai restaurant with four stars or two?

The Yelp phenomenon.

Yeah.

Okay. There's a school of thought and some very fine lawyers who think that before you start asking jurors to share that you should share something of yourself. I'll

show you mine if you'll show me yours. How do you feel, as a potential juror, about a lawyer who's going to get up and talk about some bias or prejudice of his own to get the ball rolling?

I think that's improper. I think that it's okay in a limited fashion. I'll give you an example. If an attorney gets up to do voir dire, with the understanding it's best to learn the jurors' names, and if you're terrible with names, just say, folks, I'm terrible with names. I'm going to try, but I'm going to use numbers, too; now, don't take offense. I think you're telling the jury a little about yourself. You've got the humility thing going. But I don't think it's proper to introduce a whole lot of background.

Suppose it were, folks, just to get this ball rolling, we're going to talk about things that make us biased or prejudiced. I don't happen to like bicyclists, just because of experiences I've had. Do you have any particular experiences? Maybe it should be more germane to the case, but what is your thought about that?

I think that's within bounds. As a lawyer, you could object. As a juror, if I'm hearing that, I'd probably want more.

Just hearing that, would that help you feel more willing to share?

During voir dire? Maybe slightly. You're talking to an introvert here, though. I'm hiding in the back. I'm not going to volunteer unless I'm pointed to.

What are some of the best can openers that have worked for you to get jurors talking in a meaningful way?

Here's one I would use right now: has anybody heard about the city putting in a homeless shelter without asking for a vote; without asking for community input? Has anybody heard about that? Yes, Juror No. 60, what do you think about that? Well, if I'm in that neighborhood, I would have liked to have input. So here you have a juror that wants to vote. They're getting cut off halfway through the process, which a lawsuit is, too. You want to have them pay attention until the defense case is over. So it ties into the case a little bit, too.

So they hear everything before they decide?

Exactly, and be heard. The bite is, it's a current event. And the more votes you can put in to voir dire, tying it into your case, I think that's a good way to go.

Getting back to something you talked about is the ability to remember the names of jurors. Do you think in general that is a skill that should be developed?

If possible. Voir dire happens so quickly. It is a fast-moving event, and you're going to have probably a panel of 40 people there. But 25 of them aren't going to make it. I know you have the 12 or 14 and then the first couple rows. So if you have an assistant there helping you with names, you can do it. Me, if I'm solo, I'm not going to remember 30, 40 names. It's just not going to happen. I'm not aware of any tools that can change that.

There's a thing where you make associations somebody tried to teach me. I once asked a juror, Juror No. something, may I have your name? And she said, no, you may not. Exceptions to every rule, right?

Yeah. We got the card, you know, the card ties it into the number, so you could have. But she didn't want to give it anyway. Man, that's –

I don't so much mind it with that juror as I do the pollution of the other jurors seeing me struggle.

Oh, I know. What do you do at that point in time? You have to be, I'm thinking reactive, but I'm looking for a different word. You have to adapt to the situation. Be Cool Hand Luke; don't look flustered. But that one would have got me, too.

Have you seen a team of lawyers successfully bifurcate their *voir dire* where one talks about damages and one talks about liability?

I have.

Has that been successful, in your opinion?

I was not impressed. As a juror, I don't think I'd be impressed. I'm intelligent enough to understand where things fit. I've seen a lot of lawyers double up. Not too many double up on issues as far as liability defense and damages.

You mentioned earlier a small handful of really good *voir dires* that you've seen. Without mentioning their names, are there any currents or anything special that stood out among those lawyers' *voir dires* that you can comment on?

They seemed well-prepared. They presented well. They were articulate. They were economical. They worked quickly. They asked penetrating questions. They didn't have a fear, too big of a fear, you can't have too big of a fear of offending someone. You have to dig a little bit. And they dug. Not to the point of insulting people, but they got to a level I hadn't seen. It's the exception rather than the rule.

Do you think those *voir dires*, the success of those *voir dires* shaped the result?

They were good attorneys to start with. Maybe that's part of why they're good, but I think they have success in most of the cases they handle, just high level.

Have you seen otherwise really good attorneys bomb in *voir dire*?

Many, many times.

What happens?

Some of the younger ones, even the older ones, they have a performance anxiety. Their voice shakes. They've been in court before, but something about this exercise paralyzes them and they just go through a pro forma exercise where they don't have their heart into it. They're doing it just because you're supposed to do it. And they don't show the same love for their client.

A question in my mind lately is this: is *voir dire* or jury selection a pointless exercise in the sense that, regardless of all that we go through, what we're really ending up with is the same jury we may end up with if we didn't go through all of that, with maybe the exception of one or two outliers that could creep in?

*I disagree. **I think the jury can be fine-tuned.** I've very seldom been left with a jury I didn't like. Oftentimes, I'll go to the third challenge, you know, use all of them. But it just seems to work out that when I'm done, I'm saying this is going to work. And it usually does with the jury.*

As a potential juror, when it comes to somebody inquiring to you about cause, you've been selected, you've been chosen, you've been called out, and this lawyer is asking you all sorts of pointed questions and the judge keeps bailing you out on that, how do you feel? Is there resentment building in there?

Absolutely. What's the cause?

Let's say they're insurance adjusters or people who believe that tort reform, that there's a crisis. Or let's call it a med mal case and people just don't think doctors should be held to the same standard as the rest of –

Okay. Let's leave that one there. I personally would not mind being challenged for cause. See ya later. I'm heading back to the office, going home.

Of course.

I think it can pollute the rest of the jury, for better or worse, depending on what side you're on. I think it could turn the jury even against the judge. But at that point in time, people aren't going to know this person that well. If a jury has gotten to know somebody, they're more likely to defend them. So, I'm not sure the jury would care. Now, the issue itself, it could cause some bitterness if these unknown jurors are land-mines for you.

If somebody gets to the point where you have to ask them questions to develop cause, do you think you're better off just dropping the whole cause line of questioning and save a peremptory for them?

Absolutely. Yep.

Live with it?

Yes.

On my side of the fence, there are lawyers saying, I just got five people excused for cause. I'm thinking, how the hell did they get that many people? And what must that bloodbath have looked like to the rest of the jurors?

What I do is, I ask the judge to inquire. They'll do their job, and then the judge will ask you if you have any follow-up. If the judge has been complete enough and there's cause, he'll do it right there without attorney input.

In a way that's meaningful and not just, do you think you can you follow the judge's instructions?

Judges, the ones I've been in front of, are really sharp that way. They'll do it right. If it's a close issue, the judge will hand it back to the lawyers, and then you can dig deeper trying to get cause to get that judge over the fence to help you out. But I don't think I've done that more than once or twice.

My thought is that may be diminishing marginal returns at that point. You may do yourself more harm than good. This exercise for me is about what's the most efficient way to not do harm and still get the job done?

That's a good way to approach it.

A year and a half ago, I was on three *voir dire* panels as a prospective juror. Two were PI. One was a first degree murder case. In all three panels, the lawyers seemed to be very comfortable with lawyers being jurors. I found that interesting.

I try to keep them off.

Sometimes, though, so many people are getting excused for cause, we really want to get our case out.

Yeah.

I know you understand what a burden of proof is, obviously it's a preponderance. I've asked many potential jurors what they think preponderance means, and they struggle mightily. When I tell them more likely than not; that helps. What do you think the average juror thinks preponderance and more likely than not mean?

I think they need to have it brought out more specifically like you did. And you can go one step further. If you're thinking 49% adverse to that person, you vote it's not liable, or if you have 51%, then that's more probable than not.

Do you think most jurors are comfortable with that small level of the scales being tipped?

I don't know. I've never been comfortable with it. I wish that burden was higher.

Then you need to do more medical malpractice defense. Many potential jurors talk about well, if it was just an accident, I really am hesitant to penalize the person for what was just an accident. And they always say, but if the person was drunk driving, then it would be a different story. What they're defaulting to is, they want it to be a punitive standard, I think.

I cover that in voir dire.

Do you?

Yeah. The fact that punitive damages aren't allowed.

Right. Do you ever talk about hindsight bias?

I always do in my opening and closing. I think it's something that is more appropriate in argument than voir dire. It's, whatever decision you make in this case, think about what you're going to tell your friends or family or neighbors if they ask about the case. Are you going to feel comfortable telling them you awarded this plaintiff blank, whatever the plaintiff's lawyers ask for, a day from now? A week from now? A year from now? You have to have that level of comfort. That's your hindsight, a little bit.

Got it. Hindsight with regards to the decision you're making as you're looking back. Let's talk about damages. I think special damages are pretty easy to explain to jurors. I say, anything you can put on a spreadsheet and total up, depending on what experts say and who you believe. But when it comes to general damages, I tell them, there's no fixed standard to guide you. How would you approach that?

> **Well, you know that it's three times the specials, don't you? I think jurors know that.**

Do you think so?

> **I think a lot of them do.** *They've heard, they have folks around them that have done that kind of work. As far as general damages, what I'd do is argue the facts, you know, how, if, to mitigate. If there's good medical records that show 100% improvement by eight months post-accident, you hold that up. That tells a lot about general damages.*

Then and there. I hadn't really thought or heard that juries are thinking about that three times figure.

> *I have talked to them afterwards, and had them volunteer that in a limited amount of cases; probably half a dozen cases.*

Would you want to hear how much is going to be asked for when you're in jury selection? Or some kind of a range?

> **I don't want to hear that. I'd rather wait till I hear the evidence.** *And then shifting to my attorney role, I don't like hearing that in voir dire; I'll object. He's trying his case; he's putting in evidence here and that's a no-no.*

Even if they anchor it and say, you know, this could be a case where we may ask for as much as a million dollars?

> *That's a little bit more vague. I don't like when that happens.*

Does that mean you think it's working?

> *It could be. And depending on the judge, some will let that in and some will cut it off. Can't try your case there.*

Do you think, as a potential juror, it's helpful to know or have some framing about the significance of the case? Is there anything to make you more involved or invested in wanting to be a fair juror in that case?

> **As a juror, I'd want a scouting report.** *As a defense attorney, I would try to keep that short and brief. I'd object quickly on that one.*

What I'm getting at is, so many of these cases may, in the grand scheme of things, be considered very insignificant from the point of view of the average juror. The average auto case compared to some catastrophic injury case. How do you get the jury to think other than, this is just a waste of our time?

Well, they're entitled to their day in court. Who knows why they're there? Maybe not enough money was offered. But outlining the case usually comes in.

So case selection is kind of important.

Yeah.

Do you think plaintiff's lawyers are trying too many bad cases?

There's a lot of them out there. I don't know. That's a tough question. What's a bad case?

Sure. That's not a fair question.

There are some cases out there where they're fraud, outright fraud.

I hear about that. I've personally never seen it, but I've certainly heard about it. You would know.

I've seen it, but it's very, very remote. So that's a bad case. They're fraud. But other than that, some of these cases were with light damage and – see, I'm one of those jurors that was in a worse accident. Several of them. I'm not sure I'd have a whole lot of sympathy for that kind of case. So that's not a good case. I wouldn't say it's a bad case, but as a juror, you wouldn't want me on that chair there.

As a potential juror, how do you feel about dueling experts? And do you think they're hired guns?

On the plaintiff's side, I think they have a little advantage because it's mixed treaters. Treaters will refer to another, but when you see the same usual suspects, there's a couple of them that you just – give me a break. On the defense side, they're all hired guns.

Do you think the jury knows that?

They sure do by the end of the case.

I've seen cases where highly qualified academic experts with no attachment to the case other than they were brought in, on paper, look wonderful and present well but paled in comparison to a shoddy other expert, who doesn't have that kind of a background, who's clearly been doing nothing but what you just said, being a hired gun. How do you get a potential juror or a juror to pay more attention to credentials?

On the defense side?

Or any side.

Yeah, credentials; not as good bedside manner, is that it?

As a potential juror, are you thinking that experts generally cross each other out?

It depends on the expert. I have been hammered with lack of credibility with my expert. I had one case go to trial and they show up with a box full of depositions.

Right. There are some.

And they're ready to see him say the same thing.

Is that powerful?

Against us, yeah.

It was powerful.

Sure it was.

You mean the jury really got that?

Oh, they got something out of that case. I think that the plaintiff has an advantage by that.

With that kind of a tactic?

I mean with experts. I think they have an advantage, all the way through. I think it's less of an appearance of a hired gun than on the defense.

If it's a treater, for sure.

Yeah. Even experts, they do, if they have patients; not just doing forensic work. I've been on the short end of that for a long time, but as far as accident reconstructionists, I've used a dozen of them. They could go for either plaintiff or defense. I tell them not to extend themselves or they look stupid, you know what I mean? Most of them will do that anyway.

I try to get them to be objective. We're kind of getting a little bit afar, but let me explain one thing I do. I've gotten away from using treating doctors, because I don't like to take their time. I like to find a single voice who can conduct an examination; who has their own practice, but who's comfortable in the arena. Do you think your colleagues and the insurers, are they suspicious of that?

I don't – I think they'd probably think you're doing them a favor. You know, I'd get that treater in by video tape dep or somehow get them in there. If I was a plaintiff's lawyer, I'd explain it. If you don't have them explain it somehow to the jury that that's why only this one guy's here –

Right. We're trying to minimize everybody's – these are busy people. Of course, then you don't want the jury to say, well, hey, if it's that important –

You can do it, but when you do that, I'm saying this guy hasn't even treated him. What's he here for as a witness? Why's he there? Talk about hired guns.

Do you think this is a fair question as a potential juror, and I don't know if this runs afoul of the Golden Rule or not, but if you were a plaintiff, or a defendant, what kind

of a juror would you want on your case? Do you think that's a good question to ask to a potential juror, and is it fair?

I think it's a good one.

And what sort of qualities would you like to see them have?

*I think I explained that earlier. You know, **it's open-mindedness, listening to the whole case before it's over. Using your reason, your cognition and senses to tell you where to go with it, you know? And they put away bias and prejudice.***

So, the question is, without running afoul of the Golden Rule, saying to a potential juror, if you were a party in this lawsuit, what kind of a juror would you like to see here and what sort of qualities would they have? Do you think that would be something that would get people talking and would interest them?

I think so. It's a little bit – I don't know. Something negative's coming up about it.

You've got a negative feeling about it?

It's not necessarily the Golden Rule, it's kind of like an air filler question. What if you put that in the context of your client? What kind of juror should my client deserve or – you could phrase that better.

Or, what do you think are the best attributes for a juror in a civil case? Then they can weigh in however they want to. Maybe your tech developers will say, well, you want somebody who's going to be critically thinking.

It depends on the case, I guess. Then you get back to this generic profile of who you want and who you don't want. One of the areas that I've read to stay away from as a defense attorney is potential jurors that are sympathetic. And so the question is, are women more sympathetic than men?

Or empathetic.

Yeah.

Sympathetic.

So you've asked them what kind of juror would you want. Next to women, it depends on the case, the issues. But generally, someone that is open-minded, that'll understand the issues. They toss aside prejudice, bias; actually listen instead of falling asleep during the trial. Take good notes. I hate that.

You hate the note-taking?

Yeah.

How about the questioning?

I hate that. It's brutal.

You know, I used to hate that, and it is brutal. Do you think the jurors like it?

I think they do.

You think they can sense who quashed a question if it isn't asked?

Probably. I'm usually the one that objects.

Is there anything I haven't asked that you think would be helpful?

Not that I can think of. This was really hard to do. It's hard to toss away the dual aspect of being a lawyer and a juror. I can only speculate. I've never sat on a jury.

I think it's valid, because when I was on my panels, there were lots of lawyers. We have chances of lawyers showing up on our juries. I think we have a better idea of what they're thinking; don't have to explain as much.

There's one thing I'd probably be different from than a non-attorney juror; I could put aside an incompetent attorney. I would not focus on his foibles, his (expletives). I would listen to the evidence and not hold that against his client.

If you were in a situation where you didn't know the defense lawyer, or didn't think it might get back to the defense bar, do you think you could embrace a plaintiff's case and maybe even drive the train for damages?

Yeah. The driving part might be hard. There's a phenomena with us attorneys. If you go into a bar, the drinks are always free, because everyone needs advice, you know? In a jury panel, I think they'd probably turn to the attorneys, and there may be some opportunity to drive a verdict higher, but if I thought it was too low, hell, yeah, I'd drive it higher.

If you were the foreperson –

Mm-hmm.

If any of your defense colleagues, and by that I mean the average-type of defense colleague, and maybe even some who are more on the aggressive defense side, if they ended up on the jury I was trying the case on, do you think if they were the foreperson, they would ensure a fair deliberation?

I think so, with one exception. I'm not sure they'd be able to shake their conservatism.

In terms of money?

Yeah.

Anything else?

Damages. They're thinking too, too low of a figure. The way I'd probably handle that is, you know, I've thought about what I'd tell my friends and family about this number here. And a week from now, it's the number this defense attorney wanted, and a year from now. I'd be embarrassed to tell them it was that low, based on the facts of this case. And the facts are boom, boom, boom, boom, boom. And the same if it's too high. If it's a couple hundred grand too high, I'd say, I'd be embarrassed to – I think you'd have a little bit less than an average juror with me, damages-wise. A liberal in thought process and politics, but with –

With the number.

Yeah.

I hear that a lot. We're getting away from jury selection, but since I have you here, one of the frustrations I've had is giving a number to the jury that I think is really fair, being able to look at them in the eye, and then having had them chip down at it because they think it's a negotiation. In other words, you asked for $200,000, we thought what you really wanted was $100,000. I was trying to tell them the number in my gut I thought was the most believable. How do you get around that overselling, underselling?

I've never mastered that. If you ever figure that out, let me know.

Maybe focus groups?

From my experience, as a defense attorney, they compromise. *On the criminal side, they'd drop a cause of action and maybe convict on a lesser included. That's a compromise. What I tell the jury is what I think's a reasonable number. Then I show the facts why I think it's reasonable. I tell them it's not something that I want them to split halfway. This is my number.*

This is your number. Just tell them that?

Yeah. But I've known other attorneys, and I've done this, too: not give them any number, and they end up lower than what I would have asked them at times.

Plaintiffs do that, too. They don't give a number because they don't want to anchor; don't even give them specials. Don't introduce the bills. That's a risk.

Yeah.

Thank you.

37

EMPOWERMENT AND OWNERSHIP

Caucasian female, age 39, divorced, Psychology, M.A., Psy.D. Candidate

Give them a sense of ownership. We all want a sense of ownership in whatever process we're engaged in usually.

Ladies and gentlemen, please give your attention to the attorney for the plaintiff who's going to conduct jury selection. You hear those words, you've got your potential jurors with you in the room, what are your thoughts?

I'm probably looking at the plaintiff's attorney and sizing them up. I'm trying to see what it is they're about. How are they posturing themselves? How are they looking at us? How are they sizing me up? Trying to get a gauge on where they're at, what they're thinking, what they're going for. And what the feel is.

Do you have a sense of what they might be going for at that point?

Well, if they're the plaintiff's attorney, they're going to go for someone who they think may rule in their client's favor, right? Someone who might match their client's demographic, from body type and sex to dress to how I'm sitting versus their client. Or someone who might represent someone who might be sympathetic. So any kind of those things, I would imagine, they'd be looking for in their jury and the jurors.

Do you have a sense they'd be able to reliably learn those things they may be looking for based on this group of people they are meeting for the first time, in the short period of time they have to do it? Do you think they can accomplish that job?

I think there is something to first impressions and to non-verbal communication. So how someone presents at that initial is something. But as to whether or not they'd be a good fit, because you have no idea what their experience is, what their true prejudices might be, you have no idea. They may be the exact opposite of what you think you're looking for. **Because what is presented is not the only factor, of course. So all those life experiences of that person who looks like they'd be a great juror on first impression can totally blow your case. I mean, there's no reliable way for sure. Humans are way too individual and way too unique in our experiences that we bring to the table.** *It'd be interesting to do. That would be interesting to know.*

As you're there in that moment, what are the feelings you're having?

I think there's a heightened level of anxiety, of vigilance. There's kind of an anxious feeling of, what are the dynamics? You're in that hypervigilance, you know, sizing things up, looking at what's going on. How are they looking at you?

Trying to understand what's happening. This is a new process, for me it would be. I think everything else would be pretty well-suppressed at that point.

What can that lawyer do to alleviate some of the sense of vigilance or anxiety in the moment in a way that is not manipulative?

How much are they allowed to say?

We can inquire about the individuals; can't talk much about the case.

First things first. I think being able to say, welcome everybody, glad you're here. *Can you find out if there are first-time jurors there?*

We can certainly ask questions of the group.

Like have they been?

Or of the individuals.

It would be interesting to know if there are and how many first-timers there are. So then immediately, there's a normalizing for those who are first-timers that they're not the only one in the room.

We may have that also from our demographic questionnaire that we get.

So you get this enough of ahead of time that you know?

Not enough. Almost as they're walking in.

Then for the individual, who is the first timer in there, if you can do a show of hands, it immediately normalizes, I'm not the only one. There's a lowering of anxiety just because of the commonality of a shared experience. So there's that. And then being like, oh, okay. It gives us an identity, it's formed in that. Then being able to talk a little bit about what the process is, what to expect, that it's understandable to feel anxious or not know how this is going. This is what I can tell, this is what I can't. These are some of the questions we're going to be asking you, because I'm like, what are you going to want to know? Do I need to be on the defensive? Some people wouldn't feel that way. Do I have something I need to hide? You know, depending on what you bring in the room with you. I imagine there's a real wide range of experience, besides how I would be feeling in that room, in that moment, as I imagine I am. **I think once you set the stage, then having the one-on-one conversation to be like, okay, do you have any questions for me before we get started? Letting them have some feeling of control, feeling of this is participatory, not just with you under the microscope.** Trying to build a sense of rapport and mutuality and then ask the questions you need to ask. I don't know. Having not been through it, I don't know how much you can personalize that.

Many people haven't, so they don't know either. That's helpful. I want to learn what is going through the minds of those people who are there for the first time about the process. When you're there in that moment, what are you valuing?

Valuing?

Do you value more that part of the process where you want to get to a good result or are you valuing, say, your time more and you just want to get out of there and not be a juror?

For me to be there, I'm valuing to make sure that, whatever happens, if I'm someone who's being reviewed to be selected, which is exactly what I'm there for, that whoever's reviewing me does their due diligence on behalf of their client. That's what matters to me. What I'm there for is for this process and ultimately it's not just for the plaintiff, but it's –

Right. All parties in the process.

Exactly. Is it only ever the plaintiff's attorney that does the selection?

Both sides.

Both sides do?

Have equal time.

That's good to know. Do they go in separately to review the jurors?

So the plaintiff will, there's this large group, ask questions of the group or of any individual with no order to the process. After the plaintiff's time, then the defendant will have some time, defense attorney will. Sometimes the judge will give each side a little more follow-up. Longer, major cases may have longer periods of time, but generally speaking it's very short. So you know the background, there's too many cases. And they've had to severely restrict jury selection time.

Wow, that's interesting. That makes it much more of a crapshoot.

It does.

In streamlining the process. It's all the more important.

And to not lose the case. My question then is, as the lawyer's standing up in front of you, what can they do to not alienate you?

That is a very individual question. That's such an individual question.

Maybe the better question is, what would be helpful to you for this lawyer to appear human, to establish a connection with you, the best way to do that? Or, what should they absolutely avoid to not have a broken relationship?

*I think what would allow for that to happen is **the work that attorney has done on themselves before that time. Their own self-awareness, their own worth, their own openness, their own awareness of their prejudice and bias, because we all have them.** Knowing what those are so they're not looking just at the people of color when they're talking about wanting diversity on their community or on the jury. You know, these different things that the person brings into the room unconsciously, we clue into those, right? So if somebody's coming in – like this attorney that was in my deposition. He came in, he was arrogant* *from the get-go. It was how he carried himself, it was how he postured himself in the room, how he touched his face. All of it was right there. You confirmed for me as soon as you opened your mouth, you're an (expletive), right? I mean, that's what he walked into the room with, and I knew all of that just in what he was communicating to me non-verbally. So how that person, how that lawyer walks into the room – like if you approached jury selection like they were an opposing counsel's client, that's going to alienate. That's going to put people on the defensive, right?* **You have to approach the selection process, I would hope, in a manner that was open, understanding that they're going to be in the middle of a crossfire, that there's going to be difficulties, that there are things you want to find out. I'm trying to be open. I want to be open-minded and this is a process where we need you to be open-minded and understand your own biases and prejudice and be able to communicate those to me as we talk. I have no problem with you excusing yourself; making it okay for people to excuse themselves.** *Because there's a lot of shame and guilt around what we know about ourselves and racism and prejudice and bias, and all of the different forms, from gender, sexism, all of that across the board. Making it really okay for people to excuse themselves. Because especially in our region here, we are not good about owning it.*

Really?

Excusing ourselves. Yeah. I really think that that's something like, oh, I'm not that. I'm not that. Being able to own that is not something people are good at. We have the passive kind of discrimination all over the place. So I think about those things right away in this process. Especially given personal injury, I don't know what the standard demographic is. I don't know if it's more of a privileged demographic or if it's more of an underdog demographic, in this situation. I don't know if there's more of one or the other, but that's going to play into it, the stereotype of, it's a black male who's the plaintiff. Are they just looking for a handout? You know, all these –

Right. Or a Vietnamese person; there's often suspicion that they are defrauding the system in that community, for example. This might help: generally speaking with regard to bias, I'm not too concerned about racial prejudice or sexual bias. I'm more concerned, and I think I'm right about this, the bias against trial lawyers and against sleazy lawyers and greedy plaintiffs who are out to get a quick buck and a handout –

The stereotypes of those.

– from the system. Right. And there are lots of people out there who don't like the civil justice system, think it's a runaway, out-of-control, gone-too-far system; until they need it. I'm trying to identify those people, who right off the bat, don't buy into the system.

I see. No, that makes a lot of sense actually. That's probably the better screener.

If I'm asking those questions, how can I best ask if you can be an open-minded person with regard to those kinds of issues, or any bias, really, in a way that doesn't

cause a person to be defensive? How can I get people to share their biases if they're resistant to it or if they don't even know they have them? Just to be aware?

Can you do like mock scenarios? Like that are vetted?

Not really.

No, probably not. Can you ask if they've been privy to anyone's process of a civil case?

I can certainly ask people, what is your understanding of the civil justice system?

More than that, asking, have they been privy to the process? Either involved or watched someone go through it?

Sure. Do you have a family member or close friend or your own self, have you been through that?

Right. Can you then ask them about what they thought of that?

Certainly. Of course, you never really know –

Because that's going to tell you a lot.

– what you're going to get.

But how they talk about it, what they focus on.

And some people will –

Is that true? I mean, do people do that?

Many people will be very blunt about the fact that the system is broken. That doesn't mean I can exclude those people, though. The judge will say, that doesn't mean they can't be fair.

So you have to give the judge reasons why you include or exclude?

With the exception of a fixed number of people that can be de-selected for any reason, without having to articulate a reason. Otherwise, they can only be excluded for cause. That is a judge's call. It rarely happens unless there's a demonstrated bias. So what do you personally think about the justice system? Do you think it's runaway justice? That there are greedy plaintiffs, trial lawyers, and that the system is out of control? How do you feel?

Well, largely it's based on my own experience, right?

For sure. And you know, becoming a plaintiff –

Right. Becoming a plaintiff, feeling like I was forced into it because the offers didn't cover the medical bills from the injuries I sustained. I didn't have any reserves to take care of that. If I didn't have to engage in the system, I wouldn't have, just because I don't need that level of stress and what have you. I always said if I just could get my bills taken care of, I'm fine.

It is stressful, isn't it?

I don't feel that way anymore, or all that I've been through with this. The question was, in general, what was my experience, right?

How do you feel, do you think that the civil justice system is broken? That plaintiff's lawyers are sleazy and have no credibility; that jury verdicts are too high and –

I only know my case, and then I know of some forensic cases I've been involved with professionally. Doing psychological evaluations or traumatic head injury and someone's suing where the kid fell, some things like that. I've been involved with some of those now, too. Let me speak to my case first. What was hard for me was my initial attorney and how that went through where he – I was referred to a specific person. I think he did a 30,000-foot level glance at it, didn't see that there was a lot of money to be made, passed it off to his associate, who's fairly new and she made some mistakes, underestimated some things; didn't communicate with me. I didn't review the demand letter before it went out, and out it went, with errors and not inclusive of everything. I was trying to say, no, there's more of an impact here, and they didn't listen to that. So they wanted to drop me then, because – they only offered like $13,000 – and that's not worth our time basically, without saying that. So that experience left me feeling like, okay, if I had understood, and if I had known the questions to ask; I think that was a part of it. I was naïve, I didn't know what questions to ask. I didn't know that there was a difference between someone who was going to take my case that wouldn't take me to trial. Of course, I didn't think it would go there, but they're not trial attorneys, and I didn't know there was a difference. I've never been involved in anything like this.

Do you think that's probably the norm of jurors?

It seems like it. As I talked to people about it and trying to find something more, there's the low-hanging fruit type lawyers of which they seemed to be a part of. That was very upsetting to find out; and then try and find someone with integrity, that I could feel good about engaging in the process with. It was hard to find another plaintiff attorney that I felt like could take me to trial, would want to, because now it was very complicated and it would be a long haul. They'd have to work for it.

They'd have to work hard; they'd have to spend money. Fight for people.

They'd have to invest.

Right.

They really have to invest for me.

How does that inform you as a potential juror?

As a potential juror then, I would want to know as much as I could know, are they going to be fair? I don't know how to answer that question. How do you find out if somebody's going to be fair? **And what is fair, even? It's subjective no matter what. It's an opinion no matter what.** *I think what I would want in a jury, though, is people who aren't just going to go to a quick judgment. I'd want people who are open-minded. People who can have a discourse, who can hear an opposing point of view, have that dialogue about why this is, and not just shut it down. And how do you get to that, right?*

How do we identify that?

Right. I wonder if you could ask them, what would be most important to you if someone was listening to your case? I don't know if from the plaintiff's perspective it's the best perspective to take it from, because there's a self-investment when you're going for the plaintiff, right? Like in my case. So that may not be always.

It's kind of a zero-sum game, because you have a winner and you have a loser.

You do. You really do. And yet everyone pays a price.

That's right. That's a good point I hadn't thought of before. Having been through this process as you have been, the legal system, the civil justice process, as a potential juror in that "as if" chair in that moment, what are you looking for with the plaintiff?

I am looking for how they are, how they look. Are they looking scared and nervous, which I would expect, or are they looking arrogant like, I'm entitled to this. Is there a sense of entitlement? If there's a sense of entitlement, I would be a little more nervous. I'd want to know the other side of the story. Is it something that is seemingly coming from them, or is the lawyer leading the charge? Like, the lawyers see dollar signs and pursue this for the client, you know what I mean? I've seen some of those cases, where the lawyers really misrepresent things because they see dollar signs, and then once things come to full light, like some of the forensic cases I've been involved with recently, the lawyers didn't think this through and have the education and didn't do their due diligence to know what they were taking on; really building up hopes and expectations in their clients. But they shouldn't have. But I think, looking at that person, trying to get as much of the story as I could from just how they were. What is their dynamic with the attorney in the room? Are they there when the opposing counsel attorney comes in as well?

Everybody's in there, all at the same time.

My training and what have you, I'd be sizing up the dynamics. What is it like? Because that right there is a microcosm of what it's going to be like in the courtroom, I would imagine. So how are they? Are they so nervous that they're rattled? Are they just being there and trying to be present? Are they out of their skin? Are they angry? What's going on and how are the two attorneys relating to each other? Are they decent? Are they jerks to each other? Are they curt? Are they interested in the plaintiff? Are they interested in their own – you can tell in how people approach things kind of what they're going for. For me, if there's a real negativity, a real strong bias one way or the other, I'd want to go back from that. But at the same time, I could also see myself feeling like, oh, I want to try and do right by this person, because clearly, the other side has not given them an easy time and they certainly may be entitled to something they're having to fight really hard for. How do you find that out? I think maybe it's even asking in the moment. It doesn't sound like you have a lot of time with each juror though.

We don't. Often, many jurors are not ever spoken to because they're so far in the back of the room that the chances of them being in the box are very slim.

Is it always 60 people?

It could be 40, 60. Depending on the case, it could be even more. But generally 40 to 60-ish, depending on what they anticipate, how many jurors need to go because of hardships and that sort of thing. There have been studies, one stands out, that the general public perceives lawyers, plaintiffs' trial lawyers, second only to used-car salesmen in the lowest part of the credibility scale. How do you feel about that? Do you share that? And if you do, what can be done about it?

I think those are two very different questions. I give anyone the benefit of the doubt before they show their true colors to me. Because I've met, granted, in the interviews that I did of several different plaintiff attorneys and the research that I did, there certainly was a level of, I wouldn't call them pond scum or anything, but there was a level of arrogance and entitlement, and that was a huge turn off to me. Like, if it's not the big bucks, then I'm not going to put my name on it, but I'll put my name on it and have my associate take care of it; any of that passing of the buck kind thing without there being a true presentation of the team to me was like, I'm not going to touch it. I think it takes a certain kind of person to be able to go up into the system and survive. Right? And to do well by their client. I understand that some of them really need to be that way, to a certain degree. Especially in defendants, on the defendant's side. But you're talking about plaintiff.

We're the ones that apparently the public thinks are not truthful.

Which is interesting to me. I don't know that I fully understand that other than what I can think of in that forensic case I was involved in where they saw dollar signs and didn't understand the nuance of a neuropsychology report that was not done –

Right. And that's why we have experts.

-- that was completely invalid. Then we were the experts that came in and did the other evaluation and completely blew it out of the water.

That's a whole other area, dueling experts. We won't talk about that right now. But there are lots of biases about whether experts are hired guns and –

Exactly. We had a conversation about this in my class, talking about forensic and how do you not be perceived as a hired gun and how do you handle forensic cases and these kinds of things.

While keeping your objectivity to the extent you subjectively can.

Exactly. Well said. But back to your question, I don't share that. Because I know there are people who have been severely mistreated, had horrible things happen to them, and they need an advocate.

Do you think that's because of your level of education and your level of global, broader experience to the world and people, that there are lots of scenarios in the world? That people don't just fit into boxes necessarily?

I think that's true, it does seem, in my experience, even though there were not many plaintiff's attorneys that I cared for. Just in my own process of trying to find one, there were not many that I felt good about, which was a very unnerving process, because I'm relying on that attorney so heavily and I had just gotten burned, right? So that was one of the things I used to find out: how they responded to a colleague screwing up. That was one of my vetting questions. Did they treat that person with respect? Did they give them the benefit of the doubt? Did they put context around it?

Right. Context.

Context, hugely. But I can see where, because of the cases that are publicized – I think it's also a part of how the defendant parties have the money with these corporations and companies to spin the media. I think that's a big part of it. So chicken or egg? Is it a couple of cases that got publicized and now this is a stereotype that then is embodied by the attorneys?

The McDonald's case comes up in almost every jury selection since –

Since it happened.

And there's nothing we can do about it to change people's minds.

Right. It's embedded in American culture. In American history.

Given that so much is embedded in this random group of people, and given the stresses of the moment, that we're all meeting each other for the first time, that they're forming as a group, that there's this zero-sum game where everybody has something to lose, even if they win, all of that, how do we go about finding out from you if you're somebody who can, if not have no biases, then be aware of them and work to put them aside to the extent you can for the fairest process?

I think the way to do that is to analyze an experience. So in four or five sentences, can you tell me about what is most important to you in an argument? What is a good argument to you? What makes it a good argument and how is that – is it being able to hear each other? Is it making sure that we come back and resolve it? Just off the top of my head thinking; some kind of scenario that can vet some of those ideas. When you're arguing with your partner or your kids – kids probably not, because of the power differential there.

Co-worker?

Yeah. Somebody on the same level. What is most important to you in that argument?

For example, somebody explained to me that data is so important to engineers.

Right.

Data, data, data. It's been a big eye-opener for me.

Right. The facts. Hugely. For anyone who's involved in computers, it's going to be logic. It's going to be what is the logical, the A + B + C. **The gray is not going to be a comfortable area for those who are very regimented in what they do so brilliantly. They have to be, right, because that's how computers work. Computers don't work in gray. They work within matrices and algorithms.** *That could be really telling, because they're not going to be able to get into, and I'm stereotyping here, but just doing a scenario, they may have difficulty getting into the emotional, the affective. Even in my own experience, I realize I can be very intellectual and just stay in this realm and not communicate. I think of my journey; I think okay, you have to find a way to let yourself emote what your experience has been. If this has torn you apart in these ways, then you need to be able to communicate that. And I'm like, I don't want to go there; I don't want to do that. But being able to recognize that there is an individual process and you're trying to do right by them, consider all of the evidence; it's not black and white. There is a lot of gray. There is a lot of spin. How are they going to sift through that, right? What is their framework? Maybe it's, how would they handle an argument? What's most important to them? Can you give me an example of a conflict, and even if it didn't resolve in the way that you felt was right about it, were you okay with that? What made it okay for you? Even if it didn't resolve in your favor. Questions like that would already be setting the stage if they did get selected as jurors to be like, okay, what would be important to me if I were the person there? Can they take on other perspectives?*

Can you look at things from different points of view fairly?

Yeah. And that's it.

Can you put yourself in someone else's shoes for the time being, even if it's the defendant? I mean, I want to convey – yes, I want to win my case.

Of course.

But I need to appreciate all points of view fairly. I can't win this case in jury selection. I think people will think I'm lying when I say this, I don't want all people that will vote for my client. I want a fair group of people.

Right. And for many reasons, right?

Although there's a lack of credibility, because I truly am invested and need to win this case for my client and for my own –

But what somebody else might understand is that it's not like it's necessarily said and done. There's an appellate process and other things, right? So having something be argued, and having all parties have all cards on the table as much as possible, have all of that, and having it feel like there was fair back and forth, that the information got out there so an informed decision could be made by the jury. Maybe that's it.

So that they feel good. Many of them don't want to be there; they're often hostile.

*Really? You know, I suppose that would be true. For me, when I'm going to do something, I'm all in. That's not how I would be just knowing myself. I might be concerned about the time, but once it's committed, what are you going to do? You gotta give it your all. I think that might be something to find out. It's also a statement of privilege, right? **If I'm not getting paid for two weeks of work and my family might go hungry because of it, I'm going to be a little distracted sitting in that jury box.***

Clearly.

So that's something –

And we do. Hardships are the first thing that's talked about by the judge.

That's good. I would want to make sure that's not a competing factor as much as possible and say, you know, if you are selected, we want to know that you're going to be able to attend and give your full attention to this. I'd want to know, are there people who – this is really all the information you get?

If that.

It would be interesting if you could know a little bit more about what their strengths are. Because some people are stay-at-home moms and they're not working, but they may have incredible abilities to facilitate, to project lead, to do these things that are skills that you would – I don't know. I'm really respecting the difficulty here.

A great lawyer I know has said that when he wants to ask jurors about their biases and their prejudices he says –

Flip the framework.

He says, he will share something of him, his own bias and prejudice first. I'll show you mine, you show me yours. I've gotten mixed results from people about that. Some people say, it's no business what the lawyer's personality is like; that doesn't interest me at all. Whereas others are like, oh, I can see that. How do you feel about that?

Interesting. I think that could go either way with people. Some people would immediately judge that lawyer for that bias, because they're disowning their own as well, right? So there are those people that are going to be defensive and be like, that's not me and you're a jerk. Because we see that all the time in people's response to media and response to stories that they hear in situations.

Or they could perceive it as manipulative or pandering or –

Yep.

So again, what you said earlier, that word – context, and depending on what's said and how it's said. But somebody might say, I'm going to ask if you don't like lawyers; I'm going to tell you that I don't like bankers, for example, or golfers or you know.

And you might have just alienated some people, right?

That's right. Do you feel that you can open people up by sharing something of yourself?

*Not in that situation in the same way. It's very different than me sitting across from a client and the limited self-disclosure that I would do to help build rapport and show my humanity. **That is not a normal situation in jury selection. It's a very different dynamic. There is a power differential. But it's an odd power differential, because ultimately, the jurors have the power.***

That's right.

*So it's a very interesting thing. Makes me think there's got to be a way to talk about it, to be able to say, ultimately, how you conduct yourself as jurors is ultimately the most important thing in this case. To imbue in them a sense of empowerment and ownership in the process. They're not just here for whatever reason. Of course, they were summoned and all of that, but to **give them a sense of ownership. We all want a sense of ownership in whatever process we're engaged in usually, most people do.** I think being able to be like, okay, this is not just something that you were summoned to, now you're here and how do we flip this into something that you can take your sense of responsibility and bring yourself to? And do your due diligence. I would want that communicated to me.*

Hopefully, the judge does a lot of that through colloquies with the jurors.

Do they?

Hopefully. Jurors are taking their cue from the judge who is the most credible person in the courtroom.

I know. Yeah.

That's what's happening. Since you've got this experience that many don't, your background, do you think that group formation, group formation dynamics –

Those dynamics are a huge part of this.

-- do you think that those stages are applying in the situation like jury selection? The typical group formation stages?

Yes and no.

Because we have lots of different groups here.

They're a group, and this over here is a group as well, the judge, the jury, the plaintiff, or the attorneys.

Each party is a group, the judge is a group, the litigants are a group.

And it's not like your jurors are facing each other, right?

Right.

It's a very different dynamic. So I would say in some ways, yes, but in some ways, no. Which is why I think normalizing who's there for the first time to make you not feel so –

Talk more to me about normalizing, because it sounds like giving people a sense of comfort is really important here.

I don't know how much you can do though. It's a situation where, for pretty much everyone there, people just, to a larger degree, don't want to be there, initially. So how do you get the buy-in, right?

The vast majority of the people don't want to be there. And that's a concern where some have said, I don't trust jurors that want to be there because I'm leery of anyone that wants to sit in judgment on someone else.

Well, we do that all the time. I don't know how I feel about that statement.

I think that was more in the context of a criminal case than a civil case.

Oh, okay. I can see that in a –

Where liberty is at issue and life is at issue.

I can see that being more of a concern there. But again, what would drive them to that? Or is it just a curiosity of the process? Or is it that they want to give back? But they're going to carry themselves a little differently if that's the case versus like, they have something –

Well, there's an agenda.

Right.

That's the person I'm really trying to find, the snake in the grass with an agenda. They're the most dangerous juror. Because they will act to undermine. For example, in your own case, there may be people who work for insurance companies that have been summoned that are going to show up, and those insurance companies tell their employees, you will go to jury service. We will pay your time. So you could have an insurance adjuster whose whole experience is antithetical to yours. Your lawyer will –

Can you find that out?

Sure. It'll be on the demographic.

Are any of you being paid for your time here for jury service?

Well, anybody's – their employer will pay –

Isn't it like $10 or $15 an hour?

Everybody gets paid $10 by the county or the state, but some employers will pay employees' time to be in jury service. In other words, you've got to do your civic duty, you'll continue to receive your salary. Some companies don't, and that's why we have hardships. And then other people say, I work for an important company and my project is too important. It's the snake in the grass with the hidden agenda that I'm trying to learn –

Weed out. That's tough, because often those snakes in the grass are the ones who are the most coy.

And I may not be able to get them off even if they identify themselves. The judge isn't going to exclude somebody simply because they work for an insurance company.

There's a relational aspect that might expose that, right? How they talk about, how they relate to an experience, you know? I'm sure there's a better one than asking how they would continue an argument that didn't go in their favor, but how are they okay with it? Like, what was the most important thing? There's a relational component. I just don't know how to get at that to expose their thought process, that they're an underminer. That they will take your words and twist it. That they will – you know, whatever it is. Whether it's that or their experience and they have an agenda.

The Court would allow me to inquire whether or not they can be fair and impartial. The problem is, the judge will typically rehabilitate them by asking if they can follow the law when the judge gives them instructions. I'm more concerned that if I start to pick at them, that I'm going to alienate the whole group.

Oh, so you do this in front of the whole group?

Yes.

So the one-on-one conversations aren't private?

No.

Oh my gosh, so you're standing in front of all of them. And you have to ask –

Everybody at one time.

So you can ask individual questions.

Right. I can, show of hands of the group; I can key in on any individual, any number, any person that I choose.

I don't know why I imagined it otherwise, but I guess – that's interesting. Okay. Wow. That's a lot. That's really difficult.

If it was one-on-one, not in a group setting, I would be so comfortable talking to people. But you get up and you have everybody looking at you.

Okay. That means for sure there's a lot of group dynamics in there at play then, but it's weird, because most people aren't vying for the position, right? I would imagine there are people who are trying to get themselves –

Most people are reluctant and want out. Some people want to be in because they are just interested.

*I used to feel that way myself like, I don't want to have anything to do with that. I don't want that responsibility. At some point, that's changed for me. I think really acknowledging that we understand you don't want to be here, that this is a difficult thing to ask, but think about how you would want to be treated if you were the plaintiff, and also if you were the defendant. It sounds like the judge does some of that. I think reiterating that from the lawyer, because then you know that the lawyer is interested in that level of fairness, too. That needs to be communicated, that I'm interested, and there being a discourse on jurors to get to the truth, to get to understand the facts and draw conclusions based on the facts and understand that there are people involved in this. **There's the context, right? And that you bring your experience with a level of understanding, how your experience informs your decision that you're making. So I want people who are able to do that. I want people who are able to bring their experience, understand how it's impacting their thought process and the decision that you're coming to, and have that discourse.** That's what I would want. I don't know that you can just say that. I don't know if that makes sense to say.*

You can say it.

I'm aware that how I'm approaching it and talking about it is from my own context. I may have people with just an 8th grade education in that room.

Probably the average level of education –

Is?

Well, they tell us to make our presentations for the 7th or 8th grader. But that doesn't mean that's the average level of intelligence; that's just the level we should be communicating at.

Right. Same with writing. You want it to be at that 8th grade level. I think that's where you've just got to appeal to the humanity of it. Would you want someone to make assumptions? I think being able to say that, you know, I don't want to make an assumption based on how you look, how you're acting. This is an odd kind of process – that's not the right word, but it's a unique situation. It's a unique environment.

Earlier you said you didn't want to have the responsibility. That was interesting, because I hear a lot of people say, I just don't want to be there because of the time commitment. I don't want to be bothered. But you said, I don't want the responsibility. Tell me about that. How significant is that process to you? Do you really feel that is a grave responsibility?

I do. I really, really do.

Is that because in part you're a plaintiff?

No. That was my reasoning before for not wanting. Because I did get a summons before, and it was one of those things where my employer wouldn't have compensated me, so it would have been a hardship in some of those ways. But I thought about is that hardship worth taking on because of what this process is about? And I was kind of freaked about it. I think I was 19. Is there an age range for this?

Eighteen. Voter or motor.

I think it was the first year after I registered to vote and I was like, what?

Not ready to do it.

Exactly. But I was like, that is such a grave responsibility and was something I just wasn't ready for, even for all the things I had already gone through at that point. It just didn't feel right. Like, who am I to weigh in on this? But I think that might have made me a good juror, because at the same time, I would have been questioning myself and I would have been listening more carefully. I now have awareness that I have something to offer. I know myself more; certainly know the process a bit more from a plaintiff perspective.

Yours is an unusual situation in the level of work and the degree to which that process is moving forward.

I don't know if that answered your question well enough.

There are no answers. And you're a unique interview because, your background is very different than the average juror in terms of your profession and education. And also the experience that you have. So you would probably, for all those reasons, probably wouldn't make it onto a jury. I think the defense would probably strike you for peremptory challenge because –

What exactly is that? So why would they? This is interesting.

I think, because you are a plaintiff, having been through this long experience, and also, I think, given your psychology background, you're probably more likely to identify with the victim. Not identify, but empathize with. Not necessarily sympathize, but empathize. And I think defendants generally don't want any person –

Don't want anyone who's going to – yeah.

And I want to inspire empathy.

You're in the same room as a plaintiff attorney with the defendant attorney, right?

And our clients.

If you present as looking for something more well-rounded in your jurors, so not just ones that are going to be empathetic to your client, if you present and how you are pursuing jury selection, do you think the defendants might not be as, I don't know, conflictual or contradictory or –

They can win most cases easily. They don't have to reach for the hearts and minds so much because the large insurance companies already have done the advertising for them.

Right.

We have the burden of proof.

And the people with the agenda could be wanting to stick it to the man, right? Which could work in your favor.

Unlikely. Very unlikely in our case where an individual is the defendant.

Oh, I see.

If the defendant is a corporation, a big greedy money grabbing corporation, maybe, but we've got potentially a school teacher widow who's a defendant, you know? Think about that.

That's going to be different.

The defendant is an individual that's being looked at, too. You might get a jury that says, well, we really like the plaintiff. We wanted to give them a lot of money, but we really felt that gosh, it would bankrupt this poor defendant. Well, that's an unfair thought process, but they go through it. They may not know that there's insurance when they're back there in the jury room, or enough insurance, or they're not allowed to consider that there's insurance. Now, the law has let us start suing insurance companies, so if you've got an insurance company as a defendant, suddenly the dynamic shifts.

Right.

Because we start seeing that they're all about the bottom line and they're acting against their clients' interests, and those are different dynamics. But in the average auto case, most jurors are conservative and distrusting.

Well, there you go. I can see though that, even my experience and what I know is still just a narrowed –

For all of us. You brought up that word context, and it reminds me of a book called *The Person and the Situation*. Context is so critical.

Oh, absolutely.

For example, we talked about personal injury cases, like auto cases. That's a unique context. Those dynamics shift when the defendant is a doctor.

Like in medical malpractice?

Right. Suddenly jurors embrace the defendant doctor. They don't want to see doctors sued, because –

Right. They're the healers of our society.

Exactly. And if we can't –

If we can't trust the doctors, I mean – just the implications psychologically to that are just –

I can't trust my own doctor. Right. So there's this accountability bias. It's like, if that doctor's wrong, then my doctor could be wrong and I'm not comfortable with that and I can't sleep well at night, so suddenly the burden of proof goes up. Even if it doesn't in the law, in their minds, it does. Anyway, there are no answers. There are just lots of conversations.

If it's a medical malpractice, I think finding out what do you value most in your doctor/client relationship? You know, what is it –

People say trust.

What would show you trust? What means trust to you? Or when someone's wronged you, what is most important to you?

Right. What's the most important thing?

Yeah. When someone's wronged you, what becomes most important to you? In two sentences.

We learn the more that we say, the worse our jury selection process is going to be. It's all about getting the jurors to talk.

Right. So just those open-ended questions and trying to get them to talk. Can they start discoursing between themselves?

Yes.

That's what you want to elicit then.

That's the goal. Sometimes you pick on somebody. What do you think about what they just said?

Right. And you're reading the body language, all that.

But if you can get that going, that discussion.

I would say that's what you want to do.

Easier said than done.

Easier said than done.

Because it's such an art.

Because you want to expose those group dynamics and the personalities within there. *The people who chime up on their own first.*

I'm usually leery of the talkers.

I would be too. In that case, especially in that situation. Not necessarily in others.

Is there anything you think would be helpful for me to know that I haven't asked about?

Not that I can think of.

Thank you.

38

WELCOME TO THE COURTROOM

Caucasian male, age 41, single, Firefighter/Construction, College 2 years

It could just be, welcome to the courtroom. A lot of people haven't been to a courtroom and the whole thing is intimidating. You've got a judge, you've got guys with guns standing there, you've got cameras, you've got an open arena and lots of people, and you don't know who's who. You have reporters; you have surveillance cameras as well. Just being able to say, I'm glad you made it, we're just going to ask you a few questions.

At that point the judge says, ladies and gentlemen, please give your attention to the lawyer for the plaintiff who's going to conduct jury selection. You're in this room with 40 to 60 people who are potential jurors like you. At that moment, what are you thinking, given your life experience?

I'm thinking, is this case going to pertain to me and if so, what are my answers going to be?

What does that mean?

Well, am I somebody they'll be able to choose to help in making a decision. I know with my background being a firefighter my whole life, that sometimes automatically excludes you, because there's a preconception of the judge and of the attorneys that maybe he's left or right, without even knowing the person, like a police officer. Some people just don't want a police officer.

Especially in criminal cases.

Criminal. And I know this is civil.

Assuming it didn't involve a firefighter or some sort of firefighter type of a response, given that and how you think it might apply to you, how do you feel about your ability to be fair, whatever that is in your definition?

I think most people feel they're fair in their own way. I think that's a human quality. *And I think I'd be able to weigh both sides. My family had a business; they're still self-employed. I know what it's like to be an employer, if there was an employer involved. I know what it's like to be the worker. I know what it's like to be a civil servant. I know what it's like to work for the government. I feel I'm well-rounded. I could see each side of the argument.*

What do you think you bring, given your personal and professional background? If you were to be a juror?

I have a lot of experience dealing with people; 24 years in the fire service. Much of that was for a city agency, so every shift we'd run 10, 20 to 30 calls, depending on what engine company you're on. You'd have an opportunity every day to help people and determine what their problem was and try to resolve it right there. You start getting proficient at solving problems quickly. That's something that would help me make a decision that would be fair. It's just experience in a different capacity. It's not like I was making decisions for a corporation, but I've made a lot of quick decisions that help people, and I saw instant results. Whether it was getting somebody to the hospital or food or shelter, and you get instant feedback. It's not like as a CEO of a corporation, you make a decision and it takes months to years before you see a result.

Given all the responses and all the contact you have with people, do you lean more toward feeling empathetic toward people, or do you lean more toward being critical and judgmental of them because of the situations they find themselves in?

Well, that's a good question, because I've always been empathetic and recently I've had some major life changes, and those have changed my outlook on life. Some of it makes me more empathetic than before, and some of it makes me less empathetic. It depends on the situation and what it is. If it's somebody that keeps making themselves a victim or becoming a victim, I'd have to look at the situation. **If they're truly trying to help themselves, I have a lot of empathy for that. If they just don't care and they're continuing to do it because they don't care, then I'll be less empathetic.**

The person we're talking about is the victim, the plaintiff who's been injured as a result of someone who violated a clear rule. Do you feel more strongly that the plaintiff deserves compensation because they were a victim of someone who is a rule breaker, or do rule breakers get a break too?

It all comes down to the amount or the intensity of what happened. *If they didn't put the wet floor – caution wet floor mopping and somebody slipped and fell, that's not as bad as violating somebody's civil rights and maybe terminating them without just cause.*

So we're talking about negligence versus intent.

Correct.

We're primarily talking about negligence cases. Where something happens – what we call accidents. But how do you feel about, in your experience, accidents being anything but accidents, because somebody's not paying attention or following a rule. What's your life experience or professional experience on that? Point of view?

My life experiences and my own personal feeling is, you've got to take care of yourself, and you've got to be careful. Nobody is going to follow you around and make sure you're safe. The other side of the coin is, I look at someone like my mom. She trusts people, and if anything happened to her, I'd be upset. I can see very easily her being injured one way or another because of somebody else's negligence because she doesn't have that type of lifestyle or training that I've had with my profession. Along with that, if I was injured at work and it wasn't my fault, I'd be really upset. And I'd have empathy for anybody that was in a similar situation.

You've seen a lot of people who've been hurt pretty badly; all levels of trauma.

Yes.

Can you give a description of what you've observed it's like for a person to be in traumatic distress?

Some of the ones that stand out in my mind, all the people died. I've had people upset, screaming and yelling and running around, but that was more being angry or emotional than true traumatic distress. The true traumatic distress, some of them that stick out in my mind were when I've responded to a gunshot victim and had him talking when we got there and we were doing CPR within minutes. Another one would be cutting a woman out of a car that was hit by a drunk driver and she was just catatonic. We had the roof off of the car, and she was just sitting in her driver's seat and wasn't saying a word, staring straight ahead. She died four hours later, I believe. I could give a lot of examples from over the years.

Have you had follow-up with people who've been seriously injured in, say, a car trauma, and then years later or even months later you run into them and see how they're doing?

One guy had a heart attack. My partner and I responded. When we arrived, he was in cardiac arrest. I did CPR on him while my partner drove. I did CPR for over 30 minutes, along with the medics. All parties involved, it was 45 minutes. We left him at the hospital. Two years later, I was at a market, and there was a guy buying hot dogs, chips, and soda, and he had a uniform on, and I said, hey, one of your co-workers had a heart attack a couple years ago, do you know what happened to him? And he stopped and he said, that was me.

Did you have any thoughts or comments to him about his diet?

No. At the time, I laughed when I left, and I didn't, I was just happy to meet him. He said, I've got a wife and two kids. And he shook my hand. That's not always the case, but part of it's like, what the hell are you doing? You had a heart attack and you're eating this garbage? But then I'm also glad he's alive, and I'm not one to judge. I don't know. Some people eat healthy their whole lives and still have a heart attack.

You said you're not one to judge. On the scale of, say, one who observes human behavior and is critical versus one who observes it in a laissez-faire or live and let live, where do you fall in that scale? Given that you've seen an awful lot of dumb behavior and things that just happen?

Right. That's a huge complex answer, and I wish I could just say a five. I'm in the middle, and I go on both sides.

Is it contextual? It depends?

Very much so. The thing is, the safety precautions we have with guard rails and air bags on cars and all the things, it used to be Darwinism. If you made a mistake, you were taken out of the gene pool. Now, it's not so much. So I see that point of it. But I also see the other side, which is I want my family to be protected. So it's a double-edge sword. I'd have to say I'm a five, and I deviate each direction depending on the situation.

Where does stupidity fall into that contextual shift?

Like, do they deserve it?

Stupid behavior on one side or the other?

I think stupidity's everywhere. And as far as whether or not somebody deserves it, I don't think anybody deserves to become a victim of anything because of their intelligence or lack of. So if somebody got hit by a bus because their IQ wasn't high enough and they weren't paying attention, they don't deserve it.

I didn't mean stupidity in an IQ sense: more like poor judgment. Even those of us who are bright can exercise poor judgment at times. Or just not follow the rules, safety rules.

Right. So how do you want – can you just repeat that question?

You covered it earlier on. I want to jump back to this, which is, when you're sitting there in that moment we talked about, that first "as if" moment where you and the lawyer are getting acquainted for the first time in this courtroom, what are your thoughts about the lawyer; this lawyer for the plaintiff who's representing the person who's claiming to be injured? Lots of people have very strong opinions about plaintiff's trial lawyers. Some think that the system is completely broken and these are sleazy trial lawyers who are greedy. Others are on another scale that says, well, this is what our Founding Fathers intended and this is the process and the system. It may be broken, but it's the best we've got. Where do you fit in that?

I support the legal system. I think that everybody, as soon as they walk in, they have my unprejudiced opinion until they prove me differently. If you end up being a sleazy attorney, then I'm going to classify you as a sleazy attorney. If you end up having character and prove me wrong, then I'll go that way, too. I've known several attorneys. I am still friends with them, and I remember having somebody in the fire department make attorney jokes like, the only good attorney's a dead attorney or whatever. I was offended by that. But I see both sides. Because I've also dealt with attorneys that were the kind that didn't care about helping you. All they cared about was taking your money.

You've driven emergency vehicles before. What do you think about when you hear the words "ambulance chaser"?

That doesn't affect me. I didn't even know what it was at first, and then I figured it out.

Do you think there are such attorneys?

When I was a kid; maybe back in the day. I think not so much anymore. I think now instead of chasing an ambulance, they'll either find your email or call you. But I still think that happens. I've received letters, and that's fine. It doesn't sway me either way to think they're good or bad. Maybe they just are an up and coming attorney that wants to have a challenging case.

Do you have a sense one way or the other that the civil justice system is broken? That it's out of control?

I had preconceptions and misconceptions. One of the things that was proven to me is the bureaucracy and how long it takes and how you gotta show up time after time after time for something that could be handled with a phone call or an email now. There's a running joke: that 45 minute meeting could have been an email. That's kind of how the justice system is. And what it does, too, is people that are homeless or addicted to drugs or can't hold a place down and constantly moving, they can't make these appointments. They end up getting a warrant for their arrest. Then it snowballs. They're doing something and then they get arrested for that and it doesn't fix anything and makes their life worse. As far as the justice system though, the bureaucracy's got to stop. They've got to make real changes to how they schedule and operate. If it was a business, a privatized business, they'd be out of business. Some of the things too, though, is the judges; they're people. Luckily, some of them work really hard to be fair and do their job and don't get emotionally involved. And some of them are at the end of their term; they're ready to retire and they don't care about anything. And they have a preconceived guilty or not guilty when they enter –

In the criminal realm.

– the trial.

Or maybe even in the civil realm, too.

Correct. And they may say, oh, this person's just trying to get money from this corporation or from this municipal government agency, there's a term for it, when the police or government pick a route and then everything they do, the data they gather, goes down that route. And it's like a –

Self-fulfilling prophecy?

Yeah, but there's a legal term for it that.

You've had the benefit of being in the civil justice system yourself as a litigant, as a participant, right?

Yes.

And have you ever testified as a witness or an expert in any sort of a legal proceeding?

Yes, I have.

Going back to when the attorney first stands up in front of you, what can that attorney do, right then and there, to establish a human connection with you?

So are we talking in the selection process?

I'm sorry. I was jumping around. In the selection process, when you are first introduced to this lawyer who's getting up, then and there, how does this person establish to you that they're human and genuine?

I guess it doesn't matter if it's the defense or prosecutor –

Plaintiff or defense?

*Plaintiff or defense. I think if that person just makes that connection that I think everybody has. **It doesn't have to be a car salesman, like phony. It could just be, welcome to the courtroom. A lot of people haven't been to a courtroom and the whole thing is intimidating. You've got a judge, you've got guys with guns standing there, you've got cameras, you've got an open arena and lots of people, and you don't know who's who. You have reporters; you have surveillance cameras as well. Just being able to say, I'm glad you made it, we're just going to ask you a few questions; it's not an attack against you, we just want to get to know you quickly and easily as possible so that we can either move to the next step or let you get about your day.** Something like that. I think that people will say, okay, this isn't a mechanical thing. This person cares that I have a private life and that I am nervous that I am being forced to be here or I've chosen to be here.*

How does this lawyer, who most people think doesn't have a lot of credibility, who's got an agenda to win only for their client, how do you think the lawyer can do that in a way that doesn't sound like a manipulation?

The attorney without credibility?

Who may be perceived as not having credibility from the start.

Just say basically that. We're choosing the best people that can make a fair decision and without getting into the details, we are going to pursue this the best way we can. Once you hear more about the case, I believe your perception will change. Something like that, to where they may already start thinking, maybe there's something I don't know about this, and once I get the real facts – keep an open mind.

As a potential juror, and sitting there with a group of 60 potential jurors, how do you think the lawyer can find out who can be open-minded? Or who is the snake in the grass?

*I think anybody can fake it for easily five or ten minutes. Some people can fake a relationship for years. **I think you just have to go off of that gut feeling. It may not always be right, but if you have something from a potential juror that's bothering you and you've tried to address it and you're not getting*** *the answers you want to hear, then maybe you shouldn't trust that person.*

If you were the lawyer representing a person claiming injury for negligence and a person just like you was on the jury, what question would you ask to find out if you could be open-minded? What would you ask of yourself?

I would maybe have a few pre-canned questions that fit different personality criteria. That way, if somebody seemed like they were a hardcore Democrat or a hardcore Republican or very religious and depending on the case, I would be able to ask them questions that not only exposed that, it showed whether or not they were capable of having an open mind. Because you can still be any of those things and keep an open mind. But the problem is that people go down that road and then they are not able to budge even if they know deep inside that it's right. They may hold to their values they've carried or been taught their whole life. What ends up happening is, you've proven the case, without a shadow of a doubt, and somebody's holding on to something they were taught their whole life that they had before they came in, and they are not willing to open their mind up and say, you know what? This was proven to me, and despite my upbringing, I've got to side with them because it's the right thing.

We have that situation that happens quite a bit where people, for whatever reason, believe that jury verdicts are out of control; that they're causing insurance rates to go up and good doctors to leave the community and that sort of thing. How do you feel, one way or the other, on that continuum?

I think insurance would be expensive no matter what. I think these companies still make billions and trillions of dollars despite these huge payouts. You can look at that two ways, and that is, my insurance has gone up because of this payout. Well, that's what insurance is for, and if a jury forces an insurance company to give a payout that they otherwise wouldn't pay, then it's forcing the hand of the insurance company to do what is really right. So as far as the effect it has on my rates, rates have always been expensive. I want that assurance they promise you that if something does happen to you, you'll be compensated at the very least. I have experience in that too. A firefighter I know fell down a pole hole at work on duty and was injured to the point he could never work again. He broke many bones and he had cognitive skill deficit. The city started going after his personal life and saying, he's an alcoholic. They made up all these excuses and it took years to finally get justice for that. I think a lot of times people like to complain and they have an agenda and they'll say, we have ambulance chasers. Our rates are going up because of these multi-million dollar cases, but some of them are legitimate. I'd be really upset if somebody in my family was hurt to the point they couldn't work again and nobody wanted to accept responsibility if somebody was at fault.

You've seen people at their worst and probably at their best. What are some traits about people you've observed that are relevant to your experience as a potential juror?

I've seen quite a bit of different life-changing events. I've seen multiple shootings, hangings, suicides from bridges, suicides from high rises where they've jumped. Overdoses on pills, gun shots to the chest, to the head, to any part of the body. And **the one thing I've noticed is there's always humanity. That is that when things get horrible, people step up. People band together and help each other.**

What about bias and prejudice? When we're looking for jurors, when we talk about open-mindedness, we're really trying to determine what bias or prejudice or prejudgments they might have before this case starts that would keep everybody from starting out equally. How would it best be asked of you if you had any biases or prejudices that would affect your ability to be fair in this case? What sort of ways could we get you to talk about, to open up in front of this group of relative strangers and somebody you don't know who is asking about personal information and beliefs?

Right. I think most people would be on their best behavior and it's like a first date. And you don't get to know the person until later. Some of the things maybe are interests and just that in itself is prejudiced. If somebody hunts and rides a four-wheeler, they might, according to stereotypes, listen to country music and they're closed-minded and maybe hardcore Christian. **But rather than put them on the spot in front of their peers, you could go an indirect route and get them to talk about how they feel about some other event that maybe everybody in the room knows about.** *So, do you think OJ was guilty? Or something like that, to where you get the division of people with something that simple. It gives you an idea. That by itself isn't enough to say, he's a racist or, he's not – or she – but it'll give you a building block. If there's many signs like that, and I know you don't have very much time when you're selecting these people –*

Or deselecting.

Or deselecting. I think a lot of times it's having the pre-canned questions and being able to ask the same question in a different way to another juror so that you can get the result you need. And they don't know they're being asked the same question. It's like an algorithm or a matrix; if they say this, then I go to this question. If they say that, then I go to this question, until you reach a result that you're looking for, and that is whether you want to select them or deselect them.

Do you think that can be done spontaneously?

In the fire service, we have the Incident Command System. It's something that's always there. There's certain rules that go along with it. Finance, logistics, operations, planning are at the top of the tier and then you have subdivisions of each. You have safety liaisons, things like that. It's always there and it's something you build on. And that's something that you do in jury selection; you could make up a matrix where you could say, I think this person might go against a verdict for my client and my preconception or prejudice, my profiling, tells me that this person thinks that all lawsuits are frivolous, so I'm going to go down one of my top four tiers, whether it's racist, doesn't trust people, or whatever –

Right. Whatever that is.

Whatever you end up making. Then say, okay, the frivolous, the first question is, what do you think about government spending? Or something like that, where it's not a direct question about frivolous lawsuits. But they may answer, I think everybody should pay their taxes, and I'm happy to pay taxes. Or they may say, I'm part of the Tea Party and no new taxes. It'll give you an idea maybe which way to go. You could fire off a few questions and move on to the next potential juror.

Here, you get an opportunity to be a juror. What do you think they're going through? What do you think they value? What do you think their values are? Some people tell us they absolutely don't want to be there because their time is the most important thing. Others will say, I don't think I could handle the responsibility of making such an important decision. Everybody's got some different value. What do you suppose yours is? Or what do you think the overwhelming jury values are?

My value and the value I'd like to see in a juror is that you're not only open-minded, you can still have beliefs that are strong that don't sway your decision-making skills. I think the ability to do a 180, to go into something, no matter what, whether it's a lawsuit for coffee on somebody's lap at McDonald's or somebody that got hit by a bus, to be able to go into the process open-minded. And as you are fed information and gather this and decide what you're going to do with the information, you have the ability to do a 180 if the first thing they say is McDonald's and you say, screw that corporation, and then you find out that the claimant or plaintiff has had nine lawsuits against corporations in the last five years, and they show a video where they act like they slip. You have an open enough mind to say, well, I don't like corporations or corporate America, but this is obviously frivolous.*

And vice versa.

Yeah.

As a firefighter, not only are you taught algorithms, which are rules about how to respond, but you see a lot of people who are not following rules and engaging in behavior – running a stop sign, texting while driving, whatever it may be. At the same time, you ride motorcycles and fly airplanes. How do you reconcile that? If somebody were a defendant who violated a safety rule and injured somebody, how you would take that part of you who can be a little risky, within bounds, and apply it to that person so that they're held accountable?

The first part of that would be with risk comes not only responsibility, but being able to be flexible to situations. If you're riding your motorcycle and it starts to rain, maybe it's time to park and have some coffee until the rain slows down. You have to be able to use common sense, judgment. Flying is one of the most free things you'll ever do, and it's also one of the most regulated. Between the FAA and all the government rules and regulations, it's incredibly restrictive, but it's the most freedom you'll ever experience at the same time. I think that's the same with a motorcycle. If you don't pay attention, you could end up hurt or dead quickly. That's how I was talking earlier about Darwin. So as far as applying those to either another juror or the claimant –

Claimant or the defendant.

Or the defendant, I'd have to see if they used good judgment. Just because you like to sky dive or BASE jump or ride a motorcycle, doesn't mean you're an idiot. It means that's your lifestyle and it makes you feel alive or for whatever reason you do that.

Right. And you don't necessarily have to be endangering others.

Exactly. And a lot of times you're not. If anybody's getting in danger, it's the motorcycle rider. He's not going to take out a family in a minivan; the minivan's going to take him or her out. It's all relative. You just have to have that open mind and know that if you like to stay home and read, you have to understand that people don't always have that lifestyle, and you can't use that against them. And vice versa.

We were talking about a lawyer talking to you for the first time and trying to get to your open-mindedness, to talk about your bias and your prejudice – getting you to talk about those things has helped me explain what the lawyer could do to open you up. What should the lawyer avoid doing to shut you down?

Singling you out. Asking questions that make you feel like you have to open up more than you want to in front of all the people. Because you just walked into this room and you've been there for a couple minutes. You're not used to the surroundings. You don't know the person next to you, if they're your neighbor or if it's somebody that your family knows. You're about ready to open up to answer all these questions to a person that you don't even know, and it's difficult to do that. So I think keeping it not too intense would be a good way to get the ball rolling. *Just ask little questions and maybe throw in, I was watching the game, and make a little story about yourself. It doesn't take up that much time. I was watching the game and I read in the paper about the game that night that this – how does that make you feel? It humanizes you and it opens them up, because it's more of a conversation than an interrogation.*

I'm have a working hypothesis that many lawyers are trying to do too much in jury selection. People are telling me that their number one value is time, I want to respect that. I'm getting to the point of just asking the question, open-ended, to the group, who here thinks that they can be open-minded? Who here thinks they may not be able to be and why? Just get that discussion going and accept their answers without a lot more follow-up. Do you think that would work?

Absolutely, because what'll happen is, the people that don't want to be there, they will be resentful even if they are open-minded, they'll tell you that they are not open-minded to get out of jury duty. They'll give you a reason why, whether it's valid or not, and you've eliminated a person that may just give you a judgment in favor or not in favor out of spite.

In most of my cases, with the exception of the medical malpractices cases, liability, fault is really not at issue. What's at issue is the damages part of it; how much money will the jury award? We have two kinds of damages: special damages, which are things like wages, past and future, and medical bills. Things that can be put on a spreadsheet and added up. It may take expert testimony to sort that out, but those are specials. General damages are things that you observe in your daily life as a professional: pain, suffering, disability, loss of enjoyment of life. There are no fixed standards in the law for a juror to make a determination of how much to award. How would you go about doing that? As a juror, how would you go about making a money award for an injured plaintiff?

I would do just that.

For the general damages part, the pain, suffering, disability, loss of enjoyment of life, where there's no fixed standard, and your opinion and the next person to you could be completely different?

I'd have to look at not only the injury but the person. If you're 20, it would be different than if you're 70. It depends on what your job was and what you enjoyed. If your quality of life was watching TV all day and now you still just watch TV, does it matter that you lost part of your foot or whatever the injury was? Testimony from the victim, if that's possible, helps, and having somebody from their family say, you know, he was skydiving every weekend. He'd ride his motorcycle. He loved to surf. He'd go fishing, and I never saw him idle. And now, he sits in his wheelchair and does nothing. That's a huge damage compared to, he always watched TV and now he's actually getting out of the house to go to physical therapy because it's mandated. Or maybe their life improved somehow. You don't know. But if you talk to the victim and to their friends and family, I think that's the most powerful thing. If my sister came in and testified on my behalf, it would double the award or the verdict the jury came up with, because she cares about me so much that they'd see that and people would have a whole different view.

Than if you were to talk about it.

Right. And I think it would be good to have as many people involved as you could. I think if I didn't talk at all, if my sister or somebody like that came in, it would be moving.

The general proposition has been, we tend to not want nurses on our juries; they're a little bit immune to suffering because of what they see. You've seen that and more. Are you desensitized to human suffering to the point where you might be more conservative in your money awards than someone who hasn't seen the kinds of suffering you've seen?

*That's a fair statement. I might be. But it depends. I keep that open mind. If this person worked their whole life for a company and gave all their good years to them and then there was some type of negligence or accident and that person suffered, I may be more willing to give a bigger award if they were making just enough to keep alive and they dedicated their life to this company rather than somebody that was making a lot of money and – **it all depends on the situation.** I think that's too dynamic, too complex of a question. But as far as being insensitive, when I'm at work, I'm at work, and I deal with it. I've gone to calls where you walk in and there's brains on the counter of a liquor store from a gunshot wound to the head and it's stuck in the ceiling, parts of their skull. I've gone back and eaten spaghetti. It's work. It doesn't mean that if that was somebody I knew I wouldn't grieve them, but at work you just gotta do your job and you can't get emotionally involved and that's what you do at work. That doesn't mean that I'm insensitive or I don't care about people; that's why I care about people.*

One of the questions people like to ask is, other things being equal, that is to say their income abilities and that, if it were strictly their quality of life, would some famous, important billionaire deserve more money than a person on the street for the same injury?

*I think that plays into it. In Europe, if you speed and you're a multimillionaire, your speeding ticket is tens of thousands of dollars. If you're a construction worker, it's a couple hundred bucks. It doesn't hurt a billionaire to get a few hundred dollars ticket. I think that plays into effect here, too, and I know the example is an extreme, but if you're some billionaire and you were seriously injured for whatever reason and it was found that there was negligence or somebody at fault, then maybe something higher would be appropriate. Paying him $25,000 or a hundred thousand isn't worth his time going to court. Somebody like that, leaning over to pick up a hundred bucks is losing money. But that doesn't mean if you're permanently injured and you're unemployed that you only deserve a couple hundred dollars. **It's case by case.** I think most people don't want to sue. I think most people are good and want to do a good job. If an accident occurs, as an employer, you can't protect your employees from everything. There's no training manual big enough to. I think it depends on the person and how badly they were injured from the situation. I do think that that plays into effect a little bit.*

The burden of proof in a criminal case is beyond a reasonable doubt. In a civil case, the burden of proof is called a preponderance of the evidence. What does preponderance of the evidence mean to you?

Without somebody describing it to me, just off the top of my head, I would say that would be, once I've gone through or been shown all of the evidence, I should be able to make, in my mind, the right decision based solely on that. To me it sounds like there's more leeway than beyond a reasonable doubt. If you can't prove beyond reasonable doubt, then you must acquit the person. With a preponderance of the evidence, I think there's more involved.

If the definition of preponderance were expanded to say more likely than not, does that help you? Does that change your definition of what that means to you?

> *It takes some pressure off as a juror. In a criminal case, if they said, he shot them and then the defense proves that he was in Canada, that's beyond a reasonable doubt that this person's innocent. Whatever the outcome. I think there's more at stake, too, when you take somebody's freedom as opposed to give somebody money for a damage.*

That's why we have the higher burden, because freedom and liberty are at stake rather than money. How do you feel about the notion of money as a compensating factor? We can't make people necessarily whole. Juries can give them money for medical treatment, to make up for lost wages or to pay for future wages, things like that. Can't fix them. Do you think this civil justice system, where money is compensating for injury is – how do you feel about that?

> ***I think money is a standard we've all agreed upon that everybody can relate to.*** *Whether you like it or not, once you get it, you can do with it what you will. And it gives you an opportunity now. Whether you need it for health care or if you get enough to make a difference; you could start your own business or you could donate it or you could do with it what you will.* ***But it's kind of like a Golden Ticket because you'll never be able to fix the injury.*** *That's why you're there, usually. Or your life's changed. But I think money is a good standard because you can't really punish the people. How are you going to punish them other than monetarily? Especially a corporation. Make the CEO sell his airplane or his yacht? Money to the injured is just a fair – I think the best.*

Do you think that money to an injured person that's paid by a defendant has a deterrent effect from future bad conduct or future unsafe conduct? The jury requiring a defendant to compensate an injured person by making a payment of money to them, do you think that causes a deterrent or is a teaching tool?

> *Oh, yeah. I think not so much in the government. The government will keep doing whatever they want at the loss of millions. A perfect example is intersections, stop signs. They have criteria. Going back to the algorithms and all that, but if x amount of people are injured in the intersection, then they put a light in. They don't care. If it was a corporation, they might be more proactive and preventative – or private business.*

When you use the word algorithm, does the word "rule" equate to that? Are algorithms essentially rules?

> *I think they are guidelines. It's like a key. It may fit, but it's not going to turn. If you had a juror and you said, this person may be very religious, you have to be flexible. It's a guideline. We have that in the fire service, we have NFPA. They give guidelines to firefighters. One of them is two in, two out. When you go to a fire, when two guys go in, whether it's a rescue or for fire suppression, you've got to have two guys outside so if something goes wrong, they can go in and pull them*

out. That was a long battle between the cities and NFPA and the firefighters because the cities didn't want to put four people on an engine. You'd go around with two or three firefighters on a rig and – anyhow. That's a guideline though. I think, life, there's no rules or hardcore mandatory things. You've got to be flexible. And that's the same as in the courtroom.

How about with regard to established laws that are passed down? Codes to tell us how we can and cannot drive safely, what we must and must not do?

Right. I've noticed this in the last couple of years, we already have enough laws. We're getting more all the time. I don't see these old laws coming off the books. So I think people in general are good and try to do the right thing and the more restrictions you put on people, the less freedom we have. I saw a bumper sticker and it said, "Test Your Freedom," I've thought about that every day since, probably ten years ago.

What does that mean to you?

To me, it's people keep on shoving down your throat how free you are and how America's the greatest country in the world, and how people died for your freedom. When I was younger, I believed in that. As I get older, I am questioning it more and more. Some of these wars, why are we there? And if we stopped, would they really follow us home?

What does that mean, "Test Your Freedom"?

Test your freedom means go do something that you feel you should be entitled to.

Civil disobedience, maybe?

Call it whatever you want. Some people might think riding your motorcycle is, you're out of control. You shouldn't be riding. That's crazy. I believe if you like doing it and it doesn't harm anybody else that the government shouldn't be involved. If I want to ride my motorcycle on a desolate country road that I've already driven down and there's a chain link fence on each side so a rabbit's not going to run in front of me and there's no other cars or potholes, if I want to go 170, I should be able to go 170 because the only person that's going to get hurt is me. But if a sheriff is flying over or a highway patrol or somebody witnesses it from another road and they catch you or get you on radar, you're going to go to jail for that.

For the recklessness.

Right. And that's the thing, how reckless is it if it's your own life? How much control are we going to let the government have on us when it's something that affects nobody? That's kind of what tests your freedom. A motorcycle's an easy example. But it goes to other places, too. All of our phones have GPS. If somebody wanted to find us right now in the government, they could find us right now. They wouldn't have to ask our friends or family or follow us. They can literally get a subpoena. And if you're part of Homeland Security, from what I understand, you *don't even need a subpoena. They can look us up, you know?*

If I was standing before you for the first time and wanted to get a really good sense of your values orientation, what would I ask you?

Some of the questions you've asked me and just the hot topics that get people emotional. Maybe say, what do you think about the war? I've always put trust in our government that they're doing the right thing, but I also know people that have been killed. A friend that was a Blackhawk pilot lost his legs in Afghanistan three and half years ago. So those topics that are emotional. Like, what do you feel about Donald Trump? Or something that is kind of a hot topic. You'll get a better feeling for where people lie, I think, in a shorter amount of time.

By profile, my sense is, if I was meeting you for the first time as a potential juror, knowing you are a firefighter who sees a lot of stupid activity that people engage in, government employee, working with doctors and nurses and healthcare people and seeing people break rules all the time, I might be concerned about that because I'm not sure that you'd be a person that would be giving - well, I think you'd be fair, but I think the conventional wisdom is –

Yeah. Or prejudiced.

Right. Is that you tend to be more conservative as a juror. Do you think that's probably accurate?

What's funny is a lot of people think that, and I saw that, too. I'm probably one of the most Democratic people I know or used to know, I should say, because I voted for Clinton and I voted for Obama, blah blah blah. I live here. You name it. I've got friends of all creeds, races, colors, everything. So I've broken that mold in that respect. There's guys in the department that are way more liberal than I was. But I've had a change of events in my life and that's not the case anymore.

Are you any more trustful of government as a result?

No. I'm less trustful, but that doesn't mean that I'm more liberal; it just means that I think people are emotional creatures and we – like it or not – go look on Facebook. That's some crazy stuff going on there. People are crazy. They get riled up and then you throw in the media and you throw in what really happened and what didn't happen, and before you know it, every shooting is racially motivated. And it may or may not be. So it's hard to keep track after a while. I don't put a label on myself, but I'd say if you had to label me, years ago, I was Democrat. And then I became, you show me what you've got. If I had to make a choice today, I'd vote for a Republican, almost without – I'd do the typical thing I see in our region which is, I don't care what you know or say, if you're a Democrat, I'm voting for you. I've flipped to that other side, which is, enough is enough. And I'm heading over to the dark side.

In a medical malpractice case, if a doctor were the defendant, given that nurses and firefighters tend to be kind of close, how would you be able to avoid giving the medical profession the benefit of the doubt? You work together so closely.

A lawsuit against a –

A doctor or a hospital. Let's say Harborview or a doctor at Harborview was sued. How would you put aside what conventional wisdom says would be a bias in favor of the profession that's doing what you're doing, which is helping people in crisis and trauma.

*Look at the facts and have a super open mind. I've found that even testimony isn't true. So to not have that bias for or against the same industry I'm in, I have to have an open mind and hear everything given to me, and **I weigh heavier things like photos and video than testimony from somebody emotional that was there or not there.***

How about the written record? You've filled out a lot of incident reports, I'm sure. Would you give the incident report more credence?

It would help to give an idea of some basic facts that are undisputable.

Because in the medical malpractice case realm, it's generally stated, if it's in the record, it's accurate; and if it's not in the record, it never happened.

That's totally wrong. That's 100% wrong. What happens is, we have what's called a Form 20B. Every medical incident, every person there gets a 20B. It's things like name, address, birthdate. We'll do a blood pressure, heart rate, and subjective/objective assessment. Things like that. And what your plan's going to be. So if you, for some reason, don't agree with what happened, maybe this guy was drunk and he fell down some stairs, and you're having a problem with your teenage kid drinking and you've had it with alcohol, you may be more inclined to say, this guy deserved it in your report or whatever. If you'd never seen anything like this and you weren't sure if he was drunk, you may say, this guy fell down the stairs and it's raining and it's slippery.

It's human nature.

Garbage in, garbage out. Just because it's written, it's like any other data you see or read. I remember reading a book in grammar school and there was incorrect spelling. I was like, how can this be? This is a book. This is the truth and it's always right. I couldn't believe there was misspelled words. From that point on, I questioned everything that was written. And that was good, because especially nowadays, anybody can write. I could be writing right now about something and people will believe. I could say it's raining and people would go, wow, I didn't know it was raining. They'll just take that for what's written. I think the same thing is with a report. Who wrote it? Wat's the information on it? Is it subjective or is it just data? His birthdate. Is that correct? That's a good way to cross check it, too, is that your real birthdate? Well, no it's not. What else is incorrect on this form? Is this your real name? Well, it was, but I changed my name. So those are the things that jurors will go, the weight of that went from a 10 down to 3.

In criminal cases, more so than in civil cases.

Right.

I'm thinking of one case where a client of ours was hit by a car. His head starred the windshield. The police and aid units that came assessed him but didn't give much credence to the fact that he had a brain injury. It's, he seemed okay; he talked normal. Of course our guy plummets and has a significant brain injury. Those are things that we run into.

And that makes sense. Because if you just read the report, you go, this guy's fine. Where's the report we're here for? It's like no, this is the report we're here for; this guy died or whatever.

And the firefighter or medic is even opining on the speed of the collision. Then my expert has to do a speed analysis that is different. But jurors, especially in these kinds of cases, they're cynical about what we talked about earlier, greedy plaintiff's lawyers, non-credible plaintiff's lawyers, lottery mentality victims, out of control verdicts. The pendulum has swung against us. It's harder now, especially in this community, to get jurors to award what we think are fair sums of money. We've been struggling with that for a long time.

Part of that is people "upwork". I remember hearing that. There's news articles, and you're like, this guy got five million. Perfect example: firefighter got $13.7 million and he is forever changed. He lost his career and what they don't mention when you read about it is he wanted a million.

He wanted to settle for a million.

He said, I need a million for medical, because he was out on his own. The city disowned him after a year. They said, you're on your own. He says, I need medical for this. This is an on-shift injury. And the city said no. They battled for about a decade. It went to the Supreme Court, it finally got to the point they were hiding in the bushes, videotaping him and –

The court said, I'm sorry, that's after the fact; that doesn't count.

Right. So the jury said, this is (expletive). Give this guy some money so he can live normally and without being in debt. And that's what happened. But then those are the things people don't see.

Don't see or hear.

And that's why you asked about my belief in the judicial system, and before, I thought the judicial system was totally screwed up.

Is there anything you think might be helpful at all? A last opportunity for you to add to this?

I can't think of anything off the top. I didn't have any – I wasn't sure what to expect.

That's just it. Nobody who goes to jury service knows what to expect if they haven't been through it.

Right. And I still don't really know.

Thank you.

39

AUTHENTICITY

Hispanic-Caucasian male, age 24, married, Contract Specialist–County Government, Masters Divinity and Theology

Folks these days are craving authenticity. I think people these days are able to tell whether you are being real with them or not and whether you're doing something to just be manipulative or that you really do care and are trying to be authentic.

Please give your attention to the lawyer for the plaintiff, the injured person, who will conduct their part of the jury selection process. That's usually an hour. It could be longer; it could be less. I want to learn some of your attitudes and beliefs about the system in general. When you hear the judge say those words and see the lawyer stand up before you and take in the room and all the people you're there with, what are you feeling and what are you thinking?

I'm thinking it's best to pay attention. I don't want to make a fool of myself in front of other folks, whether they be co-jurors or judges and attorneys. Just kind a mindset of focusing on what's going to be said, and try not to get distracted, especially when they're questioning, you know 59 other folks.

It's unlikely the attorneys get to people in the back because as a practical matter, with only so many challenges, it generally isn't going to get beyond the first third of the group, unless there are lots of people excused for hardships and cause. That leads me to this question: how do you feel about being there in the first place?

I think part of me would feel a sense of relief. I've lived here for like 18 years and haven't been called.

Wondering if you exist.

Yeah. And own cars, own a house. I work for –

Registered to vote.

– work for the county. I don't even get to keep a dollar of what I get.

Because they pay for you to be there.

Right. I've got to sign my check back over to the county. I've been summoned twice. One time for Superior Court in L.A., which I never got called for, and another for Federal Court in L.A. I was in school so I got excused. So I'd feel a little bit of a sense of like, wow, I finally belong.

You made it into the club.

I'm actually a peer of the community.

I wasn't selected until just last year. I'm 56, and I've been here for a long. Yet I hear stories of people who have been called many times.

I know. I lived in D.C. for a year, and there was somebody that I worked with that she, within like a year, she had been called, I don't know, four times.

It's random. Other than the sense of relief at being a part of the proceedings, what are you feeling about the participation? Your level of interest? What's most important to you at that point, to you and your values?

*I'd be interested in seeing the system, how it functions sans television. Being able to participate in that way. **I also feel a sense of burden and concern to make sure I'm going to really be engaged enough to set aside any sort of biases and render an opinion based on what the facts are, what the law states.***

How heavy is that burden weighing on you at that moment? Sure, you want to take this seriously, but do you have the burden more on the sense of dread or more something you feel fairly comfortable you can handle, but at the same time, some apprehension? Where would you fit on that continuum?

I would feel more comfortable on a civil case than criminal. It would be more, this would be something I could easily do and participate in. The apprehension wouldn't be weighing down on me that it would cripple me.

Is that because in a criminal case you've got liberty or life at stake whereas in a civil case it's just a money issue? Or have you had a personal experience that makes the civil case easier?

I want to say with a civil case, the harm has already been done. So it's about finding the compensation for that harm that's done. With a criminal case, one harm has been done. There really won't be compensation to make up for that harm. So at this point, it's more about making sure the system's fair to give this defendant their proper due process so that whatever happens is fair under the law.

You mentioned having some concern about the ability to check in to your biases and brought up being aware that you may have them and wanted to be aware of your biases. What sorts of biases do you think you might have in that civil context, if any, that would come into play?

I think the primary one would be the inequality issue, particularly when it's one person versus a corporation. I don't agree with the courts that say a corporation is a person, so I'm going to peg that as kind of a – not even David versus Goliath, but more like a David versus All of Babylon, type of thing. That's kind of my primary bias, is it something that's really being fairly handled, or is someone being so overwhelmed with pressure that it becomes not really a fair competition, you know?

Can you think of an example? A scenario that might fit into what you've just talked about?

I'm thinking of big corporation versus one of their employees, that employee who is barely getting by on the $10 an hour they're making and can barely afford any sort of lawyer, compared to the four lawyers at the table for the corporation. Something like that where it's going to be really overwhelming, because I can imagine myself in that position feeling pressure to settle, because if I don't settle, then I'm going to be run over by this big train. I would feel a little bit more toward the plaintiff in that case.

Is there anything in your background, academic or professional, that informs that feeling for you, that puts you in the sense of feeling for the plaintiff a little bit more in that situation?

Not directly.

Because you mentioned you work for the county, I wondered if there was some individual versus government kind of personal experience that you had.

No, nothing like that. I'm very pro-government. I think there are times when a big corporation may be right in what they're doing, so it's not that I'm always going to side with the individual, it's that I would start to hear things more from their perspective than I would the other perspective.

Do you have a sense if you had a case where an individual was suing a corporate defendant of some size, that if the plaintiff proved their injuries, you might make a larger award because the defendant can more easily pay it than, say, an individual who's being –

I think I would definitely weigh toward, I would. All that, the money thing, is very odd to me, because how much does something really cost? How much is it really worth? For someone, $10,000 means a lot to them. And in the context of whatever injury they've suffered or whatever it was that happened to them, for other folks, no amount of money is ever going to repair that. So the monetary thing, you have to do it big enough to where you want to convey, hey, we understand this was a big deal. That's where I think the system goes off-kilter a little bit, because there is a harm that was done, and you're just trying to compensate for that. I don't know if we can adequately do that.

How do you feel about deterrence, as something a juror should or should not consider in that context? Where you've got compensation, but there's also deterring harmful conduct in the future; teaching a lesson, if you will. And although we don't have punitive damages in Washington, how do you feel about making your award match a level that might more likely deter future harmful conduct?

I would like that. That's where you wish you had some creativity to impose some sort of penalty that could mean something. Where you could say, you're no longer CEO for the next three years or whatever. Something like that. Because

I think, at least from my perception, there's so many insurance policies that are out there, so these costs are going to be covered and it's not going to be anything that's really felt. So I wish there was something that you could do, something that would convey that message that, this is something serious and shouldn't be done ever again.

Talking about damages, let's say the plaintiff proved the case that they've been injured, and the injury was caused by the negligence of either an individual or a corporation. Doesn't have to be a corporation; it can be a person. We have different kinds of damages. We have special damages: things that can be enumerated fairly easily; medical bills and wage losses, past and future; damages to property, things there's generally a receipt for. Then we have general damages: pain and suffering and disability and loss of enjoyment of life which the Court will tell the jurors, there's no fixed standard to guide you in your decision to help you determine what that is. How would you go about determining what amount of general damages to award?

*It lies in what kind of environment they were in at the time and then trying to think what their potential would have been had that environment stayed the same. It doesn't make sense to think if someone was in a position that, for example, they were already in a wheelchair. I wouldn't lean so much that they had potential then to run a marathon by the time they were 40. I'm not going to provide in a way that would think they would do that. **But I don't know how to weigh that numerically, and that's where it comes into a problem. I really wouldn't know where to start.***

Every juror will have a different sense of what value to put on pain, suffering, disability, general damage, and you will all come together and presumably make some decision. Some lawyers will ask the jury to take a multiple, for example, of what the special damages are. Does that have any resonance to you one way or the other?

So they basically take what the special damage would be and multiple it by –

Two or three or four, whatever.

I don't think I get swung either way with that. It becomes very arbitrary, so I would want to say, why is it only two? Or why is it three and not two?

Right. It's difficult for the lawyers, too. So as a potential juror, would you want a lawyer to suggest a figure to you?

I think it would carry some weight, but I think I would rather have a range. To me, that would make sense. Because again, I don't think anybody really knows. Also, I don't know if this is included in that, but in the number that is awarded, are attorneys' fees included in that or separate? That's something I don't really know anything about. I don't know how much time you've spent on the case. You may have spent three days; you may have spent five months. So I don't know, if I award somebody $100,000, if you end up getting $50,000 of that. I may be saying, I wanted them to get $100,000. If I knew you were going to be *getting $50,000, I would have said, let's make it $150,000. I would like to see some sort of accounting of that.*

Where it actually goes.

Right.

Generally, attorneys who do this kind of work are doing it for people who have been injured to some degree or another from relatively minor injuries all the way to catastrophic injuries. Generally, none of those clients can pay the lawyer an hourly rate, so they work on what's called contingency fee, which is usually a third. It can be lower than that. I've seen it lowered to 20 to 25 percent. It can also be, in very difficult cases, such as medical malpractice cases, as high as 40 or more, percent. Generally, it's a third. That's the standard, plus whatever costs the attorney advances. Unfortunately, you're not allowed as jurors to hear that. How do you feel about that? In a given case, you don't know what the client, the plaintiff, may walk away with.

*It makes me feel a little bit not included in that. **Because again, as a juror, I'm there to make sure that there's fairness in the system and to follow through with the law as best we can.** So, not knowing that, if I'm awarding certain damages, I want to believe that is going toward the plaintiff.*

Sure. That it's meaningful?

Right. That it has meaning. I wish there was a way we could have, okay, here's the number we're giving. If whatever the attorneys are getting, that would be extra. This is what we're setting aside for plaintiff. Here's the extra.

Your background in divinity and theology, how has that informed your values or awareness of biases and prejudices in your life in a context like this?

My journey through that is both circuitous and hilly at the same time.

Isn't it that way for everybody? All the time?

Yes. Well, at least it should be. I'm not part of a faith community now and haven't been for some time.

Something about that journey has informed you and gotten you to where you are today.

Right. If I could use it this way, I'm probably more likely to be more Christ-like now than I was when I was in church, so.

Is there anything that would be helpful for me to know about why?

Not within the time constraints we have.

If there was some common current that I could take from that, just in terms of understanding people.

I wish there was, but no. I was going to say, I can imagine how hard it is for you as an attorney that you're faced with 60 people with all sorts of different backgrounds. Everybody's coming with different perspectives, because as many as me would be there, there's also those who, I work for whatever corporations or whatever.

Right. Often insurance companies.

And there's always people trying to take us for a ride, right? So, I can imagine.

You mentioned people who say that they're trying to take us for a ride. There are studies that say jurors think of plaintiffs' trial lawyers as very low on the credibility scale. They use terms like greedy lawyers and sleazy lawyers and lottery mentality victims.

More so than criminal defense lawyers?

They're kind of brothers and sisters in arms. That the system's out of control. Where do you fall in that?

I think there's probably some truth to that. I think in any profession, there are people who are out there for the wrong reasons. *Where I come from is, trying to peel that away and not even to see the defense attorneys that would be, hey, we're just trying to protect the corporation, because you know they don't make enough money. For me, it's about peeling that away and just listening to the argument. Making sure there's fairness being represented and that there's a valid argument being said. It's not about, I've seen that person's commercial three times today, or whatever. It's about here's the argument. Here's what's being said. Is this really a fair trial and is this being done in a fair manner?*

What does a fair trial look like to you? What sorts of things go into your definition of fair?

I think, one, that there is an adherence to the law, and you rely on the judge for that and that both sides get an equal representation to present their case. Obviously, a lot happens outside the courtroom that we're not privy to. I imagine that sometimes it's hard to see if it was actually fair, if each party gets their chance to say what it is that they need and have their equal representation. If someone doesn't have adequate representation, how do you make up for that? You know, once you've heard all the arguments, then just weighing it against the law and what does the law say?

In the context of fairness, where does the concept of bias and prejudice and open- and closed-mindedness fit in there for you? In the context of a fair trial?

It's hard because we can read the law and somebody can interpret it one way; another person can interpret it another way. It is a difficult journey to make. I'm not sure that there's an adequate answer for that. Because we could see the fairest of trials happen and obviously there's going to be someone that's upset and they will think that it wasn't fair at all. So I think going into it thinking that someone's not going to be happy with the results of this –

By nature of the contest.

*Right. So putting that aside, how can we make sure, that there's, I hate to use the scales metaphor, **but that there's an equal weight to both sides that are being presented.***

How do you feel about the importance of a jury that is open-minded or unbiased enough to make sure that both sides get a fair start, that they're not leaning more towards one than the other? How do you think the lawyer needs to go about asking if they have bias or prejudice or can be open-minded?

That's hard. I don't know, having never sat there. I don't know how many people say, I've got all sorts of biases. I think there are people who, for whatever reason, they want to get on the jury no matter what. It gets them out of work, they want to get their name in the paper or whatever.

Whatever it might be.

And I think people in general just don't admit to their own biases.

Why do you think that?

It's a hard question to say, what sort of biases do you have? Because people aren't going say that. I think there's got a be a different way to sort of peel that back and get what biases they –

Well, take yourself, for example. The lawyer is going to make that inquiry. How do you think the lawyer would be able to ask that question so it's a meaningful question that elicits a meaningful answer and doesn't cause you to be defensive? Would it be, do you consider yourself to be more open-minded or closed-minded with regard to some issue, or can you think of how that question could be phrased?

I don't know if you're just relegated to yes or no answers or questions.

You can expand.

Because I would say –

Open-ended questions are fine.

Describe your background with regard to blue-collar work versus white-collar work, and what kind of experience have you had with –

So asking about their background and experiences.

Right.

If someone asked you, this is a civil case where we have an injured person who's claiming they were harmed by negligence and are seeking compensation to make them whole, do you think you'd be able to approach this case in an open-minded manner, how would you answer that?

*I would say yes. **If there's a way to say, would you be able to approach the*** *case from the standpoint of the facts without consideration of who the clients are, I would think that, especially when you have one person versus a corporation, people are going to lean a certain way. But when you have one person versus one person, it becomes a little less certain. So, I think using something like, do you – in an open manner – I think people are going to say yes. They aren't going to say, no, I'm closed-minded, so I'm not going to.*

Let me frame it differently. I asked a terrible question, and violated the cardinal rule, which was I asked you a yes or no question instead of an open-ended question. Lawyers, the good ones, are looking to accomplish several things in jury selection, but first and foremost, they want to find people who, to the extent they can, be open-minded. If they have biases, and we all do, at least try to acknowledge them, work with them. We're concerned with what I call the snake in the grass, which is one or several jurors laying in wait to derail whatever cause we have because of pre-existing preconceptions about lawyers and credibility and the system being out of control. They could be people who've worked for insurance companies and have their own agenda. What do you think would be the best way for the lawyer to get those people to identify themselves in the group?

Are you allowed to ask what they do for a living?

Sure. We have the demographic questionnaire which gives us a clue as to where they work or who they work for. We'll often see aerospace or local government or large software and Internet companies.

*Right. **I guess I would say, how do you feel toward insurance companies?** And again, that's hard whether people will be honest or not. Or, how would you feel if your co-worker was injured on the job? Something like that. What sort of help would you give someone that you knew that was injured? What would you do to help them?*

You'd help them in the immediate sense or in a different sense.

Right.

Good lawyers need to establish a human connection with the jurors, which isn't easy to do when the lawyers are in this zero-sum game with each other. The jurors don't know them; may, in some cases, be suspicious of the process or the attorneys, and nobody knows anybody in this uncomfortable experience. How do you think the lawyer can best establish a human connection with you?

I think letting their guard down a little bit. Giving some sort of brief background of who they are, who the lawyer is. Being a little bit vulnerable in the sense of, I know you're here because you're summoned. I've been doing this for whatever long, and in my off time, I like to do these things. Just saying a little bit about who they are and at least making yourself a real person. And being aware, listening for when folks are giving responses, being able to listen for opportunities for sense of humor or compassion. If someone says, I had a co-worker who had a heart attack and died right next to *me, the lawyer just wouldn't say, okay, thank you, and move onto the next one, but would listen to that and offer some sort of compassion. **I think not just listening for key things like, okay, that one's not going to like me, that one doesn't like me, whatever, but listening for what's really going to make a difference here.***

And the flip side, without causing resistance or resentment or being real in a way that the jury doesn't feel manipulated; do you have any more thoughts on that?

Folks these days are craving authenticity *and so the reason why there's Trump and Sanders; a Trump and a Sanders are gaining popularity because they're real with folks, whether you agree with it or not, they're real with people. So I think **people these days are able to tell whether you are being real with them or not and whether you're doing something to just be manipulative or that you really do care and are trying to be authentic.** I think that's the best thing I can say. **People are going to know whether you're being slimy or not.***

You have more than a passing familiarity with the words you were using, authenticity and being real and that sort, have you had any training in the feeling realm or psychology or anything like that, because not everybody talks about authenticity and being real. I'm curious to know where that came from.

I think that's nothing really being trained to, but just, in following politics here and there, and probably some background. Definitely having experiences with religious folk who portrayed one thing and ended up being something else. Those words, authentic and real, become very powerful in that sense.

I'll share: I was 36 when first introduced to the concept and notion of being a real human being and being authentic; peeling away the layers of the onion and the vocabulary of feeling words. When I hear it, it resonates. But I don't hear it from everybody. Also you said, people are craving authenticity, and I'm wondering if you could share a little bit more about where and how that notion came to you and if you came to it on your own or if you'd heard that phrase before or if there's something out there that would be helpful for me to read or study up on.

*I have these waves where I kind of get into politics and then I get out of politics and get fed up with it. I'm back in it. I've been following very closely a lot of the pre-election things, because you know, we can't get into an election early enough. But a lot of what I've read regarding the reasons why certain candidates are doing better than others is about that. **In the age of social media within the Internet age, things don't get erased and deleted all that easily, and it's very easy for people to find things, so when folks contradict what they say, people are all over that.** It seems to me that people tend to be most passionate around a candidate when the candidate seems to be somewhat authentic. That's my perception as well. So it stems more toward the political landscape than it does anything else.*

Is your work data-driven, would you say?

No.

The kind of decisions that you make, are they data-driven or are they based more on some other sort of scale?

No, it's not data-driven at all. It's very much about policy and law, nothing that's data-driven.

If you're a juror going to evaluate evidence, would your decision be more emotionally-based or data-driven? What would you be looking for primarily, to determine whether or not you felt there was some truth to some fact that was offered?

I would tend to weigh the data more and really dig in, try to get to what is factual, at least what could be represented as factual within the case.

The burden of proof in a criminal trial, is beyond a reasonable doubt. In civil, it's called preponderance of the evidence. What does that suggest to you, those words; preponderance of the evidence?

*That means, in my mind, **I would probably venture to say 60% or more of the evidence would point to – kind of around two-thirds. I mean, if it was two-thirds leaning one way, then that's probably tipped enough for me.***

If the judge instructed you that a preponderance is defined as more likely than not, would your definition of preponderance stay the same or would the ratios change at all in any way?

It would stay the same.

Sixty percent?

Yeah.

Approximately.

Right. To me, it's not about flipping a coin and the likelihood has got to be a little bit above 50%, almost to the three-quarter percent figure.

If a lawyer tried to persuade you that what that really meant was just tipping the scales ever so slightly, how would you respond to that? Say, 49 and 51. Could you make a decision if that were the standard? Would you be able to go below the 60 or the two-thirds?

*No, I don't think I could. And maybe that's where emotion comes into it, **but it's gotta be something that I feel is more than just, it probably did happen. It's gotta be more.***

Gotta be more than just that.

Right.

If you were a plaintiff or a defendant in a civil case like we've been talking about, what kind of a juror would you feel most comfortable being on the jury in your case?

What qualities would that person have?

> ***Definitely someone who is fairly intelligent who can listen to the arguments that are presented and make as fair determination as possible.*** *When I was summoned the one time and was in the big pool of people and I went to take my seat next to somebody, an older gentleman, I'm not sure he was all there, and he looked at me and said, you know they're all guilty, right? I thought, if I'm ever a defendant, I hope you're never on my jury. So I don't want someone to just go in, already made their decision.*

That sounds like the very definition of closed-minded.

> *Yes. People are going to have their definitions of what fair is, but I think someone's intelligent, can listen to the cases that is made, weigh that against the evidence and against the law, whether I win or lose, I want to know that I was in a fair trial.*

Turning that question over, is there any particular quality you would want to exclude from your jury? I suppose we could just say the opposite of what we've just been saying, but can you put words to that?

> *I think people that don't care about the system; that don't care about why they're there. If they're there just to have time off work.* ***I want people who are going to be invested.*** *We live in a society where we have court systems, legal systems that have an impartial judge, two representatives of each side and 12 jurors and we're all there to work together to come up with what is supposed to be a fair result. So if you don't care about that, then I don't want you there.*

You'd like somebody who takes the system seriously enough and then, by extension, that ought to put them in the right place?

> *Right. And I know it's not a perfect system. It's not. And we have many faults. But let's not make it worse by having people sit in a jury who don't care about and don't try to participate.*

It's frustrating for those of us who try cases that a number of people do not want to participate in the system and will do anything in their power to get out of it. And they could make good jurors because they're intelligent quite often. It's hard for us to get them there. Your exposure and background in divinity and theology makes me think of jurors who say, I just don't think it's right to sue your neighbor. And that's what their religion or church dictates. What would be a way for the lawyer to acknowledge, validate and respect that; take something meaningful, a teaching moment out of that? What do you think's a good response there? Clearly, that's going to be a difficult situation for that person to be a juror, but the judge may not exclude that individual. What would be a way to connect with them?

> *If there's been an opportunity for the two parties to resolve it before they got to that point, I would point that out. Peel it back and say, as a citizen of where we're at in this country, it's not an ideal situation, but sometimes this is the*

way that we need to resolve an issue. I don't think anybody wants to be in that situation. Particularly if it really is a neighbor or co-worker or whatever. I can't imagine suing somebody I work with and then seeing them every day. It'd be a little awkward and weird. So it's not an ideal situation.

So the response is, it's not an ideal situation, is it?

Right.

Unlikely to ever bring that person around to change their mind?

*I think of religious folks I know, that really do have that belief. You could bang your head against the wall to try to bring them around, **so it's not about bringing them around, it's about helping them to set it aside for the moment.** And this is not going to, we know you're not going to change your mind about this, but can you set that aside to help us resolve this?*

Help everybody.

Right.

You work for the County. What's it like to work for a government bureaucracy that size?

It's good. I believe strongly in government, and I think when government runs efficiently and effectively, it can be a very powerful force in community and society. Unfortunately, there have been many examples of it not doing that, which is what people always point to and look at.

We always point out the negatives.

Right.

As you know, we get a number of state and local government potential jurors. If there can be any common threads, what would be important for someone who works for the County to be asked or be told or know about? As a general rule, would you want somebody who worked for the County to be on your jury? Let me explain why I ask this question. I've seen people who work at large Internet and software companies come onto juries, and for the most part, they're very data-driven and binary, and they take pride in that. But that makes it difficult to present a case to them, because there are human elements in cases that aren't binary. So I'm wondering, as a general group, county government employees, would you be comfortable trying your case to them?

Some people, yes.

And are there any particular trends?

To me it's not about where they work as much as it is that they care about the system. Unfortunately, there are people who work there who don't like it, and they are not going anywhere because they don't want to look for another job. They're just going to make everybody else's lives miserable. It's just the way things are. I wish it wasn't that way, but. I think there would be people I wouldn't like having on a jury.

I was wondering how I can connect with them.

I think people that I know from the County have gone to jury duty and it's never a good time, right?

Because of projects or –

*Right. I think it's about also having them set that aside. Being so close to work, it's easy to run over to the office during lunch and check on something, check your email, whatever it is, or being engaged in the jury room on your email or whatever. **For anybody, really, it's about setting other concerns that are going on aside so you can focus on this task at hand and not be in court thinking about, I've gotta make sure, and this needs to go, I need to email this person, this person, and this person; so that you're not really engaged in what's going on.***

That is a problem because nowadays, people are so connected to their jobs and families, they're having a hard time paying attention. Is there anything in our conversation that shined a light for you that might be helpful for me?

I wish that there was greater time to select people. I've been a proponent of professional jury systems that have people that really care about it and know what's going on. I think courtroom tricks could be done away with, because you're not going to pull a fast one over and sway the jury based on whatever; it's only going to be about weighing the facts and getting something done.

A colleague I try cases with feels the same way.

If I'm ever in need of a case of whether I would want to waive a jury trial and just have a judge trial that would always be my concern, am I going to be getting something that's really fair?

As a general rule, the defendants will always ask for the jury trial. Even though we live in a fairly liberal culture here, juries tend to be quite conservative.

Interesting.

Thank you.

40

EMPATHY

Caucasian female, age 59, married, one child, two grandchildren, Medical-Legal Case Consultant

For every challenge a person has gone through, it gives them more dimensions, more ways of empathy, more ways of looking at something. You take a single person who's had one job, who listens to one show is not very dimensional. ...Those life experiences tell you about how a person is going to look at something. Because they have a greater depth of understanding. They have more empathy. The only way you can be empathetic is to walk it. You can't read it; you have walk it.

The judge says, ladies and gentlemen, please give your attention to the lawyer for the plaintiff who's going to conduct jury selection. At that moment, how are you feeling and what are you thinking? What's going through your mind?

That they're going to now select the jury and I'm one of the 60 and I could be chosen.

How do you feel about that?

*A little excitement about being involved in something. **Concern about the time frame it's going to consume depending on what is going on in my life.** If I have kids, if I have a job that I'm the sole person that has to make the money to be able to pay the bills, if my father is not well and I'm trying to take care of that, or whatever's going on in life, all of a sudden that's going 50 miles an hour in my head. If I'm in a situation where there's more free time, it's going to take time but I am okay with it. I'm much more, interested in seeing how this all plays out and I'm more involved.*

How do you feel about the civil justice system and the process where jury trials happen to resolve disputes?

I don't trust them at all.

Can you explain?

The reason I don't trust them is that I don't trust the law anymore. I think the law is something that can be manipulated. If you've got the money and big attorneys and you can keep having the plaintiff or defense go through tons of paperwork and I can manipulate, why not? Look at TV and what's come on the news. You're going, how in the world did they get to this answer? I don't know how they did. How they could possibly? For instance, OJ Simpson. So there is times I don't think the courtroom is about finding justice and getting to the truth. It's about who can play the game best and win.

You have some experience on that based on what you do, is that how you've come to that? Because of working with lawyers?

Doing the cases I've done and realizing that the person is suing the hospital or their employer and there isn't real grounds. Somebody tripped on a sidewalk and they're suing the city because of the crack in the sidewalk. They're so trivial.

They're trivial or frivolous or –

I've seen it in family law where you have a person attack and go after another person, on unfair grounds, because an attorney can manipulate words or actions or deeds in favor of their own client and create a negative situation for someone which is not the truth. Then just what you read in the newspaper, what's on the news. It's a combination.

Given that, when the attorney gets up and wants to make a human connection with you, what are you looking for?

Truth. Truth. Which means, when I'm looking at him or her, that attorney standing before me, what kind of eye contact do I get? I think it might be more for women than for men, but it's a matter of, what am I feeling? Do I get a sense of, I'm being sent a bill of goods because you're just standing there in your suit and think I'm that naïve that I'm going to listen and your words are God's words? Or am I listening to you and I get eye contact from you and I get a sense that you believe within your soul that the plaintiff, the person you are representing, really is telling the truth and needs to be represented by counsel to get this legal situation off his back and gone. *You're representing him because you believe him to be innocent of either an action or a wrongdoing.*

What do you think the lawyer can do in his or her preparation before trial to get to that place? Is it just a matter of case selection, or is there something the lawyer needs to do in working with the client or on that case to get there? Do you have any thoughts about that?

There is a family law attorney here. She's very well-known. She's so well-known that she is very selective about her cases. She's a divorce attorney. If a client was to come to her or she was to say this is what happened and this is why I'm going to divorce, I want to take my husband or wife for whatever, there are cases in which she's said, I will not represent you because I do not believe in your actions and the vindictiveness of what you want to do. I will not be a part of. You will have to find another attorney. Whereas she will take the ones in which this person needs my help. **In fact, that's the word. Help.** *There is a person that is vulnerable that is caught up in a legal system and they're not attorneys and they don't know law. They're vulnerable as a child, as though they've been diagnosed with something. And they're coming to you for your expertise to either* *cure them or help them out. You're sort of a doctor and their lawyer because they're in mental, physical, or financial pain. If they're innocent, then that's how you need to look at them. But if you don't really want to be their doctor and cure them and take care of them, but you just represent them because they need legal representation, then you have to figure, how far do you want to go with that case?*

Do you have a sense or a feeling that a lawyer can go too far in going into the skin of the client where it's too much?

Too much; what do you mean?

I've been part of training where we learn to get into the shoes and feel a client's pain in some senses. Do you think a lawyer can overplay that?

*Yes. Same thing as a physician. A physician could get so involved that he loses perspective. That's why you don't have a family member who is a doctor work on their own children or family, because you lose a sense of perspective. You're too close to it. **So yes, you have to maintain a little bit of objectivity because with objectivity comes a clearer perspective of the case and you can handle it better.** So on another aspect of the question, let's say you have a case and you're going, hmm, I'm not thrilled about this one. I can see where he was contributing the negligence of whatever financially, criminally, whatever he was involved in. But the law states, he is entitled to counsel. Would you really take this one to trial? Because if you're going to take that one to trial then your reputation as a trial lawyer – because you're not coming across full-fledged. You have to differentiate in your heart. I take this one because legally he deserves counsel and I am an attorney and I will represent him, but I won't take it to trial. Because I don't want to lose my reputation. Other cases, I am rock solid. I am going to defend it as though I'm a physician and I'm going to try and find a cure. I'm going to take it down. I'm going to work through the whole thing. But if I go to trial, I'm still me. I'm still the same person. I believe in this one. So the next trial, five years later, that's me, I believe in this person. Believe me, because that's who I am.*

Can you envision a situation where the attorney comes with this sense of belief but you still have a disagreement with them about it? I mean, just believing in your client is not a recipe for success necessarily, right?

*True. Because like in the beginning of my opening statement, **I don't believe that the law is about finding the truth. It's about manipulation. It's about who can play the game the best.***

We've just asked the question, what are you looking for in an attorney to present or bring to the table to connect with you? In other words, I asked you, how can an attorney connect, and you said bring the truth, be honest, believe in your client.

I think that some of it, there's nothing you can do about it. It's chemistry. You can have where you have a great client, a great attorney, whatever. But the chemistry's just not there.

Between the client and the attorney or the attorney and the jury?

The client and the attorney, which can also play out where there's just not a chemistry with one of the jurors. There isn't anything you can do about it.

Let's turn that over on its head and say, what must an attorney avoid doing to keep from losing that human connection?

*When you're trying to do a jury selection, body language says a lot. **If I'm sitting back, crossing my arms, and I'm like, I want to be out of here, or you're talking and I'm not really giving you respect and the time of day that means the jury is not connecting with you.** Whether they want to be here or not, they're not connecting.*

Why do you think juries don't connect with lawyers sometimes? What is it that lawyers are doing that may cause a juror to simply tune out?

Lawyers sometimes think too much of themselves. They come across as not human beings. It's like, I know everything and I'm going to tell you what you're going to think by the end of the day. No one wants to hear that.

Can you put a word to that? I'm thinking a lack of respect, but is there something else?

*It's more than that. How would you feel if you had a doctor walk in the room and he's going to sit down with you and tell you your plan of how you're going to handle your new diagnosed disease? You're going to go, I'm listening to you. You're the specialist, **but I don't like you telling me as though this is exactly what's going to happen and this is how I'm going to think, this is how I'm going to feel and this is how it's going to go down. That does not work.** You have another physician come in the room and say, yes, you've been given this diagnosis. There are three plans. You need to think about it. I need you to educate yourself on this. I need you to work with me at reaching the goal that I see for you. **So there's a difference between leading somebody down a path so that their mind's open and the two of you are walking the path together; versus an attorney saying, this is the case. It's open and shut. It's a done deal because they're wrong, they shouldn't be going after my client this way and when it's all said and done, you're going to set my client free.***

Or give us money.

*Or give us money because we're owed it. **An attorney would be better off saying, this is the case. This is what happened. We're looking for monetary aspects of this to help my client because of what happened. How you're going to perceive this, that's what we're here for today. I want to show you what we believe would be in the best interests of this gentlemen or this gal. So we're going to go down this path together. But I'm not going to tell you what you're supposed to think.** I don't think any individual, and especially if you've got a CEO, if you've got different people that are really intelligent, they* *don't want to be told.*

We talked about the connection aspect. You know from working with lawyers on both sides, and you've probably talked to enough of them to know, and with a daughter who's a lawyer, that lawyers have a credibility crisis right now. The general public tends to perceive plaintiff's trial lawyers as fairly disingenuous, lacking credibility. Why do you think that is, how do feel about that and what can be done?

That's a lot of questions.

How do you feel about that, in general?

*I think it's unfair. That I can say in all honesty, even if my own daughter was not an attorney. I think it's a situation where someone could say one month, I don't like attorneys, they're all a bunch of – they make everything go up, cost more, they're just looking for more money, they – but the minute they get in a car accident, the minute the insurance company is not going to help pay them what they're due for their medical bills, it's the minute they want – where's that attorney? I need my attorney. Then they get involved, and it's a matter of, I could not have done this without my attorney. I think there is a lack of humanism attached to attorneys that are trying to do the best they can to help individuals. **I think TV, everything else surrounding it, has to do with creating an image that: I went to law school; I'm a big hot shot and it's about not helping that individual; it's about how many cases I can win and how much money I can make and the more prestige that goes along with it. I think Hollywood has done some of the damage.** Like I said before, if you get in an accident, you realize there's more of a human element. I don't think that's been fair for attorneys. I think there's a lot of people that don't like doctors and have a little bit of the same attitude, but by a much smaller percentage because everybody has to deal with a doctor.*

Sure. Everybody needs a doctor.

But not everybody deals with an attorney. Therefore, they're naïve. They just don't know. So they fill in their own blanks without having a true perception of what a lawyer is really trying to do. The majority of the lawyers out there are good people. And the ones on commercials are the ones to stay away from.

If you made it onto a jury and were in deliberations in a civil case with a group of 11 other people, what message would you want them to know about what you've brought to the table through your experiences with lawyers on both sides?

I would forget the lawyer completely. If I'm the jury and I'm in the room with – it would all be about that individual and what the one the case is about: the plaintiff; the party; and just digging for the truth. If I found the truth that the person was negligent or responsible, then I would try to listen to the other jurors that are opposing me and I would weigh them against and if I found that the weight and measure's mine still, then I would voice where I'm coming from, whether or not that would possibly change that other juror's perspective. And when it came to the money, then I would try to be realistic.

Let's go there. What does realistic mean to you? You know we have special damages which are the medical bills and the wage loss and those kinds of things. Put them on a spreadsheet and add them up. Then there's the general damages, the pain and suffering and disability. The law, the judge says, when you determine that, there's no fixed standard to guide you. You are your own keystone; your own decision-maker. How do you determine what general damages should be awarded? What are you looking for?

The case is now to that point and I'm being asked what I would pay out in damages and then general damages. The damages is a specific number because of the wage loss, the hospital bills, and all that kind of stuff.

The special damages.

That's a fixed number. Because that's backed up by paper, statistics. When it comes to the general damages, whether it's the pain and suffering, are jurors given a peripheral of this is high, this is low, this is medium? Or are they given no number at all?

The lawyers can certainly suggest a number, come up with a way to justify it, but in the end, their guess is as good as yours as.

Okay. You're getting a gut response, not a thought out response. This is a gut response.

That's all right.

My gut response is, that's not fair. That's not fair to the juror. *If you're the attorney, you've looked at plaintiffs that have statistically gone under, let's say, three months of rehab or had to do this or been in so many prior accidents and this is what's been paid out over the last ten years for this kind of an injury, like we had with the E.coli incidents. We took each case in which somebody had the kidney failure. Did they have surgery? Did they lose their kidney? And each case that was settled, it created a point for the next case. A benchmark. Meaning, your particular child didn't have any kidney failure, didn't have this, so therefore, you're not going to get this amount that was paid to somebody who had the full range. So for a juror to come in and say, this person should get three million dollars, I might be looking at, three million dollars is a lot of money. But then, I'm coming from a blank slate.* ***How am I supposed to make that judgment call?***

Especially when the judge won't allow the lawyers to talk about the results of prior cases. The lawyers can't say, ladies and gentlemen, jury verdicts for this kind of case fall in this range. Can't put that in. You're completely guided by your own judgment on these matters.

Which is not fair to the individual. Because my being totally naïve or coming from, let's say I'm a blue-collar worker. To me, $100,000 is a huge amount. But the CEO next to me is like, at least two million. So you get a discrepancy, and how *do we argue? It's like a paradox. We're looking at the same woman. One's an old woman, one's a young woman, but we can't see the other one and it's not fair to us that we can't see each other.*

Kind of like that elephant. You know, when you're looking at it from all these different perspectives, you don't know what you're looking at until you step back. How can the lawyer make you feel better about that decision you are ultimately going to have to make? What can the lawyer say or do?

__Put it more as humanistic as possible,__ that this person had x amount of damages done. For the medical bills, they were in the hospital for so long and we obviously want full pay. This person did not cause this accident. Or this person did not – if you find them innocent, then they shouldn't have to be paying all these bills, okay? Now, when we're talking about the damages, I'd like you to put yourself if their shoes. __They were going along with their lives, out of nowhere, this happens.__ And yet, they're going to be having – yes, they can walk. Yes, they can do this. Or yes, they're free and clear of this diagnosis. However, we want to stop this physician from doing this again, and therefore, the damages and the fact that this should have been diagnosed earlier or this person was in this auto accident and for the rest of their life – they used to be a climber and they can go on hikes, but they're not going to be able to do the things that they want to do. And let's not forget they're only 40-some years old. So that means when they're 80, it's going to be much more exacerbated. So if you were in their shoes, and this is where it changes – their income level – yes, he's a pilot. He has a plane, he flies. He skis. He does this. So even though I might not live in that world, __you have to put me into their world.__ If I lived in their world how do I get you to give me a monetary value? __Take me out of my world, put me in their world,__ what do you think I would want? You're the jury, put yourself in their shoes. What would you be looking for to make amends for what has happened? What general damages for pain and suffering would you give?

If I hear you correctly, is what you're saying that two people with the same injuries may get different amounts because they're in different circumstances in their life? We're talking about pain and suffering here, and general damages, not special. If two people each lost an arm, one was a billionaire, one was a lady in your neighborhood who didn't work. Their incomes weren't affected but their emotions are affected because they've each lost their arm. Do they get different amounts because of their circumstances?

Well, to be honest, if I was the jury right now, and that was to happen and you chose the billionaire and you chose the woman, then I would think the billionaire doesn't need a lot of money because he already has a lot of money. And he'll be given every advantage possible.

Sure. There you go. Let's say then two neighbors that live side by side. One is a middle-aged woman; one is a middle-aged man. One works; one doesn't. One takes care of the children; one's single.

*The picture I'm drawing is, they should get equal. Because one is single, one is trying to find a mate. It's going to be harder for him because he's diminished his capacity to attract women with only one arm. The other one only has one arm and is trying to take care of children; they equal out. **They're both going to have deficits, trials and hurdles in their life, just different hurdles.** And let's say one made more money than the other; it's still the same purpose. So that's where more information –*

About?

The people you're representing.

What would you want to know about the person, the plaintiff? When you're looking at the plaintiff, what is it you want to know as you're sitting there, right off the bat in jury selection?

If I was an attorney for the plaintiff, I'd be looking at the jury in the sense of how their eye contact was with my plaintiff.

And if you were the juror, what would you want to know about the plaintiff? If you could ask one question of the plaintiff as they're sitting there?

That's a hard one. I can't give you an answer to that because then it would be – if it was criminal, did you do it?

This is a civil case. You can give me more than one question if that helps. Or the things that you're most interested in hearing about.

***What are you feeling right now?** And the reason I say that is because if I'm the plaintiff, I'm sitting next to you. If I was in a situation where I needed your representation, I would look like I was blindsided. I would look like the deer in the headlights. I'd look like the frightened kid, like, oh my goodness, what's going on? Protect me. Whereas if I was sitting there going, okay, do your stuff. Make it all go away, I think there's a difference of posture. But then there's really good actors in the world; people that can fool you.*

You're asking what they're feeling. What else would you want to know about the plaintiff if you could ask them a question as a juror?

I have to think about that.

I'll come back to it.

I think it would help to give me a hypothetical case. Because on a blank slate, just saying a civil case, I don't have any emotions toward it so I'm seeing two stick figures at a bench.

Understood. No context.

Without the context, I don't know what to ask.

I understand. What do you think a lawyer would want to know about you as a potential juror?

What I do for a living. Am I single or married? Do I have any children? Do I do any volunteer work? Can you ask religion?

I can ask those questions, sure.

If you can ask if they have any religious affiliation to anything, I would ask that. Because that plays a big difference in how people will judge situations. Because they judge it from not only their own intellect, but they also judge it from the spiritual aspect.

Is that a good thing or a bad thing or can it be somewhere in between?

*It can be somewhere in between, it all depends on how fanatic, I use that word specifically regardless of what denomination or what their religion is. **If you get somebody that's a fanatic in anything, that's not good.** So what else would I ask? What do you like to do in your spare time? What kind of movies do you like to watch? What kind of books do you like to read? That's about all I can think of at the moment. But the questions deal with, do I watch TV a lot? And I'm watching the stock market all the time and I'm really into CNN or Fox all the time. I'm only into murder novels and I have no religious affiliation whatsoever and I'm single and I never want to have children. That's somebody that is not going to be very empathetic. They're pretty much into themselves and they know everything. They're not going to listen, because they have all the answers. Somebody that has a faith, they have children, and they're teenagers, there's been some ups and downs, they like country music, they like classical, they like romance, they like documentaries; it tells you they're going to listen; that they're more well-rounded. They're not closed-minded. They're not locked into one avenue. Somebody that can agree to disagree.*

That brings me to this part. I believe there are two important things that jury selection should accomplish. One is that I establish credibility and human connection with the jurors.

Agree 100%.

The other is that we learn who can be open-minded and who's closed-minded. We're talking about bias and prejudice. Who is going to keep the parties from getting an even start?

Every one of us is prejudiced.

Exactly. That being said, how do you think the attorney should approach you to learn what your prejudices are or what you're closed-minded about?

*That's where the questions come from. What do I watch? Where do I go in my off time, and some of those things. I've found that I have one very strong prejudice, and that's people that are prejudiced. I finally had to realize that if somebody was prejudiced about a religion or a race or whatever, I could not be friends with them. **Another word for prejudice would be opinionated. Because more of us are more opinionated about some things. It's not so much the prejudice.***

It's very opinionated.

So people who have strong opinions.

Yes.

May be less likely to hear other sides? Consider fairly other sides?

Yes, and again, that's the question of, what do you watch on TV? Because that's your spare time. Do you have kids? Because kids bring in a whole new personality. And how many kids do you have? If you have three kids, you have three distinct personalities and they're all going to tax you to your nth degree because they are a reflection of all your faults.

Interesting.

Yes. They basically show you, especially when they're young, they mimic you. And you're going, that's not a very good attribute. I should stop doing that or whatever. And they ask such profound questions. I know that my daughter, I learned a lot from her as she was growing up, as much as she might have learned from me.

I'm thinking of the words, the magic mirror. People have talked about that before. I'm not sure if that applies, but the insight I'm getting is, your children have learned these behaviors from you.

*Some of it. But then they come up with something completely opposite and you're going, whoa, that is unique or whatever. Every day is a challenge; every day is a new beginning. **Having children is a big change in your life that only being a parent can you really know.***

Do you feel strongly more that people who had children would make better jurors than people who haven't had children and raised children?

*Depending on the case, but on a generality, I would say those that have had children. **Because they've been taken out of their comfort zone.** They've had to deal with disciplining. They've had to deal with disappointment that their kid didn't do something, or they've had challenges that's taken them from a whole different perspective. Just like somebody who has been in a car accident has a different perspective that one day they were fine and out of nowhere, a car hit them and now they have issues; or somebody that was diagnosed with a disease that either has the potential to be cured or not. **For every challenge a person has gone through, it gives them more dimensions, more ways of empathy, more ways of looking at something.** You take a single person who's had one job, who listens to one show is not very dimensional. You take a person who's had a marriage, who's lost a wife or had a divorce or has a child, three children; has grandchildren, has had three jobs, four jobs, different bosses.*

Lots of life experience.

Experiences.

As you were talking about earlier, those facets.

*Yes. Those **life experiences tell you about how a person is going to look at something. Because they have a greater depth of understanding. They have more empathy. The only way you can be empathetic is to walk it. You can't read it; you have walk it. You have to walk the journey. You can't be told it.** I know that I've been diagnosed with cancer, I know what that felt like. But have I lost a child or have I had a child that's been diagnosed? No. Can I say that I have some concept because, I have a daughter; I've gone through it myself? In actuality, I have no idea what it's like. I can only imagine. **But the fact that I've walked what I've walked gives me a greater understanding of what I don't know.***

Compared to say a 16-year-old who's lived a sheltered life and has never had pain.

Correct. They can only presume. And let's say they're a good person, a great person. They've read; they have a love for people. But they're going to come across as, I think I know what you mean because I've read, because – whereas people that walk it –

A real experience.

We have empathy, but we also know we don't know. *We haven't walked in those shoes. Those shoes are much deeper or much different than my shoes. But it gives us a better background, a better sense of depth to take this individual who's sitting next to you who you're responsible for. You're going to hand them over to us and we have to weigh and measure what's going on. I think people that have a more complex background can weigh things a little bit better unless they've become –*

Hardened is the word.

Hardened. Thank you. That's the word I was looking for. They've become so hardened that they've shut the empathy off, they've put up the wall, and they've lost their depth because they put up the wall. It's like, anybody that does that, this is what they should get. They're not going to look at the whole story of how they got there, what the whole situation is about.

In your experience, what kinds of things might cause a person to shut down, cut off? What kinds of things in life might cause a person to do that, that we would want to be looking for?

The case I was involved in, once the opposing counsel said exactly what happened, that this person got out of the car, couldn't walk very well –

This was a DUI case?

Yes. The police had to come and take the day off to be in the room, and I'm sitting there the whole time going, let's just get this over with. In fact, I was a little bit angry because this is a waste of the judge's time, the police time, and attorney's time. This guy, he should just have not got an attorney at this point. He should have accepted the circumstances; paid his fine and done his time instead of wasting everybody's time thinking, well, if I get this attorney he can lessen it and he can get me out of here. I probably was one of those jurors that was not as respectful because I felt so bad for the defense counsel. And I felt bad for the judge. I'm thinking, I'm sitting here, this guy's guilty. I knew within two minutes of being in the room. As it went on further, I have to admit the defense did all of their due diligence to make sure there wasn't a loophole.

You mean the prosecutor or the defendant's lawyer? The drunk driver's lawyer or the prosecuting attorney?

The prosecuting attorney did his due diligence by making sure he had witnesses for everything. It was slam dunk. There was no way you could move in any way, shape, or form. But that took taxpayers' money and time. That took the police officer. As a juror, I'm looking at it going, I'm mad. Let's just get this over with.

Because it was just not worth everybody's –

Time and energy and effort. Now, if I'm in a situation where there's a car accident, something happened, and I get the plaintiff representing and saying, yes, this did happen on this day, however this person was not negligent. This was – and that's why the word is called accident, because the definition of the word accident is such and such. So this was not intentional, something fell in the car, a coffee cup, whatever. We reach down, and this person walked right in front of me. Yes, I wasn't looking ahead. But that's why it was called an accident. And this person should have looked both ways. Even if we statistically show that my client could have stopped if the piece of paper hadn't fallen on the floor, there's still no way in which this car could have stopped in time. Yes, my client hit this person. This person is either injured or this person is now dead or whatever. But please try to understand that all of us could have been in the situation where we reach down and somebody stepped off the curb right in front of us that should have waited until – at least looked for me.

To find out if there's a snake in the grass who wants to do intentional harm to my case, somebody with an agenda, how can we identify those people?

You mean in the jury?

In the group of potential jurors.

Those would have, in my opinion, have some connection some way with the case. Like we talked about, the wall. I have a wall up. I have a strong opinion about this.

So we're looking for people to talk to whether they have strong opinions about something that's related to the case?

Yes. Because if they have a strong opinion, you're not looking at reaching

*them. **You have to first tear down a wall before you can begin to reach them and have them actually hear you.** So if you feel that there's any kind of a barrier between the two of you, and I think that more or less comes from talking to people and trying to figure out, to listen to your gut. It's like if you walk into a room, and the hairs on the back of your neck go up and you're not listening to that, you're not looking around, you're not being a little bit more observant. If you are having eye contact with the juror and the words that are coming out of their mouth is everything you want them to say and you're the perfect juror, but your gut tells you, ugh, you need to listen to your gut. I would say the same thing for a mother. A mother hears the doctor say something or the teacher says they need to do what their child, but as a mother, their gut says otherwise. I would bet my life on it, 100%. You follow your gut, especially if you have been a mother a while; or you've been an attorney for a while and you have some life experiences. Then follow your gut.*

Do you think that most potential jurors think that the lawyer is trying to manipulate them?

*Of course. But that's not just one, it's both. It's equal. It's not one more than the other. I'm going to manipulate you to believe what I want you to believe and I'm going to manipulate you to believe what I believe. That's where I was saying before, **it's not about telling them what you want them to know or what they should end up knowing. It's more about, I'm taking you on a journey. I want you to see what I see. I want you to know what I know. I'm hoping that by the end of this trial, that we will come together and see this perspective.** That's why it's called a trial. I'm not going to tell you today that you're going to find my client innocent. I know he's innocent. But I know that you are all very, very intelligent and you don't like to be told. I'm not saying that's exactly how you would say it, but your thought is, I'm going to present to you all the information. Whereas most attorneys say, my client's innocent and I'm going to prove it's innocent and I'm telling you what you should think. **I don't want somebody to tell me what to think. I'll come to that conclusion after I've heard both sides, not just yours.** So regardless of the side, it's a matter of, I'm going to take you on my journey. I'm going to have you see my client. I think that's where the difference is when it comes to judges and attorneys and some of the protocol. The only way I can present this is to say, if somebody asked me a question and they want it in a yes or no. And I go well, under the circumstances… and I was interrupted and they said, I need a yes or no answer. My response back would be, you asked me to tell the truth, the whole truth, so help me God, then you're going to have to let me answer it. I cannot answer it in a yes or a no if I'm going to tell the truth. And if I'm in contempt of court for that, then I'm in contempt of court. But it is not an answer which can be answered in a yes or no. Because if I answer it in a yes or no, it can be manipulated.*

You're talking about cross-examination?

Yes.

Right. So if the lawyer's doing that to a witness –

I don't like yes or no answers. An answer should be the way they want to answer it. Now granted, it can backfire where the person is going to lie through their teeth or they're going to manipulate. They're not going to tell the truth. That's why I don't like law.

You've got a lot of experience.

*Well, it can be manipulated. It's not about the truth; it's about how to get what you want them to say and how not to say what they shouldn't say. It's not just the lawyers. It's the law in which this person has been convicted of this same crime fifty million times, but I can't bring it up. Excuse me? The jury can't know? This person has already murdered three other people but that doesn't have anything to do with this particular murder. Well, he's murdered before. Maybe he didn't murder this person. Maybe he is innocent of this one. Yes, I can understand that. That's where you need to have someone come in and explain to the jury you are getting all the information, but in giving you all this information, how would you feel if you've already paid the price? You've been in prison for something that you did and because of what you did it's like somebody turned you from a white person and made you black and all of a sudden now, the situation is that you're a black man, therefore, you're guilty. Because you got painted black when you were in prison. **I also believe that if you really want to reach people, you do it not in words or statistics, but words that create pictures. So when you're talking to a jury, they're picturing this person. They're walking with this person; they're seeing them in this incident.** They're seeing them reach down, grab the paper, and how they reacted after the accident or whatever issue happened. **They need to feel. They need to not only see the person sitting there, they need to walk in his shoes.***

When the attorney is asking people about their biases or prejudices, trying to determine who is more open-minded or more closed-minded, what do you think about the lawyer sharing something of him or herself personally, a bias, to get the ball rolling?

That's a tough one.

For example, at this point in my life, I don't seem to like bicyclists very much when I'm driving because the things I observe, it rankles me. If this were a bicycle case, I don't think I'd be a very good juror. How would you feel about hearing something like that and then saying how do you feel? Do you have anything that would make you not so suitable for this case or are you better for another kind of case?

That's very well stated. I can't articulate better than what you just said. It's funny you choose bicyclists, because I am a bicyclist. When I've been on the road I've been just as frustrated with the bicyclists. Here I am the bicyclist, you make that statement, and I see both sides, because I see the cars, it's like, I'm in this lane, hello. And you see me. And yet, I've been the driver, and I'm thinking, it's a road. It's for cars. You're acting as though you own the whole thing, and you're looking at me like I've lost my mind.

It's hit me since I moved into the city. In the suburbs, we didn't have that as much.

They've got a whole new lane down there and everything. I can't imagine. I don't even want to drive down there.

It's the running of the stop signs. That gets me the most. So I appreciate that. Maybe contextually it just depends if the attorney shares something?

*I would go with, **it depends on the case.** You're representing a client. It's a little bit tenuous as to how you're going to be able to get the truth across, because there's so many ways in which it can be shadowed, the truth. Maybe it would be one of those instances where you say something like you just said with the bicyclists, and said, we're all human. We all have political opinions, religious opinions. Whether it be something as simple as we like bicyclists or we don't or, kids these days with – depending on the jury. And if you've got younger ones in there, then you put in, these drivers they're in their 70s and you go, move it. So you can get them to tap into an emotion. They're sitting in a jury box, they're so far removed from that emotion.*

This is just to make a handshake that says, I'm going to share something. I'm going to show you something of mine; would you show me something of yours? Like a bias.

As I've gotten older, because that has been my philosophy always, I'm finding that there are those they're not comfortable with that.

Does that tell you anything about those people as potential jurors if they're not comfortable with that?

Yes. It tells you they know more than you do, or they're more closed down or more hurt or have more scars, that they're not ready to be a juror.

On that case.

It could be they're emotionally shut down because of whatever's going on in their personal life. Nobody knows. Their wife could have just had an affair. Their wife could be in the hospital. Their child could be moving back east and won't see again for years. You have no idea what's going on with each one. They could be closed down for reasons you don't know. If you'd met them a year later, they might be a completely different juror but the same person. That's why it makes your job so confusing.

And a short period of time with a large group of people and an artificial environment, where I don't have their trust to start out with. It is a difficult place to be.

And wearing a suit and tie does not help. But the law is a place of respect, and therefore, it's required.

I can't pin down how people feel about how a lawyer should dress. I have heard that the lawyer shouldn't be in a $3,000 suit.

Correct.

At the same time, I've heard that lawyers who dress like a lawyer, which means they should be in a suit, should look like they're successful.

No, it's not successful. It's respect.

Respect for?

The law. It's respect for the courtroom. Respect for justice. Respect for the United States, for our country, for all the things that have been created for us to be, for you to be heard in a courtroom; to be represented; to be tried by your peers. *It's not a matter of how expensive, and the more jewelry he wears, the more flamboyant he becomes, I would hope the less impressive people would see of him, and that he's more about the win and more about himself. He's not about his client. He's about, look at me, I'm the attorney. Aren't I great? I'm going to present to you so look at me. Whereas if you come in with somebody that is dressed appropriately, that's showing the respect of the room he's in, respect to the judge, respect to the jurors, to everyone in that room, for the freedom that we have, that's a different aspect of it. That's why I believe in the suit and tie. In fairness, to be honest, it shouldn't be a JC Penney suit either. Because that tells me, are you really qualified? Which is not fair. That would be a bias. That would be unfair, a prejudgment on that person as to whether they're really qualified, but I'm being honest.*

Given that everybody has biases and prejudices, and I'm willing to accept that, how can I get a person to be at least aware of their tendency to be biased or prejudiced so that when the time comes to decide, they can at least talk to themselves about it and say, am I really being fair? I've got this. I talked to the attorney about it, and now I at least need to –

Then I would have it as part of an opening statement. Like you mentioned about the bicycle thing. It doesn't have to be –

Maybe like loop that back; remember where we talked about –

But you don't have to refer it to you as your bias. You don't have to divulge anything about you; you do it as a generality, how there's some people – and I would look at my jury; at those that are older and saying, sometimes, you go in a restaurant and everybody's on their cell phone. At a restaurant, you're supposed to be able to talk to people, you know? So find out things that –

For example, I get turned off when I'm with a person at a meal who's looking at their phone all the time. It just bugs me because I don't feel included. That's a bias I guess. A prejudice.

I agree with you, it is. Because you could be in the same boat where somebody doesn't care about that at all. They totally get that they're at work and they've got to be connected to their phone.

Different generation.

Totally different generation. So I would look at my jurors and find out what a potential – it's like, I would Google what are the ten things that come up with ages such. What are the ten things that come up and then between those, depending on your age group, try to tap into a general bias so that you can tap into them and bring that out at the beginning. But when you're doing your closing, I would bring that back so that when they go back to the room –

It'll remind them.

It's a reminder that we all have prejudices. We all have strong opinions about things.

I'm willing to accept a lot more people than I might have tried to exclude in the past, as long as they're willing to say, you know, I do have this. I have this thing about lawyers or about the civil justice system being out of control or verdicts being too high. I'm willing to have that juror if they're willing to own up to it.

Bingo. That's exactly it.

Because then I'll trust them more.

Yes.

If the person's going to say I'll never, ever change, well then, okay. But if a person says, you know, I've got this, I'll say, can you just remind yourself of it throughout the trial. If they can look at me and credibly say yes, then I would feel more comfortable there. And I wouldn't have to try so hard at jury selection. What I'm trying to do is find a way to make this process condensed, respectful of what the jurors are valuing and to simply get them to disclose whether they can be fair in this process.

*What you are doing is so great. I agree with everything of what you're doing and I think it's wonderful. **You just have a lot of walls in front of you because of all that we've been talking about. Prejudgment.***

And my own prejudgments.

That is the whole jury process. I don't even want to go. I don't want to get a bunch of people and be bogged down with this. I don't want to take the time where we have to start from scratch. In school, you have a sense of pride for the United States. You learn about U.S. history and the flaws that came along with it but all the positives and where we are today and that part of the system that you volunteer and help out your community and the law process and the jury in which the Founding Fathers created for us to have a voice and for us to vote and you get your side heard. But we're now a generation in a situation where people don't even care about the United States. They don't look at the value of what we've got. They don't look at the freedoms of our forefathers and what they wrote in the Constitution for us. They don't value the freedoms and the privileges that we have. They just take it all for granted.

We're changing.

Yes. And not in a good way.

I'm curious if 50 years ago, 100 years ago, 200 years ago they were saying the same thing; people, things are changing, and not in a good way. I have a tendency to think that's probably what everybody says about government.

I wouldn't disagree with you at all. I'm not taking anything away, I'm adding to it; I think it's becoming more so. I think it's becoming more gray; more convoluted.

There's many more heads to this monster than before.

Yes. And the center and core of the truth or the foundation is almost to the point where you don't see it anymore. Where's the baseline anymore? Whereas before, there was all this, but the baseline existed. I think we're losing the baseline. I think the only way it would ever come back is if we had a major war that would come to the United States and bring us all together again and rally Go USA. It's respect for agreeing to disagree. But it's also respecting, even though I live in 2015, there are women that were thrown in jail. There are women that went through horrific physical abuse for me to vote. And yet, how many women don't even take the time to vote? There's people that were in the war and they fought for our freedom and we talk negative about the United States and it all goes back into this courtroom because that's where our freedoms are. If you accuse me, I have a right to be judged by my peers.

Let's talk about burden of proof. In a criminal case, the burden of proof is beyond a reasonable doubt. In a civil case, the burden of proof is defined by the words preponderance of the evidence. What does that mean to you? Preponderance of the evidence.

Keep going. I'm not drawing anything.

Okay. The word preponderance is then defined, it says, if you find by a preponderance of the evidence that this person was injured because of negligence, and the injuries were caused, then you must award damages. So the judge would go on to say that preponderance means more likely than not. Does that help you have a sense of what a civil burden of proof is to you?

It just sounds more messy and more convoluted.

What is enough for –

Then you're basically saying, it's gray. I'm looking for you to show me black and white. I have to deal with the gray because of my prejudices, my issues, me as a human being. But I'm not supposed to look at it from my perspective. I'm supposed to look at it from the judicial perspective. The judicial perspective is supposed to give me black or white. He's either guilty or he's not guilty. He did steal; he didn't steal. He lied to his insurance company; he didn't.

You've had the opportunity to review lots and lots of medical records. Have you ever had a sense where you weren't completely convinced about the person's injuries but you were a little more convinced that the injuries were genuine than the other way around?

You're saying that I have a case, and I believe that the person was truly injured –

Well, you have a question in your mind –

Oh, I have them all the time. I've had it where the person is complaining and complaining, and I know this guy is just working the system. They are totally working the system.

What if you're not so sure. The evidence is not completely clear to you, so you've got some questions that are never going to be answered because you're in the jury room having to decide.

That's a difficult question. I've had a lot of those cases and I've always said, thank goodness I'm not the attorney. I can give you the summary of the information and it is down the line or I can see pros and cons. I can see defense; I can see plaintiff. It's not my job and I just say, thank you, it's not my job.

If the attorney were to say, the judge will instruct you that the burden of proof is a preponderance of the evidence which means more likely than not, would you accept that? How do you feel about the notion that more likely than not just means tipping that scale 51% to 49%? Is that enough to satisfy you?

No.

Okay. Why – how come and what would be enough to satisfy you? What would you need?

It would have to be way more than that. If it was 50 and 49, then you're dealing with your emotions. *But then again, you're trying to pull together as all the jurors. How are you all together on this issue?*

Well, we can talk about your feelings. Just you as an individual, without having to –

I wouldn't want the burden.

You'd want more.

I'd want more proof, and I would want to come back to the courtroom and say, you have to give me more proof. You have to give me more. I'm not going to convict this person. I'm not going to make a decision one way or the other, because I'm trying to look at it as objectively as I possibly can. But you haven't given me, even with the preponderance of – I cannot. So therefore, I want more information. And if you can't give me more information, then, we're done. We're a hung trial or a hung jury. I don't think that's fair to either side. Regardless of my emotions, you know how they can go, I really want this person to be innocent, and then I'm so disappointed that after all the information, they're not. So we're all human. And we're making a human judgment call on another human being. Same thing why

I always fall back to a good doctor. When a doctor has 49/50, he doesn't make a decision; he calls in for a consultant. Not just another opinion from another person, but from another that is highly qualified to help him tip the scale.

Got it. Thank you.

41

NOBODY'S WORTH THAT MUCH

Caucasian female, age 69, married, one child, three grandchildren, Chemistry and Biology/Dental Office/Software Technician/Retired, A.A.

There was a couple people that said, nobody's worth that much. I don't care who you are. You are not worth that much. And they dropped it by another hundred thousand.

The judge then says, ladies and gentlemen, please give your attention to the lawyer for the plaintiff who will begin the *voir dire* or jury selection process. Tell me, what are you feeling in that moment? What are you thinking?

I'd like to know more about the trial and what it's about. Because a lot of it is personal. Some of it could be personal, and I have biases. And it's depending on how long the jury is and – there's a lot of factors.

You'd like to know more than they tell you in that moment.

Exactly. Because if you are chosen then it goes through a whole other gambit of –

The trial phase, which could be who knows how long.

I know. This last one, they said four weeks, period. The judge said, I'm leaving July 31st and it's going to be done by then. Period.

Which is interesting, because it tells you there's more to the justice system than justice. There's time and efficiencies and restrictions on everybody's ability to – including the jurors.

And the waste of time.

Lots of waste. I'm sure you've felt that. Tell me about that.

The two attorneys were at each other's throat all the time. It was kind of funny, like a comedian show. She kept getting on him that, you can't ask that question, we went through this before, you have the list of what you can and can't do. We were excused like every five minutes. Pretty soon, we just all stood up; we knew what was going to happen. We walked out. Tell us when you're ready. That's real interrupting, because in the back of your mind, it's like, why can't they tell us? Why can't they bring this up? What is happening? That's another thing, all the juries I've been on, after we're done, we really get the lowdown.

You hear what you weren't able to hear.

And that really is big time irritating. I was on a criminal case, he was charged with murdering somebody. We were sequestered. First degree murder was – they started – didn't get to second degree murder, because we had a hung jury and we finally quit. But we walked out of there, you should see his rap sheet. It would have been totally different if we had known in the past what he'd done, right? He wasn't the pillar of society, that's for sure.

Tell me about how you felt and your jurors felt seeing these two lawyers sniping at each other. Did it affect your decision, ultimately?

Not mine. This is what I felt. The woman attorney was great. She could just nail him every time he turned around. He acted like Columbo. He would stumble around. I think he slept in his suit. He couldn't find his glasses. They had to go back to the office to get his glasses. The two of them, it was just like, I'm going to get you. Every time he opened his mouth, she would stand up and say how about a recess, blah, blah, blah. I guess you're not supposed to ask that. We talked about the lawyers. And one juror said, he's smarter than a fox, he just is coming on that way. And I thought, well, maybe he is. Maybe that's how he's working us.

Which side did he represent? The company or –

The company.

When we are selecting juries, we need to learn who's got biases and what they are and how that might affect the trial. You said, I've got biases. Tell me about that.

I'll back up a little bit. Sometimes, I don't even know I have biases. I was on another case. I've been called oodles.

Thank you for showing up.

No, that's fine.

We appreciate that.

I enjoy – I've even been on mock juries, to see if it's even –

A case worth going, sure.

Right. So there was a Canadian, and they were young kids, and the Canadian was driving and he injured this woman and blah, blah, blah. Somebody said, do you know what a cheese head is? I've no idea. I suppose if I did, that would be a bias.

Maybe.

I don't know. I get very upset when you know that they've done it.

Sure. But we're focusing on –

And I guess civil cases are different. I was on a mock jury, which was interesting and this woman, she had surgery, she had too much anesthetic, and it burned her throat. Plus the surgeon had the wrong equipment, tools.

You were on that mock jury?

That was a mock jury. So at the end, everybody was feeling sorry for this woman. She's bedridden for the rest of her life and blah, blah, blah. So we all gave her more money. She'd already collected from the insurance companies oodles of money, and we weren't told that. I might think that's kind of unfair, that they should have listed as a bias thing.

What's a fair question that a lawyer can ask you, right off the bat without ever having met you in this setting, to learn about whether you can be open-minded or not to the case?

Interesting.

How can the lawyers say, tell me how can I know that you'll be fair and impartial and open-minded in this case? Even though you don't know much about it?

Right, I know. The wheels are going around. One question that was asked of me from the lawyer on the last civil case was, do you do jigsaw puzzles? I said, yes, we do all the time. We have one up all the time. She said, good. It's because this trial was so complicated, and so many pieces were here and there, and who got fired and why, all kind of mushed together.

You needed to get the picture.

To get the picture. So I thought that was an interesting question. It didn't even dawn on me.

If you were asked about, do you have any biases or prejudgments, how would you want to answer that?

I'd probably have judgments against African Americans.

Okay. And we all have these things.

No, I know. Just because the way I grew up.

What about towards people who are involved in lawsuits, or their attorneys who are helping them? Some people think that you shouldn't sue another person, no matter what. And some people think that the lawyers who represent these people are sleazy and unbelievable and they're ambulance chasing. How do you feel about that?

I believe it.

Do you? Okay. Tell me more.

I mean, every time you talk to somebody, the lawyers ask for millions of dollars, which I guess is okay.

Was that the experience in that last case you had? They asked for more than you thought was reasonable?

Definitely. It was like, you've gotta be kidding me.

Did they attempt to explain why that amount was chosen? I'm curious.

Nope. How we figured out her amount we thought was fair was, they gave us her W-2 forms or income tax for two years and we averaged out, because she was on not only a pay scale but a percentage. Plus, we knew what other people's service paid. We wanted it to be fair. We didn't want to get her a million dollars and the other people that were already gone –

In that company.

Right. And I don't know, maybe she had to hire a lawyer because nobody would talk to her. HR was keeping their mouth shut.

Did your juror group factor in that there might be money that the lawyer would be getting out of that as well?

*I don't think so. No, we went around and just said, how much do we think she's worth at this point? And that's how we came up with a figure. We didn't put the lawyer in that equation, because maybe the lawyer got half. I have no idea. I mean, that's never said. **But I think it's out of whack. I really do.***

You mean the system?

Yeah, the system as far as how much a lawyer can get and how much a person can get for whatever injuries.

You indicated you believed that the system's maybe a little broken –

Oh, yes.

That jury awards are too high?

Yes.

That the lawyers who represent these people maybe lack credibility to some extent? There have been studies that say among the professions of credibility, on the scale, that at the bottom are used-car salesmen and only above them are trial lawyers.

Really?

At the top are nurses. Do you think that's true that lawyers are untrustworthy or un-credible?

***I don't think all of them are.** Unfortunately, the media and what you get from – and just from me being in the system, you know, they go for the macho or whatever, the biggest, because they know they're not going to get it.*

The biggest amount of money?

Right. Hoping. And see what they come out with. I've never had to hire a lawyer for that and maybe that's just what I've heard.

Did you feel, starting out in that case you were talking about, that the lawyers were ambulance-chasers or were not credible?

No.

Was it because of the way they dealt with you from the beginning?

Right.

Okay. So you reserve judgment.

I tried, yes. You know, some days you want to –

And you said that you gave an award to the plaintiff? There was a money remedy?

Oh, yes. Definitely. And she deserved it. Everybody, all the jurors said the same thing. Money was a little bit different, how much to give her. But as far as what she deserved, yes.

How did you feel about the amount of time it took to get there?

It was horrible. Oh, you mean in the jury room?

The whole process.

It was awful. They drug it on and unfortunately, the company was kind of cleansing and it was horrible. Everybody had an affair with everybody, and they were fired. It's a big company, because they were all over the world. Then one guy said, I went to bed with so-and-so. And she was fired, and he was fired. And they were having them on the stand and I don't have to know all this. I honestly don't have to know all this.

Are you saying that there was more information provided than you really needed?

That's right. Absolutely. Absolutely. I know she did try to pull her card of being African American. I did this for the company and I did that for the company and I brought in this. Which is fine. And I'm sure she did. She was a really lovely, smart lady, I must admit. She just shouldn't have had an affair. That's the bottom line. But yes, they brought in way too many people. We didn't have to know everybody in that company and what they were doing.

What was your take on the experts and how you value the credibility of the experts on each side? I presume they had them, vocational and economist experts and those kinds of things?

Yes. They had oodles of experts. Even teleconferencing and what not. I think they were all very good. The only one that wasn't, she had mental problems, as far as she had a horrible childhood –

The expert did?

Oh, no, the plaintiff. The expert came in and it was a little weird, I thought. Whatever she was, a mental person –

Mental health person?

Yeah. No notes. Zero notes. It was the plaintiff or whatever did not want any notes taken. And I'm like, usually you have to have some kind of record. **It was all off the top of her head and that wasn't very credible.**

Were you influenced one way or another by the questions to each expert about how much money they were making per hour?

Some were pro bono, and some were making quite a bit.

Some were *pro bono* and some were making a lot of money?

Yeah.

Did the money issue affect your perception of their credibility?

Nope. You know what? I just figured, that's the way it is. **Nobody's going to take off a day or two of work and be on that stand for nothing.**

Did it enter into your sense, one way or the other, that any of those experts might have been more or less willing to go for either side, depending on who hired them first and how much they were paid?

No, because everything was documented. *Everything was read. All the emails. What date and what'd you say and what'd they say. So I didn't –*

Didn't have that –

No, not at all.

Sometimes, experts are known to be a little more objective, that is to say, they'll tell the truth rather than the truth as the side that hires them wants it.

Right, right, right.

Given what I told you about lawyers having this credibility gap, when the lawyer comes into the courtroom, how can that lawyer who has the credibility gap get to an even keel before the trial even starts? Is there anything they can do or say?

I don't know. This is interesting. We were personally taken to court one time. It was interesting what the insurance company said. We had to go through a whole bunch of stuff and it never went to trial, because the insurance company said, she hired so-and-so, and we never win.

So they decided to settle.

Yep. They settled for a lot. I'd never heard of that before.

Well, they do evaluate.

You've gotta be kidding me.

How does that make you feel? How has that affected your ability as a juror to hear a case and decide with that experience; who's credible or without having that sour you?

It did sour me. It's a hard thing to get over. *I still am a little bit soured about that.*

You had insurance, right?

Oh, yeah. Obviously it didn't come out from us personally. The insurance company paid. In fact, we didn't even know they did. And when we went to renew it, he said, oh, yeah, duh, duh, duh – you what?

They didn't tell you that they had settled the case?

No. They took depositions and whatnot, and I thought we were just waiting to go to trial. Never did. I'm going to ask you a question. Does this happen very often? For instance, the lawyers asked for more money just because they know they're going to get less or they settle out of court because they know they're not going to win?

Most cases are going to settle out of court. The vast majority.

Really?

Because they're expensive and time-consuming and risky. The risk is in part the expense, because the attorney is advancing those costs. But I'm curious to know if your experience having been sued gives you, one way or another, a sense maybe in favor with the person who's being sued in the case? So you've been a defendant; you know what it feels like to be a defendant. So that would be a question, do you have a bias towards people who had experience similar to what you had where you were sued by somebody?

Yeah.

Maybe?

Maybe.

How so?

About two years after we were sued, she was screwing the federal government, let me put it that way. They called me and said, she's been collecting blah, blah, blah for all this time. They didn't know she got a settlement.

I see. Didn't disclose.

I hope whatever happened that she had to pay it back or do some kind of something.

In your experiences in life as a child, going to school and college and having a family and doing the work you've done and having grandchildren, what's shaped you? What of your life do you think would make you a good juror?

I like people really well and I would do anything for a person. I've been on the Volunteer Fire Department for years. I've tried to help everybody out. If somebody's in trouble or they need help, I'll be there. I think that helps out. Growing up, I was in an Ozzie and Harriet type family. My mother didn't work; she was always at home. My dad worked; he was the breadwinner. I never had a babysitter. I grew up in a small town.

Good people there?

I hope so. It's changed. My mother was born and raised here, so deep down, even if I have some prejudices, I try really hard to hold them back. We were in Washington, D.C., I think it was in the '70s. We decided to take city transit. I was oblivious. We get on and we had two kids with us. I said, back of the bus. We're going to the back. And they looked at us like, why did you get on this bus? And that was the first thing – we got off at the next stop.

You felt out of place.

Yeah. I had no idea what was happening around me. And now here in this City, I was taking the bus and that doesn't bother me.

So you have an awareness of that, and you're at least able to factor that in when you're trying to reach a fair decision.

Definitely. I try to, all the experiences or whatever that has happened, I listen to other people's experiences to factor in. I'm not black and white; it's the way it is; not going to budge. I think that's horrible, especially when in a jury situation.

Did you experience any jurors on your cases that were rigid?

On the criminal case I did. One guy read the New York Times *every day; would not participate. When you're sequestered, you want to get on with it. That was not a good one.*

What's shaped you the most as a person? Has it been motherhood or grand-motherhood or anything at all that's shaped you and the way you would approach decisions in jury service?

Growing up, my father had a lot of idioms. ("N" word) rich and –

That kind of stuff.

So I grew up that way. I thought nothing of calling a black person –

Some racial bias.

So you don't even realize. Even when I was on Guam, they were Gooks. Everybody knew that. But after going through all these things, and actually getting in the big world, you know, go to college or get out, you go, oh, my eyes are opening now. This isn't the world over here that I was raised in. That really helped me open up things, to open my mind and say, these are good people.

I imagine some people, rather than open their mind, would shut down even more to hold onto their beliefs.

Values, maybe.

What is it that let you open your mind in those situations? Is that maybe you've just always been that way?

I remember in grade school, I was told what to do. It was never said, how would solve this problem? What should we do?

Your input wasn't solicited.

I was at some girlfriend's house and her mother sat down and she said, let's think about this and let's solve this. And I was like, you can?

A light went off?

Uh-huh. That was in sixth grade. I'll never forget that. And I thought, the world, there's more to it than being in this little environment I was in. Growing up, I was to be seen and not heard. It was very strict that way. They were a loving family; there was nothing wrong with that. But what I heard and only in that channel, I didn't hear anything outside that was better –

Until you did. It must have been wonderful to have that experience.

It was.

Open your mind.

It did. It just opened –

And make you hungry for more.

Exactly. Also, as a daughter, I was not to go to college. I was to get married, and I was to have two kids.

Can I ask what your father did?

*He was a fireman. And that was the way the family was raised. I asked to go to junior college and they weren't very happy. He wasn't very happy about it. So when you have no support, when I got my AA degree, I was 50 years old. I showed him the diploma, I was so happy. And he said, what are you going to do with that? He still was not proud, did not care. But that was another thing. **That really opened my eyes.** It was so much money and the kids were so young and you just want to say, honey, it's okay. It's not going to last that long. You know, they have all these things in their minds of what they're going to do and all these dreams. And you know a lot of them won't come true, but maybe they will.*

Maybe some will.

And you have to be positive.

I take it you raised a family from a pretty early age?

Yeah. I only have one daughter. I had her when I was 21.

And your husband, what did he do?

I was divorced. Her dad was in the service. I got a divorce, and I was divorced for four years before I remarried.

Those aren't totally important. But in terms of shaping you, it sounds like things that have opened your mind have been very important.

Very important. One of the dentists I worked for was a mentor to me. I followed his footsteps and figured out how he did things, financially and whatever. I paid attention.

Do you have a sense that the fellow jurors in your jury panel groups were more or less closed-minded?

When I was in another city up north, they were closed-minded. We were there for 17 years. There was one high school. There was no grocery store. There was no nothing. The people that had been there for years and years and families, they were so narrow-minded. You were either affiliated with the school or had something to do with the town.

What was that era? What time period was that?

1968 to '70. Then we moved and built a house and lived out in the country. But everybody up there, really narrow-minded. If you didn't belong to so-and-so, you didn't exist. Some of the interviews I had, who's your mother? Who cares who my mother is?

Oh, interviewing for jobs.

Yeah.

But on the jury, in jury service, did you have a sense, either in jury selection or in jury deliberation, that these people were more or less closed-minded – or open-minded than you?

They're more. They were open-minded. Number one, they're a lot younger now.

You felt the younger people were more open-minded?

Oh, yeah. Only three of us were in our 70s or 60s. One of them was just out of high school. What a shock for him. He was so cute, but so bashful.

No life experience at that point.

Exactly. This was probably a nice awakening for him.

I do motor vehicle or medical malpractice cases, medical negligence. How do you feel about cases where people are injured physically? How do you feel about those cases where people are hurt because of a car or because a doctor or some professional has injured them?

Well, if somebody else injured them, I think that they should, I shouldn't say pay the price, but be responsible for that, at a reasonable price, whatever. *I suppose, for instance, medical bills plus whatever. My brother was in a serious automobile accident. It went on for years, the court thing. His medical bills were finally paid but my father had to refinance the house because they weren't* *kicking in, you know? It was out-of-state. I found a thing in the paper when I was going through my parents' stuff and my brother got $50,000.*

Probably seemed like a huge sum of money. How much went to pay the medical bills?

Exactly. And he still has problems. He'll never be the same. **But that's another thing that's real hard to look for the future and say, you need $100,000 more ten years from now. Are you going to live that long? But I think they should be responsible at a reasonable price, but it's hard to put a price on those things.**

It is. There are people who believe doctors maybe shouldn't be sued. Where do you land, one way or the other? You sort of said it's okay. How do you feel about people who say, doctors, they're trying to help people, things happen, the insurance rates are driving them away and those kinds of things. What are your thoughts and feelings about that?

If they are really negligent – like the one I was on was definitely negligent.

And you've had that benefit of being a juror in a medical case.

It's not that they should pay the price, but something should be done, be it that he has to go back to school for a while or he has his license taken away or – the money thing sometimes doesn't really matter. Sometimes they can walk out, maybe have their license taken away and go somewhere else and hang up a shingle, I don't know.

Even if it was just an honest – an oversight.

Right.

Trying their best.

It was for the anesthesiologist – it was an oversight, unfortunately. I really felt sorry for her.

For the anesthesiologist?

Yeah. Because she gave too much whatever and it burned her lungs all the way down. She had insurance besides the hospital, but she got stripped of everything. She's gone. She doesn't have her career anymore. And I really feel sorry for her.

I'm surprised.

I don't know how that all occurred. Maybe she had three or four other ones behind her.

Maybe so.

We didn't know. Nobody said anything. One thing that happened, that was a mock jury, they came in and the doctor – we didn't know she was a doctor. And she acted like one of us. She didn't have that nose up in the air. Finally she said,

I just want to confess some of this stuff to you. And that's when she said, she's already gotten a settlement. And if you give her this settlement, that's fine, she said, because it was such a big settlement, for different parts of the hospital. You know, it was the doctor, the anesthesiologist. It was the equipment. They thought the hospital was going to close, because she got so much money.

Was this a mock jury for the defense or for the plaintiff, the injured person? Do you know?

I don't know. So you're in that and you think of things that would happen. And I don't want to see a hospital closed. I feel real sorry for this injured person. She's severely injured. What do you say, you know?

Well, let's talk about this. Our civil justice system, we can't undo what happened.

Right.

All we can do is fashion a money remedy. That's justice. Justice is money, money is justice.

Kind of.

As you know, there are different kinds of damages. You have special damages, like medical bills and wage losses and actual out-of-pocket expenses. You saw the lawyers put those up on the board, right? Then there's that other kind of damage where, you get the instruction that says, these are general damages for pain, suffering, disability, loss of enjoyment of life.

Yes.

For which there are no fixed standards. How do you go about determining what is right in those situations? Some people will lean more to say, I don't believe in giving general damages at all, because money isn't going to make the person better. I'll pay for their medical bills, and I'll pay for their wages, or we'll give them money for that, but we're not going to give them money for pain and suffering. What's your feeling about that?

If they can prove their pain and suffering; the mock jury I was in, we can tell what's going to happen. She has to have a nurse 24 hours a day. But we did ask, why we were figuring out for her for pain and suffering? The rebuttal on that was they can take her out. They can take her to any place and she has to have money to travel and money – special this and special that. I can kind of see that.

You mean money to help her do things that would help restore her quality of life?

Yes. Is that part of that?

I think so.

*You know, **I think it's individual. I don't think there's a dollar amount to say, everybody that was this, and you had a whiplash or you had this that five years down the road you'll be fine or** – you know, your body is so funny.*

I noticed you have walking sticks.

I have MS.

Are you controlled?

Pretty much.

Good.

Sometimes. The walking sticks help me balance. I walk a lot. I try to keep going, because if you don't, if you sit and go boo-hoo, you're going to end up in bed.

You know what I say? If you're going through hell, just keep going.

Yeah, right? Oh, well. It works. The walking sticks work. And we're going to take a trip, so I wanted to make sure I get – I've been swimming. I'm going to keep going. But back to the pain and suffering, another thing that pops into my mind, just because of my brother, he's the type of person that does not want to be cared for. He didn't get disability for –

For his accident?

– for Social Security. He could have done that. And maybe the government should step in at some point and say, you get disability if you can prove it. That's why I was saying the body's so different. Five years ago or ten years ago, I didn't have MS, or they didn't think I had MS. Who knew?

People's lives can change in an instant, huh?

Oh, yeah.

And that's kind of the challenge, is if somebody's enjoying their life one day and suddenly the next day, through no fault of their own, not only are they going to have all these expenses, but what they're used to, their quality of life has changed.

That's true.

And the law says that's something that's compensable by the negligent person, or entity. Are you okay with that? I guess that's the question, are you okay with the notion that the law says they're entitled to some money remedy?

I am in favor of that, but it depends on how much. How do you put a price on whatever? You know? *I go to a lot of meetings for MS and whatnot, and some of those people. And what money is going to help them? It's all attitude and that kind of thing.*

Other things. The care.

Yeah, and I think it's just like any accident, you know? You're rehabilitated, that kind of thing. I think the government can help more or somebody could help more. When you're thrown into this thing, you get six weeks of rehab. That usually doesn't do much. You understand what you're supposed to do or how it's going to work, but after that, you're thrown out in the dark. And if you don't have somebody there – so the money thing is real hard. I think it shouldn't be.

I imagine, in your experience on that employment case, you saw people come to money from lots of different value perspectives? Some more, some less?

Oh, yeah.

Tell me about that.

It was interesting. **Most of the people took her average, which was fine. It was a little high, but it was okay. And there was a couple people that said, nobody's worth that much. I don't care who you are. You are not worth that much.** *And they dropped it by another hundred thousand. So what it was, was just the back and forth, a negotiation, until you got down to everybody said, that's fine.*

Did you have a full 12 jurors in your case agree?

Yeah. **So again, how do you put money on a life, particularly?**

And that's what I'd like to hear. Because jurors sometimes say to the lawyers, I wish you would explain to us how much we should give and give us a good reason for it. Well, we struggle as much as everybody.

Oh, I'm sure you do. And do you say, okay, every five years we reevaluate your situation?

Which we can't do.

Are you walking? Good?

Right. This is the one opportunity. The biggest fear we have is the jury will go too low, because this is the one shot.

Right.

Let's talk about the burden of proof. You've been able to do criminal cases and civil cases, so you know that the burden of proof in a criminal case is beyond a reasonable doubt. In a civil case, it's a preponderance. What does that suggest to you? A preponderance of the evidence?

Do you have a dictionary?

If you could give a stab at it, then I'll give you more on that. What do you think? What does the word preponderance mean?

I don't know.

Okay. That's all right. You remember the instructions?

Yes.

The instruction goes on to read, a preponderance of the evidence is, the evidence has been shown to be more likely than not true.

What they present.

And what does that suggest to you, the burden of proof, when it's more likely than not? How much more likely than not do you need?

I would like at least over half.

Of course. Fifty-one/forty-nine?

That they can prove. In my case, there was proof, because they had all the documentation, so there was no, I wonder if.

Although there was still a lot you didn't hear, right?

Oh, I'm sure there is.

Some people say, I need to have at least 70% or 60% evidence. Whereas other people might say, a preponderance or more likely just means 51%/49%. Just enough to tip the scales. That's what you feel?

Oh, definitely.

Did you feel that the jurors in your case were that way? The case you sat on? Were they more or less like that or was that really not an issue?

I don't think it was an issue on that one. Not at all.

If the case is very, very close but there's just enough to tip it, you're okay with that?

Yes.

You indicated some experience in chemistry and biology and in technology as well. I think of those as scientific and technical fields. How have they shaped you?

I always shied away from the hard science, because I was afraid of it. And when I got into it, it was so interesting. It has opened my eyes. I had so much fun, especially in chemistry, making all these things. And that opened my eyes. As far as the technical end of it, I went into it in about 1980 so it was under DOS. I got into a company that wrote their own software under XENIX and UNIX, which is powerful. Hospitals and stuff like that use them. So I thought, I'm going to learn everything about it. I read the manuals. I read the books. I got pretty good at it. Things changed. Oh, my God, things changed. Then they ported over to Windows, because that's what everybody wanted. You don't have Windows? Forget it. You're not with Microsoft? Forget it. So I tried to start learning, and learned what I had to. Then they give me these articles and I said, not going to do it unless I have to. Sorry. There's too much. Things have really changed.

The reason I ask the question is because there are different kinds of sensibilities that are helpful for jurors to have. One is empathy. I think you show a lot of empathy and understanding. We sometimes find that technical people, engineers, software developers, scientists, may tend to be more black and white, more data-driven, less empathetic. And I'm curious to know –

That's true.

– how your scientific background has shaped you that way in terms of reliance on data as opposed to reliance on empathy and your feelings?

I was in the dental field, and they were writing dental programs. I was able to help them develop, which was really fun. And then I trained. I had empathy for these people. They don't know how to hold a mouse. This was right at the get-go. They'd call and I'd say, what hand do you have the mouse in? That helps. What are you clicking? It's really funny what I had to tell people to do. No modems. You couldn't log in. I was on the road from the border to California because we supported. If we couldn't figure it out, we were on the road seeing what was happening to keep them working. So on that part, I had empathy knowing that something new and so aggravating and –

You were on the teaching end of things and not developing.

Yes. The only development was just, I think you should do this.

There's a sense with people in software and engineering that there's only a right or a wrong because they're used to dealing with zeroes and ones.

There has to be. That's right.

They're often a challenge to reach when it comes to having them be jurors.

Do you skip them?

You can only get rid of so many. Sometimes you have people on your panel – it's the devil you know.

So next time I'm on, I'll say I'm a techie.

How about having grandchildren? How has that affected you as a potential juror?

Very interesting. They're so open-minded, energetic, go-for-it type kids. And I've tried to be a great grandmother.

Not a great-grandmother, but a great grandmother.

Right. Let's – oh, you want to do that? Let's do it. Let's try. Let's go for it. I don't say, what are you doing?

Positive.

Right. Exactly. All the kids were home-schooled. One of them graduated college, another one's in college and one of them is thinking –

Has the experience of raising a child and having grandchildren allowed you to be more open-minded in your life?

I think so. Definitely. Raising a child, it's hard. Kids are hard to raise. I just didn't realize it, in my era.

We talked about lawyers being credible and what they could do to show you they were credible, establish a human connection with you. What can the lawyer do in the very outset? I'm going to ask this question two different ways. What can they do at the outset to show you they're human, that they're developing a human connection? On the flip side, what can they do to ensure that they ruin that opportunity to show you they're human or that connection?

The most recent one, I don't know if I was biased about that she was a female, she was good. She had all the empathy. She felt sorry for her, why did this happen?

Did it appear that she cared for her client?

Yes. Yes.

Did that matter? Was that important?

I think so. And that she wasn't taking her for a ride. I had a lawyer once from my divorce. Only saw him once or twice, and it was not a big divorce. We got into court and he said, what am I here for? But she knew her client, she knew what was going on. She was really behind her. It was not like, oh, I'm not sure. She didn't come on that way.

So her relationship with the client –

Client. Helped me –

Helped you to see that she was a human?

Right. Exactly. The other guy was Columbo.

In the jury selection part, when she first gets up and you all are trying to get introduced in that short period of time, what do you think would be something the lawyer can do to establish a connection with you? Or again, what could they do to destroy that?

Well, I think instead of lecturing to us –

Is that what happened?

No. She was great. She would pick out somebody and say or ask a question and people were raising their hands. They wanted to be involved. And she wanted them to be involved.

You could tell that?

Oh, yeah.

Was she attractive?

No. She was over 60. In fact, I asked her, and she said, I'm never going to retire. She was very good, very nice.

She was experienced. Was that something that came across?

Oh, yeah. She was good. And I loved how she nailed the other lawyer all the time. And she was right.

She had the case for it.

*She was right. I felt he just bumbled around in life. I was surprised he got there. He must have had somebody drive him. I don't know. **But that helps if the lawyer talks to, not individually going down the line, but something comes up and they ask your opinion and what ifs.** Like you're doing right now.*

We're doing it. Was the jury talking back and forth to each other at some point? Did she say, Mr. Juror, how do you feel about what you just heard from your Neighbor Juror?

No. I didn't hear that at all. Maybe, when you're first kind of coming into it, you don't talk among yourselves, and I don't think she asked anybody that question.

What kind of a juror would you want if you were a plaintiff in an injury case? What personality, what traits would you like to see?

*Well, **really empathetic.***

Empathetic.

Oh, yeah. And hoping that they could bring out, if I was really injured, that I was a really good, responsible person to begin with; that I wasn't some trash coming out of the tavern, and that kind of thing.

Empathy. What would you least like to see in a potential juror sitting in judgment?

***One that doesn't pay very much attention.** Or they give you things to write on and so you see people doodling.*

How did you feel about the opportunity to ask questions, to the extent the judge actually read them.

Oh, he didn't read them.

He didn't read them?

He read them and then asked why? Now, what do you mean? He went on. He was a good judge. We always thought he was playing games on his computer. We didn't know what he was doing up there, you know? When we came to a conclusion, we all started yelling, and he came into the jury and he says, are you guys okay?

Because you all agreed and it was happy.

Right. Right.

How long did that take? The deliberations?

Two days. We had to. We had no choice.

You had to. You felt some pressure?

He was cutting it off.

Did your experience working for a dentist cause you to look at medical cases differently? Malpractice cases? Given that you worked for a dentist? How would you feel if a dentist was being sued? Could you still handle a case like that?

Sure. It depends on what it is. I feel like I have enough knowledge to know if he screwed up or not.

Maybe a little more than the average person?

Oh, I would think. But who knows? I could probably be okay with that. The thing that I don't understand nowadays is, is any medical thing is, they accuse him, and he's kind of guilty and they let him have his license and still work. I don't quite understand that.

Because mistakes are permissible, and that's why we have insurance. People don't lose their license for a mistake. That's why you don't lose your driver's license if you have an accident, necessarily. Unless there's some other factor like you've been drinking or you have a drug problem or some other issue. If a person didn't know you, such as myself, and I'm meeting you as a juror for the first time, how would you describe the person that you are? What traits would you say you possess?

I'm outgoing, I'm loveable. I hope I come on as, I'd help anybody.

Is there anything that you wouldn't want us to know but that would be important to know in a jury selection process?

One thing I've been hiding kind of – not hiding –

Other than what we talked about earlier?

I do take medical marijuana.

That's not uncommon.

And I know it's not uncommon, but it makes me feel funny. It's like, I'm a druggie.

Well, given the era we grew up in, right?

Exactly.

It's always been illegal.

Exactly. Where I grew up, everybody was toking and it was, experienced. Ooh, I've never done this before. Then when I was able to get medical marijuana, I kind of keep it under my hat.

Of course. Did it come out in the trial at all?

Well, I was having really bad spells. He was okay with that, but I had to have help getting into the jury box, I had to have help getting out. The jurors were so nice to me.

In helping you?

Everybody would go to lunch and sometimes, I'd get there by the time they'd eaten and were ready to come back. But they would have my lunch for me. Those people were absolutely wonderful on the jury.

You had a good group.

I had a wonderful group.

Tell me what you think was the quality that allowed that group to be such a good group?

I think one of the things was not only more or less their age groups, but their values were all the same. It was like a camaraderie that they'd probably be friends; everybody, very respectful.

Did you have any lightning rods on that group; people that monopolized and talked way more than other?

Oh, yes. One.

There's usually one in any group.

About the third or fourth day I couldn't stand her. And I'm not like that. I let everybody have whatever and try to choose what's the best in them, see what we can work with. Everybody was getting that vibe from me. And it was really cute. There was a young college student, he wasn't 21 yet, because we all went to drink and he couldn't go. He tried to sit next to me. One day he sat right next to me, put his computer up, so she couldn't horn in. People were taking care of me without any words. But she was older, and probably thought I was the same age. Like you said, there's always one.

There tends to be. It's the nature of groups. I was curious to know if the medication issues made it difficult for you to concentrate during the daytime?

Sure. They change them. I'm taking one medication for pain and it's for epilepsy. But it works. I'm not that bad. I guess it depends on your neurologist.

When you were in that trial or those trials, did you ever have an intention or desire to go online and look at the web pages about the lawyers that were trying the cases?

No.

Afterwards?

Yes.

Do you think any of your fellow jurors may have wanted to do that?

Oh, they did do it. During the trials.

Do you suppose that had any real consequence to the way they viewed the case?

I don't think so. I don't think there's that much information about a lawyer. Is that what you're saying? I've got the lawyers name and where they graduated –

How they present themselves online. Some very, very fine lawyers have huge results.

Fancy websites.

Lots of charitable contributions, things like that, that I think are designed to –

Impress.

-- impress their credibility online for those who don't know them. I was just curious.

No, I didn't do that.

When the lawyers are trying to find out about the biases or the prejudgments that the jurors have, that you have, would it be, in your mind, appropriate for the lawyer to say, before I ask you to share with me what your biases are, let me share something of myself. I have bias, too. For example, lately, I haven't liked bicyclists. I would have a hard time with a bicyclist case right now because they anger me. Would that, I'll show you mine, you show me yours contract be fair and appropriate?

I think so. Very fair. And that's where you get your – I think the credibility; that you'll open up and that makes other people open up. Oh, definitely.

Thank you.

42

SHADES OF GRAY

Caucasian male, age 65, married, IT Project Manager/Retired, Masters Business; B.S. Computer Engineering

When you get older, you understand that life is shades of gray. But young people, it's all black and white. That's why, when the radical people are marching down the street, it's all young people. Because they see the world in black and white.

The judge says, ladies and gentlemen, please give your attention to the attorney for the plaintiff who will conduct his or her portion of jury selection. At that point, as you sit there, what is going through your mind?

Curious what the case is all about, of course. Curious on where I am in the line, because there's a lot more jurors there than they'll actually need. I'm thinking, am I in the front, or I am all the way in back? Am I going to end up getting called? I'm calculating how many people are ahead of me and how many might get disqualified. Are they going to get to me in line? So I'm trying to guess, am I going to get called?

How do you feel about the notion of being selected if you are chosen?

*A little bit anxious. **When I was working, I was not really inclined as I didn't want to have to take a week out of my life or my busy schedule. Now that I'm retired, I was looking forward to it because I had the time.** But then I had this health issue, so I couldn't go. That's the big determinate to me. While I was working, I didn't want to. When I'm retired, I was more interested because I had the time. So those are the things I would be thinking about.*

Many people express time as a big value issue for them; time and money. When you were working, what sort of work were you doing?

Project management was my last job. Do you know what that means?

I do. In this day and age, you pretty much have to, right?

In an IT department.

Got it. So as you sit there and feel this curiosity and anxiousness, do you have any feelings or thoughts leaning one way or another towards a tendency to favor one side without knowing anymore?

In a civil case, no. In a criminal case, I would probably have a bias. But in civil case, no. I don't come in with any bias.

That's good. The overriding purpose of jury selection is to identify individuals who may have biases, prejudices, prejudgments, or inclinations to go one side or another without having heard the evidence. How do you think you'd come in on that, without hearing anymore?

Not even knowing what the case is, I wouldn't have any bias. I'd have to know what it's about to be able to take a position.

Everyone's different on the spectrum, but some lean more towards, they don't believe that people should sue other people, for lots of valid reasons. Religious reasons, for example. Some people feel that the system's out of control and there are escalating jury verdicts; that there are too many frivolous lawsuits, those sorts of things. Do you feel strongly one way or another about that?

No, I think everybody ought to have the right to sue if they feel they've been wronged.

Okay. Understanding these are generally negligence cases, where the harm is not intentional, but accidental, or as a result of some kind of negligence or even reckless conduct?

People ought to be free to sue. That's a right that everybody has.

Expressing that, do you have any feelings in your life experience suggesting that jury verdicts are out of control or that there's too much litigation in our society?

There do seem to be a fair number of frivolous lawsuits I've read about it in the paper. It's always the 1% of crazy ones that make the news. *The person who sues McDonald's because the coffee was hot. That is ridiculous. If I ended up in one of those, I would definitely throw it out. I'd say, no way. So yeah, it is possible. If I ran into a frivolous one, I would definitely be biased. But in general, there probably are more lawsuits than there ought to be. There's a lot that have no real grounds and never should have made it to trial.*

Have you had any experience where you've been either on one side or the other involved in litigation?

No, I have not. No.

Anybody close to you that's had that experience?

No. Closest thing is my wife's been on a couple of juries. She's told me. But personally, no. I've not been involved myself nor has anybody I know personally been a party to a lawsuit.

To me, the overriding purpose of this is to determine who can be open-minded and fair. I would lie if I said I didn't want people to be more open-minded toward my case, but I hope I can identify those people who can be fair-minded in general, or, identify those who have a specific bias.

You're saying how do you pick those out?

How would an attorney best ask you to express what sort of prejudgments you might have even if you didn't feel you had any? What would be the most fair way to ask you?

How much does a jury know before that point where you have the opportunity to ask? How much do they know about the case?

Just what I told you. An individual is claiming that they've been injured through some negligence and they're seeking a money recovery as a result, or a money remedy.

So what could you ask me? Well, you could ask me that question you asked a moment ago, **what are you concerned about? What are you thinking about right now when you're coming to jury? Are you worried about time away from work? Because I would think somebody who is very worried about time away from work would be wanting to expedite it** *and say, fine, guilty, whatever everybody else is saying. They'd want to just say, go ahead, I'm not going to be different than everybody else.* **So that would be a good question, if you could find out if people are anxious about their time. I can understand that a lot of people can't afford to be away from work. Other things, you could ask them if, again, following an earlier question you had, if anybody they know personally has been in a similar case and how that came out? And how did they feel about that case?** *Can you ask them that?*

I think so.

How you feel about another case that's a similar one?

That's a fair question. Let me ask this question: the bigger threat to me would be what I call the snake in the grass, the person who has an agenda, who may wish to advance that agenda against the ends of my case. That sometimes happens when we have jurors who, let's say, work for insurance companies or who are very close to doctors, for example, who have been sued. How do we identify those people? How do you think would be a fair, a non-manipulative way to ask those people in a non-threatening way?

Oh, you can't just come out and ask them?

We can, but we don't know who those people are at this point.

Well, you've got the form here that answers some of those questions, doesn't it?

Sometimes. Most often, no, because we often only get this form as they're walking into the courtroom at the same time as we're about ready to question.

Oh, you don't get it ahead of time?

We have only about an hour to talk to a large group of people nowadays.

You don't get the information about the jurors before they walk in?

Only at about the same time.

That's makes it hard if you don't have time to go through that.

Right. And often they don't fill it out as fully as we would hope.

Oh. Well, I guess I'm still wondering if, well, except you can't repeat the same, you have probably a limited number of questions you can ask, right?

You can ask almost any question of any individual or to the entire group. By a show of hands or –

Oh, so you could say, by show of hands, who's worked in the insurance industry?

I could ask that.

Who's got a friend that's a doctor?

I could ask those two questions.

Well, those seem like very relevant questions. And asking them of everybody, by showing of hands, seems like an expedient way to pick out the ones that you're trying to ferret out.

Believe it or not, in all the years I've been doing this, I don't think I've seen a lawyer ask if anybody works in the insurance industry, please raise your hands. They maybe avoid that question, but certainly it's a –

That's surprising.

In part, because we are trained that we're not allowed to introduce insurance into a case because of prejudicial concern. The law doesn't want jurors to know that insurance is possibly behind one of the parties' abilities to pay damages; the theory being that jurors may assess more damages if they know an insurance company is paying it.

I would think most jurors would always assume there's an insurance company involved in there somewhere.

You'd be surprised at how many don't think about that and how many do. Much is not known. Are you comfortable? Are you okay? It appears you have a disability.

Yes.

Generally speaking, the clients in personal injury cases are displaying some injury themselves.

Yes.

Given you have some discomfort, how would you tend to empathize more or view their case or their injuries?

My disability is a diagnosis of cancer. So it's not an injury; it's a disease I came down with.

[Brief discussion off the record]

We were talking about if you may tend to empathize more with an injured person given the condition you have now?

I possibly would. If I see somebody who's been physically harmed sitting in the courtroom, it's hard not to have some empathy for them.

I think that's fair. Another purpose of jury selection, though it's not expressed by law, is an opportunity to establish a human connection with the jurors. By that I mean, to show that we have credibility. How can the lawyer establish a human connection with you in that moment given the constraints of the situation?

That is hard, considering that lawyers in general are not liked by the public in general, because lawyers are associated with bad things like trials. Everybody hates trials. And you have a very short amount of time. So that is a huge task to do that. So how can you appear more human?

Or just establish –

A rapport?

– credibility. Show that there's genuineness.

Mm-hmm. I'm thinking.

While you're thinking, let me echo what you said, which is, studies show that plaintiff's trial lawyers are second to the bottom on the list of credibility among professions. So we're coming in already behind, having to catch up.

I guess. I think a lot of it would have to be in your manner and tone of voice and body language. In the short time you have, expressing an interest in the person and caring about them in any way you can by tone of voice and body language, I think, would be your best chance with the very limited time you have to ask any question at all. Because they say the words are only 20, 30% of what is communicated?

That's what they say. And the non-verbal is –

Is the majority of the message, so I think that's what you have to shoot for is making good use of the non-verbals in your interrogation of the jury.

Do you feel, one way or another, that it's appropriate or not for the attorney to share something of his or herself?

Sure. If that's applicable somehow. If that fits, that would make the lawyer seem more human.

In a way that is not perceived as a manipulation by a juror such that they may get defensive and dig in? Can you think of a way that the attorney could do that, at least for you, that would seem non-manipulative? Or not pandering?

I guess I have a tendency to want to believe people when they express an interest in me and my welfare, my own interests. So if a lawyer could express some empathy toward my situation as a juror, and the situation I'm in, then I would tend to want to believe them and would have some openness toward that. What else can you do?

Some people advocate validation of the potential jurors' responses regardless of what the response is, genuine validation.

Sure. That's part of good two-way communication.

As a project manager in the IT world, and I'm glad that you have this set of skills and background, because one of the most difficult jurors we have to reach are tech jurors, because they're very binary in their thinking. Or they tend to be. And tend to be less empathetic because of that. Not so much middle ground. Not so much life experience.

Everything is black and white; for tech people with a technical background, you're saying?

Yes. I have been told that throughout the tech industry, that may differ. For example, project managers tend to have a different view point than, say, tech developers.

Yes. Yes. You're right.

What subset of human skills do you bring to the table?

*As a project manager, I have to have the ability to work with people who come from different backgrounds. Some of them, a little bit like your situation, they get assigned to my project, and sometimes they don't want to be there. They have other work they would rather be doing. But their manager said they have to come to my meeting. **And developing some sensitivity to who they are and why they have to be there at my meeting and especially expressing some empathy for the fact they have other things in their work load makes it easier for them, for me to get them to do work for me.** I ask them to help me define, what's a reasonable schedule? How long do you think it's going to take to do this and this and this and this? Then they get buy-in to the project and they feel they have a voice in setting the schedules and the workload, and I get more cooperation that way. Because I just can't come in and dictate because the project managers have all the responsibility and no authority. I have no authority over the people who get assigned to my projects. So I have to reason my way into their good graces.*

And yet you also have an engineering background. So you're used to there being a solution to a problem.

Of course. Yes.

But dealing with people, that's a little different.

Again, I have to try to get them to buy in to the work.

How do you do that? Is that through an emotional appeal or is there data to back up that appeal?

Well, again, getting them to help define what has to be done makes them feel that it's their project, too.

Getting them invested.

Right. I sound like I'm repeating myself. Getting them to define what the – we have a thing called a work breakdown schedule. We break the work down into littler pieces. Getting people involved in that gets them to feel more that it's their project and they are defining all the parameters, whereas I'm usually controlling that and I'm often manipulating the way things are coming out. But I get their buy-in. In a jury setting, how does that apply? Gosh. You can't exactly – you're not laying out a project schedule in a jury setting.

Generally I know who the engineers on the jury are.

So you're just saying, how do you get them to buy in?

We often have, for example, aerospace engineers, or nowadays, computer technology, Internet or those sorts of things. They generally have, in the past, been jurors we would tend to not want on the juries. In part because when it would come to the money determination, they tended to not have the sensitivity to make awards. Let's move onto damages for a moment. Because this is really where the rubber meets the road for us. We generally are not getting to court if liability and causation are big issues. Generally, that part of it is pretty much proved or we feel comfortable about it. What we're there for is to get the jury to award an amount that is an appropriate remedy for the client. That's where the dispute usually is; the defense doesn't want to pay it and the plaintiff wants or needs it.

Oh. Is it the jury that decides how much is to be awarded?

That's right. So here's the thing: we have two kinds of damages. We have special damages which are especially identified. We can say that we have medical bills –

Oh. Quantifiable.

– and wage loss. Even though there may be some expert testimony and some differences of opinion, generally speaking, those can be penciled in.

*Yeah. **They're objective; you can quantify them in one way or other.** And then there's the other kind.*

What we call general damages, which are pain, suffering, disability, loss of enjoyment of life, for which the Court's instruction says there is no objective criterion for making a determination. In other words, it's entirely within your judgment. How would you go about thinking about general damages? Do you tend to be more conservative or more liberal in that?

*I've never actually been in a situation where I had to think that through. **That's a hard thing to decide.** My first inkling would be to go back and look at other similar cases and see what they were awarded. In project management, what you do when you have a new project is, you go back and look for a previous project* *that was similar and try to learn from it. So that's my first inclination. I don't know if you can bring that in.*

Generally, we cannot.

You cannot bring in awards from other ones?

Generally. Some people have suggested data in some form or another, some metric, if we could come up with it, could be helpful.

It can help.

Especially with data-driven individuals.

Right. People who are the engineers.

Because the binary thinkers have expressed they can't make that decision because there's no right or wrong for them in which to do it.

You're right. And they like right or wrong. I started my career as a programmer. I understand engineers, because I was one. And you're right. Everything is black and white. Either the machine works or it doesn't work.

And often, we find that these jurors tend to be somewhat younger.

Yes.

And not having the life experience.

***When you get older, you understand that life is shades of gray. But young people, it's all black and white.** That's why, when the radical people are marching down the street, it's all young people. Because they see the world in black and white.*

Idealistic.

Very. So how do you get through to them?

Do you feel comfortable being able to make a money remedy if it's proven that there was an injury caused through negligence?

*Comfortable? Not entirely, no. If I were in that position, I would obviously have to figure out some way to do it. **Thinking of a metric, I think, is a very good approach. What does it break down to, this injury to this person? How many years of their life are affected? Right? What is one year worth?***

And that's the big question, isn't it?

One year of this injury, how much is that affecting people?

What would you like to know about or hear about? What information would help you?

Well, to know what their standard of living is currently. And of course, we've talked about all the specific –

Special damages.

> *Special damages. But beyond that, what can make up for the harm that they have experienced?*

And may experience in the future.

> *You're right. What's it cost to make up for those things? What's it cost to hire somebody to do things that you can't do yourself? Right? To make up for it. If you have to hire a companion to go with you on a trip or a task. How much do those things cost? Before you were harmed, you could take a trip to Disneyland by yourself or for you and your family. Now, you're in a position where you can't do that. You would need special care. How much does that cost? How much is it worth? How much is a trip to Disneyland worth if you can't go? Compensation. How many things do you have to give up, are you giving up as a result of this injury? And how much are those things worth? And how much supplemental help do you need to do the things you used to be able to do yourself? Right?*

There are people who, when asked to think about special damages and general damages, they're comfortable awarding special damages because they can see that. They can be given a rationale. But they don't believe a person should be compensated for pain and suffering. Some people say, accidents happen; life happens; suck it up.

> *That's heartless.*

It's not uncommon. How do you feel about that?

> *That's surprising that people could have that little compassion. It just surprises me. I would have thought everybody would have some degree of compassion, it was just a measure of how much.*

Well, and they may. It may not have time to reach that in the course of the trial. I'm not sure. Maybe it hasn't been triggered yet.

> *Boy, anybody who says that is going to get some bad karma coming their way.*

To help you understand some of that, there are people who believe, for example, by awarding general damages, things like insurance rates will go up and doctors may leave the community. And there are costs associated that may come back to them.

> *I think insurance companies are in the business of handling those things. They've already got those things figured in. As long as it's not exorbitant and outlandish, I think it's very appropriate people should have some general damages. Getting awarded how many thousands of dollars for spilling hot coffee on yourself at McDonald's, no. It's your own dumb fault; you should know coffee is hot. But for someone who's suffered an injury by no fault of their own, no. To me, there's no question they deserve something, it's just a question of how much.*

Let me shift over to the burden of proof. In criminal cases, it's beyond a reasonable doubt, which is still a subjective standard. But in civil cases, the instruction says that,

if you find by a preponderance of the evidence – what does a preponderance mean to you?

That's it's highly likely. That it's 95%. Maybe it's not 100%, but it's 90, 95%; that anybody would reasonably conclude that it was what it seems to be.

If the instruction were further read to you that a preponderance of the evidence is more likely than not, does that do anything to that percentage?

I don't understand. The instruction in what context?

The instruction that was given to the jury when they go to the jury room to deliberate is, if you find by a preponderance of the evidence – which means proved more likely than not – does that number get less than 90 or 95% for you?

What the special – I mean, what the general damages are?

Any element that needs to be proved. The burden of proof is more likely than not in a civil context.

Okay. So you're asking, would I award a lower amount or a higher amount depending on how great the preponderance is?

The question really is more your threshold of decision making. When we talked about preponderance, you said you felt it needed to be proved by 90-95% or some clear reasonable amount.

Right.

Whereas, when they say, more likely than not, does that bring the weight to prove the case –

*Oh. **Well, more likely than not, that seems to be more like a simple majority.***

Okay.

Fifty-one percent.

How comfortable would you be with that if that were the burden of proof?

*That it only had to be 51%? **Less comfortable if it were closer to 50/50, very close to that. Fairly less comfortable in awarding damages if it's that far off. So there is some kind of correlation between the degree of the preponderance and the degree of the award. In my mind, there's going to be some kind of correlation there.***

The bigger the award, the more you'd want to feel comfortable about it?

Yeah. That it was with great certainty.

How do you feel about professional negligence? Cases that are brought against doctors or other professionals that have a higher degree of experience and also trust with their patients?

I think that's pretty bad.

How so?

I expect professionals to be able to make the right call at the right time. I don't have a lot of patience for professional incompetence.

If a case were brought against a physician or a medical facility the physician worked for, there are many people that are very uncomfortable with those kinds of cases, which can be demonstrated by the fact that nine out of ten times when a doctor is sued, the doctor will win.

He does, huh?

Very, very difficult cases to win.

Interesting. I'm pissed off at one of my doctors, but I'm not suing him because of that same reason.

Are you feeling that there was a misdiagnosis or failure to treat?

Yeah. I had a low back problem starting in October, and tried my usual going to chiropractors, and it didn't work. I went to my doctor. He did an x-ray in December, and said, nope, nothing, everything's fine. Have some physical therapy. I went to a couple rounds of physical therapy, and it didn't fix my back problem. Finally in June I got an appointment, with a different doctor – my regular doctor wasn't there that day – and I insisted on an MRI. I want to know what's going on with my back. At that point, they looked at it and said, Stage III cancer. So I am angry that my doctor didn't find something six months earlier in December when he did this x-ray and said, everything's fine.

Or referred you to a specialist for the MRI at least.

I wish I'd had the MRI in December, six months earlier; could have caught this.

Given your staging profile perhaps differently.

[Brief discussion]

We were talking about burden of proof, and that being, more likely than not, maybe something closer to that 51/49%, and your level of comfort with that.

*Yes. Right. And the degree of the award. **I would probably bias my opinion on the size of the award according to the degree in which the evidence was a preponderance.** It is just a little? Is it 51% or is it 99%?*

These kinds of cases are often very expert-driven. In other words, both sides are bringing in experts to talk about relevant areas because they're beyond the province of the individual - medical, technical skills. How do you feel about experts in these cases and do you feel that experts tend to be more or less biased given who they're working for?

Yes, I would say they are biased; that you can find an expert to attest to

almost anything if you really want to. If you look long enough, you can find somebody to support whatever thesis you have. I take any expert opinion with a grain of salt.

We find that jurors, generally speaking, are not critical of one expert making huge amounts of money for their time and an opposite expert making very little. They don't attribute a bias because of the amount of money the expert may be earning. In fact, they say, good for the expert, and the other one needs to up their game. How do you feel about that? How would you detect who's more objective?

I would be surprised that the juror would know how much the expert was being paid.

We're allowed to elicit that in cross-examination as a potential bias.

Oh, I see. Sure. For enough money –

Or they've testified for the same side time and time again. Generally speaking, jurors are not too affected by that. What's your thought?

I would be more suspicious of somebody who's paid a huge amount, yes. I would discount their testimony. I'd be more interested in the credentials of any so-called expert. What's the basis for his alleged expertise? That weighs more heavily to me than what they're being paid.

We find that there are experts, in both sides, that there are highly credentialed experts whose opinions may be, at least we feel, less objective than others. But we do try to find credentialed experts. Credentials these days, I don't think jurors really understand a lot about that.

There's a whole lot of initials people have after their names and it's hard to know what they all mean.

And they can have written dozens of papers, but in an entirely different area than what they're testifying about.

That's possible.

Very difficult. If you were a plaintiff in a civil case, what kind of a juror would you like hearing your case and making an ultimate decision?

Someone who's been in the same spot that I find myself. *That would be ideal.*

What are those traits?

Whatever that injury is, somebody who's had the same injury. I probably go more for female than male, because in general, females I feel are more empathetic. I'd probably, as you alluded, avoid the technical people, because they don't see things in shades of gray. ***Likewise, older people; I think older people make better jurors, because they have the life experience.***

Do you think older people are more or less conservative in their money determinations?

Yeah, they are.

Although we find that young wealthy people are no less conservative.

Interesting. But just, having been around longer, I think people understand the shades of gray; that life is not black and white. And hence, there'd be more empathy for the plaintiff's position, I would think.

If we had never spoken before as we have in this short period of time, what would be a good question of an attorney to ask, what are your values? What are the important values you hold in your life, in a way that wouldn't be intrusive, and that you'd feel comfortable answering?

What's wrong with that question? What are your values? It's not a bad question. Or what's important to you in your life?

What's important to you in your life?

That seems like a fair question just as it stands. You ought to be able to ask that.

What's important in your life? What are your values and principles that guide you?

Well, I'm a Christian, so the basis of my values and morals and ethics is my Christian belief.

Has that been long-held, in your life?

It has been. I have particular areas of concern. I have particular empathy for people who are hungry. I've done a lot of work with hunger organizations, made a lot of contributions to organizations that try to feed people. That's a particular interest of mine. I'd say that's pretty much it. That's where it all comes from, for me.

Is there anything in the discussion I haven't touched on that might be helpful for me or my readers?

As far as jury selection in general?

Jury selection or juror attitudes, biases, beliefs, prejudices, open-mindedness, closed-mindedness, credibility issues.

*I just, in my limited experience of juries, **it surprises me that so many times, questions are asked of just one individual instead of asking questions of everybody, all the prospective jurors.***

When you've been in that selection pool?

Yes, in the pool. Right.

And the attorneys have zeroed in on one person rather than the entire –

Right. They'll spend much of their time, which I guess, there's a limit, asking one individual about a series of questions, instead of asking questions of the whole pool in general. **Because that question that they're spending a lot of time on with this one individual might be extremely relevant to this other person over here whom they've not asked anything. So I've always thought it curious that they didn't ask more questions of, hold up your hand. What do you feel about this? What do you think about this? And try to screen people that way. It would make a lot more sense to me, if I were a lawyer, to do it that way, then you can slip any kind of question in there if you're asking questions of everybody in general. If you see one person who's raising their hand consistently on all the questions that are contrary to your case, then that seems like a good way to screen them out. But spending all your time on just one or two individuals at a time seems a waste of your precious time.**

Our very precious time. Thank you.

43

THE BAD GUYS – A MATTER OF PERSPECTIVE

Caucasian female, age 61, married, two children, OB-GYN/Retired, M.D.

In the medical profession, there's this cone of silence around the bad guys.

The judge then says, ladies and gentlemen, please give your attention to the attorney for the plaintiff who's going to conduct jury selection. What are you feeling or thinking about the process or just being there?

It's unfamiliar, and I'm very interested in how it's going to proceed.

As a medical doctor, how did you feel about the convenience or inconvenience of being called for jury service?

*It was before I retired. Now it would be fun. But before I retired, I'd been called before, and I just couldn't go because I was either on call or somebody was due; I promised to deliver. Then the last time I was called, I was winding down. I had stopped delivering babies. I was just doing surgery, and I was in the office so I could carve out the week. I thought, finally, I can do this. I wanted to be there, because it's part of being a citizen. I was interested in the experience. So I was able to. **But it still was terribly inconvenient.***

Nearly everybody feels that way.

*I'm sure. **Plus, if I don't work, I don't make money. I gave up a week's pay and I have family and staff and rent in my office and all that to support. So it was quite a sacrifice as well.***

A lot overhead for sure. Was this a criminal or a civil case?

Criminal.

Since we're imaging that we're here for a civil case, how do you feel, given your background, about the civil justice system and what it seeks to accomplish?

Well, I think every story's different. There certainly are categories of stories. I think there are so many people who are injured in so many ways who need this avenue for justice, for sure. And I think there are lots and lots and lots of cases where there's fraud, insurance fraud, and there are acts of God that are attributed to personal negligence. So it runs the gamut.

It sounds like you're open-minded enough, and many people express that they don't feel that way, but that you're open-minded enough to appreciate each situation as being different.

I hope so.

That's our goal, to identify those people who can be unbiased and unprejudiced going in. How do you feel that question would be best asked of you, to determine whether or not you'd be suitable and open-minded for a case?

Well, you kind of got what you were looking for, so the way you asked it was good. I think if people are really single-minded about, it's all ridiculous or whatever, they would say that. So I'm not sure how else you could ask it.

So more or less just directly?

Yeah. I think people will say. I hope.

Everybody is very different. Some people are very hesitant to even speak up. Other people want to speak up.

Everybody's so different. I'm used to talking, and talking directly, so.

In a position of trust, as well. What can be frustrating is we often have to talk to as many as 60, 80, or 100 people in a very short period of time.

I know.

Have colleagues told you about that?

That I could tell from when I was sitting in there. But also, I have talked to thousands and thousands of people, and I have ten minutes to figure out everything about them. I'm asking about what's going on in their vaginas, you know? I gotta get to it.

Have you developed any particular skills that you think help you to get to it; to whatever the issue is that is most important?

Probably. I developed what worked for me, but it's very different from asking questions in front of lots of people. I'm in a room that two people are. Usually I have a little intake form, and you do, too, right? You know what their profession is and blah, blah, blah.

It's not often filled out completely or accurately. But some demographic –

I usually start with something demographic. Oh, you live there? I used to live close by there. Or, you have three kids? You know, whatever, some rapport thing that has nothing to do with what they're there for. I start there. But as I said, it's professional, but you still have to establish a personal connection.

That leads into my next area, which is, as a trial lawyer who the general public does not perceive very well or very credible, I feel at a disadvantage.

Really?

Yes. Plaintiff's trial lawyers are viewed as being the least credible person in the room going in.

I would think criminal defense lawyers would be. Just because whatever the crime is, it's usually bad.

My job, probably even before identifying bias, is to establish a connection with the people, a connection of trust. How do you think the lawyer can do that best without it being manipulation?

I think here, it's different from everywhere else I've lived. Everywhere else I've lived, plaintiff's lawyers did not look like you. They were pointy toe, slick back hair, shiny suit kind of guys. I've been deposed by them several times. It helps that you look like you do. So being one of us is sort of the first step. That's big. Because you don't really get to know the person. So the way you present –

You're seeing me, of course, in a casual get-up.

I know. But you have a little beard, and when you talk, you look people in the eye and you talk kindly. You know, and all that stuff.

I see.

So that makes a huge difference.

Well, thank you for that. I appreciate the feedback. Tell me, since I have the benefit of a medical doctor here, and I'm so grateful for this, tell me how the medical profession views the –

Trial lawyers?

Trial lawyers.

Well, I can't represent all medical professionals, because –

Those who you know –

Different from the average.

You're in a high-risk profession.

*Very. **Most doctors are conservative Republicans,** even here. And I'm not. I'm progressive, liberal, Democrat. So right there, I don't represent most doctors. **The conservative Republicans think everything that's wrong with the medical profession are the trial lawyers. For those of us like me, we don't want to feel that way, because we know that there are a few bad apples.** Kind of like the police, you know?*

Sure. And again, I think any profession.

*Right. **So we're torn. In the medical profession, there's this cone of silence around the bad guys. And given that, the party line is that they're out to get us because they think we have very deep pockets. Which we do, because we spend enormous chunks of our income on insurance, which drives us crazy.** Because here, in this city, there are so many doctors because it's such a great place to live that we do not make anywhere near the average salary of the* *rest of the country, depending on your specialty. But even in my specialty, which is fairly well remunerated, we make about a fifth to a third of what other areas of the country make. I mean, it's significant.*

Is that the region as well?

Oh, especially. Because this is where the doctors live. In the rural areas, you'll make more because you'll see more patients. There's nobody else for them to go to, especially in the specialties and sub-specialties. So we don't make very much money, and sometimes we're paying more for our malpractice than we actually take home. We're very, very angry about that. But it's our own fault, because we chose to live here. We want to live here just like everybody else wants to live here. So there's that. We're paying for people to take potshots at us, basically. And all of us, in my specialty, the average number of suits is between three and four a career.

I didn't know that.

So none of us escapes. Not one of us escapes. And that's not counting what happens in residency where you aren't – I mean, you're personally but you aren't really – so many people have had a hand in whatever you did. It's usually not you. You're in training, so people know you're going to make a mistake. Everybody goes through it. It's horrible. We want to kill ourselves, basically. I mean, literally, you make a plan. It's pretty awful. And most doctors, the vast majority, are doing the best they can every single second, to much detriment to ourselves, our lives, our families, our health, our pocketbooks; all that stuff. So when you get hit, it's like, what's the point? I did a lot good; I saved this person's life, but I'm going to make the same decisions with the same information every time, and then somebody's going to tell me I didn't read this right or there's some – so it's pretty awful. We're sure that trial lawyers have no idea what we're going through; and they don't. So it's awful. That's how we feel. That's how I felt. It's very personal. It's unfair, almost all the time, especially for somebody who feels like they are really doing the very best they can at every moment. And every moment outside of our 8 to 5 in the operating room or the office is shortening our lives, you know?

High stress.

Yeah.

Did you feel the insurance company treated you well or that your lawyers hired in those instances were –

Pretty much.

You felt that –

Pretty much. They understood. They seemed to understand more; quite a bit. They didn't actually get it, but they did. There's a lot of pressure to settle. Lot of pressure.

The insurance companies put a lot of pressure on you to settle?

They wouldn't say that, but it was definitely under the radar. Because it's so much cheaper.

I don't know if you're familiar with this general statistic, but roughly nine out of ten times, doctors will win at trial.

I do know that. I'm aware of all that. But at that point, it doesn't matter. You've already lost so much income from the time you've had to give, and it's the accusation; it's not the verdict. I never went to trial. It's not that. That, we could not care less.

Since we're talking about medical negligence cases, what would be a better solution? What would be a way to minimize the impact on your profession?

I don't know for sure. First of all, we should not be working in any organization that's for profit. It should be a single payer, well-run – so I guess it can't be the government. But that's the dilemma. It should be totally different. There should be no-fault, just physician-only group stuff where you talk weekly, monthly, about hard cases and what you did and I mean, that's been tried and some hospitals do it. But doctors don't want to talk. First of all, you're not supposed to talk about it once you get a suit. You're not supposed to talk to anybody. So there you are with your accusation, by yourself in your bed at night, thinking about killing yourself. So there needs to be support where you can talk about it as much as you want.

Of course, not all outcomes are necessarily as terrible as say, maybe what happens in your profession.

Well, no. There can be outcomes like, I couldn't urinate for five days after my hysterectomy, and I had to have a catheter and that was terrible.

Miss a broken bone, or something.

They're not all tragic, but that doesn't matter.

And of course, those are *de minimis*.

Those are what we call nuisances. You show the patient, or the lawyer shows the patient the consent they signed where I explained it in depth and had the person initial next to, there may be urinary injury and explained thoroughly, and she signed it. I never signed that. So it doesn't matter. They're calling you a liar. They're calling you negligent; they're calling you inept. They're calling you – you know, it doesn't matter. It's worse when the baby dies or something, but still, it's like –

Or has a bad outcome and then lives, which is –

Even worse.

In terms of the economic –

And even worse for the parents, in my view. And much worse for the doctor, because it costs a lot more. And they can bring the baby in the wheelchair and the respirator.

Do you have a sense one way or the other that lawyers who make medical negligence a large part of their business are careful to screen cases that tend to be more legitimate than –

I don't know about that. I have done a little bit for the insurance company, a little bit of expert review.

Peer review. How did you feel about that? Did you enjoy that process?

It was really interesting, because again, we're so solitary, except within our own practices that – I mean, we have hospital QA stuff that we serve on, but you really don't get the whole story. It was interesting to me. A lawyer can only take the reviewing doctor's word for it. My lawyer once said, I am an amateur obstetrician. And she laughed. And I know what she meant, but she's not an obstetrician.

Because we have to rely on experts.

I know.

On our side as well as yours.

Probably they do a lot of screening, as I'm sure a lot of cases never come to – but even then, we know. Because the records are requested. And we know. It's usually when something happened and then we lose sleep over that.

Probably every time the records are requested, some committee at the hospital or –

Not necessarily. We don't always hear about that, but we've heard about it in our own practices, because they request the office records. And that's another thing I don't think hospitals do a very good job of communicating with doctors. There have been suits about cases where I was involved that I never heard about until much later and by chance. You know, something where I was called in at the last minute. Because everybody thinks they can deliver babies. So no, I don't know about those. I assume they screen them, and a lot of things I never hear about. But I don't know about them.

I'd like to impart my experience is that any lawyer who attempts to do medical negligence work would be very, very cautious about the cases they take, given the risks and the costs.

I would think. Because it's contingent.

And the costs are so enormous.

Their fee is contingent. Of course.

Yes.

No, I understand that. But it doesn't make it any easier for me.

And thank you, for sharing with me a side that I never heard before, which is the personal impact on the individuals. I can presume and imagine it, but I haven't heard about it directly. How do you feel about institutional negligence? Where the facility doesn't give the doctor – well, how about credentialing cases, for example, where the institution has known physicians who have issues that maybe predispose them?

Impairment?

Yes, of some sort.

I think that's terrible. I know they have some protocols, because I've known a few doctors who had addiction problems. I've never been in the operating room where I heard that so-and-so came – I've never heard that or been involved in that. They have huge responsibilities when they know. Huge. And I do know that in this State, there is a program. Where we can call –

Through MQAC and –

Yeah. And there's a – I forget the name of it, because I've never had to call. But one hospital would bring in this guy every once in a while or I'd go to conferences and he was in charge of the physician impairment program. It bypassed everybody. You could just call and report somebody and they would call outside of all repercussion organizations. They would get a hold of the doctor and offer help and that kind of stuff, which I thought was really important.

I think so. You can't have an –

Anonymous reporting. I think it's obligatory. But, you really have to weigh, do I really know? And if you didn't have that avenue. So I feel like the State has done something that is helpful for patients.

If there is an instance where a colleague of yours has done something that was negligent that caused a bad outcome that likely would not have happened otherwise, how would you feel would be the best way for the family to seek justice?

Justice meaning?

I guess the only justice we are able to provide, or that juries are able to provide, is a money remedy.

Money. Well, first of all, the family would not be the only party that knows about it. I feel like if it's in the hospital, the hospital, the employees, the colleagues, and the family should have a place to go which should be like the risk management area of the hospital to start an investigation. And certainly, the patient's family's lawyer should be able to be involved in that at some point.

With the enormous amounts of money at stake, how can it be that both sides come to it, especially say, the side that this physician's insurance or the hospital that's self-insured is looking at a six to ten million dollar potential verdict? How can they be trusted to conduct an investigation that's –

No, there needs to be some sort of –

– objective?

– body that judges.

I guess we call that the jury.

But I don't know that that's the best, because it's hardly a jury of the peers of the physician or the institution. *So it needs to be experts who are not at risk of losing their money, outside of the parties. But it needs to be some – I mean, the patient has a lawyer and experts, and everybody else who was involved has lawyers and experts. And then the body that decides is composed of physicians, hospitals, patients, and medical-legal experts who usually are lawyers or doctors.* **I just think it should not be in this adversarial court system with Joe Blow who knows nothing about what happened. I mean, they can have empathy for the outcome. But injury equals negligence is not the case, in a lot of cases.**

I'd like to represent that I think that the vast majority of trial lawyers know that.

Oh, I'm sure.

I think, as you talked about the conservative trend, I think this City tends to be a very conservative place when it comes to trial outcomes, awards.

Probably.

Relative to other parts of the country.

No, probably.

We were talking about a process that would be something less impactful than the trial would be. I share your frustration as well for those on our side. These cases can last for year upon year, especially at the very high level, where there are appeals and lawyers doing everything they can.

Just getting to trial is years. And getting to the request for records can take a long time.

Sure. With a three-year statute of limitations, or in your case, even longer, because -

Forever. Twenty-one, eighteen plus three. I have the charts in my garage. Not the patient charts; they're at the hospital. But I have to keep them forever. You have a bad outcome from six years ago, and you can't relax. I still am expecting suits into my seventies. The potential. You know, it's like, you're never really retired.

Fortunately, you've got an insurance tail.

Yeah, but. As I said, it's not – I mean sure, they can't come after my –

It's the emotional.

– paltry assets, but yeah. It's all about the internalization of potential

incompetence.

If you found yourself on a civil jury that was a non-medical negligence case.

Do you think I really would ever? Once they know who I am?

Well, you know, I would be more open to it.

Really?

I'll tell you why. Because you've expressed to me that you're open-minded to the situation and you're intelligent. I would trust you would do what's fair, as you see it. You said you think you're open-minded in a non-medical negligence type case. How would you see yourself on a jury, in an automobile accident case with serious injuries?

I'm not sure what you're asking.

That was a poor question.

I mean, I can see myself being on that jury.

Do you think you'd be able to weigh the facts without –

I think so.

Burden of proof is, in a criminal case, beyond a reasonable doubt. In a civil case, as you know, is a preponderance of the evidence. I like to ask people what comes to mind when the word preponderance –

Majority.

Majority. Okay. I've had people say, well, it's gotta be 90% or 60% or something. Then I explain that a preponderance is more likely than not. Many people have difficulty with that notion of just tipping the scales being enough to meet the burden of proof. How do you feel about that? Or is that your standard?

It is. I mean, that's what that word means to me, preponderance. How do I feel about that in terms of making a judgment on that?

If that was all the proof –

That you needed?

Yes.

*I feel okay about it. **There needs to be some standard, and if that's the standard that's there, that's the standard that's there. Should it be different? I don't know.***

And of course, it's a subjective standard.

Right.

As people want to view it.

Yeah.

Which leads us to: every element, the negligence, the causation, and the damages parts need to be proved by a preponderance in a civil case. Most jurors, I find, struggle not with negligence, not even so much with causation in non-medical cases, but with the damages part, especially the general damages, which is the pain and suffering, the disability, the loss of enjoyment of life, because there's no fixed standard. How would you go about evaluating or making a money remedy in that instance? What would you look for?

That's really tough. So you're talking about over and above the –

The special damages.

– lifetime care and medical and –

The care. Whatever the care –

– the care –

Medical, wage, *et cetera*.

– and wage.

Out-of-pockets.

Caretaker who has to quit her job and –

If it's that serious, and they're not all.

Right. I think there should be guidelines, you know, that are given because –

Like a multiplier or some other sort?

Possibly. Some kind of guideline; multiplier of the care-taking damages or whatever?

Multiplier of the special. Some people say, two times the specials or three times the specials. Other lawyers like to suggest a dollar figure per day – but nobody really has the answer. It's very difficult for lawyers to help the jurors get there. What are your thoughts?

Well, we can't just make it up and have it be right on the spot. I'm sure there's volumes written about this.

Every 12 people are different. You can have the same trial presented to different groups of people with vastly different outcomes.

Right. So there need to be guidelines with some basis, some research, some agreement on it before. Not based on the case, but just sort of general guidelines for the judicial system, I would think.

If you were on my jury in a civil case, and I had an injured client, and wasn't worried about negligence and causation issues, I would think you have a lot to add because you've seen people, through your medical training, who have experienced disabilities. You know that everybody is different. Do you think you would be a leader in that aspect with the jury? That people would look to you?

It depends on who else is on the jury, you know? Of course, I think my judgment is right, because it's me. Plus I'm a surgeon, and we have to think we're right or we can't even do anything. So we're very good at making decisions.

Very good at making decisions. And one thing my surgeon used to tell me was, recovery is not a linear process.

That's right.

I've struggled with getting juries to understand the concept that there are fluctuations and swings in that. And also long-term, sometimes permanent residuals. You're nodding your head yes.

Oh, yeah.

You indicated three or four instances where you've had a case brought against you. Did any of those go to trial?

No.

You were deposed?

Oh, yeah. I've been deposed many times. Not just on my own cases.

If you were a plaintiff or defendant, what are the traits and qualities you would like to see of the jurors that are sitting there potentially in judgment?

Intelligent.

What does that mean? People say that, but what kind of intelligence? Because we have empathetic intelligence. We have data-driven intelligence. There are lots of kinds of –

Every kind of intelligence.

Every kind of intelligence.

Every kind. I mean, I don't want some data person who doesn't have a heart, you know?

Data is very difficult for us. They're very binary and there tend to be no gray areas, especially young, white, male, data people.

*Yeah, **all-around intelligence. People don't have to have advanced degrees to be intelligent. But a certain level of intelligence in every way; that primarily, and some life experience.***

What sort of life experiences do you think tend to be more valuable?

Not a solitary person. Somebody who's been self-supporting and out in the world and has care-taken for other people, in any capacity.

Right. Children, grandchildren.

Or parents. Or anything. Somebody who has close relationships with other people for whom they feel responsible.

How about political leanings? Conservative –

It depends. Like the anti-abortion person who killed a doctor, you know, I probably don't want somebody who thinks that's just fine. One life for many, that kind of person.

Sure. Tea Party people who believe that the system is entirely broken and that there are runaway verdicts and runaway juries and that the system's in chaos; how do you feel about that?

I don't think it's the greatest system in the world. I'm thinking of my particular profession, but there has to be some system, and this is what we've got. Do I think there are some runaways, sure.

Do you think that's more or less the case, that there are more excessive verdicts –

Than not?

– than fair verdicts?

*I have no way to know that evidence-wise, but no. **I think they're not very common, but I think they exist.***

People like to talk about the McDonald's case. That comes up in every jury selection as being a –

The hot thing?

Yes, the hot coffee.

I have brothers who are in insurance. They're not in personal liability stuff, but one of them, who's in fast food, this was his take: just turn the temperature down on the coffee burner.

Right.

It's not rocket science. It's ridiculous. But I do also have, these are so anecdotal, so it's not usually how I make judgments, but I know of cases that they haven't seen a penny. A penny. And it's been decades. I don't know how much the judgment was, but you know, the Tea Party-ers don't have to worry too much about that, because the judgment does not mean they were paid that money, which I didn't know, because I thought judgment equals payment; not necessarily.

Quite the opposite. The larger the judgment, the longer the haul it is to collect. A very accomplished lawyer once said to me, you don't get paid on those cases.

Oh, no. It's just for looks, basically. I had no idea that you don't get paid a lot of the time and it goes on forever.

Is there anything the attorneys in the cases involving you could have done differently?

Oh, God, yes. So many things.

I'd like to hear it. Because as an attorney, I'd like to know how to be a better person in all phases of –

I had like a 20-year case from my first year of residency where the guy flew out here. And he asked me –

To depose you?

Uh-huh. I barely – I didn't remember the case. All I remembered of it was it was –

It's in your notes, right?

A blur. Residency. I didn't sleep for five years. Some woman that I happen to see in triage when she came in and thought her water broke or something. Then he started to ask me about my personal experience with childbirth and, have you ever experienced your water breaking? I looked at my lawyer, I said, can this possibly be okay?

Is this relevant at all?

There must be a rule about this, because this is ridiculous. I'm sure he wanted to piss me off.

I'm not surprised.

He was that kind of guy, and it certainly did, because I thought, first of all, when I was a resident, that was a time where 5% of OB/GYNs were women. So I felt persecuted from the day I started medical school and 10% of my class was women. And now it's still happening, you know, so that. Unless that's your goal, to make somebody really angry at you, which –

So unfair questioning.

Really unfair.

Disrespectful questioning.

Disrespectful. Disrespectful questioning.

It's frustrating for me, that this is an adversarial process. And it's a zero-sum game, right?

Exactly. And you know, first of all, I remember in that case, nothing bad happened. Doesn't there have to be damage in order to sue? I mean, there has to be –

There has to be a harm.

Harm. So really, there wasn't any. The kid wasn't going to go to Harvard, and he was slow, but he wasn't like – his IQ was not below 100, or below 90 or some average. Later in the case, a friend of mine who's a lawyer did some looking into it and found that the father of the baby flunked out of school in 8th grade. There's this family history of not very bright people. And the kid now is 11 or 20 or something. It probably wasn't me with a negative test for ruptured membranes that caused the kid to have trouble in school. I mean, she came back the next day and the test was positive. All I had to go by was the test, you know? So probably her membranes were ruptured, but there's no fluid, there's no positive test, the ultrasound shows plenty of fluid, you know, evidence. I can only go by the evidence.

So the lawyer and respect in the deposition and throughout the process. What else do you think you would like to say to lawyers?

Plaintiff lawyers?

Or defendant lawyers, too, because some of them may read this. I have colleagues on both sides that will certainly be getting this book. I know people in the medical malpractice defense bar. Many of them are very good lawyers.

My experience with them was good. They were very kind.

Your lawyers?

Uh-huh. They knew it was horrible for me. They were blindly respectful, which helped. But I knew it was blind. I was under no illusion that they were the judge and the jury and they had decided I was innocent. They were like, non-judgmental friends, which is helpful. The lack of awareness of the emotional turmoil and toll on the plaintiff's lawyer's part and how devastating it was –

Do you think an attorney could actually represent that genuinely in that –

Probably not.

– in that context?

I mean, but if –

Because I'm trying to think of how could I do that if I were taking anybody's deposition and trying to let them know that it's not personal. I understand there's a big turmoil here, and yet, I'm the person that caused that turmoil.

Well, not really. First of all, the turmoil is caused by the damage, and that I was present for it. That's the turmoil. The turmoil is not that the plaintiff's attorney made me feel bad.

I see.

*They just are rubbing salt in the wound. The wound is there. It starts from when the baby's died. It's not necessarily what they've said. **So acknowledgment of that would help.***

Acknowledgment of how you must feel about the incident regardless of –

Right. I feel just as bad. I truly believe that at the time, I've made the best decision I possibly could. Every time. And sometimes, something bad happened and something bad didn't. Somebody said, your job must be so happy in terms of babies. I said, it's only happy when it's over. You know? Because if it doesn't turn out well, it doesn't matter. I've had patients who have called me and said, I really don't think the baby's been moving. I say, you've gotta come right in. Well, don't you think it's probably okay? And, shouldn't I just wait until tomorrow? I say, I can't possibly know. And then they don't come in, and then they come in the following – this has happened twice, you know, but of course I remember. I listen for a heartbeat; the baby's dead. I feel just as bad that that happened even though I said, do this, do this, do this. But I don't want to say, well, you should have come in. Because perhaps the baby's already dead. What good is it making them feel guilty about not doing what I said? And yet, I did say the right thing. So I lose sleep over that as much as if the baby dies in labor and I'm right there. So there is the factor of, I'm going to get sued for this, because I was there when the baby died. So it has nothing to do with what happens after, but the plaintiff's lawyer can make it a lot worse. But it's already bad.

In those instances where you were sued, I know that contracts with malpractice insurance companies generally have a consent to settle clause where they can't settle without your permission.

Right.

How did you approach those when you were having the decision-making process about whether I should consent or not to consent? How did you weigh that?

It had entirely to do with how much time I would be away from my practice and how much money I would lose by not working, *because, as my brothers who own insurance companies say, what you do is piecework. It's like a factory. If you're not there, you don't make any money.*

I don't think the public thinks that.

No. But anyway, how much time, how much pain I would go through. It had nothing to do with the likelihood of winning. And also, the insurance company presenting me the two scenarios: this will cost this much to us, and this trial will cost us this much. But we will do it if you want. This will cost you this much, and this will cost you this much in lost time.

Did you feel pressured one way or the other?

I know that they don't care if they go to trial and lose the suit – or win the suit. What they care about is how much money it'll cost to defend. So I knew what they wanted. I didn't care about their – I've paid them plenty of money over the years. Not as much as they could possibly lose, but you know. They've got all those dermatologists who've paid, too, and don't get sued. But it was entirely what I would have to go through. I could have some closure here. And yeah, I could admit to whatever they want me to admit to, but at least I won't have to continue to dread showing up and losing money.

Do you feel that your colleagues share a similar mindset?

Oh, yeah.

Did you ever feel exposed in a lawsuit in terms of a financial personal exposure?

No.

Coverage was always adequate for you?

Well, I mean, no. I had a one million dollar per case limit, cap.

Your clinic probably had something, and the hospital has something.

Yeah, but they apportion blame; hospital, doctor. There's no way for my portion we could have covered millions of dollars. So yeah, to that extent, but I didn't have very much.

As a general rule, plaintiff's lawyers tend to not go beyond the insurance.

Well, not in OB. We've had hundred million dollar judgments.

That's true. It's not in anybody's interest to put somebody out of work is what I'm saying.

Well, that's what happens. Not necessarily because of the monetary value of the judgment. People quit after being sued. They can't be insured, a lot of the time. They can't find anybody to insure them if there's a multi-million dollar suit; your career is over. I had a friend, downtown, one of the best OB/GYNs and there was a multi-million dollar suit and he quit. He had to. He couldn't do anything. He was uninsurable.

After just this one – just because of the –

Amount. It was fourteen million dollars.

Did you feel pitted against your clinic or hospital or those other entities that were part of the suit?

No. We were all in it together. There was another doctor involved. I was out of town when everything happened, but I was her doctor, and he was covering for me. I got 66% of the liability and he got a third. I was really angry.

Because they didn't keep –

He didn't tell me.

– each side –

They didn't even tell me what percentage would be applied to me. It had nothing to do with the money, because it's insurance money. It had nothing to do with anything, but that I wasn't told. I thought I wasn't liable at all because I wasn't even there, you know? So that really made me angry, not at him, but the other doc and the insurance company. But not pitted against from the start, no. I wasn't ever sued after that, so I couldn't watch out for that or something with the next time.

You mentioned that you tend to be a little more politically leaning on the different –

Way more.

– way more than most of your physician colleagues. Do you think those who lean the other way would look at that in a calculated monetary way, the decision whether to consent to settle or not? Do they look at it as a function of how much they may lose?

Not necessarily. Possibly people on my side look at it differently, too, because there's such ego involved. In my case, I gotta make some money. They always think we're guilty anyway, so I don't care. But –

Who's they?

The person for whom something bad happened.

I see.

They – you can't live with yourself if you're a woman who didn't go to the hospital when –

Right. So you have to find –

So you have to blame the doctor. But there are docs for whom being right, and I don't know that is a politically correlated thing, the ego; it's probably both sides.

Let's talk about experts, because as you know, certainly in the medical litigation context and in almost all personal injury contexts, any negligent case now, these are expert-driven cases, for the most part.

Right.

Certainly the negligence aspect, the causation aspect, the damages aspect, we find that jurors are all over the board about who they find credible and who they don't find credible.

How can they know? I'm sure it's personality.

Because we'll have what we perceive as a less credible expert who's making a ton of money for their time and who we perceive to be a more credible expert not making much. The jury will say, that person needs to up their game and start charging more. What would you say to potential jurors to help them determine which expert is more credible than another?

I do think in evaluating an expert's testimony that intelligence comes into play. I do think that substantiation of the expert opinion is crucial. And the understanding of what makes what they're saying credible is somewhat education-driven and somewhat intelligence-driven. So that's hard because statistics can say anything. So you have to be able to parse that out. The vast majority of people have no concept of that. That needs to be taught in high school. What's real and what isn't. What's the difference between anecdotal evidence and the scientific method? Vast swaths of our country don't believe in the scientific method, you know? Who said this – shoot. Oh, Tyson, the astrophysicist.

Neil deGrasse Tyson.

He said, just because you don't believe it does not mean it's not true, like about evolution or whatever. So I think juries, you know, just the population has no idea of how to evaluate.

Well, we don't. We can look at a 60-page CV and we can look at a 12-page CV, but that doesn't necessarily tell us that –

Right. That that person knows more. He's on a few more councils or – so it's impossible. It's impossible for me to trust anything without going back to the original article. And then it's only one article. You have to go back further and read them all. I have a friend who was a physician and then he got out; he couldn't take it. He developed video games and wanted to patent something, so he went to a patent lawyer. Then he had to read the patent law textbook, because he wanted to make sure that that patent lawyer knew what he was doing. So that's like me. I married and got these step-children. I know nothing, except how I was raised. I wanted to take classes. I got the textbook. I read the textbook before the classes. That's how I am. And I just don't see how other people can make a good decision without all that information. So that's my bias. I think I'm right about that because we think we're right. So I don't know how you do it. That's why I think that all the people on this outside the jury system council should have read all the books so they can make a good judgment.

Or at least be more familiar.

Yes. It's an imperfect system. The jury system. But we don't have anything better.

It truly is. And inefficient.

Oh, my God. The money that's spent. It's terrible. The money, the money. Ugh. Makes me sick.

I know colleagues who have risked millions.

You have to be passionate about what you're doing. And it just doesn't matter about the money. It has to be a passion.

It is hard. Thank you.

44

MANIPULATION

Caucasian male, age 55, married, Investment Property Manager/Accountant/Auditor/Retired, B.S. Marketing

I like people who come across as very honest and sincere and not manipulative and – I don't know. When I feel like somebody's putting on a show or immediately trying to get me to say things, I become a little bit defensive and wary of the person.

At this point, the judge says, ladies and gentlemen, please give your attention to the attorney for the plaintiff who's going to conduct a portion of jury selection. As you're sitting there, surrounded by your potential jurors and not knowing anything more, what are you feeling in that moment?

I don't know. I guess I'm kind of excited. I'd like to be on a jury, and it would also worry me a little bit about the type of a case. It could be kind of complex and maybe not real clear. It might be difficult to accurately calculate fair damages if there was damages due. So it's not a straight up guilty/not guilty. You'd have to somehow come up with a formula to calculate damages so that would concern me a little bit.

How do you feel about being called for service in the first place?

I think it's a great idea. I feel it's an important civic duty, and I'd be excited about it. Especially not knowing how it works.

A lot of people express that they'd really rather not be there for time concerns or money concerns. How do you feel about that?

*Absolutely. If I was making a lot of money, that would be a concern of mine. **But I would be really curious how the whole thing works since I've never been on a jury,** so I'd be very open to it.*

How do you feel about civil lawsuits in general?

In general, I know they're absolutely important to a society that functions properly, but in my opinion, I think there's a lot of abuse in civil lawsuits. But I'd certainly be able to keep an open mind and be objective.

One of the goals for the lawyer is to identify people who may have some preconceived notion or prejudgment or a bias against one side or the other. How do you think the lawyer can best ask the people there whether or not they can be open-minded in a way that will get a reliable answer?

*I do not know off the top of my head. **I guess kind of the first question you***

would ask, what's your opinion of civil lawsuits? That can tell a lot about a person's opinion. Just kind of like what I said is when you asked that question, I immediately said I think there is a lot of abuse in those types of lawsuits, but I also think they're a very important – I don't know. I'd have to think about that a little bit.

That's okay. We can come back to it. If an attorney were to ask whether or not you had any sort of beliefs or opinions, maybe based on the fact that you were in the insurance industry, that might have you lean one way or another, how might you react to that?

I guess maybe if you just ask the person, what is your opinion? Do you think there is a lot of abuse in civil lawsuits? Do you think it's just a money grab where people are trying to take advantage of a situation and try to make a lot of money? That might ferret out some people who feel very strongly that way.

How about you and your experience in insurance? You probably have a lot of insight. I would imagine you do. Do you have any insights into the –

I know of cases when I was in workers' comp insurance, and I know of cases where people would come up with fake injuries and get big awards. Everybody's heard of these cases where the guy's got the bad back and he can't work and he's out lifting a big heavy object and putting it into his truck and there's a hidden camera watching. There's definitely things like that going on. We had investigative people out looking for that sort of thing. But anyhow, I know for a fact there is abuse, and that does concern me. Especially when you have soft tissue injuries or headaches and, I can't sleep at night and I can't work anymore and those things that are very difficult to measure. I become very suspicious of those.

How prevalent was that?

There's no way I could ever put a percentage on that. But there's little things that you hear in those cases and you know everybody talks about so it gets a lot of attention. You know, if someone gets busted for abusing the system. I just don't have any idea of how prevalent it really is. I would imagine it's pretty small.

If you're on the jury, with that awareness and that experience and knowledge you've gained, would you be more or less critical of the evidence if it were, say, a case like a soft tissue injury case?

Like I say, I would be suspicious. The only way you can measure damages is by one person's opinion and his suggestion of all this pain. You don't have a way to independently verify what he's claiming. So I would definitely discount what they're saying somewhat, because there's no one on the planet but that person and they're about to benefit with a large award. Obviously there's a huge incentive for someone to exaggerate their condition.

That's interesting. This is the first time the word incentive has come up, but that's a really great observation. Do you think money awards by their nature are incentives for people to be more or less truthful?

> **Absolutely to be less truthful.** *Usually with somebody that's really upset about something, they're going to exaggerate the bad things and make it sound a lot worse than it really is.*

How about on the other side?

> *I think you just run wild with claims. Like I said, about I can't sleep anymore and this and that. There's just no way to confirm any of that.*

How about the motivations of the other side who may have to pay an award? Do you think they might also have more or less reason to be untruthful?

> *Yeah. I believe insurance companies, for example, will be very aggressive at denying somebody what they're really due. I would definitely discount claims that they make as well, yes.*

We try to ferret out people that have beliefs that may cause one side or the other to not get an even start. For example, there are studies that show many people, a majority of people, believe plaintiff's trial lawyers are not credible. They're about as low on the scale as used-car dealers. That's something that we have to overcome even before we walk into the courtroom. How do you feel about that one way or the other? Do you think that's honest or truthful or a fair assessment?

> *Yeah. I definitely also would discount plaintiffs' motivations as well. I believe they can easily exaggerate things and work things to their advantage by not necessarily worrying about the truth.*

Are you referring to the lawyers for the plaintiffs?

> *Yeah.*

Got it. Now, I think you, probably more than the average person, are aware that many, if not all, of the plaintiff's attorneys advance costs and have a contingent fee arrangement. How do you factor that into the attorney's role of screening cases carefully so they don't take a loss?

> *I guess I don't understand the question.*

Let me rephrase that. Lawyers who do personal injury work get paid on a contingent basis. They only get something if they win, and they generally are advancing all the costs for some period of time. So there's a lot of risk there. Given that there's an awful lot to lose, does that change your evaluation of plaintiff's lawyers more or less with regard to credibility?

> *I would never really think about that. I don't think that impacts me at all as to their motivation. Obviously they want to get paid. But even if it wasn't a contingency, I don't think it would really affect my opinion of the plaintiff's attorney.*

Are you comfortable with the notion that in our system it's difficult for people of lesser means to bring a case to trial without lawyers who operate on a contingent basis and advance costs?

> *I understand that. It definitely makes sense. I guess that is a good thing for society.*

Coming back to this notion about the lawyers trying to find people that make the best group of jurors that are open-minded, how do you think an attorney could best identify a snake in the grass juror who has a real agenda to do some harm to the plaintiff's case? Or anybody's case?

> *I don't know.* **You just try to get them to talk as much as possible and answer questions rapidly, not give them a chance to really think about it too much.** *I suppose you have to be kind of like a police detective. You ask a question one way and then you ask it another way, and if the answers aren't consistent, you might catch them lying somehow. But I don't know. That's kind of a complicated strategy you'd have to come up with.*

Are there any questions you think would be off-limits in terms of somebody asking about your personal beliefs and opinions about these kinds of cases and the system?

> *I don't know. I don't know if it's fair to ask about someone's politics, you know, if you're a Republican or who you voted for or –*

It actually is allowed. Let's say the question is asked, do you lean more toward the liberal side or more toward the conservative side? Where do you sort of fall there?

> *You want me to answer about me?*

Does that feel like a fair question to you?

> *I don't know.* **I don't think I would like to answer that.**

Okay.

> **I don't know if that's really relevant, answering personal questions in front of a large group of people.**

It wouldn't be so comfortable or fair to have to answer personal questions?

> *Yeah. I mean, if someone asks you, are you a racist person or something like that;* **if you ask them really personal questions, you're not going to get probably an honest answer anyway if you're asking in front of a large group of people. I think if you ask those kind of really personal questions, you may get lies or non-truthful answers.**

Right. So the objective is to get the most truthful answer in the least offensive or manipulative way. One of the other goals is to establish a human connection with the jury as early as possible. What do you think that looks like? What would you think a lawyer should do to establish a human connection with you in this kind of an environment?

I like people who come across as very honest and sincere and not manipulative and – I don't know. When I feel like somebody's putting on a show or immediately trying to get me to say things, I become a little bit defensive and wary of the person. But just real, sincere, honest, like a friend talking to you.

That's what I hear from most people. How do you make allowances for what's probably a feeling of anxiety among everybody in that room at that time, given there's a large group of people who are coming together; there are adversaries down there, there's a judge's bench, a lot of unfamiliarity and a lot on the line. How do you make allowances for individuals showing a little of that stress or tension?

You mean the jurors? Potential jurors?

I was thinking more the attorneys or their clients. But even the jurors, too, because everybody's new in that setting.

So you said, do you make allowances? You wouldn't be as critical?

How can you make allowances? I'm coming into this environment knowing that as a lawyer I'm perceived somewhat poorly, at least not credibly, that there is a large group of people that have different beliefs and that's okay, and I have to elicit those in a non-threatening way and at the same time, as you say, be friendly and open and honest. How does a lawyer recover from a misstep, let's say?

I don't know. For me, I'm a very objective person. That stuff isn't going to impact me as much. I fully understand that you've got a very important job to do, and I'm not going to be terribly critical of that.

So when you make a decision about something important, do you value more data evidence or do you value more your empathic, intuitive gut feeling?

*I would always go with the data first. But you know, you have to weigh – I would say for me the data is much more important – from an independent source. **Data from an independent source would be absolutely very high on my list of something that I would rely on.** And not so much the intuition at all.*

Would you consider expert witnesses or witnesses on either side to be considered independent sources?

No, not at all. I have very little confidence at all in the expert witnesses.

Can you explain why?

I just know that you can get an expert witness to say anything you want and the other side can get an expert witness to say anything they want, and I just don't have much confidence in them at all. I mean, they're there to make a lot of money and to make their particular side happy. So no, I don't feel that they're independent in any way.

Do you feel that there are ranges of credibility and objectivity among paid experts?

I guess I don't know enough about it to really give you any useful information. I just have a very negative view of them. However, I know that they must be important to the case, but boy, it would be very hard for me to be swayed by them. You'd have to of course listen to the counter-arguments against what the expert says. So in those types of – that would be really important to evaluating the expert witness' credibility. But once you start to get into real technical things, then it gets extremely difficult as you're talking about it. Medical malpractice, you've got an expert witness talking about a really complicated subject, and then another guy on the other side saying something opposite that. You just wouldn't know what to do.

It's a difficult role for the jurors, isn't it?

Yeah.

Do you think it's fair to ask jurors to make these kinds of decisions?

I don't know. **I have pretty big doubts that the jury of your average person could actually handle a really complicated case like that. I think they would end up being swayed by things other than the data, just because it's too complicated. And I think they could be swayed by other factors.**

What are the kinds of data – I mean, I've heard people say data can be manipulated too.

Absolutely.

What kinds of data present the most objective picture for you?

I don't know. Can you give me some examples of what type of data we're talking about?

Medical records, for example, are data, but they're subjectively written often. You could have measurements or income flows which track somebody's earnings, but there might be difference of expert opinion about what that means going forward.

Right. Remind me of what the question was.

I was just trying to ask are there certain kinds of data that you would find more trustworthy, valid, and objective than others?

Obviously things like earnings records in the past are very easy to measure and it'd be hard to argue with certain things like that. But anything that involves estimates and assumptions into the future, way off into the future for earnings, obviously I would be very suspicious of. And they can easily be manipulated.

You use the word assumptions and that is really where the rubber meets the road.

Yeah, you can make a tiny change in an assumption and over 30 years or the life of somebody's – it could make a huge difference.

Not all data is created equal.

Yeah.

Nor are the conclusions. So how would you describe who you are and what you value?

In the context of a case?

What we're talking about here.

Honesty and integrity are very important to me, and people who are not trying to manipulate the system and game the system for their advantage. *I have a very negative outlook about that sort of thing. I also have a strong belief that we have a certain amount of self-responsibility to be careful about what somebody does. I think one of the negative things about me for being picked on a jury is, I really have strong feelings that people have a certain amount of responsibility to be careful.* **And just because something bad happens to you doesn't mean that someone else is always to blame and you should be awarded massive amounts of money.**

When you say you have a strong sense of self-responsibility, personal responsibility, how do you feel about people who are rule breakers or rule violators that cause some kind of injury as a result? What do you think is the cost of that?

The cost of – I guess I don't understand.

You've got a strong sense of personal responsibility. Do you feel that accidents happen, but some people cause accidents or harm because they simply weren't following the rules.

Right.

Where do you fall on the line of enforcing other people to be responsible? What I'm getting at is, plaintiffs sometimes get a rap that they need to accept that not all harms are compensable because maybe there was no negligence; accidents happen. By the same token, being someone who has a strong sense of personal responsibility, how do you feel about it when others break the rules and cause harm?

Obviously that makes it a lot worse, if you're being negligent, if that's what you're saying. Or are you saying that the plaintiffs broke the rules and they got injured themselves?

I was talking about the defendant's side. In general, do you tend to view people who don't follow rules or who violate rules in an unfavorable way?

Certainly.

Okay. Let's talk about the compensation part of things. You know, we have damages that are called special damages which are specifically itemized like wage loss and medical bills and things of that nature. And then we have general damages, which are pain, suffering, disability, loss of enjoyment of life. For those, there's no fixed standard. How would you go about making a remedy for money when there's no fixed standard for doing that?

It would be difficult. I kind of assumed there was a standard way to calculate the damages. Don't you get instructions from the judge or something on what to do on these types of things?

What the judge basically says is, with regard to these general damages – now specials, of course, are itemized and those can be basically recovered dollar for dollar. But general damages, the judge will only say you are to be guided by your own decision-making process. So everybody's different.

*Right. **I guess I'm kind of impacted by things I see in the news all the time where juries award just fantastic sums. I find that really offensive and I really don't like that part. I hate to see that. I just think it can really be abused. It's so easy for someone to give away a lot of money to an injured person; it's going to make them feel good.** But fairness maybe doesn't come into play at all. That does worry me a lot.*

You think then that you'd tend to lean more on the conservative side than on the –

***Absolutely. Unless there's like terrible, gross negligence.** But if it's just sort of an innocent thing that happens and someone gets hurt, I wouldn't want to be awarding huge sums of money.*

Would it matter to you if the defendant was an individual as opposed to an institution?

I'd hope that wouldn't matter to me. I don't like that attitude of, they're a big rich corporation; they can afford it. Send them a message. I don't really like that sort of thing.

How do you feel about the notion that jury remedy awards both compensate and deter future rule breaking?

You said to compensate or deter?

Right. How do you feel about those being twin purposes and do you feel that they do that?

I don't like the whole notion of the deterrent thing. I think somebody should be penalized for what they did and not penalized for something that they – or try to prevent them from doing something into the future. I think it should be based on actual damages. So I don't like that deterrence thing.

Talking about the burden of proof; in criminal cases, it's beyond a reasonable doubt. In civil cases, the instruction is that you make a decision if the evidence has been proved by a preponderance. So the question is, what does that mean to you when you hear the word preponderance?

You said if the judge asks you to judge based on the preponderance of the evidence?

Right. And what does a preponderance mean to you when you hear that word?

It does worry me a little bit. I know how sometimes there's a criminal case and someone might be found innocent and then they go back and have a civil case and all of a sudden they're guilty and they have to pay a lot of money. That kind of thing concerns me and obviously it makes it more subjective.

Right. When you hear the word preponderance does that suggest any standard or numerical percentages?

*I've never really thought about it, but yeah, it **just sounds like it's a majority to me.** I don't think it shows overwhelming evidence. It's just more of a majority or for the most part.*

If the judge were to give you further information that a preponderance means more likely true than not true, does that help clarify it for you?

That's kind of what I was thinking is, you know, the majority of the evidence.

How do you feel about that being the burden in a civil case?

That's not very high at all. It just seems like there could be some injustice with that sort of instruction.

How would you apply it if that were the law?

I guess I'd have to follow the instructions. I wouldn't like it, but I'd guess you'd have to follow the instructions that the judge gives you.

Right. So you like lawyers any less now that we've been talking for 40 minutes?

I actually find it really interesting.

What do you think is the role of insurance in the majority of these civil cases?

What do you mean the role of insurance? It's just to spread risk around among a large group of people buying into the system.

What I'm getting at is, the courts generally will not allow attorneys to talk about the fact that one side or the other does or doesn't have insurance for the reason that they don't want the juries to take that into account and give an unrealistically high verdict.

I can see how a jury would maybe award more money if they thought some insurance company was going to pay for somebody's problems or damages.

As you sit there in that hypothetical courtroom, do you have a strong sense one way or the other that the individuals are insured and that insurance may ultimately pay?

I would assume pretty much everybody would have insurance. There probably wouldn't be a case if there wasn't some insurance backing it up.
If you're suing a driver who hit your clients and you know they didn't have a lot of insurance, I'm sure there wouldn't be a case in the courtroom. I would have to

assume there's insurance involved. Unless it's a big company.

And even the big companies often have self-insurance and supplemental insurance, right?

Yeah. But they're going to have enough resources to pay something like that whether they have insurance or not, most likely.

As we've been talking, has your sense of identification for one side or the other crystallized or come to the fore at all or are you still, as you say, objectively open-minded?

*I still think I'm pretty objective about it, but like I described, I'm pretty wary of both sides. I'd have to have some pretty good evidence to sway me one way or the other. **I'm definitely suspicious of the motivations of both sides.***

If you were one of the parties, the plaintiff or the defendant, in a case like that, what are the qualities you would most like to have in the jurors hearing your case?

If I was the plaintiff – plaintiff's attorney, what would I like to see on the jury?

If you were the party, the plaintiff or defendant, what are the qualities and traits you'd like the jurors to have?

You want somebody who's probably emotional and maybe somebody who cheers for the underdog and doesn't like big corporations and thinks they're inherently evil and doesn't like insurance companies and that sort of thing.

Pretty good chance that those people won't make it on if they express those beliefs.

Of course.

Do you have any personal biases as we've talked that have come up; personal strong opinions or beliefs that would be something the attorneys should know about with regard to your view of these cases?

*I think I've explained it, **but I do have a lot of biases, preconceived notions of motivations of people and all that.***

And everybody does.

However, I do want to hold myself to being objective and make sure I don't get swayed. But I guess I do have some real preconceived biases.

One of the things I'm exploring is being okay with as long as people understand they have them and are willing to at least consider those as they're going through the process. What do you think about that?

I guess that's just a reality. I suppose everybody's like that. Most people maybe wouldn't admit it, but everybody's got their biases. So I guess that's just something you have to deal with in the jury selection.

We've got such limited time to do jury selection, especially in the garden-variety cases. Major cases, there's more latitude. But in that time frame, there's not a lot I can learn. I think some lawyers go a little too far and get a blow-back from the juries if they intrude. My thought is, hey, what if I just asked people to raise their hands if you think you can be open-minded? If you say you will, that's good enough for me and leave it at that, and trust people to be honest.

I guess if you don't have a lot of time that certainly could work. I mean, do you evaluate people and how they look and how they dress?

To some extent we do that. But the goal here is to get people who are willing to say that they are or they're not open-minded and kind of just go there and not be intrusive. That's something I'm testing out. A number of people have said they thought that might be an okay way to go; because I'm not so sure I'm going to learn anything meaningful other than just asking that question.

No, I think that's a good idea to ask the juror questions. Because you can cover a lot of ground in a hurry that way. But I would be worried about people – people are always afraid to raise their hand and admit something. That's because there's certain personalities that would be afraid to be really honest in front of a group of people.

Any group, you get different things, from people that won't stop talking to people that won't talk.

Yeah.

One of the skills they've taught us, in order to get juries to open up to our questioning is – some have suggested maybe start out by sharing something about ourselves that might be appropriate for the context. What do you think about that?

*I guess that would be fine. **Again, I'm kind of leery of someone trying to be too manipulative. If it doesn't sound natural and sincere, you kind of feel like they're trying to manipulate you.***

Right. Is there anything that's come up that you think would be helpful for me to know?

One more comment about what I just said. It's like if you go to buy a car and the salesman just starts acting in a certain way, is really nice, and it just immediately turns me off. He's following a script. He just got out of his training course on how to be salesman and he's using all these certain points, and that kind of thing turns me off.

What do you suppose it is about that script process that turns you off?

Well, it's just not honest and sincere.** He's been trained to do that in order to achieve a goal. **And he's trying to work me over to his advantage. I'm just really wary about that.

Sure. Disingenuous, dishonest or –

He's just trying to manipulate me to do a certain thing that will basically take money out of my pocket and put it into his. I don't like that at all.

Do you feel like jury awards take money out of your pocket?

No, no. I was using the analogy of the car dealer.

I get that. I was just wondering if – you know, some people, many people, say that jury awards just make the costs of living go higher.

I wouldn't really think about that at all. I mean, I know that that's true, but no, I look at it on a case-by-case basis, unless it's going to be like a hundred million dollar award or something. But if it's fair compensation for some real damages, no, I wouldn't think about anything other than just that case.

Are there any kinds of cases where a harm has happened or a rule has been broken where you might feel strongly that you would want to make the defendant pay a lot of money?

If it was really gross negligence or if somebody was like – when you hear about these car – I think it was General Motors, where they're aware their ignition devices were wrong and they completely ignored it and continued to produce the cars. That's really bad; kind of something I could see being really bad or a really big award for something like that.

So that's a little bit more of a punishment.

If it's a casual thing, if someone slips and falls, you know, comes to work, dropped a grape on the floor, and somebody else walked along and stepped on it, it's, I mean, that's bad, but what could the supermarket reasonably have done to have picked that grape up within a minute of it dropping on the floor? I would not feel compelled to give a really outrageous award for something like that.

If you're in that situation and get on a jury and you're considering making some money award or verdict, would you factor in that the lawyer is taking a contingent fee?

No. I don't think so. No. I know it's very common and you guys have to take a lot of risk and you're advancing a lot of costs and all that. So I think you're fairly compensated. So no, that wouldn't impact me.

Let me ask it a little bit differently: would you make a higher award so that the plaintiff got the amount you thought they should get knowing the attorney will take a percentage?

I don't know. I've never even thought about that until you just mentioned it, so it certainly wasn't something that I would be thinking about. I don't think I would be impacted by that.

I wish more people were.

Maybe people really are thinking about that?

Definitely not the majority.

Yeah.

Is there anything else on these issues of biases or attorney credibility that you think – any more thoughts you might want to add?

I can't really think of anything off the top of my head.

Okay. Thank you.

45

CORPORATE DEFENDANTS

Caucasian female, age 60, married, two children, Homemaker/Parent/Educational Writer, B.A. Psychology

If the corporation is wrong as an entity, though, then I would want more from them for the same damage.

At this point, the judge says please give your attention to the lawyer for the plaintiff who's going to conduct that part of jury selection. It generally will last an hour or so and then the other side gets to talk. At that moment, as you're sitting in the courtroom with your potential jury peers and the lawyers and their clients and the judge, what is going through your mind and how are you feeling about the process?

I would feel a mixture of things. And I'm putting myself there. I'd be curious. I'd probably be feeling a bit anxious and depending on the nature of the situation and the vibes and stuff, I might be very anxious. I also would have a concern, because this has come up for me around how am I going to handle this? It's not criminal. And I would know that it's not criminal? Okay. I don't hold a value around penalizing people. I have a value around people learning to be better in the future. I realize that sometimes consequences – that the victim or whoever should be compensated and all of that. So I think it would be less of an issue in a civil.

Because in civil cases, there is no loss of liberty. As there is in the criminal case.

Right.

In civil cases, the remedy is essentially a loss of money or a gain of money, depending on who the person is that's receiving or giving. So you're feeling this mixture of feelings depending on what's happening. How do you feel about the lawyers?

It would depend a lot on how they presented themselves, like you. I would probably feel comfortable. You have a very comfortable – of course, you're not wearing a suit and – but even the suit, you know. There is something a little off-putting about suits, for me, not living in the corporate world, I mean, not being in a corporate setting in my life. I've certainly been around lawyers. My friend is a great friend and she's not scary. But I've definitely been around lawyers who have very big egos and you can feel it emanating off of them as they walk. So it would vary.

Do you have any feelings that one might call a bias or a prejudice or some kind of a prejudgment about lawyers who do plaintiff's work, lawyers who sue on behalf of people who are claiming an injury?

Not in a general, overall way. It would depend, again, on the case. I might have some sense of like what are they going after? It would depend maybe on the content. At this point, I don't know what that content is? That it's civil?

A civil case that's seeking some sort of money recovery. People talk about sleazy trial lawyers. That's something I hear quite often. Is that a hot button issue for you in any way?

I think they exist, but I don't think all lawyers are like that. I wouldn't say it's a hot button issue, but it might be a hot button issue in a particular case where I feel like this is a sleazy lawyer.

As you go in, are you feeling more or less neutral?

*I'm kind of wait and see. Let's see how this plays out. That's part of what my anxiety is. **What's this going to be? Am I going to be out of integrity with myself participating in this? That is a huge concern for me, civil or criminal. I don't want to be out of integrity.** So that would always be the place where I would say – you know, they ask whatever that question is, is there any reason you shouldn't be on this jury? That would be like a place where I would say that if I knew enough about it and I was picking up whatever.*

If they asked that question?

So that makes me a little nervous knowing I have this question, because I have to put myself out there and buck the trend, maybe.

Would it be all right if I did ask that question that you just posed? Which is really the ultimate question. Is there anything, to paraphrase, that you think may make you more or less suitable to be a juror in this kind of case?

I might not want to not be on a jury if I had some concerns myself that maybe there is an injustice kind of thing going on, then maybe I would really want to be on the jury. I don't know if then the question would mean that because I already have some ideas that I shouldn't be on the jury or not. I'm not totally clear on that.

Some people are very expressive and very clear and say, I don't believe in these kinds of cases or I believe the jury system is broken and run amok and we have too many crazy verdicts and I just don't want to participate in that. Others are more towards, I'm interested in this process, I believe in it, and I'm willing to do my part. Everybody falls in that continuum.

Well, I will say that I like the jury process as – I don't know if in fact the way it works it's a good system, but I love the idea of random selection. How random it actually winds up being, I can't really say. But certainly, there's a lot of self-selection out. For example, I myself have done that. At least twice.

Those were issues that had to do with, I need to be home?

Be with my kids. Be there for my kids.

And the inconvenience of having to go a long distance?

When I didn't have a car.

Right. For some who-knows-how-long period of time.

Right. Exactly. And it wasn't like, it might just be a day. It could be weeks or – because I had no idea.

You said that your value was this personal integrity. I'm sorry if I don't remember the exact word, but that was the value that you keyed in on earlier. Were those the right words?

I would not want to be out of integrity, so, for example, going into a jury situation, you don't even know whether it's civil or criminal. I would be concerned about, am I going to be asked to make a decision to punish someone rather than help them learn a better strategy or simply keep society safe or both. Because there are times when they're not going to learn, very likely, and we need to keep society safe. But it's not about making them pay or the punitive approach.

We don't have punitive damages in our State. Although in criminal cases, certainly all of that is a punitive – I suppose there's a goal of rehabilitation, too. What is your sense of the role of civil cases to teach correct behavior?

*I think it's fair. I don't know that I even knew there was no such thing as punitive damage in civil cases here. So that's kind of nice. I like learning that and I like knowing that. I'm a parent educator. **I believe in consequences.** Consequences can maybe disguise punishment, but if someone's taking a car and riding over someone's lawn for whatever reason, well, it makes sense that they would compensate the lawn owner with something that would allow them to make repairs and for whatever pain and suffering. They now have to do something that wasn't on their plate before and I've been there. Busy, now I have to do this other thing; compensated for their time and turmoil. So that seems reasonable. It fits. **I like the idea of it fitting the nature.** The consequence feels appropriate. It seems more like a well-placed consequence in that sort of situation. How it really shows up in courts, I don't really know.*

The primary goal of jury selection is to identify individuals who are more or less appropriate for a case because of bias and prejudice. How do you think is the best way to ask you or your group that will generate meaningful answers in a setting where we don't really know each other; we're all in high states of alertness?

*I do a lot of reading on brain research so it depends on how you set the questions. What's coming to mind, based on more recent readings I've been doing – to ask the question, **what are your deepest values?***

What are your deepest values?

And allow the jury to have a conversation, perhaps facilitated or not, among each other to talk about what their deepest values are. Not only does it seem to get at part of what you're asking or all of what you're asking, but also, because we're these living systems, right? And then we're in a group and the group itself is a living system, so it starts to create a living system of, I think, more likely fairness. So it's not, where are you at right this second, but what's possible for this group to gel in a way that serves justice; to have their highest values in mind? Connecting around that, and the likelihood of the jury or individuals on that jury being able to actually live into that is higher. **So the question can actually develop the group.**

You have some expertise here, so I'm going to ask for a little help. If a question is asked of this group about their values, is there a way to put it into a context that's something that they don't feel so overwhelmed by?

That's kind of a core question, what are your deepest values?

They may not quite know what the purpose is and the context.

I think you could preamble it with, for the purposes of understanding how you all will function together as a group and to have a sense of – the research that was done around this question, they found it was more productive when they asked the question in a very open-ended, sort of unsettling way, that it helped people get into a deeper place. Just have it really open-ended. It is somewhat unsettling. Knowing group process, sometimes these juicy questions, it takes maybe a couple, three go-arounds. It takes some time, at least an hour, I think, so that people could circle, go around the group two or three times. The first pass, they're not going to go there. But it does this spiral-y thing.

And they tend to model each other's behavior and push a little bit.

Well, someone will share something. **It could be something like, please share from your own experience. You have the right to pass if you want to. Sometimes people will pass, and then second time they'll share. If they pass the whole time, maybe that's a reason not to have them on the jury. And maybe there will also be something around, my reason for being here is to help you have a conversation or whatever.** *We're trying to filter out – we want the right people, so we are listening.* **But we want you to feel like you're making a contribution. It's not a bad thing to say. We want you to feel like you're making a contribution.** *We want to feel like justice is served. Something like that.*

Do you have an opinion or a feeling one way or the other about the attorney leading off by sharing something of his or her values?

I think that sounds really nice. It's also a model. The facilitator is often in a place where they can model how it's done by doing the first share.

Do you have a sense that would be perceived as manipulative by anyone in the group?

I don't know what people think a lot of times. I'm always surprised. I'm used to circles and conversations. I did Conversation Café for a while and facilitated that.

How many were in those conversational groups?

It varied, like eight, ten. So kind of smallish, but a fairly consistent core of us. Probably always at least five.

We're talking about getting people to identify their core values. Once you've identified your core values to the group or talked about that, where would you feel comfortable with the lawyer taking that?

So it would be the lawyer that's facilitating this group and you're imagining starting out the sharing?

You've just shared and then –

And you've given permission to pass –

Right.

– if you don't have anything in any particular round.

What would the lawyer do to follow up that would be comfortable for you? What would you expect?

Well, if you've stated in the beginning, we've got 40 people in the room and what we want is a jury of twelve so we are filtering, and there is a filter here. It's kind of emergent. It's kind of like, we're making judgments or – I don't know if you want to use that word, but something – we're making assessments or something maybe less threatening.

We're learning about you.

We're learning about you. *Yes, that's better.* **And learning about how this group can work together.** *I don't know exactly like what the filter is. That would be for a group of lawyers to figure out, or for people to figure out what. But some of it, I would think, would be somewhat emergent and you would make some choices, clearly. If it's done well, everyone walks away feeling like they got something, even though they're not on the jury. Some people are going to be disappointed. Some people are going to be totally relieved. I think.*

Some who are at the very back won't have a likelihood of being on anyway. They generally know that and maybe are less likely to participate and are often less selected to talk.

Right. Does that answer the question?

I think so. So you're okay with talking about your values and potential – how about if I said this: is there anything you think about this kind of a case that would make you feel more or less suitable to be here? Is there a different kind of case you'd rather be on?

No, not necessarily. I think I'd be open. As I said, in the early stages, some anxiety. If I knew there was a process like this then I'd be like, this is cool. Then I'd be excited about it.

What I'd like to see, ideally, is the jury lets both sides start at the same point. So those people who think that for whatever reason, somebody is going to start out having to make up ground – for example, trial lawyers are deemed in some studies as being second only to used-car dealers in terms of credibility. I walk into this courtroom already behind. I would like jurors to let me start out from an even place with the other side. Do you share any of those feelings or concerns about lawyers?

Like I said, I think lawyers are different. I not only know my friend, I know other people who are very fine people. There are some that aren't so fine. I don't hang out with them.

We were talking about starting out.

Oh, keep them at the same – so I think that the process I'm describing is part of what could help lawyers be more – because you're participating. You know, the circle goes around again, you share a second – **and it's real. It's not canned.** *I mean, you might have a sense of what a canned starting point is,* **but it's like, what's up in the moment? Someone might say something that sparks another comment, or whatever. So I think there is something very equalizing about a circle process, which is what I'm describing, or circle conversation.**

Do you think, given your education, background and experience, that you are a good fit for justice? That you feel like you can participate with a group and reach a result you can live with?

I think in a civil situation, yes, more likely, especially because it's a not penal civil system here. In a penal situation, I think it could be very challenging to work with people who are wanting to mete out punishment and suffering.

How do you feel about the fact that this is an adversarial process with the parties; that one side is going to win and one side is going to lose? Does that color your feelings about the potential credibility of the attorneys and their clients because they have so much to gain or lose?

Right. I have a question and it relates to this fantasy process. Where's the other lawyer in this? The opposing lawyer?

The other lawyer, the defendant's attorney, then gets an opportunity to do their questioning –

With the jury?

Questioning of the jury.

Separate?

Yes. Then sometimes the judge gives me another bite at the apple, and then the same with the other lawyer.

Are you witnessing?

Yes.

Oh, you are?

We're all there.

Both lawyers are watching. So it's a fishbowl-type of thing.

We're all observing each other.

Got it. Okay. So the question is, because it's adversarial and there's going to be a winner and a loser, at least within this case; the way that I'm thinking of it is, that there was a loser, because there is a victim, someone that something happened to because of someone else's actions.

Right. Or inactions.

*Or inactions. For whatever reason. **So to me, it's making it even again. It's taking the loser and putting them back to as close to where they started from as possible.** I'm thinking the loser is the person that did or didn't do something. It's not always that way, but anyway, I'll just run with this: they've lost the case, but in life, hopefully, over time, they'll kind of go, that was the right thing. In the moment, they might not feel that at all.*

They may not feel that having been accused or sued.

*Certainly lots of people, including the winner, feel resentful for their whole lives. They didn't get exactly what they wanted; the compensation wasn't enough, whatever. That's the part where you can't control what other people feel or think. So that part you let go. **You do whatever you can to bring people to a place where justice is served and people can walk away more comfortable with the decision at some point, looking back on it.***

Would you feel differently about the case if the defendant was an individual as opposed to a corporate entity?

Probably.

How so?

I do have some prejudices against. Not every corporation is, but our system is built in a way that corporations are always about growing, growing, growing, growing. There's the triple bottom line sort of stuff.

Profit.

It's a system designed to make ogres of corporations, even though that might not be the original intention of when a corporation begins and I'm not as involved as I used to be in all that stuff. So I don't know where we're at. But I know we're plundering our earth, and I have a lot of concerns about the corporations are people; they're not. That makes ogres out of corporations.

The reason I ask that is that you may have a person and she may be a school teacher who's a defendant, but you may also have a corporation whose employee caused the same kind of harm. Let's say a teacher drove her car negligently and caused a permanent injury to a person, or a corporation's employee did the same thing. But one defendant is the corporation; another defendant is an individual that we revere as a school teacher. How would you be able to mete out the same or a different kind of justice for the same injury?

Same injury, same costs involved? I don't know. Typically, in a situation like that, are people looking at the corporation and saying they have deeper pockets so we should be able to be compensated without penalizing them more? Or is that –

You can only sue the individual or entity that injured you. I guess the question I'm getting at is, would you do different justice, and by that I mean, would your award be less if the defendant were a revered individual as opposed to an entity?

Well, what I would want to know with the entity is, with an individual, they're not beholden to – they're driving themselves as themselves. With a corporate entity, it's like they're an employee. Is the employee trained well? Are they maintaining the vehicle properly? **To me, there's always going to be other questions that are more systemic. Because it's a system as opposed to an individual.** *I would start wanting to know more with a corporation. It seems more straightforward than an individual. Are they doing drug testing of their employees? Was this an employee who was drunk? If the teacher's drunk, that's one thing. You deal with that. If it's a corporation whose employee is drunk and maybe all other corporations regularly drug test, but this corporation isn't or they have a policy to drug test but they're not, it gets more complicated. It's not a simple answer.*

No, it isn't. And it's a difficult issue.

Because corporations aren't people.

What I'm getting at is, if you perceived the corporation had deeper pockets than an individual, the schoolteacher, for example, would that cause you to award a different amount? Given the ability of the defendant to pay when it's all said and – for the same injury and the same –

Let's say that everything's on the up-and-up with the corporation. We have asked these questions and have gotten answers that are reasonable. Yes, they've trained the employee. It was clearly the employee's fault. It was clearly not the corporation's fault, in that they've done everything they were supposed to do within training and drug testing and all of their things. That's all in place. They've maintained the vehicle, blah, blah, blah. So it seems like you would just get the same amount. You would ask for the same amount. **If the corporation is wrong as an entity, though, then I would want more from them for the same damage, so to speak.**

Got it. Some people have said, for the same injury, because I don't think the schoolteacher can pay it, I don't want to bankrupt the school teacher. I'm going to probably award the plaintiff less because I don't think the defendant can pay it.

Okay. Well, then that's a different thing.

That's a concern because then we wonder –

I might. I don't know. I'm not really sure. But I could see wanting to go down that road at least and look at that. If this is a person who's like – I mean, I suppose there's a lot of things you're not allowed to consider.

Insurance.

Insurance. I don't know. Like, there have been witnesses that have said this is a great teacher. I love this teacher. Am I a teacher? Or done all this wonderful work in the world and she doesn't really – I can see that the money isn't really there, but I might be inclined to not necessarily screw the corporation in a similar thing, but to make it fair. To me, it's like, she did this thing, but it wasn't on purpose. You know, it wasn't manslaughter, or it probably was manslaughter if she had killed somebody. But it wasn't intentional.

Just negligent.

Wasn't violent. So I might opt to look for what's the most fair thing that's possible for both. Again, it's not trying to punish. It's trying to meet each situation where they're at, I guess.

Each case being uniquely different.

Yeah.

We talked about biases, and I never liked the words bias and prejudice; I'm always looking for something different there. But one of the other goals I feel strongly about is how can the lawyer establish a human connection with you?

In that jury context?

In that context, given the limitations of time and the numbers of people there and this unfamiliarity we have.

I think again, just going back to that, the one that occurs to me, values; I think there's many layers of value to that sort of thing. I think it would definitely establish some human – as much as is possible within a short time frame.

Are there any values you'd like to see in the lawyers?

If you're asking that question, what's your deepest core value, kind of thing? Then what I'd like to hear a lawyer say when they're asked that or sense about them? Integrity. And not wanting a punitive, retaliatory sort of lawyer voice or intention.

Is that a stereotypical thing, do you think, that you're keying in on?

It can vary. My friend who's a lawyer is a mediator so I'm tapped into the whole mediation thing, at least in family law.

Alternative dispute resolution.

Exactly. So in other words, in that teacher situation, if she really doesn't have that much money, you know, it's like you don't want to make it so she can't be a teacher anymore or can't live in this City anymore or whatever. That seems like something I'd like to see, whatever that positive quality is. I guess fairness.

Fairness. Okay. What about a passionate belief in the client and the case? How would that be best expressed in a way that's not manipulative or that would create any defensiveness?

Well, some types of people are going to be defensive. It's just – that's their stuff, and my stuff, sometimes.

It's great when we can all acknowledge that at least, right? What I'm looking for are people who have what they come with but can acknowledge it and be mindful of it through the process. That, I think, is the best I can hope for.

*I think the passion is like caring. It's like, I care about your values, whether you're winding up on the jury or not. I don't know exactly what gets said to convey that, but – and so I care about the client I'm representing. I'm passionate in that way, but again, not passionate about screwing over the other party. It's about, let's solve the problem. To me, it's a problem that needs to be solved, and we're here to solve it together, and solve it, the bigger problem of the whole case. **Obviously, you're advocating for your client, but you're not advocating in a way that's hurtful or mean-spirited,** if that makes sense.*

In some senses, that's really what it is. It's just coming at it from lots of different points of view. Let me come back to the schoolteacher for a minute. She sits there with her sweater on and doesn't really talk other than when she's given an opportunity to testify, but what nobody knows is that she has a million dollars in insurance. It's never talked about.

Wouldn't that be obvious?

The courts do not allow anybody to consider insurance. You are instructed specifically that insurance is not to be speculated about nor is it brought out in evidence.

Wow. That's weird.

How then do we know that we can do the right amount of justice?

So we can't ask the teacher under penalty of perjury whether she carries insurance and what the amount is?

That's right. It doesn't come in. And the reason for that –

Wow.

– is the courts don't want people to award more just because insurance is there.

Oh, the insurance industry doesn't want this to come up in court.

Right. And the courts also, and I think fairly so, say, if every jury knew there was insurance in every case, they would award more.

Got it.

When the issue is not – fairness isn't necessarily the ability to pay, it's what should the individual receive for their injuries? Compensation rather than –

That's interesting. I didn't realize that.

Most people assume that businesses have insurance.

But isn't our State – like aren't you required to carry insurance if you're driving?

Mandatory minimums, 25/50/10.

So in other words, you might be inclined to award the victim more than what the mandatory minimum is and this teacher may only have the mandatory minimum or you could assume that or you would hope that's true, because of course, people can blow up their insurance. I know people that drive without it.

Lots of people.

I don't know lots of people, but I do know people. So, that's an interesting question.

And we don't have an answer to it, it's just something –

So then you'd just have to go with the value. Then you can't really figure out, because you don't know whether they have insurance or not. So then you can't take it into account what they're able to pay.

Right. That's what the judge's instruction would be.

Then that seems that's the way it is, according to the rules of the game. I guess I can kind of see that with insurance. There's some value in having an insurance industry and we don't want to have to pay $5,000 a month premiums because all these things are getting awarded, so. It's sort of the industry of insurance is holding a lot of tension in it.

Big industry. Big. And they are constantly at odds with trial lawyers because insurance takes the brunt of these kinds of awards when there's a verdict. Generally, an insurance company is there to pay it, and they want to pay as little as possible. So there's a lot of tension in this process. This project is to get a sense of where people fit.

Our culture's a lot of punishment. People like that. And that's how they associate it with justice. But I think when you start asking people what their core values are, some of that starts to dissolve somewhat.

What core values would be most helpful in this context? Or let me turn that question upside down. What are some core values I would want to identify that we would not want to have participating?

My guess is if they're really getting to their core values, it's all good. But my guess is, part of the filter is they're not in touch with their core values.

What does that look like?

I don't know. That's just how I see it. It looks like meting out punishment rather than, this is my values, right?

Right.

So it looks like, screw that other person or, I don't believe in your client and obviously they're not going to be on – you know. It's like I have a value to this, your client is bad.

Or greedy?

Yeah. And the other client is bad or greedy or both. I have a question. Do you have the power or authority as a lawyer in a civil case to run jury questioning in this manner? Is that an option for you?

We question openly to the entire group - individually or to the group.

So you could conceivably do a round.

I could ask for a show of hands. Generally we key in on the first 20 or so. We may ask an individual juror to please talk about something. And maybe ask another person, what do you think about that? There really are no rules about how we do it, only some rules about what we can and cannot talk about.

So you could run a circle process if you chose to? Not saying you should, it might not be the best method.

Sure.

I keep going there, because I'm elaborated on that so much.

With a group of, say, 60 or 80, that can be time-consuming. Maybe a smaller group, I can see that. Or as we've narrowed them down, because I like what you say. That would be the approach I would ideally want to do; every person participating in this, and knowing that their turn is coming if they wish to participate, or opt out.

So I would say, I don't know about this exactly, but if they're not able to tap into their value, in the sense that they're not really connected even with themselves, they're disconnected with themselves for any number of reasons. They're not able to find a place of compassion in themselves. You're not picking up compassion; sensing that they're not going to be a team player, which is probably something you filter for anyway.

Look for.

*And I don't know that it could be. **Some of these things aren't necessarily going to be explicit, it's just how they're showing up.** They're not going to say, my core value is to not get along with other people. They're not going to say that. They may pass or they might say the right words, but you're not feeling that connectedness to themselves. Hatred. We all carry some of that stuff anyway, but if it's really alive and animated kind of thing –*

Some people will be very honest because they want to get out of jury service.

Or dishonest to get out.

To get out. And we can use that sometimes to get people to keep talking more about that issue. If somebody says, I just hate trial lawyers. Well, okay. Great, thank you. And how does everyone else feel about that?

Yeah, that's great.

Let's talk about damages. In civil cases we have to prove negligence caused harm. So three things: an injury that was caused by negligence. Let's assume we've proved negligence and causation and we're talking about the harm. The harms are compensable. You have two kinds. Special damages: those are wages, medical bills, things that can be specifically enumerated.

Financial.

Right. Generally speaking, you can look for receipts and numbers. They may be past, they may be future. But we also have general damages, which may be pain, suffering, disability, loss of enjoyment of life, for which there is no fixed standard for determination. How would you approach a way of thinking about compensating somebody?

__That's a big mystery to me.__ I've been in auto accidents where I've negotiated that with my insurance company.

They had a different point of view, I would guess.

I approached my insurance company as, this is a problem, let's solve it. I didn't take their first offer. I'd made a counteroffer and we would somewhere figure it in the middle. We're not talking huge amounts of money here, maybe $2,000 of medical damages and maybe three for car, but stuff you could put the money to.

Did you negotiate for the pain and suffering part?

*Yes. Yes. Yes. And I'm trying to remember. **It seems like it would be one to three times as much as the dollars,** I was told in one situation with the insurance company that because I was okay, so my car Blue Book value is like five hundred dollars. But I was driving it, and I can't replace it for five hundred dollars. It was in good mechanical shape. In order for me to get a replacement car, it's going to cost me several thousand dollars. And they're like, we can't, there's these two parts. I negotiated with two different people, or in two different contexts or something. They were like, we can't count it as – what you said, compensable* *or whatever they called it – but when it comes to this other part, then you can kind of pad it. So that's how I worked it in my mind. My main thing was, I want to replace my car. I spent like forty hours of my precious time in this last month dealing with this. So that sucks. So I kind of figured, and I wasn't working, what's my time worth?* **I'm thinking double to triple the costs on paper was the pain and suffering part.**

You had that as a guideline going in?

Yeah. I was always like, I don't want to do a lawyer. No one was horribly hurt. But there would be some medical stuff. A couple times, three times it's happened. So that seemed reasonable to me. I don't know in a civil case of someone else's. I just knew that I wasn't there to screw over my insurance company, and I also knew that if I'm approaching them like they're my enemy, I'm going to probably get less.

Was this your insurance company or the insurance company for the person who hit you?

I think I've done both. One time, it was a friend's car, this was many years ago, and it was her insurance. I wanted, obviously, all my expenses. That was the worst accident I was in. The car was front-ended and it was bad. I was only in my early 20s, so I don't think I knew how to advocate as well. I would have asked for more now. But at the time, it just seemed like, oh, boy, I get this money. That was probably the time that I got maybe the same amount in pain and suffering. They just offered it to me, and I'm like, two thousand dollars? Sure, I'll take it.

Did you have any permanent injuries as a result of those accidents?

I don't think so. I mean, all the things that happen to us in our lives we store in our bodies. So in some sense, yes. But in other senses, I've been able to work with it. I have some medical providers in my life and have done a lot of personal stuff around posture, so I'm sure it's in there. It's in me, but it certainly wasn't serious stuff that some people – you know, broken bones and – it was more like neck and back, shoulder stuff.

I've wondered if posture is something you unconsciously or consciously use as a filter to determine if somebody's credible or not?

Well, probably unconsciously, because we all do, don't we?

I think so.

Looking you in the eye, for the most part, it's pretty accurate except for those people that are very good at knowing how to lie. There are those people. But yes, I'm sure unconsciously I do.

Let's talk about that for a minute. Lying. Do you have a sense that people who have something at stake in the courtroom are being truthful or have a tendency to be less truthful because there's so much at stake to win or lose? Is there anything you have experienced?

Yeah, they probably have a stake in coloring it in a certain direction. I think that's human nature. It's almost like, how could you not? Right? Lying – I'm sure some people do. What the percentage is, I have no idea. But there's probably statistics on that sort of thing. And there are sociopathic people. If they're highly intelligent, and not all of them are, and make a study of facial stuff, they certainly can intentionally lie and not feel the guilt and not show it, so you don't pick up on it.

Coming back to the human connection, I like to turn questions on their head and say, we've talked about what a lawyer could do to establish a human connection with you. What might they do that would serve the opposite end?

To break it? I think it's probably just slightly under consciousness. Maybe sometimes it rises into consciousness a little. When there's someone on a hot seat, I am really noticing body language. So, breaking eye contact, especially when they're saying something that you're not quite sure, like you're trying to assess, is that real?

Breaking eye contact with the person who you're questioning?

Right. Or, well, with questioning, I don't know. That's a little different. Because sometimes you give them space so you're not looking directly at them. I don't know. You're not talking about on the witness stand, you're talking about in this jury process.

As a juror, what would turn you off?

There's something about body language there, probably in part because you brought it up. I can't tell you exactly what it would be. That, again, punitive kind of – this party, that party. Or maybe, not giving a sense that I care about my client. It's just another, I'm bored. That kind of stuff.

Just things that we all – common sense.

I would think so. Common sense.

Not being fully engaged in a genuine way.

Yeah, it's being real as different from not being real, like trying to hide your tiredness or antsy-ness as opposed to being able to say, gosh, I think I drank too much coffee this morning or, I didn't drink enough coffee this morning. My child kept me up all night.

Burden of proof in a criminal case, as most people know, is beyond a reasonable doubt. In a civil case, we have a different burden of proof, called a preponderance of the evidence. When I say preponderance, what does that suggest to you? We have a burden of proof standard that's different. In criminal cases, we call it beyond a reasonable doubt. The reason that's so high is because liberty is at stake. Civil burden is somewhat less; a preponderance, because liberty isn't the issue. Money is the issue, property. What does the word preponderance suggest to you considering what amount of weight must carry the day?

*I have to say our culture – money is so important, it's such a high value and a high necessity. We don't have this great safety net. **To me, it's almost the same weight because it's almost like, you don't get liberty without money in our particular culture, unless you have a lot of money.** But then you can afford to lose a million.*

The instruction the judge gives to the jury at the conclusion of the case mentions a preponderance of the evidence for all the elements that need to be proved. But then goes on to say, a preponderance of the evidence means more likely than not. Does that inform you more one way or another from what we just talked about?

More likely than not? As opposed to beyond a reasonable doubt? Does the judge say, this is different from beyond a reasonable doubt, or does he or she just say more likely than not.

The judge reads the instruction to the jury and says, if you find, by a preponderance of the evidence each element has been proved; then a separate instruction says, a preponderance of the evidence simply means more likely true than not true. Does that suggest a different amount of weight to sway you one way or another?

*Somewhat depends on whether I'm a deep thinker or not and whether I'm really paying attention in this moment and whether or not I can make those distinctions of vocabulary. Even me, who tends to be a deep thinker and pay close attention to words and definitions, even I might not catch it. **I might just be thinking, it's gotta be proven or I might not hear it if it was only said once and it wasn't said as a contrast to and by the way it's different from a criminal thing,** which is blah, blah, blah. So, if I didn't have something directing my attention in a very specific way on the weight of that, especially in our highly text-y, high-tech-y culture, my sense is most people wouldn't pick up the difference. That's my sense. And I might not even. But now, having this conversation, I would really pay attention. Now we're focusing on it and assuming I have really paid attention. I don't know. It's like I need the actual example.*

Let me ask you this: you've seen the statue of the blindfolded lady with the scales. That's the statue of justice.

I didn't know she was blind.

Justice is blind.

I've heard that, but I didn't know that the statue with the scales was blind. Are her eyes like kind of staring?

Just covered with a –

A cloth. I didn't know – see? All these details.

What's so great about this process for me is, it helps me understand that people don't speak the same vocabulary or live in the same world. That helps me be more aware of what I need to do to explain.

I think, now more than ever, we live in very different worlds.

Exactly. A lawyer that I admire greatly says, if you want to know what a jury is thinking, don't ask a lawyer. Because we have a different frame. We're trained to have a different frame.

> *Absolutely. Because probably, at some point in law school, you were talking about blind justice and what that means and looking at that picture. I don't know how many people would know. **I've heard justice is blind. I know that, and I can assume; I can kind of figure out what that probably means based on my own thinking.** But I didn't even connect. I don't think I've ever noticed the scarf or thought of it that way.*

She's holding the scales. If the scales were tipped 51 to 49, how do you feel about that being an adequate burden in a civil case?

> *Off the top of my head, seems reasonable. We're not going to get perfect.*

If the lawyer argues that a preponderance or more likely than not means just this (gesturing with hands to indicate 51/49), are you comfortable with that as the standard if that was all the proof on an issue?

> ***Probably. Of course, it's dependent on my group.** I probably wouldn't hold an opposing line of the whole group if it was that close.*

If you felt it was different than the group, you'd want to talk about it, right?

> *Yeah, but I'd be willing to concede if – I work in groups a lot in unanimity, proper consensus process. But it doesn't have to be a hundred percent. **Like, don't let the perfect be the enemy of the good or whatever.***

Exactly. If you were a party in a civil case, had been injured or had injured someone, what are the traits of individuals you would like to see as jurors in your case?

> *Again, back to not trying to mete out punishment as opposed to trying to just solve the problem **so it's fair for everybody.** I would want to feel like I could trust them. I would want to feel like I could trust them together, because I am a big believer in the value of collective, thoughtful process, especially when it's a random group. This is not exactly random with juries, but approaches it somewhat; one of the things that approaches it most in our system. So I'd want to feel like I could trust them to make the best determination.*

If you were able to ask each juror independently one question that would get to whether or not they might have an agenda one way or the other that would impair the process of the group, what would that be?

> *Well, the surface one is, is there anything you think would recuse you from or – that's so frontal, and you're probably not likely to get a very good answer. I'm wondering if the question, what's your deepest core value is what I would want to most ask.*

I can answer that question for me, but it took me nearly 50 years to identify my deepest core value. And that was based on some very significant circumstances. I am wondering, do people really know what their core values are?

No. That's the thing. They don't know at first. It takes a process. That's why the open-endedness is much more valuable. They may not get to it in a session. This experiment was set up is, they were asked to write it 10 days in a row. It's a book called Words Can Change Your Brain. *I think Newman is one of the authors. It's two authors. One's a neuroscientist and the other is a business consultant. See what you make of it. The other instruction is, when you wake up, the first thing you do is write the core value, right before your conscious brain starts kicking in and filtering all that out. But my thought is, in a round kind of group process, it shortens that length of time. I don't know if it's going to get you the same place an individual writing it is going to get you, but you can get deeper for sure through a process, like Conversation Café, where you go around in a couple rounds. This is my experience. And the more diverse the group, the more likely they're going to go deeper. The more broad, and the more different places people are coming from when they answer that question, the better – I mean the deeper.*

What kind of individuals would frustrate those ends in that process?

That's a good question. Someone maybe who is on drugs at that time, actively using. Being in some huge crisis in their personal lives. Somebody that is not physically able to be present. Maybe mental illness. Probably sociopathic personality. I don't know how easy it is to find them. People that really just can't show up. But still, there have been experiences recording a group process with people who are homeless and at the bottom of society and still having some really good conversations.

Conversations.

I don't know if that's informative to this.

Some training advocates that the lawyer identify their biggest fear about the case and go straight to the jury with it. What do you think about that? Some lawyers who are very successful say that their approach to jury selection is, identify what I fear most about the case and go straight to the jury with that fear. Share that fear.

Right. I think if you're coming from a place of fear, you're likely to push away some people that might be very good on your jury. They talk about fear-based in Words Can Change Your Brain *and this comes up in other writings, coming from a place of value, this is what I want, or this is my vision, even being able to say that and prepping yourself in a – this is going be a really amazing jury. Not that it's concrete necessarily, but you're coming in with an energy, an attitude around positivity. **It's like justice will be served and I'm participating in the best possible way that I can, and I believe that everyone here is doing the best they can. It's my job. Part of my job is to find the ones that are going to help justice be served the best for the sake of my client or whatever.** So* *my sense is that would be more effective because I'm thinking, that's a scary question or statement.*

If you're afraid of something.

And there's a lot of people that have enough self-doubt that they're going to go, oh, well, that's probably me, so.

I appreciate that perspective. That resonates with me. Is there anything in our discussion that's come up that you think might helpful?

I think we've been pretty thorough.

I appreciate it. Thank you.

46

YOU CAN'T FAKE GENUINE

Asian-Caucasian, female, age 47, divorced, Researcher, Ph.D. Clinical Psychology

Too polished, too rehearsed. There is just a sense that there is something they want from you. They're shining up their presentation to be appealing to you, but yet you know, at the very bottom of that, they want a sale. It's just a little too friendly, over-friendly, kind of schmoozy.

Ladies and gentlemen, please give your attention to the attorney for the plaintiff who will conduct their part of jury selection. In that room with those people, the judge and the lawyers and their clients, what are your primary thoughts and feelings?

First, I'd probably be wondering whether or not I would be selected, and then what the criteria would be about, whether or not they would want to include me or exclude me from being one of the jurors.

Given your professional background?

Yeah. I wouldn't know what they were looking for or what they wouldn't want because at that point, you wouldn't have any idea what the case actually was, right? You would just have, based on what you just told me, very general information about what it is. I would be wondering if the plaintiff was in the right, if they really did deserve to get a settlement. I'd probably be wondering who was the person or the company that was perhaps negligent. And I'd be thinking about the lawyers' experience as well.

That's a lot of thought about other people. In that room, are you comfortable about your ability to be a juror, then and there, in the case as you've heard about it?

*I think so. I've always been a fairly analytical and logical type of person, so **I think I would be able to weigh the evidence soundly.** But who knows? Who knows what they're going to present? **Is there something that's going to strike me in an emotional way?** And would that then somehow play into how I thought about the case?*

In jury selection we want to find people who can be open-minded, they use the words bias and prejudice, so people who can identify their biases and prejudices can come forth and say, because of those, they can or can't be good jurors in that case. How do you think it's best to approach you to ask the question, can you be fair and impartial in a case? If you have any biases, can you put them aside? How do you think it's best to bring that up, given that I'm a stranger and these are all strangers coming together for the first time as a group for this purpose?

That's a hard question to answer, because you don't know what potential
bias could come into play in that particular case. I think you can certainly
ask people if they think they have any biases or prejudices that may come
up that they couldn't set aside. That may be the way you do it already. I would
like to think I could set those aside and be objective as a juror, but I know that I
do have some biases and prejudices, yes. And it is very possible those would come
into play somehow; if not affecting me emotionally, then it would affect maybe
my judgment even a little bit. That's very possible.

Thank you for articulating and acknowledging that. Given that you've mentioned
you may have some, would you be willing to share what some of those might be that
you think would or potentially could get in the way or be a part of your thinking?

So I'm going to imagine that it's maybe a corporation versus an individual.

As the defendant?

Yeah. The plaintiff would be an individual; the defendant would be a corporation.
Maybe in that situation one bias would be that a corporation's not a person.
They're an entity, which I see needs to be responsible for a lot of different things.
And corporations can't, I suppose they can't attend to every single detail, so
there's the potential there could be something that they did or didn't do which
caused injury. As far as people go, I can tell you right away, Republicans, this is
probably too blunt for the interview, but I have a thing about Republicans, ultra-
conservatives, people who are racist. Those are pretty strong biases.

Biases that you have already coming in that you're aware of, that you think there's
a possibility could affect the way you think, one way or the other, for one side or
the other?

Mm-hmm.

That's what we want to hear from people. Often, it's pretty hard to get people
talking about their own biases and prejudices for lots of reasons. They want to be
on the jury, and they don't want to let people know about it. They're not sure what
people are looking for. Maybe they're blissfully unaware that they have them. Given
you have those feelings or biases or predilections that you acknowledged, how do
you think those might affect your weighing of the case, one side or the other?

I think the most basic would be whether or not any of those factors had
any bearing on the case. Are they relevant? That would be part of it. But it
could also make me feel or think differently about whoever that person is if they
revealed themselves in that way. For instance, if they were a member of NRA.
Those things may never come up, and I'm guessing that I might never hear any
of that, but if I did, I wouldn't forget it. It would be stuck. I would definitely try to
put it aside, of course, because that would be my job.

I guess that is the question, when you've identified those, and then it becomes, how
strongly do you feel you could let this side start out evenly and wait until you've
heard all the evidence to make a decision?

*Mm-hmm. So your question earlier about how would you ask somebody about their biases that way, and you may already do this, **but it could be that you describe scenarios and ask a person, if you were in this scenario, what would you do or what would you think? In that way, it's less direct.***

Can you think of anything that might be a way to approach that without coming right out and saying, hey, folks, what are your biases and prejudices?

It would really be specific to the case, though, right? Because as a lawyer, you would be wondering if certain personal biases would affect that juror. You would know what the case is all about, right. If you couldn't talk about the case at that point, which you probably couldn't –

Can't really talk about the details. What we often face, and what we're getting people to say is that there are too many frivolous lawsuits. I don't believe that people should be suing as much as they're suing. I don't think people should get money damages for pain and suffering, that lawyers are dishonest and greedy and sleazy; ambulance-chasers. Those are the attitudes we like to hear, because then at least we know those are potentially people that may not let us start evenly. That's the number one thing I like to explore: how can I get people to talk about their attitudes and beliefs without being threatened by it or feeling manipulated?

*So you can't just directly ask about that? You couldn't just directly ask, **what do you think about the state of things today where people are suing for a lot of different reasons?***

We can. And we can address not only any individual juror, but we can ask people to raise their hands.

But you're trying to figure out a way to finesse it, so that you can get the information, but that people don't feel threatened or that they're not –

Or manipulated.

– or influenced to not say that, you know what I mean?

Right. And it's not like a therapeutic group where you're sitting in a circle. It's kind of us versus them in a sense. Especially because I'm coming in already with a lack of credibility as a plaintiff's trial lawyer.

Really? Why is that?

Well, the general public doesn't perceive trial lawyers, especially plaintiff's lawyers, very well.

*That's something that wouldn't have occurred to me. **I know people think negatively in general about lawyers; not everybody, but many do.***

We're perceived as very incredible. So we're catching up as we come in there. And for the reasons you talked about earlier, and by Fox News and the McDonald's verdict and those things, where people hear about the lady who spilled coffee on herself and she gets, they think, millions and millions of dollars and that just isn't right. What kind of a lottery system is this? Or, this is causing our costs to go up. Insurance is going up, doctors are being driven out of the country; that's what many people believe. How do you feel about that?

> *I'm sure there are frivolous lawsuits, but in my mind, I don't categorize, I don't see them all that way. To me, there's a lot of differences between every single case. I would want to weigh each case individually, so I don't have that kind of bias. As far as spilling hot coffee in your lap and getting burned, sure, there can be some compensation, but a limit on that. If you're seriously talking a million, that seems like way too much, right? So I think there's a reasonable amount that people should be able to get. Tell me if I'm not answering your questions.*

There are no right or wrongs.

> *Some of these questions are, I really have to think about.*

It's okay because in the *voir dire* process you'd be as cold to these questions as we are now. You'd be hearing them for the first time, just like at this point. The spontaneity is good here. The next important thing, and maybe more critical than identifying bias, is how can an attorney who you don't know establish a human connection with you in that environment?

> *I think I'm the kind of person who reads body language and facial expression very well and very accurately. So for me, at least, **I don't think you can fake being genuine. I think people would be looking for a genuine humanness about you, a genuine humanity, and that you're really interested in them. I think some people may be fooled. The one thing that comes to mind right now is that salesman demeanor. If you have that, I mean, that's an immediate turn off.***

One of the reasons why I'm doing this project is, I tend to be comfortable in this jury selection process, but I have not gotten the kinds of money awards I've been seeking from the jurors. I'm wondering, is there something about me there or is it just maybe case selection? It's hard to say. I feel generally comfortable talking to jurors, but I'd like to be better at it. What does the salesman demeanor look like to you?

> ***Too polished, too rehearsed. There is just a sense that there is something they want from you. They're shining up their presentation to be appealing to you, but yet you know, at the very bottom of that, they want a sale. It's just a little too friendly, over-friendly, kind of schmoozy.** Do you know what I mean?*

We all know when we're being sold. Some people have said, make sure you acknowledge what I'm saying. Don't just listen for what you want to hear and then if you don't hear it, move on. He said, I'll know that and I'll be unhappy about it. At the same time, we can't connect with everybody. We have such a limited time to address so many people in a fairly nerve-wracking environment with a lot at stake.

So I'm trying to find a way to hear what people have to say about what they think the experience is like and what their needs would be.

I think right off the bat, when you're walking into a room of 40 or 60 people, you can notice who makes eye contact with you. You can really get a sense. So if you're going up and speaking in front of this group, right away you notice who's really paying attention and who seems interested. Are they playing on their phones? Are they looking out the window?

Right. There are clearly people that just want to get out and they're going to probably find a way. It's often the snakes in the grass that are the hardest, because they may have an agenda and don't want to talk about or articulate, but they want to be there. People who work for insurance companies or what have you.

*Right away, I think of eye contact. I work with people who don't like to make a lot of direct eye contact, and I had to learn a different way of communicating with them. So I think it depends. You have to feel out who you're with, too, and whether or not it's threatening. Some people have told me that my eye contact is too intense. But that's partly because when I'm listening, that's where I get the most, that's where I think I learn the most when I'm talking to somebody. But in the tribal communities where I work, people typically don't look directly at you. They look in this direction while they're talking, and then they'll turn and look at you, then they look away. Anyway, **I think in a person's body language you can read so much.***

It would be dangerous to try to do that without – I mean, I know there are schools of thought about reading body language and facial expressions and those sorts of things, but in the moment, we don't really have time to chart that or figure it out.

Right. Exactly.

We can hire people. What would you suggest would be helpful to tune into the first thought, right thought, the gut approach or – really what we're doing is de-selecting. We're trying to find those who are most dangerous to the case. Maybe that's easier than we make it out to be sometimes.

I don't know. I find these questions hard because it's hard to imagine being in your position.

It's kind of unfair because I'm asking you to be in a position and you're trying to get into my position so we're both jumping around a little bit.

Well, a lot of your questions are, what would you do? What should you do to have a certain effect on me? And I'm really not sure.

I've found it helpful in these conversations to turn it on its head and say, what would really turn you off as a potential juror sitting there in that environment? What would cause you to have some real pause about the credibility or the importance of the case or your own wanting to be there or sharing genuinely?

When I think about being in that situation, I know the people who are going to be talking to me are prepared, or they're supposed to be prepared, so I can't imagine them making many mistakes. But I think if they seemed impatient or seemed kind of fumbling over their words. If they, like you mentioned earlier, have that underlying motive; which you do, right? Like you said, you're de-selecting. I guess if I got a sense that was what it was all about, I might be turned off by that. **I think what you said earlier about really being interested in the person – that would be important. That would need to come across.**

How do you do that without it getting creepy?

So are you talking group or one-on-one?

Both. Because we're talking sometimes to an individual but the group is watching. They're paying attention. Ultimately, we want to get everybody talking. The fewer words I say the better, because I want to hear people talk. But everybody has a different comfort level with eye contact and being put on the spot. I'm going to put somebody on the spot and they may not like it or they may not want to be. How do you go about doing that? How would it work for you to be called on?

I think it's better to ask a question for the whole group and then see who wants to respond to it. *And I don't know, you probably already do this –*

That's a good point.

– but as you said, **facilitate conversation among people. You could pose a question, whatever it may be. You could describe a scenario, and then you could say, what I'd like to hear is all of you talk about this particular topic. What do you think of blah, blah, blah? In that way, they're talking to each other more, and also talking to you.** *I actually do this a lot. I run groups quite a bit. I do focus groups.* **What I do is, I may pose a question, but then I try to facilitate. So if somebody says something, I'll reflect something back. If the room is quiet, I'll say, so what did you think of what this person said to try to keep the conversation going.** *Do you already do that?*

We do that. From my experience, and what I've heard related is that, because of who we are as a profession, because of that environment that's foreign to most people, not ever been in a courtroom, sometimes scary, people have a hard time being themselves like they might be in a therapeutic group. First, there's so many of them. Nobody really wants to be there. They're worried about their time and money and they know that the lawyers are just out for the clients and so those are the issues that are percolating that I've found make it difficult to have that comfort I think you were talking about in the groups you facilitate. If it wasn't so much at stake in that moment - maybe that's an issue I have to work on.

So you're saying that doing something like that could be harmful to the process?

I think what you're articulating is absolutely the way the process has to happen, the way you just suggested.

Because out of that conversation then, or the discussion that various people have, you'll see who comes forward, right? Who actually wants to speak up? Then you'll be able to start picking up on the nuances of whether or not there is bias with regard to what you're doing. But I was also going to say, I think a really important beginning would be, how do you frame the whole process that you're going through? When you walk through the door and you start talking to people who are in that room, what do you say? **There's got to be something, some way of framing it so people don't feel as threatened, that they feel more relaxed and comfortable and free.**

Right. Somebody said, how can I normalize the group, initially? And as you say, framing it. They tell us in our training that you want to have jurors talk about the things you're most worried about doing damage to your case. I mentioned earlier, those are attitudes about – people don't think that the court system works, that it's out of control and they're suspicious. So trying to get folks like you who are on juries to open up about that. Your level of education and experience, I think, makes it easier for you to open up than maybe some.

True. Do you talk about that when you start talking to potential jurors? Do you bring up the whole idea of the system? Have you done that?

We don't have a lot of time; maybe an hour to an hour and a half – each side has.

Okay. I had no idea of what your time frame was.

They come in. The judge has given them an instruction about the system and what they're expected to do. But it's often not enough.

So you take that big group of people and talk to them over an hour to an hour and a half and then you whittle it down to a small group?

The other side has their time and each side maybe a short follow up. Then we do the process where we're able to excuse. We have a number of challenges where we can excuse for no reason. We can also attempt to excuse for cause, but that's tantamount to getting a person to say they can't follow the judge's instructions regardless, and that's often hard to do. People may have biases, but they're like, I really think I can follow the judge's instructions, as they sharpen the knife that's going to cut your client's head off. But no. It's not that bad.

So in the end, both sides agree to a certain number of people? Is there a set number of people?

You'll have 12 people plus one alternate or two from that large group; you're essentially de-selecting.

I don't know. Is this helpful for you at all?

Absolutely.

I don't feel like I have a lot of good information to share.

Every person has something valuable to say. You have said a number of things that are important that have helped me. What do you think would make you comfortable and at ease in that situation in that moment? What do you think you could hear or see that would put you at ease?

I think just a really good honest description about the process that you're going through.

About the process.

Because like I said, I've never been on a jury before, so walking in the room, I really wouldn't know what to expect, which is partly why I've asked you a lot of questions, because it's hard for me to imagine.

And that's a good question: who has and who hasn't had experience as a juror in the past? Because I think that would help me get a sense of comfort levels. Those who've been there are probably a little more comfortable than those without that experience, right?

Do you ask that question? Who has and has not been on a jury before?

We get this questionnaire. The problem with the questionnaire is we get it almost literally as they're walking into the courtroom.

*Oh, well, but you wouldn't need to look at that. That's kind of an ice breaker-like question. **Just by a show of hands, how many people have served on a jury before? How many have not?** I think that would make me comfortable, too, just to have some ice-breaker questions where you get participation because you've got to raise your hand for something.*

You've got to raise your hand.

It's a real simple thing, but I think it starts to engage people.

Right. And they don't have to share anything verbally at that point that will expose them to ridicule or make them feel nervous. And if you were asked, by show of hands, if you've not been on a jury, raise your hand and you do, what would you want to hear next?

*I think a good introduction of who you are. Or maybe you do that before you ask the jury a question. **I guess it's just describing the process. Also, I think you would be saying, we have this much time and this is our goal during that time, so why don't we start with – we just want to start out with some general discussion of blah, blah, blah, you know, and go from there.***

To say, this is our goal, which I like that, then we don't have to disguise it. Would it be comfortable for you if the lawyer said, our goal is to identify the jurors who can be the most open-minded or who can be open-minded to all of the evidence or something like that? Because we are trying to get those who aren't open-minded to identify themselves.

You could say that. I don't know if open-minded is the best way of phrasing it, but it might be. I don't know. Let me think about that for a second.

I'm afraid of the words bias and prejudice and attitudes because they have negative connotations.

So what do you think about – this is one way I phrase it sometimes when I'm talking to people is, we're looking for the best match. Maybe that sounds too much like you have this idea in mind of the exact person that you want. I don't know if match is such a good one, but –

Match or fit?

A good fit.

A good fit for this case.

Mm-hmm. Yep.

We're looking for those jurors who are a good fit for this kind of case.

Mm-hmm. That could be.

That gives them a sense of it, but it may not tell them yet what that good fit is.

Right.

Then taking that one layer further, and by a good fit I mean, you know, those folks who aren't prejudging or something like that?

You could say that. That would be okay.

That would be okay with you?

Yeah.

Because you can only really speak for yourself.

Exactly.

Is there anything that would turn you off about somebody asking you about your own personal beliefs?

You mean just in general, or –

In that setting. Say the attorney just called on you, and some are less subtle than others, and said, Juror No. 12, do you think there's anything about you that - you think you have any biases or prejudices that we ought to know about? That's not too far from how it goes sometimes.

*Aye, yi, yi. **That would be difficult, because you're in a group of a bunch of people and they would hear what those are.** If you really want somebody to list them and talk about it, it almost seems like that should be communicated privately, if it needs to be. You don't ask them to tell you what the biases are, or you do? I mean, not in the big room, right?*

We don't get one-on-one time.

Oh, okay. You don't get any one-on-one time.

Only one-on-one within the locus of the whole group being present.

So you may want to talk about biases or prejudice and you might want to just put it right out on the table at some point and describe what it is you have in mind and why. Why are we going through this process of talking with you for an hour and a half? I don't know if that's a good way to do it or not, just to kind of put it all out there. Because maybe, at some point after you've warmed up with people and made that connection, then that's when you would talk about it and you would say, **one reason we ask these questions and we wanted you all to talk about this, whatever it was, this topic, was because we are concerned about potential biases and that we want people to be as impartial as they can be and look at the actual evidence.** *There's got to be a way of describing it that's non-threatening.*

We have the Blindfolded Lady of Justice. She holds the scales and the scales are evenly balanced and she's blindfolded so that the decision is made without there being prejudice and bias. Do you think concretizing that by showing a picture or referring to that would be helpful? Or is that too schmaltzy or smarmy or –

No, I think that would be actually not a bad thing.

Invoking the Constitution and a greater purpose.

Mm-hmm. **Because what it does, it speaks to a person's sense of duty and patriotism to show something like that, and to explain the whole idea of justice and how you're trying to achieve justice for your client.**

As is the other side. Would it seem self-serving if the lawyer then went on to say, I'd be dishonest if I told you that I wanted anything but favorable jurors for my side.

Don't say that. No, that immediately would – to me that's a red flag. Even though it may be true, I think just by saying it makes me know that you're thinking about that and here you're trying to be even and find a good fit, but then when you talk about that, then I know right away you're totally one-sided and – no, I would never say that. But I do like the idea, and **one reason I like the idea of The Blindfolded Lady of Justice, is many people are more visual. It'll give them something to think about.** *I think it's more understandable than just speaking in many ways. So that's a good idea.*

Like has anybody heard the expression, justice is blind or something like that. One of the schools of thought about jury selection is, if you want to get people talking about their biases, you should open up first and share something of yourself. I've asked a lot of people, how do you feel? Do you think it would be appropriate for the lawyer to do that? I've gotten all kinds of answers. Some people say, I don't care about the lawyer. I don't want to hear anything about them. Other people have said, I think that would help me. How would that work for you if the lawyer said, I have a real problem with bicyclists. I just couldn't be on a case with bicyclists, because I don't think I could give them a fair shake. Is there anything that you think might be an issue for you in a case like this?

I think you could share something of your own as an example, but I would make sure it's not something that's going to offend anybody. It's going to have to be a real moderate example. You might even want to take it out of the arena of law and jury selection and make it something like food, food preference.

Right. Somebody said, you can talk about the difference between a bias and a preference. I prefer this kind of food, but it doesn't mean I'm biased against the one that I don't have as often. So there's that. I still haven't figured out if I am comfortable sharing my own biases and prejudices.

I would have to think about that. The way I would think about that is, I would envision myself in that situation and it would be like, what could you say that would help me understand what you were getting at, but yet wouldn't give me some negative personal idea about you?

To feel that you're being manipulated by me somehow.

Exactly.

Because some study has said that lawyers are second to the bottom only next to used-car salesmen in terms of perceived credibility. This is a very real thing we lawyers are facing in courtrooms today. A lot of cynicism, a lot of distrust. Not only in us, but in the system. Much of it I think perpetuated by big business and certain political leanings and maybe TV. A lot of stereotypes.

So how does it feel to be a lawyer then and to know that you're thought of that way?

It's not something I ever imagined when I was a young boy wanting to be a lawyer. That was never a part of what I thought the profession would be about.

I remember wanting to be a lawyer also at one point. I've wanted to be a lot of things. That is something that in some way dissuaded me from going in that direction because I just know how people feel about lawyers. The difference for me, though, is I know some lawyers, and it takes that part of it away. But before I knew any, I did have, I would say, some negative feelings about lawyers.

Such as?

That they charged exorbitant amounts of money, so much more than anybody else. And I've heard it talked about when lawyers work a case, they get a certain percentage and a client not receiving their full award because such a big percent of it goes to the attorney. I think that's what it's all about, it's about the money.

And that is the end game, always. My side wants to get as much for the client as we can and the defense wants to get as little or save their client as much. In this realm that I'm in, that's how we measure justice. While we're talking about the damages and the money, how do you feel about the fact that we have these cases where people seek a money remedy for injury? That they're being compensated for – there are two kinds of compensation. We have what we call compensatory damages; we call them specials, but they're out-of-pocket costs, medical bills, wage losses past and future. And then we have general damages for the pain, suffering and loss of enjoyment of life, things for which there's no fixed standard. I would think in your profession, you could understand that impact a little more than the average individual. But notwithstanding that, how do you feel about the law having a process where people can seek a money remedy for things that can't be measured or felt?

> *I think it's important. If you didn't have that process, then I think there would be less accountability. I think people would be suffering. And as you said, there would be no remedy. It can't take away the original injury, but it can compensate for, as you said, pain and suffering.*

Some people think it's okay to compensate for things like medical bills and wage losses and car damage and property damage and that, but pain and suffering shouldn't be compensated. Some people feel very strongly about that, don't think somebody's pain and suffering deserves to be compensated. First of all, it can't be measured. There's no metric for it, because every single person's idea of that is different. Therefore, it's unfair. You could have twelve people on this jury reach one decision and twelve people on this jury reach an entirely different one. So why bother with it? How do you feel about that and where do you fall?

> *Well, we have brains, we can think. We can make judgments about these sort of things. So even if you say you can't measure it, there's going to be some information that you're processing to come to an amount that you think is fair, right? No, I absolutely believe in compensation for pain and suffering. Because if there was negligence and something happened to you that affected your life that caused you pain and suffering, none of that would ever be there, right? Period. So basically, it disrupted your life. I think that's enough, right there. So it wouldn't be even.* **It wouldn't be justice just to be compensated for medical bills and the actual expenses that you incurred, because there's the cost of your mental health and your emotional health. And then there's the cost of your relationships with your family and other people because of it.** *So anyway, that's how I feel about it. And I think any reasonable person would think the same way.*

Prior to your having the professional experience you've had, had you felt that way?

> *Yes, definitely. I have friends who've been in car accidents and have back injuries, et cetera, and it's years later. Maybe they got a small award in the beginning; it should have been bigger, because this is affecting many, many years of their lives. My own example would be when I had blood drawn from my arm, the woman didn't stop. I told her she hit my nerve, and she didn't stop drawing the blood.*

She was very inexperienced, I think, and I had this shooting, hot pain down my arm, down my nerve, and it stayed that way for a couple of weeks. And now it's numb along here and I still get little shooting pains down my arm. I've never done anything about it. I may do something someday, but I can put a ballpark figure and it would be a small amount because it's not impairing my work or anything like that.

For me, it comes down to, people have to feel. They have to feel what's right to them. How do we identify those people who don't feel good about awarding money for pain and suffering or do I just ask them, is there anybody here who thinks that remedies for pain and suffering and damages that you can't see are improper?

You could ask that directly. Another idea would be to ask people to talk about whether they've known anybody who's been involved in a situation like this where they did receive compensation or seek compensation for pain and suffering from a car accident or something. Maybe use that as a lead-in, then, is there anybody who thinks that it's not right for a person to seek that extra compensation? That may be a good way of introducing it.

What we're finding is, people are awarding, but the amounts seem to be very small. We have a conservative jury pool in this community. Even though it's a liberal environment, it's a conservative fiscal environment. Do you have any thoughts about that?

I don't know what that would be exactly. I'm trying to think about how I would be if I were in that situation. ***I guess the word reasonable comes to mind. What would be a reasonable amount?***

We have to suggest what we think is a – we don't have to, but they're looking to us to tell them why we think a certain number is the right number.

I don't know. I wonder if there's something about the social climate of this area. In some ways, it's a less friendly, less warm environment than other places, so maybe it's that jurors feeling emotionally connected to the plaintiff; that they're much more standoffish or emotionally separated from that person. Maybe that's why. That's the only thing I can think of around here.

I've got a couple theories. One is that there's a strong Norwegian influence here, and that Norwegian people tend not to complain about their pain and suffering. I don't know if that's true or not.

I've also heard this.

Another is that we've got a lot of tech-type people, engineer-type people, who are binary thinkers, who don't necessarily see things in shades of gray, especially since many of them are very young and haven't had life experiences.

Could be. Both of those factors then do tie in with that whole, I guess, lower social emotional connection with other people.

Right. And a lack of minorities may be an issue here as well. But when you say – the term of art that you just used, a lower social connection? Is that what you said?

Social and emotional connection or both, to other people.

How do we get a random group of people to socially and emotionally connect with one's client? And there's one thing we're not allowed to do; we can't say, put yourselves in the shoes of our client. That's called the Golden Rule, and we're not allowed to violate that.

*On your jury, **you would want to select the people who have that quality who do appear to be more emotional, more socially adept, maybe. And part of that is, how do they communicate with you? How do you see them interact with other people in the room?** Another way you could do that would be telling a story and then getting people to give you feedback about that story. Maybe it's a story of somebody who had an injury and received compensation. I don't know, just tell a little short version of that and see what people's reaction is.*

The story that comes up in almost every jury selection process is the McDonald's case. I can't remember a jury where it hasn't been brought up by them. Almost to the person they think it was too much and we don't – nobody disagrees with that necessarily.

That's such an extreme example, which is why I probably wouldn't use that example. Because it's too extreme that most people, if 98 out of 100 people are going to say that was too much, what did you just accomplish by asking?

Well, they bring it up.

Oh, the jurors bring it up.

The jurors bring it up.

Okay. I get it. I don't know. Maybe you could counter after somebody brings that up with another example. There are so many examples out there of people who legitimately sought for damages and received them for very good reason.

Could you think of good reasons why damages would be appropriate?

Particularly, I think about head injury cases. That's altered you for the rest of your life. And the cases where people need medical attention and nursing care or something for the rest of their lives.

People are okay with that, because those are money damages that can be penciled out for something. When we talk about these emotional damages, people say, that's just a golden ticket. And it's often a function of who the defendant is. If the defendant is, I like to use this example, a single schoolteacher versus a corporate entity with deep pockets. People fashion justice as they will. Whatever feels good to them, I think. How about your own values? Someone said that if you know what they value, you can really understand them. You have a better chance of learning about people. How would somebody want to learn about your values in a non-threatening way?

I don't know. Just maybe by asking, what's important to you? I mean, think about your life and just the simple question of, what's important to you?

Would you need to have a context if it were asked of you in that court setting? Just what's important to you could be a –

Right. That's pretty broad.

– broad question. Here you are, in this courtroom environment, is there anything that's important to you now or is there anything you'd like to know or are there any questions you'd like to ask? I want to empower people. I want to get them talking. I don't want them asking me questions, necessarily. Do you think people are comfortable with talking about what's important to them or what their values are? Think people even know? Because I didn't know what my values were until – I had a sense, but it wasn't until certain uncertain things were said to me that I knew what mattered. Of course, that was then. Maybe there was a different set of values before that.

I don't know how I would feel if, in that situation, somebody asked me directly about my values. I can imagine maybe. I have to think about that. How could you ask that? How could you pose that question? **You could rephrase it into something like, a lot of people in life, at this point in your lives, you know what's important to you. Other people are still searching for what's important to them. And you could just say, so where do you all feel that you fit into that spectrum** *of – I mean, do you know? Maybe just pose that question? I don't know if people would answer that. I think they would, but I don't know.*

That's okay. Because every person comes at it differently. If you were a plaintiff or a defendant in a court case similar to what we're talking about, what would be the attributes and attitudes and beliefs you'd like to see on a juror sitting in a case, essentially judging you?

I think **somebody who's a good listener, who's really going to pay attention, who's really going to think about it; not just in the courtroom, but who will go home and go over the details in their own minds. I would put that probably at the top of the list, somebody who is a good thinker. Somebody who has empathy,** *so can relate to whatever I'm going through. I think that's part of it, a big part of it, actually. And then, if you're the plaintiff, you want them to rule in your favor, right?*

Sure. But we're looking for a fair jury.

Right. I would never be a plaintiff if I didn't think I had a good case. So I think a quality in a juror is to be able to weigh the information on both sides, to come to the correct decision. Because if they did, and I knew I had a good case, they would be in my favor whether I was the plaintiff or the defendant.

Suppose winning wasn't so much the issue but it was, what kind of a juror would you want that you feel could step up and fight to get you the most money for your injury?

Probably somebody who would relate – who could relate to me. I would want a multiracial – I personally would want a multiracial jury. I would feel uncomfortable if it was primarily Caucasian. If it were all Caucasian people, I wouldn't feel comfortable at all because I don't identify myself that way. I feel Asian, Asian-American, mostly. And I know from experience, people have treated me differently because I look different in a way. They're not sure why I look different, but I just do. So for me, a jury that can relate to me as a person.

As an Asian woman, how do you feel perceived by the people in this region?

Things have definitely changed around here. It's much more mixed racially and ethnically than it used to be. I grew up in a very Caucasian neighborhood, and as a young person, not being in that neighborhood, but going outside that neighborhood to other areas around here, people always ask me questions like, what are you? I don't get asked that much anymore. Maybe it's just because I'm an adult.

Were they asking what are you to determine if you were Chinese, Korean, or Japanese?

Yeah. Or something else.

If you're in the courtroom and none of your jurors are anything other than Caucasian males and females, you would not feel comfortable with that?

No, definitely not.

What biases do you think they bring to the table that would make you uncomfortable?

I think when you're of a mixed ethnic background, you just see the world differently. And I think my experience or experiences are vastly different from say, an African American person; also vastly different from a Caucasian male. So I have no trust that those people can understand where I'm coming from. *For instance, if I were the plaintiff, why I'm asking for those damages. Just to me, the mindset would be very different. It would be. And I would be worried about that.*

That's hard for me too, because I think of all people as the same. I think they're entitled to the same justice no matter what their skin color is or their sex or anything else. And I'm hearing you say that's not your experience. Is that right?

I shouldn't say these things to you, but I think it's a white person's privilege to not even think about these things.

Right. I've talked to several black people and I've gotten their perspectives on this. I would like you to talk about that as freely as you can.

Particularly when you look at all of the positions of power, right? They're mostly all white men. I'm not a racist person. I would, though, say that I feel more comfortable with people of color in general. Obviously I have friends of all different backgrounds. But if I were to be faced, for instance by a jury that was all

Caucasian people, it would feel threatening, almost. I would almost be sure that they wouldn't judge in my favor. I hate to say that, but I think generally, people who are in a privileged position don't think about the, plight is too strong a word, but the lives of people who are not in that privileged position, as evidenced by things like the killings of African American people. American Indians as well. They have twice the suicide rate or more. I just read that 1% of the country is American Indian, yet 2% of the killings by police are American Indian. So things like that.

Disproportionate.

I think most people, if you're in that privileged position, you don't even think about those things. You're not interested in them, in general.

Even with your high level of education and enculturation and all, that still persists. You still feel that, even though you are not say, stereotypical of an Asian person?

Do I still feel different? I feel different.

Different as perceived.

Yes. I do feel like I'm perceived differently, that people notice. A good example would be going to the coast. I felt like people looked at us oddly. I didn't see another person of color in that whole place. It could have been, hey, there's a good looking couple. But no, I'm being looked at differently; that's the first thing that came to mind. And even though I know that I'm half-Caucasian you don't see me first as an Asian female. I feel like I relate to other people of color more closely than I do Caucasian people.

How about male versus female? I've heard it said that women jurors might be more critical of women litigants. On the one hand, you say you're not too comfortable with a male jury, let's say white males, but what if it were all white females? Would you feel comfortable with that more than say –

I think it's less about the gender than it is about the ethnic background.

Ethnicity isn't something I generally worry about in jury selection because I'm doing civil cases. In criminal cases, you often have that as an issue – how do you feel about race? Do you automatically convict somebody because they're black? But if you were my client, do you think that would be an issue that would need to be talked about with jurors? That that would be one of the biases I'd want to elicit from people?

I do. I think absolutely that it would. It would be much more important in a criminal case than in a civil case, too, because you want jurors to be sympathetic to you. I think people who are most sympathetic would be a mixed group of people.

You think a single person in the jury would ever cop to having a racial bias?

Probably not. So that would be a difficult thing to accomplish, unfortunately.

When I was on a jury selection panel, we had a Black man who was accused of first-degree murder. When it was talked about, race, in that instance, I went the other way and said, I have a greater sense of empathy towards people of color than the other way around. I'm going to give him more of the benefit of the doubt.

And there are people like you. There are people like that. But then there are people who you would never guess have these biases. One woman in my exercise class – we started to become friends. We were eating one time and she started talking about how African Americans should be able to pull themselves up by their bootstraps.

She didn't see you as a minority.

I don't know. So we had a conversation about that, and that was pretty much it. I mean, we didn't argue, but – we argued civilly. I was explaining to her, but do you understand that if you're born into this kind of family and you're of this racial background that you don't even have to think about racism and how you're treated differently? So, no. They've had centuries of injustice, and this other influence that has kept them from succeeding as much as others.

It hasn't been a fair contest.

Yeah. So even a person who seemed to be open-minded, there was that.

The last issue has to do with burden of proof. In civil cases and criminal cases, there's a different burden applied. In criminal cases, the burden is beyond a reasonable doubt, however the jury interprets that. In a civil case, you'll hear the judge instruct that the burden of proof is a preponderance of the evidence. What does that mean to you, a preponderance of the evidence?

The biggest proportion of the evidence, so that most of the evidence points in that direction and a small amount of it is not consistent with that.

The judge's instruction goes a little further and says, more probably true than not true is what preponderance means. Does that change for you the meaning of preponderance in isolation? So preponderance is – you've given me that – what you think that is. And then having heard, more likely true than not true, does that change how you view a decision?

*More probably true than not true? It does in my mind. **This may seem silly, but if I'm thinking about a whole pie, and you say preponderance, I'm thinking about, there's maybe a slice of that pie, that part doesn't match the rest. But when you say the next phrase, which is more probably than likely, I'm thinking more 50/50.***

Some people go to a 49/51.

Yeah, well, actually, I should say 60/40. It moves it from being this big giant piece of evidence to 60/40.

A lot of people aren't comfortable making decisions when the burden of proof is explained to them that it doesn't have to be as great. How do you feel about that's what the burden of proof is?

That there's just a little bit more information that's favorable one way or the other?

If that's how you understand the instruction. If that's how you understand preponderance and more probably true than not true. I like to think that's what it means, 51/49, but there's no further instruction that says it's 51/49. It's just however the individual chooses to interpret it at that point. But some people have said I can't feel comfortable making a decision when it's that close. I'm going to need more. Sometimes, there isn't more.

I could definitely see that. So then it's more like, it could go either way. And I think that's when your connection with one or the other defendant or plaintiff comes into play.

Right.

Absolutely. It's not clear-cut. So it might be a little more of, well, this person can afford it. This person needs it. Or this person doesn't really need it, and they can't afford it. You know what I mean?

People will get to the decision they need to get to. Although now, we're hearing that they've made their decision long before they've heard the evidence, and they're picking and choosing that which confirms their gut level choice or reptilian brain decision. Safety.

So that's what most people do, you think? They have a preconceived idea of which way it's going to go or what the truth is, let's say?

I think a lot of people go in, make a gut level decision and then sift for those things primarily that support that. I'm not saying people will always go that way; there may be something that brings them back. The theory being – evolutionary psychology or evolution of our brains – we've evolved from this organism that was used to making decisions instantly for self-preservation. And only then, through the neocortex, have we then learned to explain why or why not. But at that point, you can lie to yourself. Reptiles probably don't lie to themselves.

I think you're right. Because people do make, or come to conclusions pretty quickly, and then hear the evidence. Definitely, there's intuition. If you were to meet them or receive the plaintiff and the defendant in the courtroom once you've been selected for jury duty, you already form ideas about them. So when you're doing jury selection, though, those people are not present or they are?

Everybody's in the courtroom. The clients are, the lawyers are, the judge is, and then –

Oh, but – no. When you're doing the – with the room with the 40 or 60 people?

Everybody's there. You have 12 of them that get seated in the box, and then the rest of them line up in the pews, and everybody has a number and we start working.

Oh, I get it.

The ones in the box are the ones who are there until they're asked to be excused and then somebody will take their place, the next one in line. People at the back often aren't going to get into the box and you want to concentrate on the first 20, 25 or however –

I was envisioning just a big empty room with folding chairs.

There's no room for people to sit and watch jury selection because the courtroom's full of potential jurors. Is there anything I haven't talked about that you think is helpful to know? Talking about race was interesting, and I'm intrigued by your professional background and understanding more about human nature than the average individual.

Mm-hmm. But I also think, absent the education, people go into a field for certain reasons, right? So I think before I ever started going to school for psychology, I was already thinking about people a lot. I can't think of anything else to add.

Thank you.

PART TWO – **THE JUDGES**

47

SEE HOW IT'S DONE

For a newer practitioner, someone who hasn't tried an awful lot of cases, I'd really recommend coming to the courthouse and watching some criminal cases that are doing *voir dire*. Because the prosecutors and the defenders do this week in and week out, and they're really, really good at it. They're not a bundle of nerves because this is old hat; they do it all the time. And watching how they do it, I think, can be really, really helpful to civil practitioners who, frankly, get into trial very rarely these days. ... And you see a lot of different people, so you're going to see a lot of different styles. You're more likely to find one that feels comfortable.

I have been asking people to put themselves in an "as if" place. Some have been jurors, and some never have. I always ask them to imagine they've been summoned, they've been convened, brought upstairs and the judge has explained that it's a civil case where a person's claiming injury from negligence caused by some entity. And then the judge says, ladies and gentlemen, please give your attention to the lawyer for the plaintiff who will conduct jury selection. At that point I ask what are they thinking and feeling and valuing, right then and there. I'd like to ask you, what do you think, at that point, is important to jurors?

> So you're asking me what, as a trial judge, I think jurors are thinking about and concerned about and perhaps worried about?

Exactly.

> Okay. In those circumstances. Well, what I've observed, and it's probably no surprise the lawyers who do tort cases, is that **jurors seem very suspicious of those kinds of claims.** They're not inclined to be generous, either in terms of determining liability and apportioning responsibility, if there's a claim for apportionment or comparative fault or whatever. I can only speculate as to why. I don't have any inside information. But one gets the impression that whatever's out there in popular culture that most people in the community that get summoned for jury service have been exposed to has been very critical of these kinds of cases. **I think a sizable percentage of the venire does walk in expecting to be scammed.** In that regard, lawyers representing plaintiffs

in those kinds of cases are starting a step back or perhaps more than a step back. Now, that's not true for everyone, and I've heard very compelling stories from some potential jurors about how they or someone they're very close to was involved in a system and was injured and had an awful lot of difficulty getting their claim resolved and the insurance company was mean to them or whatever. Some of them will describe situations that the insurance wasn't mean to them and they were able to resolve it. So this stuff comes up, but it just seems like a really sizable percentage comes in negatively disposed to claimants.

Right. And in addition to that, what I've heard is, they are valuing their time above their service. Many of them have said, time is more important to me than actually doing my civic duty. I found that's something to honor as well.

Oh, you mean like asking to be excused for hardships?

Exactly. They come in and they're very concerned about the time. They're very concerned about, some of them, even whether or not they're qualified to sit. I find it interesting.

*I haven't seen too much of that in tort cases. I do the court voir dire. I have started just in the last couple of years doing a little bit of an ice-breaker where I ask people to introduce themselves to us, tell us their occupations and the occupations of other adults in their household, tell us the neighborhood they live in, and tell us about an activity they enjoy. **It gives everybody a chance to speak up about non-threatening kinds of things, gives them a chance to relax. And it gives the lawyers a chance to get a feel for – very briefly – what kind of person is this?** Because there's so little information in the bios. After they do that, and I've already done the introductory stuff –*

And you're doing this with all –

I do it with the whole venire.

– 40, 60, 80 people? However many it may be?

It's not really that many. The courtroom won't hold much more than 50, but –

True.

So, we do it with everyone and with the standard group of 35 or 40 people, it usually gets done in about 20 minutes. It doesn't take too long. Then the first question I ask them is about hardship. But before I do that, I always talk to them about the constitutional right to a jury trial which includes the right in a civil case. I always talk to them about how our justice system is the best in the world, but it only works when people like them are willing to make themselves available and take time away from their busy lives. I explain to them I can't do my job without them. And so I call it waving the flag. I try to wave the flag for them some.

Sure. And it gives them a context and a framework for feeling good about *voir dire*.

Yeah. I mean, this is really important. So I will do that with them before I ask *about hardships. And I will also then define for them what a hardship is and explain it's not just inconvenience, because this is probably inconvenient for every one of them. I tell them a little story about that ten dollar a day jury fee being set in 1957 when it was probably not an unreasonable day's wage. I really try to get them involved in the system before I ask about hardships. And then of course, I will describe for them in my introductory remarks what the schedule's going to be so they have an idea how long the case will be. I have found that by doing all of that, it does cut down somewhat on the number of people who ask to be excused for hardship. But in a trial that is slated to go longer than a week, it's still really tough. It seems like the great majority of employers who are not government or really big corporations will not pay people for jury service. **So people are really, really concerned that they're not going to be able to pay their rent if they take time off from work.** This is probably extraneous, but one thing that I would really love the legislature to do is pass a law requiring employers to compensate their employees at least for a certain amount of jury service, two weeks, three weeks, whatever. I realize that would be an expense to them, but perhaps make it neutral by letting them take some kind of a credit against their B & O tax obligations for doing that. Now, realistically, that's going to result in a loss of revenue. And I don't know how much, because I'm not a statistician, but it seems to me that it's really unfair for people to ask them to forego a significant amount of compensation in order to do their civic duty. For a couple, three days, maybe, **but for more than a week, it's really hard on most people. And so what that translates into is that our actual jurors who sit on the case are disproportionately unemployed people, retired people, and people who work for the government or large corporations that pay for jury service.** So they're not truly representative of the community for that reason. Or people who can just afford to take the time off.*

Who can do it, right?

So I guess I'm digressing a little bit from what you asked me, but that's a real concern to me. I wish we could adequately pay jurors for jury service, or I wish that we could require employers to pay them for jury service.

Even some of those, I've found, who are working for companies that are willing to pay are, and this is more common with tech and data people, is that they believe, for example, that their project is so important that it can't survive without them.

*And sometimes, they've got deadlines coming up and so on that, I'm sympathetic to, and other times, what goes through my mind is, well, what happens if you get sick? Or what happens if you decide to take a vacation? I mean, I've had people tell me, I haven't had a vacation in five years. **Pretty much everyone who's self-employed manages to get themselves off the jury. Pretty much everyone who works on commission manages to get themselves off the jury.** Because I can't force people to stay if it's going to be a significant financial hardship for them. It wouldn't be fair. And they'd be distracted, so they probably wouldn't make good jurors.*

I served for three weeks. I had been on two *venire* panels and then I was in a panel on a first-degree murder case. I was in the box and was the seventh peremptory used by the prosecuting attorney.

Oh, my. Was that disappointing or was that a relief?

It was a relief to not be. I was excited about the opportunity to be there, and to go there every day for three weeks and be a part of several *voir dires* was fun from that perspective. But what I became of aware of is there seem to be far more attorneys who were being accepted onto panels or accepted into the box, than I had seen on my side of the –

Interesting. Interesting.

I would accept lawyers, myself. I wouldn't be afraid of them. I used to think we would not want to have lawyers on our juries. Well, with that in mind, the first thing I would like to do as a plaintiff's lawyer is to put these jurors at ease and make them comfortable. I'm wondering what you've seen or what thoughts you have that might be important for me to know in accomplishing that.

That's difficult. **I think that jurors are very suspicious if they think someone's trying to lead them somewhere.** *You know?*

So to put them at ease and to make them comfortable after you have done what you can do?

Right. I'm not sure exactly what works. **I think getting them talking; asking an open-ended question and really getting them talking, even if it's about tough issues is useful, especially if you can get a dialogue going.**

Maybe it's easier asked this way: what should the lawyer avoid doing? What definitely should you not do?

I think arguing your case is a bad idea even if the judge lets you do it because I think the jurors are kind of steeling themselves against that.

They're not ready.

Yeah. You know, the reason why I'm hesitating so much is because I'm not sure what makes them feel at ease exactly, you know? Some lawyers are really good at it. Some I remember going, wow, they really got them going.

Got a way.

Yeah. Not everybody can do what some do, because we all have different personalities. **And I think trying to pretend you're someone who you're not is probably death.** *So that's not a good idea.* **But just – I think one thing is, they can pick up if the lawyer's really nervous.** *I've seen lawyers who seem to have carefully prepared for voir dire, but it's really obvious they're just a bundle of nerves. And jurors will pick up on that. But telling someone, well, you should relax and not be a bundle of nerves is not very helpful advice.*

Well, it's important to know that you should be somewhat spontaneous and as calm as you can be.

And just kind of tell them what you need to know in a candid sort of a way and get them talking about it. And find out if anyone disagrees. Once they start talking, they'll talk.

They will talk.

The difficulty is getting them to start talking. For a newer practitioner, someone who hasn't tried an awful lot of cases, I'd really recommend coming to the courthouse and watching some criminal cases that are doing voir dire. Because the prosecutors and the defenders do this week in and week out, and they're really, really good at it. They're not a bundle of nerves because this is old hat; they do it all the time. And watching how they do it, I think, can be really, really helpful to civil practitioners who, frankly, get into trial very rarely these days.

That's in part why I'm doing this project, because the last case I tried was over two years ago. How can you get good at something that you do so rarely?

You can't practice.

Even with work-shopping, it's tough.

So I think it really helps to watch the criminal cases just because some of them are good lawyers and some of them are great lawyers; very few of them are bad lawyers because the bad ones wash out usually before they get to felony court. So they're all people who are really good at voir dire, and I think a lot can be learned from that. And you see a lot of different people, so you're going to see a lot of different styles. You're more likely to find one that feels comfortable.

Maybe this is the same question packaged a little different way, but is there anything you've seen good attorneys do that makes a positive impression or a positive connection with the jurors? When we think of the really good attorneys, what sorts of things are they doing or not doing that –

With juries?

Right at the outset in this abbreviated time that they have.

They're ready. They know what they want to ask. They know how they want to follow up. They don't argue with prospective jurors. When they say, thank you for sharing that, they actually mean it. A lot of them say, thank you for sharing that, and you can just tell they really don't mean it. And I don't blame them. You hear a lot of bad stuff, but the truth is, you want to hear bad stuff, because you want to know who shouldn't be on your panel or whether you have a challenge for cause. So I think you have to invite people to talk about things that are going to be not good and then hopefully see whether someone else disagrees and why and be able to be relaxed about it. But that's much easier said than done.

I think lawyers try to do too much in *voir dire*; I know I have. So I've thought, maybe what I need to do is abbreviate it and simply get up and with some context ask the entire group, is there anybody here who thinks they're not a suitable juror? And accept that and be done. I wonder what you think, other than the economy, the savings of time there is, if you think that would be something to consider.

*Well, I guess what comes into my mind is, **are you going to get some hands going up? And if you do have hands going up, then you can say, well, why do you feel that way? Then you can get people to say they agree or disagree or whatever. People are just really uncomfortable talking about a lot of these issues. They really are. A lot of plaintiff's lawyers ask about awarding money damages for intangibles like pain, suffering, loss of enjoyment of life, and people are like, huh?***

That's what I've found, is that nobody wants to do it. They don't. They don't know how to do it. Nobody can show them how to do it. They're fine with specials.

Sure. That's easy, because you can do that on a calculator.

Exactly. So I'm not even sure I want to talk to them about that in *voir dire*, but maybe I would have to in the right kind of case.

*I guess it depends. **You're going to have some people who will say, there's just no way, and I wouldn't do it. I don't care if the judge tells me I'm supposed to do it, I won't do it. I just wouldn't be able to do it. And then there are other people who will say, well, you know, I'm not comfortable with that or convey to you somehow that they're not comfortable with that.** But maybe there are some ways to talk about it.*

Right. I've gotten some help from people on that.

If I can, if you want me to share a long-ago war story which sticks in my mind because it was the last trial that I tried as a lawyer before I went on the bench, and it was a wrongful death of a woman who apparently everyone in the community just adored. I mean, we had to keep the lay witnesses away with a stick. But she had never made – had mostly made money in the teens. I think one year she made thirty thousand dollars. And it was a rural county. Oh, and she had no surviving spouse. She had three children, all of whom were adults. So the case was really just about non-economic damages except for funeral expenses because it was an accident; she died on impact. It was just horrible. I spent an awful lot of time thinking about, how am I going to talk about general damages and how am I going to convey this? So I started talking about – and I had a slide show – I'm not sure I'd do that today, but PowerPoint wasn't that ubiquitous then – and so I showed them a picture of a Monet painting that had recently been in the news as selling for, I don't know, fifty million dollars or whatever it was. And I say, you know, what is this? It's paint on a piece of canvas, that's what it is. Now, is that worth fifty million dollars? Of course not. Why is it worth that? Well, it's a Monet. It's unique. It's beautiful; there will never be another one. And then I showed a picture of Alex Rodriguez. This was just after he went to Texas.

For two hundred and ten million or something like that.

And we talked about that. And it's like, he gets paid to swing a baseball bat and to catch balls, right? **But he's worth all this money because of intangible things. And so I talked about various ways that our culture puts a dollar value on intangible things. And we all do it, and we all understand it in that context. And then, move that context over to valuing life.** *And it's really, really hard, but if we don't do it, then it means there's no value to it, and we know that's not true. So that seemed to work. Would it work in every case? I have no idea. I only used it in that one case.*

Since you talk about damages, there's a question in my mind, and there seems to be a mixed sense among the people I've interviewed, whether to talk about damages in *voir dire* or not. Particularly a number.

No.

Some have said, I don't want a number. Some have said, it would be helpful. So I'm curious to know what you have observed that has been helpful or not.

I haven't seen very many lawyers do it. **And I've never seen it done in a way that seemed helpful or effective.**

Because some want to anchor early on and –

I'm not sure exactly why, just usually – you know, it's never a small number, right? It's always a really big number. And it just depends. If what you're trying is a case where somebody was rendered quadriplegic, then I think throwing out a really big number in voir dire may be a lot less problematic than if it's a soft tissue neck strain case – which we get an awful lot of those, an awful, awful, awful, awful lot of those – and I suspect it's because they're not settling, and that's why we get them. I don't think it's because of something the plaintiffs' bar's doing wrong, but there's an awful lot of them, and they very rarely go well from the plaintiff's standpoint.

That has been my experience, more or less. Every now and then, we're emboldened by somebody who's done something spectacular.

And that does happen.

Now and again. But you're right. I think case selection – and that's a sub-theme here.

Yeah.

Looping back, as far as talking about the money, it may be okay to talk about the notions of damages, but not necessarily amounts, in your estimation?

I wouldn't want to say absolutely one way or the other. **I'm just saying that the times when I've seen it done in non-catastrophic injury cases, the results don't seem to have been very good.**

A number of trial attorneys and one or two very great lawyers say that they like to approach the jury panel with the, I'll show you mine; will you show me yours.

And that's, of course, a Spence thing.

The Spence thing. Do you think jurors want to know anything about the lawyer? Because some have said to me, I couldn't care less about the lawyer. And others have said, I think that would be okay. Again, I think there are no absolutes here, but I'm curious what your thoughts.

So in terms of the lawyer sharing what exactly? Like things about his or her life or –

Some sort of a bias, generally. Something in the context of the case that helps get the jurors to talk about bias and prejudice. Because I have come down to two goals: one is to identify high-risk jurors or to get people to talk about their biases, and the other is simply to show them that I'm a credible person, to establish a human connection. Those are my goals. I have successfully talked about my own biases. For example, if it was a bicycle injury/MVA case, I think I would get up and say, you know folks, I really have issues with bicyclists myself. And a lot of people do. But not go beyond that.

That's probably a good idea if there's something like that, where you've got good reason to believe there's going to be jurors that just don't like something that's relevant to your case.

Or don't want to talk about their biases because they may not want to open up, may be more inclined to open. Do you sense that lawyers who do that might get people to open up a little bit more?

I think that's certainly possible. I guess, again, it depends on the subject matter. I've seen lawyers – and I wish I could come up with a concrete example and I can't. **I've just seen lawyers kind of mention things, you know, preferences they have or don't have that just seemed silly and extraneous. At least, I'm wondering why they're talking about it. The trouble is, I don't necessarily think like a juror either.**

Of course.

So I don't know, but it does strike me as a little waste of time. But yeah, you've got a case involving a cyclist, you need to do something to get people, you know those damn cyclists and they're always running through the stop signs. And I almost hit one the other day because they were wearing dark clothing at night with no lights and – yeah. You want them to talk about that for sure. **And you can say, well, I had this experience and who else had the experience like that? I don't think that's a bad idea at all.** *You know, if you start talking about you like turkey better than pastrami – which I've seen some lawyers do – it's like, please.*

Let's be relevant. Exactly.

And there's a difference between preferences. You know, my favorite color is blue versus your favorite color is green. There's a difference between that and prejudgments about certain things or certain people or certain roles that people are in.

Open-mindedness and closed-mindedness.

Yeah. In a criminal case where I'm expecting law person officers to testify, one of my standard questions that I ask in judge voir dire is whether there's anyone who has strong feelings, either on the positive or negative side about law enforcement. I'll usually get a lot of cards going up. Then I usually leave it to the lawyers to follow-up. And if the lawyers don't, I always wonder. But when they do, usually you'll get some story about some cop that was really mean to somebody and really unfair, and then you'll get a whole bunch of people who have friends or relatives who are in law enforcement who – they're going to believe anything that comes out of the mind of somebody wearing a uniform. And you really need to know that, right?

For sure. Well, certainly in the criminal context. Is there something similar in a civil context, something that – you know, you talked about law enforcement, and obviously we want to talk about insurance in *voir dire*.

Usually the jurors will bring it up.

They usually do. And I'm curious to know, though, if they don't, can the lawyer in your court bring it up? Even though we're instructed not to talk about insurance throughout the trial, it seems to me that's something we ought to be able to talk about. I don't want to have you go on record saying something that would be regretful, but –

Well, a couple things. One is, I've never heard a lawyer bring it up directly, but if you're talking about an automobile accident case, then 90% of the time somebody on the jury will bring it up. Because you ask, has anybody, you or someone close to you, been injured in an automobile accident? And you will always get some cards, right? So when you start asking them questions about it, they will talk about the insurance company inevitably, so it comes in. I think I'd be a little uncomfortable if a lawyer brought it up, even though I'm very well aware of the rule. I will also mention that there is a Court of Appeals decision from Division I that originally came out unpublished, but it's my understanding that Division I just granted a motion to publish that affirmed the then judge giving a preliminary instruction about insurance to the jury when a number of members of the venire brought it up and it was a situation where it was a one-car accident and it was – I don't think they were actually married, but they were essentially domestic partners – they were the equivalent of being married. So the passenger was suing the driver who was her domestic partner. A lot of jurors expressed a lot of confusion about, why would anybody do that? Because what's his is hers and vice versa. So the judge actually gave them an instruction that insurance doesn't have anything to do with the case. They're not to consider it in determining either liability or damages, because liability was contested in that case, but that there was insurance and that the suit was necessary to access the insurance. But then in the same instruction, she told them it shouldn't enter into their decision making on either liability or damages. And at the conclusion of the trial, she gave the standard WPI instruction on insurance. And that was a basis of an appeal of what was a pretty good plaintiff's verdict. Division I just affirmed recently. I think they're going to be publishing.

If we could talk for a moment about these can opener questions and the things that can help jurors open up authentically about things like their bias or their prejudice. I'm hesitant to use words like bias and prejudice, because they have negative connotations.

They do. And I will tell you, and maybe the lawyer should do it if your trial judge isn't doing it, what I have added to my introductory remarks in every case is that, yes, the words bias and prejudice – and I do it in the context of challenges for cause and explaining that to them – I'll say, you know, they have ugly connotations in our culture and they're used synonymously with words like bigotry. And bias certainly includes that. But in the legal sense, it's much broader than that, and it's just having some philosophy or some belief or some life experience that would make it difficult or impossible for you to consider the evidence objectively and impartially. And I will usually give them an example. I will say, for example, in our courts here, we sometimes have trials where the defendant is accused of sexually molesting a child. And inevitably, when we get a large group of prospective jurors, unfortunately, there will be people in the panel who have had the experience of being sexually abused as a child or someone they love has had that experience or has had the experience of someone they love having been unjustly accused of sexually abusing a child. And those experiences tend to evoke very powerful emotions. For many of those people, it would be extremely difficult to consider evidence in this kind of a case and be able to be fair and impartial. And it doesn't mean they wouldn't be perfectly wonderful jurors in a different kind of a case, but they may not be well-suited for this kind of a case. And so that's why we ask you these questions, because inevitably there will be some of you who, because of your life experiences or your beliefs or whatever, just aren't a good fit for this particular case. And I'll tell them about affidavits of prejudice and they can be filed against judges and we don't take offense or, we at least try not to when that happens. And so I kind of try to soften it for them that it doesn't mean that they're bad people, it doesn't mean they're unfair people, it just means that they may be a little too close to some of the issues for both sides to get a fair trial. And what we want is, we want a jury that will give both sides a fair trial.

Right. And that leads to challenges for cause. I know lawyers have talked about having five or six excused for cause in a single jury selection. It doesn't work for me, and I've found that the more I dig, the more, the judge doesn't like me, and, it seems, that the rest of the jury doesn't like me either.

Really?

I'm getting to the point where, if I have to go down that road, I'm better off to just tag that juror in my mind as somebody I don't want to probe further with.

So what are you finding? Are you finding judges quote/unquote "rehabilitating jurors" or – can you give me a for instance?

I had a medical malpractice case I was trying, this is quite a while ago. The person didn't have a strong sense that she could be fair, but thought that she maybe could be. It wasn't an obvious case where I thought the judge should have excused her, but –

And did she give a reason?

Not really. She was a nurse, and she had lots of comfort with the medical profession.

Well, she works with doctors all the time.

In that *voir dire*, it felt I was swimming upstream, and not only was I potentially alienating this one individual, but if she stayed, was never going to like me. I had a sense the jury might turn against me too, because here's one of theirs that I'm trying to get to say the golden words but she wouldn't do it. And the judge, a fine judge, did as much as he could, but I guess my question is, how far do you think lawyers can go with for-cause challenges without alienating the rest of the group?

*Well, I think you can't be accusatory, right? **Usually, when it's successful, the juror kind of excuses herself. You know?** If it's a juror who, for instance, in a medical malpractice case, she's someone who really highly respects doctors and would never question the judgment of a physician. You can sometimes get them to say, you know, this isn't the right case for me, I don't think. And I mean, usually, if someone is ambivalent about their ability to be fair, I will ask them. And I will say, well, this is hard stuff, and I realize it's really hard stuff, and you know yourself a lot better than we can possibly get to know you in the short time available to select a jury, so can you assure us with confidence that you're going to be objective and you're going to be equally fair to both sides. Usually, if they have a significant doubt about it, they will tell me that. And they will say, you know, I just – I'm not sure. I really can't. Well, for me, that's enough to excuse someone for cause. I don't know about all of my colleagues, but for me, that's enough. Because I don't want to put somebody on the spot.*

And that's my difficulty, because especially in front of the group, it's so difficult, as you're standing there in this scary environment for these people.

It is.

I had a sense that this individual – delightful young woman – I think she really just wanted to have the experience.

Yeah.

You know? But –

*And you know, she might – it goes back to, she might be a great juror in a different kind of a case. This one is making her uncomfortable. One of the other things that I've added to my remarks – I keep building on them – **is that there are no right or wrong answers to questions that are asked during voir dire, and that this is the one – and I would urge lawyers to do this if the judge doesn't – this is the one place in our culture where we really are asking them not to tell us what they think we want to hear, not to say what they believe might be politically correct, but really tell us what's going on in their minds and in their hearts.***

Right.

***And so don't tell us what you think we want to hear. Don't tell us what you think might be politically correct.** And I realize that's really hard, because this is the only place in our culture where we take a bunch of strangers and put them in a room and say, don't be politically correct. Really tell us what's going on in your minds and your hearts. **So I think that's more effective coming from the bench, just because, for better or for worse, I'm the authority figure.** So they're paying attention to what I'm telling them. But I do urge them to really – I say, you know, as long as what you're telling us is really what's in your mind and in your heart, then it's the right answer.*

No question.

So I really try to prime them to be forthcoming.

Some have said that the judge's ability to put it that way made all the difference in the world.

Really? That's good to know.

Some wished that they would expand the orientation film that everybody watches when they first come in. Well, we've talked about money. I guess if we could talk about the word context, and what do you think that the lawyers can do to give the case context to help the jurors?

What do you mean by context?

Well, it's one thing to ask somebody, do you think you can be fair and impartial – but really, what I'm hearing is, they need to have a context.

Sure. I mean, no one's going to come out and say, I'm not a fair person. At least, I would hope so.

We want to put it in terms of the case itself, but we're hamstrung by how much we can say and talk about the facts of the case. That's always been very difficult for me. I speak with a potential juror and the juror says to me, I don't know, I haven't heard the facts. So then it becomes very difficult to get them to talk when I can't give them more.

So what is it that you want them to be telling you?

What their thoughts, feelings, impressions, beliefs, prevailing beliefs are about plaintiff's lawyers, about plaintiff's injury cases, about runaway verdicts, McDonald's. Do we have a crisis? Sleazy trial lawyers. All of those things.

Well, I saw a movie years and years ago, I think it was called – was it called Legal Eagles *or something like that? I forget. It had Robert Redford in it when he was younger. And there was a clip that stayed in my mind from voir dire where he gets up, pretty much at the beginning of voir dire, and says, how many people think there's too many lawsuits? And he raises his hand and then people raise their hands and then he says something like, how many people think that this is one of those lawsuits? And that might not be a bad ice-breaker. You know, get them talking about that.*

I've done that. I once said, how do you all feel about lawyers? They laughed, and immediately opened up.

And then where did it go from there?

I don't recall. It was a long time ago.

Because remember, there's a lawyer for each side. So I'm wondering how you thought them telling you, you know, lawyers are all scumbags, how that translated into helping you pick the jury? Or helping you de-pick the jury.

De-select the jury. I interviewed a friend of mine who's had 250 jury trials as a civil defense and criminal defense lawyer, and I was surprised when he said that even his friends and people that he meets, when he says he's a defense attorney, he gets the same sort of thing that we plaintiffs' do, initially, the knee-jerk.

Well, in a lot of people's minds, they're defending the rapists and the murderers. And you know, what a sleazy thing to be doing. And of course, you know, people in popular culture don't think about it so much in the context of presumption of innocence and constitutional rights and the prosecution doesn't always charge appropriately and the prosecution doesn't always have the right person. And so – again, this is a matter of popular culture. When I was growing up or when I was a young adult, we had shows on like Perry Mason *and* Matlock, *where the heroes were defense lawyers. Everything now is – the heroes are all law enforcement and prosecutors. Right? All the* Law and Order *and all of its spinoffs and everything like that. And they tend not to portray criminal defense lawyers in a very flattering light. So again, that's what's going on in people's minds because that's what they're exposed to in terms of the popular culture. So I think you have to get people talking about that. I've had criminal defense lawyers during voir dire say things like, well, what does everybody think my role is? And somebody will say, well, you know, you're supposed to prove your client's innocent. And there'll be some discussion about whether he has to – whether the defendant has anything to prove and why that is. And it's amazing, actually, how people kind of come around and go, oh, and start thinking about things in a new way.*

Have you seen lawyers talk about burden of proof successfully in *voir dire*? Because I've had some interesting comments from people about it. Most of them, when the word preponderance is used –

Nobody knows what that means.

— are 60-, 70-, 80-, 90%. Then hearing more likely than not, some of them will get that it's a majority. But others are still very high up on that scale. I'm curious if you think that's something that should be talked about in *voir dire* and if you've seen it done well?

I think it's not a bad idea to talk about it in voir dire, because you may have some people there who just will not accept that it's a little more than 50/50 and that it's not fair. They're going to carry that feeling with them into the jury room. And finding out who those people are wouldn't be a bad idea. A lot of them are going to say, I'll follow the judge's instructions, but at least you know who they are. But I would get them talking, hopefully, about, well, why do we have that as a burden of proof? And should it be higher? And why should it be higher? And should it be as high as it is in a criminal case? Why or why not? And usually you'll get someone who starts to talk about, well, loss of liberty is a lot more important than money and those kinds of things. So I don't know that it needs to be done in every case, but I certainly wouldn't discourage someone from doing it.

It's particularly important in medical malpractice where the default position seems to be more than a preponderance.

Especially when you get those error in judgment instructions.

Especially with that. Is there anything else that you think as a catchall would be important for readers of a book like this who want to get a sense of what the jury might be thinking and what works and doesn't work?

Well, generically, I would say, figure out what scares you about your case and try to get people talking about it. You know? If your case involves injuries that can't be seen on an X-ray or a CT or quote/unquote "soft tissue" injuries, find out who thinks that's all a scam. Especially with limited time and limited peremptory challenges and so on, I think if I were an advocate, I would really want to know about whatever it is in my case. If it's a med mal case, would you ever presume to substitute your judgment for that of a physician? I wouldn't ask it that way, but that would certainly be something that would concern me as an advocate. So really go after the stuff that's important to your case and that's important for you to know. And people will talk. They really will. If they feel like they're not being shut down and it's a safe space for them and they've been assured that we just want to know what they really think, I think they will usually start talking. Unless for some reason, they're just made really nervous because counsel's so nervous.

Have you observed when a lawyer can memorize juror's names.

Oh, yeah.

Do you think that if it can be cultivated, is worthwhile?

I don't allow it. *And the main reason I don't allow it is because if I have a court reporter, it makes the court reporter crazy.*

Oh, of course.

And if I have FTR (For The Record – Digital Court Reporting), which is what I have 90% of the time or more, it's even worse. Because if you think about it, if somebody has to listen to that recording and produce a transcript, what are they going to do with a long complicated name that gets said quickly and perhaps not even all that audibly. My job – one of the things that's really important to me as a judge is that there be a clear record. Okay?

Right.

So I tell the jurors that the only time we're going to use names for them is when they first get up and introduce themselves. And frankly, they should introduce themselves in any way they feel comfortable. They can say, hi, my name is Jane. They don't have to give us their last name unless they want to. And I tell the lawyers, I want you to refer to them by number because it just makes for such a – and I always get a laugh, because I say, well, there's several reasons for that. One is, it's a little more protective of your privacy. Second, it prevents me from horribly mispronouncing your name. I always get a chuckle from that one. And then I explain about the record and how it's produced. So I tell the lawyers ahead of time, please, when you're talking to a juror, refer to them, Juror No. 7, Juror No. 32, whatever it is. Some of the lawyers don't like it, but.

I had an experience once where I thought I would try to get some rapport with the jury and I chose a woman several rows back and I said, Juror No. 24, may I have your name please? And she said, no you may not. And I was like, oh, goodness. Here we go. That told me something about her, but at the same time, you know, these things throw us.

And again, I think it's easier coming from the bench, explaining to them we're going to use numbers and here's why we're going to use numbers so they understand. *I tell them, we mean no disrespect. I've never had jurors be unhappy about that.* **So I have found, in general, that people, whether it's lawyers, litigants, pro se litigants, jurors, whomever, that if they understand the reason for something, they are much more likely to feel okay about it. And they're much more likely to follow the direction or the order or whatever it happens to be if they understand, this isn't arbitrary; there's a**

reason for this, and here's what the reason is. I think that's human nature. I mean, if someone tells me, thou shalt not x, and it strikes me as arbitrary, I'm a lot more likely to say, to heck with that. I'm going to do x, than if someone says, don't do x because if you do x, these bad things are likely to happen. Then I'm like, oh, okay, that makes sense. I won't do x. So I think that's just human nature. And I always, if I'm going to be telling jurors something or even if I'm making a ruling as a judge, I always try to explain to someone why. Not just what, but why.

What else drives you crazy about plaintiff's lawyers during *voir dire*?

During voir dire? I don't know. People who have no idea what to ask and they're kind of fumbling around.

I've heard it said by a defense attorney who's tried, as I said, 250 significant cases, that even very fine lawyers he's observed have done very poorly in *voir dire*. Only a small handful have done what he thought was a very superb job.

It's hard. It's probably the hardest part of trying a case, because you can prepare and prepare and prepare for your direct and your cross and you could have your outlines and you can script your opening and your closing and you can memorize it and could practice it so it doesn't sound like you're reading and you can do all that, but you can't script voir dire, because it's like Improv.

Exactly.

You don't know what's going to happen. And actually, I don't know this is a fact, but it occurs to me that really good training for voir dire for lawyers might be getting involved in Improv. Okay? Because you have to be able to think fast on your feet, you don't know what's going to be coming from this other person, and you have to be able to react to it and move on. That's a thought that just occurred to me. But that might be really good practice for voir dire.

I know some of the people who have done the Trial Lawyers College, and others, they've followed up in some Improv training in San Francisco and other places.

And was it helpful for them?

Those who have done it, I've heard, have thought it was helpful. I think everything that you do, it's like your boots on the ground; every step will help you on that journey.

Yeah.

Thank you, Judge. If there's anything else you think I haven't covered here while I still have you –

Now I feel like my deposition's being taken.

Exactly. It's interesting, you said that people don't generally like to speak too much in jury selection. I've found that when I met people, they really wanted to talk. I think it was the space. Sitting one-on-one and having a cup of coffee with somebody is so much different than coming into this scary - some people have said, it's scary to be here.

It's intimidating.

You've got the police and the metal detectors and the cameras and you don't know what's the right thing to say and what's the wrong thing. So I've really gained a respect -

And it's very formal.

And it's very formal. And they don't like us. Many of them don't. Or -

Or they don't trust –

– don't trust us.

I think it's more – well, maybe not. I was going to say, I think it might be more lack of trust than lack of liking, but maybe it's lack of liking of the stereotype that they have come to expect, which is usually an unfair stereotype. But, what are you going to do?

What are you going to do? Thank you.

48

GOING TOO FAR

There's a danger that lawyers may go too far, ask for too much, push the bounds of reasonableness, and I think jurors can react, and often do, with a bit of vengeance if they really think the lawyer is asking for too much. And ultimately, it's not just how they're asking, but the bottom line is, are they asking for reasonable compensation or are they hearing a message of windfall, greed, all those attributes that will, I think, not just cause a jury not to agree, but cause a jury to start heading in the other direction.

So what I'm primarily interested in finding out, from the view from the bench, is what works and what doesn't work. I've been focusing on how do I get jurors to identify that they're open-minded or not? Quickly, without manipulation, or the feeling that they're being manipulated, and a way to connect as a human with them. That's what I'm looking for, initially. What thoughts do you have, in general, about getting jurors to talk about bias and prejudice and closed-mindedness?

I think the key is not so much the issue of bias, because we all have biases. It is getting jurors to be able to see if they can recognize their biases. And if they can, you're probably further along in keeping those folks because they recognize what they have to work against, particularly if those biases may not help your case. That can help to diffuse the natural proclivity to get rid of jurors who aren't saying the right thing. They may be identifying their bias and so be a good juror to keep. So those would be, I think, the questions to ask to try to see if jurors are able to identify what biases they have. In a criminal case, if a former law enforcement officer is asked if that would make a difference or affect their view of the case and they say, of course not, they're probably just not recognizing a bias that they naturally have. But if that same prospective juror could say, that's a problem for me, and you talk about that a little bit, that's a juror who's going to be more consciously aware of that bias and work to overcome it, in jury deliberations. In my view.

I share that view, that if you can get them to be aware of it, they're more likely to work to keep it from getting in the way of a fair deliberation.

Sure.

Hopefully.

So I think productive voir dire is a conversation with jurors. And hopefully you know something about the sorts of people or personalities you'd like to have on your ideal jury, and then you can ask the kind of questions that may help to reveal what sort of folks these are; as trite as it may seem, the TV shows they watch, the books they read, the magazines they subscribe to, the bumper stickers that are on their cars. If you can get all of that information, you have the information then to make some informed decisions about what sort of jurors they are. But those are often the questions that aren't asked, and then lawyers have a habit of not listening to the answers, so they're not making the connection of what information they've received.

Years ago I had a case where some of those questions were asked and one of the jurors, a woman, said that she belonged to Plant Amnesty. I thought, what an interesting answer. What the heck is Plant Amnesty? And there was no follow-up question. And I'm thinking, you got the question, you got the answer, and it just fell into a black hole.

It's been echoed by jurors that one of the things that frustrates them, is being asked a question but not having their answer heard because the attorney didn't get what they were looking for and moved along. One person said, just spend even a moment with me.

*Sure. And that's where the process can be helpful, if lawyers use the process by asking for comments on answers given by other jurors. But with limited time, in State Court we provide, I think, more time than Federal Court, I try to provide what time the lawyers would like. **But so often, it's viewed as an effort by the lawyers to help sell their case or explain the law and that will come through jury instructions or opening statement or things of that sort.** So the voir dire is a very limited opportunity to learn as much as you can about the jurors. I think there's a natural bias by lawyers to think they have an intuitive sense of discerning who's a good juror and who's not.*

I've learned not to trust myself on that, unfortunately.

*Well, I learned, in the one case where I'd hired a jury consultant, and it was an extremely difficult decision for me to let go of the authority and the power of choosing a juror and accept the recommendations of my consultant, but the fact was, he was spot-on. That case was a criminal prosecution where the first juror was a kindergarten teacher. The case was a sexual molestation case involving a ten-year old. She belonged to the county rape relief program, acknowledged that she would be more inclined to believe a child over an adult and didn't want to serve. I was more than ready to excuse her, but after a recess, I had time to talk with my consultant who said I should keep her on. He said, if I keep her, it will be an ordeal, **but she will work very hard to be a fair juror.** I was intending to strangle my consultant midway through the trial when the youngster was testifying and I noticed that juror, whom I chose to keep, was crying. Then when my client testified, I saw she was crying again. It finally occurred to me, maybe he knew what he was talking about. And he absolutely did. But it was very much against my instincts and intuition to keep the people he recommended and not excuse them and to excuse some of the people I would have gladly kept, because*

I didn't realize that, while they're answering all the questions the way I would hope, that was telling me nothing about them. It was really masking biases they had. And once in a while, I will see lawyers really do a good job of connecting with jurors, eliciting information, and maybe helping in the process to steer them in the right direction if they don't understand fundamental concepts or are swayed by the media. But that's also an issue with what many jurors will talk about of the McDonald's coffee case or things like that.

Every single one.

That is difficult for lawyers in a limited time to try to explain to them why what they've heard is not accurate.

You mentioned you've seen some do better than others. What do you think it is, tangibly or intangibly, that they're bringing to the table to engage these prospective jurors in a way that's meaningful to them, that's likely to get them to be more trusting of us who are coming in with a deficit of trust?

I would say it involves some measure of humility and honest desire to connect with the people, whether they're kept as jurors or excused. If you know it's somebody that has to be excused, move on, don't spend too much time with them. But really spend time with the others. Try to find areas of common ground, places of connection with the facts of your case or the personalities that they're going to hear from. And it can be in a positive way, so they can identify with your client or your witnesses; or in a negative way, where they may be distrustful of an expert who's coming in is not going to be helping your case at all. But I think that effort to engage them in a conversation and try in as little time as you have to learn as much as you can starts to create a little bonding. Especially if there are facts or themes that you can go back to in closing argument that can reaffirm that connection you may made in voir dire, then I think you hope to have jurors who are, if not with you, at least open-minded and willing to hear your case and give you a fair shot.

I'm tumbling to this notion that *voir dire*, as we're practicing it, or many of us are, could be shortened to asking the group, who among you thinks you may or may not be suitable for this particular case? Tell me why or why not, and be done with it. Honor their time. They seem to value time more than anything else. What's the most important thing to you? Time, number one. A commitment to doing good service, maybe not their top priority. That's been illuminating to me. So could I gain their trust and connect with them by honoring that and keeping that process very, very brief?

I think you gain trust and appreciation, but you don't learn much about the jurors. So the risk is that you may excuse someone who has time commitments or stress at work who would be an outstanding juror for your case because they just say they don't have the time or aren't interested or whatever. And then you may keep a juror, who for the same reason says, no, I'd love to be of service and I'm anxious, you know, who is tickled to, and I got my notice, and none of that tells you whether they're going to be a good juror.

There'd be some follow up, but it would be briefer, hopefully, because they would be honest. You would hope that you ask people to raise their hands so they don't have to speak and maybe be embarrassed by the answers they have to give. Some people have related that they're really uncomfortable having to relate in front of people they don't know, in this foreign environment, what their biases might be.

I still go back to the notion that, if you have someone who believes that if someone is injured in an accident should get their expenses paid, but anything else is a windfall, that sort of question doesn't ferret that out. I think you need to know that sort of information as a lawyer before you can exercise informed challenges. I don't see that there's anything wrong with that, because I think it's helpful to know if jurors don't think they should sit and why and if they have conflicts or can't pay attention or something else is on their mind, that that's all important and may be enough of a basis to excuse them. You certainly don't want people who start with a chip on their shoulder. I recently had a jury where a juror asked to be excused because she'd been recently hired on and had training or something going on. I didn't feel that was a legal basis to excuse her; didn't get quite to the place where I was going to give her a break. But I frankly thought one of the lawyers, given that we had enough jurors and enough challenges, could have excused her and gained favor with the rest of the panel. Instead, they both kept her and she started with a chip on her shoulder. I'm not sure if it was against the judge or which lawyer or all of us, but she wasn't happy to be there. And she did a job, but I think it would have been better had one of the lawyers given her a break and let her go. Because she didn't say anything that made me feel that she was going to be a particularly good juror for either side.

That gets to this notion of talking to jurors and getting them to give you the words you need to hear to excuse them for cause, and I am not very good at it. Whenever I do it, I feel as if I'm alienating that juror. I don't think I'm going to get that juror excused because of the rehabilitation potential from the bench, so I'm alienating this juror and possibly even the group. I'm almost of a mind that it's not worth it to pursue those jurors to get them to say the things they need to say to be excused for cause. Just take your peremptory, unless it's very, very obvious.

But another way to approach it, and I hadn't thought about it particularly, is because the critical issue is, can they be fair and impartial? And you can ask leading questions, of course. **It sounds like I'm hearing that you don't think you could be fair or impartial. Do you think it would be better that the judge go ahead and excuse you? That takes the heat off you as the lawyer and it makes the judge seem a little awkward if he then tries to keep somebody who's acknowledged that they can't be fair or impartial. Let the other side try to rehabilitate them if they want, but I don't think you alienate yourself if you choose later to exercise a peremptory challenge if they're not excused for cause.** *But I think it's often awkward, and if the* *questioning of jurors – and it comes about sometimes in the, I think, misguided effort to educate the jury – if they don't know what a reasonable doubt is, for example, in a criminal case and are asked and say, well, it's beyond any doubt, you know beyond the shadow of a doubt or something that's not quite accurate, well now, you're off. It's awkward. They may feel bad if they didn't get the answer right. Those kinds of questions are, I think, not very helpful and have the risk of alienating jurors because they go, well, jeez, I took Civics in high school, but I guess I got that one wrong, because now he's lectured me about what reasonable doubt is –*

That's helpful.

— or even politely corrected me. **But we don't take correction well sometimes. So I think having a conversation instead of that sort of question and answer goes a lot further in making the best use of the limited time that you have for voir dire. If you don't know what sort of jurors you want, then it's of less use.** *And I'm reminded of the trial a long time ago of – it was a relative of the Kennedys, Smith, who was accused of rape in Florida.*

Right. The doctor, and was represented by Roy Black, if I'm not mistaken.

Right. And the interesting thing was the prosecutor was seeking out conservative, Republican, middle-aged jurors that most prosecutors would like on most of their cases. And because there was the question involving the victim and whether she had brought about some of this conduct on her own, through focus groups and things like that, Roy Black learned that this is the sort of juror that would do well for his case. So the irony was, they were both paring down the jury panel to get the same jurors; the difference being that Roy Black knew it would be helpful for his case. The prosecutor presumed wrongfully that they would be the same type of people helpful for the prosecution. So that involves some homework, and maybe in a major case, learning from focus groups or things like that what sort of personalities will be most receptive to the case you're going to present as a lawyer. I thought that was a good example where that preparation work – that was a case, in my view, in hindsight, was decided with jury selection.

It's interesting when you talk about burden of proof. I've asked everybody that I've spoken with what to them is meant by the words preponderance of the evidence? I get a very interesting response that it's often as high as 60- or 70- or 80- or 90%, and then I go on to say, it would be further defined as more likely true than not true. Then that brings them back down. It's something I feel they need to know going in. But what you've just said is, that may be a difficult conversation to have if you're correcting them on that, because they may feel bad when they think preponderance is 90% but then they hear it's not. How would you – would you even talk about that in jury selection in a civil case, for example?

You can, but instead of asking them what they would define a legal concept to be, in that example, a different approach is simply to say, if the judge tells you that a preponderance of the evidence means that a proposition is more likely true than not true, is that something you can apply?

I see.

Is that a standard that you're comfortable applying to my client's case? Then you're helping to inform them without correcting them. And you can also ask for a preliminary instruction from the Court at the outset of the case, either before or after voir dire. But usually, the beginning instruction, if I'm ever asked to give one, follows voir dire. And I'm thinking, that sort of road map about what they're going to hear and burden of proof and proximate cause might be better given before jury voir dire commences so that the jurors understand, have that framework, going into it. But I've never been asked to give that instruction until after the jury's been impaneled.

One of the frustrations I've had in *voir dire* is asking jurors questions but not being able to apply a context, because they haven't heard enough about what the case is going to be to say that they can be fair. Well, I haven't heard the evidence, so I don't know if I can be fair, Counsel. That's frustrating. I try to tell them a little bit about the case, and opposing counsel objects because I'm giving the jury too much. What can a lawyer do?

I don't know without thinking of more concrete examples. I think you can, and typically the judge will paint a very broad outline of the case. You can try to make that a little more detailed to put a little more flesh on the bones than the usual summary statement. But I think most judges will allow you, as groundwork for a question, to lay out some of the facts. For example, soft tissue injuries. For a layperson, being asked to return a verdict for damages for soft tissue injuries may think, well, it's hocus pocus. It's just, we all have a sore neck or back from time to time, but if it's put in the context that soft tissues include things like a brain or your kidneys or your heart or your muscles or tendons and it only distinguishes between bones, there are some vital parts of our bodies that involve soft tissues. So if they're damaged, they should be willing to compensate for the damage to those injuries, especially if they haven't resolved or healed up. So those are different ways to try to help to educate and get jurors thinking that what they, as a layperson, may think we're thinking about may really not be what they should be thinking about when they're back in deliberation.

Talking about damages as we have a little bit, and the end game, which is the verdict – or a word that seems to work better is "remedy" – better than award or judgment or verdict. Most people are not comfortable with the notion of general damages for pain and suffering. They really struggle with that. I understand why, because I struggle with it. Because there's no fixed standard, and we can't really give them a metric that's all that helpful, what's your thought about talking to jurors about general damages in *voir dire*?

Well, my experience tells me that if there are cases involving intentional harm, it's a lot easier, because jurors are much more willing to impose damages intended to punish what they view as intentional misconduct. It's in the cases where the harm is not intentional, and worse yet, if you have a policeman, fireman, teacher as a defendant, it's going to be tougher, **because they don't want to be interpreted as punishing a good citizen for an accident.**

And don't want to bankrupt them, that good doctor or that teacher.

Yeah. So part of the process is to let them know that's not what's at issue. And when we're talking about compensation for expenses and for pain and suffering, we're trying to restore the plaintiff to the condition they were in before this ever happened. In a lot of cases, that's going to be impossible. And if the jury understands that our compensatory system is intended to do the best we can to place a dollar value on what's been lost, and it has nothing to do with the accident per se – I mean, we have to prove liability – but if we meet that burden, then the focus shifts to compensating the plaintiff for what they've lost; it doesn't have anything to do with punishing the defendant. That's not their concern. They shouldn't be concerned with whether an award will be paid or who will pay it or how it will be paid. **Their focus is to compensate the plaintiff for what's been lost. And if they understand in cases where there's residual pain and that, there may not be a dollar value that will be capable of compensating the plaintiff.** If I lost an arm in an accident, I don't think there is a dollar value I would accept and say, well, that's a fair trade-off. I would much rather have the arm. So whatever they award is going to fall short of the mark of really trading what I've lost in terms of a dollar value, and that may **posit the case in a way that they realize their task is still to do the best they can to come as close as they can to adequately compensating a plaintiff for what's been lost.** I think in some cases, it's a lot easier for jurors to do that. And in some cases, lawyers can put the case in a context that brings that home to jurors in a way that they want to step up to the plate.

Even in *voir dire* you can plant those seeds?

I think you can plant the seeds. But you drive it home in closing argument.

Have you seen anybody successfully use a metric of some sort, whether it's a dollar figure per day or an *x* specials? Some people have said, that would be helpful to me. But what I'm getting a sense of is that every case is different for every group.

They are, but there are ways to put things in a perspective that I think is permissible. The argument about having a stone in your shoe and how painful that could be and if it would be worth five bucks to have somebody take the stone out of your shoe so you can walk without discomfort, we'd think, there's no – we wouldn't think about it; of course we'd pay five bucks to be relieved of the pain. But if it persists, when we would be able to take our shoe off, remove the stone, and fix the problem in an instant, when that is so persistent but it continues minute by minute and hour by hour – if that's a fair dollar comparison, I don't know whether a jury would respond to that and say, that puts it in a different perspective, and this is a major loss to this person.

I've also learned you need to take cases that justify being in a courtroom for some length of time. A lot of cases being tried aren't getting very good results, and I think the jury public is just not wanting to give that kind of money to people. They don't think the case is worth it, and so I'm not going to fight that tide. Just take better cases.

It is. And I think, especially in medical malpractice cases, when I was practicing, I learned hard and unfortunate lessons of why experienced lawyers generally didn't take those cases unless the damages were, back then, over $100,000. The risks of losing were too high and the costs to present the case were also too high. And while I didn't fall flat on my face with some of those cases, I had a couple that I did take; I look back and wished I hadn't, because the results weren't worth the time and effort that I had to spend on them. So that's always a problem. But every case is different, and I think if you can identify or have jurors who can identify with the loss that a plaintiff has sustained – and sometimes it's apparent.

I struggle with what is the right amount. I'm curious to know what your thought is about talking about a specific dollar figure in *voir dire* or a range. Some people like to do it as an anchor. What have you seen that works or doesn't work in that regard to get them thinking about money?

I think it's probably best to let them know within some parameters in voir dire. Because if you're going to ask for a million dollars or five million dollars, and you have a juror who is incapable of understanding or agreeing to award that much, you probably need to know that in voir dire. I think it also helps to set the stage. They know what's coming, and it's not going to come as a big surprise at the end of trial. It doesn't preclude you from reevaluating and asking for more or less. And I think it can help to let the jury know this is an area that's difficult as lawyers to tell them what a case is worth. That's their job, and you may have undervalued the loss to your client. They can certainly – they don't have to accept what you're asking for; they can go above and obviously they can go below; we usually see that more often than the other. I think it's probably better to let them know. **If it's a lesser dollar value case, something in the range of 50-, 60-, $70,000 and there's $10,000 or $15,000 of medical specials, I don't know that you need that discussion ahead of time.** They're going to be looking to see, what are the losses and how do you tie it together and justify the claim for whatever you're asking for. I don't think those numbers are so high as to cause jurors to naturally say, whoa, really? **But I think, even jurors who are not prepared to award millions of dollars in damages, can be prepared to do so and willing to do so if the case is properly presented.**

I've learned a lot by asking not what works or what people think will work, but what absolutely doesn't work and hasn't worked? That's become a more instructive question for me. Are there things you've seen attorneys do routinely that don't serve the purpose or the needs of the jury selection process or turns the jurors off to them?

One of the things that works is recognizing that if you've got twelve people on the jury, collectively, they have the skill set to answer a lot of unanswered questions and fill in a lot of blanks. So you can touch on topics; you don't need to spoon feed them everything, because they're going to be capable, and perfectly capable, in their deliberations of making the connections and links and answering the key questions. You need do little more than point them in the right direction. **What doesn't work, I think, is when lawyers speak down to the jury or argue or take on the view that they are the expert and they're informed and here's what the jury needs to do. I don't think jurors like to be told what they must do, and I think they probably react a little bit to a lawyer who's overbearing or pompous or just comes across in an essence of not valuing their intelligence, their life experiences, and their ability to connect the dots.**

Speaking from the heart, it can be difficult when you're looking at a panel of jurors to believe they can do that. Given you have this group that in some cases may not be very educated, may not be very motivated, certainly may not want to be there and might not be paying attention, do you still feel that somehow this group is going to find the right way?

If the case is properly presented, for the most part. I think there are some cases where judges may do a better job than jurors, particularly in cases that involve a lot of technical information that jurors who aren't well-educated may not really be very able to grasp, I think, **given that our usual experience here in this county is that jurors are often much more conservative than we as judges would think they should be on a given case.** I think there are many times that lawyers might have fared better with a judge than a jury. **But there are lots of things that one can do to bring around that hodge-podge of jurors. One is obviously not to use words they don't understand, even if they're very bright and you're very bright, simple words – and Paul Luvera's a good example of breaking it down to get away from terminology and just get to the basics – so, my client hurt. Very simple. People do understand when something hurts or it doesn't move right. That's a very hard place to check yourself as a lawyer, because with the education we bring to the table as lawyers, we tend to speak in a vocabulary that someone with a high school or not having a high school education isn't really, that's not their comfort level, and you really want to be in their wheelhouse in terms of a comfort level, and that begins with being very mindful of the language you're using as a lawyer and the language that your witnesses are using. The other touchstone, I think, is the recognition that they could be sitting there. They could have suffered this injury.**

How do you talk about the Golden Rule when you can't talk about the Golden Rule in jury selection?

I think there are still ways that you can do so. You can certainly elicit from them that if they were seriously injured, would they want to be compensated? Would they want to be fairly compensated? Would they be comfortable hiring a lawyer to navigate a very complex system that might provide the opportunity to get that compensation? Those are ways I think lawyers can, in essence, get jurors to identify that they would like to be treated fairly, if not generously.

That's helpful. I would have skirted around that more safely, because that almost is getting them to put themselves in the shoes of the plaintiff or the defendant. But if I get you accurately, you think you can get to those –

I think you can elicit that information, and you may not even get an objection if you're having that conversation in the course of voir dire. The worst case is, you get an objection that's sustained, and I think the lawyer who raises the objection doesn't look particularly good if it seems like a very natural discussion to have with somebody. One of the biases, I think, particularly in medical negligence cases, is the notion that this whole process and suing doctors and damages awards is going to drive the cost of medicine through the roof. The reality is, at least for me, I'd rather pay a few bucks more when I see my doctor and, if something goes wrong, there is a remedy. There is compensation that I can have available. The notion that if a doctor cuts off the wrong leg that I have no recourse but my office or hospital visit was $100 cheaper, is little solace. And I think most people would feel that way. But they're taken by the notion of – and these are broad concepts that often do affect bias and do come up in voir dire, just as the McDonald's case or other high profile cases will be commented on by jurors.

Almost universally.

And I think if there are ways that those issues can be addressed, I think judges will allow some latitude, because those are things that affect bias and the point of voir dire is to find that out.

Insurance. I find people all over the board on whether or not they know that insurance is at play, that they don't know, they never thought about it. Some people, we immediately talked about it in deliberations. I think it's important. I've had instances where jurors have brought it up in *voir dire*, but I've been reluctant to bring it up because I wasn't sure if I could or how to do it. It seems like a double standard. If the juror brings it up, it's fine, but the lawyer shouldn't bring it up or maybe can't in some courtrooms. I don't know.

*It's very awkward. They will be instructed typically that they're not to consider insurance. **Certainly, if it comes up, and if the word gets mentioned, I would think it would be proper to say, there may or may not be insurance in play; that's not your concern, the judge will deal with that. And as much as I might like to talk with you in great detail about insurance, I can't do that. So trust that that's not going to be an issue for their consideration. I don't know of a better way than we have of addressing that issue.** I find it's awkward every time it comes up and every time it's mentioned by a juror, the lawyers tend to look at me as a judge like, okay, now what do I do? And I don't have a good answer.*

It sounds as if we shouldn't or can't bring it up in *voir dire*.

> *I don't think that you can. And I think if you have a judge who's on the ball, he or she may be able to explain to the jurors the fact that they're not going to be allowed to consider it, and it may or may not be something that's there. It's just not going to be for their consideration.* **I tend to think the twelve jurors, especially if it's an auto accident case, are going to assume that there's insurance here and the money isn't going to come out of somebody's pocket, but I don't know.** *I haven't been back there to know the nature of those discussions.*

What do you think jurors value and want from the lawyers in civil cases? What are they looking for that they're not getting?

> *I think one issue certainly is, that they're looking for competency as a lawyer. I don't think they warm up to lawyers that they know are doing a bad job. I think they look for honesty in the presentation. I think they react very favorably if they understand there is a connection between the lawyer and his or her client, and some empathy there; that the lawyer cares about the client personally as well as professionally.*

Have you seen that go too far?

> *I don't think so. I think for the most part, as long as it comes across as genuine. And if it doesn't come across as genuine, the lawyer needs to take more acting classes.*

Or spend more time with the client.

> *Exactly. But I do think there's a danger that lawyers may go too far, ask for too much, push the bounds of reasonableness, and I think jurors can react, and often do, with a bit of vengeance if they really think the lawyer is asking for too much. And ultimately, it's not just how they're asking, but the bottom line is, are they asking for reasonable compensation or are they hearing a message of windfall, greed, all those attributes that will, I think, not just cause a jury not to agree, but cause a jury to start heading in the other direction.*

Have you seen lawyers successfully in *voir dire* share something of themselves in order to get the group a little warmed up?

> *Mm-hmm.*

We've been taught - certain schools say, show them yours and they'll you show theirs. But I'm learning that there's a limit to how far you should go with that, that it should be contextual.

> *Mm-hmm.*

There is some information that's too personal.

I agree that there have to be appropriate limits. But I do see that. I guess hypothetically, if a juror mentions that they have a dog, whether you have a dog or not, it's, I suppose, appropriate to mention that you too own a dog of the same breed or things like that. It's technically not permissible and it may prompt an objection, but I think if it's not the predominate theme of your voir dire, is, look folks, I'm just like you, there's a place where some of that can come out and those connections can be made. If the jurors are asked if they have children, knowing that the lawyer has children, can be a place of connectivity that I think is okay. Whether you have kids or not probably has nothing to do with voir dire, whether the juror can be fair or objective, but it's still going to look stupid for the other side to object to some comment like that.

What about articulating a bias that you may have in order to get them to understand that biases aren't such a bad thing? I have been frustrated, since I've moved to the city from the suburbs, that bicyclists tend to not stop at stop signs. That to me is a little bias and gets people talking. Do you think that's a good thing for lawyers to do?

I think it can be in a way that, with the theme that, we all have biases, but we need to find a way to identify them and recognize them. *That can be helpful if there's a relatively benign bias that you identify that you're working on. For us it may be learning to put the toilet seat down or something that's innocuous but still reflects the kind of issue that we need to be mindful of it and work on it.*

The awareness is really half the battle, isn't it?

Yeah. Sure.

How do you do that with snakes in the grass; the ones that don't want to talk about, don't want to identify, frequently may be working for insurance companies, and those kinds of things?

I don't know how you can elicit that information from people who don't want to share that information with you. Then I think it's a matter of trying to identify whether they're leaders or followers. If they're leaders, then you need to be proactive enough to not let them sit on your jury. *Either they're going to be bad or it's an unknown quantity, neither of which I think you want to take a chance on. If it's clear that they're a follower and not a leader, having some of them on the jury isn't going to hurt, if the balance of your jurors are better. And I do think there are some things that, while it's possible that a juror who works for an insurance defense firm could be a fair juror for a plaintiff, I don't know how difficult it would be to find that out.* ***And the time it would take to learn that they would really be a good juror is probably more time than you have, so why spend time? They would assume that they would likely be excused, so move on. Spend your time with people that are less transparently apt to have a bias that's going to be hurtful to your case.***

Right. One juror type that has become prominent on my radar are what I call the tech jurors, or the web developers, what we used to call the aerospace engineers. In our region we have young, very data-driven jurors who tend to not be so empathetic. What do you think is a way to reach them, both in jury selection to get them interested in participating – because they generally don't want to – but also to understand that the world isn't black and white as it so often is when you're working with computers and software and data and that kind of thing?

> *I don't know. I'm not sure that they can't do a good job. In other words, the question is, how much of that is itself a bias, that they do look at things black and white or data-driven or aren't empathetic or would not return a generous verdict? I don't know if that's accurate.* **I recognize our verdicts are often low in cases that I think they should be higher, but I've not necessarily made the connection that it's because of retired people or elderly people or high-tech folks or aerospace engineers and workers or any class of people that may be over-represented on a jury panel.** *And I don't know that there's – there probably are good ways to appeal to those people in a data way, but I can't think off the top of my head how to present things in a way that appeals to people who are going to be more motivated by mathematical formulas and data and things of that sort.*

I have had a few people in the field talk to me about ways they'd like to have the trial presented to them. But we're talking about *voir dire* here. Is there anything that you absolutely would like to see all of the plaintiff's lawyers in your courts do that would make your job and their job and the jury's job a lot easier, especially in *voir dire*?

> *No, nothing that I can see other than,* **I think having a conversation with jurors and eliciting as much information and then listening to what you're hearing and knowing how that will impact your case is probably the best overall thing that I'd like to see more of.** *Usually, with good lawyers, I see good voir dire. And sadly, with less competent lawyers, I sometimes think, this was a waste of time. I learn nothing and worse yet, the lawyer learned nothing from the process. So while it might have been or might not have been engaging, it wasn't productive.*

One of my colleagues on the civil defense side who's had close to 250 trials in his career was interviewed and I asked him, have you seen very good lawyers do very poor *voir dire*? He said, oh, I see it all the time. But he said, when it is done right, it's – and he named a few people who are very good at it. That was a little disappointing to hear there are very good lawyers not making any progress in their *voir dire*, but they can do well in other parts of the trial. One of the reasons why I'm doing this project is because I haven't tried a case in some time. Where do you get the opportunity to practice these skills?

> *In the courtroom.* **I don't think there's a substitute for the experience that comes from trying cases coupled with ongoing education.** *But it's very difficult, because if our goal is to get the best results we can for our clients,*

that doesn't always lend to going to trial every few months. When I tried cases, because there were long gaps between jury trials, the anxiety in preparing for a jury trial was overwhelming because I hadn't been in the pit for a while. Once I got going, then I was looking forward to the next opportunity to have a jury trial, but it wasn't waiting in the wings. And I think that's a difference often between plaintiff's counsel and defense counsel.

Boots on the ground.

And it's a small group of lawyers that are regularly doing trial work; not just going to court, but jury work, and probably more on the defense than the plaintiff side. So it's a natural limitation, but I think that there are lots of avenues to practice and take more cases to trial. If it's a close call on settling a case for a host of reasons, as long as it's the client who's making that ultimate decision, because we don't have a crystal ball, we don't know what a jury's going to do, but if we think we're close but it's worth a shot and a client who's willing to do it, it gives us experience. Some of the cases that I appreciated the most were hopeless cases where I had a client who just wanted to go to trial. That was nice, because I didn't have the anxiety of expecting a successful outcome. I was more relaxed, but I could practice some of the skills we learn in seminars and training and things like that. I think nothing is more rewarding than to learn some new technique and have an opportunity to put it to work and see that it actually does work.

Especially without a lot of outcome-based thinking pressure. And that's, I think, the most difficult part. We care. We're invested in these cases. I wish that the juries could know how much the lawyers are invested in these cases.

For sure.

Thank you.

PART THREE – **THE TRIAL GREATS**

49

BEYOND A REASONABLE DOUBT

Jurors naturally believe the standard of proof is beyond a reasonable doubt. That's their starting point. You need to disavow them of that. You need to talk about what the burden of proof is and are they going to be able to do that? Do they understand it? Will they follow it? Because a lot will say, you know, I just don't think that that's a high enough burden of proof.

What I'm trying to find out here – and it may have been Paul Luvera who said, if you want to know what a juror's thinking, don't ask a lawyer. I didn't want to believe that at first, but the more I practice –

Really true.

I thought, maybe I need to talk to people and find out what they're thinking; a cross-section. I had conversations with people who opened up to me and it was enlightening and it was concrete. I started out by asking, how do you feel about lawyers and lawsuits? How do you feel about being in the courtroom? What do you think about economic damages and non-economic damages and burdens of proof and all that? And I got some great stuff that helped me understand what I'm up against.

The other people who would be great sources of information are jury consultants, especially the ones who debrief juries.

If they'll give that stuff away.

Depends on who they are and your relationship. But that's been a great sounding board for me over the years, because they have so much more contact and interaction with them. For example, I think lawyers are terrible at debriefing a jury. Paul Luvera – I think he's the best at voir dire I ever saw.

Can you tell me why?

He understood what he was doing. He understood what he was trying to identify. He didn't challenge jurors. He shut up. He let them talk. He knew what would be important ultimately for their decision making process and what type of jurors to avoid. We don't pick a jury; we un-pick a jury.

We de-select.

Yeah. And there's also something special about Paul. His values of the legal system and his humanity run deeper than the rest of us. He's able to draw on that in ways that the rest of us can't. And we can talk about and we can see, but we can't implement. He operates at a different level; it's not fair. But he can argue damages in a way that is so sincere. And he can talk to potential jurors about role and everything else, of a jury, that's just at a different level.

You mentioned damages. It seems that, by and large, nobody wants to give general damages unless it's one, a corporate entity of some sort, or two, a heinous act, partly because they don't know how to calculate them. And we can't give them a lot of help.

I don't know if I agree with that. I mean, if you look at cases that produced large verdicts or verdicts that had a substantial amount of non-economic damage, you know, if it's a case that has real merit and they're behind you, they'll award that. And they'll award that in spades.

If the damages are there?

Obviously there's got to be some there, but they've got to feel strongly enough about the liability to get to it. But if they're in your camp on liability, I think they'll award the general damages. You'll run into some jurors, but usually you can weed them out, who don't agree with general damages or whatever. Or they'll want to be excused. Some will say, well, gee, I just can't award that much money. And there'll be some negotiating, but I think by and large, if your case is solid, you're okay. I just don't agree that jurors do not want to award general damages. I wouldn't agree with that proposition. I'd agree with the proposition that in certain types of cases, it's hard to win. I think it's really tough against just a doctor to win, period.

I've heard them say, we just don't want to bankrupt this poor doctor. Of course, they don't know.

They just don't want to tarnish them, whether it's bankrupt or tarnish them or whatever. It's just tough. They're just not going to, even when all the merit and logic and evidence is in your favor, they just won't pull the trigger. And I think that's the difficulty in those types of cases as opposed to a reluctance of awarding general damages.

Sure. Definitely in that context. Let's talk about jurors. We know that they, generally speaking, don't want to be there. They value their money and their time. They're reluctant, for the most part, to do jury service. But what connects with jurors or what doesn't connect with jurors in that first hour or so of *voir dire*, in your experience?

You mean how do you make the connection or what resonates with them?

That's sort of one in the same, isn't it? I mean –

Maybe.

Show them that you're a human being and that they're going to connect and have some trust with you.

There's a great difference between doing voir dire as defense counsel and doing it as plaintiff's counsel.

Right. And this, of course, is a book for plaintiff's counsel.

Yeah. But this is what you have to understand. If you – oh, your book will also be read by defense counsel. If you're defense counsel, what you really striving – I didn't have to worry too much about credibility. The biases are all in my favor at that point as defense counsel, and what I'm really driving at are, what are my themes? I would talk to jurors about listening to all the evidence, that's of course a standard one. But I always use stuff about being falsely accused and how do you clear your good name? Holy smokes, did that ever hit traction. And then I'd talk about some other things. But there were two or three things like that that you could put in.

Hindsight bias can be a big one.

*It might, if it's peculiar to the case, but clearing your good name, that was one that I thought really, really had traction and people could identify with. I'd ask them about their circumstances and had they ever been falsely accused? Maybe at work or in a social setting. You get some great stories, and talk about how would you clear your good name? Well, this is a place where you can do that. That creates a nice theme for defense counsel that he's here to clear his good name. He's been falsely accused. That's a great theme for the defense. **On the plaintiff's side, they hate you. And you're not going to establish credibility in the first hour. You're not. That's not enough time, and they think you're just putting on a show and trying to be nice to them anyway. And what you're saying and asking is just part of the charade. You're a lawyer and you represent patients suing their doctors. Even middle of the road people are pretty skeptical of you, because I think, in large part, due to at least 30 years of propaganda from the far right.** It's just nuts. And the plaintiff's bar can't get traction with the press to publicize stories. As a quick aside, there are more doctors and more office space for physicians and more healthcare providers than we've ever had in this state. We can't get that published. But if a doctor left town because he said, oh, gee, my malpractice rates went up, that's a front page story. So the truth and the counter to it and the ability to publicize it just doesn't happen. We can't get it published in* The Times. *The reporters say, my editors have no interest in this. And I'm like, well, thanks a lot. We're getting the short end of this stick. I don't think you can establish your credibility that fast, but you can certainly start to lay the foundation early in voir dire.*

The foundation for your case or for the connection with you?

*The credibility. Look, to me, **credibility is the key to persuasion.** If they don't believe me – you know, that was always my mantra as defense counsel. I'd say,* *this is what the case is about, and they'd listen and I didn't expect them to believe me. But if I proved, through the rest of the story, the rest of the trial, that's what it was about and here were the facts that supported that, and they go, you know, he was right. That was the story and his facts were supported and the evidence is there to support that. That story says, the doctor doesn't have to pay. That's how I tried them on the defense. And I think it's similar on the plaintiff's in that you're not going to establish your credibility. **It's important in opening statement not to over-promise and under-deliver. Don't make statements that you can't prove. And with the jury, you want to – what you're really trying to do – I mean, one, be nice and just be yourself. That's going to be credible unless you start BS-ing them. Don't try to schmooze them; it's just not going to work. Just be nice and be reasonably friendly but don't try to kiss ass. Get them talking. Find out the jurors that you want off. That's what you're driving at. You've got to figure out who those jurors are that are going to be death to you and can really drive the decision in the wrong way.***

That's where your jury consultant helps you, right? Because then you can help identify a –

There are two parts to that. There are certain good questions to ask that'll give you – well, let me slow down. I think in the old days, we relied on demographics a lot more. All people of this class or this ethnicity were, not all, but were, by and large, pointed in a certain direction. I think we've gotten away from that, which is good, although I still don't like engineers or CPAs or actuaries. They're just death because their orientation is very specific to always having solid proof instead of –

Data, data, data.

But you can ask questions that identify attitudes. And that can be really important to you. Those types of questions really help you.

If you can't get credibility, can you get a human connection at least, to where they're neutral about you?

Well, you start. It's too early. I think you start making your connections and stuff, but I'm just saying it's too early to be able to do that. They're not going to get done with an hour of talking with you and an hour of talking to your opponent and say, you know, I really like that guy; I believe what he says. As long as you haven't put yourself in a vulnerable position or stepped in it and ticked anybody off, that's as much as you can hope for at the beginning, I think. You establish your credibility and your persuasiveness as the case goes. You have too many biases working against you. *If you've tried med mal cases and tried PI cases, jurors treat you totally differently. It's just totally different. In a PI case, they're like, well, somebody got hurt and somebody believes that something was done wrong and well, let's see what the evidence is. That's by and large where they come from. You don't have this push back that you get in a med mal case.* ***In a med mal case, there are some that will be openly hostile to you. There are some that will be very defensive to the***

medical community. There are some who will attempt to appear neutral, and really, they just want to skewer you.

Snakes in the grass.

And they really are lying in wait for you. The ball-game's just totally different. You're dealing with a lot of bias.

What can you do to avoid stepping in it? Maybe that's the better question.

One, don't talk much; listen. Two, ask open-ended questions. Follow your outline about, this is what I need to know, and so I'm going to ask these questions, because those are important factors in determining how to get through jury selection and identify the jurors that you don't want. I had to watch one fine attorney do certain things and he had like two or three themes or, areas of interest would be a better term. And he'd focus on those and that would help really determine which way it was going to go in his voir dire, in his jury selection, and in his challenges. He was real good about that. But they were key themes about how people hold others accountable or how people deal with the legal system and money. He would focus on certain things, and he was outstanding at it. You can step in it if you try to tell the jurors what to think or to try to change their views on things. They're not going to do that.

I felt I stepped in it by trying to establish cause. When I started probing about cause, I felt like the juror was resentful and the group was resentful. Now I'm thinking that maybe I ought to not go there; too much push back.

Depends on the situation and what happened. I don't know enough about that case to offer...

I couldn't have been more polite to her either, it's just that –

You are going to talk about that sometimes. In the context, you can ask the juror, what do you think should happen if the doctor doesn't follow basic rules of practice and injures somebody? What do you think should happen? Some people would argue well, bad stuff happens, and even if they didn't give you good care, that's the end of the discussion. Done. And others say, you know, you're supposed to follow that and this helps. And that person should be compensated and the doctor should be reminded that this isn't going to happen in the future because there're consequences; what do you think? You want to see where they're coming from. In med mal cases, what most plaintiff's lawyers don't grasp, they'll give lip service to it, is that 70% of the defense is causation. They'll say they get that. They don't get it. But it's true. That's where the defense is, and a lot of times the analysis will go by the jurors. I don't know if you did anything wrong. I don't really like the care, but I'm not sure if it was negligent, but it didn't cause the injury; therefore, he wasn't negligent. They loop back like that. It's kind of a funny detail.

It's a great out for them as well. I mean, they can satisfy one prong but without having to –

Well, but you get a verdict form back and it says, no negligence.

Or there was negligence but no causation.

You'll see that sometimes.

In medical cases, it can be really tough with these dueling experts.

Most of the plaintiff's attorneys, how do I say this, they don't really grasp causation. I mean, all they can focus on is the negligence part and that it caused the injury. They don't go through an analysis that says, okay, so he didn't do x test or didn't do y action, so what? What difference did that make? They don't ask themselves that question. I would get phone calls from people or I'd be talking with potential clients and say, okay, well, what difference did that make? And then they don't approach it at trial by saying, well, what difference did it make? You said the doctor should have done x? Well, what if he had done x? What difference would that have made? You know, what were the consequences of him following the course that he did? They don't ask those questions. They don't get it. It's really rare that causation is real simple. There are some cases, yeah, but causation is just, you've got to just overwhelm them in those cases.

How do you talk about causation in *voir dire*? Or do you?

You know, that's probably not something I'm going to talk about in voir dire. It's too complicated. And it's too hypothetical. I've also got a limited amount of time.

Would you talk about burden of proof?

Yes.

I've asked people to tell me what preponderance means to them. I get everything from 60- to 90%. When I go on to explain that preponderance is defined as more likely true than not true, well, they tumble a little better, closer to a 49/51, whatever. But I think that's something that probably ought to be talked about in *voir dire*, because I think you want to know where people are starting from.

Yes, it needs to be talked about in voir dire. The best analysis or best format for discussing it is stuff from David Ball. *There was stuff published about 10 years ago that was really good. It was one of the articles I kept.* **There are lots of examples that you can give that show that preponderance wins.** *Basketball game, 91 to 90. You got one more point; that team wins. An election, all sorts of things. I do know lawyers who do med mal work who do not understand how scales work. It was mind blowing. And I thought, that probably explains why you've never won a trial. But they did not understand how a scale works and that more weight on one side means that side goes lower.* **I think the key, the reason you want to discuss burden of proof at length is multi-fold. Jurors naturally believe the standard of proof is beyond a reasonable doubt. That's their starting point. You need to disavow them of that. You need to talk about what the burden of proof is and are they going to be able to do that? Do**

they understand it? Will they follow it? Because a lot will say, you know, I just don't think that that's a high enough burden of proof.

They say that.

I know a lot of lawyers that give jury instructions to their focus groups, and I know some that will include a burden of proof instruction. I never give them a burden of proof instruction. I want to see what they do when it's a – because they're going to operate under their default standard. That's what I want to see, what's the default standard in how they resolve that case that way? That's better for the defense. I don't want to win my focus groups; I want to win at trial.

One of the reasons I've been hesitant to talk about burden of proof in *voir dire* is the argument that, well, if he's talking about it already, he must be worried that he's not going to meet it.

I don't buy that at all. Look, the defense is going to talk about it, but you have the burden of proof. And they're going to go on and on. They will try to use words like, you must be convinced. That's not what the burden of proof is and should be objected to at every phase. You need to tell them, look, all your decisions are going to be made on a more likely than not basis, kind of a majority rules. I think it's important to have that orientation early that says, this is how you go about making your decision. This is the threshold. And once you reach with each decision, you then address the next question anew. There's no carryover. *It's not like, well, gee, at the end of the first inning it was 2 to 1 and now we're starting the second inning. No. The second inning is a separate game. It's who's going to win that inning? What issue was being decided? And it's by that burden of proof. I think you have to talk about it.*

Those are good analogies. The sporting one that you just said, I'd never heard that.

Yeah, though I always worry – that's why I'll also use like an election or voting or something else. Maybe it's a board decision and we're going to have a decision by the board members and the majority decision wins. Because you know only 35% of the population is interested in sports. It's really a lot smaller than you think. But they tend to be, if you look, they're much more interested. If you look at, what are the most read stories? Go read that list. There'll be top ten stories whether you're reading The New York Times *or* The Seattle Times. *And one of the top most popular stories in Seattle, particularly, it'll be sporting game stories. Well, you got 35% of the population's going to read those four sport stories that are high on the totem pole. So they'll all be listed in the top ten.*

While we're talking about Seattle and King County and the Northwest, it always pains me that I selected the Pacific Northwest as my base to be a trial lawyer when I hear about some really crazy numbers that come out of other jurisdictions around the country. The jury eligible public around here: pretty conservative.

Depends on where you are. One, I wouldn't agree that this is a bad place to be a plaintiff's lawyer. At least about half the states have tort reform.

There's that.

*So that takes out half the states. In a lot of other states, they're just so conservative anyway that you're not going to win. I mean, good luck with a plaintiff's case in Oklahoma, North Dakota, Wyoming. **So when you look at the legal landscape, this is a pretty good place to practice law and I think it's relatively safe from erosion from the far right.** You know, we got past everything 10 years ago. God, other states. Ten years ago Idaho moved their caps from 250 to 150 because 250 was too high. Are you kidding me? You can kill somebody and the damages are capped. You can injure somebody. I could take your arm off; general damages limited at 150. When it comes to trying cases in Washington, depends on the county you're in, and in fact, can depend on what part of the county you're in. I think South King County is very different from North King County.*

You mean trying cases in Kent as opposed to downtown?

Yeah. It has to do with income and education. Look at average income and education south of I-90 versus north of I-90 which is the dividing line; it's a big difference. It's a big difference. I will not try a case in Lewis County.

Somebody has to try those cases.

*You know, that's true. But when I'm advising the client, my job's to help them. **If I can't really get a fair trial for them, then what sort of job am I going to be able to do for them?** I tried a case down there and I think 20% didn't have a full set of teeth. A third, 25- to 30% of the jurors had been out of work at least a year. And this is before the recession happened. Their numbers on I 330 were really high. I think over 60%. You can look up what the voting record was on that, and that's a great way to evaluate counties if you want to try them.*

Look up the voting record on –

I 330. If you look at Lewis County, it was very pro I 330. I think they were 60-some percent. Remember, that thing lost like 58 to 42 or something. It was at least 55% against it. If you looked at Cowlitz County, it was much closer compared to Lewis. So it varied.

I think that a lack of minorities is making a difference in some of the conservative verdicts. I think that tends to drive verdicts lower.

*I don't know. **I don't think the judges enforce Batson as well as they should. The lawyer needs to, and the court needs to articulate this and the judges just don't enforce the rules enough, by and large, including stuff like that.** I don't know. It's hard to say whether certain things are driven by race and ethnicity or driven by just social attitudes. I mean, the people you get in one part of the region, they're going to have a different view of the world than what you're going to get here. I just know that culturally, that's different, but I don't know how much is driven by ethnicity. I'm not sure.*

I've spoken with some black people in this study and they to a person agreed that they think black people will award more money, generally, than white people, because they want to give back something. They've been not getting it and they want to see somebody else get it.

> *That may be true. Here's my caution: your sample size is really small to get a valid number. You can do the math. My jury consultant that I used, to a large extent, since '88, had interviewed hundreds of juries; not just jurors, but juries, early in his career. He's also a trained psychologist. But he's drawing on hundreds and hundreds of debriefings and jury exercises. When he would say x, I listened really closely. Doesn't mean he's infallible, but he was my favorite jury consultant by far. I got to work with a number of them. There were many of them who were very good, but I just really trusted him and I thought he had the experience to back it up. He and I worked together well. Part of the reason I like talking with him is, he had so much more jury experience and people experience and tried cases lots, had handled cases all over the country, had a good idea that it was reliable information.*

A colleague has had 250 defense cases, and he said it's not uncommon to see very fine lawyers otherwise do very poor *voir dire*.

> *I think voir dire – from the plaintiff's side, voir dire is so much harder than you imagine. I used to like voir dire on the defense side. I used to think I was pretty good at it. I'd ram my case right down their throat by the end of voir dire. I got an hour I get to talk to the jury? Watch this. I'm going to cram it halfway down to their stomach.* **On the plaintiff's side, (expletive), it is an uphill slog in the sand. It is really, really tough. The attitudes and how you're able to talk with jurors is totally different, especially in med mal.**

What do you think about the Spence, identify your fear in *voir dire* and go there; share something of your own fear and vulnerability?

> *I think there's some value in that, but here's the thing to remember: I've read two or three of Gerry's books, I've seen him on TV a few times. I did not go to the three-week camp. Here's the thing about Spence: he can do what the rest of us mere mortals can't do. He's out of a different cut of cloth. I've seen him just do small points, like on a panel discussion or whatever; I can't do that. And you know what? I really don't know anybody else who can.* **So what works for Gerry isn't going to work for anybody else. Look, a lot of what he says and does has really been helpful. I think being open with the jurors is fine, and I think it's important, you know, if you want to share, here's what I'm really worried about. I'm worried that you won't like my client because he's abrasive and you're going to hold that against him when it comes to the merits. I think that kind of stuff is fine. I think there's good value for this. I think sometimes lawyers share something that's really personal and not germane to the decision making process.**

No context.

It isn't really going to help them on the whole thing. But they think, well, I'm doing the Spence method and I'm sharing this and this was personal to me and I was really embarrassed when this happened to me in junior high school. **You know, I would go watch just about everybody that I could that I thought was pretty – especially if it was nearing the end of their career.** *And if I could borrow – I mean, we're all plagiarists. And we call it – we give it a fancy Latin name and so we can justify stealing from everybody. There were things I saw done where I thought, I could use that, but I can't use it for another 30 years; I'm too young to use that. Or that would work for him; won't work for me. That's particularly true for men versus women. There's stuff I watch women do and I'm like, I'm never going to be able to do that. And by the same token, there are things that they would see me do effectively and go, I can't do that.* **So everybody's got to work within their skills and their assets.** *Spence, I just watched that stuff and I thought, I can't do any of that.*

There's one exceptional lawyer who comes at it from the brutal honesty approach. He's out of California, has had outstanding results and wrote a book, *Trial by Human* was the title of the book. His approach is that he starts out from the beginning with a jury and says, I'm going to just be brutally honest about every aspect of this case.

I think that's a – I mean, I don't think that's new.

Right. Because you're talking about credibility and genuineness.

Yeah. **This has always been the path to success. It's always been the cornerstone of persuasion.** *Telling the jurors this is what I'm going to do, you know, I don't know that that really helps you. It may work for him.*

Right. Another of these dynamic individuals who just exudes in a way, innately, that we can't copy.

That's far more easy to copy. Look, we have one lawyer here, he's had the most success in the last 15-plus years. Why?

Case selection?

In part. But his willingness and ability to – his willingness to try cases and his ability to relate to jurors. Because he's very credible. But he will be the first one to tell you, look, he's bald, he's short, he can be abrasive at times, he is high-strung, not things that generally endear you to a jury, **but he's really credible. That's a big key to his success and he's had fabulous success.** *He's gotten more eight-figure verdicts than anybody in the last 15 years. He's done a great job. He's really a magnificent attorney and just a great guy and really done great things for his clients. Really has. But he's just credible. He doesn't BS the jurors. And you can get up there and say, I'm going to be really honest with you, and the jurors are going to say, baloney. You're a lawyer. And you're a plaintiff's lawyer and you have a stake in this outcome. So they're not going to believe you.*

Well, you've got both sides coming in there with no middle ground agreed on.

See, there's some things that both sides agree on. There are key things that they disagree on. A lot of times it's just, is this crappy care or not? Is this something that you want to tolerate in the community or not? **If you're plaintiff-ing and over-promise or say things that can be refuted easily, a smart defense lawyer will attack that immediately.** *A lot of times, they'll just say, I disagree with everything anyway. Well, they really don't. There's a lot of stuff they do disagree with, but key points they may disagree with. It's far easier to be defense counsel than a plaintiff. People don't have a clue. They really don't have a clue. But the magnitude of the difference and the difficulty of doing plaintiff's work is under-appreciated by the defense bar in spades. I remember being at one defense office and some of the lawyers were standing around and one of them said, oh, I could do plaintiff's work. It wouldn't be that much different. And I politely said, you know, I'm the only one on this floor that's done both sides; it is day and night difference, and it's ten times harder than I thought it would be. There are a lot of people on the defense side that would look at the plaintiff's guys and say, it's like clipping coupons. It's fish in the barrel, blah, blah, blah. Oh, God, was that wrong.*

One lawyer of experience told me that was the case 40 or 50 years ago. He said it was a different ballgame then.

It was a different ballgame, but it wasn't easy. Not by any means. Look at the number of plaintiff verdicts back in the – there weren't that many people doing med mal in the 70s and you couldn't get experts. It was a mess for plaintiff's attorneys. It was a lot easier to do defense work. If you looked at all trials or even all verdicts – I'm sorry, all results – the numbers still vastly favored the defense. You know that two-thirds of all cases filed have no money paid on them? Did you know that? Two-thirds of all. Those numbers were true prior to '06. After '06, the number of filings dropped from 400 to about 250 or something and no one's really sure why. I don't have a good answer for you. But I know that average number of filings in med mal cases was around 400 prior to '06. There's a lot of cases that are screened out. They can't get a lawyer, it's not a good case, it's not a big enough case, whatever. Two-thirds of those cases filed had no money paid on them. And 90% of the cases that went to trial were defense verdicts. And the rest, well, some money was paid. Was that a good amount or was it not a good amount? That's a case-by-case analysis. Most people don't know those numbers. It was a different game then. There were different challenges. I think it's harder now. I think the 80s and part of the 90s were pretty good for plaintiffs. But you know, the last 20 years has been really tough.

Tell me what you think about jurors and experts? They tell me they don't really care if an expert makes money or they don't; they've got to get paid. What do you tell them in *voir dire* or hear from them in *voir dire* about experts?

Nothing. Why would I waste my time talking about that? I have an hour. I have much bigger fish to fry. That isn't where I'm going to make any

headway in evaluating that juror for this case. I wouldn't talk about it. You wouldn't get any information. It's not going to move the needle. How you deal with it through the trial and how you argue it in closing can depend on the case, and it may have traction. I think most lawyers think that experts play a bigger role than they really do. By and large, they cancel each other out.

I can think of exceptional lawyers who move the needle with lay witnesses.

Much better.

Really work hard to develop those.

Much better. And most of the people we have been talking about would tell you the same thing. Experts? I think insurance companies are impressed with an expert's credentials. I think sometimes jurors are. In defending cases, I would much rather have what we would call a Henry Kastner expert than some guy who was chair of the department, might look really good on paper and have a 20-page CV. A Henry Kastner expert was somebody who was in the same position as the defendant. I'm a surgeon, I work in this hospital, I work a hundred hours a week. This is what life is really like in the trenches.

From the defense perspective?

Yeah, but the same thing from the plaintiff's perspective, otherwise I've got some ivory tower guy. That's not going to work. But I wouldn't spend a moment on experts and what jurors think about them. That isn't going to help you analyze what to do in voir dire. I wouldn't take the time.

How about pretrial questionnaires? Do you feel that's a necessity in every medical case?

Probably. I think they have high value. In all of those types of cases that are going to probably take two to four weeks to try, I'd use one. If it were a different case and shorter, I don't know whether I'd use one or not. That's why I say, probably valuable. Can be no longer than two pages.

Part of the problem in *voir dire* is, you get the juror's bio sheet and you don't have time, as they're walking in, to look these things over and conduct a meaningful *voir dire*.

You know, I think there are two things that you can do to work with the judge. If they've ever tried a case, they'll understand the value to the bench, to the lower bench, and to the parties and the jurors. One is, set a firm start time for evidence, which is probably going to be Wednesday morning. The other thing is, get your pretrial schedule done so that you can get things done. In other words, motions in limine are done before the first day of trial when the jurors walk in. Get the jurors in, talk about hardship, get the questionnaires answered, get them copied, and you get an hour or so over the lunch hour to review them and then come back and start working on it. That probably makes some sense. If you plan ahead like that and work with the judge and talk to him about the difficulty scheduling witnesses and how I can't just call them up and have them come in, they're flying in from out of state, and this is true for both sides. So if we start at a particular time, I think we can probably be on schedule. Otherwise, we're going to have problems. Every time I've explained that to a judge, one, I don't always get agreement from defense counsel because they don't care. They want me to be disjointed and out of order and stumble and stuff. And I'd probably just tell the judge that if I'm getting much resistance from the other side. But it helps their scheduling. So I'll probably get some cooperation. But every time judges have agreed with that. **And I think it's important because I think being efficient is important. It helps with your credibility. And your sequence is really critical.**

Spence, and this may be applicable only to criminal cases, has said, if you ask the question, who really wants to be on this jury and people raise their hand and say they do, he's very skeptical of any juror that wants to sit in judgment on somebody else. I presume that translates over to civil cases, but I'm not sure.

I think that's true. I think you'd want to ask, well, why? You know, if I were called as a juror, I think it's a really important service.

Me, too.

And I'd be real – and that's why I would want to be on the jury. **The next question is, whether it would be a good case for me.**

Right. Probably, you'd be able to put your biases aside in the case. Because I think we, as attorneys, understand the importance of doing that.

Yeah, but my experiences are going to play such a huge role.

And your leadership.

That's a whole separate issue. But my experiences, I mean, I'm watching some witness testify or some argument from the defense and I would know exactly what that was. What is that code for? Let's take this concept. Do you believe in personal responsibility? I was with a doc on vacation and he was at the same table and found out what I did and he goes, do you believe in personal responsibility? I said, well, if personal responsibility is code for (expletive) happens and tough luck buddy, then no, I don't agree with that. If personal responsibility means you take responsibility for your decisions and that applies to both plaintiffs and defendants, patients and doctors, then I do totally support it.

How do you evaluate group dynamics when you're doing *voir dire*? If you can.

I don't know. **What I'm worried about are really strong-willed, obstinate jurors; the juror who says, well, I'll only vote for the plaintiff in this case, but the damages can't be over $100,000 or someone who's going to really drive the decision making process or who's going to talk about their own stuff all the time and not listen to the evidence.** *It's going to be all from their own point of view about their own experiences.*

Are you cautious of people who talk a lot? Lightning rod types?

Yeah. There's the person who wants to draw attention to themselves, a lot depends on what they're saying. They may talk a lot, but if they're saying things that make sense and they sound like thoughtful people, I'm okay with that. If they've got an agenda, if they've got lots of opinions and no basis for it, I don't like dogmatic thinkers. They scare me because the facts don't matter.

Good point.

That kind of person I don't like in general, and particularly on a jury. I'm real cognizant of, like I said before, I don't like engineers and CPAs, and you have to be real cautious about leaders.

And engineers as well. No empathy for the most part.

Yeah.

Binary, data-driven, no empathy.

Hands down.

And CPAs, well, they understand the value of a dollar a little too much. What about – I think nurses may be a little more critical of bad medical care than anyone else nowadays.

*I'd have to go back to my notes. There's a series of three questions that you ask when it comes to nurses. I think what you say is true in part. **You can also get a whole lot of nurses who may not like what doctors do and know that mistakes happen, but they're not going to find against a colleague and they're not going to go back and face their peers for finding in a patient's favor.***

There's that.

Those are much bigger hurdles and much bigger factors in general. *If you're plaintiff-ing a med mal case you don't want a nurse on there or any healthcare provider on the jury.*

Particularly if they're young in their career.

Yeah. As a friend described, another doctor, he's a bit too young to be so opinionated. I thought that was a great way to phrase it.

Meaning?

That someone who's inexperienced is in no position to have such strongly held opinions. They don't have the value and the insight that's acquired with time and seeing that, well, things don't quite work that way.

You definitely, seems to me, make a better juror if you've got some significant life experience.

Mm-hmm.

For example, having had children or having had some care-giving experience in your life.

There are lots of things like that that'll play a big role. But you get some 26-year-old nurse who thinks she's got it wired and she's the new charge nurse because she wanted the job, she knows everything; that's a tough spot to be in.

Could you give me a sense of what your preferred demographic profiled juror would be in a med mal case?

*You know, no. **I can't do it on demographics, because I think demographics are overemphasized and erroneously relied upon too much.** So I don't think that's the way I would measure it. **It's mostly the things I want to avoid and by corollary the things that I like. I don't like dogmatic thinkers. I don't like people who do not have experiences regarding empathy in life. But how they've dealt with difficult situations will play a big role, and often one that's really surprising.** Let's assume that I represent a plaintiff who's had a spinal cord injury, not paralyzed, but has injury. And I've got a potential juror up there who's had a similar injury. Do you like that person as a plaintiff's attorney and how do you feel if you're defense counsel? The defense attorneys are scared to death because, quote, "that person will identify with the plaintiff and be a strong plaintiff's juror" blah, blah, blah, blah, blah. Invariably, the defense will get rid of that juror. As a plaintiff's attorney, I'm scared to death of that juror, because their reaction more likely is, this happened to me and nobody gave me any money, so why would I give this guy any money? Nobody gave me any money. They didn't do that in my case. They didn't do this in my case. They did this and I didn't get any money. That person is death. And all they're going to do is talk about their own experiences and stuff.*

And it's not that bad, *et cetera*.

As plaintiff's counsel in that setting, I learned, save your third peremptory for that one. The defense will probably bump them before you get to them and you won't have to use your peremptory, even though that may be the person who scares you the most. But that's an example where, quote, "the demographics" or certain events lead you to a different conclusion than well, what are their attitudes and stuff? I've gotten much better over the years at, well, what are your attitudes about certain things? I may have a schoolteacher who's just really conservative. Usually a schoolteacher would be somebody who'd –

Right. Somebody who's a member of the NEA.

There could be lots of reasons, that's why I try to and really admire how some can do it in trying to find key attitudes that will help identify jurors as to who are preferred and who are definitely wanted off.

Some have talked about asking jurors what their values are. I'm struggling with that

concept for this reason: it wasn't until I was 49 years old and had gone through an ordeal – I had no idea what my values were or at least, couldn't articulate them.

I would never ask that question. I don't think you're going to get a good enough answer.

It's abstract, isn't it?

How would you? What are your values? Truth, justice and the American way? What kind of an answer are you going to get that would help you do your job, either in exercising your challenges or in trying the case?

Does the word attitudes closely parallel the word values? I mean, when you ask people what their attitudes are, what's a good can opener word that you like to use to get people talking?

What do you think?

What do you think? Because sometimes, when you ask them, how do you feel, they think they're being psychoanalyzed.

What do you think about this? Or, tell me your thoughts about this. Here's the situation. Some people would say this, some would say the other, tell me what you think.

You're there with anywhere from 40 to 60 or more people, depending on the size of the courtroom and the case, that have looked at you for the first time and you've got to decide who to talk to right then and there. Some have said, find the juror that you're most uncomfortable with and go right there. I don't know. Where do you start? Who do you start with?

It's not going to be the person I'm least comfortable with. I'm going to get to them, but I don't – it's like Twain said, "It's regrettable we have but one chance to make a good first impression." I want a little easier path.

Are you going to stay within your first 20?

Initially. You can't treat all of them equally, because they're not equal. The odds of the people in the first 18 getting on the jury is far greater than the next 18 people which is exponentially higher than the next 18.

Do you tell them that if they're feeling excluded in the back?

Sometimes, just depends on how the conversation's going. I may look at the guy at the end. I've seen one lawyer look at a juror near the back of the group and ask him a question and it was basically like, what do you think the odds are of you getting on this jury because we're all in order? Pretty low; you're right. So I won't take any more of your time. And it was a nice chuckle. You know, I think people who expect to have success of a Paul Luvera or Gerry Spence, that's unrealistic. That shouldn't be your assessment or your yardstick to measure whether you did well or not. They both have tremendous gifts as a lawyer; most – some of which cannot be replicated or learned. There are things you can learn or acquire or this is how I'm going to do things at the office. You can be a slob at home, but you're organized at the office. I mean, those are things you can learn. But certain other skills, I think that's unrealistic. I think you need three things to be a successful plaintiff's lawyer. One, you've got to have the skill to do the work.

You mean the pretrial work as well as the trial work?

The whole thing. If you work hard, you'll be okay. That's going to take care of that. Number two is, you've got to have money. If you're going to do med mal and try to do it on a shoestring, you're in trouble. So are your clients. They're not going to get the service they deserve and you're going to be in big trouble. And then you've got to have the cases. That's the part you don't have control over. You don't have control over whether you're going to get the cases or not, and that's the thing that really impedes most defense lawyers from switching even though some of them want to. Who's going to call? And your ability to get cases is dependent on a lot of things, but bottom line is, do people have confidence that you'll represent the referred client well? I mean, that's really what it's all about.

My good friend, now deceased, Dan Cullan MD, JD out of Omaha was my roommate at the Trial College in '96. I never thought I would do a med mal case in my life, and he said, you ought to do it. You can do it. And remember, take only good cases. But there are lots of good cases. What do you think about that? Do you think there are lots of good cases out there?

Yeah. The problem is, I think most people can't identify them. You've really got to limit your cases to ones that have merit and ones that suit you that you can do.

Do you have a sense that jurors are moved by lawyers who are true believers in their client's case and have spent more time with them and identified with them and love their client and that sort of thing?

I don't know if I'd phrase it like that. **I think if you don't believe your case, you've got no business being in a courtroom.** *You made a mistake taking the case to trial or you got pushed into taking it to trial when you wished and should have settled it. You know, a good defense lawyer will believe just as strongly in his clients, the righteousness of his position or at least give that impression.* **I think what's more important is that you're credible, not that you're best buddies with your client. I think little things will come clear to the jurors that you care about your clients.** *I think that's true on both sides; that it's more than just a job, that this is important. I'll tell you a funny story about, oh, this is an important case. A lawyer was over arguing on an asbestos case. He was arguing about how important the case is and on and on and on. The defense lawyer stands up and says, this case isn't that important; I'm only in practice, this is my second year. Do you think my firm would have sent me over here to defend this case if this case was really important? They'd send one of the senior guys. You know?*

There's an argument against everything, I suppose.

Well –

Some are better than others.

But the point is that lawyer took a case that put an argument on a situation, that's often very good, and wanted to apply it in every case, without thinking about, does it really apply here? That was the mistake, and it made him extremely vulnerable. If he hadn't lost the case already, he lost it then, because not just was the defense attorney right, but it showed that the plaintiff's attorney had no sincerity and no credibility. It really wasn't that important of a case. If he had said something different that said, look, I know this isn't the biggest case in the world, but it's really important to these people, and I'm sure it's important enough to the defense who spent the time and money to come in here to defend themselves and so on, and your decision is always important. That would have been credible. But to whoop it up, nah. He lost all credibility when he did that.

Thank you.

50

IT DEPENDS

The problem with talking about jury selection is that everyone, every jury selection is different.

I've been asking people to imagine they've been called to jury service in a civil injury type of case. I'm trying to find out what matters and what doesn't? What I'd like to know first and foremost is, in that moment that you're standing up addressing a jury for the first time in a major case, what do you think they're thinking and need and value? And what are you doing to establish a credible human connection with them?

> *Well, I think they're nervous.* **They're nervous or scared.** *Most people are not real good at public speaking. Most people live their lives within pretty narrow confines, so now they're hauled out of their normal life; they're put into a courtroom.* **In large part, I think they're looking for what all of us want when we're under stress or feel threatened, which is some avenue to safety. So without saying it explicitly, I try to help them feel more comfortable in the situation and try to establish as quickly as I can that I will be a trustworthy source of information. So I will help to orient them, here's what we're doing, here's why, a little bit, if the judge hasn't done a good job of that, and then kind of let them know really early on, there's no threat here. They're not going to get hurt. They're not going to get embarrassed.** *That sort of thing.*

What do you think is the most important thing to not do, to avoid doing? Because I've found that some of the best lessons really aren't what to do but what not to do.

> **Well, lecture, cross-examine, be boring. Those are the big three,** *I would say.*

Jurors who've spoken to me, or potential jurors, have said they really value their time and they value their money, it seems, more than they value their commitment to public service, at least initially. Do you agree with that?

> **Well, yeah. It's like how do you get them out of their what we all have, kind of a self-involved focus on our lives, our own issues, and take them outside themselves to something else? From a plaintiff lawyer perspective, if you can't get them to do that, you're going to lose most of the time. It takes energy to move money from one side of the courtroom to the other, and so why should they expend the energy?**

Somebody said, I'm getting paid $10 a day to listen to your dog and pony show and you're going to get a third of it.

Right. Exactly.

You know, what's in it for me?

Right. So, you have to find something that's in it for them.

Do you feel case selection is a big part of that?

It could be. Certainly, some cases are easier to engage jurors on than others. You have an injured child, people are more open-hearted and more responsive. You have something different, they're less likely to be open and responsive.

If you've got a corporate entity defendant –

Yes. Right. Right.

– as opposed to an individual doctor.

*Mm-hmm. Yeah. So there're different things that can engage them easier, but no, **I think assuming you have a meritorious case, there's something to hook them on with just about any case.***

What do you think they're most ready to have addressed to them early on? Some say they're not ready to hear about money or the facts of the case. Judges don't want them to hear about the facts of the case. Are they ready to talk about bias and open-mindedness and those sorts of things?

***The problem with talking about jury selection is that everyone, every jury selection is different.** And you could say every cross-exam is different, every opening is different, but I think the variation is greater in jury selection than just about any other stage of the trial because you know, literally, some judges won't let you ask a single question; other judges will let you go on for days. So that's an obvious one. But some judges do a beautiful job of explaining to jurors public service and why they are here. Other judges do a terrible job of it, and kind of encourage jurors to feel alienated and disengaged from the system. So I don't think there is a – **there's not a single way to talk about jury selection. If a juror's just heard a beautiful speech from a judge about the importance of jury selection or about the importance of trial and jury service, they're going to be in a very different place than someone who's just brought in on a cattle call, told to sit down, given a number, asked about where they live, and then turned over to you to ask questions or not turned over to you to ask questions.** There's such a variety of factors in a voir dire that there's just no way to generalize. I think that's the danger is, for people trying to learn about this, you can say to them, here are the things you should accomplish in opening, because there's always certain things you always want to try to do in opening or closing or cross or whatever. But in jury selection, there's just no way to say ahead of time. You're going to have 20 minutes for voir dire, the judge is going to say x, you can start to put together, okay, here's what needs to be done. But –*

If you had an hour to speak to a panel of 40 to 60 people in a major case, where do you think you would go, right off the bat?

I don't think anyone has improved upon Spence's thing of, find the issues you're afraid of and just start talking about them. You know, it is by far the best thing I've ever found.

I've spoken with lawyers and judges who say they've seen that misused in that Spence also says, share your fear with the jury and share something of yourself, but sometimes people have taken it a little too far and a little out of context. Can you speak to that at all?

*Well, in part, that goes back to what I was saying before about what's appropriate in one setting is not appropriate in another. **What's appropriate with a group of people that has been warmed up properly by the judge is one thing. And in another courtroom, it'd be the exact wrong thing to do.** So you need a certain amount of – I mean, I wouldn't want to speak for Spence, but I think his point is, **stop trying to pose as a lawyer and ask the lawyerly questions. Try to get a dialogue going.** It's like, you know, at one cocktail party, you're trying to get a conversation going, you might try one thing. At a different cocktail party, you might try another. And at church, you might try another.*

Do you have any thoughts about who to talk to right off the bat when you're facing this group of people that you've never met before? Someone once said, find the person that you're most uncomfortable with and talk to them first. Well, I tried that, but I wasn't so sure that was the best way to do, you know?

*I like to start with someone I think will be the most talkative, so you can kind of get a sense of that, because the judge usually has asked some questions or you get some sense of how relaxed people are. So then I'll try to start with someone who I think will be the most talkative, whether friendly or not, you know. **It's more just to get the expectation going. Break the ice; get the conversation going.***

How about talking about money? Some say they like to talk about money to inoculate the jury to a potential big number; others have said they don't think it's the best thing to do. I'm curious to know what your thoughts are about talking about money in *voir dire.*

Again, I think it depends on the case. *You know, the kind of cases I do often don't have much in the way of hard damages. When that's the case, I usually don't talk about money.*

You mean, hard damages in terms of specials?

Like life care plans, right. Lost wages. I guess my tendency is not to talk numbers in front of the jury in voir dire. If I had a catastrophically injured person with a big life care plan, I might talk about that early on. You know, the experts say, she's going to need $10 million in care in the future, I'd probably drop that.

Because that's a solid anchor, isn't it? When you've got –

Big specials. Right. On the other side of the equation, if it's like the wrongful death of a six-year old boy, I usually do not bring up money. But it certainly – I don't think it's wrong to do it. **I like to bring them along slowly but again, it kind of depends on your goals, I think. You know, there's one school of thought of, the primary objective is to identify the bad people and get them off.**

De-selection.

Yes. Now, another school of thought is, I'm going to form a relationship with these people.

Build a tribe.

Build the trust, build the tribe. And those two things run at cross purposes to some extent. So, I tend to be more of the build a tribe view, although I certainly try to identify the bad people and get them off, but I think it kind of depends where you are on that spectrum. *I've certainly gone in with idea of just knocking as many people off. And then I'd be more inclined to talk money, because I think you'll get people – and so without talking about my own hopes of money at the end, I'll often say, some people have a mental idea that a case of a certain sort should never be more than – you know, you've heard the judge describe this case; do you have an amount of money beyond which you couldn't go just based on what you've heard so far? And that'll often get them to self-identify.*

I was both surprised and not surprised to hear most of the lay people I talked to say they really didn't feel the general damages were appropriate. I think it comes down to the fact that they don't know how to calculate them just as much as we don't know how to calculate them.

That's right. That's right.

Do you talk about that in *voir dire*?

Again, no. **When I'm in state court, as to the non-economic damages, I'd rather get the momentum going and the trust built and all of that. Which is not to say – I mean, I've certainly asked the question, how do you feel about non-economic damages? And get them discussing that. And some people will say, I just can't do it. So there's a good way to get people out.**

How about burden of proof? That's always an interesting one. I was surprised when person after person would tell me that they thought a preponderance meant 60-, 70-, 80- to 90%.

Wow. Interesting.

And of course, when I explained to them that it was more likely than not, they move more closely to what we want to hear, but what are your thoughts about – and the reason I ask is, somebody once said, I don't want to talk about burden of proof in *voir dire* because I don't want the jurors to think that I'm worried about it.

Yes. Or that I just have 51%. I would never talk about burden of proof for that reason until I heard David Ball talking about it. But I don't talk about it for educational reasons. **I talk about it – it's a really good way to identify conservative jurors, you know, ones who are going to be resistant to our case. Because I'll talk about it in terms of – and other people do this too, obviously of – you've heard the judge describe this case, you've heard him say preponderance of the evidence. That means we just have to prove by just the slightest bit more, 51%, to prove our case. Some people think in a case such as this one where millions of dollars are at stake, it should be a higher level. What do you think? And a lot of the conservatives will practically jump out of their seats saying, no, if you want millions of dollars, I need to be really certain. It's a really good way to get rid of them.** *So I use it for that reason rather than educate them, well, if we only had – if we only prove our case for 51%, will you still rule our way? I think that's a big mistake for the reason I said.*

At the same time, what you've just done through that method, that way of talking about it is, you've educated them anyway while you've –

You've educated, them, right. But, the purported and the real purpose is more about – and then I'll return to the 51% in closing. Years ago I found this brilliant argument Spence had of saying I'm sure there's been times in this trial where you've been really confused. You think you've figured it all out, and then a different lawyer gets up to ask questions and all of a sudden, it's all confusing again. And then you think you've figured it out and a different witness comes up, and it's all confusing. Well, there's a tool that the Courts use to help with that, and it's this jury instruction, preponderance of the evidence. And then you explain that, and then you explain you don't have to get certainty. And the reason we have this is not to be sloppy, but you realize this could go on forever. One person talking and another and – you know, a good lawyer can make anything seem upside down and confusing, so you don't have to figure out all the little details and tie up all the loose ends, you just have a sense of which is more right than the other and that's all you need, and judges use this standard themselves when they decide cases as fact finders.

For the last several hundred years of our nation's history.

Exactly. So anyway, I only use it in voir dire to kind of help identify the conservatives.

How about telling the jury that there are going to be experts with lots of differing opinions? Do you talk about experts with jurors in *voir dire*?

No. Really my goals are just to get to know them, let them get to know me, knock off the really ugly ones, and if I get that done, I'll feel like I'm way ahead.

Are you using a jury selection assistant when you're in big trials?

I haven't. This is my bias, I just don't think anybody really knows. I mean, you can tell the obvious ones, and there will be a consensus on those, but you don't need somebody to tell you about that the guy who's foaming at the mouth over verdicts being too high or whatever. In this last trial I had, there were three people who went on and on about lawsuits are ruining the country and too many too big verdicts and so, you know? I can't tell you how many times I thought oh, these jurors or these four or these two are totally in my camp, even after watching them for a six-week trial, I think I know who's on our side and who isn't, and it's the exact reverse. It happens so often. Some people are better than others at getting the bad ones to come out to the front and then knocking them off. I don't feel like I've got a particularly great skill at that.

The times I've tried to establish cause challenges, I felt like I've alienated the potential juror and the group. And the judge sometimes.

Yes.

Then I'll hear some stalwart friends of ours say, I got five people knocked off for cause on this trial. I could never do that.

Well, it's a different skill set, I think. And you give up something by approaching – I mean, to take those two mission statements I was describing of forming a group, forming a tribe, gaining trust, making them feel safe with you as the leader, or I'm going to target these people and knock them off. They're not necessarily inconsistent, but it's awfully hard to accomplish one while you're also – it's very hard to do an optimal job at both of those things. *You're going to give up something depending on which way you go, I think.*

I agree. What are you doing in advance of your trials to identify a juror profile? Are you doing that through focus groups or having consults, or do you just establish your themes and -

We probably do focus groups maybe in – 25% to a third of our cases.

Some people go into a trial with their preferred demographic or their preferred juror profile.

You know, I never – I mean, the short answer is, no.

I wonder if sometimes we complicate this too much.

Right. Well, there's stuff that goes on in the moment with this particular group of people that's just hard to orchestrate ahead of time. So, yeah. I mean, certainly I get a lot out of focus groups, but we don't usually do a demographic type, you know, we're not usually looking for a profile of jurors.

Right. Christian, white, male.

Yeah. There've been some cases where I've assumed women would be more on our side than men, like I just kind of intuitively felt women would be more open to our case.

I intuitively feel that about almost every case I'm in, women or minorities.

Yeah, that's probably true. Although it's not hard to imagine, with a woman plaintiff, I might be more inclined to get men. So again, I wouldn't have an across the board thing. It's always going to be different, I think.

Always going to be. Do you use written jury questionnaires?

Same answer; it depends.

What would it depend on for you?

If I'm doing insurance bad faith cases, I don't want a questionnaire, because I think it's more likely the hidden juror is going to be an anti-insurance company juror than a pro-insurance. Even the most conservative people tend to not like insurance companies that well. So in a lot of these insurance cases, I'd be much more inclined to not have a questionnaire. Sometimes, we're trying cases against huge firms with huge power and resources. Now, we've used them very effectively. In the example I just gave, the judge nevertheless gave a questionnaire and we did fine in jury selection and in trial. But those would be my preferences. **They're obviously very helpful in identifying bad jurors, but helpful to the defense in identifying bad jurors, too.**

We're near the bottom of the barrel in terms of the perception of the jurors with regard to credibility and truthfulness and honesty. How do you steel yourself emotionally before a trial going in to, say, I'm going to connect with these people, even though they know, or think they know, that I'm a non-credible person? Is there something you do to buy in to your case or to buy in to your client in a way that your credibility is integrated and biological?

I think it comes from, if you honestly believe in your case, you've got nothing to be defensive about. So it's kind of that, I guess. Does my case have weaknesses? Yes, my client has a burglary conviction or whatever. Does my client still deserve to win? Yes. So what do I have to be – he's the guy who got the burglary conviction, not me. You know, I'm not trying to hide.

Do you think defensiveness is something that's sniffed out and works against us?

Absolutely. Yeah. I think a big part of my CLE work is to try to get plaintiff lawyers to be less defensive, but not self-righteous. *I mean, that's the walk. So many plaintiff lawyers get either defensive and angry or self-righteous and angry and you know, I really think having gone to many different places, tried many different kinds of cases, I think for sure there are differences, but a lot of the differences are an inch deep. So the things that get to people get to them. I* *wouldn't be in court if I didn't think the client deserved to win. And I've thought about all the bad stuff, and I still think the client deserves to win, if not, I would have settled it.*

What do you think makes you different and accounts for your success in the courtroom? You're very calm and relaxed, and you appear to enjoy what you're doing.

Right. I think I have a type of emotional detachment that allows me to see the strategic implication. I think a lot of plaintiff lawyers get so emotionally wrapped up, either their own ego, you know, I don't want to lose because it'd be so humiliating, or they identify so much with their client that they can't really separate what's a valid point on the defense versus what's not a valid point from the defense. And if you can't figure out what's valid and invalid from the defense standpoint, you're going to run into trouble.

I think as great as the Spence training has been, for me and many others, I've seen people take it a little too far.

Right. And that's the danger, I think, is that they so identify with the – I mean, just like so many things, Spence is completely right, and too much of a good thing, and you're now in the wrong again. You know, he corrected what was this sort of antiseptic professional detachment that lawyers cultivated. He corrected that appropriately, but then some people took it to mean, and I've heard him speak about this a little bit, you know, that you can take it too far. If you identify so much that you can't see the flaws in your case and the flaws in your client and the strengths of the defense, then you're like a kamikaze. So I think partly, I've been able to be detached. I think my problem is, I'm sometimes too detached. But I can be detached from my client and their problems and sort of see kind of objectively what's going to appeal to people and what isn't.

This notion now of, caring is contagious, is a big buzz that's going around, and people tell me that they think that they want to see the attorney care.

Right.

I'm trying to determine, what is the sweet spot there?

Right. I think it's going to be different for each personality, too. You know, we've all seen lawyers who can emote and it's genuine. I've seen people do it really effectively. I don't know if you've ever seen Tommy Moore from New York, but he's about the most emotive lawyer I've ever seen, you know, pounding the table and screaming and he's gotten more multi-million dollar verdicts than any lawyer in the history of the world. He's very, very effective. He does mostly birth injury med mal cases and in New York, so he's in a different venue and different dynamics going on that I don't know that would be effective in a commercial case or a car crash case, but for his cases, it's very effective and we've also seen people who seem to have no emotion and can be very effective, too.

Are you talking to jurors in *voir dire* about lay witnesses that they'll be hearing from?

No. I'd never get down to that kind of level of detail.

Jurors always say, I need to hear it in context. I spoke to some judges about that, and the difficulty I have is, we can't often talk about enough of the facts of the case to give jurors the context they need. So that's pretty frustrating.

Well, I think that's, again, even by asking the question that way, the assumption is that the facts are what's going to drive the verdict. And to some extent that's true, but I think they also need, what they're also saying, maybe without knowing it, is they need emotional context. What's the real story here? And who am I going to identify with? What and how am I going to feel about this when I hear the whole thing?

I'm frustrated at the emote your own personal fears, share something of yourself, your vulnerability, to get them to then open up and then honor the share. You don't have a whole lot of time in that environment to do that with these people. And I don't think judges are letting us do it either.

I've been working on doing psychodrama. I started doing psychodrama and learned so much. But part of what I learned from it was not even the psychodrama part, but watching the sociometry in forming groups. I was really struck by there are ways to get the jury to be a cohesive group.

That's a whole other level of jury selection that's difficult to focus on, the group dynamic, when you're trying to determine –

Exactly. That's what I've gone to. Spence is a trial genius, and a genius in a variety of ways. A lot of the stuff he does, he does kind of instinctually. He's absolutely 100% right in what he's saying, and so I was really taken by, because I've heard him speak for decades, you know, form a tribe, form a group, make your client part of – well, how do you do that? Well, there are group dynamic principles about how to make someone a – you know, bringing a newcomer into a group, how to get people to form a group. So after the last few trials, that's what I've really focused on is how to form a group.

And have you been paying mind to that during the *voir dire* process?

Oh, yeah. That is the time.

I was talking to a psychologist about that and wanted to know if the stages of group dynamics apply to jurors. But the problem is that there're so many different groups.

Yes.

They come into the big group –

Right.

— and then there's our group in the courtroom with them –

Yes.

— and subgroups and then they become a smaller group and it – I just don't know what to do other than to be aware of the stages of group formation.

Right. Well, there are things you can do to foster it and things you can do to have them regard you as the leader and a variety of things. With an hour or more, it can be done pretty effectively; if you get less than an hour, it starts to get hard, although with this last trial I tried it a little bit, and I think it was helpful. Well, the first time I tried it, I actually lost the case. But the jury was formed so tightly, they kept having picnics together for months afterwards. They kept getting together. The defense lawyer was totally freaked out by the time I was done with my part of the jury selection. He told me afterwards he really worried and he'd never seen anything like it. So I'm encouraged by it.

Do you have any final thoughts?

Well, we sit somebody here in this seat and ask them questions and try to decide if they'll be a good juror, that's very different than putting them in a courtroom and asking them if they'll be. Or even putting them in a focus group is different than having them in the courtroom. So that's the confounding factor is, everybody sits and tries to pre-orchestrate how their jury selection's going to go and all that. The real answer is, it all depends. And you don't know what they had for breakfast, if they fought with their wife, if the guy next to them has body odor. I mean, all the infinite number of things that can influence how a person's going to react. But, we can be part of that. If we're conscious of those kinds of things, we can hopefully – and I think that's Spence's whole – I mean, to me, the big things are, talk about the weak points in your case, the stuff you're afraid of, get them to see you're not going to waste their time, you're to the point. I think that's more and more important as time – I mean, compared to when you and I started practicing. It's sure changed a lot that way that they would put up with more slowness and –

I came in in the tail end of the multi-day *voir dires*.

They won't put up with that anymore.

I appreciate it. Is there anything I haven't touched on.

No, I don't think so.

Thank you.

PART 4 — **CONCLUSION**

WHAT I LEARNED

It is no easy task to summarize all of the lessons and takeaways from a project of this magnitude. Every participant came to the conversation table with personal insights about what matters to them, our prospective jurors in the jury selection process, and many of them reiterated what we already know to be helpful. For my part, I found it particularly enlightening to ask about and learn what might not be helpful or important to them, a form of "addition by subtraction". Too often we're instructed to "do something", "do something different" or "do something better" but I have found there can be great improvements made by knowing, simply, what not to do and then, simply, not doing it. Many of the questions and answers that make up the 50 conversations in this book are a result of that approach.

The reader will note that the titles and the quoted material that begin each chapter reference a distinct theme worth emphasis. By no means is that necessarily the only or even the most important theme touched upon in any given conversation. Indeed, throughout the book, within each chapter and conversation, I have highlighted, in bold for emphasis, many comments that the reader will be well served to study, digest and comprehend, preferably in the context of the entire conversation.

Still, throughout the process, it became apparent that some themes were touched upon with more frequency and emphasis than others and they bear further mention, with the *caveat* that the only rule is that there are no hard and fast rules. In every situation it can be said, "It depends".

With that in mind, the following summarizes some of the essentials of what I learned throughout the process of conducting these 50 conversations.

WE ARE ALL BIASED

I believe that the primary goal of jury selection is to identify those potential jurors that may have a bias or biases that they cannot or will not put aside, and that will prevent our clients from getting the fair trial that is their right. This book provides many examples of safe approaches to asking about, uncovering and dealing with juror bias, prejudice, prejudgment and close-mindedness.

However, it is important, in my view, to understand that we lawyers are no less biased than our most biased juror. Think of this: our values, i.e. our economic livelihoods and professional reputations, our comfort and safety and our egos, all depend on us winning in the courtroom. Our self-interest, particularly for those of us risking our precious time, efforts and money on contingent fee cases, literally depends on our success as measured by wins and losses and, ultimately, on jury verdict amounts large and small for our clients and, dare I say it, for ourselves. We simply cannot, by virtue of who we are, in our chosen profession, ever be unbiased and we do ourselves, our clients and all participants in the civil justice system, including our adversaries, a disservice if we claim to be.

We were taught to think differently and about dull grey topics the average person cares little or nothing about beyond the vague notions of "right", "wrong", "justice" and "responsibility". We speak a different language and routinely use words that are beyond the comprehension or interest of many, if not most of the individuals we entrust with the facts, law and arguments we make for and against. The word "preponderance" comes to mind as one notable example. We passionately support organizations that advance our professional if not our personal agendas. And, if we're empathetic, we care and feel for our clients, sometimes deeply, at times to a point where we risk losing perspective. All of these things make us not just different from our prospective jurors, but very different. And they, the prospective jurors, come to us uniquely as well, with their own very different experiences, beliefs, and values orientations, each no less or more right than any other. Let me repeat this with emphasis: each of us is no more or less right in our beliefs and values than any other individual. We all have the right, whether God-given, by Natural law, or by the rights enumerated in the Constitution of the United States and its Bill of Rights, to be who we are, ourselves.

This project gave me the priceless gift of respect and appreciation for and a celebration of the differences between and among the people who are our prospective jurors. It gave me the gift of appreciation for and acceptance of those jurors who may have inherent biases, who may be close-minded or inclined to pre-judge. Behold, they are not the enemy. The enemy is our own reflexive hatred or revulsion or fear or anger toward them for the beliefs they hold and the values they espouse that differ from our own. To paraphrase my good friend Eric Fong who wrote the Foreword to this book, right minds will always differ. I will add that right minds will always differ rightly, for I am not right and they are not wrong, we are only different. I believe a firm understanding of this concept is the cornerstone to the foundation of good and effective jury selection.

CONNECTING WITH THE JURY

I approached this project believing that the next primary goal of jury selection is to establish a credible human connection with our potential jurors. Whether this goal is more or less primary or important than identifying and de-selecting jurors with deeply-entrenched biases may be debated and, I imagine, depends on the context and the unique situation of any given case at the moment.

We know that the general public in our culture, with an assist from mass media, certain members of the political right, business interests large and small and the insurance industry, already views our profession, particularly trial lawyers, with the suspicion, skepticism and disdain typically reserved for used-car salesmen. Pity the poor used-car salesman. Jurors are sensitive to greed and wary of people taking advantage of the system and often assume that the plaintiff is doing just that and they, perhaps rightly, discount our clients' credibility, believing it to be compromised by self-interest. Many of them believe that the law is about manipulation, not truth. But in my view the news is not all that bad. Yes, our potential jurors, or many of them, are skeptical of such things as general damages for emotional pain and suffering, of runaway verdicts, needless windfalls, Golden Tickets, bogus and fraudulent lawsuits and a litigation crisis that is driving up the costs of insurance and medical care and sending our doctors, the healers of society, packing. And we will likely always have the McDonald's coffee case or some version of it to swim upstream against. But what I take from the conversations here is that while all of the foregoing concerns exist, to some extent in the public consciousness and in the minds of our jurors, the majority of them believe that there are many more good and decent lawyers who are representing good and decent people for good, valid and just reasons that help make society better and safer. To be sure, justice will always be fluid and unpredictable, shaped by the unique situations, persons and entities involved and by the events of the day, may be more-than-occasionally disappointing and will be determined on a case-by-case basis. While the lessons of this book can help lawyers do a better job in jury selection and can certainly help level the playing field, they cannot guarantee a favorable verdict in a poorly selected, poorly prepared or otherwise poorly presented case. No lawyer ever won a case in *voir dire*, though some, most certainly, may have lost there.

THE FINAL ANALYSIS

This book will help the reader identify what he or she needs to be, if not most then at least well-aware of when preparing for and doing jury selection. Awareness of what we need to accomplish and awareness of what jurors need and want is the first step on the path to success. Without awareness, without context, we are less likely to know how to "be" and less likely to know how to appreciate and properly use the tools we are given. What follows is intended to summarize what jurors need and want, what lawyers will be well-served to understand about how they themselves ought to be (i.e. the personal qualities they present) when doing jury selection, and what to do and what not to do to in order to best accomplish the primary goals identified above.

JUROR NEEDS AND WANTS

So then, what are prospective jurors thinking? What do they need and want and what matters to them in those moments when they first receive a jury summons in the mail, when they go through the indignity of security screening performed by armed Sheriff's Deputies, when they first assemble at the courthouse and when they are literally marched into the unfamiliar, serious and imposing confines of a courtroom? What doesn't matter? What do they need to have happen, to see and hear there in order to have a sense of ownership and feel good about trial lawyers, our clients and the process? How do we help them feel included, normal, validated, valued and respected? How do we help them form a cohesive well-functioning working group?

The answer is that they need what matters to them in the situation and at the moment. They need their concerns to be addressed and to be heard if jury service is a hardship, real, perceived or otherwise, for them and their families and to be excused with thanks and without embarrassment. They need us to value their time and sacrifice, to be professional, look professional and speak in normal tones of voice and in words they can readily understand. They need to be trusted to do the right thing and not talked down to, not told what to think or feel and not be manipulated. They need eye contact and body language that shows them the lawyer is genuine and they need humor too. They need us to listen, meaningfully and to accept and appreciate that they come from different places and with all manner of experience and they need us to appreciate how difficult and embarrassing it can be to talk about one's closely-held beliefs before a roomful of strangers. They need us to not waste their time with frivolous cases or ask for outlandish amounts of money when such is not warranted in the circumstance and to explain, as best we can, what is meant by the burden of proof and how also to come up with a way, any sensible way, and a "why" that helps them fairly fashion a remedy for general damages for unseen pain and suffering. They need us to understand that there is often a difference between what may be important to them in their decision-making process ("juror proof") and what may be important to us ("lawyer proof"). This bears repeating and is well-covered in the literature on focus groups. They need us to understand the kinds of evidence that will help them make the best decisions they can feel good about and find ways to present the evidence so that it makes sense to them. They need us to understand that not all cases, in their minds, are created equal, that right is relative and fairness is subjective and that the justice they determine to be fair and appropriate will depend on who the parties are, how they are perceived in the moment and the nature and degree of the wrong and the severity of the resulting harm, and that, in their minds, there are such things as honest mistakes. Each and all of these needs and wants are expressed throughout this book.

HOW TO BE

Throughout this book I asked the participants what qualities they would most like to see, hear and emanate from attorneys in the courtroom. Not surprisingly, they tell us attorneys should be honest, authentic and persons of integrity. We should be interested in the jurors as well as understanding, respectful, caring and non-judgmental. We should be accepting, inclusive, empathetic and reassuring; calm, humble, reasonable and fair; and prepared, focused, direct and concise. Doubtless there are many more qualities or many other words to describe the qualities listed here and this is not intended to be comprehensive.

Also, it is not for me or for this book to teach the reader how to be a person. Instead, it is up to each of us to do the work necessary on ourselves, in whatever form or process that takes, to become the best we can be in service of ourselves, our clients and our profession.

WHAT TO DO (AND WHAT NOT TO DO)

In the course of this project I learned many things, some of them new and surprising and some reminders of things forgotten. It is no easy task to read a book of this length and, as an assist to the reader, I was encouraged to share what I believe are the most important Do's and Don'ts of jury selection in summary form. I urge the reader to keep in mind that lists and admonitions like the ones that follow are only a guide and are by no means exhaustive or exclusive. Books like this one can be helpful, even necessary, to engage our minds in thought but as I learned twenty years ago at the Trial Lawyers College, there is no substitute for the experience that comes when we engage our bodies in action.

In keeping with my belief in the value of the efficient model of "addition by subtraction", listed first are the Don'ts, the "no-no's", those things I believe attorneys must not do if they wish to transcend from ordinary to great.

DON'T

     ☒   Patronize, condescend or talk down to jurors;

     ☒   Dig or pry too deeply;

     ☒   Manipulate;

     ☒   Argue your case;

     ☒   Sell your case;

     ☒   Explain the law;

     ☒   Force emotion on the jurors;

     ☒   Tell the jury what they are supposed to think;

     ☒   Ask boring, monotonous or repetitive questions;

☒ Exaggerate or be overly-flamboyant;

☒ Over-embellish or oversell;

☒ Lose perspective;

☒ Go too far or ask for too much;

☒ Paint a juror into a corner;

☒ Be defensive; or

☒ Be self-righteous;

DO

☑ Find the issues you are afraid of and just start talking about them;

☑ Think about what will be important to the jurors in your case;

☑ Think about what the issues are that may be of concern to the jury;

☑ Learn safe and inoffensive ways to ask about bias, prejudice and close-mindedness;

☑ Invest the time to listen so the jurors feel heard and validated;

☑ Smile;

☑ Make eye contact;

☑ Have good posture;

☑ Be aware of your non-verbal messages and tone of voice;

☑ Go with your gut feelings and instincts;

☑ Share something of yourself, in context;

☑ Ask simple open-ended questions;

☑ Use plain ordinary language;

☑ Use humor if the circumstance permits;

☑ Understand that justice is not an absolute in the minds of the jurors;

- ☑ Explain "why" when introducing the importance of concepts, notions and approaches that jurors may not be familiar with;

- ☑ Educate the jury about the process and provide a road map or checklist to help jurors understand what may be expected of them;

- ☑ Provide a brief synopsis of the case;

- ☑ Put the jury at ease and orient them to comfort and a feeling of safety;

- ☑ Craft a method to normalize first-timers and experienced jurors alike;

- ☑ Watch accomplished trial lawyers do *voir dire*;

- ☑ Have a way to explain the burden of proof (e.g. "concretize" for visual learners with "Justitia", otherwise known as the statue of Lady Justice);

- ☑ Ask for a show of hands to general questions;

- ☑ Understand that jurors are generally uncomfortable with the concept of general damages for pain and suffering;

- ☑ Let the jurors do most of the talking. You won't learn about them otherwise;

- ☑ "Honor the share" by thanking and appreciating a juror who answers a question;

- ☑ Provide context for the process and the questions you are asking;

- ☑ Focus the presentation;

- ☑ Consider the use of written questionnaires;

- ☑ Provide reasons for the "remedy" of money;

- ☑ Put jurors in the world of your client;

- ☑ Understand that documentation, especially from an independent source, generally beats argument;

- ☑ Give jurors the right to pass;

- ☑ Have an appreciation for the experiences and feelings of minorities and people from different ethnic backgrounds;

☑ Move on if a juror is reluctant to answer or openly hostile.

☑ Educate the judge on race issues and the *Batson* case when minority jurors are being unfairly excused without "cause".

☑ Encourage all responses, especially those that are hostile to your case;

☑ Let the jurors know that there is no right or wrong answer;

☑ Determine who is more likely to work to "overcome" a bias;

☑ Appreciate the desire of most jurors to do the right thing;

☑ Think about what qualities and attributes might best to have as a juror in a given case;

☑ Learn how to use the example of a "scale" (i.e. do you lean more one way or more another way? On a scale of 1 to 10 would you consider yourself closer to 1 or 10 or somewhere in the middle? Are you more for or against or closer to neutral about a given issue?); and

☑ Select good cases for trial, use focus groups and prepare thoroughly or fail to do so at your peril;

PARTING THOUGHTS

The trial greats are great at jury selection because they try a great many cases. While some may have inherent gifts of charisma, personality, intelligence, drive, or some other intangible that makes them naturally more proficient, likable or credible it is important to appreciate that none of us becomes an expert overnight. There is always work to do, more to learn and experience to be gained.

CONTINUING THE CONVERSATION

Meaningful dialogue and thoughtful feedback are encouraged and appreciated. You may post comments and criticism about any part of this book at **conversationsjuryselection.wordpress.com.**

APPENDIX

Demographic Data

Fifty individuals participated in the conversations that are transcribed and printed in this book. Of those fifty, two are sitting Superior Court judges, one male and one female, each with more than ten years of experience on the Superior Court bench, and two are attorneys, both males, with demonstrated excellence, as measured by results (wins and jury verdict amounts), in major civil injury cases.

- Of the remaining forty-six individuals, the "jury-eligible" cohort:
- 54% are male; 46% are female.
- 54% are married; 31% are single; and 15% are divorced.
- 60% of males are married; 24% are single; and 16% are divorced.
- 48% of females are married; 38% are single; and 14% are divorced.
- The average age is 47.82.
- 49.16 is the average age of males; and 46.24 is the average age of females.
- The age range is 24-78.
- The average number of children is 1.13 and 59% have children. Of those with children, the average number is 1.93.
- 24% have grandchildren.
- 85% of the participants are Caucasian; 7% are Black; 4% are Asian; and 4% are Hispanic. There were no American-Indian or Pacific-Islander participants.
- 37% report some connection to law enforcement.
- 70% report some connection to the legal profession.
- 61% report some connection to the medical profession.
- 28% report some connection to the insurance industry.
- 30% report some connection to civil and/or criminal case experience.
- 50% report having prior jury experience. Of those, 17% report having been forepersons.

Resources

- *Trial by Human,*
  Nicholas Rowley & Steven Halteman, Trial Guides 2013

- *Connecting With the Jury* (DVD),
  Nicholas Rowley, Trial Guides 2013

- *Reptile, The 2009 Manual of the Plaintiff's Revolution,*
  David Ball & Don Keenan, Balloon Press 2009

- *Paul Luvera on Trial Strategy* (DVD),
  Paul Luvera, Trial Guides 2008

- *Winning Medical Negligence Cases, A Guide for the Plaintiff's Lawyer,*
  William Trine & Paul Luvera, ATLA Press 1993

- *A Day With David Ball On Damages* (DVD),
  Washington State Trial Lawyers Association 2004

- *The Elements of Trial,*
  Rick Friedman & Bill Cummings, Trial Guides 2013

- *Trial Tactics* (DVD),
  Rick Friedman & Roger Dodd, Trial Guides 2014

- *What Makes Juries Listen Today,*
  Sonya Hamlin, Glasser LegalWorks 1998

- *The Culture Code, An Ingenious Way to Understand Why People Around the World Live and Buy as They Do,*
  Clotaire Rapaille, Broadway Books 2006

- *Gerry Spence on the New Seven Steps to Voir Dire* (DVD),
  Gerry Spence, Trial Lawyers College 2005

- *Win Your Case, How to Present, Persuade, and Prevail – Every Place, Every Time,*
  Gerry Spence, St. Martin's Press 2005

- *Courtroom Power: Communication Strategies for Trial Lawyers,*
  Paul M. Lisnek & Eric Oliver 2001

- *Adjust Your Focus Early,* Phillip Miller & Paul Scoptur, *Trial* January 2016

About the Author

David Crump is a nine-time Super Lawyer (*Washington Law & Politics*); a nine-time Top 100 Trial Lawyer in Washington (The National Trial Lawyers Association); a four-time Top 100 Litigation Lawyer in Washington (The American Society of Legal Advocates); a lifetime charter member of the Best Attorneys of America; a Premier 100 Trial Attorney (The American Academy of Trial Attorneys); AVVO rated 10/10; an Eagle Gold member of the Washington State Association for Justice; contributor to WSAJ's *Trial News*; and a graduate of the Gerry Spence Trial Lawyers College. He is currently working on his next book, *Why This Matters*, and makes his home in Seattle, Washington.